IOM International Organization for Migration

Academic Foundation New Delhi

WORLD MIGRATION 2008

MANAGING LABOUR MOBILITY IN THE EVOLVING GLOBAL ECONOMY

VOLUME 4 - IOM World Migration Report Series

IOM is committed to the principle that humane and orderly migration benefits migrants and society. As an intergovernmental organization, IOM acts with its partners in the international community to: assist in meeting the operational challenges of migration; advance understanding of migration issues; encourage social and economic development through migration; and uphold the human dignity and well-being of migrants.

This edition is published in India in 2009
by: ACADEMIC FOUNDATION
4772-73 / 23 Bharat Ram Road, (23, Ansari Road),
Darya Ganj, New Delhi - 110 002 (India).
Phones : 23245001 / 02 / 03 / 04.
Fax : +91-11-23245005.
E-mail : academic@vsnl.com
www. academicfoundation.com

World Migration 2008:
Managing Labour Mobility in the Evolving Global Economy
(Volume 4 — IOM World Migration Report Series)

ISBN 81-7188-769-4

Printed and bound in India.

IOM EDITORIAL TEAM

Editors-In-Chief and Concept	Gervais Appave, Ryszard Cholewinski
Editorial Board	Michele Klein Solomon, Frank Laczko, Sophie Nonnenmacher, Jobst Köhler, Nilim Baruah
Steering Committee	Juan Artola, William Barriga, Jean-Philippe Chauzy, Shahidul Haque, Jill Helke, Bernd Hemingway, Irena Omelaniuk, Robert Paiva, Richard Perruchoud, Jillyanne Redpath-Cross, Peter Schatzer, Irena Vojackova-Sollorano, Thomas Weiss
Editorial Assistance	Juan Artola, William Barriga, Shahidul Haque, Jill Helke, Michele Klein Solomon, Frank Laczko, Sophie Nonnenmacher, Irena Omelaniuk, Robert Paiva, Irena Vojackova-Sollorano, Elizabeth Warn
Publications Assistance and Layout	Clara Francia Anaya, Anna Lyn Constantino, Valerie Hagger, Caroline San Miguel, Alma Sy, Carmelo Torres
Executive Assistance	Dominique Jaud-Pellier, Antoinette Wills
Regional Overviews	Verónica Escudero, Claudia Natali
Cartography	Jana Hennig
English Language Editor	Ilse Pinto-Dobernig

ACKNOWLEDGEMENTS

The Editorial Team wishes to thank all contributing authors and is especially grateful to Brunson McKinley, former IOM Director General, for his vision and encouragement to produce this publication.

The Editorial Team wishes to thank the following persons, principally current and former IOM staff, for their kind assistance and support:

Christine Adam, Christine Aghazarm, Serhan Aktoprak, Carmen Andreu, Jorge Baca, Diego Beltrand, Andrew Billo, Philippe Boncour, Rosilyne Borland, Peter Bossink, Andrew Bruce, Cynthia Bryant, Anne-Marie Buschman-Petit, Audrey Carquillat, Laurentiu Ciobanica, Ricardo Casco, Sarah Craggs, Luca Dall'oglio, Richard Danziger, Anita Alero Davies, Priyanka Debnath, Alexandre Devillard, Flavio Di Giacomo, Françoise Droulez, Sylvia Lopez-Ekra, Disha Sonata Faruque, Berta Fernandez, Stephanie Fitzjames, Jorge Andrés Gallo, Nicoletta Giordano, Mary Haour-Knipe, Laurence Hart, Janet Hatcher Roberts, Dina Ionesco, Nayla Kawerk, David Knight, Sarah Költzow, Umbareen Kuddus, Lucy Laitinen, Kerstin Lau, Chris Lom, Marina Manke, Kristina Mejo, Ugo Melchionda, Susanne Melde, Françoise Moudouthe, Günter Müssig, Alina Narusova, Ndioro Ndiaye, Pierre Nicolas, José-Angel Oropeza, Paola Pace, Jemini Pandya, Niurka Pineiro, Carina Raisin, Felix Ross, Redouane Saadi, Ovais Sarmad, Scott Schirmer, Meera Sethi, Frances Solinap, Lucie Stejskalová, Alma Sy, Yorio Tanimura, Lalini Veerassamy, Galina Vitkovskaya, Shyla Vohra, Vassiliy Yuzhanin, Zhao Jian, Jennifer Zimmermann.

The input of the following external experts to the concept of *World Migration 2008* at a workshop in Geneva in January 2007 is also much appreciated:

Ibrahim Awad (International Labour Organization – ILO), Luca Barbone (The World Bank), Johannes Bernabe (International Centre for Trade and Sustainable Development – ICTSD), Scott Busby (Intergovernmental Consultations on Migration, Asylum and Refugees – IGC), Antonia Carzaniga (World Trade Organization – WTO), Verona Collantes (United Nations Conference on Trade and Development - UNCTAD), Jeff Dayton-Johnson (Organisation for Economic Co-operation and Development – OECD), Carla Edelenbos (Office of the United Nations High Commissioner for Human Rights – OHCHR), Lisa Eklund (United Nations Population Fund – UNFPA), Raquel Gonzalez (International Trade Union Confederation – ITUC), Geneviève Gencianos (Public Services International – PSI), Bela Hovy (Population Division of the United Nations Department of Economic and Social Affairs – UN DESA), Robyn Iredale (Australian Demographic and Social Research Institute, the Australian National University), Azfar Khan (ILO), Eleonore Kofman (Social Policy Research Centre, Middlesex University), Christiane Kuptsch (ILO), Virginia Leary (Emeritus Professor of International Law, State University of New York at Buffalo), Lindsay Lowell (Institute for the Study of International Migration, Georgetown University – ISIM), Frederick Muia (International Organization of Employers – IOE), Edmundo Murrugarra (The World Bank), Kathleen Newland (Migration Policy Institute – MPI), Pierella Paci (The World Bank), Dilip Ratha (The World Bank), Martin Ruhs (Centre on Migration Policy and Society, University of Oxford – COMPAS), Brigitte Suter (Malmö Institute for Studies of Migration), Siri Tellier (UNFPA), Sabrina Varma (United Nations Development Programme – UNDP), Stéphan Vincent-Lancrin (OECD), Martin Watson (Quaker United Nations Office – QUNO), Vincent Williams (Southern African Migration Project – SAMP).

Several organizations generously shared their data and other research materials:

Canadian Permanent Mission to the United Nations (Geneva), Centre for European Policy Studies (CEPS), COMPAS – University of Oxford, IGC, International Institute for Sustainable Development (IISD), International Migration Programme of the ILO, Internal Displacement Monitoring Centre (IDMC) – Global IDP Project, Norwegian Refugee Council, OHCHR, OECD, Pan American Health Organization (PAHO), Platform for International Cooperation on Undocumented Migrants (PICUM), Population Division of UN DESA, PSI, SAMP, Thai Ministry of Interior, Thai Ministry of Labour, United Nations High Commissioner for Refugees (UNHCR), UNFPA, The World Bank, WTO.

The Editorial Team is especially grateful to the following donors for their generous financial support towards the development and publication of *World Migration 2008*:

Governments of Australia, Denmark, Switzerland and the United States, The John D. and Catherine T. MacArthur Foundation, Agence intergouvernementale de la Francophonie (specific financial contribution towards the translation of the French version).

TABLE OF CONTENTS

LIST OF FIGURES AND TABLES

OCEANIA

SELECTED ACRONYMS AND ABBREVIATIONS

ABS	Australian Bureau of Statistics
ABTC	APEC Business Travel Card
ACP	African, Caribbean and Pacific countries
ADB	Asian Development Bank
APC	Intergovernmental Asia-Pacific Consultations on Refugees, Displaced Persons and Migrants
APEC	Asia-Pacific Economic Cooperation
APMRN	Asia Pacific Migration Research Network
ARGO	Action programme for administrative cooperation in the fields of external borders, visas, asylum and immigration (European Commission, 2002-2006)
ASEAN	Association of Southeast Asian Nations
AU	African Union
AVRR	Assisted Voluntary Return and Reintegration (IOM)
BLA	Bilateral labour agreement
BMET	Bureau of Manpower, Employment and Training (Bangladesh)
CAFTA	Central American Free Trade Agreement
CARICOM	Caribbean Community and Common Market
CARIM	Euro-Mediterranean Consortium for Applied Research on International Migration
CCRALC	Canada-Costa Rica Agreement on Labour Cooperation
CDMG	European Committee on Migration (Council of Europe)
CECA	Comprehensive economic cooperation agreement
CEECs	Central and eastern European countries
CEPS	Centre for European Policy Studies
CERI	Centre for Educational Research and Innovation (UNESCO)
CeSPI	Centro Studi Politica Internazionale (Italy)
CFO	Commission on Filipinos Overseas
CIC	Citizenship and Immigration Canada
CIREFI	Centre for Information, Discussion and Exchange on the Crossing of Frontiers and Immigration
CIS	Commonwealth of Independent States
CMA	Centre for Migrant Advice
COMESA	Common Market for Eastern and Southern Africa
COMPAS	Centre on Migration, Policy and Society (University of Oxford, U.K.)
CREAD	Centre de Recherche en Economie Appliquée pour le Développement (Algeria)
CSME	Caribbean Single Market and Economy
DAC	Development Assistance Committee (OECD)
DDA	Doha Development Agenda
DETE	Department of Enterprise, Trade and Employment (Ireland)
DFID	Department for International Development (U.K.)
DHS	Department of Homeland Security (U.S.)
DIAC	Department of Immigration and Citizenship (Australia)
DOL	Department of Labor (U.S.)
DOLE	Department of Labor and Employment (the Philippines)
ECLAC	Economic Commission for Latin America and the Caribbean (UN)
ECOSOC	Economic and Social Council (UN)
ECOWAS	Economic Community for West African States
EEA	European Economic Area
EECA	Eastern Europe and Central Asia
EIB	European Investment Bank
EIU	Economist Intelligence Unit
ELM	Education labour market
EMN	European Migration Network
EPA	Economic partnership agreement
EPZ	Export Processing Zone
ESCAP	Economic and Social Commission for Asia and the Pacific (United Nations)
EU	European Union

EUROPOL European Police Office
Eurostat Statistical Office of the European Communities

FDI Foreign direct investment
FERME Fondation des entreprises en recrutement de main-d'œuvre agricole étrangère (Québec, Canada)
FMS Federal Migration Service (Russian Federation)
FRONTEX European Agency for the Management of Operational Cooperation at the External Borders of the Member States of the European Union

GATS General Agreement on Trade in Services
GATT General Agreement on Tariffs and Trade
GCC Gulf Cooperation Council
GCIM Global Commission on International Migration
GDP Gross Domestic Product
GFMD Global Forum on Migration and Development
GMG Global Migration Group
GNP Gross National Product

HIV/AIDS Human Immunodeficiency Virus/Acquired Immune Deficiency Syndrome
HLD High-Level Dialogue on International Migration and Development (UN General Assembly)
HRD Human resource development
HRSDC Human Resources and Social Development Canada

IACHR Inter-American Court of Human Rights
IADB Inter-American Development Bank
IAMM International Agenda for Migration Management
ICMPD International Centre for Migration Policy Development
ICT Information and communication technology
ICTSD International Centre for Trade and Sustainable Development
IDB Islamic Development Bank
IDM International Dialogue on Migration (IOM)
IDMC Internal Displacement Monitoring Centre (Norwegian Refugee Council)
IDPs Internally Displaced Persons
IGC Intergovernmental Consultations on Migration, Asylum and Refugees
IISD International Institute for Sustainable Development
ILO International Labour Organization
ILOLEX ILO database of international labour standards
IMES Institute for Migration and Ethnic Studies (University of Amsterdam, The Netherlands)
IMF International Monetary Fund
IMI International Migration Institute (University of Oxford, U.K.)
INS Immigration and Naturalization Service (U.S.)
IOM International Organization for Migration
IPCC Intergovernmental Panel on Climate Change
IPEC International Programme on the Elimination of Child Labour (ILO)
IPPR Institute for Public Policy Research (U.K.)
ISIM Institute for the Study of International Migration (Georgetown University, Washington, D.C., U.S.)
ISSER Institute of Statistical, Social and Economic Research (Ghana)
ISTAT Istituto Nazionale di Statistica (Italy)
IT Information technology
ITUC International Trade Union Confederation
IUSSP International Union for the Scientific Study of Population
IZA Institute for the Study of Labor (Bonn, Germany)

JPEPA Japan-Philippines Economic Partnership Agreement

LDCs	Least Developed Countries
M&As	Mergers and acquisitions (cross-border)
MDGs	Millennium Development Goals
MENA	Middle East and North Africa
MERCOSUR	Common Market of the South
MFN	Most Favoured Nation
MIDA	Migration for Development in Africa
MIDSA	Migration Dialogue for Southern Africa
MIDWA	Migration Dialogue for West Africa
MLDR	Migrant Labour Dependency Ratio
MLSA	Ministry of Labour and Social Affairs (Czech Republic)
MOITAL	Ministry of Industry, Trade and Labour (Israel)
MOU	Memorandum of Understanding
MPG	Migration Policy Group (Brussels, Belgium)
MPI	Migration Policy Institute (Washington, D.C.)
MRU	Market Research Unit
MSR	Market Situation Report
MWF	Migrant Welfare Fund
NAFTA	North American Free Trade Agreement
NAMA	Non-agricultural market access
NBER	National Bureau of Economic Research (U.S.)
NESC	National Economic Social Council (Ireland)
NGO	Non-Governmental Organization
NHS	National Health Service (U.K.)
NRB	Non-resident Bangladeshi
NRI	Non-resident Indian
ODA	Official Development Assistance
ODI	Overseas Development Institute (U.K.)
OAS	Organization of American States
ODIHR	Office for Democratic Institutions and Human Rights (OSCE)
OECD	Organisation for Economic Co-operation and Development
OFW	Overseas Filipino Workers
OHCHR	Office of the High Commissioner for Human Rights
OPF	Overseas Pakistani Foundation
OPT	Occupied Palestinian Territories
OSCE	Organization for Security and Co-operation in Europe
OWWA	Overseas Workers Welfare Administration (the Philippines)
OWWF	Overseas Workers Welfare Fund (Sri Lanka)
PAHO	Pan American Health Organization
PEA	Private employment agency
PICUM	Platform for International Cooperation on Undocumented Migrants
PIELAMI	Cooperation on preventing illegal employment of labour migrants with a view to promoting legal employment opportunities (IOM Helsinki ARGO project)
POEA	Philippine Overseas Employment Administration
POLO	Philippine Overseas Labour Officer
PPP	Purchasing power parity
PRSP	Poverty Reduction Strategy Paper
PSI	Public Services International
RCM	Regional Conference on Migration (Puebla Process)
RCPs	Regional Consultative Processes
RTA	Regional trade agreement
S&T	Science and technology
SAARC	South Asian Association for Regional Cooperation
SADC	Southern African Development Community
SAMP	Southern African Migration Project
SAMReN	South Asia Migration Resource Network
SAWP	Commonwealth Caribbean Seasonal Agriculture Workers Program (Canada)
SAWS	Seasonal Agricultural Workers Scheme (U.K.)
SIEMMES	Statistical Information System on Migration in Mesoamerica
SLBFE	Sri Lanka Bureau of Foreign Employment
SMEs	Small and medium enterprises
TNCs	Transnational corporations
TOEA	Thailand Overseas Employment Administration

TOKTEN	Transfer of Knowledge Through Expatriate Nationals
UN	United Nations
UNCTAD	United Nations Conference on Trade and Development
UN DESA	United Nations Department of Economic and Social Affairs
UNDP	United Nations Development Programme
UNECE	United Nations Economic Commission for Europe
UNEP	United Nations Environment Programme
UNESCO	United Nations Educational, Scientific and Cultural Organization
UNFPA	United Nations Population Fund
UNGA	United Nations General Assembly
UNHCR	United Nations High Commissioner for Refugees
UNICEF	United Nations Children's Fund
UNIFEM	United Nations Development Fund for Women
UN-INSTRAW	United Nations International Research and Training Institute for the Advancement of Women
UNODC	United Nations Office on Drugs and Crime
UNRISD	United Nations Research Institute for Social Development
UNRWA	United Nations Relief and Works Agency for Palestine Refugees in the Near East
UNSD	United Nations Statistics Division
UN-WIDER	United Nations World Institute for Development Economics Research
UNWTO	United Nations World Tourist Organization
UP	Unió de Pagesos
U.S.-CAFTA-D.R.	United States-Central America-Dominican Republic Free Trade Agreement
VoTs	Victims of Trafficking
WHO	World Health Organization
WMO	World Meteorological Organization
WTO	World Trade Organization

FOREWORD

World Migration 2008, the fourth in a series which started in the year of IOM's 50th anniversary in 2001, shares with its predecessors a threefold purpose: to provide policymakers and the general public with up-to-date and authoritative information on international migration trends; to identify major policy issues as they arise; and to discuss available policy options.

It is one thing to acknowledge that migration has become a matter of great interest or concern to the international community; it is quite another to address it with the purpose, determination and coherence that have been achieved in other, comparable spheres of international affairs. Unfortunately, a balanced understanding of migration – how to live with it, manage it and benefit most from it – has not always kept pace with its growth or changing nature. As a result, the global debate on migration is often confused, and action piecemeal.

World Migration 2005 looked principally at the impacts of migration in terms of social, economic and political costs and benefits. *World Migration 2008* surveys the same migratory landscape from the reverse perspective. It considers how the intricately woven social, economic and political realities, collectively referred to as "globalization", are giving rise to and shaping contemporary patterns of mobility with particular attention to economically-motivated mobility.

The first part of the Report consists of a series of studies produced by independent researchers invited to offer individual perspectives on different facets of economically-related mobility, including the movement of highly skilled, semi-skilled and low-skilled workers, student mobility, short-term travel for tourism and business purposes, family migration, internal migration and irregular migration. The second part, intended especially for policymakers and programme managers, discusses broad policy strategies for the management of international labour mobility, focusing on the development of an adequate knowledge base, the most appropriate policies for countries of origin and countries of destination, the migration and development relationship, and cooperation at the global, regional and bilateral levels. A separate section presents overviews of migratory activity in six major regions of the world.

Once again, we have drawn on the expertise and experience of IOM staff based at Geneva headquarters and in the field throughout the world, as well as external scholars, researchers and government practitioners. We hope that this volume will be of interest to the reader and make a valuable contribution to the debate on international migration.

William Lacy Swing
Director General

INTRODUCTION*

The Challenge of Migration Management

At the beginning of the 21st century, migration continues to loom large as a subject of media interest, of community preoccupation and of political controversy. Nevertheless, the discourse has evolved significantly in recent years, both in terms of substance and tone, and is now conducted with noticeably less acrimony than before and with much reduced levels of distrust between developed and developing countries. For instance, at both the UN General Assembly High Level Dialogue on International Migration and Development (HLD), held in New York in September 2006, and the Global Forum on Migration and Development (GFMD), held in Brussels in July 2007 (see Textbox Int. 2), participants were, in general, disposed to agree that migration holds considerable potential for economic and social development (UN, 2006b). At the same time, however, it was apparent that there is much more to be done before agreement can be reached on appropriate management strategies to be put in place, both nationally and on the international level, for that promise to be realized.

* This introduction was written by Gervais Appave, Co-Editor-in-Chief.

The task of formulating a workable global approach to the management of international migration remains a formidable challenge, and one that will require both time and effort over the coming years. The word "management" has occasionally been criticized as a euphemism for "restriction" or "control" and for giving insufficient attention to human rights concerns. As used in *World Migration 2008*, it refers to a planned and thoughtful approach to policy development; and to the careful selection and implementation of appropriate policy responses to the key questions confronting the international community:

- What should be the scope and content of a comprehensive migration management strategy conducive to coherence of action across countries and policy fields?
- What are the organizing principles to be adopted?
- Is there a conceptual point of leverage to move the debate forward?

The dual purpose of this volume - reflected in its structure - is, first, to explore the nature and extent of the need for more comprehensive, coherent and purposeful action through the study and analysis of a wide range of contemporary migratory patterns linked to economic purposes (Part A) and, second, to canvass policy elements that might contribute to the development of a strategic response (Part B).

Globalization and Mobility

Part of the problem is the difficulty of reaching consensus on the fundamental nature of migration and its outcomes. Underlying the current and welcome inclination to acknowledge the potentially beneficial outcomes of migratory phenomena are many questions that are yet to be fully resolved:

- Should migration be considered an entirely "natural" part of human behaviour that has occurred throughout history, or rather as "unnatural", in the sense that it involves the often painful uprooting of individuals from their places of birth and their equally difficult relocation in other countries?
- Is it a process through which nations are built and strengthened, or rather divided and weakened?
- Does it further economic growth in countries of origin through the flow of remittances and the transfer of skills and technology, or lead to stagnation through the loss of talent and inadequate attention to development and the creation of job opportunities at home?
- Are migratory flows being sustained primarily by a complex interplay of push and pull factors or by social communication networks?
- Would migration management be made more effective if the primary policy concern were to be directed at the protection of national interests and the securing of borders or rather by allowing considerable leeway to the free interplay of market forces?

In the midst of such uncertainties, it is worth exploring suggestions that **contemporary** migration, in contrast to earlier migratory phenomena, is uniquely related to, and defined by, the processes of economic and social integration that are collectively known as globalization. It is true that what might properly be called the formal or organized aspects of globalization have focused on the elaboration of legal and administrative mechanisms to facilitate, to the largest extent possible, the movement of capital, goods and services,[1] not people. But, whether by design or not, these developments appear largely responsible for the creation of an unprecedented context in which **human mobility seeks to find expression on a genuinely global scale**.

In 2005, there were some 191 million international migrants[2] worldwide, nearly two and a half times the figure in 1965, a pace of increase well in excess of the global population growth rate over the same period (UN DESA, 2006). The number of migrants is likely to be in excess of 200 million today. Even more striking, however, are the widely different origins and distribution of those migrants. Fifty years ago, only a handful of industrialized countries - mainly those that had established formal immigration programmes in the aftermath of World War II, such as the United States, Canada and Australia – were identified as "countries of destination", while the "countries of origin" were mostly in Europe. Today, the patterns of movement are such that most countries are simultaneously countries of origin, of transit and of destination, albeit to varying degrees. At the same time, there has been a diversification of migratory behaviour to include short-term relocation, longer-term temporary assignments, permanent migration and even multi-stage migration itineraries leading back to the point of origin.

The particular conditions identified as contributing to these trends are too numerous and too familiar to be dealt with here at length; suffice it to say that

1 The movement of services does cover some movement of "natural persons" as incidental to trade (see Textbox Int. 1).

2 Defined as persons residing in a country other than their country of birth for a period of 12 months or more, both in regular and irregular situations.

they may be grouped into two very different but inter-related sets.

One set consists of **enabling** factors such as macro-political changes including the collapse of the Soviet Union and the opening up of China to the world; the advent of affordable air transport; the creation of real-time global communication networks; and the redefinition of individual and family identities in transnational terms. In combination, they add up to almost-unlimited networking possibilities, knowledge sharing and awareness of opportunities. The other - and arguably more important - set of **causal** factors arises out of the interplay of large, not fully understood, socio-economic variables that form part of complex international equations. Pritchett (2006) identifies five such driving forces.

The first of these factors consists of disparities in income and employment opportunities across and within countries and regions, particularly the steep economic gradients between developed and developing countries. According to Pritchett, wage gradients of between 2 to 1 and 4 to 1 between countries of origin and destination were at the root of mass worker movements in the 19th century. Today the real wage gaps are often as high as 10 to 1.

The second factor is the increasing global demographic imbalances. In brief, while the populations of low-income countries will grow significantly over the next 50 years, the populations of high-income countries will grow at a much slower rate. Simultaneously, the populations of the latter will continue to age. The proportion of persons above 60 years of age in more developed regions is expected to grow from 21 per cent in 2007 to 32 per cent in 2050, while the number of children is expected to decrease from 17 per cent to 16 per cent. In other words, in 2050 there will be in industrialized countries twice as many people over 60 than children (UN DESA, 2007). Demographic disparities are expected to generate migration from two opposite directions: on one hand, shrinking and ageing populations in industrialized countries will stimulate demand for migrant labour and on the other, large numbers of young workers in developing countries will seek work and life opportunities abroad (Lawson et al., 2004).

The third factor is linked to the liberalization of flows of goods, capital and services - including communication - across virtually all parts of the world. In such circumstances, pressures for labour mobility are bound to increase, all the more so when the international community stands to gain very significant economic benefits from the lifting of constraints on worker mobility.

The fourth factor lies in current and expected future demand in developed countries and mid-income developing countries for low-skilled services (for instance, in home care or hospitality sectors) that come to be required as a combination of increased productivity, greater access to higher education, rising incomes, reluctance of nationals to perform certain jobs perceived to be of lower status, ageing populations and the globalization of manufacturing. Technological advances (especially automation) may go some way towards countering that phenomenon, but, as Pritchett (2006) points out, the capital/labour substitution process has obvious limitations: while it is conceivable that devices endowed with artificial intelligence will increasingly replace human service providers, such developments are unlikely to completely replace nurses in hospitals or serving personnel in restaurants and hotels.

Finally, account must be taken of increased pressure for population movement through shifts in the desired population of specific countries or regions. In brief, a large decline in labour demand in a given location (and this has been the experience of many developing countries in recent times, for instance as a result of changes in agriculture, in climate or in resources) creates substantial pressure for outward migration.

The net impact of all these factors is a global context where migration is increasingly seen (a) at the individual level, as a choice worth including in life plans (although not one that is necessarily exercised by a majority of people – since roughly 97 per cent (IOM, 2003) of the world's population consistently opts **not** to migrate[3]); and (b) at the national level, as a significant factor to be taken into account in economic and business planning, whether by governments or the private sector. At the centre of these plans is the concern for employment.

In summary, globalization offers almost unlimited awareness of opportunities and networking possibilities. A world that is spanned by fast, real-time communication lines and connected by research webs, where large information databases are available at a click of a mouse, is also one that offers near instant access to information on job market openings. At the same time, globalization gives rise to powerful socio-economic dynamics that play across borders: income disparities, population imbalances and labour market discrepancies combine to produce migratory flows that are increasingly dominated by the search for a better life through improved employment opportunities.

Labour Migration, a Key Aspect of Human Mobility and the Global Economy

The current focus on migration for work-related purposes, clearly discernible, for instance, in the evolving policy preoccupations within the European Union, is all the more noteworthy because of the predominance of asylum and irregular migration issues on the policy agendas of many countries during the last three decades of the 20th century. The global migration landscape and the attendant international deliberations were dominated by a succession of refugee and humanitarian crises: in Asia, the exodus from Viet Nam, Cambodia and Laos, by land and sea; in the Middle East, large numbers of people displaced by the Gulf War; in the Balkans, massive outflows from Bosnia and Herzegovina and Kosovo; and, in Africa, displacements and flights out of Rwanda, Sudan and the Democratic Republic of Congo, for example. Between 1992 and 2001, in western Europe alone, over four million people sought asylum (UNHCR, 2002). As a natural consequence, the international community was called upon to act primarily on issues of protection and humanitarian assistance. As often as not, these were caught up in related migration policy concerns such as integration, border control or trafficking in persons, but these were of subsidiary or tangential interest. There was little policy space available for the consideration of broader and comprehensive approaches to migration management.

The gradual shift in policy perspective towards a broader grasp of the nature and the prevalence of human mobility can thus be attributed, at least in part, to a decline in the numbers of asylum claims lodged in industrialized countries. Since 2001, applications for asylum in industrialized countries have declined by 49 per cent, the total number of claims in 2005 being the lowest since 1987 (UNHCR, 2006).[4] Another contributing factor may have been the realization that tackling migration issues such as integration or return in isolation had not been particularly effective. Of greater moment, however, was the rediscovery, at the turn of the millennium, of the economic impact of labour migration on countries of origin, first through the magnitude of the global remittance flows and, second, the extent to which these were embedded in the fabric of global economic activity. Labour migration is now acknowledged as an integral part of the global economic landscape.

[3] As in n. 2 above, migration here is understood in the context of moving to a country other than one's country of birth for a period of 12 months or more.

[4] However, this declining trend was reversed slightly in 2006 and in 2007 (UNHCR, 2007, 2008).

Powerful global production dynamics now help ensure that patterns of labour supply and demand operate across international borders. There is, first of all, the constant search for productivity and the place of migrant labour in the complex equations that are meant to yield the best economic outcomes. Another significant factor is the growing need for human services, especially in developed economies, where ageing populations require continuous personal assistance and affluent working age parents can afford to pay for child care and general household help. Account must be taken of the increasing scarcity of workers willing to engage in low- or semi-skilled employment in industrialized economies, not only in the care sector but also in agriculture, construction, hospitality as well as other service sectors. Finally, there is the emphasis on information and knowledge management, exemplified in multiple ways through fierce international competition for expertise in data management and processing fields, through appreciation of the value of multilingual and multicultural workforces, and through the recognition of adaptive capacity as a valued work skill.

Major Policy Issues and Challenges

This rapidly evolving situation poses policy challenges that require innovative thinking and, most importantly, renewed cooperative efforts among the numerous parties involved if workable solutions are to be found. Three separate but closely interwoven clusters of policy challenges are of central interest to this Report.

The first, already stated in the title, concerns the identification of effective strategies for the management of international labour mobility, at national, regional and global levels. To do so presupposes an understanding of the characteristics and magnitude of current and future labour migration flows and of how they fit into the global economy – clearly demonstrated through the existence of international niche markets in such sectors as information technology and health services; but also evident in low-skilled sectors such as hospitality industries, construction or domestic services where migrant workers fill labour market gaps to satisfy the service requirements of affluent societies. It also raises multiple questions about the assessment of the types and levels of need; about the setting up of policies and programmes to match labour need with appropriate supply; about training both for work competencies and adaptation to work environments abroad; about streamlined and fair recruitment practices; and about the evaluation of programme activity. Given the newness of such enterprises to many countries, issues of administrative infrastructure and of capacity building also become major considerations.

The second cluster of challenges lies in the relationship between migration and trade: 40 years ago the international community embarked on the negotiations of the General Agreement on Tariffs and Trade (GATT), which led, in due course, to the establishment of the World Trade Organization (WTO) and the General Agreement on Trade in Services or GATS, negotiated under WTO auspices. It is interesting to note that the international community could have gone the other way; the nation states of the world **could** have decided to opt for highly self-sufficient, enclosed and highly protected economies. They **could** have decided that economic insularity was a small price to pay for the retention of strong national identities, social quiescence and harmony and for a maximum of security within their borders. They opted instead to aim for the global networking of production systems and increasing facilitation and streamlining of trade flows.

Global trade liberalization negotiations have resulted in a substantial reduction of barriers to trade in goods and capital, opening up significant, albeit unevenly distributed, global economic gains. Barriers to the movement of people, however, have been identified as a continuing and considerable impediment to further global economic gains from trade, gains which are predicted both to exceed both the gains from further liberalization in other sectors and to benefit developing and developed economies alike. There are many promising lines of action to be explored in this area, ranging from broad multilateral initiatives such as those offered under GATS Mode 4 (see Textbox Int. 1), and opportunities for worker mobility linked to regional trade liberalization efforts, to bilateral labour mobility schemes and more open unilateral policies. In each case, a fundamental question concerns the extent to which progress on international trade arrangements, alone or through complementary initiatives external to the trade talks, can facilitate the orderly, predictable, safe and mutually beneficial movement of people.

Textbox Int. 1

The State of Progress in GATS Mode 4 Negotiations

A new round of multilateral services negotiations began in 2000, as foreseen in Article XIX of the General Agreement on Trade in Services (GATS). With the launch of the Doha Development Agenda (DDA) in November 2001, services became part of a broader negotiating round.

Mode 4 is defined in Article I.2(d) of the GATS as "the supply of a service... by a service supplier of one member, through presence of natural persons of a member in the territory of another member" (i.e. a person who is a service supplier, such as a banker or an architect, is present in a foreign country to provide the service). A "natural" person is a human being as opposed to a merely legal entity, such as a business. Mode 4 is an important component of the negotiations on services and has been identified by a number of World Trade Organization (WTO) Members, particularly developing countries, as one of the areas where they seek improved market opening commitments.

Up to the end of 2005, negotiations on Mode 4, as on all other services areas, proceeded on the basis of bilateral request-offer exchanges. At the end of March 2003, Members began to submit, this time to the entire membership, initial offers of improved commitments and these initial undertakings were followed by the submission of revised offers as of end of May 2005, based on an ongoing process of bilateral consultations.

However, most commentators deemed that this bilateral negotiating process had yielded very modest results. The Chairman of the Special Session of the Council for Trade in Services, the WTO body overseeing the services negotiations, summarized the prevailing sentiment on the progress after two rounds of offers by stating that, "it was widely acknowledged that the overall quality of initial and revised offers is unsatisfactory. Few, if any, new commercial opportunities would ensue for services suppliers".[1]

This was generally true for all services areas and, particularly so for Mode 4, a traditionally sensitive domain. Out of some 70 offers (counting the European Community as one entity), less than half proposed upgrading Mode 4 commitments. All improvements would apply horizontally, i.e. in the same manner for all services sectors covered in Members' schedules. While this reflects the horizontal nature of many immigration regimes, in practice it also implies that the lowest common denominator will determine the conditions for access across the whole services economy.

The main improvements to Mode 4 commitments offered concern additional categories of natural persons not associated with a commercial presence abroad (e.g. self-employed service professionals); greater clarity in the application of "labour market tests" or "economic needs tests" and/or reduction in their scope of application; removal of discriminatory measures, such as nationality or residency requirements; and extended periods of stay. However, such improvements are unevenly spread across individual offers and most schedules continue to significantly restrict Mode 4 access, particularly for persons whose movements are not directly related to a commercial establishment. Finally, very few offers include additional commitments on issues such as transparency of regulations or administrative procedures, and visa requirements affecting Mode 4.

In spite of the somewhat disappointing start, services talks were given fresh impetus by the Hong Kong Ministerial Declaration of December 2005, where Members agreed to intensify the negotiations in accordance with a set of objectives, approaches and timelines. In particular, Members agreed to be guided "to the maximum extent possible" by a number of objectives, some of which related specifically to Mode 4, while ensuring appropriate flexibility for developing countries (improvement of commitments on categories of persons both linked and de-linked from commercial presence, the reduction/elimination of economic needs tests and the extension of the permitted duration of stay).[2] Concerning approaches, the Declaration also foresees the possibility to pursue the request-offer through multilateral negotiations.

In keeping with this mandate, over 20 collective requests were submitted, including one on Mode 4, and two rounds of multilateral discussions were held in early 2006. The Mode 4 collective request, sponsored by some 15 developing countries, is addressed to nine developed Member countries. As may be expected, the focus of the request is on better commitments for categories of natural persons whose movement is not linked to a commercial establishment abroad. In particular, access is sought in a number of services sectors for "contractual services suppliers", i.e. persons moving abroad to supply a service pursuant to a contract between their employer, who does not have a commercial presence in the host country, and a services consumer; and "independent professionals", i.e. self-employed service professionals.

The results of the multilateral discussions were to be reflected in a second round of revised offers, due by 31 July 2006. However, all negotiations under the Doha Development Agenda were suspended just one week before, reflecting mainly a stalemate over agricultural and non-agricultural market access (NAMA). It was not until February 2007 that the negotiations were fully resumed. As a result of the suspension, however, there is at present no timeline for the submission of second revised offers. Members seem to agree that a new timeline should be set only after a breakthrough is achieved in the agriculture and NAMA negotiations.

Notes:

1 WTO document TN/S/20 of 11 July 2005.

2 WTO document WT/MIN(05)/DEC of 22 December 2005, Annex C.

Source: *Antonia Carzaniga, WTO.*

A third large cluster of issues revolves around the complex relationship between migration and development, the subject of discussions of the Global Forum held in Brussels in July 2007 (see Textbox Int. 2). The increasingly significant contribution of labour migration to the global economy has been very thoroughly researched and commented upon in recent years (IOM, 2005; World Bank, 2006; GFMD, 2008), with one of the major topics of interest being the substantial contribution of migrants to home country development through the transfer of knowledge, skills, investment and remittances. In 2007, recorded remittance flows were estimated to have reached USD 337 billion worldwide (in nominal terms a staggering 99% increase over what they were five years earlier), with USD 251 billion going to developing countries (Ratha et al., 2008). However, four major policy formulation questions remain:

- What can be done to lower the transfer costs of remittances and to encourage their flow through formal channels?
- What conditions ought to be created to encourage the application of remittances to sustainable development endeavours, bearing in mind that they are private funds?
- What strategies are needed to ensure labour migration does not lead to the depletion of the skill base in developing countries of origin?
- What kinds of partnerships can be forged between governments and diasporas to enhance the positive impact of remittances on development in countries of origin?

While these questions are intrinsically important, they carry additional significance because recent experience has shown that they represent a unique meeting platform where countries of origin, transit and destination can work together towards common objectives. As such they have appeared on the agendas of many Regional Consultative Processes (RCPs), for instance those of the Ministerial Consultations on Overseas Employment and Contractual Labour for Countries of Origin in Asia (Colombo Process), the Abu Dhabi Dialogue, the Regional Conference on Migration in North and Central America (Puebla Process) and the Migration Dialogue for Southern Africa (MIDSA).[5]

[5] An overview of the major RCPs with a specific reference to labour mobility is provided in Textbox 13.4.

Textbox Int. 2

Global Forum on Migration and Development (GFMD)

The Global Forum on Migration and Development (GFMD), launched in Brussels in July 2007, set the tracks for a new international consultation process on migration and development policy and practice. The Belgian Government took up the call of the UN General Assembly High-Level Dialogue on International Migration and Development (HLD) a year earlier for an informal, non-binding, government-led forum on migration and development. The forum was intended to be outside the UN system, but linked to it via a Special Representative of the Secretary-General.

The Brussels meeting engaged more than 150 governments and a range of international and civil society entities in team-led debates around themes of common interest and good practices. One of the key roundtable themes, "Human Capital Development and Labour Mobility",[1] addressed the policy environments that could maximize the beneficial effects of labour migration and minimize the risks to migrants, their families and development efforts of home and host countries. Often, the best policies are not specific to either migration or development: for example, more coherent skills training and employment distribution and retention strategies can help avoid brain drain from poorer countries.

The meeting confirmed that migrants who are socially and economically protected and empowered are likely to bring the greatest potential contributions to development back home and in the host country. This can be best achieved through policies that tie migration planning more to labour market planning; ensure decent, standard labour contracts; inform, orient and train the migrants; regulate recruiters, employers and other non-state agencies; address gender and family issues; and strengthen diaspora engagement with home country efforts.

New policies were explored, including on how to lower the often prohibitive up-front costs of migration, which can be higher than the back-end transaction costs of transferring remittances and can adversely affect the potential gains from migration. Some market-based solutions were offered and, beyond the July meeting, governments will study the efficacy of financial intermediation services offering affordable loans and credit to migrants to cover the costs of migrating. Circular migration was discussed as an innovative way to combine the interests of developed countries in meeting labour needs flexibly and legally with those of developing countries in entering richer labour markets and benefiting from the migrants' accumulated capital and skills, as well as the circulation of diaspora skills.

A number of concrete actions to follow up on these issues will be carried forward by teams of governments and expert agencies to the next GFMD meeting to be hosted by the Philippines Government in Manila in October 2008. See also the GFMD website at http://government.gfmd2008.org/ and GFMD, 2008.

Note:

[1] The three key Roundtable themes were "Human capital development and labour mobility", "Remittances and other diaspora resources" and "Policy and institutional coherence".

Source: *Irena Omelaniuk, Senior Adviser to the GFMD.*

Important as they are, these three major challenges cannot be considered in isolation from a wide range of very significant and sensitive cross-cutting issues, addressed in this Report not as separate topics but as matters informing the discussion wherever appropriate.

Foremost among them, and of immediate concern to both countries of origin and destination, are the human and labour rights and status of migrant workers. The issues to be addressed extend well beyond the unquestionably important formulation and implementation of minimum standards of protection. In a globalizing labour market, migrant workers seek to move across international borders in part because they have, at the very least, potentially competitive assets in terms of skills, wage expectations, and cultural attributes. The difficult challenge here is to have a policy regime that allows this competitive edge to be put to advantage and enables the realization of these assets, while precluding the "commodification" of migrant workers.

Separate from questions of rights proper, but closely related to them, are matters pertaining to the management of the interface between migrants and the host community. Once relatively homogenous and cohesive societies are increasingly characterized by multiple layers of social diversity and, in such contexts, policy issues such as assimilation, integration and multiculturalism, the fight against discrimination and xenophobia and the delicate question of entitlements to social benefits and services need to be revisited in the light of evolving migratory circumstances. Even very solidly grounded concepts such as citizenship invite fresh reflection in the light of trends towards dual citizenships and the phenomenon of transnationality. In such circumstances, it is no longer possible for countries of destination to simply pick off the shelf one of the policy models that has been used in the past. They face the challenge of having to keep their core values and social structures at the very least under review to achieve an effective equilibrium between the maintenance of national identities and adjustments in response to changing social dynamics often exacerbated by the arrival of permanent or temporary newcomers.

The management of security issues is another underlying, multifaceted policy issue of major interest. It is the sovereign prerogative of each country to determine who enters and remains in its territory, for what purpose and under what conditions. Open societies face the question of how to regulate and facilitate legitimate entry while protecting themselves from threats of international terrorism and criminality, including trafficking and smuggling in human beings. The problem is worldwide. According to one estimate, the irregular migrant contingent may constitute between 10 and 15 per cent of the total migrant population (ILO, 2004). However, given that the vast majority of irregular migrants either enter countries through unofficial channels and take up unauthorized residence and employment or lapse into irregularity after regular entry, this figure is impossible to verify on the strength of currently available official data. What is certain, however, is the vulnerability of irregular migrant workers to exploitation, victimization and abuse.

Often misused or misunderstood, the term "feminization of migration" points nonetheless to an important issue in contemporary migration. The proportion of women in global migratory flows has not fluctuated markedly over the last few decades, but their role in and impact on migratory processes have certainly changed. On the one hand, migration can empower women by giving them access to international employment opportunities, providing them with an independent income and enabling them to contribute to the welfare of their families through the remittances they send back home. On the other hand, as women and foreigners, they are often engaged in gender-segregated, low-skilled and often unregulated or informal sectors such as domestic/household services, and are therefore vulnerable to multiple forms of discrimination on the labour market and may have limited access to adequate social and health facilities (see Textbox Int. 3). There is therefore a clear need for the gender dimension to be factored into migration policy making.

Textbox Int. 3

Female Labour Migration and Gender Issues

About half of all migrant workers are now women, with more women migrating independently and as main income-earners rather than accompanying male relatives (Martin, 2005). Although women can be found in practically all professions, skilled women have tended to go into what can be broadly classified as the welfare and social professions (education, social work and health, particularly nursing) (Jolly and Reeves, 2005). At all skill levels, female labour migration is concentrated in occupations associated with traditional gender roles. Demand is increasing for care services in less-skilled and under valued jobs, such as domestic work and caring for children, the elderly and disabled persons. Many women migrant workers also hold jobs as contract and hotel cleaners, waitresses and in hospitality and entertainment industries (Moreno-Fontes Chammartin, 2006), while others are active in retail sales, in labour-intensive factory work such as the assembly of microelectronics or the manufacturing of clothing and textiles, and in the informal sectors. In many instances, women may replace male workers who have left to work in richer countries.

Migration can provide a vital source of income for migrant women and their families, and earn them increased autonomy, self-confidence and social status. At the same time, female migrants, especially if they are in an irregular situation, are doubly exposed to exploitation – as migrants and as women. In countries of origin and also in countries of destination, female migrants may be victims of negative attitudes about women working at all, attitudes that affect their right to leave the country without permission, to receive further education or training and to engage in certain occupations.

Globally, the ILO reports that the most frequently encountered issues regarding the working conditions of women migrant workers are low remuneration, heavy workloads with long working hours and inadequate rest periods, limited training facilities and poor career development. In some countries such workers also lack freedom of movement. Women migrant workers' jobs are normally located very low on the occupational ladder and are usually not, or only inadequately, covered by labour legislation or other social security or welfare provisions (ILO, 1999). The best example is domestic work, where protection is flimsy and psychological, physical and sexual abuse has frequently been noted (UNESCO, 2002). Female domestic workers may be required to undergo mandatory pregnancy tests and face immediate deportation if they are found to be pregnant (Engle, 2004; CARAM Asia, 2004). Domestic workers often experience inadequate healthcare or face denial of medical care and treatment. Those who seek help may find that agencies accuse them of refusing to work and of creating problems (Mughal and Padilla, 2005). Measures to protect such workers may have unintended and paradoxical consequences: for example, when the Bangladesh government placed a ban on female migration for domestic work with the objective of protecting the dignity of women abroad, many women continued to migrate through unofficial channels to fill the strong international demand for female domestic workers, thereby increasing their vulnerability (UN-INSTRAW and IOM, 2000).

Hew (2003) carried out a particularly interesting anthropological study of women workers and their families in Sarawak, Malaysia, interviewing 50 women who had migrated internally from rural to urban regions to work in the service sector (in restaurants and coffee shops, as domestic workers, cleaners, hotel housekeepers and at petrol pumps). The reasons they gave for migration were partly economic, but a major motivation was also "to become modern". Although their work was repetitive, dirty, "dead-end" and frequently involved shift-work, the women rarely complained: their main aim was to live in the city, to be independent, to send money home. Work was simply a means to accomplish this – they did not expect it to be fulfilling and were quite pragmatic about it. The women gravitated to gendered employment sectors, certainly because of discriminatory employment practices, but also partly because of their own images of what constituted appropriate and safe employment. They did not feel tyrannized by their employers or by oppressive employment practices.

Carling (2005) also uses the example of migration from the Philippines to protest against the "suffering and sacrifice" approach to gendered migration. For Filipina domestic workers in Italy, migration may provide a possibility to balance self-interest and self-sacrifice vis-à-vis their families: migration is an opportunity to see the world, to move away from rigid gender roles within the household and possibly to escape an unhappy marriage. He also elaborates on a global care chain in which female migrants are involved: women in rich countries pursuing professional employment need help to care for their families and households. The demand for domestic work is met by female migrants from developing countries such as the Philippines. In the home country, the migrant caregiver in turn hires a live-in domestic worker from a poorer, non-migrant family to care for her family during her absence, or turns to her mother or other family members for help, while the absence of the mother in the non-migrant family in turn creates a demand for the care for her own children – as she cannot afford to pay a domestic worker, that task is often taken on by an elder daughter while the mother is away.

Source: *Mary Haour-Knipe, Independent Advisor, Geneva, Switzerland.*

Finally, there is the question of migrant health that stems from the recognition that the expansion and diversification of population flows creates bridges between very diverse living and working environments. As modern transport and communication conquer physical distance, the international community moves towards a globalized community where health risks and benefits are to a certain degree shared. Inclusion of a migrant health dimension into public health systems is therefore increasingly becoming a priority for governments and health activists worldwide. Public health strategies now increasingly seek to address the issue of migrants' rights to health services; to adapt mainstream health services to the needs of culturally diverse populations in response to specific mobility-related medical challenges such as tuberculosis, HIV/AIDS or avian flu; and to provide information on health stresses and risks associated with migration. At the centre of all these preoccupations lies the need to better understand the changing physical and psychosocial health situations of individuals as they move through different stages of their migrant experience from preparation, through travel, arrival and adaptation to new work environments, and, finally, reinsertion into the home context on their return.

All of these challenges are being tackled ad hoc by the international community, but the need remains for **a broad and coherent global strategy to better match demand for migrant workers with supply in a safe, humane and orderly way**. *World Migration 2008* has been designed to gauge the nature and magnitude of that need and to canvass available policy responses.

Structure of the Report

This World Migration Report differs from preceding editions in some key aspects of construction and content. The first is the choice of a closer focus on economically-induced and especially employment-related movements; the second is a greater emphasis on **mobility**, incorporating a wider set of migratory behaviours than subsumed in **migration**, narrowly defined. The reasons for this should be obvious: in the past, migration has been predominantly linked to a type of movement leading to a permanent change of residence in another country. That association was so strongly felt that for the last third of the 20th century, certain countries were often described by their governments as being "migration" or "non-migration" spaces. Today, migratory behaviour, especially when it is employment-related, is acknowledged to be far more complex than implied by this all too simple classification. Shorter-term movement is now the choice of a very large number of workers. Multi-stage movement is another commonly exercised option, as migrants move from one location to another rather than staying at their initial point of arrival. Return migration to the country of origin is also much more frequent, as is the circular or pendular movement between two countries. It is also the case that many persons viewed administratively as students or visitors are in some instances indistinguishable from migrants. In the midst of all that diversity, traditional administrative distinctions continue to be maintained – for instance between those who have permanent or temporary visas, or between those who have authority to work and those who do not – but category-bridging or category-switching options are nonetheless often available.

Part A. The Worlds of Contemporary Mobility for Economic Purposes

Part A of the Report is an exploration of contemporary mobility, presented in the form of a mosaic of independent studies developed by specialist researchers invited to offer individual perspectives on different facets of economically-related mobility. While they are not identical in structure, in general terms they all deal with issues of definition, attempt to map out the magnitude and distribution of movements, address major issues that arise, discuss possible policy responses and identify priorities for further research.

All too often, the impact of globalization on labour mobility is studied and discussed from separate and isolated domestic and international perspectives, as though each of these two realms of work existed independently from the other. **Chapter 1** argues instead that workers, irrespective of their geographical location, are now living, by and large, in the same world of work, one offering a wide range of opportunities but, at the same time, characterized by increased competition and calls for greater flexibility in work practices. It looks at how the forces of globalization are changing the way enterprises do business, giving rise to more integrated labour markets and, consequently, creating demand for increased labour mobility. The chapter provides an overview of the forces that determine the nature and patterns of employment worldwide, especially the globalization of financial flows, trade and production. It considers how these dynamics affect employment in terms of both jobs and wages and goes on to look more closely at how international labour migration features in the global economy, as a strategic response to the demand for increased efficiency in production on the one hand, and, on the other, as an increasingly important contributing factor to the development of the economies in the South. Finally, the chapter discusses what might be meant by the concept of a "global labour market" and calls for greater attention to be given to the labour factor in theoretical studies on globalization and trade, to provide a clearer and stronger basis for decisions by policymakers.

While migrant workers are to be found in a wide range of employment sectors and at all skill levels, it is possible to discern some distinct patterns. Clustering is obvious at the extremes of the skills spectrum, with a strong, and officially recognized, demand for highly skilled migrants at the one end and a noticeable, but often officially ignored, demand for low or semi-skilled migrants at the other. **Chapter 2** surveys the first of these patterns. Highly skilled migrants appear on the migration scene in various guises. Most of them are permanent residents, but a growing number is admitted under various temporary migration schemes, which, in due course, may provide an opening to permanent residence status. At the same time, the foreign student population is increasingly seen as an attractive source of talent. The chapter outlines the major trends in highly skilled migration across the regions of the world, identifies the main geographical poles of attraction and lays out the different sets of policy issues facing the two major global constituencies, which are, respectively, the countries of origin and of destination. For countries of destination, the challenge is to beat the competition through the formulation of policies that will attract the "best and brightest" (Kapur and McHale, 2005). For their part, countries of origin feel the need to protect themselves against the loss of their highly skilled citizens and/or to secure their return or at least the return of the resources, both financial and in terms of skills, know-how and networks, acquired by their expatriates. In that connection, key policy options are canvassed and attention is drawn to the importance of bilateral and multilateral efforts.

The focus of **Chapter 3** is on the re-emergence of low and semi-skilled migration programmes – a seemingly surprising development considering the economic and socio-political problems that brought large-scale temporary worker programmes in both western Europe and the U.S. to an abrupt halt more than 30 years ago, but one which reflects the recognized need for foreign labour as spelled out above. While this type of movement occurs predominantly between developing and developed countries, it also affects a wide range of middle-income countries. The chapter maps out broad global distribution patterns before addressing the triple challenge of ensuring positive outcomes for countries of origin, countries of destination and for the migrants themselves. It argues that for "win-win-win" solutions to be achieved, policymakers must resolve problems of distortion, or unevenness, in labour supply, dependence or undue reliance on migrant labour, and address the difficult question of possible trade-offs between human rights and numbers. Carefully designed economic incentives may be a promising means to encourage employers and migrants to maintain programme integrity.

A distinction has long been made between permanent migration and short-term admission policies. Though these two categories are not necessarily mutually exclusive, the migration policies of countries of destination almost always distinguish between those who arrive with the intention of staying and becoming part of the host community and those who come with the main intention to study or to work for a limited period of time before returning to their country of origin. Chapters 4 and 5 focus on the often overlooked migratory objectives and itineraries of students and visitors and their increasingly felt impact on global employment trends.

Chapter 4 tracks patterns of student movements and policy developments since the 1990s, and highlights the shifts in both government motivations and the design of educational programmes during that period. Broad academic, political, cultural and development goals of an essentially humanitarian nature have not completely disappeared, but they are now overshadowed by sharper-edged economic objectives. Governments see their education programmes as a convenient and effective means for the subsequent recruitment of highly skilled migrants, while for foreign students they offer an entry to the international job market. The chapter outlines major trends in student mobility and discusses the underlying factors, while pointing to new forms of cross-border higher education offers where establishments or programmes move to meet the demands of student populations. The identification of four major strategies characterizing government policy stances that reflect the different motivations at work in this field (mutual understanding, skilled migration, income generation and capacity building) opens the way for an assessment of the increasingly close interplay between student mobility and migration policies and a discussion of the need for international cooperation and harmonization in this area of mobility.

In terms of sheer numbers, short-term travel, generally not exceeding 6 to 12 months, occurs on a much larger scale than for any other form of mobility, although this type of movement is not usually addressed in migration-related research and is, in fact, generally dealt with as an entirely separate policy category. **Chapter 5** sets out to investigate the complex, often overlooked bidirectional relationship between tourism and migration. It points out that many flows for leisure and business purposes are related to, or are inspired by, earlier migratory movements and that, in turn, tourist movements may, subject to certain conditions, lead to longer-term migration. More importantly, it reveals that, on closer inspection, short-term travel does have important ramifications for labour mobility and that governments are now inclined to see short-term travellers as possessing skills, experience and knowledge that can be put to good use in very flexible ways to meet temporary labour market needs – as in the case of the increasingly popular working holiday schemes. The movement of tourists can also affect employment opportunities and practices of countries of destination in different ways, a point that is illustrated by the reference to medical tourism.

Family-related migration in all its diverse forms has often been a major component of migration intakes. It has long been a dominant mode of entry in many countries of destination, especially in traditional countries of immigration such as Australia, Canada and the United States and, more recently, the European Union. It is all the more surprising, therefore, that family migration has been relatively ignored by academics and policymakers. **Chapter 6** begins by considering the reasons why family migration has traditionally played a marginal role in international migration research and flags recent developments that have generated more interest in the role of families in migration. A survey of the trends and types of contemporary migration then provides a platform for the discussion of both international conventions concerning the right to family life and national developments in family migration policy, as part of the wider context of comprehensive approaches to migration management. The chapter points out that the sharp distinction that is all too easily made between socially oriented family reunion programmes and economically induced labour migration programmes is often misleading. It argues that there is a need to acknowledge the labour force participation of family migrants and to reconsider the outdated perception of the woman and dependent family migrant with little personal interest or possibility to work.

A great deal of labour migration occurs not across but within national boundaries. Such movements are perhaps easily overlooked when the focus of discussion is on **international** migration, but can hardly be ignored when the intention is to map out a comprehensive **global** picture. **Chapter 7** explains that the labour migration flows in many countries occur inside the country and, taken together with proximate cross-border flows, are far more important than outmigration to more distant destinations, both in terms of the numbers of people involved and of the value of remittances they eventually send back home. This is especially true of countries with marked regional inequalities, but it is not limited to the developing world. Given the richness and complexity of the topic, the chapter focuses on five issues of current academic and policy interest: the rising incidence of such internal movement; the impact of internal remittance flows on development; the migration of women, children and ethnic minorities, and the resulting segmentation of migrant labour markets; links between international and internal migration; and irregular cross-border migration. Finally, the chapter offers an analysis of emerging policy strategies in this relatively new sector of migration management, with particular reference to those that are directed to the management of patterns of supply and demand and those that focus on support to and protection of internal migrants.

Chapter 8 deals with the paradoxical world of irregular migrants, who may be invisible in administrative terms and often absent from official statistics, but who are a prominent and sensitive topic in the political debate. They operate at the edge or outside the limits of formal labour markets, but often become an established feature of the economy, although opinion is divided as to whether they contribute to or detract from the health of the economy. Given its clandestine nature, irregular migration is hard to describe or define, but an attempt is nonetheless made to clarify the language used in reference to it and to draw attention to the many types of movements involved, including migrant smuggling and trafficking in human beings. The focus of attention falls next on its many interrelated economic and social determinants and on the complex trends and patterns of irregular migratory activities around the globe. The chapter reviews and assesses policy approaches used to respond to irregular migration, including control-oriented solutions, prevention through development in countries of origin, repatriation and return mechanisms and regularization programmes, highlighting throughout the necessity of partnerships in any action between countries of origin, transit and destination.

Part B: Managing Labour Mobility in the Evolving Global Economy

Part B of the Report consists of six chapters that complement the analyses presented in Part A by outlining and discussing broad policy strategies that can contribute to the effective and appropriate management of contemporary labour mobility.

Migration management is a policy domain where both policymakers and researchers decry the lack of up-to-date, comprehensive and comparable data, especially in relation to employment-related movements. **Chapter 9** outlines the case for the development of a comprehensive knowledge base as a prerequisite for the formulation of effective and transparent policies at the national level. Attention is first of all drawn to the diverse needs for reliable data of officials working at different levels in public administrations, before discussing the most commonly available and useful data sources. Their relative advantages and limitations as well as the ways and means of improving overall data accuracy and reliability are discussed. Given the changing nature of migratory phenomena and related issues, the chapter identifies several policy areas that invite fresh attention, including transnational communities, return and circular migration, and remittances. A final section deals with the importance of establishing appropriate bridging mechanisms between research and policy making.

Chapters 10 and 11 are complementary units. **Chapter 10** focuses on the elaboration of effective foreign employment policies and their integration within the human resource development strategies of countries of origin. While job creation at home remains their first priority, an increasing number of countries of origin find it attractive to complement this strategy by seeking opportunities for their workers on the international labour market. The chapter argues that this can be best made to work within the context of a carefully planned approach to human resource development. An examination of a number of basic policy tools, including quality standards and indicators, and facilities for both formal and informal training, leads to a detailed discussion of the constituent elements of an optimally functioning foreign employment policy framework covering, inter alia, the regulation of private recruitment agencies, the protection of workers, the provision of support services, including the dissemination of accurate and authoritative information, marketing techniques, administrative structures and international cooperation. In relation to this last point, emphasis is placed on the important role that can be played by Regional Consultative Processes.

Chapter 11 offers a complementary perspective from the standpoint of countries of destination. It discusses various options to balance the facilitation of regular migration with the prevention and reduction of irregular migration within a managed migration programme. Given the importance of cross-border movements for the purpose of employment, the development of appropriate policies in countries of destination is widely acknowledged as a key component in a comprehensive framework for the management of international labour mobility. However, there is no "one-size-fits-all" formula. The challenge for each country of destination is to develop a planned and predictable labour migration policy that will also be sufficiently flexible to contribute to its workforce requirements. The chapter reviews the key policy issues confronting countries of destination in this area. It then identifies elements of good practice to achieve specific goals pertaining to needs assessment, the design of foreign labour admission policies, in respect of both temporary labour migration and employment-based immigration, and post-admission policies, including labour market regulation and protection, migrant worker rights and responsibilities, the economic and social integration of newcomers and the maintenance of social cohesion. Policies aimed at the prevention and management of irregular migration receive separate treatment. The chapter concludes with an overview of means of productive cooperation and partnership among countries of origin, transit and destination as well as with other stakeholders.

There is, arguably, no migration-related policy issue that currently attracts more political and academic scrutiny than the migration and development relationship. It is, however, all too often the case that the locus of investigation is drawn much too narrowly around the impact and value of financial remittances. **Chapter 12** offers a much broader perspective to the reader. It lays out, first of all, the elements of a framework for the appraisal of the varying impacts migration can have on economic growth when it is tied to the history of a country's emigration experience, from the time of initial outflows through periods of adjustment, consolidation, networking and eventual return. This analytical grid is then used as a reference to meaningfully address the manner in which countries of destination can contribute effectively to global development through targeted interventions aimed at the orderly recruitment of workers, mitigating the brain drain, and the facilitation of the transfer and mobilization of remittances. The chapter goes on to consider, in a similar manner, the policies countries of origin can formulate and implement to maximize the developmental impact of migratory flows, including through sound macroeconomic policies, the encouraging and support of higher education, investment in infrastructure and participation in bilateral and regional labour migration initiatives. On account of the aggregate financial resources at their disposal, the skills they possess and the information they hold, migrant diaspora networks are seen as potentially important agents and a valuable resource for the realization of such processes.

The focus of **Chapter 13** is on international cooperation. It provides an overview of the principal modes of cooperation on issues related to labour mobility that may take place in both formal and less formal settings at the bilateral, regional and global level. The chapter examines the means of cooperation found in applicable human rights and labour law instruments adopted under the auspices of the United Nations and the International Labour Organization (ILO), and in the multilateral agreements regulating international trade, such as the commitments entered into on the movement of natural persons in the context of service provision under GATS Mode 4 (see Textbox Int. 1). Binding arrangements at the regional and bilateral levels include regimes for the free movement of persons, such as exist in the European Union, and the temporary labour migration agreements concluded between countries of origin and destination. Informal dialogue mechanisms, such as the Global Forum on Migration and Development (GFMD) and the Regional Consultative Processes referred to earlier, as well as IOM's International Dialogue on Migration (IDM), also form an important part of the chapter.

Finally, **Chapter 14** offers a number of concluding observations on the essential features of the contemporary migratory landscape surveyed in this Report, and of the broad policy strategies that could contribute to international efforts to realize the social and economic potential of international labour mobility. These can be summarized in ten brief points:

1. In its many and varied forms, human mobility within and across borders is one of the characteristic and perhaps even defining features of our contemporary world. To a large extent, it is both part and consequence of the complex and interacting social and economic processes involved in the phenomenon of globalization.
2. People seek to move for a large number of personal, family, social, business or work reasons, often in varying combinations,[6] but the opportunities to move are frequently limited, particularly for low and semi-skilled workers.
3. In view of the choices made by the international community to facilitate the movement of capital, goods and services, human mobility or, more specifically, the movement of human resources, at all skill levels, is now being increasingly factored into the equations intended to yield new economic gains. In other words, labour market dynamics are increasingly operating across international borders.
4. The policy implications of this steadily evolving situation are yet to be fully understood, but it is already apparent that avoiding the issue, ignoring this trend or a passive laissez-faire approach are unlikely to lead to the policy stances needed to realize the social and economic potential of mobility.
5. What is required, therefore, are planned and predictable ways of matching demand with supply in a safe, legal, humane and orderly manner. Given the diversity of labour market needs and of available skills, policies and procedures will have to display commensurate flexibility and adaptability to enable modes of labour mobility that may be short-term, circular, long-term or permanent.
6. Countries of origin and destination are increasingly engaged in the formulation of policies to meet their particular labour mobility objectives, namely, to train and prepare migrant workers for employment abroad on the one hand, and to identify labour market needs and seek recruitment of appropriate personnel on the other. Optimal outcomes will be achieved when the two sets of policies are complementary and mutually supportive elements of a coherent whole, directed towards the achievement of mutual development goals. To be successful, more cooperative approaches to human resource development are needed to meet national, regional and global objectives. Policies and appropriate means are needed as well to secure the participation in this shared endeavour of non-state stakeholders, including employers, recruitment agencies, trade unions, migrant and disapora associations, and relevant inter-governmental organizations.
7. This pleads for the identification and development of clear linkages between the domains of migration proper and those of development, employment and trade within the broader framework of established global economic interests.
8. To reach that objective, the international community requires a common and accurate understanding of the many important issues at stake, including economic growth, managing social change while maintaining cohesion, upholding social justice and the protection of the human rights of the workers concerned, the pursuit of which amply justify the maintenance and further development of consultations and cooperation at regional and global levels.
9. A closely related need is the enhancement of global, regional and national knowledge of labour market trends, labour force profiles and labour migration trends through the establishment of appropriate databases and analytical work.
10. Of relevance to all of the above is the recognition of capacity-building requirements of all governments, in particular those of

[6] The focus here is on movements that are essentially voluntary, but there are obviously persons who are forced to move and for whom there is an established international protection regime.

developing countries, to assess the levels of need, formulate policy and legislation, improve labour migration and related human resource development programmes through experimentation and innovation, and to monitor and evaluate outcomes.

A new spirit of partnership in outlook and action is both possible and essential to realizing beneficial outcomes for the international community as a whole, including countries of origin, countries of destination and migrants and their families.

REFERENCES

Global Commission on International Migration (GCIM)

2005 *Migration in an Interconnected World: New directions for action*, Report of the GCIM, October, SRO-Kundig, Geneva, http://www.gcim.org/attachements/gcim-complete-report-2005.pdf.

Global Forum on Migration and Development (GFMD)

2008 *Report of the first meeting of the Global Forum on Migration and Development*, Belgium, 9-11 July, Bruylant, Brussels.

International Labour Organization (ILO)

2004 *Towards a Fair Deal for Migrant Workers in the Global Economy*, Report VI, International Labour Conference, 92nd Session, International Labour Office, Geneva, http://www.ilo.org/public/english/standards/relm/ilc/ilc92/pdf/rep-vi.pdf.

International Organization for Migration (IOM)

2003 *World Migration 2003: Managing Migration - Challenges and Responses for People on the Move*, IOM, Geneva, http://www.iom.int/jahia/Jahia/cache/offonce/pid/1674?entryId=4992.

2005 *World Migration 2005: Costs and Benefits of International Migration*, IOM, Geneva, http://www.iom.int/jahia/Jahia/cache/offonce/pid/1674?entryId=932.

Kapur, D. and J. McHale

2005 *Give us your Best and Brightest: The Global Hunt for Talent and its Impact on the Developing World*, Center for Global Development, Washington, D.C., http://www.cgdev.org/content/publications/detail/4415.

Katseli, L., D. Papademetriou, J. Dayton-Johnson, G. Maniatis and R. Münz

2007 *Gaining from Migration: Proposals for Managing a New Mobility System*, Final Report, March, Organisation for Economic Co-operation and Development (OECD), Paris.

Lawson, S., R. Purushothawan and S. Schels

2004 *Making the most of Global Migration*, Global Economics Paper No. 115, Goldman Sachs.

Pritchett, L.

2006 *Let Their People Come: Breaking the Gridlock on Global Labour Mobility*, Center for Global Development, Washington D.C., http://www.cgdev.org/content/publications/detail/10174.

Ratha, D., S. Mohapatra, K.M. Vijayalakshmi and Z. Xu

2008 *Revisions to Remittance Trends 2007*, Migration and Development Brief 5, July 10, Migration and Remittances Team, Development Prospects Group, World Bank, Washington, D.C., http://siteresources.worldbank.org/INTPROSPECTS/Resources/334934-1110315015165/MD_Brief5.pdf.

United Nations (UN)

2006 High-Level Dialogue on International Migration and Development, UN General Assembly, 14-15 September, New York, http://www.un.org/migration/statements.html.

UN Department of Economic and Social Affairs (UN DESA), Population Division

2002 *World Population Aging 1950-2050*, United Nations Department of Economic and Social Affairs (UN DESA), Population Division, New York, http://www.un.org/esa/population/publications/worldageing19502050/.

2004 *Trends in Total Migrant Stock: The 2003 Revision*, UN DESA, Population Division, New York.

2006 *World Migrant Stock: The 2005 Revision*, UN DESA, Population Division, New York, http://esa.un.org/migration/.

2007 *World Population Prospects: The 2006 Revision*, UN DESA, Population Division, New York, http://esa.un.org/unpp/.

United Nations High Commissioner for Refugees (UNHCR)

2002 *UNHCR Statistical Yearbook 2001: Refugees, Asylum-seekers and Other Persons of Concern – Trends in Displacement, Protection and Solutions*, October, UNHCR, Geneva, http://www.unhcr.org/home/STATISTICS/3dcb7f666.pdf.

2006 *Asylum Levels and Trends in Industrialized Countries, 2005*, 17 March, UNHCR, Geneva, http://www.unhcr.org/statistics/STATISTICS/44153f592.pdf.

2007 *2006 Global Trends: Refugees, Asylum-seekers, Returnees, Internally Displaced and Stateless Persons*, 16 July, UNHCR, Geneva, http://www.unhcr.org/statistics/STATISTICS/4676a71d4.pdf.

2008 *Asylum Levels and Trends in Industrialized Countries, 2007*, 18 March, UNHCR, Geneva, http://www.unhcr.org/statistics/STATISTICS/47daae862.pdf.

World Bank

2006 *Global Economic Prospects 2006: Economic Implications of Remittances and Migration*, World Bank, Washington D.C., http://www-wds.worldbank.org/external/default/WDSContentServer/IW3P/IB/2005/11/14/000112742_20051114174928/Rendered/PDF/343200GEP02006.pdf.

Textbox Int. 3 - Female Labour Migration and Gender Issues

Coordination of Action Research on AIDS and Mobility (CARAM) Asia

2004 *The Forgotten Spaces: Mobility and HIV Vulnerability in the Asia Pacific*, CARAM, Kuala Lumpur.

Carling, J.

2005 "Gender dimensions of international migration", GCIM, Global Migration Perspectives No. 35, May, Geneva, http://www.gcim.org/mm/File/GMP%20No%2035.pdf.

Engle, L.

2004 *The World in Motion; Short Essays on Migration and Gender*, IOM, Geneva.

Hew, C.S.

2003 *Women Workers, Migration and Family in Sarawak*, RoutledgeCurzon, London and New York.

International Labour Organization (ILO)

1999 *General Survey on Migrant Workers*, Report III (1B), International Labour Conference, 87th Session, June, International Labour Office, Geneva, http://www.ilo.org/public/english/standards/relm/ilc/ilc87/r3-1b.htm.

Jolly, S. and H. Reeves

2005 *Gender and Migration: Overview Report*, Institute of Development Studies, Brighton, U.K., http://www.bridge.ids.ac.uk/reports_gend_cep.html#migration.

Martin, S.

2005 *2004 World Survey on the Role of Women in Development: Women and International Migration*, UN DESA, Division for the Advancement of Women, New York.

Moreno-Fontes Chammartin, G.

2006 "Female Migrant Workers in an Era of Globalization" in *Female Migrants: Bridging the Gaps Throughout the Life Cycle*, Selected Papers of the United Nations Population Fund (UNFPA)-IOM Expert Group Meeting, 2-3 May, New York, 77-84, http://www.un.int/iom/final%20report%20Sept%202006.pdf.

Mughal, R. and L. Padilla

2005 "Regulatory Frameworks for Recruitment of Migrant Workers and Minimum Standards in Employment Contracts: A Comparative Study of Pakistan, the Philippines and Sri Lanka" in IOM, Department for International Development (DFID), U.K., Asian Development Bank (ADB), *Labour Migration in Asia*, Geneva, 13-83.

United Nations International Research and Training Institute for the Advancement of Women (UN-INSTRAW) and International Organization for Migration (IOM)

2000 *Temporary Labour Migration of Women: Case Studies of Bangladesh and Sri Lanka*, UN-INSTRAW/IOM, INSTRAW/Ser.A/47, http://www.un-instraw.org/en/downloads/final-reports/index.php.

PART A

THE WORLDS OF CONTEMPORARY MOBILITY FOR ECONOMIC PURPOSES

INTERNATIONAL LABOUR MOBILITY IN THE EVOLVING GLOBAL LABOUR MARKET*

CHAPTER 1

1. Introduction

The aim of this chapter is to place the debate on international labour mobility within the wider context of the impact of globalization on employment. All too often the discussion on globalization deals with the impact it has on economic growth and employment in the domestic labour markets of developed and developing countries without also considering how it might be affected by, or have an impact on, international migration.

Addressing the issue of the impacts of globalization on the domestic aspects of employment in isolation from its effects on the international dimensions is particularly unfortunate for two reasons. Firstly, both globalization and migration are areas generating considerable interest and passion, with a wide gap between public understanding of the issues involved, policy positions and academic research. Consequently, public opinion often focuses on the phenomenon of deteriorating job opportunities and labour conditions along a developing/developed world dividing line. Labour movements at the global level are often wrongly perceived by the public as a zero sum game, where the gain of one is the loss of the other, with only winners and losers. For example, it is assumed that workers from developing countries can only gain at the expense of their developed country counterparts through the transfer of either jobs or workers. Secondly, while there has been a recent impetus from international organizations and researchers focusing on development to include migration considerations in their work on the impact of globalization on labour, inequalities and poverty, the general inclination among many policymakers is still to treat labour migration and employment as two separate issues, a position reflected in the insufficient integration of migration issues in national and regional labour market policies.[1]

This chapter looks at how the driving forces of globalization have affected the way enterprises do business and created more integrated labour markets. It observes that workers, independently of their location, now find themselves in situations

* This chapter was written by Sophie Nonnenmacher, Migration Policy Specialist, Migration Policy, Research and Communications, IOM, Geneva.

[1] For some labour market analysts, migration is simply an expression of distortions in the domestic labour market that need to be addressed through appropriate labour market policies resulting, in due course, in the suppression of migratory flows. This argument ignores the existence of pull factors such as wage differentials, or non-economic related factors such as the social networks that play an important role in the decision to seek job opportunities abroad.

characterized by increasing competition and flexibility, but equally offering an unprecedented range of job opportunities with mobility emerging as an important career and skill development strategy. The costs and benefits of this new environment and the opportunities for better jobs and mobility have not been evenly shared either between or within countries. To date, the main beneficiaries have been persons endowed with capital and/or needed skills.[2] However, policymakers are increasingly faced with the challenge of managing the mobility of labour contingents of varying skills profiles.

The first part of the chapter provides an overview of the forces driving employment worldwide, namely the globalization of trade, financial flows and production. The next section examines how these trends affect employment in terms of both jobs and wages. The third section looks more specifically at how international labour migration features in the global economy as a response to changes in employment opportunities, as well as a contributor to the growth of economies in the developing world. Finally, the chapter discusses the meaning and significance of a "global labour market", calls for a stronger focus on the labour factor in globalization and trade analysis to better inform policymaking, and suggests some directions for the development of strategic approaches that would reduce the risks and maximize the beneficial impacts of globalization on international labour mobility.

[2] It is commonly accepted that globalization places a premium on skills, with more open markets leading to increased demand for skills where new capital is invested, or to support technological development/innovation. Skills act as an incentive for foreign direct investment (FDI), while increased FDI also raises the demand for skilled labour. According to the International Monetary Fund Balance of Payments Manual (BPM), "FDI refers to an investment made to acquire lasting interest in enterprises operating outside of the economy of the investor. Further, in cases of FDI, the investor's purpose is to gain an effective voice in the management of the enterprise. ... Some degree of equity ownership is almost always considered to be associated with an effective voice in the management of an enterprise; the BPM suggests a threshold of 10 per cent of equity ownership to qualify an investor as a foreign direct investor". See UNCTAD's website at http://www.unctad.org/Templates/Page.asp?intItemID=3146&lang=1.

2. Globalization and its Key Drivers

2.1 What is Globalization?

Globalization entered the common vocabulary in the 1980s. Although there have been other peaks of intense global interaction in the past (see Textbox 1.1), the current manifestations of globalization are often considered to have more far-reaching consequences and impacts. In its broadest sense, globalization refers to a multitude of interactions and growing interdependence among governments, organizations, businesses and people across the world. These processes are very diverse in nature and encompass a wide array of social, cultural, technological and political developments, but in this chapter the focus is on **economic globalization** and, in particular, its implications for international labour mobility.

Three key determinants are considered to be of crucial importance in the globalization of economic endeavours: movements of capital; international trade or the exchange of goods and services; and the production of these goods and services. The theories mapping out and interpreting the relationships among these determinants, as well as their current and potential impact on labour markets and migration, are as diverse in their conclusions as they are numerous.[3] However, the core of conventional trade theory supporting the free movement of mobile factors of production (i.e. labour, capital) rests on the factor proportions model of the Heckscher-Ohlin theory and its extensions. It is based on the idea of countries gaining from specializing in the production of certain goods depending on the available factors of production (including a non-mobile factor: land) and their best use. Trade liberalization is promoted as a means of maximizing global economic welfare in

[3] They nonetheless recognize that the relationship of these three key determinants with a non-uniform (in terms of income, exploitation and opportunities, etc.) global labour market is a major driver of change in the world of work.

Textbox 1.1

Three Waves of Globalization

Three waves of globalization have been identified. The **first wave** took place between 1870 and 1914 and was triggered by a combination of falling transport costs and a reduction in tariff barriers. It opened up the possibility of using abundant land and resulted in the intensive production and export of primary commodities. People immigrated to land-abundant countries such as Argentina, Australia, New Zealand and the United States, and capital was invested in manufacturing in those countries. The **second wave** of globalization lasted from 1950 to 1980 following the Second World War. Transport costs continued to fall and, by 1980, trade in manufactured goods between developed countries was essentially free of barriers. However, barriers facing developing countries were removed only for those primary commodities that did not compete with agricultural goods in developed countries. Most developing countries still had trade barriers in place, and agglomeration economies (country specialization from agglomerated clusters) existed in manufacturing production in developed countries. There was also a redistribution of manufacturing within developed countries to lower-wage areas. The **third and current wave** of globalization began in 1980. Many developing countries changed their policies and broke into global markets for the first time (including Bangladesh, China, India, Indonesia, Mexico, Morocco, Philippines, Sri Lanka and Turkey) thus making globalization truly more "global". Transport costs continued to fall and this wave has been characterized by the development of information technology.

***Sources**: Various. See for example World Bank (2002; Ch. 1: "The New Wave of Globalization and Its Economic Effects").*

accordance with the theory of comparative advantage and specialization in the most cost-efficient production of traded goods.[4] This assumption concerning the benefits of free trade is extended to capital and labour where, it is argued, higher gains could be obtained if free movement were allowed.[5]

Globalization occurs because of the possibility of freer movement of various commodities, resources and goods and the existence of these freer flows leads to further globalization of the world economy.[6] These free movements or their absence are reflections of technological, social and economic realities as well of legal frameworks regulating them at national, regional and global levels.

The general trends apparent in each of these domains are examined before addressing their impact on labour.

2.2 Globalization and Trade

World trade has expanded significantly since 1960 with global exports growing from just under USD 1 trillion a year to about USD 10 trillion, an average annual growth of some 5.5 per cent. During that period, global exports also grew significantly faster than global output – or gross world product – which grew by some 3.1 per cent per year. While in 2006 the GDP growth rate in high-income economies was 3.1 per cent, it grew by seven per cent in developing countries.[7] Although developing countries generate only 22 per cent of global GDP, they account for 38 per cent of the increase in global output (World Bank, 2007).

The share of exports relative to global output has more than doubled since 1970 to stand at over 25 per cent. This increase is due to economic reforms that followed the collapse of the former Soviet Union, the opening up of the Chinese and Indian economies and, more generally, trade liberalization occurring within the framework of the World Trade Organization (WTO) and the proliferation of regional trade agreements.

[4] Resulting in the production of goods at a lower cost and sold at a lower price for the benefit of selling and buying countries, and consumers.

[5] For a recent review of trade theories and employment, see Jansen and Lee (2007).

[6] Free movement should not be understood solely in terms of physical crossing of geographical borders and territories (e.g. of wine bottles from France to the U.S.), as some important movements are virtual and invisible (e.g. movement of information, money transfers, etc.).

[7] But only 5.5 per cent when China and India are excluded.

The composition of global merchandise exports has also changed with trade in manufactured goods and related employment fields exceeding growth in primary goods (e.g. fuel, food).

World exports in trade in services reached USD 2,009 billion in 2004, while the share of service exports as a proportion of total exports of goods and services stood at 17.5 per cent. For developing countries, the growth of service exports as a share of GDP rose from two per cent in 1984 (USD 54 billion) to 4.7 per cent (USD 400 billion) in 2004, with the countries in East Asia, the Pacific, Europe and Central Asia the main contributors (World Bank, 2007).

Though, in the past, trade expansion mainly benefited developed countries and only a number of developing countries[8] (World Commission on the Social Dimension of Globalization, 2004), future trade expansion is projected to benefit developing countries more significantly with the result that, by 2030, they will account for nearly one-third of global output (as compared to one-fifth today) (World Bank, 2007).

2.3 Globalization and Capital

Globalization is also fuelled by foreign direct investment (FDI), which has accelerated since 1980 to reach USD 916 billion in 2005, with 36 per cent directed to, and 13 per cent originating in, developing countries (UNCTAD, 2006). FDI flows to Africa amounted to USD 31 billion in 2005 (3% of global FDI), although much of it was concentrated in only some countries (with South Africa attracting the bulk of these inflows) and in certain sectors, mainly natural resources and banking. In South, East and Southeast Asia, FDI inflows accounted for 18 per cent of global FDI inflows. According to UNCTAD (2006), the top developing recipients are Brazil, China, Hong Kong SAR, Mexico and Singapore.

The job-creating potential of FDI is one of the main reasons governments seek to attract transnational corporations (TNCs).[9] Measures to attract them range from reducing control of inward financial flows and the repatriation of profits, to the establishment of Export Processing Zones (EPZs).[10] TNCs are at the origin of approximately 10 per cent of international investment (gross capital formation). TNCs located in developed countries generate the largest share of global FDI, although TNCs from developing and transition economies are also increasingly investing abroad. FDI flows from the latter play an important role in many least developed countries (LDCs), amounting to more than 40 per cent of total FDI in some of them (e.g. FDI from South Africa accounts for more than 50 per cent of FDI flows to Botswana, the Democratic Republic of the Congo, Lesotho and Malawi (UNCTAD, 2006). However, FDI between developing economies remains primarily within the region.

While FDI for the creation of new assets (or greenfield FDI[11]) was for long the privileged method to enter a foreign market, cross-border mergers and acquisitions,[12] or the utilization of existing assets, have also increased in significance to achieve the same goal, reaching USD 716 billion in 2005 (an 88 per cent increase over 2004) (UNCTAD, 2006).

---

8 The developing countries that were successful are those that managed to move away from primary commodity exports to manufactured exports.

9 "Transnational corporations (TNCs) are incorporated or unincorporated enterprises comprising parent enterprises and their foreign affiliates. A parent enterprise is defined as an enterprise that controls assets of other entities in countries other than its home country, usually by owning a certain equity capital stake". See UNCTAD's website at http://www.unctad.org/Templates/Page.asp?intItemID=3148&lang=1.

10 Export Processing Zones (EPZs), as defined by ILO, are industrial zones with special incentives set up to attract foreign investors in which imported materials undergo some degree of processing before being re-exported. See http://www.oit.org/public/english/dialogue/sector/themes/epz/epzs.htm.

11 Greenfield FDI refers to investment projects that entail the establishment of new production facilities, such as offices, buildings, plants and factories, as well as the movement of intangible capital (mainly in services) (UNCTAD, 2006).

12 Cross-border M&As involve the partial or full takeover or the merging of capital, assets and liabilities of existing enterprises in a country by TNCs from other countries. The impact of M&As on employment will depend on the motivation behind them, leading either to expansion (potential creation of jobs) or rationalization (potential loss of jobs).

Foreign portfolio investments[13] have also accelerated globally and contributed to the financing of local companies. However, compared to FDI, these flows are rather more volatile and short-term and can have a negative impact on exchange and interest rates as, for example, in the financial crises in Mexico in 1994-1995, in Asia in 1997-1998 and in Argentina in 2001-2002.

The actors behind portfolio investments, investment firms or collective investment institutions and schemes, including private equity firms and various investment funds (e.g. mutual funds, hedge funds and similar constructs), have recently become major sources of FDI.[14] Indeed, while their engagement is generally of a more short-term nature, some of these funds manage their investments over a longer period thus acquiring some of the characteristics of FDI and blurring further the distinction between the different investment tools. Private equity-financed FDI (which is generally longer-term than FDI from hedge funds) was estimated to amount to at least USD 135 billion in 2005 (UNCTAD, 2006).[15]

2.4 Globalization and the Production of Goods and Services

While the impacts of the liberalization of the flows of capital, goods and services have been profound, according to Castells (1996: 92), what makes contemporary globalization really different from previous efforts at the internationalization of economies is the possibility "to work as a unit, in real time, on **a planetary scale**".[16] This includes the development of means of communication, and technologies underlying modern production and distribution at the global level. Cheaper and faster communications facilitate economic transactions around the world, while policy decisions to reduce the barriers for such transactions were a pre-condition for the emergence of globalization processes.

Globalization, in other words, has resulted in new ways of connecting workers, producers and consumers. "The network enterprise is a unit of business operations made up of different companies or segments of companies, as well as consultant and temporary workers attached to specific projects" (ILO, 2007: 10). Large companies, especially multinationals, rely on vast networks of suppliers and engage in strategic alliances with other companies in specific processes or product lines. This encourages the development of a diversity of contractual arrangements between labour and capital (ILO, 2007). The number of long-term employees decreases while that of workers under alternative employment arrangements increases, with the result that labour relations are increasingly characterized by flexibility and the individualization of labour conditions and labour contracts.[17]

(a) The global assembly line for goods

Production and delivery services are undergoing profound changes through the adoption of flexible, real-time production systems, where production is organized to respond rapidly to market stimuli with limited inventories; at the same time, production is located as closely as possible to the local market and consumer.[18]

[13] These are distinguished from FDI by the degree to which foreign investors exercise management control in a company. Portfolio investors' involvement is financial while direct investors have a more long-term and management interest in the company in which they invest. Portfolio investments comprise the acquisition of financial assets, including stocks, bonds, deposits and currencies.

[14] When cross-border investments of private equity and hedge funds exceed the 10 per cent equity threshold of the acquired firm, they are classified, according to the IMF Balance of Payments Manual (BPM), as FDI.

[15] While the sum of worldwide gross private capital flows (the sum of absolute values of foreign direct, portfolio and other investment inflows and outflows) since 1990 represent more than 20 per cent of world GDP, this did not necessarily translate into an increase in investment in infrastructure and productive capacity in the world (ILO, 2006b).

[16] Emphasis added.

[17] Flexible forms of work also pose new challenges for social security systems in determining entitlement to benefits as workers move in and out of employment, work for different enterprises with fluctuating working hours, and in a variety of different work arrangements. Similarly, the rise in self-employment creates conditions in which workers may be exempted from many provisions of labour legislation, including limits on maximum working hours.

[18] Whereas previously businesses introduced their goods into a market through exports, today they use FDI to produce directly the goods in the target country.

Computer-based information systems have been instrumental in the development of flexible production methods (e.g. computer-integrated manufacturing)[19] and, more broadly, facilitated the management of companies with units located around the world. Reductions in the costs of transport and telecommunications and the lowering of trade and FDI barriers have also contributed to the emergence of global chains of production taking advantage of lower labour and material costs and more favourable policy environments.

According to this scheme, the production process of goods is divided and each segment located where it can be carried out most efficiently and at minimum cost. A considerable proportion of employment in manufacturing has thus been relocated to low-wage countries, including to Export Processing Zones (EPZs), creating job opportunities that often attract low-skilled workers, including women, from rural to urban areas.

The strategy of "outward processing for reverse importing" is, at least in part, responsible for the transformation of corporate structures and activities. Some companies send materials, components and supplies for processing or assembly abroad for which, when returned, duty will be charged only on the value added abroad. This approach has been widely adopted by developed countries, especially in the textile and electronic industries, and has helped secure an important share of import business in the U.S. and the European Union.

While the share of the industry sector (mainly composed of manufacturing processes) remains at about 21 per cent of total global employment, reflecting a decrease in developed countries and an increase in developing countries, total global employment in industry rose by 83 million between 1995 and 2005, half of which occurred in East and Southeast Asia (ILO, 2006b).

(b) Global resourcing of services

Offshoring or outsourcing of services to lower-wage locations is a recent phenomenon that has been encouraged (as with manufacturing) by lower telecommunication costs, as well as by decreased risks in locating services in developing countries (e.g. by the introduction of intellectual property protection measures).

The McKinsey Global Institute (2005: 14) defines "global resourcing"[20] as the "process a company goes through to decide which of its activities could be performed anywhere in the world, where to locate them and who will do them". According to the McKinsey study (2005), offshoring of services to emerging markets was expected to grow at 30 per cent annually between 2003 and 2008. It argued further that, in 2008, 11 per cent of worldwide services employment (160 million jobs) could in theory be performed by people located anywhere in the world (undertaken, for instance, by engineers, finance professionals, accountants and analysts). However, it is estimated that, in practice, companies will offshore far fewer jobs, growing from 565,000 to 1.2 million for the eight sectors of the economy covered by the study.[21]

Global resourcing can have positive outcomes for developed and developing countries through reduced costs, repatriated profits and new markets for home country goods and services. Indeed, the McKinsey

[19] A computer-automated system in which individual engineering, production, marketing and support functions of a manufacturing enterprise are organized; functional areas such as design, analysis, planning, purchasing, cost accounting, inventory control and distribution are linked through the computer with factory floor functions such as materials handling and management, providing direct control and monitoring of all process operations.

[20] "Global resourcing", "offshoring", "international outsourcing" are terms often used interchangeably when referring to the transfer of services operations or production processes to a foreign country.

[21] Automotive services, health care, insurance, IT services, packaged software, pharmaceutical products, retail and retail banking.

Global Institute (2003) estimated that for one dollar spent on outsourcing, the U.S. economy gained USD 1.12 to 1.14, while the foreign host country received USD 0.33.

(c) The role of TNCs

The globalization of production is largely carried out by TNCs. According to UNCTAD's 2006 World Investment Report, *FDI from Developing and Transition Economies: Implications for Development*, the EU, Japan and the U.S. still host most of the world's dominant TNCs. However, more than 20,000 TNCs have their headquarters in developing countries and there is a growing and significant presence of FDI by firms from developing and transition economies. Significant differences exist nonetheless between the top TNCs from the developing and developed world, with the former in general having fewer foreign assets and a less extended global outreach and presence.

In 2005, TNCs generated USD 4.5 trillion in added value, employed some 62 million workers and exported goods and services valued at more than USD 4 trillion (UNCTAD, 2006). Three per cent of global trade is intra-firm. TNCs have not only played an important role in directing FDI flows, but also contribute to more labour market openness. Specifically, the internationalization of the activities of firms for the production of goods and services is accompanied by increased international mobility of their workers among branches in different countries to perform services or undertake business visits abroad.[22]

3. Impact of Globalization on Employment

Starting with some key global figures on employment in 2005 (see Textbox 1.2), this section examines the impact of globalization on wages and job security, the way the structure of economies are modified and the predominance of certain economic sectors, and the repercussions on the movement of jobs (offshoring) and workers (labour migration).

22 For the link between business visits abroad and labour mobility, see Chapter 5.

Textbox 1.2

Some Key Figures on Employment in 2005

- **The global labour force[1] comprised over three billion workers.** Of these, 84 per cent lived in the developing countries of Asia and the Pacific region, Africa, Latin America and the Caribbean, as well as the transition countries of the Commonwealth of Independent States (CIS) and south-eastern Europe (ILO, 2006b).
- **Women represented around 40 per cent of the world's labour force (1.22 billion).**
- **2.85 billion individuals aged 15 and above were employed.** However, about half did not earn enough to raise themselves above the poverty line of two U.S. dollars a day. These figures are the same as those of ten years ago. Agriculture had the highest employment share (40.1%)[2] as compared to industry (21%) and services (38.9%) (ILO, 2006a).
- **The global unemployment rate was 6.3 per cent** (ILO, 2006a), affecting some 191.8 million people,[3] with young persons accounting for approximately half of the unemployed, a relatively high proportion given that they represented only 25 per cent of the total working age population (ILO, 2006a).
- **86 million persons were identified as migrant workers** (ILO, 2006c).
- **TNCs** comprised 77,000 parent companies with over 770,000 foreign affiliates, the latter **employing some 62 million workers** (UNCTAD, 2006).

- **66 million workers were employed in Export Processing Zones (EPZs)**,[4] mainly women. (Singa Boyenge, 2007).
- **565,000 jobs were offshore** (Farrell et al., 2005).

Notes:

1 The "labour force" includes the portion of the population above 15 years of age, either working (employed) or looking for work (unemployed).

2 But there are important regional variations. While in the EU and the U.S. agriculture accounts for less than four per cent of the workforce, it accounts for 50 per cent in developing countries (ILO 2006b).

3 To be employed does not necessarily mean to have decent and productive work that would enable a person to sustain a living (see also Textbox 1.4).

4 See footnote 10 in this chapter for a definition of EPZs. The figure provided is for 2006.

3.1 Impact on Labour Markets in Terms of Wages, Job Security and Upgrading of Skills

In general, globalization has increased pressures on domestic labour markets in terms of wages, job security and the upgrading of skills for movement between jobs. Yet, end results are not always straightforward.

In broad terms, those who have benefited most are investors, entrepreneurs, managers and workers associated with internationally competitive national enterprises and TNCs. Workers with internationally sought after education, skills and managerial ability have been particularly advantaged. Conversely, workers in sectors previously protected by trade barriers, subsidized state enterprises, and small and medium enterprises (SMEs) that have not been able to adapt to the rapid liberalization of the economy have suffered the most through reduced job security, the relocalization of jobs or downward pressure on wages (World Bank, 2007).

The impact of globalization on employment will be amplified as more countries participate in the global economy and open their markets to international trade and capital flows. This effect will be particularly felt with the entry of large numbers of (mainly low-skilled) workers from China and India into the global labour force. By 2030, they are projected to account for 40 per cent of the global workforce.[23] Their entry will have an impact on manufacturing production and trade balances, with concerns already being expressed by other developing countries that they will struggle to attract investments and manufacturing enterprises given their less favourable general conditions (social, economic or political) and higher wage levels,[24] and that their domestic markets will import large quantities of goods from these two countries. On the other hand, while it is foreseen that China will dominate world trade, least developed countries (LDCs) might still be able to produce low-skill labour intensive products, as export growth in China and India is expected to raise wages as well as create the need for the import of intermediate inputs.

High-income countries, for their part, are conscious that the emerging Asian economies are increasingly characterized by high skills and modern technological know-how, a combination which will make them increasingly competitive in high-tech markets.[25]

23 The entry into the global workforce of workers from China, India and the former Soviet Union represents a doubling of the global labour force (Freeman, 2005).

24 For instance, the entry into the global workforce of lower-wage workers from China and India might negatively affect the jobs of low-skilled workers in higher wage developing countries. Wages in Peru, for example, are three times higher than in China (Freeman, 2006).

25 And therefore in competition with highly skilled workers in developed countries for performing high tech work.

3.2 Shifts in Employment Sectors and Internal Migration

Changes in economic priorities worldwide have led to a shift from agriculture-based economies to more diversified platforms of economic activity, accompanied by corresponding rural to urban migration.

While two-thirds of the world's poor rely on agriculture for their livelihoods, its share in total global employment is declining rapidly with manufacturing failing to compensate for this decline. Indeed, in all regions of the world, except East and Southeast Asia, employment growth in manufacturing is declining as well. In developing countries, workers leave agriculture to move into services and informal petty trading. In Africa and Latin America, this is the employment segment with the highest growth rates. Formal work is still rare in developing countries, with 72 per cent of jobs in sub-Saharan Africa, 65 per cent in Asia and 51 per cent in Latin America in the informal economy (ILO, 2006b).

Job opportunities linked to capital investment and, more generally, to patterns of trade transactions may significantly impact on the geographical distribution of workers within a country, as is the case with EPZs. For instance, as early as 1995, one in five manufacturing jobs was found in the *maquiladoras* grouped at the Mexican border with the U.S. (*Migration News*, February 1996).

3.3 Increasing Resort to Foreign Workers through Offshoring

Global resourcing and increased trade in services[26] will make this current phase of globalization quite different from previous ones that were dominated by trade in goods (see Textbox 1.1). Global resourcing will create new opportunities in developing countries, while highly skilled workers in high-income economies will face competition for their jobs.

Global sourcing is, of course, not new, but what is new is the change in direction it has brought about from the provision of skilled services from developed to developing countries to developing countries performing both lower and highly skilled tasks for developed economies. This change in direction will put highly skilled workers from both developing and developed countries in direct competition, with a risk of job losses in the more advanced economies. Indeed, developing countries host twice as many skilled workers as developed countries, even though these workers represent a smaller share (one quarter) of the workforce than is the case in developed countries (World Bank, 2007).

On the other hand, global resourcing in manufacturing and services can cover any activities not constrained by the need for customer contact or local knowledge. This feature makes global resourcing different and in a way more limited than migration as migrant workers can fill any jobs in any sector.[27]

3.4 Impact of Globalization on International Labour Migration[28]

Given the amount of political attention it attracts, the total knowledge about the nature and magnitude of the international labour force, which represents around three per cent of the global workforce (ILO, 2004a), is remarkably limited (see Chapter 9 and Textbox 1.3). This is particularly the case in relation to irregular migration, which by its very nature is difficult to measure (see also Chapters 8 and 11).

---

26 Services employment has been on the rise in all regions of the world with the exception of the Middle East and North Africa where it has remained at constant levels (World Bank, 2007).

27 Workers in developed countries enjoy a higher level of capital per worker, a more productive infrastructure, and are generally seen as more skilled and productive. Developed countries employ an important number of workers in service industries, but not in manufacturing. Therefore, there is potentially less competition between developing and developed countries in terms of jobs in this sector.

28 The impact on international labour mobility is covered more thoroughly in Section 4 below discussing whether there is a global labour market.

Textbox 1.3

Some Key Features of International Labour Migration[1]

- Approximately one-third of the world's migrant workers live in Europe, with slightly fewer residing in Asia and North America. Africa hosts approximately eight per cent of migrant workers, while Oceania, Latin America and the Caribbean are each home to three per cent of migrant workers (ILO, 2004c). The majority of migrants move from one developing country to another rather than from a developing country to a developed one. This is often seen as a consequence of restrictive immigration policies in developed countries; however, it is also worth bearing in mind that in regions where rights to free movement of persons are granted and promoted, such as in regional integration frameworks (see Chapter 13), the movement is limited. For example, in 2004 in the EU only two per cent of EU citizens actually took advantage of these rights (European Commission, 2006).[2]

- Low-skilled migrant workers still represent the bulk of labour migration flows, but between 1995 and 2000 in a number of countries (e.g. some OECD countries) the arrival of highly educated migrants exceeded that of the low-skilled (ILO, 2004a: Executive Summary). Among highly skilled workers, the majority move to or within the developed world (see Chapter 2). Although labour migration flows are becoming geographically more diverse, the largest share of labour movements takes place within regions.

- Almost half of all migrants are women (49.6%), with only slightly more living in developed than in developing countries. More women are migrants than men in every region of the world, except in Africa and Asia (UN DESA, 2006, and Map 5). It is also notable that more women are now migrating on their own as the primary bread earners for their families. In the labour market, women migrants are generally concentrated at opposite ends of the skills spectrum and often occupy jobs in which women generally predominate. Accordingly, many migrant women are skilled workers in the health and education sectors, while the majority of women migrants find work in low-skilled sectors such as domestic service, manufacturing and entertainment (see also Textbox Int. 3 in the Introduction).

- During the 1990s, most developed economies experienced a significant growth in temporary labour migration and again since 2000 (see Chapters 3 and 11). But the number of temporary foreign workers is in general relatively small compared to the size of the destination country's labour market, with the exception of the Gulf Cooperation Council (GCC) States. Home and host countries are both developed and developing countries. Indeed, developed countries (e.g. United Kingdom) are both major countries of destination and origin of migrant workers (see also Chapter 11). Similarly, some developing countries such as South Africa or Thailand are simultaneously significant countries of origin and destination.

- Both skilled and low-skilled migrant workers seem to work predominantly in the service sectors of major developed countries, notably in construction, commerce, catering, education, health care, domestic and other services. In developing countries, migrant workers tend to be found mainly in primary activities (agriculture, fishing and mining) and in manufacturing, although the share in services (particularly tourism-related) is rising in several countries (UNCTAD, 2001).

Notes:

1 More detailed analyses of patterns of international migration are offered in the Regional Overviews in the last part of this volume.

2 In 2004, only 1.7 per cent of EU citizens from the former 15 EU Member States, and only 0.3 per cent of EU citizens from the ten new EU Member States, exercised their right to free movement. However, the latter percentage is now likely to be higher because more former EU Member States have lifted the transitional arrangements on the free movement of workers from the new Member States (see Textbox 13.3).

The reasons that stimulate people to migrate are numerous and operate in complex and interactive ways at individual, family and socio-economic levels. The dissemination of information and lower transport costs facilitate increased labour mobility and the creation of transnational communities. Workers move to find better employment opportunities and working conditions (see Textbox 1.4). While wage differentials are an important incentive,[29] access to higher levels of health and education services, more personal security and generally better quality of life can also be important elements affecting the decision to work abroad.

29 See the Introductory Chapter and Chapter 3 for a discussion of wage differentials between developed and developing countries.

The impact of globalization on international labour migration is highly diverse and related to other determinants than merely the internationalization of trade, financial flows and production, making it difficult to draw a clear and simple picture. The extent or degree of such impact depends on a country's economic situation, and will vary according to the group of workers in question. However, trade liberalization is generally said to increase outward labour migration in the short term until domestic economies adjust to the new environment (the "migration hump").[30] Indeed, more free trade and open markets may lead to job losses in some sectors where domestic firms are unable to compete with foreign TNCs or foreign goods, while it takes time to adequately strengthen the capacity of enterprises to respond to new opportunities. In a similar vein, FDI can lead to both the creation and elimination of jobs and, by the same token, act as a push factor or a deterrent to labour migration.

For instance, FDI can lead to the creation of jobs in host economies, directly in companies benefiting from FDI and indirectly in businesses which complement the activities of these enterprises, thereby contributing to economic growth in general. In addition, through the transfer of technologies and know-how and access to foreign markets, FDI can lead to temporary movements for the provision of services or other forms of movements of workers, who, now being more knowledgeable, are able to find jobs abroad more easily.

Trade and FDI liberalization can also lead to an increase in wages in absolute terms in countries of origin. If wages rise, but more slowly than in destination countries, this may increase the propensity and the actual ability of persons to emigrate. If they rise more rapidly than in destination countries, while the propensity to move may increase as well, the pressure to move may decrease (with a decrease in the wage gap).

[30] The Stolper-Samuelson theorem of factor price equalization postulates that trade can substitute for migration in the long term, while migration will continue in the short term and may actually increase as a result of developing countries facing strong exogenous shocks and receiving more foreign investment. For the "migration hump", see Martin and Taylor (1996).

Textbox 1.4

Decent Work and Migrant Workers

> The primary goal of the ILO today is to promote opportunities for women and men to obtain decent and productive work, in conditions of freedom, equity, security and human dignity.
> *Juan Somavia, ILO Director-General.*

The goal of the ILO Decent Work Agenda is to promote access for all workers to freely chosen and productive employment, the recognition of fundamental rights at work, an income to enable people to meet their basic economic, social and family needs and responsibilities and an adequate level of social protection for the workers and family members. The ILO works to promote decent work through its work on employment, social protection, standards and fundamental principles and rights at work and social dialogue. The ILO's Decent Work for All Agenda covers all workers, including migrant workers.

People throughout the world face deficits, gaps and exclusions in the form of unemployment and underemployment, poor quality, precarious and unsafe jobs, insecure income, denial of rights at work, gender and other discrimination, lack of representation and voice, and inadequate social protection and security. Decent work deficits are a major driving force in international migration, where people seek better jobs and standards of living in foreign countries. Globalization has served to increase these disparities across nations, thereby contributing to additional migration pressures (Stalker, 2000).

There are two distinct aspects in discussing provision of decent work opportunities to migrant workers. The first relates to countries of origin, where the need is to provide decent work opportunities for potential migrants (internal or overseas) and for returning migrant workers. The ILO Action Plan, adopted by the International Labour Conference in June 2004, contained a resolution concerning a fair deal for migrant workers and pledged support to countries for the implementation of the ILO Global Employment Agenda at national level, which can serve to mitigate the circumstances driving migration by generating decent work opportunities in countries of origin (ILO, 2004).

The second aspect requires a commitment on the part of countries of destination to adopt national policies aimed at equal treatment of migrant workers with nationals in respect of local labour laws and access to applicable social protection, combatting the exploitation of vulnerable migrant workers, including those in irregular status, and the promotion of basic human rights for all migrants. The ILO position is that all labour standards apply to both national and migrant workers in the workplace, irrespective of their status.

Decent work is an issue for both national and foreign workers. Yet migrant workers everywhere, especially low-skilled workers, face relatively greater problems in realizing decent work. These disadvantages may arise from their skills profile, temporary status, irregular status, gender, manner of recruitment or sectors of employment.

One good example of lack of decent work is the situation of the bulk of low-skilled migrant workers, especially construction workers and female domestic workers. Migrant domestic workers in a number of countries experience highly exploitative working conditions and abuse, including the confiscation of passports, excessive working hours, low wages that are sometimes not paid at all, violence and harassment, and relative isolation. In many countries they are often not covered by national labour laws. Similarly, migrant workers in the informal sector in developed countries are often subject to abuse and exploitation in the workplace. OECD studies clearly show a concentration of migrants in seasonal, low-paid and precarious jobs in sectors such as agriculture, construction and hotel and catering, which are often shunned by national workers. Discrimination and xenophobia add to decent work deficits. Often migrant workers are not allowed to form unions or are bypassed by national unions.

The promotion of decent work for migrant workers should be pursued on several levels. First and foremost, their basic human rights and core labour rights should be respected by both countries of origin and destination. Second, migrant workers should benefit from all applicable labour standards and national labour laws in equal measure with national workers. The ILO Multilateral Framework on Labour Migration (see Textbox 10.4) is a tool available to countries in promoting decent work for migrant workers, as it has synthesized the main principles and guidelines on the treatment of migrant workers contained in international conventions and practice. Ratification and enforcement of the three international migrant worker conventions (ILO Convention on Migration for Employment, 1949 (No. 97), ILO Convention on Migrant Workers (Supplementary Provisions), 1975 (No. 143) and the International (UN) Convention on the Protection of the Rights of All Migrant Workers and their Families, 1990) should provide a solid foundation for ensuring decent work for migrant workers at the national level. It is important to note that 79 countries in the world have ratified at least one of these three conventions.

In destination countries, extension of coverage of labour laws to migrant workers, equal treatment with national workers, gender-sensitive migration policies, combating discrimination, effective labour inspection systems to monitor workplaces and access to redress mechanisms would be essential to ensure decent work for migrant workers. In countries of origin, the ILO Decent Work Country Programmes provide a mechanism to bring migrant workers within the goal of Decent Work. At the same time, expansion of regular labour migration opportunities for low-skilled workers and protection of their rights should be promoted as advocated by recent global forums, such as the ILO International Labour Conference, June 2004, the Global Commission on International Migration, the United Nations High-Level Dialogue on International Migration and Development, and the Global Forum on Migration and Development.

Source: *International Labour Office.*

4. Is there a Global Labour Market?

Does the greater integration of the world economy and the predominance of market economies create a global labour market? At its simplest, a labour market is where the **demand** and **supply** of labour interact. This interaction has an impact on employment, wages and income.[31]

[31] E.g. if an enterprise experiences difficulties in finding workers, a decision may be taken to invest in technology and automation (i.e. to raise the capital:labour ratio). While this investment will lower the enterprise's profit in the short term, it may represent a saving in the longer term if the new system reduces production costs.

The answer to the question of the existence of a global labour market varies depending on the research referred to and which aspect of the global labour market is being considered: on the supply side the focus is on the global offer of labour for companies; on the demand side, attention is directed towards the required skills, or certain goods and services (and the workers' ability to produce them); finally, consideration may be given to the mechanisms that make it possible for the workforce to respond to employer needs.

One convenient, frequently used measure of the extent of labour market integration is the degree of convergence in real earnings across countries (according to the classical trade theory of factor price equalization[32]). Though comparable data on real wages are not easy to come by and are moreover interpreted differently by researchers, many of them have concluded that there is no readily discernible convergence in wages. For some, this simply highlights the fact that labour is not yet sufficiently liberalized (thus impeding wage convergence through the relocation of labour surpluses to locations with a labour deficit).[33] For others, it signifies that wages are mainly determined by domestic factors, such as the cost of living.

Despite limited actual labour mobility, however, the globalization of trade in goods and services, the existence of international network enterprises using global assembly lines for the production of goods, and their recourse to global sourcing of services are all elements that contribute to the emergence of a more integrated global market for labour.[34]

[32] See n. 30 above.

[33] Some commentators argue that the flows of migrants from developing to developed countries might contribute to the global convergence of wages, and that the return of migrants to their country of origin can lead to an increase in local wages (IMF, 2000).

[34] Even if this is not reflected by wage convergence.

4.1 The Supply Side

For some commentators, the emergence of a global labour market is related to the entry of more countries into the world economy, with their markets being more open to international trade and capital flows, and to the number of countries increasing the ratio of trade to their GDP. As a result, their workforce is said to be more integrated into the world economy. This results in competition for jobs, which leads employers to consider on one hand offshoring or outsourcing options and on the other the hiring of migrant workers.

TNCs are tapping into opportunities offered by a labour force supply more readily available and accessible in more countries than before. The capacity of countries to have their workforce considered for outsourcing or a supply of migrant labour will depend on a series of factors such as wage levels, taxes, facility to import and export goods, services regulations and geographical location, as well as the workers' respective skills, education and productivity. Some of these factors, such as education, recognition of qualifications, and geographical proximity will also interact with the capacity of workers to provide their labour through emigration.

However, the global pool of workers is unevenly spread and demographic changes suggest an accentuation of this trend (see Textbox 1.5). Most of the increase will come from developing countries, while many developed countries will continue to experience ageing populations and declining workforces.[35] As a result, imbalances in the capacity to supply labour will favour the developing world and will concern different countries over time, as developing countries will experience their own demographic transitions, with negative or zero population growth and population ageing.

[35] In some European countries, the population would have declined without migration: net migration counterbalances the excess of deaths over births in Austria, Bosnia and Herzegovina, Greece, Italy, Portugal, Slovakia and Slovenia (UN DESA, 2007).

Textbox 1.5

Global Population Trends and Their Impact on International Migration

Introduction

According to the *2006 Revision* of *World Population Prospects*,[1] the most recent version of the official United Nations population projections, the world population is likely to increase by 2.5 billion from the current 6.7 billion to 9.2 billion by 2050. This increase will be absorbed mostly by the less developed regions,[2] whose population is projected to rise from 5.4 billion in 2007 to 7.9 billion in 2050. In contrast, the population in the more developed regions[3] is expected to remain virtually unchanged at about 1.2 billion, and would have declined were it not for the projected net migration from developing to developed countries, which is expected to average 2.3 million persons annually after 2010. International migration is the component of population change most difficult to measure and project reliably. Not only does the quality and quantity of migration data vary considerably by country, the movement of people across international borders is also subject to a high degree of volatility.

Population trends and international migration in developed countries

Since 1960, the average annual net number of migrants moving to the more developed regions has generally been increasing, with the highest value of 3.3 million persons annually reached in the period 2000-2005 (Figure 1.1). For 2005-2010, the projected value is close to the average net migration level estimated for the 1990s (i.e. 2.5 million persons annually), but the long-term level projected for 2010-2050 is slightly lower at 2.3 million persons per year. Although this projected long-term level is about a third lower than the peak reached in 2000-2005, it is also 40 per cent higher than the average annual net migration flowing to developed countries witnessed between 1960-2005 (1.6 million).

Figure 1.1:

Average Annual Net Number of Migrants to the More Developed Regions, 1960-2050

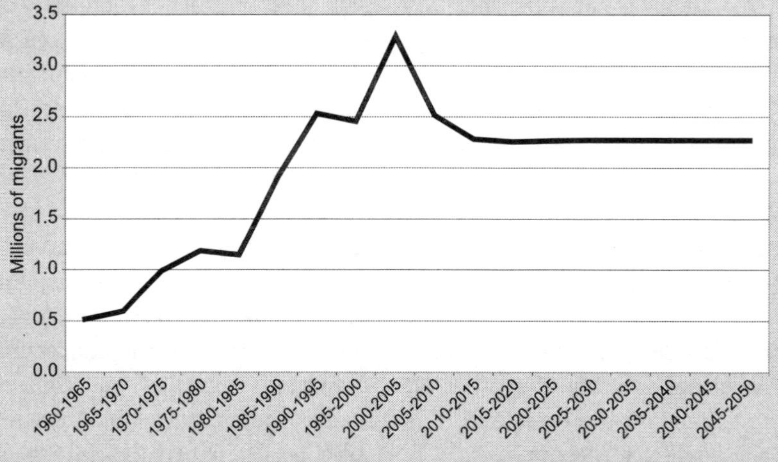

The population of developed countries is ageing rapidly. In most developed countries, fertility started to decline already more than a century ago and, since the 1980s, their fertility levels have been very low. As a result, the number of children[4] in developed countries is declining and there are already fewer children than persons aged 60 years or more. Furthermore, their working-age population is poised to decline despite the expected gains from net migration (Figure 1.2). In the absence of international migration, the population aged 20 to 64 in developed countries as a whole may be expected to decline from 741 million in 2005 to 571 million by 2050, a reduction of 23 per cent. On the other hand, if the projected moderate levels of international migration were to be realized, the expected decline in the working-age population would be just 10 per cent.

Figure 1.2:

Population Aged 20-64 in More Developed Regions Projected With and Without Migration, 1950-2050

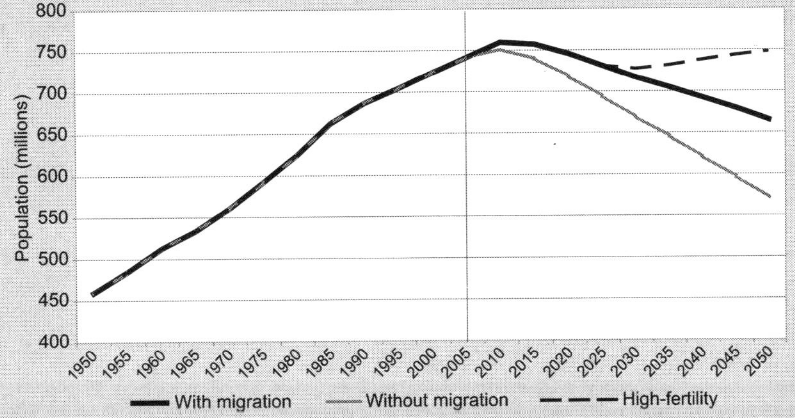

If fertility levels in developed countries were to increase more rapidly than those assumed in the medium variant plotted in the graph above (see the "with migration" and "without migration" scenarios in Figure 1.2), international migration would still be necessary to avoid the decline of the working-age population since most of tomorrow's workers have already been born. In the high-fertility projection variant, for instance, fertility is projected to be half a child higher than in the medium variant and, as shown in Figure 1.2, in combination with the projected levels of net migration, such fertility levels are sufficient to ensure that the population aged 20-64 in developed countries remains within two percentage points of the number it reached in 2005.

Therefore, for developed countries to avoid a rapid reduction in the size of their working-age population, maintaining average net migration levels similar to those prevailing during the 1990s will be necessary, even if fertility levels were to increase more than those projected in the medium variant.

Population trends and international migration in the less developed regions

During most of the period starting in 1960, the three major areas in the developing world, namely, Africa, Asia[5] and Latin America and the Caribbean, have been experiencing net emigration, that is, their net migration levels have been negative. As Figure 1.3 shows, until the early 1980s, all three major areas experienced modest levels of net emigration but, starting in the 1980s, their magnitude increased markedly, first in Latin America and the Caribbean and later in Asia. In contrast, Africa has not experienced a marked increase in net emigration over the past three decades.

Figure 1.3:

Average Annual Net Number of Migrants, Africa, Asia and Latin America and the Caribbean, 1960-2050

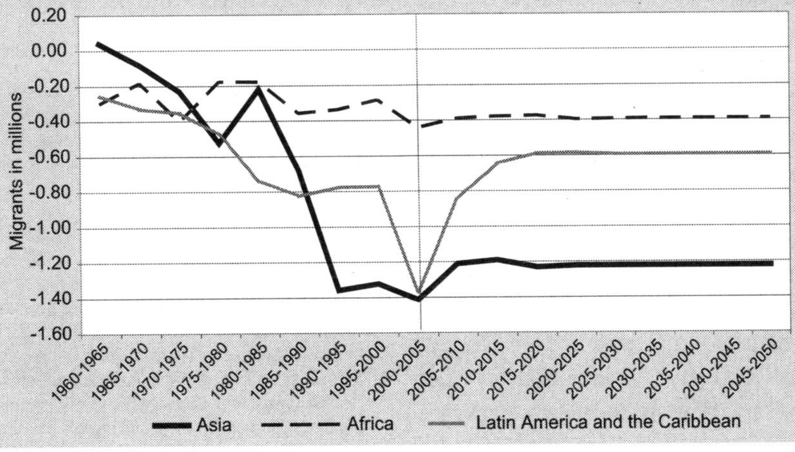

According to current estimates, for Asia and Latin America and the Caribbean the period 2000-2005 was characterized by historically high levels of net emigration, though as regards Asia high levels of net emigration were also noticeable in the 1990s. During 2000-2005, on average, nearly 1.4 million persons annually were lost through emigration by each region. Net emigration from Africa was considerably lower, averaging 0.44 million persons per year. Except for Africa, net emigration levels projected for each of the other two major areas in the developing world are lower than the peak reached in 2000-2005. For Latin America and the Caribbean, in particular, the expectation is that net outflows will be more moderate in future since the rapid increase of expatriate populations of Latin American origin in North America and southern Europe that occurred during 2000-2005 is unlikely to be sustainable over the long term from the perspective of the countries of destination.

In contrast with developed countries, where the working-age population is expected to decrease, the major areas of the developing world expect substantial increases in their working-age populations and the moderate levels of emigration projected produce only small reductions in those populations. Thus, the population aged 20-64 in Africa is expected to nearly triple from 408 million in 2005 to 1.12 billion in 2050. Without emigration, it would rise to 1.14 billion. For Asia, the population aged 20-64 is expected to rise by 40 per cent from 2.21 billion to 3.08 billion and without emigration would stand at 3.12 billion instead. Lastly, the increase expected in Latin America and the Caribbean amounts to 45 per cent from 303 million to 441 million which, without emigration, would be 467 million. These figures underscore a key point: over the next four decades, the developing world can easily be the source of as many persons of working age as are likely to be in demand in countries with decreasing populations of working age.

Notes:

1 UN Department of Economic and Social Affairs, Population Division, *World Population Prospects: The 2006 Revision*, Vol. I, Comprehensive Tables (New York, 2007), http://www.un.org/esa/population/publications/wpp2006/wpp2006.htm.

2 The less developed regions include all countries in Africa, Asia (excluding Japan), Latin America and the Caribbean, and Oceania (excluding Australia and New Zealand).

3 The more developed regions comprise Australia, Europe, Japan, New Zealand and North America.

4 Persons under 15 years of age.

5 Asia including Japan.

Source: *Population Division of the Department of Economic and Social Affairs of the United Nations Secretariat.*

4.2 The Demand Side

Demand exists at both ends of the skills spectrum. Firstly, there is global demand for skills. The global economy is supported by the spread of technologies and characterized by rapid economic transformation. As a result, more workers capable of mastering these technologies and demonstrating flexibility and adaptability to changes in the economic and work environments are required globally. This is particularly true in the information technology (IT) sector. However, a wide range of professionals, scientists and managers able to further raise the quality and productivity of local companies and enhance a country's comparative advantage are also sought after. Scarcity of highly skilled workers creates a global competition for talent (see Chapter 2) and induces the relaxation of immigration rules together with the creation of incentive packages for such workers by employers and governments (e.g. tax reductions, higher salaries, access to good research facilities, etc.). The mobility of such workers is facilitated by the internationalization of education (see Chapter 4) and the development of international standards for professionals, for which a global market already exists, such as accountants, engineers, lawyers and architects.[36]

[36] E.g. see respectively: Intergovernmental Working Group of Experts on International Standards of Accounting and Reporting (ISAR) Guidelines on National Requirements for the Qualification of Professional Accountants (1999); the Washington Accord (1989), which facilitates recognition of equivalence between accredited engineering degree programmes by accrediting professional institutions party to the agreement, and the Sydney Accord (2001), which covers recognition of engineering technology programmes; the International Bar Association (IBA) Standards and Criteria for Recognition of the Professional Qualifications of Lawyers provided to the WTO in the framework of the GATS; and the International Union of Architects (UIA) Accord on Recommended International Standards of Professionalism in Architectural Practice (1999) and related policy guidelines, which define good practices and provide guidance for governments and agencies willing to enter into mutual recognition agreements (Nonnenmacher, 2007).

At the opposite end of the skills ladder, demand also exists for low-skilled workers, although low or semi-skilled migration remains highly regulated and restricted in most countries.[37] The global demand for low-skilled workers is likely to be boosted by growing labour market gaps in developed countries where, on account of rising education levels and accompanying wage expectations, workers are turning away from low and semi-skilled occupations. While some of these jobs may simply be phased out through improved work organization or advances in technology such as automation, there are many work sectors that will continue to depend to a great extent on human resources, especially construction, agriculture and hospitality.[38] These market needs are structural, the demand may fluctuate, but is unlikely to be erased entirely. The Asian financial crisis of the latter part of the 1990s demonstrated that even in times of hardship such workers are not easily replaced by native workers.

Depending on actual circumstances, migrants may be clustered at both ends of the labour market or more evenly distributed across the jobs ladder.

4.3 Labour Market Clearing Mechanisms: Moving Jobs or People?

For some observers, the existence of a global labour market is conditional on the existence of clearing mechanisms operating at the global level. There is currently no established **global** framework to facilitate the mobility of labour and no mechanism for the systematic matching of labour demand and supply. Compared to capital and trade, therefore, which have been significantly liberalized, labour mobility is lagging far behind and is still heavily constrained by national regulations.

Economic theory would suggest a different approach. The free movement of labour would appear to be a natural corollary to the principle of competitive efficiency. In the real world, however, political imperatives commonly dictate the imposition of restrictions, although it is far from clear that the latter are economically beneficial in the longer term.

There are, nonetheless, different kinds of clearing mechanisms for matching labour supply and demand in active operation to facilitate either the mobility of jobs (clearance through mobility of capital) or workers (clearance through mobility of labour).[39] In the case of mobility of jobs, the global labour market might be seen as emerging from trade and investment which act as proxies for international mobility of labour (Mehmet et al., 1999). In the absence of free movement of labour, labour markets are integrated through trade and investment where the decision of firms to invest and locate their production is based in part on the labour costs and standards of different investment locations, while states respond by adjusting them to be more attractive.

In the case of workers, it is important to note that the fact that mobility is regulated does not mean that movements are necessarily marginal or discouraged everywhere. For instance, in some countries, such as those in the Gulf region, more than 40 per cent of their workforce is made up of foreigners. In addition, a number of mechanisms are currently in place to facilitate the movement of workers between

[37] On the other hand, temporary labour migration programmes are increasing and there is a growing interest in both developed and developing countries in making such programmes work more effectively (see the discussions in Chapters 3 and 11).

[38] For instance, in some countries of Latin America, a combination of rapid urbanization, rural-urban migration, growth of the informal sector and emigration abroad, compounded by growing expectations of improved education and income by large numbers of young persons, has resulted in a relative shortage of workers in specific rural areas or regions, or for particular seasonal products. This has created a growing demand for migrant workers to fill these positions in what is being labelled as "replacement migration", i.e. migrants who mobilize to take over jobs previously occupied by nationals who have moved away. This is the case, for instance, of Nicaraguans and Hondurans, who take over agricultural jobs in the south of El Salvador, and of Bolivians and Paraguayans in Argentina. This trend seems set to increase in Central America and southern Mexico and probably also in other parts of the continent (Gammage, 2007).

[39] However, the effects produced by these two modes are frequently very different in terms of wages, as a worker moving to a developed country will, in most cases, benefit from a higher salary than if hired by a foreign company to perform the job locally (outsourcing).

countries: at the bilateral level (e.g. bilateral labour agreements, bilateral agreements for the recognition of qualifications); at the regional level (e.g. the EU free movement regime, facilitated movement of skills under the Caribbean Community (CARICOM) Single Market and Economy) or at the global level with the General Agreement on Trade in Services (GATS) Mode 4.[40] Finally, matching demand and supply also occurs through irregular labour migration (see Chapters 8 and 11), despite the adverse consequences of such movements.

Domestic labour market dynamics, therefore, are far from operating in a wholly self-contained and insular environment and are affected by two principal questions with an international dimension:

1) where and how labour demand and supply match (in developing countries of origin – through offshoring and based on free movement of capital, or in developed destination countries – through labour mobility/migration); and
2) where wages are determined (in the domestic labour market in which workers perform their activities, or on the basis of international labour demand and supply).

As La Palisse[41] might have said in answer to these questions: "The more economic outcomes are determined outside domestic labour markets, the more domestic labour markets will function globally or in a global context".

5. Is there a Case for Free Movement of Workers? Who will Benefit - Developing or Developed Economies?

In purely conceptual terms, it is possible to identify the removal of current constraints on the mobility of one main factor of production (labour) as the "tipping point" that would make labour markets truly global, thus enabling the international community to take globalization to its fullest realization. Under this approach, the movement of workers across international borders would be dependent on their assessment of market opportunities rather than subordinated to individual country regulations.

One of the striking and even paradoxical features of the current globalization phase, however, is the relatively minor role played by international migration in a world that is more interconnected than ever before.[42] Economists point out, for instance, that while the international trade's share of output is around 13 per cent (Freeman, 2006a) and foreign equities in investor portfolios stood at approximately 15 per cent at the beginning of 2000, the stock of migrant workers in the global workforce does not exceed three per cent. This stands in marked contrast to previous phases of globalization, in particular the first phase during the late 19th and early 20th centuries when human mobility closely accompanied the boom in trade, an explicit historical demonstration, if indeed one was needed, that governments can and do open their labour markets when they are convinced that they stand to benefit substantially. This, it must be admitted, is far from being the case at the moment. In most instances there is, at best, cautious interest in weighing impartially the costs and benefits of migrant worker programmes;[43] at worst, suspicion that costs are likely to substantially outweigh benefits.

[40] Mode 4 covers the temporary movement of service providers (see Textbox Int. 1). These bilateral, regional and global mechanisms are discussed in more detail in Chapter 13.

[41] Jacques II de Chabannes, seigneur de La Palisse, was a warrior known for his soldiers having said of him in a song that "15 minutes before he was dead, he was still alive". Since then "a truth from Lapalisse" refers to an affirmation which is self-evident.

[42] Currently, the only free movement regime operating on a large scale is found in a regional setting, i.e. the EU. While labour mobility is covered in bilateral labour or trade agreements or regional integration frameworks (see Chapter 13), such movement occurs mainly on the basis of unilaterally devised immigration policies.

[43] For an analysis of the costs and benefits of migration, see IOM (2005).

Clearly, there are some fundamental questions that have to be worked through before convincing policy advice can be put forward, including the nature of the relationship between migration and trade, and the nature and magnitude of the purported gains, the eventual distribution of these gains among the major actors, the non-economic or social and political considerations involved, and the prospects for a global framework to manage labour mobility.

5.1 Migration and Trade: The Case for Liberalization

Investigation into the relationship between migration and trade is ongoing and unlikely to be concluded without much further research, analysis and debate. One question often addressed at the theoretical level is whether migration and trade are mutual substitutes or complements. Responses vary considerably. For instance, according to Mundell, migration and capital mobility, or both, are substitute/s to trade mobility. Other models consider migration as a complement, with migration increasing with growth in trade flows (e.g. Markunsen).

Textbox 1.6

Migration and Trade Models

Maurice Schiff provides an overview of the different migration and trade models. He demonstrates that many assumptions in these models are insufficiently grounded in reality as the interrelations between migration, investment and trade are complex and depend on a whole range of factors: the skills of prospective migrants; the distance between countries of origin and destination; the basis for trade (endowment, technology, imperfect competition, other distortions, increasing returns, etc.); the level and changes in tariffs and other forms of protection in countries of origin and destination; whether trade involves goods or services; whether FDI is vertical or horizontal; whether FDI is between developed and developing, developing and developing or developing and developed countries; regional trade agreements (RTAs); the impact of exogenous shocks which vary according to whether these shocks involve trade costs, migration costs and income tax; and the role of diasporas in promoting trade and FDI.

Source: *Schiff (2006).*

A second line of investigation explores analogies between trade and migration in terms of their potential to enhance global economic growth. As a general rule, economists are inclined to believe that the international community stands to derive considerable aggregate benefit from the freer movement of labour across international borders. As Chang (2007: 1) sees it,

> recent increases in the international migration of workers are but one facet of globalization, which economists understand to mean the development of a global common market, that is (...) evolution towards a world economy that is integrated across national boundaries.

He takes note of the improvements achieved both in global economic welfare and in national economies through the liberalization of international trade in goods, and argues that similar if not greater progress can be made through the facilitation of the movement of workers across national boundaries.

According to this view, constraints on worker movement create market distortions resulting in the inefficient allocation of human resources at the global level, as witnessed by labour shortages in developed countries and oversupply in developing countries. In contrast, the facilitation of movement would trigger a flow of workers from low-wage origins to high-wage destinations, with resultant global welfare gains potentially higher than those that would be obtained from further liberalization of trade in goods or capital. Walmsley and Winters (2003) estimate that a relaxation of the movement of temporary workers corresponding to three per cent of the labour force of high-income countries would lead to global income gains of USD 150 billion annually (using a 1997-based comparative static model).[44]

Rodrik estimates that since wages for similarly qualified workers in developed and developing countries differ sharply – by a factor of 10 or more as against a difference for commodities and financial assets that rarely exceeds a ratio of 1:2 – the gains from free movement of labour could be as much as 25 times larger than the gains from the liberalization of movements of goods and capital (Rodrik, 2002; see also Pritchett, 2006).[45] Free movement would, in theory, also have a positive impact on the global distribution of income by creating a convergence in wage rates for the same class of workers.

The issue of the impact of migrant remittances (see Chapter 12 for a fuller treatment) on global economic activity is not unrelated to this discussion. It is now fully recognized that remittances have become a key source of global finance. Remittances sent through official channels were estimated to have reached 318 billion in 2007, up from USD 188 billion in 2005 and considerably more than double the level in 2001. Nearly USD 240 billion of these funds went to developing countries (Ratha et al., 2007), an amount far larger than Official Development Assistance (ODA) and representing the second source of external funding for developing countries after FDI (World Bank, 2006). It is believed that the real value, when including remittances sent through informal channels, may be 50 per cent higher. In most developing countries, remittances are on average larger than ODA and are proving to be more stable than either ODA or FDI.[46]

5.2 How will Benefits be Shared?

From a theoretical perspective at least, there is little reason to doubt that the freer movement of workers would benefit the world economy by creating significant efficiency gains. However, as scholars look more closely at how those gains might be distributed across the world economy, they have to grapple with many uncertainties.

The case is often made that, in comparison with the liberalization of trade and capital, which, it could be argued, benefits most countries, the benefits from free movement of labour would mainly be oriented towards developing countries. This is because movements from developing countries are currently more constrained (especially for low-skilled workers) and the highest wage differentials are to be found between developing and developed countries.[47]

Nonetheless, possible scenarios are in reality numerous and not infrequently contradictory. On the one hand, it is claimed that in a world economy increasingly dominated by technology, freer movement may lead mainly to more skilled migration between and

---

[44] For an analysis of the potential gains of international migration and the elaboration of models to capture evidence, see World Bank (2006).

[45] The fact that wages vary more than the costs of goods and capital around the world, and that higher barriers to mobility are found to affect workers, leads economists to assume that the gains from the liberalization of labour would be greater than any additional openings in trade and financial markets, which have already been liberalized significantly.

[46] However, each of these flows has its own particular dynamics. ODA is development aid money from the members of the Development Assistance Committee (DAC) of the OECD to developing countries, directed towards the economic and welfare development of these countries. As observed earlier, FDI is defined as investment of foreign assets into domestic structures, equipment and organizations. It does not include foreign investment in stock markets which is considered an indirect investment. This money is directed towards the private sector and responds to the objectives of private actors. Finally, remittances are private household funds which are mostly used for consumption, even if more and more measures are now being taken to encourage these flows to be directed towards productive investments.

[47] This is recognized to a certain extent by the fact that GATS Mode 4 negotiations are part of the Doha development agenda (see Textbox Int. 1).

towards developed countries with a positive impact on economic growth in developed countries and an increase in the scarcity of such human resources in developing countries with all the risks this holds for their economic and social development.[48]

The allocation of gains and losses turns out to be quite different if the focus of attention is on low and semi-skilled workers. Outflows of such workers could alleviate labour surpluses in developing countries in addition to providing them with a valuable source of foreign currency in the form of remittances;[49] in developed countries their arrival could set them up as competitors to local workers. The latter might then find themselves in the unenviable position of either having to accept lower wages to remain competitive or resign themselves to seeing their jobs offshored (which is a risk every time there is a push for a wage increase beyond gains in productivity).

Closer analyses (e.g. World Bank, 2007) suggest even more complex scenarios: while an inflow of low or semi-skilled workers to a developed country might reduce the real wages of its own low-skilled workers, their presence might at the same time be to the advantage of highly skilled workers and the economy more generally, as both stand to benefit from lower prices for goods and services provided by the migrant workers; on the other hand, skilled movements from developing to developed countries will increase income disparities between skilled workers and low-skilled workers in countries of origin (with a trend towards an increase in the wages of skilled workers who remain).

[48] As Ghose (2002: 26) points out, international migration in the first phase of globalization was "a force of convergence because it led to equalization of resources endowment across trading countries. Today it is a force of divergence because it accentuates the inequality of skill endowments between industrialized and developing countries".

[49] From a global economic perspective, the gains from liberalizing the movement of workers are expected to be greatest with respect to the liberalization of low-skilled workers, and this is because of the importance of wage differentials for these categories of workers, the current significant barriers to these movements and the abundance of these workers in developing countries (Chapter 3 provides a fuller discussion of this point).

It is important to note that in all of the above equations the actual outcomes for the countries of origin, the countries of destination and the migrants themselves may vary significantly depending on whether the migratory movements are of a permanent or temporary nature. Policymakers and other stakeholders increasingly argue that circular forms of movement (see Chapters 11 and 12), if managed successfully, could do much to optimize the benefits of labour mobility for all concerned, because they represent the best trade-off between the prospective interests of the three parties.

While there is therefore considerable theoretical work backing up the hypothesis that massive aggregate gains would accrue from the lifting of current constraints on the movement of workers across international borders, the realization and actual distribution of these gains will depend ultimately on how the movements are actually channelled and managed, and management choices will rest in turn on policy considerations that extend well beyond the economic sphere.

5.3 Looking Beyond the Economic Dimension

Prospects for the freer movement of labour should therefore be envisaged not only from the perspective of economic gains and losses but also from social and political angles.

From the perspective of countries of destination, economic benefits will always be weighed against social implications (such as provision of social services, welfare coverage or, less tangibly, impacts on social cohesion) and security concerns, all of which are politically sensitive issues. From the perspective of countries of origin, there are issues of brain drain, family dislocation and community disruption.

Less obvious perhaps are the social costs of non-openness. They include the development of informal labour markets where migrants work under conditions that are at best unfair, at worst equivalent to forced labour or slavery. There are also smuggling and trafficking networks, which are often in the hands of organized crime. These adverse effects show how inefficient administrative barriers can be at keeping people out, and lead to questions about how such flows should be managed to ensure, at a minimum, that national labour market policies reconcile the competitiveness sought by employers with the protection of workers' rights and interests.

At the individual level, as well, the decision to move is driven by both economic and non economic considerations. Differences in wages and general economic prospects between countries of origin and destination are obviously important, but other matters such as political stability, freedom from conflict, levels of human rights protection, labour standards and access to social services, such as health and education, can also play a role. The existence of a diaspora providing support to new migrants and acting as an information network (see Chapter 12) enters into consideration in the selection by the migrant of the destination country, together with employment prospects and possible access to secure or permanent residence status. Geographical proximity also plays a role, especially for low-skilled workers, as it affects their travel costs unless these are taken care of by the employer. Finally, elements as disparate as the possibility of being accompanied or joined by a family member, the difficulty of severing connections with one's community and life style in the country of origin, the costs of living, exchange rate differentials, taxation, the climate, language and the rules relating to recognition of qualifications will, in the end, all be weighed in the individual worker's decision to opt for mobility or not.

5.4. Prospects for Enhanced International Cooperation in the Management of Labour Mobility

Given the complexity of the economic, social and political equations that have to be resolved before significant progress can be made, the slowness and cautiousness of inter-governmental negotiations in this field is hardly a surprise. With regard to mobility, the unequal balance powering the supply/demand equation between countries of origin and destination creates no strong incentive for the latter to enter into a multilateral framework encompassing the admission of migrant workers. Destination countries are still largely in a position to satisfy their labour market needs through unilateral policies, and adjust them according to changes in their labour markets. This is clear from the limited commitment made under GATS Mode 4 to date and the absence of a significant outcome in the current negotiations.[50]

The General Agreement on Tariffs and Trade (GATT) and its successor, the WTO, were created to ensure that the negative and positive impacts of free trade would be shared equally, and are supported by the economic reasoning that, through specialization in production, most countries, both developing and developed, could gain from the establishment of such a regime. The IMF and the World Bank have been given a role in managing international finance, and there is widespread support for the development of a framework which would ensure more stable exchange rates and strong currencies. On the other hand, the case for an international regime establishing freer movement of workers does not yet attract a critical mass of support because of the perceived asymmetries of supply and demand, the lack of reciprocity in potential gains and the social and political implications that remain to be addressed.

[50] Major developed and destination countries have made only limited offers under GATS Mode 4, principally for top managers, highly skilled professionals and intra-corporate transferees.

While prospects for a global regime opening the way to the freer mobility of workers remain guarded, there are concrete indications of progress in regional settings, where economic disparities are often more limited and consequently less likely to act as obstacles to liberalization (see Chapter 13). Even in such restricted settings, however, it is the more highly skilled who are most likely to benefit from movement facilitation arrangements.[51]

Countries are more interconnected through trade, capital flows and the global production system than ever before. Changes in the economic situation and regulations in countries that are the most important economically have repercussions for the rest of the world. Therefore, increased globalization requires the elaboration of new ways of approaching the world of work in its domestic and international dimension, with renewed emphasis on consultation and cooperation.

Coordination among the actors involved in the formulation of policies impacting on employment (i.e. labour market policy, but also labour migration, social security, education policies, etc.) is first required at the national level, while national actors also need to devote more attention to the international dimension of this phenomenon both at the regional and global levels. This could be facilitated by the creation of a roadmap on "globalization and labour mobility" to guide discussion in international fora and maximize the potential for collaboration between global agencies with mandates in this area (e.g. ILO, IMF, IOM, World Bank, WTO, among others).

An important objective of such a roadmap would be to recognize the interrelationships between globalization, the world of work and the international movement of workers. It could provide an analysis of the challenges arising from these interactions in terms of creating new work opportunities in the developed and developing worlds while protecting the most vulnerable individuals who are not in a position to tap into these opportunities. It could look at what can be done at the national level, but also how regional and global frameworks as well as institutions mandated to address trade, finance, employment and migration issues could help countries to better manage these challenges by creating more synergies in their endeavours in these different fields.

6. Conclusion

An examination of the place, present and future, of international labour mobility within ongoing processes of globalization leads to three main observations. First, workers in the developing world provide a pool of human resources that can respond to demand in the developed world now and well into the future, although much remains to be done to realize this in practice and to make it beneficial for both countries of origin and destination; for instance, through the elaboration of human resource development strategies and the creation of effective mechanisms to match demand with supply.

Second, the relationship between trade and migration needs to be better understood. There is a greater need to focus on labour in trade theory than in past globalization phases, because the current phase is characterized by an increase in trade in services and knowledge-based trade, both of which rely heavily on human resources. New trade theories (and supporting evidence) are needed to better inform policies that seek to address the need for increased international labour mobility.

Third, policy coherence needs to be improved on a number of levels. The transformation of the world of work has led to a change in the roles of traditional stakeholders (e.g. public authorities, employers and

51 From a purely economic perspective, there is a paradox here as movement is liberalized in a setting (i.e. of the highly skilled and between countries that are at a similar economic level) where the gains from the liberalization are not the most significant.

trade unions) or at least in their ability to perform the role traditionally assigned to them. They face the task of having to formulate and implement policies and protect interests at the national level in the face of global economic forces.[52] The state also tends to have a more limited role in the regulation of the economy than before as new prominence is given to enterprises as regulators.[53] As roles and relationships change, there is a challenge in ensuring that the mobility of workers and the role of key players, including TNCs, are properly integrated within employment and migration policies and strategies at the national and international level.

At the broadest policy level if, as it is likely, the gathering forces of globalization – as evidenced and implemented through trade reforms that have already taken place with respect to liberalizing the movement of goods and capital – increase the pressure for greater labour mobility, but systems of migration management are not adjusted accordingly, a serious disconnect will be created between policies and realities. There are manifest social costs to be paid for this in terms of irregular migration and the related exploitation involved.

To date governments have chosen to manage migration essentially from a domestic perspective.[54] This is unlikely to change radically but, in so doing, governments are confronted with the challenge of maintaining their sovereign prerogative to manage movements across their borders, while having to cope with the inefficiencies of regulating a transnational phenomenon with national level policies. Regional processes may provide helpful consultative and experimental platforms for the exploration of approaches that may reconcile needs for security, mobility and worker protection. Attention is now focused on building interstate cooperation in the migration field from the bottom up rather than the top down and, in particular, with respect to labour mobility. In parallel to the pursuit of legally binding international instruments regulating the movement of persons and protecting the human rights of migrant workers at the global level,[55] bilateral cooperation, regional dialogue and consultation, and even non-binding global consultative mechanisms are exploring means to achieve greater cooperation in managing migration and labour mobility. A period of confidence building in the ability to manage labour mobility to mutual benefit is needed – at national, bilateral, regional and global levels – and may pave the way in the future for more comprehensive and coherent approaches to labour mobility that would be more supportive of freer movements.[56]

[52] As a result, some actors are modifying their strategies. For instance, some trade unions are developing more international strategies (setting up international branches, or creating international networks) or recognizing new realities with the inclusion of migrant issues in their agendas and/or opening their membership to migrant workers. See the Global Union Research Network (GURN) website at http://www.gurn.info/topic/migrant/index.html.

[53] Not only through the impacts of their economic weight but also, for example, through the adoption of corporate social responsibility norms.

[54] One evolving exception is the migration law and policy of the European Union.

[55] E.g. temporary movement of persons through GATS Mode 4; the 1990 International Convention on the Protection of the Rights of All Migrant Workers and Members of Their Families (see Textbox 13.1).

[56] See Chapter 13 for a fuller discussion of interstate cooperation.

REFERENCES

Castells, M.

1996 *The Rise of the Network Society: (The Information Age: Economy, Society and Culture, Volume 1)*, Blackwell Publishers, Oxford.

Chang, H.

2007 "The Economic Impact of International Labor Migration: Recent Estimates and Policy Implications", *Temple Political and Civil Rights Law Review*, 16.

Commission of the European Communities

2006 *Report on the Functioning of the Transitional Arrangements set out in the 2003 Accession Treaty (period 1 May 2004-30 April 2006)*, COM (2006) 48 final, 8 February.

Farrell, D., M.A. Laboissière and J. Rosenfeld

2005 "Sizing the emerging global labor market. Rational behavior from both companies and countries can help it work more efficiently", *The McKinsey Quarterly*, No. 3 (August), http://ce.mdic.gov.br/SOFTWARE/McKinsey%20-%20Labor.htm#foot4up.

Freeman, R.B.

2005 "What Really Ails Europe (and America): The Doubling of the Global Workforce", *The Globalist*, 3 June, http://www.theglobalist.com/DBWeb/printStoryId.aspx?StoryId=4542.

2006a "People flows in globalization", National Bureau of Economic Research (NBER) Working Paper No. 12315, June, Cambridge, MA.

2006b "Labor Market Imbalances: Shortages, or Surpluses, or Fish Stories?", Boston Federal Reserve Economic Conference on Global Imbalances – As Giants Evolve, 14-16 June, Chatham, MA, http://www.bos.frb.org/economic/conf/conf51/papers/freeman.pdf.

Gammage, S.

2007 "El Salvador: Despite End to Civil War, Emigration Continues", *Migration Information Source*, July, Migration Policy Institute (MPI), Washington, D.C., http://www.migrationinformation.org/Profiles/display.cfm?ID=636.

Ghosh, B.

2005 "Managing Migration: Whither the Missing Regime?", Draft Article of the UNESCO Migration without Borders Series, Doc. SHS/2005/MWB/4, 15 February, http://unesdoc.unesco.org/images/0013/001391/139149e.pdf.

Ghose, A.K.

2002 "Trade and international labour mobility", Employment Paper 2002/33, ILO, Geneva, http://www.ilo.org/public/english/employment/strat/download/ep33.pdf.

Global Commission on International Migration (GCIM)

2005 *Migration in an interconnected world: New directions for action*, Report of the GCIM, October, SRO-Kundig, Geneva, http://www.gcim.org/attachements/gcim-complete-report-2005.pdf.

International Monetary Fund (IMF)

2000 "Globalization: Threat or Opportunity?", IMF Issues Brief 00/01, 12 April (corrected January 2002), http://www.imf.org/external/np/exr/ib/2000/041200to.htm.

International Labour Organization (ILO)

2004a *Towards a Fair Deal for Migrant Workers in the Global Economy*, Report VI, International Labour Conference, 92nd Session, June, Geneva, http://www.ilo.org/public/english/standards/relm/ilc/ilc92/pdf/rep-vi.pdf.

2004b *Trade, Foreign Investment and Productive Employment in Developing Countries*, Governing Body, 291st Session, November, ILO, Geneva.

2004c "Facts on Migrant Labour", June, International Labour Office, Geneva, http://www.ilo.org/public/english/region/asro/bangkok/child/trafficking/downloads/migrantsfactsheet.pdf.

2006a "Global Employment Trends", Brief, January, International Labour Office, Geneva, http://www.ilo.org/public/english/employment/strat/download/getb06en.pdf.

2006b *Changing Patterns in the World of Work*, Report of the Director General, Report I (C), International Labour Conference, 95th Session, June, Geneva, http://www.ilo.org/public/english/standards/relm/ilc/ilc95/pdf/rep-i-c.pdf.

2006c "Facts on Labour Migration", June, International Labour Office, Geneva, http://www.ilo.org/public/english/bureau/inf/download/ecosoc/migration.pdf.

2007 *Labour Market Trends and Globalization's Impact on Them*, Bureau for Workers' Activities, ILO, Geneva, http://www.itcilo.it/english/actrav/telearn/global/ilo/seura/mains.htm.

International Organization for Migration (IOM)

2005 *World Migration Report 2005: Costs and Benefits of International Migration*, IOM, Geneva, http://www.iom.int/jahia/Jahia/cache/offonce/pid/1674?entryId=932.

Jansen, M. and E. Lee

2007 *Trade and Employment: Challenges for Policy Research*, A Joint Study of the International Labour Office and the Secretariat of the World Trade Organization, ILO/WTO, Geneva, http://www.ilo.org/wcmsp5/groups/public/---dgreports/---dcomm/---webdev/documents/publication/wcms_081742.pdf.

Martin, P.L. and J.E. Taylor

1996 "The anatomy of a migration hump" in J.E. Taylor, (Ed.), *Development Strategy, Employment and Migration: Insights from Models*, Organization for Economic Co-operation and Development (OECD), Paris.

McKinsey Global Institute

2003 "Offshoring: Is it a win win game?", Perspective, August, McKinsey Global Institute, http://www.mckinsey.com/mgi/publications/win_win_game.asp.

2005 *The Emerging Global Labor Market*, June, McKinsey Global Institute, http://www.mckinsey.com/mgi/publications/emerginggloballabormarket/.

Mehmet, O., E. Mendes and R. Sinding

1999 *Towards a Fair Global Labour Market: Avoiding a new slave trade*, Routledge: London and New York.

Migration News

1996 "Mexican Maquiladoras", *Migration News*, 3(2), February, University of California at Davis, http://migration.ucdavis.edu/mn/more.php?id=872_0_2_0.

Nonnenmacher, S.

2007 "Recognition of the Qualifications of Migrant Workers: Reconciling the Interests of Individuals, Countries of Origin and Countries of Destination", *IJMS: International Journal on Multicultural Societies* (UNESCO), 9(1): 91-112, http://unesdoc.unesco.org/images/0015/001538/153803E.pdf#page=93.

Panos

1999 "Globalization and employment: New opportunities, real threats", Panos Briefing No. 33, May, London, http://www.panos.org.uk/?lid=272.

Pritchett, L.

2006 *Let Their People Come: Breaking the Gridlock on Global Labour Mobility*, Center for Global Development, Washington, D.C., http://www.cgdev.org/content/publications/detail/10174.

Rodrik, D.

2002 "Feasible Globalizations", July, Harvard University, Cambridge, MA, http://ksghome.harvard.edu/~drodrik/Feasglob.pdf.

Ratha, D., S. Mohapatra, K.M. Vijayalakshmi and Z. Xu

2007 *Remittance Trends 2007*, Migration and Development Brief 3, 29 November, Migration and Remittances Team, Development Prospects Group, World Bank, Washington, D.C., http://siteresources.worldbank.org/EXTDECPROSPECTS/Resources/476882-1157133580628/BriefingNote3.pdf.

Sachs, J.

1996 "Globalization and Employment", Public Lecture, 18 March, International Institute for Labour Studies, ILO, Geneva, http://www.ilo.org/public/english/bureau/inst/papers/publecs/sachs/index.htm.

Schiff, M.

2006 "Migration, Investment and Trade: Substitutes or Complements?", World Bank, Universidad de Chile and IZA, October, http://www.eudnet.net/download/Schiff.pdf.

Singa Boyenge, J-P.

2007 "ILO database on export processing zones (Revised)", WP.251, April, Sectoral Activities Programme, International Labour Office, Geneva, http://www.ilo.org/public/english/dialogue/sector/themes/epz/epz-db.pdf.

United Nations Commission on Trade and Development (UNCTAD)

2001 "Movement of Natural Persons under the GATS: Perspectives for the New Negotiations", Mimeo, UNCTAD, Geneva.

2006 *World Investment Report – FDI from Developing and Transition Economies: Implications for Development*, UN, New York and Geneva, http://www.unctad.org/TEMPLATES/webflyer.asp?docid=7431&intItemID=2068&lang=1&mode=toc.

United Nations Department of Economic and Social Affairs (UN DESA), Population Division

2006 *World Migrant Stock: The 2005 Revision*, UN DESA, Population Division, New York, http://esa.un.org/migration/.

2007 *World Population Prospects: The 2006 Revision*, UN DESA, Population Division, New York, http://esa.un.org/unpp/index.asp?panel=2.

Walmsley, T.L. and A. Winters

2003 "Relaxing the Restrictions on the Temporary Movements of Natural Persons: A Simulation Analysis", Centre for Economic Policy Research, Discussion Paper No. 3719, January, London.

Winters, L.A., T.L. Walmsley, Z.K. Wang and R. Grynberg

2003 "Liberalising the Temporary Movement of Natural Persons: An Agenda for the Development Round", *World Economy*, 26(8): 1137-1161.

World Bank

2002 *Globalization, Growth, and Poverty: Building an Inclusive World Economy*; The International Bank for Reconstruction and Development / The World Bank, Washington, D.C.

2006 *Global Economic Prospects 2006: Economic Implications of Remittances and Migration*, The International Bank for Reconstruction and Development / The World Bank, Washington, D.C., http://www-wds.worldbank.org/external/default/WDSContentServer/IW3P/IB/2005/11/14/000112742_20051114174928/Rendered/PDF/343200GEP02006.pdf.

2007 *Global Economic Prospects 2007: Managing the Next Wave of Globalization*, The International Bank for Reconstruction and Development / The World Bank, Washington, D.C., http://www-wds.worldbank.org/external/default/WDSContentServer/IW3P/IB/2006/12/06/000112742_20061206155022/Rendered/PDF/381400GEP2007.pdf.

World Commission on the Social Dimension of Globalization

2004 *A Fair Globalization: Creating Opportunities for All*, February, ILO, Geneva, http://www.ilo.org/public/english/wcsdg/docs/report.pdf.

Textbox 1.4 - Decent Work and Migrant Workers

International Labour Organization (ILO)

2004 Resolution concerning a fair deal for migrant workers in the global economy, adopted at the 92nd Session of the International Labour Conference, Geneva, in: *Report of the Committee on Migrant Workers, Provisional Record 22*, International Labour Conference, 92nd Session, International Labour Office, Geneva (pp. 55-64), http://www.ilo.org/public/english/protection/migrant/download/ilcmig_res-eng.pdf.

2006 *ILO Multilateral Framework on Labour Migration: Non-binding principles and guidelines for a rights-based approach to labour migration*, International Labour Office, Geneva, http://www.ilo.org/public/english/protection/migrant/download/multilat_fwk_en.pdf.

Stalker, P.

2000 *Workers without Frontiers: The Impact of Globalization on International Migration*, International Labour Office, Geneva.

HIGHLY SKILLED MIGRATION*

CHAPTER 2

1. Introduction

The major countries of destination have admitted increasing numbers of highly skilled migrants since the early 1990s. At the beginning of the decade, the traditional countries of immigration had already put into place policies pitched to increase their intake of highly skilled migrants, though most European countries did not review their policies to attract skilled migrants until the latter part of the decade.

This trend towards skilled migration is continuing today and appears to be a composite result of evolving government policies and changes in the nature of the global labour demand and supply.

Highly skilled migrants are involved in various migration scenarios. The largest stock of skilled migrant workers consists of permanent residents, even though the flow of short-term migrants is increasing and often exceeds the yearly admission of skilled immigrants on a permanent basis. Various countries admit increasing numbers of skilled workers under temporary worker schemes, and continued to do so even during the post-2001 economic recession. Indeed, in some countries temporary migration schemes are of a more transitional nature because they either permit, or do not impede, the eventual acquisition of permanent resident status.

The other notable change is what has been referred to as the spectacular increase in the flow and stock of foreign students (OECD, 2004). In fact, foreign students are increasingly seen as an integral and advantageous component of policies to attract highly skilled migrants. Some countries are developing specific policies to attract and retain students. Other forms of highly skilled migrant mobility include step migration from one country to another, and the return of often long-term migrants to their home countries, which some observers liken to circular migration.[1]

The increase in the migration of highly skilled workers raises the issue of brain drain and demographic indicators show that this concern may be warranted. About 10 per cent of all highly skilled persons from the developing world live in either North America or Europe. This proportion across

* This chapter was written by Lindsay Lowell, Institute for the Study of International Migration, Georgetown University, Washington, D.C.

[1] Step migration refers to mobility from an original residence to first one and then another destination, e.g. in a "stepwise" or sequential fashion. Circular migration is variously defined, but generally refers to recurrent movement between two countries (see also Chapter 11).

the board would appear to be about right in terms of the numbers necessary to generate linkages to the global economy and to yield positive feedback effects from the diaspora. But many Latin American, African and Caribbean countries have a much larger share of their highly skilled nationals living abroad, which poses a serious challenge to their own socio-economic development.

This chapter first reviews some of the trends in highly skilled migration in major countries of destination. The distribution of highly skilled migrants in different countries is reviewed, as well as their share of migrants from different source regions. Next, data on permanent immigrants are presented together with a brief discussion of the limited data available on temporary skilled foreign workers and foreign students, a subject addressed in more detail in Chapter 4. This is followed by a discussion of the major elements in admission policies associated with the trends in highly skilled migration. The chapter then turns to the impact of highly skilled migration on countries of origin. A brief discussion of the literature dealing with such impacts then leads to a discussion of policies that could contribute to optimizing highly skilled mobility for the benefit and development of countries of origin. The chapter concludes with some observations on policy and research implications.

2. The Increasing Mobility of the Highly Skilled

In recent years, new data sets based on the collection of national census data have revealed the patterns of highly skilled migration. They demonstrate that skilled migration is indeed increasing and that there are many and complex relations between major countries of origin and destination. Student migration also shows a marked increase and is likely to significantly influence the future volume, composition and destination of highly skilled migration (see also Chapter 4).

Migratory movements tend to be influenced by regional affinities. While policymakers and researchers have focused their attention mainly on migration from developing to developed countries, there are other types of flows that deserve attention. According to Ocampo (2006), South-North, South-South, and North-North migration flows account for roughly one-third each of the global distribution of migrant stocks. Moreover, the growing share of tertiary educated migrants in migration movements is notable, accounting, for instance, for a 46 per cent increase in migrant flows in OECD countries between 1990 and 2000.

2.1 Defining Highly Skilled

It is not always clear just who the highly skilled are. The most obvious indicator is either the level of education or occupation. Depending on the objective to be achieved, one or the other is preferred. If relevance to policy is important, most governments typically use a combination of both education and occupation to select the highly skilled. Ultimately, data availability often constrains the definition used for the purpose of analysis.

The most basic definition of highly skilled migrants tends to be restricted to persons with tertiary education, typically adults who have completed a formal two-year college education or more. This is also the most readily available international statistic and, by default, the most widely studied measure of highly skilled mobility. When possible, additional information regarding an academic or professional degree would be desirable. The National Science Foundation of the United States, which has some of the most complete international data on the stock of scientists and engineers, tends to focus on data for holders of doctoral degrees.

The Manual on the Measurement of Human Resources of 1995, or the "Canberra Manual", is a response to the work of both the OECD and the European

Commission's efforts to prioritize standardized data on human resources devoted to science and technology (S&T). It draws on best international and national practice and classifications and provides definitions in terms of qualifications (levels and fields of study) and occupations (Auriol and Sexton, 2002). While it is, perhaps, one of the most detailed definitional guidelines for comparative international statistics, its focus on S&T occupations limits its general usefulness.

Most frequently, governments define highly skilled migrants not in terms of either/or, but in terms of both education and occupation. For example, the United States' well-known "specialty worker H-1B visa" is based on a list of specific occupations and a minimum academic requirement of a Bachelor's degree. The definition of "highly skilled" depends on both an educational component and a threshold defining minimum competence in a knowledge-based society.

Professional activity and experience are important as selection criteria as this allows to filter out workers with little education and to target desired skills. The S&T occupations defined in the Canberra Manual are an example in point as they focus on technical skills regarded as crucial for research and development (R&D) and the engineering requirements of knowledge-based economies.

However, to restrict the meaning of highly skilled to S&T occupations would be too narrow an approach as it would disregard other high-skill categories that are in significant demand, such as business persons, managers, teachers or healthcare providers. Of course, it is possible to go beyond narrowly defined immigration policy interests by extending it to include a "creative class" that includes S&T workers as well as writers and artists (Florida and Tinagli, 2004). Arguably, such an expanded definition goes beyond the domain of immigration policy, as creativity has, or should have, deeper endogenous wellsprings, although it raises an interesting point about what might be considered as most important for national productivity — education, skills or creativity? Other than for the specific purpose of constructing international norms in statistics, occupation is important precisely because it points to what is being done; and what is being done is ultimately of critical importance. Highly skilled persons are mainly in high value-added and high productivity activities that are essential to the global knowledge society. S&T workers, physicians and business persons bring different competencies and their professional activities at various levels combine to advance economic and social development and national wealth.

2.2 Flows and Stocks of Highly Skilled Migrants

The existing data on the mobility of highly skilled individuals are limited to the assessment of persons with tertiary education and have only recently been compiled for the World Bank and the OECD using national censuses. Putting these estimates together is a substantial task requiring the collection of data from national censuses in destination countries, which often work with different definitions. More refined estimates, for instance regarding more detailed levels of education, or for the mobility of men versus women, or by occupation, have yet to be developed.

Using tertiary education, Figure 2.1 shows that the growth of highly skilled migration to EU countries already started in the early 1990s, preceding the "New Economy" and the boom in the information, communications and technology (ICT) sectors. Once underway, the percentage of highly skilled migrants increased until the end of the ICT-led cycle in 2001. From just under 15 per cent of all migrants in 1991, the share of the highly skilled grew to just over one-quarter of all migrants by 2001.[2]

[2] For the EU, the new immigrants are those who arrived in the respective year. For the United States, new immigrants are those admitted during the past five years.

In contrast, the share of highly skilled migrants to the United States initially accounted for about one-quarter of all recently arrived immigrants, increasing to around 30 per cent already by the mid-1990s. Compared to European countries, the United States started the 1990s with a substantial share of highly skilled immigrants attributable to the Immigration Act of 1990, which increased both permanent and temporary visas for highly skilled workers.

Figure 2.1

Percentage of New Immigrant Adults Aged 15-64 with Tertiary Education

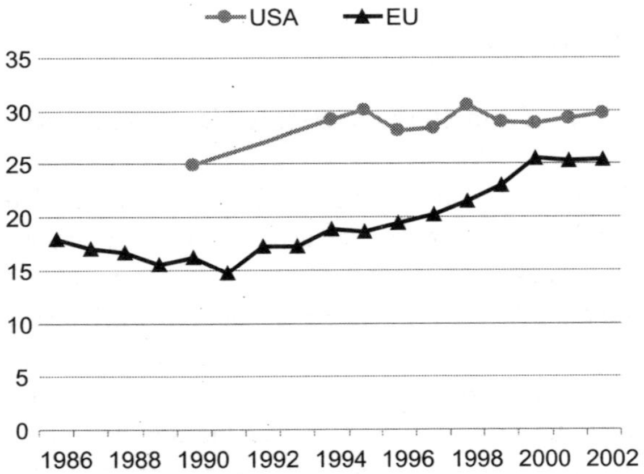

Sources: *European Commission (2003: 197, chart 139); tabulations U.S. Census microdata.*

As from the mid-1990s, however, the share of skilled migrants in the U.S. intake stabilized while it increased in Europe. The sharp increase in the European intake in the late 1990s appears to have stabilized around 2000, or just at the peak of the ICT boom, despite the fact that many countries had introduced policies to attract the highly skilled. This would indicate that, while policies can have a significant impact on the intake of highly skilled migrants, economic conditions strongly influence trends.

Table 2.1 shows the distribution in 2000 of the tertiary-educated, foreign-born individuals by country of residence. Asian-born migrants are the largest contingent of the internationally mobile population, making up 35 per cent of the world total. They are closely followed by European migrants, who make up 34 per cent of highly educated individuals living outside their countries of birth, the vast majority from the EU-25. They are followed by migrants from the Western Hemisphere, i.e. North America, Latin America and the Caribbean, who account for 23 per cent, and African migrants who account for about seven per cent of the total. It is not surprising that Asians predominate among the highly skilled migrants as they are mostly from developing countries and therefore strongly attracted by opportunities to improve their prospects. However, it is less well recognized that Europeans are also highly mobile as they move mostly within the region. Such moves are less driven by policies designed to attract migrants per se, than by a common history, contiguous borders, cultural affinities and the most recent EU enlargement.

Table 2.1:

Percentage of Tertiary Educated Foreign-born Adults by Region of Birth, 2000

Country of Residence	Region of Birth							
	Asia	Europe-EU25	Europe-Non EU	Africa	Latin American and the Caribbean	North America	Oceania	Total within Country
Australia	35	39	5	6	2	3	10	100
Austria	13	57	21	4	2	3	0	100
Belgium	11	68	4	13	2	3	0	100
Canada	35	35	7	6	11	5	1	100
Czech Rep.	8	64	24	1	1	2	0	100
Denmark	28	37	19	8	3	5	1	100
Finland	11	65	13	6	2	4	1	100
France	17	35	7	34	4	4	0	100
Germany	25	43	20	4	3	5	0	100
Greece	11	44	19	11	1	14	1	100
Hungary	5	30	61	1	1	2	0	100
Ireland	8	72	3	6	1	9	3	100
Italy	16	32	22	14	10	6	1	100
Japan	77	2	0	1	16	4	1	100
South Korea	86	2	0	0	0	11	1	100
Luxembourg	0	95	4	0	0	1	0	100
Mexico	7	25	3	1	34	31	0	100
Netherlands	28	36	6	10	17	3	1	100
New Zealand	24	47	3	7	1	4	15	100
Norway	23	49	9	6	4	9	1	100
Poland	4	28	67	0	0	1	0	100
Portugal	0	16	0	79	4	0	0	100
Slovak Rep.	3	79	17	1	0	1	0	100
Spain	6	39	8	8	35	4	0	100
Sweden	23	45	18	5	6	3	1	100
Switzerland	10	65	9	6	5	5	1	100
Turkey	6	56	33	0	0	5	0	100
U.K.	33	27	0	21	6	7	6	100
United States	41	16	5	4	29	4	1	100
Total OECD	**35**	**27**	**7**	**7**	**18**	**5**	**2**	**100**

Note: Adult population ages 25 and older. North America is Canada and the U.S. and the rest of the hemisphere is included in Latin America and the Caribbean.

Source: *Docquier and Marfouk (2006).*

A large proportion of migration occurs within a particular region. Although the United States and Canada receive most of their highly skilled immigrants from Asia, their prominent position as immigration countries is mainly due to their substantial intake of highly skilled residents from within the western hemisphere, with 33 per cent of highly skilled migrants moving to the U.S. from within the region, in particular from Canada and Mexico. Likewise, most European countries receive a large share of their highly skilled migrants from other European countries. The two Asian countries in Table 2.1, Japan and Republic of Korea (South Korea), equally draw the largest share of their highly skilled migrants from other Asian countries.

Former colonial or other historical ties also play an important role. Even though Australia is much closer to Asia and actively promotes policies to attract highly skilled migrants from that region, its most important source of highly skilled migrants is Europe. Similarly, 34 per cent of France's highly skilled migrants come from Africa, as do 79 per cent of highly skilled migrants to Portugal. Japan draws 16 per cent of its highly skilled migrants from South America, primarily because of historical links arising out of previous Japanese immigration to Brazil.

Thus, highly skilled migrants tend to move within regions or close to home. The supply of workers is more readily available in neighbouring countries where familiarity, the reduced cost of moving and historical linkages between countries facilitate mobility. At more distant removes, as when Asians migrate to the geographically distant Americas, previous migration or historical linkages to particular countries may come into play, for example owing to Chinese and Japanese labour migration in the latter part of the 19th century and the beginning of the 20th century, or later military interventions in Korea and Viet Nam. Such linkages help establish beachheads of immigrants who sponsor family members and establish networks that facilitate the movement of their compatriots.

Employers are eager to hire highly skilled migrants to offset local labour shortages or to respond to the "just-in-time" requirements of knowledge-based economies and tight production timeframes. Today's labour markets remain regionally clustered but are obviously extending further. Local labour shortages are not the only reason why employers hire immigrants; they do so also because, in a globalizing economy, they can. It is ever easier to advertise for and identify potential workers in other countries, and international recruitment agencies arrange to bring workers and employers together. At best, expanding labour markets make for more productive enterprises that benefit all stakeholders. The challenge is to implement policies that inhibit unscrupulous employers from hiring foreign workers at low wages and displacing local workers.

2.3 Temporary Workers and Foreign Students

It is widely recognized that increasing numbers of temporary workers and foreign students, courted by policies designed to attract them, are part of the evolving mobility of highly skilled migrants. Several European countries, in particular, are further developing their policies aimed to attract highly skilled migrants. Unfortunately, there are no systematic data on these movements and the numbers can only be inferred from comparative collections in the annual migration reports of the OECD (OECD, 2006a). Such data indicate that at least 650,000 highly skilled temporary workers are admitted yearly by OECD countries, a threefold increase since the early 1990s.

The trends in student numbers are described here to provide a fuller picture of new mobility patterns and are discussed in depth in Chapter 4. From 800,000 in 1980, the number of foreign students rose to 1.2 million in 1990; by 2000 their numbers had increased to 1.9 million and reached 2.7 million in 2004 (OECD, 2006b). The origins and destinations of students are broadly similar to that of all tertiary-educated migrants, but they are even more likely to come from

Asia or Africa. The reason why student mobility is important is because it may be the leading edge of increased migration by highly skilled persons from these source regions.

The reasons for the long-term increase in numbers are numerous and include more aggressive policies introduced in many countries since the late 1990s. Major European and English-speaking countries have implemented policies explicitly designed to attract students.[3] These policies fall within three general areas: (1) facilitating student admission policies; (2) student outreach and university marketing programmes; and (3) (in most new policies) providing for easier transition from student to worker status, especially for science and engineering students (Suter and Jandl, 2006).

3. Attraction and Admission Policies

What are the specific features of immigration policies that have led to the increasing flow of highly skilled workers and students to the major destination countries? A complete and final analysis is difficult because of the variety of policies involved, the variations in their timing and the fact that the nature of international mobility continues to change. Any quick and simple answers are unlikely since the issues involved are transitional and complex by nature. But it is desirable and should be possible to compare national policies according to their various regulations that can be changed independently or in concert to affect the composition and/or level of admissions.

In recent years, there have been many changes in the admission policies of major countries of destination, perhaps most notably the United Kingdom, but also France, Ireland and Germany. The Canadian and Australian admission systems have also recently introduced several changes; however, these countries have courted skilled migrants for nearly two decades. Arguably, most of the important changes or numerical increases concern temporary admissions (Zlotnik, 2005), with fewer changes in permanent admissions.[4]

What components of policy attract greater numbers of highly skilled migrants? Obviously, the contingent reserved for a given visa by implication regulates the potential volume of migrants, but numbers may be capped, uncapped or set by some impartial mechanism. Similarly, variations in different elements make a visa more or less attractive to either the potential employer or migrant worker. The policy elements in these countries often differ, but they tend to include at least the following seven components (Lowell, 2004).[5]

(i) Visa numbers: Some countries are creating new working visas with large or even unlimited numerical caps, while others adjust numbers periodically. Large or uncapped numbers tend to favour increasing immigration.

(ii) Labour market test: Often migrants are allowed entry only if there appears to be a shortage of local workers. This protects the local workforce from undue competition, but if stringently applied, labour market tests favour less immigration and may encourage employers to raise wages.

[3] The United States has over a fifth of all international students and about half of those in the English-speaking world. The number of students going to the U.S. dropped markedly during 2001 and many observers argue that the U.S. became more "restrictive" and lost out in the new competitive environment. But what changed post 9/11 was the implementation of pre-existing regulations, such as consular interviews for all applicants, but at such short notice that this led to backlogs. Also, steeply rising U.S. tuition costs, cited by students as the major deterrent, along with other factors inhibited student applications. Sharply rebounding student visa issuances since 2005 suggest that recessionary impacts and administrative bottlenecks have abated (Lowell and Bump, 2006).

[4] As recently as 2002, McLaughlan and Salt (2002: 3) studied admission policies for the highly skilled in 31 countries concluding that "[m]ost European countries, together with developed Asian ones, have not introduced special measures to recruit highly skilled workers. They continue to rely on their existing work permit systems".

[5] These rankings were undertaken in 2004 and there have been some notable changes since then. However, the countries that have instituted changes, and the nature of those changes, make it unlikely that the ranking of these admission regimes would change markedly.

(iii) Labour protections: After a visa is issued, requirements may be set concerning the wages, working conditions or employment of migrants.[6] This protects both migrants and local workers, but requires oversight and may be objected to by employers.

(iv) Enforcement mechanisms: Admission systems are increasingly interwoven with security concerns and their bureaucracies. Stringent admission processes can slow admissions and/or deter migrants. Some countries attribute post-admission enforcement responsibilities to ministries responsible for employment, though others mandate no agency. Generally speaking, lax systems favour increased immigration (and abuses).

(v) Employer portability: Temporary or transitional work visas may require migrants to stay with a sponsoring employer for a set period. Employers tend to favour this arrangement, but workers prefer the possibility to negotiate new employment at any point.

(vi) Restrictions on dependants/working spouse: Often the spouse has not been permitted to work if the principal holds a transitional visa. Many countries are relaxing this regulation, a move which potential highly skilled migrants find attractive.

(vii) Permanent residence rights: Many highly skilled migrants work on temporary work visas and initially do not intend to stay permanently. By encouraging a transition to permanent residence, countries offer a strong incentive to potential highly skilled migrants (see Portrait 2.1).

[6] The employment of migrants may be contingent on the notification of domestic workers, unions and/or regulations that bar employment if local workers are laid off.

Portrait 2.1

Working as an IT Specialist in the Czech Republic

Stojanco is 28 years old and comes from a small town in the Former Yugoslav Republic of Macedonia (FYROM) where his family has lived for several generations. Since November 2005, he has been working as an IT engineer for IBM in Brno in the Czech Republic. He is also a participant in the Government's Pilot Project on the Selection of Qualified Foreign Workers,[1] which enables selected skilled foreigners who have obtained employment and temporary residence in the Czech Republic to qualify more rapidly for permanent residence.

Stojanco began his undergraduate studies in FYROM before leaving for Bulgaria to study electrical engineering. He recalls: "After four semesters in a school at home, I had the choice of either continuing my studies in Skopje or to go to Bulgaria to study. Because of the war, and also because I wanted to see more of the world, I went to Bulgaria. My decision to study there was also influenced by the fact that it was less expensive to study in Bulgaria than in my home country. I did not have to pay tuition fees and the cost of living was also lower."

Four years later, Stojanko completed his studies in Bulgaria and returned to FYROM, where he stayed for some time before deciding again to leave: "I was back in a community context where everybody knew everybody and I did not have the right connections to find employment. In the Czech Republic, a person who has knowledge and skills and is good at what he does can find a job."

He learnt about the Czech Pilot Project on the Selection of Qualified Foreign Workers from newspaper articles and a TV programme. He was aware that foreign workers were needed in the Czech Republic: "Generally, I knew that the Czech Republic needed experts from other countries as Czechs were leaving to work abroad and that there was a lack of young people and young professionals".

When Stojanco found that IBM was looking for skilled workers in the Czech Republic, he applied through a company in Bulgaria that had organized a tender for jobs and advertised this at the university where he had studied. In the final round of interviews Stojanco was successful, and his application to work for IBM in the Czech Republic was accepted. IBM made the arrangements for his employment in Brno and organized all the necessary documents so that he could move to work there.

Once in the Czech Republic, Stojanco began to look for more information on the Pilot Project and found some useful indications on the website of the Ministry of Labour and Social Affairs. After spending three months to assemble the necessary documents, which included not only the work and residence permit but also documents confirming his education and language skills, he was interviewed and informed that he met the selection criteria for participation. While Stojanco does not speak the Czech language very well, he understands it quite well, and his employer also paid for him to attend a two-month Czech language course. He is keen to improve his language skills, but finds it a challenge as English is the main language spoken at work.

When asked why he joined the Pilot Project, he explains: "Mainly because it is an easier and faster way to obtain permanent residence in the Czech Republic, which I consider the greatest advantage of the Project. When I'm granted permanent residence, I will have the chance, for instance, to acquire a mortgage to buy a flat."

Since Stojanco arrived in Brno, much has changed in the city where only few migrants had lived before. IBM alone employs about 1,000 migrants. Stojanco observes: "Many of them are from my home country and Bulgaria, but there are also people from India or South Africa working in our company. In fact, from all over the world."

Stojanco does not intend to return home just yet: "I am not yet ready to return home. Before I do so, I would still like to get to know the world. I now have many friends in Brno. But I'm not here only to earn money. I also like to be here and enjoy the style of life." However, he remains uninterested in politics: "That is one thing I prefer not to be interested in. If you are from the Balkans, as I am, then you know that there are at least as many different and often politicized versions of each historical event, as there are peoples affected by them. Each country tends to develop its own interpretation of history. That is why I prefer to just concentrate on my work as an IT specialist and use my skills, without becoming too involved in politics and other sensitive issues."

Note:

1 The Pilot Project (2003-2008) provides selected qualified foreign workers, who are already in lawful employment in the Czech Republic, with the opportunity to apply for permanent residence within a shorter period of time, after one and a half years (in the highly qualified workers category) or two and a half years (in the standard category of qualified workers) of uninterrupted stay and work (as compared to the current standard period of five years).

The project is open to citizens of Belarus, Bosnia and Herzegovina, Canada, Croatia, FYROM, India, Kazakhstan, Moldova, Montenegro, the Russian Federation, Serbia and Ukraine; graduates of Czech universities coming from all countries (except those who studied in the Czech Republic as part of development assistance projects organized with their home country), who graduated in 1995 or later; and graduates of Czech secondary schools from all countries, who finished their studies and passed the school leaving exam in 2000 or later. In order to qualify for participation, applicants must obtain at least 25 points in the computerized selection procedure reflecting various criteria (e.g., qualifications, practical experience, language skills, family situation). Family members of project participants are also allowed to settle in the Czech Republic and obtain permanent residence there.

The Project is implemented by the Czech Ministry of Labour and Social Affairs in cooperation with the Ministry of Foreign Affairs and the Ministry of Interior. The office of the International Organization for Migration (IOM) in Prague, together with IOM missions in the qualifying countries, assist the Czech Government to disseminate information on the Project.

Source: *Adapted from Pilot Project Selection of Qualified Foreign Workers (Reporter: Martina Křížková, Faculty of Social Sciences, Charles University, Prague, 18 July 2007) http://www.imigrace.mpsv.cz/?lang=en&article=media2&mm=4176.*

The application of these regulations may vary significantly among countries. However, there has been little national or comparative evaluation of the success of admission programmes. In fact, there is rather little international effort to evaluate programmes, other than all-too-often perfunctory administrative/legislative reviews, and very few countries have attempted to either collect the necessary data or carry out rigorous analyses.

Certainly, countries have different criteria for measuring success and particular countries may even have conducted experiments with different programmes intended to achieve different ends. However, it appears that there is very little interest in policy evaluation when it comes to the impact of admission policies on highly skilled migration. According to McLaughlan and Salt (2002), the five approaches most often used to determine success are qualitative assessments to see whether policy objectives have been met; measurement of work outputs; level of complaints lodged by stakeholders; surveys of public opinion; and research conducted internally or externally. The authors note that only Australia, Canada, Germany and the United States have carried out such systematic research. Comparative frameworks for programme evaluation are therefore still at the development stage.

In fact, most international policy studies to date do little more than specify criteria deemed important for comparative purposes. The most detailed comparative study so far, completed in 2000 (Christian, 2000), covers some 15 countries and compares them in terms of class of admission (type of migrant/business stream), the use of quotas, the type of employment authorization (employer or employee-based), and application procedures (employer or employee-based). Rollason (2002), whose main focus is on the United Kingdom, remarks on the comparative features of temporary or permanent programmes in 11 countries in terms of the categories of workers, general/specific admissions, tests for the availability of domestic workers, quotas, period of stay and possibilities for renewal, and the permissibility of family reunification. Having constructed major criteria for comparison, however, none of these studies goes on to draw firm conclusions about effective practices. Even the regular reporting on policy changes in the OECD's annual *Trends in International Migration*, rarely draws any strong conclusions.

One exception to this tendency to make systematic comparisons while drawing few conclusions is found in Papademetriou (2003), who identifies four major strategies to admit skilled immigrants: employment-based admissions where employers apply to hire a worker under conditions that safeguard domestic labour; labour market testing where government agencies identify sectors with labour shortages; talent accrual where points are awarded for characteristics like education or language ability; and "filtration systems" where permanent residence status is awarded to students or temporary workers who first demonstrate their value. He suggests that a combination of the best of these strategies might be a good approach and might be accomplished using a points system, similar to those used in Australia and Canada, awarding points for sub-elements of each of the four strategies. In this regard, he starts with an evaluation of the strengths and weaknesses of various strategies, not recommending one or the other, but rather a combination of the best elements of each.

In addition, there have been policy recommendations for the orderly management of migration on a worldwide basis that are in some ways supplementary to legally binding standards, such as those found in international trade agreements. They offer ideas for the cooperative management of highly skilled workers between developing and developed countries. Such projects include the Transatlantic Learning Connection (1999) or the International Regime for Orderly Movements of People (Ghosh, 2000). In partnership with the International Organization for Migration (IOM), the Swiss Government launched the Global Consultative Process for Inter-State Cooperation on Migration Management in 2001 (Berne Initiative), which contributed to the development of the International Agenda for Migration Management (IAMM) (2005) containing a set of common understandings and effective practices for a planned, balanced and comprehensive approach to the management of migration.

The Global Commission on International Migration was launched by the U.N. Secretary-General and a number of governments in December 2003. The Commission's final report in October 2005 makes recommendations on how to improve the national, regional and global management of international migration (GCIM, 2005). In the European Union, the recent enlargement to 27 members has renewed pressure to go beyond the harmonization of national policies to a common legal migration policy (Van Selm and Tsolakis, 2003), including a proposal for a EU Directive on the conditions of entry and residence of highly skilled workers from non-EU third countries (European Commission, 2005). In October 2007, the European Commission published a Communication introducing this draft directive. The proposal establishes a fast-track procedure for the admission of highly qualified workers from third countries, based on a common definition and criteria. Workers admitted would be provided with an "EU Blue Card", essentially a residence permit allowing them to work and also affording them a set of rights, including favourable family reunification conditions. The proposal envisages restrictions on access to the labour market for the first two years in the Member State of residence. Thereafter, such workers would enjoy equal treatment with nationals as regards access to highly qualified employment. Moreover, after two years of lawful residence in the first Member State, the proposal would enable the migrant to move for work to another Member State subject to certain conditions (European Commission, 2007). While there has been progress in the development of common policies on asylum seekers and refugees and on the treatment and movement of long-term third-country residents, the achievement of consensus on the establishment of common criteria for the admission and residence of highly skilled migrants in EU Member States will require a great deal more work.

4. Policies that Address Brain Drain[7]

It is fair to say that the greatest competition has been for highly skilled migrants from the developing world, the source of the largest and growing numbers of highly educated persons. Despite Europe's increasing intake, the United States remains the dominant destination country for highly skilled workers from developing countries. Already at the outset of the 1990s, the U.S. had just over half of the world's highly skilled migrants from the developing world (Carrington and Detragiache, 1999). In fact, Table 2.2 shows that the traditional North American destinations of the United States and Canada have been the place of residence of nearly two-thirds (65%) of the world's tertiary educated foreign-born adults in 1990 and 2000. The traditional countries of immigration, along with Sweden and Norway, are the most successful countries relative to the size of their own populations in attracting highly skilled migrants (Lowell, 2006).

These figures translate into substantial losses of highly skilled populations for the developing world. As of 2001, nearly one in every ten tertiary educated adults born in the developing world resided in North America, Australia or western Europe. About five per cent of the developing world's emigrants with secondary education live in industrialized countries and the figures for the upper echelons are even higher. It is estimated that 30 to 50 per cent of the developing world's population trained in science

[7] See also Chapter 12, which discusses some of these policies.

Table 2.2:

Percentage of All Tertiary Educated Foreign-born Adults by Region of Residence and Region of Birth, 1990 and 2000

Region of Birth	Region of Residence					
	Europe	North America	Latin America and the Caribbean	Asia	Oceania	Total from Region of Birth
	2000					
Europe	36.7	49.9	0.6	1.6	11.3	100
North America	24.9	62.1	4.6	2.3	6.1	100
Latin America & Caribbean	8.0	88.3	1.3	1.4	1.0	100
Asia	14.5	73.1	0.1	4.2	8.0	100
Oceania	22.4	27.2	0.1	0.7	49.6	100
Africa	47.8	44.5	0.1	0.1	7.6	100
Total OECD	23.6	64.8	0.7	2.4	8.5	100
	1990					
Europe	27.2	57.2	0.8	0.9	13.9	100
North America	19.1	67.2	4.8	2.9	6.0	100
Latin America & Caribbean	7.9	87.3	2.2	1.2	1.5	100
Asia	13.5	69.0	0.2	7.7	9.6	100
Oceania	15.3	28.5	0.1	0.8	55.3	100
Africa	46.8	43.2	0.1	0.1	9.8	100
Total OECD	20.3	64.9	1.0	3.2	10.7	100

Note: Adult population ages 25 and older. North America comprises Canada and the U.S. and the rest of the hemisphere is included in Latin America and the Caribbean. Includes mobility across national borders and within the region. Data collected for OECD destination countries.
Source: *Docquier and Marouk (2006) (authors' tabulations of online database).*

and technology live in the developed world (Lowell, Findlay and Stewart, 2004).

Still, a brain drain can only be said to have occurred where there is clear evidence that migration flows have had adverse consequences for the source economy. The growing research literature finds that a relatively large-scale emigration of highly skilled workers relative to their populations, particularly from least developed economies and smaller developing countries, has adverse impacts on national economic growth. The difficulties caused by the increasing emigration of health workers from developing to developed countries are illustrated in Textbox 2.1. However, some observers argue that a certain degree of highly skilled emigration is required for source countries to benefit from links to the global economy. Also, highly skilled migrants may reinvest human and economic capital in their home countries. Indeed, emigration rates of some five to ten per cent may benefit economic growth, but higher rates can be detrimental and, unfortunately, are not uncommon for many Caribbean and African countries (Docquier, 2005).

Textbox 2.1

Globalization and the Mobility of Health Workers

Globally, health workers are on the move. Although they move to many parts of the world, their migration is increasingly asymmetrical, from developing to developed countries, reflecting a broader dynamic context in which labour markets for skilled professionals are becoming global. The main destination countries of health worker migrants are indicated in Table 2.3. The United States currently employs the greatest number of foreign-trained doctors and nurses, followed by the United Kingdom. Of all regions, sub-Saharan Africa suffers the greatest shortage of health workers, yet doctors trained in this region represent close to one quarter (23%) of the current foreign-trained doctor workforce in OECD countries (Pond and McPake, 2006).

Table 2.3

Health Workers moving to OECD Countries from Developing Countries

	Doctors from abroad		Nurses from abroad	
OECD country	Number	% of total	Number	% of total
Australia	11,122	21	-	-
Canada	13,620	23	19,061	6
Finland	1,003	9	140	0
France	11,269	6	-	-
Germany	17,318	6	26,284	3
Ireland	-	-	8,758	14
New Zealand	2,832	34	10,616	21
Portugal	1,258	4	-	-
United Kingdom	69,813	33	65,000	10
United States	213,331	27	99,456	5

Note: - = not applicable
Source: *WHO (2006: 98).*

In addition to emigration, many developing countries continue to experience the internal movement of health workers from rural or under-served to urban areas. With increased international private health investment and "medical tourism", they are also witnessing a flow of health workers from public to private healthcare systems. The result of these migratory flows has been diminished access to healthcare and services for individuals who depend on the public healthcare system – the system used by the large majority of poorer populations in developing countries (Marchal and Kegels, 2003). Low health worker density and diminished service access and availability, in turn, correlate with increased mortality among infants, children under five years of age and women during childbirth.

Globalization contributes in various ways to the conditions which lead to all three forms of health worker migration: rural to urban, public to private, low-income to high-income country. First, there are generally applicable enabling factors. Professional credentials are increasingly recognized across borders particularly where free trade areas have been formed, the European Economic Area (EEA) serving as the best example. Eased migration and mobility (including, for instance, through cheaper, faster and easier travel, multilingualism, post-colonial ties and common academic curricula) have contributed to a veritable sense of "global citizenship" worldwide, with professional credentials serving as passports. The opportunity to accumulate savings and remit portions of incomes to family and communities back home is another incentive for health workers to migrate. The Internet – one of globalization's primary tools – has increased access to recruitment agency and employer websites. Diasporas established in the developed countries have also become another factor of attraction.

Second, deteriorating economic, social and environmental conditions "push" health workers to seek a better life abroad (Dovlo and Martineau, 2004; UNFPA, 2005). In many countries, economic deterioration has, in part, resulted from poorly sequenced or overly rapid global market integration; financial crises arising from increased flows of speculative capital; loss of public revenues due to trade liberalization and a decline in tariffs; and requirements for privatization, cost recovery or expenditure ceilings associated with loans or debt relief from international financial institutions (IFIs), all of which limit the ability for governments to pay adequate salaries or to provide incentives for health workers to remain (Joint Learning Initiative, 2004).

Finally, globalization is making it easier for rich countries to "pull" in health workers. A number of regional trade treaties incorporate specific measures designed to encourage the free movement of labour within their defined geopolitical areas. Border barriers in many rich countries are being actively lowered for professional and highly skilled immigrants but raised for lesser skilled individuals. These same countries often experience shortages in their domestic supply of health workers and the increased demand of an ageing population. They rely heavily on the immigration of foreign-trained professionals to fill the supply/demand gap – even while enjoying better health status and a much higher ratio of health workers to the population than many of the countries from which foreign-trained health professionals migrate. Their ability to offer higher pay, better working conditions and greater opportunities in safer environments will continue to pull in foreign health workers until supply exceeds demand (Mullan, 2005; Wilbulpropraserl et al., 2004).

Short of an end to "globalization-as-we-have-come-to-know-it", this flow will continue. The policy challenge is one of reducing both the "push" and the "pull" factors. Since this "push/pull" flow is inherently global, managing it to ensure that health does not suffer will require multilateral agreements and strategies.

Source: *Ron Labonté and Corinne Packer, Institute of Population Health, Faculty of Medicine, University of Ottawa, Canada.*

In short, high levels of skilled emigration can unfavourably affect local development, even though it may simultaneously generate benefits. Most studies find that adverse impacts are most commonly associated with permanent as opposed to temporary migration of the highly skilled. Otherwise, the benefits of highly skilled labour migration flows are neither automatic nor inevitable. The extent to which these migrant flows benefit developing source countries will depend on the development and implementation of appropriate policies that optimize the benefits and minimize the costs. To be effective, these policies are best developed in both countries of origin and destination, both separately and in partnership with one another. There are at least three policy arenas which have the potential to generate a regulatory environment that benefits source countries: adoption of multilateral and bilateral agreements to harmonize policies; managing return migration; and fostering the transfer of knowledge and remittances by diasporas (Lowell, Findlay and Stewart, 2004). A fourth approach, which would consist of restricting outflows, is sometimes put forward, but it conflicts with individual rights, such as the human right to leave one's own country and, given the contemporary interplay of labour dynamics, is unlikely to be effective.

4.1 Migration Agreements and Policy Harmonization

Multilateral and bilateral agreements are among the best means to manage the exchange of workers, especially where a chronic shortage of labour in host countries can be met by a surplus of appropriately skilled labour from a country of origin. But, just as it took decades for the construction of international regimes to regulate trade, it may take years before there are equivalent multilateral migration regimes. In the meantime, adopting appropriate bilateral and regional agreements may be both more feasible and, in some cases, preferable for other reasons.

Intergovernmental agreements enable national authorities to agree on the elements that govern the exchange of workers and occupations, or the types of workers concerned. They are an alternative to the damaging practice of "head-hunting" by international recruitment agencies, which often seek migrant workers from developing countries where high-skill endowments are scarce and who can least afford to lose their professional and scientific elite. At the same time, bilateral agreements can stipulate that foreign workers must be trained in the destination country in the skills appropriate to the needs of the developing country. However, bilateral and multilateral agreements may not be able to meet short-term or cyclic shortages, and they may place developing countries at a disadvantage in certain bargaining situations (Koivusalo, 2003).

The General Agreement on Trade in Services (GATS) is seen as the most promising approach towards a broad multilateral framework to govern the mobility of skilled persons. The Mode 4 elements of the GATS (see Textbox Int. 1) can reduce the risks of a loss of scarce skilled human resources because it offers a managed approach to the temporary movement of service workers. Developing countries with the highest initial barriers to trade in services stand to gain the most from the liberalization of this type of movement. Developing countries like Brunei, China, the Philippines and Thailand are aware of this and made more commitments under Mode 4 delivery of services by "natural persons abroad" than under other Modes. Future progress requires the adoption by all parties of clear definitions and transparent regulations (Findlay and Warren, 2000).

4.2 Managing Return Migration

Return migration is often referred to as capable of generating significant benefits for the country of origin (Ellerman, 2003). The return of highly skilled expatriates with their newly acquired skills, taste for innovation and the potential to create networks can be especially advantageous (see Textbox 2.2). Certainly, highly skilled returnees offer benefits that are often overlooked when foreign advisors or business persons are called upon in their stead, while temporary or short-term movers have been shown to maintain a commitment to send money back home. Return can be facilitated, if not always permanently, then with targeted programmes that benefit the country of origin.

Textbox 2.2

Impacts of Return Migrants on the IT Industry in India

Labour migration from India has been slowly changing over the last few decades; whereas the 1970s and 1980s saw a large outflow of Indian workers to the Middle East, since the 1990s the new wave of labour migration has been of highly skilled migrants, particularly working in the information technology (IT) sector (Chishti, 2007).

The United States has emerged as the most popular destination for engineering graduates and IT professionals. Indeed, migration from India to the United States doubled in the 1990s, and its contribution to the U.S. IT boom is now well established (Chishti, 2007). In 2001, out of 331,206 H1B visas granted, 49 per cent went to Indian professionals of which 92 per cent concerned IT-related jobs (Hira, 2004).

Originally, this outflow occurred not only in response to the growing demand in countries of destination, but also owing to a lack of opportunities for IT specialists in India itself (Vinutha, 2005). However, the situation has since changed. The impact of the growing number of foreign firms investing and establishing themselves in the Indian economy (Kalita, 2006), together with the saturation of the IT job market and strict immigration and visa control in the U.S. (Babu, 2003), has brought about unprecedented opportunities. Furthermore, India has also experienced rapid growth in its own IT industry and developed strong business connections between India and Indian IT professionals in developed countries (Chishti, 2007). This environment has encouraged IT expatriate professionals, especially in the U.S., to return to India for business opportunities thereby generating a phenomenon of "reverse brain drain" (Vinutha, 2005). According to one estimate, between 30,000 and 40,000 expatriate professionals have returned to Bangalore, India's major technology hub, of their own volition in the last ten years alone (Kalita, 2006).

One of the most important impacts of return migrants on India's IT economy, besides any capital investments, has been the transfer of knowledge, expertise, market information and work culture to the Indian economy. This development has, in turn, generated what may be referred to as "chain migration", as the environment created by return migrants makes the IT industry increasingly attractive for other IT expatriate professionals to return. In addition, global economic and work practices are becoming increasingly established in Indian companies increasing further their attractiveness for expatriate Indian IT professionals.

The returning migrants show a highly diverse professional profile, ranging from recent graduates from American institutions who return to India for their first jobs to those who return to retire in India (Weisman, 2005).

Making the most of the IT boom in India, many young non-resident Indian (NRI) professionals have become eager to return. Many of these highly qualified returnees now occupy top and mid level positions in India. Although the figures vary, it is estimated that between five and 12 per cent of applications for such positions are received from NRIs (Menon, 2003), and this trend is expected to increase further.

The contribution made by such highly skilled returnees to the growth of the Indian IT sector is also confirmed by the rapid growth in revenues from software exports of 33 per cent in the year 2005-2006 (Chishti, 2007). Thus, today India's so-called brain drain has come full circle. The popularity of "career fairs" held in the U.S. to attract Indian expatriates back from the Silicon Valley to a prospering Indian IT industry attests to this development (Shiels, 2003).

Source: *IOM Dhaka.*

For countries of destination, the most direct and honest means of achieving return is to create temporary worker programmes with short durations of stay and mechanisms that facilitate return (Martin, 2003; see also Chapter 3). Assuredly, the longer migrant workers stay abroad, the lower the likelihood of their return to their places of origin. In developmental terms, there are strong reasons to encourage return at the end of fixed-term contracts. However, for that to occur there must be political acceptance and commitment. In fact, as previously discussed, many "temporary" work permit programmes in Europe permit a transition to permanent residence status after a period of several years (see also Chapter 11). And U.S. temporary programmes place few obstacles in the way of workers who ultimately choose to apply for permanent residency.

It is therefore a great challenge from a policy development point of view to find the appropriate balance between protecting the rights of highly skilled temporary workers, circumscribing opportunities for permanent residency without eliminating them altogether **and** creating incentives for return. This is an area where effective practices are yet to be elaborated. In broad terms, however, it could be argued that what is needed is a new, systematic approach, where conditions are created to enable the ethical recruitment of workers (including through private employment agencies adhering to equitable and professional standards); prevent exploitative practices (Jones and Pardthaisong, 1997); facilitate the movement of such workers; encourage the maintenance of linkages with their country of origin; and to create attractive options for return. Each of these steps has been experimented with, but they are rarely found together in a purposeful combination. It is fairly obvious that such a programme cannot be attempted in isolation by either the home or host country, but calls for close cooperation between them.

4.3 Diasporas and the Transfer of Knowledge and Remittances

A country's expatriate populations, or diaspora, can transfer knowledge, technology and capital back home (see also Chapter 12). Exercising the so-called diaspora option is a relatively low-cost means of capturing tangible returns from expatriates, other than through their return. The exchange of knowledge from a diaspora draws primarily upon networks, often informally constituted, of professionals, intellectuals and scientists abroad. Networks can also be fostered by government programmes and through the establishment of ongoing contacts with source country academic and other relevant institutions.

One of the leading proponents of diaspora management argues that this networked approach turns brain drain into a brain gain, and that it overcomes institutional barriers to the flow of information (Meyer, 2001). Studies indicate that international cooperation in academia and research bolsters economic growth. For instance, a study of Columbia's "Caldas" network established expatriates' involvement in oversight committees and active collaboration in areas of scientific research. The diaspora option can be a low-cost approach to leveraging expatriates' knowledge without permanent return. Research also finds evidence of the growing strength of electronically linked diasporas and different institutional forms of diaspora organizations (Sami, 2006). In recent years, considerable attention has been paid to the establishment of communication networks by governments (for example, the South African Network of Skills Abroad or the Mexican Talent Network) or private institutions (e.g. Red Caldas in Colombia, or Chile Global) to promote and facilitate the involvement of highly skilled migrants in the economic life of their countries of origin (Kutznetsov, 2006).

Remittances are another means by which workers can boost development at home. The global volume of remittances is significant and increasing rapidly. Remittances represent a sizable share of GDP in many countries and almost always exceed foreign aid. It is estimated that each remittance dollar multiplies into two to three dollars of GDP, and there is evidence that remittances can help to alleviate poverty. However, the impact of remittances by highly skilled workers should not be overstated. Such workers integrate rapidly into the society of the host country and, because they often tend to bring their families with them, are less likely to remit over time (Faini, 2003). Rather, highly skilled migrants could have a more powerful impact by way of investments, business partnerships and more sophisticated financial flows to foreign currency accounts or to remittance-backed bonds.

4.4 Policies for Democracy and Development

Finally, the successful management of migration requires the adoption of a holistic approach, which includes tackling the causes of migration. Highly educated individuals often emigrate not because of fundamental demographic and economic factors, but because of a lack of basic freedoms. The loss of highly educated persons can undermine the foundations of democracy and the institutions needed for well-run economies. Human rights abuses and lack of democracy are at the root of what are, in most respects, non-pecuniary brain drains. Investment in the protection of human rights and the promotion of democracy should take into account the role of intellectuals, seeking means of retaining them, as well as ways of benefiting from the diaspora. Expatriate organizations can and do play a political role in actively promoting free speech and democracy.

In the same vein, emigration may occur not simply because of basic economic disparities, but because of the constraints on R&D and educational institutions. In many developing countries, public budget allocations to research, science and technology are limited, and young professionals find it difficult to remain motivated. Highly educated or skilled individuals often wish to operate in challenging environments. The crux of the theory of optimal brain circulation is that emigration of highly skilled individuals can induce those remaining behind to pursue higher education. As elegant as that may sound, educational institutions of countries experiencing brain drain face severe problems. Human resources are one of the key factors leading to economic development, and policies that strengthen educational institutions and promulgate training are likely to have a beneficial impact. General cooperative ventures between developed and developing countries are, perhaps, some of the more policy-relevant tools available. For example, schemes that aim to strengthen the capacity of specific educational institutions in countries of origin may provide one effective strategy for compensating skilled emigration.

5. Policy Implications

While most policymakers believe that policies help shape the flow of skilled migrants, their precise role, or the role of individual policy elements, has not been systematically studied. Some researchers see admission policies as a response to the prevailing political economy or as unnatural impediments to international mobility. There is little interest here in breaking down the nuances of various policy elements. Surprisingly, most formal migration theories - and there is "no single, well-developed theory" of the determinants of migration - do not even include admission policy in the mix (Russell, 1995; Massey et al., 1994). More to the point, comparative research is lacking on how **policy elements** shape the size and composition of highly skilled migration. So, the impacts of labour market tests, consular interviews, rejection rates, retention offers, and the like, have tended not to be studied as part of a system.

Analysts tend to agree that general features of admission policies have profound impacts on the skill composition of immigration. The long dominance of family admissions in the United States and Europe, for example, is thought to have reduced the skill levels of immigrants over time. The decline in the average skill level appears also to have been a key factor underlying research findings concerning the somewhat poor economic integration of newcomers (Borjas, 1999). The outcomes of policy choices are never fully predictable, however, since Canadian immigrants, purportedly selected for their likely economic success, integrate no more readily than Latino immigrants to the U.S. (Antecol et al., 2004). In turn, the integration prospects of Latino immigrants are affected not only by poor average levels of education, but also by the fact that many of them are undocumented and have no prospects of regularization under current policies. At any rate, it can be argued that the declining skill levels of individuals admitted only on the basis of their family ties may be one reason for the introduction of policies in so many countries during the 1990s that tend to tilt more towards admission on the basis of labour market skills (Chiswick, 2005) (see also Chapter 6).

Economists raise some interesting points about the causes of the level of immigration. They do not necessarily agree on whether policies impose a cost affecting the decision to migrate, or are a quantity constraint that conditions the impacts of push/pull factors. But empirical analyses find that policies matter. Analysis of emigration to the United States finds that quota consolidations reduced Asian immigration in the 1970s, while the legalization of nearly three million workers doubled Latino migration in the 1990s (Hatton and Williamson, 2003). However, these policies are seen as operating within a structure of restrictive immigration policies and the dominant impacts of economic variables on the flows are interpreted accordingly. In fact, highly restrictive policies could well make various push and pull factors irrelevant, or at least make extrapolating the empirically measured impact of push/pull factors difficult, if not impossible if policies were to change. At the same time, an analysis of emigration to 14 OECD countries found that pull factors are the dominant driver and that push factors play no substantive role (Mayda, 2005). While other research finds that push factors do play a role in emigration, this analysis, based on a substantial sample of countries, suggests that pull factors are the driving force of international flows. In fact, an interaction of restrictive policies with pull variables suggests that laxer admission policies increase the power of pull factors in the host economy (Orrenius, 2003).

These analyses suggest that the level of immigration depends heavily on economic conditions. As long as those conditions favour migration, reducing restrictions on immigration by either lifting caps or easing admission requirements should increase overall levels of immigration. This may not be a terribly provocative observation, but it is consistent with recent trends in the mobility of highly skilled individuals. Most observers agree that globalization is now the dominant force driving this type of movement (see also Chapter 1).

The ICT revolution appears to be one force of globalization, an observation reinforced by the timing of increasing migration during the New Economy boom of the 1990s and the fact that many new policies explicitly target ICT workers. The ICT revolution has fuelled globalization by helping to further flatten the differences between national markets. It also feeds agglomeration economies and helps link those major cities where skilled immigrants reside (Sassen, 2006; Smith, 2003). The ICT revolution favours highly skilled workers and may continue to do so, unless what appears to be the complexity of using today's ICT technologies changes and becomes accessible to lesser skilled workers. Secondly, economic development in transitional economies has altered the international specialization of production, enhancing demand for highly skilled workers in the advanced economies. There are, however, transitional economies that have a growing educated class and increased R&D capacity that may alter this scenario. Some observers think the most likely prognosis is for decreasing migration between industrialized countries and increasing migration between developing countries (Hatton and Williamson, 2003; McLaughlan and Salt, 2002).

6. Conclusion

The huge and growing differentials in the demographic profiles between developed and developing countries, coupled with persistent economic disparities, make it a certainty that there will be a plentiful supply of potential migrants for many years to come. No competing for migrants via ever laxer policies will be necessary, as the number of migrants may be expected to increase and satisfy demand; rather, the challenge will be to design policies with the right balance of elements to attract the best and the brightest, while also including incentives for the optimal return of migrants to encourage their participation in the economic development of their countries of origin.

At the same time, these forecasts do little to ease concerns about the potential effects of brain drain. Despite the surprisingly widespread belief that highly skilled migration is either benign or clearly beneficial to the development of the country of origin, the research literature suggests adverse economic consequences follow losses of more than 10 to 20 per cent of a source country's college educated population. Particular countries experience losses well above this range, while certain sectors, such as health services or information technology, also experience losses several times this amount. Moreover, the social costs of highly skilled migration to migrants and their families are hardly negligible (see Textbox 2.3). Given the foregoing speculation about future trends, the potential adverse effects of highly skilled migration are likely to remain a potent challenge to economic and social development.

Fortunately, there are a number of proactive policies that might be able to address those challenges and even generate optimal benefits from highly skilled migration.

Textbox 2.3

Social Costs of the Migration of Women Health Workers

Health care workers around the world are increasingly looking to migration to find employment. While health professionals may move abroad to pursue further training and career development, for many health workers, in particular for those moving from developing to developed countries, the main reason for migration is to find better pay and improved working and living conditions.

Public Services International (PSI), a global federation of public-sector trade unions representing more than 20 million workers, has documented many cases where the work in women-dominated labour market segments, such as the health sector, continues to be seriously undervalued and discriminated against. For example, a nurse with qualifications up to degree-level, plus five years professional experience and who supervises a team of 15, will earn only two-thirds of the salary of a craft supervisor, who, for instance, has completed an apprenticeship, has three years job experience and supervises two people. Similar examples of wage discrimination between female-dominated labour segments, such as nursing and caregiving, and jobs predominantly performed by men could be cited.

Moreover, the participatory research conducted in developing countries of origin by PSI in 2003-2004 demonstrated the effects of structural reforms and the reduction of public health services on women health workers, as they struggle with heavy workloads, low and inequitable wages, violence in the workplace, inadequate resources and the added responsibility of caring for their families. As a result, many women health workers have migrated or are considering migrating to find work in developed countries. However, when asked what their preferred choice would be, a majority of the workers interviewed during the research replied that they would prefer to stay in their home countries if they could earn a living wage.

The book published by PSI, *Who Cares? Women Health Workers in the Global Labour Market* (Van Eyck, 2005), presents the histories of women health workers as they struggle to cope with the difficulties of migration, gender disparities, deteriorating working conditions in the health sector and the undervaluing of women's work. Migration flows oriented towards the health care and health services sector are increasingly dominated by women migrants. Within what scholars refer to as the "global care chain", women increasingly migrate to find work overseas, allowing other women to participate in the local labour market (see also Textbox Int.3).

Hoping to find better paying jobs, health care workers leave health sector employment in their home countries to take up work abroad. Unfortunately, for many of them that hope does not always translate into reality. Private recruiters and unscrupulous employers prey on migrant workers and their vulnerability and desperation, charging exorbitant fees that could lead to a form of bonded labour. Several documented cases reveal breaches of work contracts, threats of deportation, health care professionals whose qualifications are ignored and who work in jobs well below their skill level, denial of trade union rights and various forms of exploitation and abuse. Women migrant health workers pay a high social cost as they face gender, class and race discrimination in their host societies, are subjected to heavy workloads, isolation and separation from their children and families, particularly in cases when family reunification is not possible. Separation of families due to migration has been known to lead to other societal problems, such as the eventual break-up of the family unit, alcoholism, drug abuse, juvenile delinquency and children's failure at school.

As the global union organizing and representing workers in the health sector, PSI launched in 2005 a project on *International Migration and Women Health Workers*, engaging public-sector trade unions in both home and host countries in bilateral partnerships to provide information to potential migrant health workers on their rights and the realities of migration; organize and defend women health workers' rights to better pay and working conditions through adequately funded public health services; denounce cases of violations; and call for the application of ethical recruitment guidelines and internationally established human rights norms and standards in the employment of migrant health workers.

One example of an information and organizing tool developed by PSI is the *Pre-decision Kit for Migrant Health Workers*, which consists of a package of information and facts about the realities of migration, employment conditions and legal rights in the destination country, contacts to union resources and how to join unions, as well as other basic information explaining the issues surrounding migration in the health sector. It is called a "pre-decision kit" because trade unions aim to provide information at the pre-decision stage, when a health worker is still considering the option of migrating for employment. PSI believes that with proper information and trade union support and in cooperation with civil society organizations, governments and the private sector, various migration pitfalls and the abuse of migrant workers can be avoided.

Source: *Geneviève Gencianos, Public Services International, http://www.world-psi.org/migration.*

REFERENCES

Antecol, H., D. Cobb-Clark and S. Trejo
2004 "The History of Selective Immigration in Australia, Canada, and the United States", *Brussels Economic Review*, Special Issue on Skilled Migration, 47(1): 45-56.

Borjas, G.J.
1999 "The Economic Analysis of Immigration" in O.C. Ashenfelter and D. Card (Eds), *Handbook of Labor Economics*, Vol. 3A, Elsevier, Amsterdam, 1697-1760.

Carrington, W.J. and E. Detragiache
1999 "How Extensive is the Brain Drain?", *Finance and Development*, 36(2), http://www.imf.org/external/pubs/ft/fandd/1999/06/carringt.htm.

Chiswick, B.R.
2005 "High Skilled Immigration in the International Arena", IZA Discussion Paper No. 1782, September, Forschungsinstitut zur Zukunft der Arbeit (Institute for the Study of Labour), Bonn, http://ftp.iza.org/dp1782.pdf.

Christian, B.P.
2000 "Facilitating High-Skilled Migration to Advanced Industrial Countries: Comparative Policies", Working Paper, Institute for the Study of International Migration (ISIM), Georgetown University, Washington, D.C.

Docquier, F.
2006 "Brain Drain and Inequality Across Nations", IZA Discussion Paper No. 2440, November, Institute for the Study of Labour, Bonn, http://ftp.iza.org/dp2440.pdf.

Docquier, F. and A. Marfouk
2006 "International Migration by Educational Attainment (1990-2000)" in C. Özden and M.W. Schiff (Eds.), *International Migration, Remittances and the Brain Drain*, Palgrave-Macmillan, London, 151-200.

Ellerman, D.
2003 "Policy Research on Migration and Development", World Bank Policy Research Working Paper 3117.

European Commission
2003 *Employment in Europe 2003. Recent Trends and Prospects*, Directorate-General for Employment and Social Affairs, September, Office for Official Publications of the European Communities, Luxembourg, http://ec.europa.eu/employment_social/employment_analysis/employ_2003_en.htm.

2005 *Policy Plan on Legal Migration*, COM (2005) 669 of 21 December.

2007 *Proposal for a Council Directive on the conditions of entry and residence of third-country nationals for the purposes of highly qualified employment*, COM (2007) 637 of 23 October.

Faini, R.
2003 "Is the Brain Drain an Unmitigated Blessing?", United Nations University, World Institute for Development Economics Research (UN-WIDER) Discussion Paper No. 2003/64, http://www.wider.unu.edu/publications/working-papers/discussion-papers/2003/en_GB/dp2003-064/.

Findlay, C. and T. Warren
2000 "The GATS and developing economies in the ESCAP region", *Studies in Trade and Investment*, 37: 11-60.

Florida, R. and I. Tinagli
2004 *Europe in the Creative Age*, February, Carnegie Mellon Software Industry Center, co-published in Europe with DEMOS, http://www.demos.co.uk/files/EuropeintheCreativeAge2004.pdf.

Ghosh, B. (Ed.)
2000 *Managing Migration – Time for a New International Regime?*, Oxford University Press, Oxford.

Global Commission on International Migration (GCIM)
2005 *Migration in an interconnected world: New directions for action*, Report of the GCIM, October, SRO-Kundig, Geneva, http://www.gcim.org/attachements/gcim-complete-report-2005.pdf.

Hanson, G.H. and A. Spilimbergo
1996 "Illegal Immigration, Border Enforcement, and Relative Wages: Evidence from Apprehensions at the U.S.-Mexico Border", Inter-American Development Bank (IADB) Working Paper Series 328, Washington, D.C.

Hatton, T.J. and J.G. Williamson
2003 "What fundamentals drive world migration?", National Bureau of Economic Research (NBER) Working Paper No. 9159 (September), Cambridge, MA.

International Organization for Migration (IOM) and Swiss Federal Office for Migration
2005 *International Agenda for Migration Management*, IOM and Swiss Federal Migration Office, Geneva/Berne.

Jones, H. and T. Pardthaisong
1997 "The commodification of international labour migration", Centre for Applied Population Research Paper 97/4, University of Dundee, Dundee, United Kingdom.

Koivusalo, M.
2003 "The Impact of WTO Agreements on Health and Development Policies", Globalism and Social Policy Programme, Policy Brief No. 3 (January), http://gaspp.stakes.fi/NR/rdonlyres/3000F54A-DDCF-48C4-AFFE-056867902724/0/policybrief3.pdf.

Kutznetsov, Y. (Ed.)
2006 *Diaspora Networks and the International Migration of Skills: How Countries Can Draw on Their Talent Abroad*, The World Bank, Washington, D.C.

Lowell, B.L.
2004 "Policies and Regulations for Managing Skilled International Migration for Work", United Nations, Department of Economic and Social Affairs (UN DESA), Population Division, New York, http://www.un.org/esa/population/meetings/ittmigdev2005/P03-LLowell.pdf.

2006 *An Evaluation of an Extended Index on Pro-Development Migration Policies*, Report to the Center for Global Development, Washington, D.C., http://www.cgdev.org/doc/cdi/2006/lowellMigration.pdf.

Lowell, B.L. and M. Bump
2006 "U.S. Competitiveness: Foreign Students in Science, Technology, Engineering and Math", ISIM, Georgetown University, Washington, D.C.

Lowell, B.L., A. Findlay and E. Stewart
2004 "Brain Strain: Optimising Highly Skilled Emigration from Developing Countries", Asylum and Migration Working Paper 3, Institute for Public Policy Research (IPPR), London, http://www.ippr.org.uk/ecomm/files/brainstrain.pdf.

Martin, P.L.
2003 "Highly Skilled Labor Migration: Sharing the Benefits", May, International Institute for Labour Studies, ILO, Geneva, http://www.ilo.org/public/english/bureau/inst/download/migration2.pdf.

Mayda, A.M.
2005 "International Migration: A Panel Data Analysis of Economic and Non-Economic Determinants", IZA Discussion Paper No. 1590, May, Institute for the Study of Labour, Bonn, ftp://repec.iza.org/RePEc/Discussionpaper/dp1590.pdf.

McLaughlan, G. and J. Salt
2002 *Migration Policies Towards Highly Skilled Foreign Workers*, Report to the Home Office, Migration Research Unit, University College London, http://www.geog.ucl.ac.uk/research/mobility-identity-and-security/migration-research-unit/pdfs/highly_skilled.pdf.

Meyer, J-B.
2001 "Network approach versus brain drain: Lessons from the diaspora", *International Migration*, 39(5): 91-110.

Massey, D.S., J. Arango, G. Hugo, A. Kouaouci, A. Pellegrino and J.E. Taylor
1994 "An Evaluation of International Migration Theory: The North American Case", *Population and Development Review*, 20(4): 699-751.

Ocampo, J.A.
2006 "International Migration and Development", presentation to the United Nations International Symposium on International Migration and Development, 28-30 June, Turin, http://www.un.org/esa/population/migration/turin/Turin_Statements/OCAMPO.pdf.

Organisation for Economic Co-operation and Development (OECD)
2004 *Trends in International Migration: Annual Report*, SOPEMI, OECD, Paris.

2006a *International Migration Outlook*, SOPEMI, OECD, Paris.

2006b *Education at a Glance 2006*, Chart Box C3.1, www.oecd.org/dataoecd/46/0/37368660.xls.

Orrenius, P.M.
2003 "Do Amnesty Programs Reduce Undocumented Immigration? Evidence from IRCA", *Demography*, 40(3): 437-450.

Papademetriou, D.G.
2003 "Innovation in the selection of highly skilled immigrants", presentation at the Athens Capstone Conference on Managing Migration for the Benefit of Europe, sponsored by the Greek Presidency of the European Union, 15-17 May, Athens.

Price, M. and L. Benton-Short
2006 "Counting Immigrants in Cities across the Globe", *Migration Information Source*, January, Migration Policy Institute (MPI), Washington, D.C., http://www.migrationinformation.org/Feature/display.cfm?ID=567.

Rollason, N.
2002 "International mobility of highly skilled workers: the UK perspective" in OECD (Ed.), *International Mobility of the Highly Skilled*, OECD, Paris, 372-342.

Russell, S.S.
1995 "International Migration: Implications for The World Bank", Working Paper No. 54, May, Human Capital Development and Operations Policy, The World Bank, Washington, D.C., http://www-wds.worldbank.org/external/default/WDSContentServer/WDSP/IB/1995/05/01/000009265_3961019111203/Rendered/PDF/multi0page.pdf.

Sami, M. and P. de Guchteneire (Eds.)
2006 Transnational Knowledge through Diaspora Networks, Special Issue, *International Journal on Multicultural Societies*, 8(1).

Sassen, S.
2006 *Territory, Authority, Rights: From Medieval to Global Assemblages*, Princeton University Press, Princeton, NJ.

Smith, H.
2002 "Global Migration: New Zealand and European Union Experiences and Challenges", paper delivered at the Inaugural New Zealand European Studies Conference, 31 May, National Centre for Research on Europe, University of Canterbury, Christchurch, New Zealand.

Suter, B. and M. Jandl
2006 *Comparative Study on Policies towards Foreign Students: Study on Admission and Retention Policies towards Foreign Students in Industrialised Countries*, International Centre for Migration Policy Development (ICMPD), Vienna, http://www.icmpd.org/774.html?&F=2&tx_icmpd_pi2%5Bdocument%5D=548&cHash=10fde5b0ec.

Transatlantic Learning Community
1999 *International migration in Europe and North America: policy recommendations for the new millennium*, Final Report of the Transatlantic Learning Community prepared for the Cooperative Efforts to Manage Emigration (CEME) Project, University of California at Davis.

Van Selm, J. and E. Tsolakis
2003 "The Enlargement of an 'Area of Freedom, Security and Justice': Managing Migration in a European Union of 25 Members", Policy Brief No. 4, May, MPI, Washington, D.C., http://www.migrationpolicy.org/pubs/eu_enlargement.pdf.

Zlotnik, H.
2005 "International Migration Trends Since 1980" in *International Migration and the Millennium Development Goals: Selected Papers of the UNFPA Expert Group Meeting, Marrakech, Morocco, 11-12 May 2005*, United Nations Population Fund (UNFPA), New York, 13-28, http://www.unfpa.org/upload/lib_pub_file/487_filename_migration_report_2005.pdf.

Textbox 2.1 - Globalization and the Mobility of Health Workers

Dovlo, D. and T. Martineau

2004 "A Review of the Migration of Africa's Health Professionals", Working Paper 4-4, Joint Learning Initiative on Human Resources for Health, Harvard University, Cambridge, MA.

Joint Learning Initiative (JLI)

2004 *Human Resources for Health: Overcoming the crisis*, JLI, Harvard University Press, Cambridge, MA, http://www.who.int/hrh/documents/JLi_hrh_report.pdf.

Marchal, B. and G. Kegels

2003 "Health workforce imbalances in times of globalisation: brain drain or professional mobility", *International Journal of Health Planning and Management*, 18/S1: S89-S101, http://www3.interscience.wiley.com/cgi-bin/jissue/106561850.

Mullan, F.

2005 "The Metrics of the Physician Brain Drain", *The New England Journal of Medicine*, 353/17: 1810-1818.

Pond, B. and B. McPake

2006 "The health migration crisis: the role of four Organisation for Economic Co-operation and Development countries", *The Lancet*, 367/9520 (29 April): 1448-1455, http://www.thelancet.com/search/results?search_mode=cluster&search_cluster=thelancet&search_text1=Pond+and+McPake&x=15&y=12.

United Nations Population Fund (UNFPA)

2005 *International Migration and the Millennium Development Goals*, UNFPA, New York, http://www.unfpa.org/upload/lib_pub_file/487_filename_migration_report_2005.pdf.

Wilbulprasert, S., C. Pachanee, S. Pitayarangsarit and P. Hempisut

2004 "International service trade and its implications for human resources for health: a case study of Thailand", *Human Resources for Health*, 2(10), http://www.human-resources-health.com/content/pdf/1478-4491-2-10.pdf.

World Health Organization (WHO)

2006 *Working together for health. The World Health Report 2006*, WHO, Geneva, http://www.who.int/whr/2006/whr06_en.pdf.

Textbox 2.2 - Impacts of Return Migrants on the IT Industry in India

Babu, M.

2003 "Do NRI techies need motivation to return home?", *IT People Evolve*, http://www.expressitpeople.com/20030818/abroad1.shtml.

Chishti, M.

2007 "The Rise in Remittances to India: A Closer Look", *Migration Information Source*, February, Migration Policy Institute, Washington, D.C., http://www.migrationinformation.org/Feature/display.cfm?id=577.

Hira, R.

2004 "U.S. Immigration Regulations and India's Information Technology Industry", *Technological Forecasting and Social Change*, 71(8): 837-854.

Kalita, S.M.

2006 "A Reversal of the Tide in India: Tech Workers Flow Home to More Success", *Washington Post*, 28 February, http://www.washingtonpost.com/wp-dyn/content/article/2006/02/27/AR2006022701513.html.

Menon, R.

2003 "NRI techies head back home", *The Times of India*, 30 October, http://timesofindia.indiatimes.com/articleshow/258117.cms.

Shiels, M.

2003 "IT professionals return to India", BBC News, 23 July, http://news.bbc.co.uk/2/hi/business/3083817.stm.

Vinutha, V.

2005 "India beckons", Express Computer Online, 21 March, http://www.expresscomputeronline.com/20050321/technologylife01.shtml.

Weisman, R.

2005 "High-tech talent flows back to India: those who helped fuel US boom may spur brain drain", *The Boston Globe*, 8 August, http://www.boston.com/news/world/asia/articles/2005/08/08/high_tech_talent_flows_back_to_india/.

Textbox 2.3 - Social Costs of the Migration of Women Health Workers

Van Eyck, K. (Ed.)
2005 *Who Cares? Women Health Workers in the Global Labour Market*, Public Services International (PSI) and UNISON UK, Ferney-Voltaire, France, http://www.world-psi.org/Content/ContentGroups/English7/Publications1/Who_Cares.pdf.

LOW AND SEMI-SKILLED WORKERS ABROAD*

CHAPTER 3

1. Introduction

The world appears to be on the threshold of a new era in temporary labour migration programmes, characterized by more sources and destinations of migrant workers at all rungs of the job ladder (Martin, 2003b; Abella, 2006). Current temporary labour migration programmes aim to add workers temporarily to the labour force, but not settlers to the population. This may seem surprising, since programmes such as the Mexico-U.S. Bracero and the German *Gastarbeiter* (guest worker) programmes ended when destination country governments were persuaded that large numbers of temporary migrant workers adversely affected local workers and could result in migration getting "out of control".[1]

In a world of persisting demographic and economic inequalities and better communication and transportation links, young people in particular want to cross national borders for higher wages and better opportunities. There is general agreement that the world is about to enter a new stage in international labour migration, with more labour migration sources and destinations and migrants employed in a wider range of industries and occupations.

The improved management of labour migration in the 21st century is likely to require temporary migrant worker programmes that include economic incentives to encourage employers and migrants to abide by programme rules. For example, employer-paid taxes on migrant earnings that finance the restructuring of migrant jobs can allow the programmes to shrink over time, while the refunding of worker-paid taxes can encourage migrants to return home as programme rules require while providing funds to stimulate economic development and to reduce the incentive to emigrate in the future. Adding such economic mechanisms could help to better align temporary labour migration programme objectives and outcomes, and convince industrialized countries that such programmes will not turn into furtive "side door" or de facto permanent immigration, but lead to more border gates being opened for regular migrant workers.

---

* This chapter was written by Philip Martin, Professor, Department of Agricultural and Resource Economics, University of California, Davis, California, United States.

[1] It is generally agreed that the Bracero programme sowed the seeds for later irregular Mexico-U.S. migration (Martin, 2004: Ch. 2), and that Germany faces major integration challenges with settled Turkish guest workers and their families (Martin, 2004: Ch. 6).

This chapter focuses on low and semi-skilled[2] migrants moving from developing to industrialized countries, such as from Mexico to the U.S. There is also a significant flow of low and semi-skilled migrant workers to a wide range of middle-income developing countries, including Argentina, Costa Rica, Malaysia, South Africa and Thailand. These labour flows are similar to those that take workers to developed countries, but differ in that many migrants sometimes fill jobs that are vacant because previous workers emigrated to richer countries, for instance when Poles migrate to the United Kingdom and their jobs at home are then taken up by Ukrainian migrants.

The chapter begins by addressing some key definitional issues, such as the notion of low and semi-skilled migrants and temporary labour migration. It then provides an overview of global and regional distributions of temporary migrants with particular reference to low and semi-skilled workers. The remaining parts of the chapter discuss some of the key policy challenges for temporary labour migration programmes to operate effectively in the 21st century and on a larger scale, and to increase their economic gains for all stakeholders, namely for migrant workers and countries of origin and of destination. Such challenges include the problems of economic distortion and dependence that can be traced to migrants and the "numbers versus rights" conundrum. These questions are also considered in more detail in Part B of the Report, especially in Chapter 11.

2 See also Section 2 on definitions.

2. Definitions

While it is fairly straightforward to define skilled or highly skilled migrants by reference to university or tertiary education and years of professional experience (see Chapter 2), the notion of low or semi-skilled employment is more nebulous and more difficult to define in any meaningful way. Put simply, as such workers fall outside the definition of skilled and highly skilled, this often means that in the immigration context they do not qualify under ordinary work permit schemes or points systems regulating admission to a country for the purpose of employment.[3]

This chapter and the Report in general use the terms "low" or "semi-skilled", but the notion of "unskilled" is deliberately avoided on the grounds that most workers, regardless of the nature of their tasks, have some basic skills, or that, indeed, as some commentators argue, the skills they have acquired are being grossly undervalued, as illustrated in Textbox 3.1 in relation to labour migration to Southern Africa. Yet, the positive correlation between the level of education and income can be observed on nearly all labour markets and is universally acknowledged.

3 For example, under the ordinary work permit scheme in the UK, this means determining **either** that the job requires the following qualifications: (i) the equivalent of a UK degree-level qualification; (ii) the equivalent of a Higher National Diploma (HND) qualification relevant to the post to be filled; or (iii) a HND qualification not relevant to the post on offer plus one year of relevant full-time work experience at National/Scottish Vocational Qualification (N/SVQ level 3 or above - **or** the job requires the following skills: 3 years full-time specialist working experience for the type of job for which the permit is sought (UK, 2008). To apply as a skilled worker under the Canadian points system, the applicant must have work experience of Skill Type 0 (managerial jobs), A (professional jobs) or B (technical jobs and skilled trades) as determined by the Canadian National Occupational Classification (NOC) (CIC Canada, 2007).

Textbox 3.1

Labour Migration in Southern Africa: A Case for the Review of the Concept of Low and Semi-skilled Migration

Cross-border migration for the purpose of employment in the Southern African Development Community (SADC) region is a long-standing historical phenomenon and continues to be one of the primary features of migration in the region generally. Since the mid-nineteenth century, the countries of Southern Africa have been sending and receiving migrants primarily to work in the mining industry. While most migrants initially moved independently, this was considered unprofitable by the mining industry, and a system of contract labour migration was set up to ensure a regular and reliable supply of migrant workers to the mining centres in the region, including Namibia, South Africa, Zambia and Zimbabwe. While the mining industry was and continues to be the major employer of migrant workers, commercial farms and plantations, as well as the construction, domestic and services sectors are also employers of significant numbers of migrant workers. In some cases, the contract labour system had been extended to these sectors as well.

Most of the migrant workers in these sectors fall into the categories commonly described as "low- skilled" or "semi-skilled". However, not only are these categories perhaps outdated as descriptive of the nature of and the level of skill often required by the migrants employed in these sectors, but they also devalue the contributions of migrant workers to the economies of the countries in which they work.

It is often assumed that temporary or contract migrant workers only supply manual labour to make up the numbers of people required to work in the mines and in the agricultural, construction and services sectors. However, in part due to the nature of the contract labour system and also as a general phenomenon, many of these migrant workers return at least annually to work in the same sectors and have over time, developed considerable skills and expertise in their jobs. For example, when the South African Government attempted to reduce the number of migrants working in the mines, the mining industry protested against this move, making the argument that it would be difficult to replace the accumulated skills and experience that have been built up amongst regular migrants who return to the same jobs year after year.

The inherent danger in describing temporary and contract migrant labour as "low-skilled" or "semi-skilled" does not only have to do with devaluing the contribution of migrants, but it also implicitly suggests that the migrants themselves are inferior, which in turn, feeds into the perception that migrant workers are poor and uneducated manual labourers who compete unfairly with nationals for available jobs. It is true, of course, that many employers prefer to hire migrant workers because it is cheaper to do so and migrants are generally more exploitable, but this has to do with the lack of protection mechanisms and measures for migrant workers, rather than being a reflection of their actual levels of skills, competencies and experiences.

Despite the deeply entrenched nature of labour migration in the SADC, governments have tried and continue to try and put a stop to it, if not in practice, at least rhetorically. In most cases, however, attempts to curb regular migration in these sectors have had unintended consequences and in particular, have led to increased irregular migration and heightened anti-migrant sentiments.

Perhaps the time has come for a reconsideration of the concept of "low-skilled" or "semi-skilled" migration. At some point, it may have been a useful classification or description of particular categories of jobs held by migrants, but it has now become equated with the devaluing of these jobs and the contributions of migrants. It also has the connotation that the migrants who occupy these jobs are themselves inferior and less deserving of the protection and opportunities afforded to migrants who are considered "highly-skilled".

This is, of course, not just a problem in Southern Africa, but is in fact magnified when the arguments presented here are considered and applied on a global scale, particularly in terms of migration from developing to developed countries.

Source: *Vincent Williams, Southern African Migration Project (SAMP).*

There seems to be no widely accepted definition of temporary labour migration. Abella (2006: 4) suggested a definition based on a destination country's perspective and considers "temporary migrants" as "those whose legal status is temporary, regardless of the amount of time they may actually have stayed in a country". It goes without saying that this is a very wide definition and would apply to an

> extremely broad array of different movements, conditions and durations, [including] *au pairs*, seasonal workers,[4] trainees, intra-corporate transfers, contract workers, working holiday makers, exchange visitors, highly skilled professionals, cross-border service providers, installers, performing artists and sportspersons, etc. (OECD, 2007: 51).

3. Global and Regional Distribution of Temporary Migrants with Particular Reference to Low and Semi-skilled Workers: Flows and Stocks

3.1 Global Distribution

Today, the world community consists of some 200 countries with their respective annual per capita incomes in 2004 ranging from less than USD 250 to over USD 50,000 (World Bank, 2006b). Such economic differentials provide a significant incentive, especially for young people, to migrate in pursuit of higher wages and better opportunities.[5] In 2004, one billion people, or one-sixth of the world's population, lived in the 30 high-income countries with a gross national income of USD 32 trillion, representing four-fifths of the global wealth of USD 40 trillion.[6] The resulting average per capita income of USD 32,000 in high-income countries was 21 times the average USD 1,500 in low and middle-income countries, and this 21:1 ratio has remained stable over the past quarter of a century (Martin et al., 2006).

Migration is an age-old response to variations in economic opportunity, security and other factors, but the crossing of international borders is a relatively recent phenomenon, as international borders have multiplied along with the sharp rise in the number of independent states making up the international community as it is known today.[7] The number of international migrants has also doubled during the past two decades to 191 million in 2005 (UN, 2006). As shown in Table 3.1, some 62 million migrants moved from South to North, i.e. from a developing to a developed country; 61 million moved from South to South; 53 million from North to North; and some 14 million migrants moved from North to South.[8]

Table 3.1:

Migrants in 2005 (millions)

Origin	Industrialized country	Developing country
Industrialized country	53	14
Developing country	62	61

Source: *UN, 2006.*

Given that about half of these migrants are absorbed into the labour force of the destination countries,

4 Seasonal labour migration is also by definition temporary in nature, and many of the policy issues discussed below and in Chapter 11 in relation to temporary labour migration, apply to mobility for the purpose of seasonal employment, which, however, has certain distinguishing characteristics. Importantly, seasonal labour migration comprises particularly short-term movements (3-9 months), which are dependent on the natural rhythm of the seasons, such as sowing and harvesting time in agriculture, and demands for workers in the hospitality sector especially during peak periods in the year (e.g. ski resorts in the winter, coastal resorts in the summer months in Europe).

5 Young people are most likely to cross borders as they have invested the least in jobs and careers at home and have the most time to recoup their "investment in migration" abroad.

6 At purchasing power parity (PPP), which takes into account national differences in the cost of living, the world's gross national income was USD 56 trillion, including 55 per cent in high-income countries.

7 From only a small number of recognized independent states at the beginning of the 20th century, the number of countries making up the international community as we know it today has risen to 193 by 2007, when the CIA World Factbook listed 193 "independent states", one "other" and six other entities (CIA, 2007).

8 These are stock estimates in 2005, meaning that migrants may have arrived recently or decades ago.

the 60 million migrant workers in high-income countries account for an average of 12 per cent of the local labour force (ILO, 2004). The labour force distribution of the 31 million migrant workers moving South-North is quite distinct from that in destination countries: 40 per cent of the 3.2 billion workers worldwide are in agriculture, 20 per cent in industry and construction, and 40 per cent in services (World Bank, 2006b), and migrant workers from developing countries largely originate from societies characterized by this 40:20:40 distribution. In industrialized countries only about three per cent of the total workforce is in agriculture, 25 per cent in industry and 72 per cent in services (OECD, 2005). However, a look at the distribution of migrant workers in these countries shows 10 per cent to be in agriculture, 40 per cent in industry and construction, and 50 per cent in services (OECD, 2006) (Table 3.2).

Table 3.2:

Migrants and Local Workers by Sector, Percentage Distribution

	Agriculture	Industry	Services
Industrialized countries	3	25	72
Developing countries	40	20	40
Migrants in industrialized host countries	10	40	50

Note:
Industry includes construction.

Sources: *OECD (2005), (2006), World Bank (2006b).*

The difference in migrant worker distribution reflects the three types of employers and respective demands for migrant workers in: (a) sunset industries – e.g. agriculture, light manufacturing, garment industry; (b) industries that cannot be moved – e.g. construction; and (c) services at all levels of the skills ladder, from IT and health care to domestic work and janitorial services.

Migrant workers from developing countries who move to industrialized countries also have personal characteristics that differentiate them from native-born adults. The best single determinant of individual earnings in industrialized countries is years of education. In most developing countries, the distribution of adults by years of education has the shape of a pyramid, a few well educated persons at the top and most workers with less than a secondary-school certificate or high-school diploma grouped near the bottom.

A graph showing native-born adults in high-income countries by years of education has a diamond shape. About 25 per cent have a college degree, 60 per cent a secondary-school certificate and 15 per cent have less than a secondary certificate or high-school diploma. Migrants from developing countries in industrialized countries differ from both adults at home and abroad, as their distribution resembles an hourglass or barbell shape when arranged by years of education. About 35 per cent have a college degree, 30 per cent a secondary school certificate and 35 per cent less than a high-school diploma (Figure 3.1). International migration from developing to industrialized countries takes persons from the top and bottom of a pyramid distribution and adds them to the top and bottom of a diamond-shaped distribution.

Figure 3.1:

Native-born and Migrant Adults in Industrialized Countries by Education, 2005 (percentage)

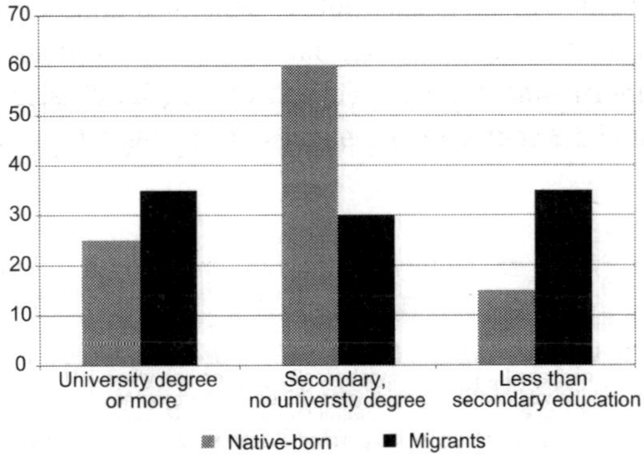

Migrants from developing countries drawn from the top of the education pyramid are often professionals and students, and most have become legal residents of industrialized countries. Over the past two decades, almost all industrialized countries have made it easier for foreign professionals to enter as students (see Chapter 4), temporary workers and settlers. However, most of the world's workers and most of the world's migrant workers have low skills, and a crucial labour migration issue is whether and how to move more low-skilled workers from developing to industrialized countries.

3.2 Regional Distribution

While most temporary labour migration flows are from developing to the developed OECD countries in Europe, North America, Australia and New Zealand, and in East Asia, i.e. Japan and the Republic of Korea (South Korea), significant regular movements also occur between developing countries, particularly from the countries of South and Southeast Asia to the oil-producing Gulf Cooperation Council (GCC) States (UN DESA, 2004) and within Southern Africa, and Latin America.[9]

According to OECD statistics, the number of temporary work permits issued to foreign workers admitted for employment in a number of OECD countries has increased steadily since 2000. From 2003 to 2004, temporary entries for work increased by approximately seven per cent (OECD, 2006), and these levels remained largely unchanged during 2005 with the admission of some 1.8 million temporary migrant workers into OECD countries (OECD, 2007).[10] Table 3.3 indicates the entries of temporary workers to selected OECD countries in the principal categories. While highly skilled migrants are more likely to be found in the intra-company transfer and general temporary workers category, low and semi-skilled migrants dominate in the seasonal workers, working holiday makers and trainees categories. Working holiday makers are a specific group of short-term entrants essentially to Australia, New Zealand and the United Kingdom, and are discussed in Chapter 5. As far as trainees are concerned, traineeships in Japan and the Republic of Korea have often been considered "a disguised form of lesser skilled migration" (OECD 2007: 52). In Japan, a growing number of such trainees stay for further employment after their traineeship ends (32,000 in 2005), while in South Korea the introduction of the employment permit scheme, which is mainly aimed at low-skilled occupations, means that admissions for temporary work are now taking place through this channel (60,000 in 2005) (OECD, 2007).[11]

Except for GCC States, where the foreign population outnumbers citizens,[12] stocks of temporary foreign workers are generally small relative to the size of the destination country's labour market (Nonnenmacher, 2007).

While globally the ratio of female to male migrants is almost 50:50, the ILO (2003) observes that, in recent times, the majority of women migrants are engaged in temporary labour migration, with the Middle East (including the GCC States), East Asia and Southeast Asia as the major poles of attraction. Female labour migration is characterized in particular by its concentration in a very limited number of female-dominated (essentially lower-skilled) occupations associated with traditional

[9] A snapshot of temporary labour migration trends and data in specific world regions with a focus on low and semi-skilled workers is provided in the sub-sections below. Supplementary information is available in the Regional Migration Overviews in the final part of the Report.

[10] These figures, however, do not cover the free labour mobility of EU nationals within the EU, including the recent large movements from the new accession countries, or temporary movements associated with the free movement of workers agreement between the EU and Switzerland (OECD, 2007).

[11] See also Chapter 8, which discusses the historical problems with the industrial trainee system (since phased out and replaced by the employment permit system) in South Korea in terms of increased irregular labour migration.

[12] For example, Ruhs and Martin (2006) observe that migrants constitute over 95 per cent of Kuwait's private sector labour force (citing statistics of the Kuwait Institute of Banking Studies; see http://www.kibs.org/eco/ecokmain.htm).

gender roles, such as domestic (see Textbox 3.2) and "entertainment" activities. Moreover, "while these jobs do not necessarily have to be exploitative, the circumstances of the job itself often lead to a high degree of vulnerability to abuse and exploitation, even forced labour and slavery." (ILO, 2003: 11).

Textbox 3.2

Women Migrants in Domestic Work

To give an idea of the significance of women migrants in domestic work, some figures are quoted here: in Hong Kong SAR, migrant domestic workers numbered more than 202,900 in 2000; between 1999 and June 2001, 691,285 Indonesian women left their country (representing 72% of all Indonesian migrants) to work mainly as domestic workers abroad; in Malaysia, there were 155,000 documented (and many more undocumented) migrant domestic workers in 2002; in Italy, 50 per cent of the estimated one million domestic workers are non-EU citizens, and in France over 50 per cent of migrant women are believed to be engaged in domestic work.

Source: *Adapted from ILO (2003:11) (footnotes omitted).*

Table 3.3:

Entries of Temporary Workers in Selected OECD Countries by Principal Categories, 2003-2005 (thousands)

	Trainees			Working Holiday Makers			Seasonal Workers			Intra-company Transfers			Other Temporary Workers		
	2003	2004	2005	2003	2004	2005	2003	2004	2005	2003	2004	2005	2003	2004	2005
Australia	6.9	7.0	7.0	88.8	93.8	104.4							56.1	58.6	71.6
Austria	1.7	0.8					17.5	15.7		0.2	0.2		10.5	9.8	
Belgium							0.4	1.0	2.7				1.2	0.5	2.8
Canada							18.7	19.0	20.3	3.8	4.2	4.5	52.1	55.8	
Denmark	1.4	1.5	1.9										3.6	3.4	2.6
France	1.0	0.5	0.4				14.6	15.7	16.2				10.2	10.0	10.5
Germany	2.3	2.3					309.5	324.0	320.4	2.1	2.3		43.9	34.2	21.9
Italy				0.1	0.3	0.4	68.0	77.0	70.2						
Japan	64.8	75.4	83.3							3.4	3.6	4.2	143.7	146.6	110.2
Republic of Korea	55.8	46.7	51.6							7.8	8.5	8.4	7.2	8.3	11.9
Netherlands													38.0	44.1	46.1
New Zealand	2.0	2.4	1.8	20.7	21.4	29.0			2.9				40.3	43.7	44.3
Norway	0.5	0.5	0.3				17.9	25.4	20.9				2.5	2.1	1.1
Sweden							7.3	4.9	5.9				2.6	3.4	2.2
Switzerland	0.4	0.4	0.3							14.4	7.5	1.8			
United Kingdom				46.5	62.4	56.6		19.8	15.7				98.0	113.4	111.2
United States[13]	1.4	1.4	1.8				29.9	31.8	31.9	57.2	62.7	65.5	192.5	221.8	218.6

Note:
The categories of temporary workers may differ from one country to another. Only the principal categories of temporary workers are presented in this table. Data on temporary workers generally do not cover workers who benefit from a free-circulation agreement.

Source: *OECD (2007: 52), compiled from residence and work permit data.*

[13] Author's note: Temporary migrant-trainees in the U.S. are not comparable to trainees in other countries, particularly Japan and South Korea.

(a) East and Southeast Asia and the Middle East

The growth in the numbers of temporary migrant workers can be seen across East and Southeast Asia and the Middle East. In Japan, 146,000 temporary workers were admitted in 2004 compared with 114,300 in 2000, although in 2005 admissions dropped to 110,200 (OECD, 2007). However, the numbers of trainees admitted has risen steadily (54,000 in 2003; 75,400 in 2004; 83,300 in 2005) (OECD, 2007). Stocks of temporary foreign workers in East Asia have also risen, particularly in South Korea and Taiwan Province of China, where they rose by half, and then doubled respectively between 2000 and 2004 (Abella, 2006: Table 3.4). In Japan, however, the total number of foreign workers, including various categories of temporary migrants, is relatively low and estimated at around 650,000 by the end of 2005, or less than one per cent of the labour force (OECD, 2007). Table 3.4 includes estimates of undocumented migrants who are prevalent in many low and semi-skilled employment sectors (e.g. construction) in Malaysia and Thailand.

In the GCC States the number of overseas contract workers rose by 2.5 per cent annually between 1985 and 2000, though this rate of increase is relatively small compared with the rates of expansion from the mid-1970s to the mid-1980s (Abella, 2006; Table 3.4).

Table 3.4:

Temporary Foreign Workers in Asian Destinations (stock estimates)

Country of Employment	1985	1997	2000	2004
East Asia[1]				
Brunei			80-90,000	
China		82,000	60,000	80,000
Hong Kong SAR		171,000	217,000	217,000
Malaysia		1,720,000	800,000	1,359,000
Republic of Korea		245,000	285,000	423,000
Singapore			612,000	580,000
Taiwan Province of China		246,000	327,000	600,000
Thailand		1,126,000	1,103,000	1,624,000
Viet Nam			30,000	
West Asia[1 2]				
Bahrain	99,000		180,000	
Jordan			35,000	
Kuwait	574,000		976,000	
Lebanon			75,000	
Oman	91,000		55,700	
Saudi Arabia	2,722,000		3,060,000	
United Arab Emirates	784,000		1,300,000	

Notes:

1 For East Asia, the figures include work permit holders and estimates of undocumented migrants. For "West Asia", only work permit holders are recorded.

2 "West Asia" is the region referred to in the original Table – it denotes Arab Mashrek countries and GCC States covered in the Middle East Migration Overview (see the Asia Overview).

Source: *Adapted from Abella (2006), citing sources from the Gulf Cooperation Council (GCC), OECD (2003) and Hugo (2005).*

Israel is also a significant destination for temporary foreign workers, who, since the early 1990s, have been admitted to replace Palestinian workers. At the end of 2003, official estimates counted approximately 189,000 such migrants, with many employed in low-wage and low-status jobs. Over half of the migrant workers in Israel come from Southeast Asia: about 50,000 from the Philippines, employed mainly in home healthcare, 30,000 Thai migrants mostly working in agriculture, and 15,000 Chinese migrants in construction. There are also approximately 65,000 foreign workers from eastern Europe, with over half from Romania working by and large in construction. One third of the migrants are women employed chiefly in the home healthcare sector (Kruger, 2006).

(b) Established countries of immigration: Australia, Canada, New Zealand and the United States

In the admission systems of established countries of immigration, which are primarily geared towards permanent migration for employment, temporary labour migration remains nonetheless an important feature with the objective of filling labour shortages in specific sectors (Table 3.5). In the periods 2004-2005 and 2005-2006, these countries received approximately 1.14 and 1.24 million temporary migrant workers (including dependants) respectively, and their numbers are rising steadily.

Table 3.5:

Temporary Migration for Employment to Australia, Canada, New Zealand and the United States, 2004-2006

	2004-2005	2005-2006
Australia[1]	100,758	118,181
Canada[2]	93,481	99,141
New Zealand[3]	118,460	142,536
United States[4]	831,715	883,706

Notes:

[1] Figures for fiscal years 2004-2005 and 2005-2006, respectively, relating to the issue of temporary resident visas (skilled visa, social and cultural, international relations and other), but excluding working holiday visas (see Chapter 5).

[2] Figures for 2004 and 2005, respectively.

[3] Figures for fiscal years 2004-2005 and 2005-2006, respectively, relating to work applications and including young persons employed under Working Holiday Schemes with specific countries, which are described in Chapter 5. These include principal applicants and secondary applicants. The applications also include individuals who apply for more than one visa or permit in a given year.

[4] Figures for fiscal years 2004 and 2005, respectively, including spouses and children, but excluding intra-company transferees (L-1 visas) and foreigners coming to the U.S. for work-and-learn experience (exchange visitors – J-1 visas).

Sources: *DIMA (2006), CIC Canada (2006), Immigration New Zealand (2007), U.S. Office of Immigration Statistics (2006).*

Although seasonal labour migration is not a common occurrence in the Asia-Pacific region, in April 2007 the New Zealand Government started a bilateral Seasonal Labour Scheme for Pacific Islanders, in partnership with the World Bank. It aims to enable up to 5,000 low-skilled and semi-skilled Pacific Islanders to take up specific agricultural jobs left unfilled by local workers (see Textbox 3.3).

Textbox 3.3

Expanding Job Opportunities for Pacific Islanders through Labour Mobility

In a world of rapid globalization, the economic competitiveness of a number of countries is coming under increasingly severe strain owing to their limited territory market size and remote location, while rapidly eroding trade preferences also no longer suffice to support competitiveness. Furthermore, international economic aid, which had enabled the development and construction of local infrastructure and the delivery of important services, may no longer be able to mitigate their growing cost disadvantages. Hence, for small and remote island economies to be viable, economic integration and export diversification – particularly in niche markets able to overcome the limitations of small size – are important. Facilitated labour mobility may be considered as responding to such a niche market.

Indeed, labour mobility is important and also urgent for the Pacific Island countries, where unemployment and population growth are high and job creation is limited by the combined challenges of demography, size and geography. With burgeoning youth populations (now nearly 40% of the total) and scant employment opportunities, the risk of social instability is also growing. Better opportunities for local labour, particularly at the lower segment of the labour market, would expand available job opportunities for Pacific Islanders and help to provide development benefits to the country of origin. Migration policy is no longer a matter of domestic policy, but an international development issue with potentially very positive outcomes for the poor if appropriately designed and implemented.

The recent migration report by the World Bank (2006) provides a detailed analysis of the opportunities and constraints to labour market integration in the Pacific region. First, the report makes demographic projections that indicate a coincidence of excess supply of labour in the Pacific Island economies with an excess demand for labour in many industrialized countries in and around the Pacific region. This can set the stage for the potentially mutually beneficial movements of labour in the region.

New household data collected for the report show that remittances have helped to reduce poverty and improved income distribution in Fiji and Tonga. Remittances are used to finance education and to seed fund the launch of a business activity, as well as serving as a form of social protection and providing a consumption cushion for the poor and vulnerable populations. Non-migrant sending households also benefit from incoming remittances through the expansion of the local economy and productive capacity. In addition to being a source of remittances, evidence from other parts of the world shows that low-skilled labour mobility may help to improve social equity in countries of origin, reduce social tensions and create a larger constituency for economic growth and governance reform.

While the economic benefits of immigration to destination countries are increasingly acknowledged, more immigration to industrialized countries, especially of low-skilled labour, is still a sensitive socio-economic and political subject. Most of these concerns can be successfully addressed through carefully designed labour schemes. The analysis in the report therefore draws on global experience and concludes that, for temporary worker schemes to be successful, especially for low-skilled labour, they should best be part of bilateral agreements, which allow a high degree of flexibility and can be adjusted to the needs of the parties involved. For such schemes to operate successfully, due attention will have to be paid to the '4 Cs': **Choice of workers** to ensure that their skills correspond to the jobs available, and avoid the hiring of overqualified workers likely to misuse the scheme; **Circular movement of workers**, allowing workers to go home, then return to their old or new, jobs, which helps to limit the incentive to violate the arrangement by overstaying; **Cost-sharing** by employers to reduce the financial burden of, for example, travel costs, for migrants and thereby making overstaying less attractive; and **Commercial viability** to ensure that the schemes remain private-sector driven (and not to fill quotas) and reflect labour market conditions in host countries.

The findings and recommendations of the report have been widely disseminated in the Pacific region following its release in August 2006. The New Zealand Government has taken the lead in launching a new Pacific Seasonal Labour scheme in April 2007. The new policy allows up to 5,000 low and semi-skilled Pacific Islanders to take up seasonal jobs in the horticulture and viticulture industries left unfilled by local labour. The World Bank has been working closely with the main stakeholders on the operational design of the bilateral arrangements and pilot schemes that incorporate and reflect best practice and the experience gained globally from similar temporary worker programmes. The World Bank, together with other donors, is currently coordinating technical assistance projects to strengthen the institutional capacities of member countries from the Pacific region to enable them to facilitate, regulate, manage and benefit from temporary labour migration. The Bank is also providing technical assistance to facilitate trade in the region; however, the liberalization of labour movements may actually be far more beneficial to some of the small and remote island economies than further trade liberalization alone. As a follow-up to the report, the World Bank is also leading a steering group with key stakeholders from the public and private sectors with the aim of further reducing the cost of remittance transfers that remain unduly high in the Pacific region.

Source: *Manjula Luthria, Senior Economist, World Bank, East Asia and Pacific Region.*

In 2005, most temporary migrant workers in Canada came from three EU countries; out of an EU-total of 17,447 migrant workers in Canada, 7,582 came from France; 7,263 from the U.K. and 2,602 from Germany; while 16,332 came from the United States and 12,610 from Mexico (CIC Canada,

2006), the majority of Mexican migrants being low-skilled agricultural workers employed under the Canadian Seasonal Agricultural Workers Program (Brem, 2006).[14] Moreover, the Canadian Government recently introduced a new global Low Skill Pilot Project under its Temporary Foreign Worker Program, allowing the admission and employment of low-skilled workers for up to two years to fill pressing labour shortages, particularly in Western Canada. Employers have to obtain a positive Labour Market Opinion (LMO) (discussed in Chapter 11) that includes paying the same wage to migrants as is paid to other workers, generally more than the minimum wage. Furthermore, employers have to pay travel expenses to and from Canada and health insurance for their workers, in addition to confirmation of the availability of affordable and suitable accommodation (HRSDC Canada, 2007; Bart, 2007).[15] While the changes to Canada's Temporary Foreign Worker Program have been welcomed by employers and their representatives, obstacles still remain to securing the rapid deployment of workers into jobs where there is a shortage of labour, such as backlogs in the processing of labour market opinions and visas, the difficulties for employers to find suitable low-cost accommodation for their workers and the costs of advertising the jobs to be filled and the paying of travel expenses (Carlson, 2007).

In the United States, the two largest entry categories of persons with temporary work visas[16] in fiscal year 2006 were 431,853 persons in high-skilled specialty occupations (H-1B visas)[17] and 180,503 seasonal workers, comprising 46,432 agricultural workers (H-2A visas), 97,279 non-agricultural workers (H-2B visas) and 36,792 returning H2-B workers (H-2R visas) (U.S. Office of Immigration Statistics, 2007); these data record admissions, not individuals, so that the same person entering and leaving the U.S. within a year is counted more than once. In contrast to admission for permanent residence, where women predominate, men accounted for the majority of non-immigrant admissions in 2006 (53%) (U.S. Office of Immigration Statistics, 2007).

(c) Europe

In Europe, significant temporary labour migration flows are also taking place within the European Union, largely from the new central and eastern European Member States to Ireland and the U.K. The vast majority are from Poland, but significant numbers come also from Slovakia and the Baltic States, especially Latvia and Lithuania, with many taking up employment in low and semi-skilled occupations. Between 1 May 2004 and 31 March 2007, the U.K. registered a cumulative total of 630,000 work applications on the Workers' Registration Scheme. The highest share of approved applicants came from Poland (65% of the total), followed by migrants from Lithuania and Slovakia (10%).[18] The largest share of registered workers were young (82%, aged 18-34), with a male:female ratio of 57:43. Over the same period, the top five sectors in which registered workers were employed

[14] In 2004, 11,494 temporary workers from Mexico came to work in Canada (CIC Canada, 2006), and 10,777 were seasonal agricultural workers (Brem, 2006).

[15] The Project was amended in February 2007 to enable employers to retain workers for a maximum two-year period instead of one year before the workers are required to return home. After a four-month interval at home, the worker may apply for a new work permit (CIC Canada, 2007; http://www.cic.gc.ca/English/work/low-skill.asp).

[16] "Non-immigrants" in the U.S. are foreigners seeking to enter the country temporarily for a given purpose (e.g. tourism, business, study, temporary employment) (U.S. Office of Immigration Statistics, 2007).

[17] In 2005, 65,000 H-1B visas were available for issue to first-time applicants, plus 20,000 visas for foreigners with advanced degrees from U.S. universities, and an unlimited number for non-profit institutions, such as universities. The H-1B visas are normally used up well before the end of the fiscal year. An Immigration Bill rejected by the Senate in June 2007 (the SKIL bill – Securing Knowledge, Innovation and Leadership) would have raised the cap for H-1B visas to 115,000 and then by another 20 per cent if all the visas were used up in the previous year (*Migration News*, 2007). As observed in Chapter 11, many H-1B visa holders are also sponsored by their employers for immigrant visas (i.e. Green Cards) (*Migration News*, 2006a; 2006b; 2007).

[18] In 2006, 227,710 initial applications for registration were approved: 162,390 from Poland, 21,725 from Slovakia, 17,055 from Lithuania and 9,485 from Latvia (U.K. Home Office, 2007).

were administration, business and management (37%), hospitality and catering (20%), agriculture (10%), manufacturing (7%), and food, fish and meat processing (5%). "Administration" in the above list may be slightly misleading, as the majority of workers in this sector work for recruitment agencies and can therefore be employed in a broad range of occupations (U.K. Home Office, 2007).

A principal feature of temporary low-skilled labour migration in Europe is seasonal employment (Table 3.3), particularly to the southern European countries, Austria, France, Germany, Norway and the U.K. Germany, for example, has a relatively large-scale scheme that, on the basis of bilateral arrangements, provides over 300,000 seasonal jobs annually for a period of up to four months in the agriculture, forestry and hospitality sectors to migrant workers from central and eastern Europe (German Federal Ministry of Interior, 2007; Table 3.3). A recent development, undoubtedly related to the considerable out-migration from the new EU Member States to the former EU-15, is the growing labour shortage in central and eastern European countries, particularly in the low and semi-skilled sectors. The shortages of agricultural workers in Poland have led to the introduction of a policy in 2006 allowing farmers to recruit seasonal workers from neighbouring countries (Belarus, Russian Federation and Ukraine) for a period of thee months within a six-month period without the need for a work permit (OECD, 2007).

In recent years, Italy has implemented labour migration schemes covering both temporary and seasonal workers. In the 2006 quota-setting decree, provision was made for the entry of 45,000 temporary migrant workers in the domestic and personal assistance sectors, and for an additional 50,000 seasonal workers in agriculture and tourism out of a total migration contingent of 170,000.[19]

[19] Decree by Prime Minister DPCM No. 7 of 15 February 2006, published in the *Gazzetta Ufficiale* (Official Journal) on 7 March 2007.

(d) Africa

In sub-Saharan Africa, most temporary labour migration is across borders and circular, involving also irregular movements (see Chapters 7 and 8). More reliable information is available concerning specific types of regular movements in the Southern African Development Community (SADC), such as contract labour migration to the principal mining centres in the region (Textbox 3.1). While labour recruitment figures for mines in South Africa for 1990-2000 show a decline in the number of migrants from all countries except Mozambique, there was an increase in foreign workers in the mining industry, from 40 per cent in the mid-1980s to almost 60 per cent in 2000. Lesotho, Mozambique and Swaziland are the three main countries of origin. In 2000, the numbers of migrants from these countries stood at 58,224, 57,034 and 9,360, respectively (Crush and Williams, 2005). According to more recent figures provided by officials from Swaziland, 13,000 of their nationals were working in South African mines in 2005 (MIDSA, 2007). In addition to mining, the principal sectors employing migrants in South Africa are construction, domestic services and factory work. Commercial agriculture is another important sector employing migrants both with and without authorization (Crush and Williams, 2005). Botswana and Namibia, both of which are experiencing rapid economic growth, are also important destination countries in the region, mainly for skilled migrants from other SADC countries (MIDSA, 2007).

The numbers for both regular and irregular Asian migrant workers in the Southern African region are increasing, such as for Chinese workers in Lesotho's textile industry and Chinese, Indian and Pakistani workers in Swaziland and Tanzania, who appear to be filling jobs left vacant by both skilled and less-skilled nationals who moved abroad for employment. Mauritius is a country of both origin and destination for migrant workers (MIDSA, 2007; see also Textbox

12.2).[20] Labour migration in West Africa is more complex, and movements have fluctuated in recent times because of economic downturns in what were until recently relatively prosperous countries and destinations for migrant workers (e.g. Côte d'Ivoire and Nigeria) and because of conflicts in others (e.g. Liberia and Sierra Leone) (Adepoju, 2005; see also Textbox 13.2).

Labour migration is also occurring within and to the Maghreb from sub-Saharan Africa, and it appears that most of these workers are either low or semi-skilled (see Textbox 3.4).

[20] In Mauritius, labour shortages exist in the manufacturing and hotel industries. In March 2007, 29,400 work permits had been issued in Mauritius, mostly to Chinese and Indian nationals. However, the country is also undertaking a major 10-year reform programme to restructure the economy, which, according to World Bank estimates, will result in the loss of 12,000 low-skilled jobs. Consequently, the Mauritian authorities are looking to offer employment abroad for some of their nationals through bilateral temporary (circular) labour migration programmes (MIDSA, 2007).

Textbox 3.4

Mobility of Skilled and Low-skilled Workers from, within and towards the Maghreb

In the immediate post-independence era, most Maghreb countries faced an unbalanced labour market due to a surplus of relatively low-skilled and a shortage of qualified and highly skilled workers. Owing to geographical proximity and social and historical links, a number of Maghreb countries pursued an emigration policy with Italy, France and Spain, which went hand in hand with the recruitment of skilled foreign personnel to develop and manage services and enterprises. This arrangement was terminated in the context of Franco-Maghreb relations in 1973 against a backdrop of global recession. One year later, other European countries also ended the Maghreb labour migration programmes.

As concerns migration towards the Maghreb, 2006 United Nations data (Figure 3.2) show that out of a total Maghrebin population of 90 million, over one million were migrants. This represented 1.23 per cent of the population in 2005, with female migration accounting for 40.3 per cent. Since the 1970s, Libya has been the country with the largest number of foreigners on its territory. In 2005, they numbered just over 600,000, or five per cent of Libya's population. Libya is still the leading destination country for migrants from other Maghreb countries.

Figure 3.2:

Evolution of the Foreign Population in the Maghreb from 1960 to 2005 (thousands)

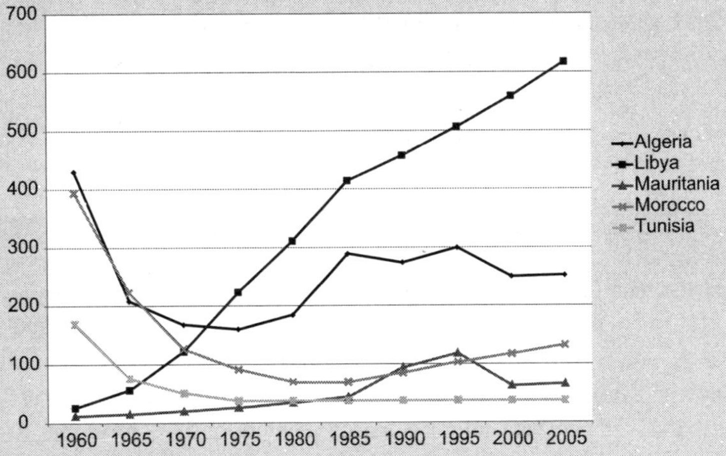

Source: *UN, Department of Economic and Social Affairs, Population Division 2006, Country Profile, World Migrant Stock: The 2005 Revision Population Database, http://esa.un.org/migration.*

The 1989 treaty Establishing the Arab Maghreb Union (l'Union du Maghreb arabe) provides for the free movement of workers among the countries of the Maghreb. These countries have also ratified the Arab League agreement on the social protection of workers. But labour flows within the Maghreb are still limited (excluding cross-border movements). As there are no detailed statistics for Libya and Mauritania, the analysis that follows focuses on the central Maghreb: Algeria, Morocco and Tunisia.

Estimates of migration within the Maghreb can be read in two ways. Data on the foreign population in the Maghreb indicate average mobility. Of an estimated total of 210,000 migrants in 2003, intra-Maghreb migration was estimated at an average of 42 per cent, though with fairly wide variations from one country to another: 59 per cent in Tunisia, 45 per cent in Algeria and 25 per cent in Morocco. Relative to the total Maghreb population abroad, the level of intra-Maghreb migration was very low. Out of an overall emigrant population of 4.7 million from the Maghreb, only 321,000 migrants had migrated to other Maghreb countries, or an average of 6.8 per cent. Tunisia had the largest (9.2%) and Algeria the lowest (3.3%) proportion of its migrants in the Maghreb.

Although no reliable data exist regarding the profiles of Maghreb workers in these countries, empirical observations made during the course of university exercises show that workers migrating to one of the countries in the Maghreb generally have an intermediate to low level of skills.

Workers migrating to Maghreb countries show two contrasting profiles and fall into two categories: those migrating from sub-Saharan Africa and those arriving from developed countries. Migrants from sub-Saharan Africa go mainly to Libya and, as a second choice, to Algeria, more particularly to the *départements* of the Sahara. A recent study (CISP, 2006) on sub-Saharan migrants in Algeria shows that the migration patterns of sub-Saharan workers vary with their level of education. Those with lower levels of education choose to work in the Maghreb, while those who have completed secondary education are mostly in transit.

Migrants from developed countries, i.e. Europe and the United States, and from Asia or the Middle East, are usually qualified or highly skilled workers. The bulk of the European migrant workers are from France. Statistics on French citizens abroad show a renewed surge in French migration to North African countries. From 70,000 in 1984, the number of French migrants in North Africa fell to 46,000 in 2000, to rise again to almost 85,000 by 2005. The majority went to Algeria, where they currently number around 40,000, up from a mere 8,000 in 1995. Some 83 per cent of French workers are employed in the tertiary sector, 46 per cent are in top management or academia, and 18 per cent are entrepreneurs.

In recent years, Algeria has been recruiting skilled and highly qualified human resources, more specifically in connection with Asian enterprises engaged in construction and public works, and for its infrastructure building programme. As of June 2007, Algeria had 32,000 foreign workers, of whom 23 per cent were senior executives, 21.7 per cent managers and senior technical staff, 27.7 per cent technical staff, 25 per cent highly skilled workers and 1 per cent low-skilled workers. It is expected that at least another 20,000 foreign workers will be recruited under the scheme to build a highway linking the Tunisian and Moroccan borders.

This unprecedented pull effect of the Algerian economy on foreign workers may, in the right circumstances, lead to a further increase in intra-Maghreb mobility.

Source: *Mohamed Saïb Musette, Centre de Recherche en Economie Appliquée pour le Développement (CREAD), Algiers, Algeria.*

(e) Central America, the Caribbean and South America

In Central America, the Caribbean and South America many low and semi-skilled workers migrate in an irregular manner (e.g. Nicaraguan migrant workers to Costa Rica, Haitian migrants to the Dominican Republic and the Bahamas, and seasonal workers from Bolivia and Paraguay to Argentina).[21] There are approximately 500,000 migrant workers in Costa Rica (17% of the labour force), half of whom are there irregularly. Many of these workers come from neighbouring countries, particularly Nicaragua, and

[21] Some of these movements are also described in Chapter 8.

are concentrated mainly in agriculture,[22] but also in other low-skilled employment such as construction, tourism and domestic work. An estimated 50,000-80,000 women migrant workers work irregularly as domestic help in Costa Rica. In the Dominican Republic, there are a reported 500,000 to 700,000 mainly irregular Haitian migrant workers, the majority employed on sugar plantations, but increasingly also in the construction sector and, to a lesser extent, in service sectors such as tourism (Achieng, 2006). In the Bahamas, there are an estimated 40,000-50,000 Haitians or Haitian descendants, mainly in low-paid, lower-skilled employment in agriculture/landscaping, construction, domestic service and informal trading (Fernández-Alfaro and Pascua, 2006). Some of the labour migration in this region, however, is occurring on a regular and documented basis, such as the seasonal employment of Guatemalan agricultural workers in southern Mexico. Movements also occur from within the region to Spain, particularly from the Dominican Republic, Colombia and Ecuador, facilitated by bilateral arrangements (see Chapter 13). Regularization programmes are also a common feature across the whole region (see Textbox 8.3).

4. 21st Century Temporary Labour Migration Programmes

The major difference between past and current temporary labour migration programmes is their scope and purpose. During the U.S. Bracero and German guest worker eras, the general practice was to admit migrant workers under one major national programme. Today, most high-income countries have multiple programmes to admit foreign workers, front doors for immigrants, side doors for temporary workers and back doors for the unauthorized. The rationale for these programmes is straightforward: welcome skilled workers and allow them to settle, but rotate low-skilled migrants in and out of the country.

The "front doors" are for foreigners invited to reside permanently, mainly highly skilled or economic migrants. Australia, Canada and the U.K. select economic migrants primarily on a supply-side basis that emphasizes personal characteristics such as age, education and professional qualifications, while Germany and the U.S. favour a demand-side approach, selecting economically motivated migrants who have job offers. There has been some convergence between points-based or supply-side selection systems and employer-based or demand-side selection systems, as Canada awards points to foreigners with job offers and the U.S. makes it easiest for college-educated foreigners to obtain immigrant visas. Germany, on the other hand, requires payment of a threshold salary to obtain permanent residence on admission.[23]

"Side doors" admit migrants for a specific time and purpose ranging from a few days for tourism to several years for work or study. Side doors were traditionally not explicitly linked to "front door" settlement channels, as reflected in rules requiring foreign students to return to their country of origin upon graduation. This has changed, and most industrialized countries now allow foreign student graduates to work after graduation and eventually to settle (see Chapter 4). Similarly, these countries often permit foreign professionals to enter as temporary workers and later settle as immigrants, making them in effect probationary immigrants. Migrants using the "back door" are foreigners who either enter a country without authorization, or who enter legally and subsequently violate the terms of their entry, e.g. a tourist accepting paid employment. In the U.S. and southern European countries such as Italy and Spain, many of the foreigners who eventually obtain the right to reside permanently (for instance through regularization programmes) arrive clandestinely or as authorized temporary entrants.

[22] According to the Costa Rica Ministry of Labour and Social Security, in 2002-03 there were 50,400 seasonal migrants working in agriculture, of whom 40,900 (or 81%) were undocumented.

[23] These admission policies are discussed in more detail in Chapter 11.

Temporary migrant worker programmes in the mid-20th century were usually "macro" in the sense that there was one major programme per country, and the overall unemployment and job vacancy rate played a determining role in deciding the need for temporary migrant workers. Today's multiple programmes are "micro" in aiming to respond to specific labour market needs, such as filling job vacancies in nursing and IT. Overall unemployment and job vacancy rates play only a small role in determining admission to these specialized sectors. Government employment services, which have shrunk in size, have less credibility in determining whether foreign workers are "needed" to fill job vacancies.[24]

With admission procedures giving employers more say in deciding whether foreign workers are needed, employers have gained an important voice in admission policy. In many industrialized countries, if an employer decides that a college-educated foreigner is the best person to fill a vacancy, the hiring and admission procedure is relatively straightforward. For example, available H-1B visas in the U.S. are generally exhausted well before the end of the year, in part because the admission process is easy – most employers simply "attest" that they will be paying at least the prevailing wage to a college-educated foreigner who is filling a job normally requiring a college education. As a general rule, the admission procedures are more stringent for low-skilled workers. For instance, in Canada, employers wishing to hire low-skilled workers for employment in agriculture or under the new Low Skill Pilot Project discussed in Section 3.2(b) above, are still required to obtain a Labour Market Opinion from Human Resources and Social Development Canada (HRSDC). However, in some regions, where labour market information indicates that the demand for labour in particular occupations exceeds the available supply, the labour market test is relaxed considerably. For occupations found on Regional Lists of Occupations under Pressure, developed by HRSDC and Service Canada, employers do not need to conduct lengthy or comprehensive job search efforts before obtaining permission to hire foreign workers (HRSDC, 2007), with Labour Market Opinions issued for the number of workers required by a specific enterprise.

[24] In the U.S., there are two major ways of determining whether an employer "needs" migrants. Under certification, the U.S. Department of Labor (DOL) controls the border gate, not allowing migrants to enter until the employer conducts recruitment activities supervised by DOL. Under the alternative attestation process, the employer controls the border gate, opening it by attesting that she is paying the prevailing wage, and DOL responds to complaints of violations.

5. "Win-Win-Win" Migration: The Economic Argument for More Low and Semi-skilled Labour Migration

Moving low and semi-skilled workers from lower to higher-wage countries can be a "win-win-win" situation, with migrants benefiting from higher wages, destination countries from more employment and a higher GDP, and countries of origin from jobs for otherwise unemployed workers, remittances, and returns. The first two "wins" are well established, as migrants demonstrate a strong desire to go abroad by taking considerable risks to move to higher-wage countries. Most studies in destination countries conclude that the major beneficiaries of economically motivated migration are the migrants who receive higher earnings, and that the presence of migrants slightly expands economic output, albeit by depressing wages slightly (Smith and Edmonston, 1997).

The third "win", the effect of emigration on countries of origin, has been in the spotlight as migrant numbers and remittances are rising rapidly. The Global Commission on International Migration (GCIM, 2005), the World Trade Organization's GATS Mode 4 negotiations,[25] the UN High-Level Dialogue on Migration and Development[26] and the Global Forum on Migration and Development (GFMD)[27]

[25] See www.wto.org/english/tratop_e/serv_e/serv_e.htm.

[26] See http://www.unmigration.org.

[27] See Textbox Int. 2.

have recently lent support to the belief that more temporary labour migration from developing to industrialized countries can enhance "win-win-win" outcomes, citing remittances and the contributions of migrants who return and create new jobs at home, and the diaspora that maintains links to the country of origin (see Textbox 3.5).

Textbox 3.5

Promoting Temporary Labour Migration: Policy Response of the International Community

Global Forum on Migration and Development (GFMD)

"**Temporary labour migration can work to everyone's advantage if it is legal, protective and linked to real labour needs.** It is a flexible way of meeting labour surplus and shortage across countries. Assuring legal access to a varied labour market, protecting the basic rights of migrants, especially women, and assuring temporariness of the migration are key to maximizing the mutual benefits. In the absence of a functional multilateral system, bilateral arrangements have been found to operate effectively in certain countries. Individual countries can also adopt institutional and policy frameworks that contribute to realizing the objectives of temporary migration. Joint arrangements between origin and destination countries, particularly for lower-skilled migrants, can help enforce the laws to protect temporary migrants and enhance their contribution to their families and home communities."

GFMD (2008: 65).

UN Secretary General's Report on International Migration and Development

"84. Temporary migration programmes are becoming more numerous. They are a response to the rising demand for labour in receiving countries. Although the number of migrants admitted under the more recent programmes is modest, there is potential for these programmes to result in beneficial synergies for migrants, countries of origin and countries of destination. Under such programmes, migrants benefit from having a legal status and countries of origin gain from remittances and the eventual return of migrants, provided the experience they gain abroad can be put to productive use at home. Receiving countries secure the workers they need and may enhance the positive effects of migration by allowing migrants to stay long enough to accumulate savings."

UN (2006: 18).

World Bank

"Greater emigration of low-skilled emigrants from developing to industrial countries could make a significant contribution to poverty reduction. The most feasible means of increasing such emigration would be to promote managed migration programs between origin and destination countries that combine temporary migration of low-skilled workers with incentives for return."

World Bank (2006a: xi).

ILO Multilateral Framework on Labour Migration

"Chapter IX. Migration and development

...15. The contribution of labour migration to employment, economic growth, development and the alleviation of poverty should be recognized and maximized for the benefit of both origin and destination countries.

Guidelines

The following guidelines may prove valuable in giving practical effect to the above principles:

...

15.8. Adopting policies to encourage circular and return migration and reintegration into the country of origin, including by promoting temporary labour migration schemes and circulation-friendly visa policies."

ILO (2006).

Global Commission for International Migration

"States and the private sector should consider the option of introducing carefully designed temporary labour migration programmes as a means of addressing the economic needs of both countries of origin and destination."

GCIM (2005: 16).

International Agenda for Migration Management (IAMM)

Temporary migration

... "The effective management of temporary migration offers States the opportunity to channel migration to address a range of domestic needs and policy priorities, such as short-term labour market requirements or the acquisition or improvement of skills, knowledge and resources through training and work abroad. Different criteria and conditions may be developed for each temporary migration category. The key elements of a comprehensive and balanced temporary migration programme are that it is transparent, non-discriminatory, orderly, efficient, reliable and safe.

Effective practices in regard to temporary migration:

- Promotion of the use of certain forms of temporary migration, such as short-term and project-related migration, as a means of meeting labour market needs, improving the skills of nationals of countries of origin, especially developing countries and countries with economies in transition.
- Facilitation of regular consultations on a bilateral or multilateral basis to identify and meet temporary migration needs through orderly channels, including through conclusion of bilateral or multilateral agreements.
- Identification of employment sectors that would be designated as suitable for temporary migrant workers.
- Definition of categories for temporary migrants according to specific intended objectives, for example business, family visit or study.
- Implementation of measures to enable and facilitate temporary migration and multiple short stays, including through efficient registration systems and delivery of multi-entry visas based on available technology and information sharing for tourists, business visitors, family visits and other temporary purposes.
- Provision of clear, accessible and user-friendly information on temporary migration opportunities and procedural requirements, migrant rights and responsibilities, as well as means to access such information, including through such services as migrant information centres.
- Implementation of temporary migration programmes which provide temporary migrants with a secure legal status, with rights and responsibilities that reflect their temporary status.
- Promotion and implementation of measures to ensure that temporary migration remains temporary, such as conditioning subsequent re-entry on timely return.
- For those States utilising temporary migration programmes as a possible route to permanent migration, articulation of clear conditions under which those who qualify can gain permanent status.
- Promotion of data collection and analysis regarding temporary migration."

IOM/Swiss Federal Office for Migration (2005: 35-36).

UN Department of Economic and Social Affairs (World Economic and Social Survey 2004: *International Migration*)

"It is widely recognized that a liberalization of the movement of people (workers and services providers) that is not for resettlement purposes would result in gains to the world economy and especially to developing countries. ... Improving the way temporary migrant flows are managed is a promising option. A step forward would be to implement such arrangements for the less skilled. (...) The movement of [less-skilled] workers from developing to developed countries promises to yield the greatest gains because this is where the difference between factor prices is largest and where there is considerable scope for movement."

UN DESA (2004: 139).

Economists estimate that more workers moving across borders could significantly increase global economic output as workers would be placed where their productivity is higher. One of the first studies was conducted by Hamilton and Whalley (1984), who estimated that global GDP could double if migration were to increase sufficiently to equalize the marginal productivity of labour (and wages) between seven world regions that included 179 countries.[28] Even if migration were insufficient to equalize wages, global GDP would still increase significantly if there were more migration, since the initial migrants face the largest gaps in marginal productivity or wages and thus gain the most by moving.

In its Global Economic Prospects Report 2006 on *Economic Implications of Remittances and Migration*, the World Bank (2006a) estimated that if an additional 14 million migrants were to migrate from developing to high-income countries that would generate a global income gain of over USD 350 billion, exceeding the anticipated USD 300 billion gain from completing the Doha round of trade negotiations.[29] The press release accompanying the report argued that more

> managed migration programs, including temporary work visas for low-skilled migrants in industrial countries (...) would contribute to significant reductions in poverty in migrant sending countries, among the migrants themselves, their families and, as remittances increase, in the broader community.[30]

If more labour migration produces "win-win-win" outcomes, how should it be organized? "Carefully" would seem to be the answer. The GCIM (2005: 79, para. 1.3) recommended "carefully designed temporary migration programs as a means of addressing the economic needs of both countries of origin and destination". The need for a careful design of temporary migrant worker programmes is especially urgent in countries such as the U.S. and Germany, where governments have not had a great record of keeping temporary worker programmes true to their design as past programmes did not function as expected. An understanding of why

[28] In Hamilton and Whalley's simulation, massive migration to equalize wages would have added USD 5 - 16 trillion to global GDP in 1977, when it was USD 8 trillion. Their simulation relied on a number of assumptions, including full employment of the world's workers, who produced a single output with a CES production function (i.e. constant elasticity of substitution between labour and capital). They estimated differences in 1977 in the marginal productivity of labour across seven multi-country regions and assumed that these differences were due to migration restrictions. Migration that equalized marginal productivity and wages (factor price convergence via migration) would result in workers in destination countries losing and capital owners in these countries gaining, and the opposite distributional effects in countries of origin. (The full employment assumption is necessary to justify equating wages and marginal productivity; they assume that the wage:profit ratio is one in both rich and poor countries before migration barriers are lifted and that capital does not move even as labour migrates.)

[29] Two-thirds of this USD 300 billion gain would come from liberalizing farm trade.

[30] World Bank, "Migration Can Deliver Welfare Gains, Reduce Poverty, Says Global Economic Prospects 2006", Press Release, 16 Nov. 2005, citing Uri Dadush, Director of the Bank's Development Prospects Group.

temporary labour migration programmes tend to get larger and to last longer than originally intended is a prerequisite to designing programmes that can come closer to fulfilling the goal of adding workers temporarily to the labour force, but not adding settlers to the population.

6. The Problems of Distortion and Dependence and Possible Solutions

Temporary migrant worker programmes tend to get larger and to last longer than intended because of distortion and dependence. Most employers in the majority of host countries do not hire temporary migrant workers. Distortion means that the minority who do have access to a supplementary labour supply – those hiring temporary migrants – face generally limited supplies of low-skilled workers at home and almost unlimited supplies abroad.

Employers hiring temporary migrant workers often do so assuming that migrants will continue to be available and make investment decisions reflecting this assumption. Thus, farmers who depend on migrants may plant fruit trees in areas with few people, assert that they will go out of business without migrants to pick their crops, and resist efforts to reduce the number of migrant workers because doing so would reduce the value of their investment. This is economic distortion in that some employers face more stringent labour supply constraints than others. Employers relying on migrant labour can either avoid raising wages when local workers are no longer available or willing to do the work, or they can expand production because they are able to recruit migrant workers.

Dependence reflects the fact that some migrants and their families as well as their regions and countries of origin may assume that foreign jobs, earnings and remittances will continue to be available. If the opportunity to work abroad legally is curbed, but the "3 Rs", i.e. recruitment, remittances and returns, have not been set in motion to remove or reduce migratory push factors, migrants may continue to migrate to avoid a reduction in their income. Most researchers conclude that the U.S.-Mexico Bracero programmes sowed the seeds of subsequent unauthorized Mexico-U.S. migration, via distortion in rural America (the expansion of labour-intensive agriculture) and dependence in rural Mexico (population and labour force growth without economic development) (Martin, 2003b: Ch. 2).

The realities of distortion and dependence should encourage governments considering new temporary labour migration programmes to proceed cautiously, and to include economic mechanisms to minimize distortion and dependence. These mechanisms include taxes to encourage employers to look for alternatives to migrants and subsidies to encourage temporary migrant workers to return to their countries of origin as their contracts require.

Dealing with distortion requires recognition that employers always have choices when they make investments and fill jobs. By the time government is involved in a request for temporary migrant workers, the employer has usually found the migrants desired, so that a supervised period of recruitment usually fails to find local workers. Government employment services are ill suited to second-guess employers in such situations, which is one reason why labour certification processes (i.e. labour market/resident worker tests) can become very contentious, especially if unemployment rates in the areas where migrants will be employed are high.

Once the employers who turn to guest workers learn how to have their "need" for migrants certified, most assume they will be able to continue to hire foreign workers. As a result, investments in alternatives to migrants can dwindle, and distortions may increase as migrant-dependent sectors become isolated from national labour markets. For example, agriculture may not offer workers' health insurance to its employees because the young male migrants who dominate the seasonal workforce prefer cash wages to costly benefits, but this also makes farm work less attractive to local workers who are interested in benefits. Networks linking migrants and work places soon span borders as current migrants refer friends and relatives to fill vacant jobs. One result is that labour market information may flow far more freely from a migrant workplace to migrant countries of origin than to pockets of unemployment nearby.

International norms and local laws usually call for migrant workers to be treated equally, receiving the same wages and benefits as local workers. One way to minimize distortion is to realize that social security and health insurance payments increase the overall payroll expenditure of employers by 20 to 40 per cent. These amounts could be collected on migrant payrolls to level the playing field between migrant and local workers.

The employer share of migrant payroll taxes could be used to combat distortion through the restructuring of migrant jobs, such as promoting labour-saving mechanization. For example, in an industry such as agriculture, it is often hard for one farmer to finance or implement mechanization, since peach packers and processors want fruit that is either picked by hand or mechanically, but not both (Martin, 2003b: Ch. 8). Thus, a mechanization programme funded through payroll taxes could help to provide alternatives to migrants.[31]

Mechanization is not the only alternative to migrants. Sometimes local workers may be attracted to "migrant jobs" once they have been restructured, as has been the case with garbage collection in the U.S., whose labour force has been "renationalized" by switching to large containers lifted by a truck operator. In other cases, subsidized research could develop alternatives to migrants, as when some elderly persons have in-home migrant caregivers and others use technology such as cameras linked to computers to live alone but under video monitoring that can summon help quickly. The universal truism is that wages held down by the presence of migrants will lead to more labour-intensive ways to get work done, and pressures to increase wages by the absence of migrants will encourage the development of alternatives to high-wage workers.

The other half of the equation involves giving migrants incentives to abide by the terms of their contracts, which usually require them to leave when jobs are no longer available or their work contract ends. To encourage returns, the worker's share of payroll taxes can be refunded when the migrant surrenders his/her work visa upon return in the country of origin. Given the increasing global interest in using remittances to hasten development, governments and development institutions could match payroll tax refunds to support projects that create jobs in the migrants' home country.

Minimizing distortion and dependence with taxes and subsidies will not have the desired effects on employers and migrants if unauthorized workers are readily available and labour laws are not enforced. Some employers hire unauthorized workers to save payroll taxes, and some migrants will resist departing when their work visas expire despite refund offers if they believe that they can continue to work abroad in an irregular status and have only few options to earn income at home. Thus, the enforcement of immigration and labour laws is a prerequisite to the development of temporary labour migration programmes that minimize distortion and dependence.

7. Numbers vs. Rights

The new approaches to the management of temporary labour migration give rise to a difficult discussion

[31] To recognize that each sector is different, boards representing employers, workers and governments could decide how to spend the accumulated funds to reduce dependence on temporary migrant workers over time.

about possible trade-offs between migrant numbers and migrant rights. The demand for migrant workers depends in part on their cost, which in turn will partially depend on their rights. If migrants enjoy the "full rights" laid down in ILO and UN conventions, including the right to work-related benefits and family unification, their cost will be typically higher, and fewer will be sought by employers (Hasenau, 1991). On the other hand, fewer rights and lower costs can expand migrant numbers but also lead to a layered labour force and society (Ruhs and Martin, 2006).

Most international discussions call for more numbers as well as more rights, that is, more channels for temporary migrant workers to enter developed countries as well as securing all the rights provided for in the relevant ILO and UN instruments concerning migrants. In fact, most destination countries have not ratified either the ILO or the UN conventions protecting migrant workers; therefore, the call for "more" migrants and more rights provides little guidance on how to deal with the trade-off in practice. For example, should the international community encourage the movement of more overseas contract workers to oil-exporting Gulf States even though the conditions of their employment may fall short of what is prescribed in ILO or UN conventions? Overseas contract workers earn more in GCC States such as Saudi Arabia, Kuwait and the United Arab Emirates than they would at home, with the result that they may be able to improve significantly the welfare of their families in countries of origin (see Portrait 3.1), although they do not, as yet, enjoy equal treatment with nationals. Recent reforms in the United Arab Emirates aimed at improving working conditions have introduced summer sun breaks during the hottest part of the day, increased the number of labour inspectors and imposed financial penalties on companies that fail to pay their workers (DeParle, 2007).

Portrait 3.1

Dates for a Better Future

On a sunny morning in March 2007, two-year-old Fatema is seeing her father, Anwar, for the first time in her life.

Anwar left for Saudi Arabia for the first time in 2000. He is one of those fortunate enough who get to take leave to visit their home country every couple of years. His last visit to Bangladesh was in 2003.

He initially took the decision to seek work abroad after years of hardship in his village, where he struggled to make a living with a small piece of land he inherited from his father. Like thousands of Bangladeshis, he opted for temporary employment opportunities in Saudi Arabia.

Anwar remembers the first time he left Bangladesh. He arrived in Saudi Arabia and joined a *Khejur* (dates) packaging company. It gave him very little pay to start with, but it provided him with the hope of a better future for himself and his family.

Although living so far away from his wife, children and mother has been very difficult, he feels that this opportunity abroad has helped him raise and educate his four children, which he values greatly.

Being illiterate himself, he understands the importance of educating his children, particularly his daughters.

Anwar has been fortunate that his salary at the *Khejur* (dates) company increased over time. His employer, satisfied with his work, gave him additional responsibilities at the factory. With this he has repaid all his debts incurred to take up work in Saudi Arabia. It had cost him approximately USD 2,200 to first travel to Saudi Arabia for work.

In addition, with the money he has saved over the years, Anwar has also been able to rebuild and repair his home.

Although Anwar will have to leave Bangladesh again in three months, he hopes that some day he will be able to return to Bangladesh permanently, buy arable land in the village and live comfortably with his whole family.

***Source:** IOM Dhaka.*

The presence of migrants in countries that restrict the rights of migrants demonstrates that many workers are willing to accept the trade-off between higher wages and fewer rights. The fact that overseas contract workers may pay up to 25 per cent of what they will earn to obtain a two-year contract to work in GCC countries suggests that the international community may want to focus more on the effective implementation of core human and labour rights in respect of migrant workers as well as the development of more comprehensive migrant rights conventions.

The fundamental dilemma is that inequality motivates migration, but migrant conventions and norms call for equality after arrival. This dilemma lies at the core of the WTO's General Agreement on Trade in Services (GATS) negotiations, which aim to liberalize the movement of "service providers".[32] If achieved, there could be "hundreds of millions" of additional migrants crossing borders to provide services.[33]

In 2000, about one per cent of global trade in services involved GATS Mode 4, the "movement of natural persons" over borders. Many developing countries would like to see more Mode 4 movements, with some envisaging the goal of a "GATS visa" that would allow access to any WTO member country national for one to three years (Chanda, 2001: 648), so that refusal to allow entry and employment would be a reason to file a complaint with the WTO.

The "numbers versus rights" trade-off becomes clear when dealing with wage standards for GATS service providers. ILO Conventions Nos. 97 and 143 call for wage parity for migrant and local workers. However, Chaudhuri et al. (2004) assert that equal wages would limit numbers: "Wage-parity (...) is intended to provide a non-discriminatory environment, [but] tends to erode the cost advantage of hiring foreigners and works like a de facto quota". Chanda (2001: 635) goes further, asserting that wage parity "negates the very basis of cross-country labor flows, which stem from endowment-based cost differentials between countries". In other words, if GATS opened new channels for migrants, would they be paid local minimum or prevailing wages, which may limit their numbers, or could they work for lower wages, which would presumably increase numbers?

"Numbers versus rights" raises other questions as well. Ruhs (2005) emphasizes that it is a human right to leave one's country, but there is no corresponding right to enter another country. As a result, the balance of power in determining whether either numbers or rights receive higher priority lies mostly in the more affluent destination countries, which have to answer questions such as whether to enforce the return of skilled migrants to avoid brain drain from countries of origin, or welcome skilled migrants to generate the maximum benefits from migration. Countries of origin largely react to these policies, making decisions about whether to facilitate labour emigration or attempt to prohibit or discourage migration to particular countries.

8. Conclusion

Economic theory suggests that workers who move from lower to higher wage countries are the major beneficiaries of temporary labour migration programmes, and that such labour migration increases global economic efficiency. There are many types of temporary labour migration programmes, ranging from those that admit temporary workers to fill temporary jobs, to those that admit temporary workers to fill permanent or year-round jobs, and those that admit probationary immigrants.

---

[32] Services move across borders in four major ways or modes: Mode 1 (cross-border supply) occurs when the service rather than the supplier or consumer crosses national borders, as with call centres; Mode 2 (consumption abroad) occurs when the consumer travels to the supplier, as when a tourist visits another country or a patient travels abroad for medical services (see also Chapter 5); Mode 3 (commercial presence) reflects the movement of capital, as when a bank or insurance company establishes a subsidiary in another country; and Mode 4 ("movement of natural persons") involves the supplier travelling to the consumer of a service.

[33] In answer to the question, "Are we looking at tens of millions of people moving around in the future?" [under Mode 4], Abdel-Hamid Mamdouh, Director of Trade in Services at the WTO, said "Ah, yes - it could be hundreds [of millions] if we liberalize" (Zarocostas, 2005).

Governments with large numbers of unauthorized foreign workers often see temporary labour migration programmes for low and semi-skilled workers as the best compromise between the extremes of "no borders" and "no migrants". The arguments for having such temporary migrant workers admitted via regular channels rather than unauthorized foreigners seem compelling. Employers argue that they cannot find local workers to fill vacant jobs at prevailing wages and working conditions, and many migrants want to work abroad for higher wages. To avoid having non-integrated second and third-generation foreigners, governments are often attracted to the concept of simply "borrowing" workers from lower-wage countries.

Earlier "guest worker" programmes ended under a cloud, as they lasted longer and became larger than anticipated, and resulted in significant settlement and family unification. To avoid the same fate with 21st century temporary labour migration programmes, it is important to develop more effective approaches to programme management to help ensure that temporary migrant workers do not become permanent features of the labour landscapes in countries of origin and destination. This could be done, for instance, by introducing economic incentives for return or offering attractive opportunities for investment in countries of origin.[34] Such policies might encourage industrialized countries to open more gates for low and semi-skilled migrant workers.

Well-managed temporary labour migration programmes benefit migrants and destination countries, but while remittances can contribute to poverty reduction (see also the discussion in Textbox 12.3), it is less clear whether such programmes taken as a whole can be a positive force for sustainable development in countries of origin. The ILO (2004: 30) reviewed the migration and development literature and concluded that "migration can, in some cases, contribute positively to development where a country is already poised to develop; it cannot, however, create such conditions." The World Bank's 2006 Global Economic Prospects Report similarly asserts that "migration should not be viewed as a substitute for economic development in the country of origin [as ultimately] development depends on sound **domestic** economic policies." (World Bank, 2006a: xi). These messages were also strongly echoed in the government-led discussions of the Global Forum on Migration and Development (GFMD) (see Textbox Int. 2).[35]

Potential conflicts of interest between countries of origin and destination highlight the need for dialogue and cooperation. Destination countries prefer the best and brightest workers, such as IT and healthcare professionals. Professionals earn more and can remit more, but may also find it easier to settle abroad, which is likely to reduce remittances in the longer term. It is not yet clear whether the advice being given to developing countries, "Don't worry if your best and brightest leave because you will get remittances", will eventually be as discredited as was the advice of half a century ago to speed up development by creating and protecting basic steel and other heavy industries behind high tariff walls.

Governments and international institutions advocating more 21st century temporary labour migration programmes for low and semi-skilled workers have not yet dealt with the fundamental dilemma that inequality motivates people to move, but most legal norms in developed countries as well as international standards call for equal treatment after arrival. Countries in which the equality norm receives least attention have the most migrants, as in the Middle East, while countries which adhere to the equality norm have fewer, as in Scandinavia. There are no easy or universal answers as to whether numbers or rights should receive higher priority, but one way forward is to think in terms of core rights that all migrants should enjoy. These issues are addressed again in Part B of the Report focusing on policy responses.

[34] See also Chapters 11 and 12 where these policies are discussed in a little more detail.

[35] These questions are discussed further in Chapter 12.

REFERENCES

Abella, M.

2006 "Policies and Best Practices for Management of Temporary Migration", paper presented at the International Symposium on International Migration and Development, United Nations Department of Economic and Social Affairs (UN DESA), Population Division, 28-30 June, Turin, Doc. UN/POP/MIG/SYMP/2006/03, http://www.un.org/esa/population/migration/turin/Symposium_Turin_files/P03_SYMP_Abella.pdf.

Achieng, M.

2006 "Managing Haitian Migratory Flows to the Dominican Republic: The Challenges and Opportunities" in T. Lesser, D. Fernández-Alfaro, L. Cowie and N. Bruni (Eds.), *Intra-Caribbean Migration and the Conflict Nexus*, Human Rights Internet in collaboration with the International Organization for Migration (IOM), the Association of Caribbean States and The University of the West Indies (Center for Latin America and the Caribbean), Ottawa, 343-367.

Adepoju, A.

2005 "Migration in West Africa", paper prepared for the Policy Analysis and Research Programme of the Global Commission on International Migration, September, Geneva, http://www.gcim.org/attachements/RS8.pdf.

Australia, Department of Immigration and Multicultural Affairs (DIMA)

2006 *Annual Report 2005-06*, October, DIMA, http://www.immi.gov.au/about/reports/annual/2005-06/pdf.htm.

Bart, J.

2007 Presentation on Canada at the Session on Examples of Law and Practice of Receiving Countries in Facilitating Temporary Labour Migration, Swiss National Centre of Competence in Research (NCCR) – Trade Regulation (Individual Project on Services) and International Centre for Trade and Sustainable Development (ICTSD) Workshop on Trade and Labour Migration: Developing Good Practices to Facilitate Temporary Labour Mobility, 20-22 April, Jongny, Switzerland.

Brem, M.

2006 *Migrant Workers in Canada: A Review of the Canadian Seasonal Agricultural Workers Program*, The North-South Institute, Ottawa, http://www.nsi-ins.ca/english/pdf/MigrantWorkers_Eng_Web.pdf.

Canada, Citizenship and Immigration (CIC Canada)

2006 *Facts and Figures. Immigration Overview 2005: Permanent and Temporary Residents*, September, CIC Canada.

2007 Skilled workers and professionals, http://www.cic.gc.ca/english/immigrate/skilled/index.asp.

Canada, Human Resources and Social Development Canada (HRSDC)

2007 Temporary Foreign Worker Program, http://www.hrsdc.gc.ca/en/workplaceskills/foreign_workers/index.shtml.

Carlson, D-L.

2007 "Ontario lawyers help Western Canada recruit: New foreign worker measures not perfect", *Law Times* (Focus on Immigration Law), 5 March, http://www.siskinds.com/pdfs/Foreign_Worker_program_comments.pdf.

Chanda, R.

2001 "Movement of Natural Persons and the GATS", *World Economy*, 24(5) (May): 631-654.

2004 "Movement and Presence of Natural Persons and Developing Countries: Issues and Proposals for the GATS Negotiations", Trade-Related Agenda, Development and Equity (T.R.A.D.E.) Working Paper 19, May, South Centre, Geneva, http://www.southcentre.org/index.php?option=com_content&task=view&id=234&Itemid=67.

Chaudhuri, S., A. Mattoo, and R. Self

2004 "Moving People to Deliver Services: How can the WTO help?", *Journal of World Trade*, 38(3): 363-394.

Cornelius, W.A., T. Tsuda, P.L. Martin, and J.F. Hollifield (Eds.)

2004 *Controlling Immigration. A Global Perspective*, Stanford University Press, Stanford, CA.

Crush, J. and V. Williams
2005 "International Migration and Development: Dynamics and Challenges in South and Southern Africa", UN Expert Group Meeting on International Migration and Development, Population Division, UN DESA, 6-8 July, New York, http://www.un.org/esa/population/meetings/ittmigdev2005/P05_Crush&Williams.pdf.

DeParle, J.
2007 "Fearful of Restive Foreign Labor, Dubai Eyes Reform", *New York Times*, 6 August, http://www.nytimes.com/2007/08/06/world/middleeast/06dubai.html.

Fernández-Alfaro, B. and G. Pascua
2006 "Migration Management Challenges in the Caribbean" in T. Lesser, B. Fernández-Alfaro, L. Cowie and N. Bruni (Eds.), *Intra-Caribbean Migration and the Conflict Nexus*, Human Rights Internet in collaboration with the IOM, the Association of Caribbean States and The University of the West Indies (Center for Latin America and the Caribbean), Ottawa, 70-87.

Germany, Federal Ministry of Interior
2007 Labour Recruitment, http://www.zuwanderung.de/cln_108/nn_1070222/EN/ImmigrationPast/LabourRecruitment/labourRecruitment__node.html?__nnn=true.

Global Commission on International Migration (GCIM)
2005 *Migration in an interconnected world: New directions for action*, Report of the GCIM, October, SRO-Kundig, Geneva, http://www.gcim.org/attachements/gcim-complete-report-2005.pdf.

Global Forum on Migration and Development (GFMD)
2008 *Report of the first meeting of the Global Forum on Migration and Development*, Belgium, 9-11 July, Bruylant, Brussels.

Hamilton, B. and J. Whalley
1984 "Efficiency and Distributional Implications of Global Restrictions on Labour Mobility", *Journal of Development Economics*, 14(1): 61-75.

Hasenau, M.
1991 "ILO Standards on Migrant Workers: The Fundamentals of the UN Convention and Their Genesis", *International Migration*, 25(4): 687-697.

Hugo, G.
2005 "Migration in the Asia-Pacific region", Report prepared for the Global Commission for International Migration (GCIM), September, Geneva, http://www.gcim.org/mm/File/Regional%20Study%202.pdf.

International Labour Organization (ILO)
2003 *Preventing Discrimination, Exploitation and Abuse of Women Migrant Workers. An Information Guide. Booklet 1 – Introduction: Why the focus on women international migrant workers?*, Gender Promotion Programme, International Labour Office, Geneva, http://www.ilo.org/public/english/employment/gems/download/mbook1.pdf.

2004 *Towards a Fair Deal for Migrant Workers in the Global Economy*, International Labour Office, Geneva, http://www.ilo.org/public/english/standards/relm/ilc/ilc92/pdf/rep-vi.pdf.

2006 *ILO Multilateral Framework on Labour Migration: Non-binding principles and guidelines for a rights-based approach to labour migration*, International Labour Office, Geneva, http://www.ilo.org/public/english/protection/migrant/download/multilat_fwk_en.pdf.

International Organization for Migration (IOM) and Swiss Federal Office for Migration
2005 *International Agenda for Migration Management*, IOM and Swiss Federal Migration Office, Geneva/Berne, http://www.iom.int/jahia/Jahia/cache/offonce/pid/1674?entryId=8005.

Kindleberger, C.
1967 *Europe's Postwar Growth - the Role of Labor Supply*, Harvard University Press, Cambridge, MA.

Kruger, M.
2005 "Israel: Balancing Demographics in the Jewish State", *Migration Information Source*, July, Migration Policy Institute (MPI), Georgetown University, Washington, D.C., http://www.migrationinformation.org/Feature/display.cfm?ID=321.

Martin, P.L.
2003a *Promise Unfulfilled: Unions, Immigration, and Farm Workers*, Cornell University Press, Ithaca, NY.

2003b *Managing Labor Migration: Temporary Worker Programs for the 21st Century*, September, International Institute for Labour Studies, ILO, Geneva, http://www.ilo.org/public/english/bureau/inst/download/migration3.pdf.

2004 "The United States: The Continuing Immigration Debate" in W.A. Cornelius, T. Tsuda, P.L. Martin and J.F. Hollifield (Eds.), *Controlling Immigration. A Global Perspective*, Stanford University Press, Stanford, CA, 51-85.

Martin, P.L., M. Abella and C. Kuptsch

2006 *Managing Labor Migration in the Twenty-First Century*, Yale University Press, New Haven, CT.

Migration Dialogue for Southern Africa (MIDSA)

2007 Workshop on Human Capital Mobility, Labour and the Millennium Development Goals in Southern Africa, 26-28 March, Victoria Falls, Zimbabwe (various presentations).

Migration News

2006a "H1-B, Day Labor, Wal-Mart", *Migration News*, 13(2), April, University of California at Davis.

2006b "Immigrants and Wages, H-1B, Nurses", *Migration News*, 13(3), July, University of California at Davis.

2007 "Labor, H-1B, Trade", *Migration News*, 14(1), January, University of California at Davis.

Miller, M.J. and P.L. Martin

1982 *Administering foreign-worker programs: Lessons from Europe*, Lexington Books, Lexington, MA.

New Zealand, Immigration Statistics

2007 WI – Work applications decided, January, http://www.immigration.govt.nz/NR/rdonlyres/95F88B05-F496-4DDD-83C5-FCB74D50E383/0/W1.pdf.

Nonnenmacher, S.

2007 "Overview of Global Trends in Temporary Labour Mobility: A Policy Perspective", paper presented at the Regional Workshop on Temporary Labour Mobility and Mode 4, 9-11 May, Nadi, Fiji.

Organisation for Economic Co-operation and Development (OECD)

2005 *OECD in Figures*, July, OECD, Paris.

2006 *International Migration Outlook – SOPEMI 2006*, OECD, Paris.

2007 *International Migration Outlook – SOPEMI 2007*, OECD, Paris.

Ruhs, M.

2005 "Designing Viable and Ethical Labour Immigration Policies" in *World Migration 2005: Costs and Benefits of International Migration*, IOM, Geneva, 203-220, http://www.iom.int/jahia/Jahia/cache/offonce/pid/1674?entryId=932.

Ruhs, M. and P. Martin

2006 "Numbers vs. Rights: Trade-offs and guest worker programmes", The Centre on Migration Policy and Society (COMPAS) Working Paper, December, University of Oxford, http://www.compas.ox.ac.uk/publications/Working%20papers/wp-06-40.shtml.

Smith, J. and B. Edmonston (Eds.)

1997 *The New Americans: Economic, Demographic, and Fiscal Effects of Immigration*, National Research Council, Washington, D.C.

United Kingdom, Home Office, Border Agency

2007 *Accession Monitoring Report. A8 Countries (May 2004 – March 2007)*, U.K. Border Agency, http://ukba.homeoffice.gov.uk/sitecontent/documents/aboutus/reports/accession_monitoring_report/.

2008 Business and Commercial work permit arrangements, U.K. Border Agency, http://www.ukba.homeoffice.gov.uk/workingintheuk/tier2/workpermits/workpermitarrangements/businessandcommercialworkpermits/.

United Nations

2006 Report of the Secretary-General, *International Migration and Development*, UN General Assembly, 60th Session, UN Doc. A/60/871, 18 May.

United Nations Department of Economic and Social Affairs (UN DESA)

2004 *World Economic and Social Survey 2004: International Migration*, UN DESA, New York, UN Docs. E/2004/75/Rev.1/Add.1, ST/ESA/291/Add.1, http://www.un.org/esa/policy/wess/wess2004files/part2web/part2web.pdf.

United States, Central Intelligence Agency (CIA)

2007 *The World Factbook 2007*, CIA, Washington, D.C.

United States, Office of Immigration Statistics, Department of Homeland Security

2006 "Temporary Admissions of Nonimmigrants to the United States: 2005" (by E.M. Grieco), *Annual Flow Report*, July, Office of Immigration Statistics, U.S. Department of Homeland Security, http://www.dhs.gov/xlibrary/assets/statistics/publications/2005_NI_rpt.pdf.

2007 "Temporary Admissions of Nonimmigrants to the United States: 2006", *Annual Flow Report*, July, Office of Immigration Statistics, U.S. Department of Homeland Security, http://www.dhs.gov/xlibrary/assets/statistics/publications/NI_FR_2006_508_final.pdf.

World Bank

2006a *Global Economic Prospects 2006: Economic Implications of Remittances and Migration*, The World Bank, Washington, D.C., http://econ.worldbank.org/WBSITE/EXTERNAL/EXTDEC/EXTDECPROSPECTS/GEPEXT/EXTGEP2006/0,,menuPK:1026834~pagePK:64167702~piPK:64167676~theSitePK:1026804,00.html.

2006b *World Development Indicators*, The World Bank, Washington, D.C.

Zarocostas, J.

2005 "Migration helps export services", *Washington Times*, 3 January, A10.

Textbox 3.3 - Expanding Job Opportunities for Pacific Islanders Through Labour Mobility

World Bank

2006 *Pacific Islands At Home & Away: Expanding Job Opportunities for Pacific Islanders Through Labor Mobility*, Report No. 37715-EAP, September, The World Bank, Poverty Reduction and Economic Management Sector Unit, East Asia and Pacific Region, http://www-wds.worldbank.org/servlet/WDSContentServer/IW3P/IB/2006/11/15/000090341_20061115095505/Rendered/PDF/377150EAP.pdf.

Textbox 3.4 - Mobility of Skilled and Low-skilled Workers from, within and towards the Maghreb

Comitato Internazionale per lo Sviluppo dei Popoli (CISP)

2007 La migration sub-saharienne en Algérie, Summary report prepared by M.S Musette for the Comité international pour le développement des peuples, Algiers, Algeria.

STUDENT MOBILITY, INTERNATIONALIZATION OF HIGHER EDUCATION AND SKILLED MIGRATION*

CHAPTER 4

1. Introduction

The dynamics of student mobility and the internationalization of higher education have changed profoundly since the 1990s. Twenty years ago, the primary motivations to study abroad were related to academic, political, geo-strategic, cultural and development aid issues and considerations. At the time, countries took a favourable view of the mobility of students and academics as an opening to the world, in the hope of creating international networks of elites. Universities received foreign students and academics but made no special effort to recruit them. Today, even though the original motivations remain valid, cross-border education – that is, all that entails the international mobility of students and teachers, educational programmes or institutions of higher learning (Knight, 2004) – is being increasingly driven by economic considerations. Governments see it as a fulcrum of economic development and as a means of improving the quality of their higher education and their institutions of higher learning, an element of prestige (and sometimes a source of income), giving them a competitive edge. Individuals see it as a further boost to their career both in their home country and on the international job market, or even as an investment towards possible future emigration.

A growing number of persons either go abroad to study, enrol in foreign programmes or establishments present in their country, or simply turn to the Internet to follow courses run by universities or other institutions of higher learning at a distance from other countries. Between 1998 and 2004, the number of foreign students enrolled worldwide rose by 52 per cent to 2.7 million, with the OECD countries hosting 85 per cent of the total.

This trend results from a range of different, not mutually exclusive factors: greater mobility of skilled individuals and workers in a globalized economy; the falling costs of transport and communication; the desire of countries to encourage university and cultural exchanges and to attract highly qualified personnel; the wish on the part of tertiary institutions to generate additional income or increase their prestige and raise their profiles, both nationally and internationally; or the need for a better educated workforce in emerging economies where local capabilities are often quantitatively and qualitatively insufficient.

* This chapter was written by Stéphan Vincent-Lancrin, who is an analyst at the Centre for Educational Research and Innovation (CERI), a division of the Directorate for Education of the Organisation for Economic Co-operation and Development (OECD). The analyses given and the opinions expressed in this chapter are those of the author and do not necessarily reflect the views of the OECD and of its members.

Cross-border higher education has evolved differently across countries and regions. In very general terms, student mobility has been induced by political action in Europe and by strong demand in the Asia-Pacific region. North America, for its part, has been a magnet for foreign students, although it is only in recent years that the United States has adopted a policy of more active recruitment. Though South America and Africa receive relatively few foreign students, and then mostly from within the same region, student mobility in general is also increasing in those parts of the world. However, only limited statistics are available for these regions.

The major trends in cross-border higher education and the implications for educational policies are set out and examined in two OECD publications (2004a and 2004b): *Internationalisation and Trade in Higher Education. Opportunities and Challenges*, and *Quality and Recognition in Higher Education: The Cross-border Challenge*. Also, detailed data on foreign and mobile students are collected and published each year in *Education at a Glance* (OECD, 2006a) and by UNESCO (2006).

This chapter retraces the predominant trends in student mobility and highlights the major strategies for the internationalization of higher education, while underscoring the main implications for migration. Section 2 examines the major trends in student mobility, the causes of this mobility, and describes the emergence of new forms of cross-border higher education – viz. the mobility of both programmes and educational establishments. Section 3 proposes a typology of the main strategies in the internationalization of higher education. Section 4 discusses the interplay between student mobility and migration policies, and examines the link between student mobility and brain drain. Finally, the conclusion underlines how the internationalization of higher education further complicates the link between student mobility and skilled migration.

2. Main Trends in Cross-border Higher Education

The main trends in cross-border higher education may be summed up in two words, namely growth and diversification: **growth** in the number of students enrolled in foreign education programmes (or abroad); **diversification** of the supply of cross-border education, as new forms of international mobility emerge. This section outlines the main trends in student mobility and argues that, like student mobility, the new forms of cross-border education can facilitate the migration of highly qualified professionals or skilled migration (i.e. of graduates from institutions of higher learning).

2.1 Student Mobility: Main Trends

International student mobility is the main form of cross-border higher education. In 2004, there were 2.7 million students worldwide studying outside their own countries; in other words, almost three times as many as 20 years ago.[1] OECD countries receive some 85 per cent of all foreign students, two-thirds (66%) of whom were nationals of non-OECD countries in 2004. Thus, such student flows show a strong South-North orientation, with five OECD countries hosting over half of the total (58%). In 2004, 22 per cent of all foreign students worldwide were in the United States, 11 per cent in the United Kingdom, 10 per cent in Germany, 9 per cent in France and 6 per cent in Australia. The top five English-speaking host countries (United States, United Kingdom, Australia, Canada and New Zealand) alone receive almost half (47%) the total number of foreign students (Figure 4.1). Of the ten countries hosting the largest share of foreign students (75% of the world total) only Russia and South Africa are not OECD members. The 35 leading host countries for foreign students listed in Figure 4.1a account for 95 per cent of all foreign students enrolled throughout the world.

[1] Unless otherwise indicated, the figures used in this chapter are from the OECD education database for all members and non-members covered in it (OECD, 2006a), and from UNESCO for all other countries (UNESCO, 2006). In the absence of 2004 data, the last available year was taken as an estimate.

Textbox 4.1

Foreign and International Students in International Statistics

Despite constant efforts to improve international statistical data on student mobility, some imperfections persist. Although these efforts attempt to list non-resident foreign students who have entered a country for study purposes, the national data for some countries include both resident and non-resident tertiary students (ISCED[1] 5A, 5B and 6). Hence, "foreign" students are generally an over-estimation of genuinely mobile international students. In 2006, the OECD published for the first time data on mobile international students as distinct from data on foreign students. The **foreign** students are identified by their nationality, while the **mobile** students are identified by the country where they had previously studied or by their residence. For the 12 countries for which data are available, mobile students account for an average of 70 per cent of foreign students, although there may be large variations. In Norway and Spain less than 40 per cent of foreign students are mobile, as compared with over 80 per cent in Australia, Austria, Canada, Hungary, Japan and the United Kingdom. In principle, the data do not reflect the fact that foreign students who enrol in programmes for at least one semester count as full-time students. Students sent abroad for short periods (i.e. less than a full academic year) and who remain enrolled in their institutions of origin and/or are still paying their tuition fees to that institution should not be recorded as foreign students in the host country. Lastly, a student from country A, registered in a programme offered in country B via distance learning, should, in principle, be counted as a foreign student of country B, which is not always the case in practice. The variations between the national and international data for a given country stem from the adjustments needed to make country data comparable internationally. Although foreign students may not be (mobile) international students, this chapter often uses the data on foreign students as an approximation of student mobility. This is done for practical reasons as such data are available for a greater number of countries.

Note:
[1] ISCED - International Standard Classification of Education.

Figure 4.1:

Numbers and Percentages of Foreign Students in the 35 Main Host Countries, 2004

4.1a: Numbers

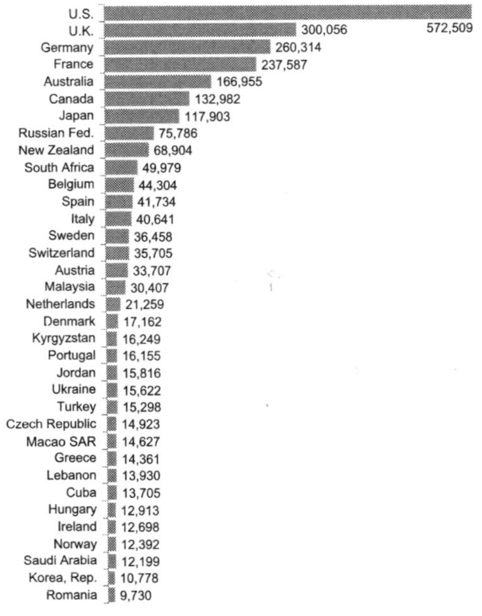

4.1b: Percentage enrolled in higher education

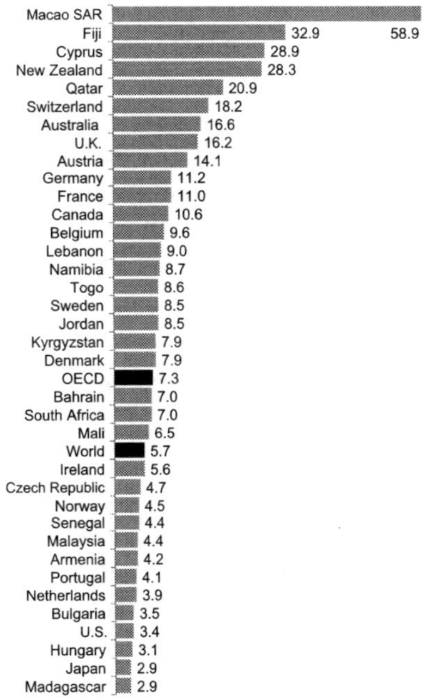

***Sources:** OECD and UNESCO.*

In relative terms, i.e. as a percentage of the size of the higher education systems of various countries, the situation varies somewhat. Cyprus, Fiji, New Zealand, Switzerland and Macao SAR are among the countries and regions with the largest proportion of foreign students in their national higher education systems, while the United States drops from first place (Figure 4.1a) to rank thirty-second among host countries (Figure 4.1b). Against a country average of 5.7 per cent of foreign students worldwide, the average for OECD countries stood at 7.3 per cent of their total student body in 2004 (up from 4.5 per cent in 1998). In 2004, the overall student body in nine smaller, English-speaking countries included at least 15 per cent international students. Generally speaking, the fewer foreign students a country receives, the greater the tendency for those students to come from neighbouring countries or from within the same continent. Hence, 99 per cent of foreign students studying in sub-Saharan African countries are themselves from sub-Saharan Africa, and the percentages are about 80 per cent for the countries in Latin America, South Asia and the Pacific, and almost 70 per cent for the Arab and Central Asian countries - as against a mere 27 per cent for western Europe and North America taken together (UNESCO, 2006).

In the OECD area, Europe is the main destination with 1.2 million, or 52 per cent of foreign students on record there (see Table 4.1). It is the leading host region for students from Europe and Africa and is also attractive to students from the Americas and Asia. North America is host to 31 per cent of foreign students, and the Asia-Pacific region to the remaining 17 per cent.

The geographical distribution of foreign students varies across the major OECD regions (Table 4.2). While North America receives fewer foreign students (707,000 in the United States, Canada and Mexico in 2004), it is the most attractive region for Asian students (Table 4.1). Accordingly, over half (61%) of all foreign students in North America come from Asia, compared to Europe (14%), South America (12%), Africa (8%) and North America (5%). In the European OECD countries, students come first and foremost from Europe (44%), followed by Asia (29%), Africa (18%), and the Americas (8%), while Asian countries receive 85 per cent of students from within the Asian region.

Asia ranks first in terms of students going abroad to pursue higher studies. In 2004, almost half (48%) of the foreign students in the OECD area came from Asia, followed closely by Europe (27%), Africa (12%), South America (7%), North America (4%) and Oceania (1%).

International students choose their study destinations according to their region of origin. As Table 4.1 shows, student mobility in Europe occurs largely within Europe. Among European students registered abroad, 81 per cent are studying in another European country, while among Asian and North American students registered as studying abroad, 28 per cent and 44 per cent, respectively, remain within their continent. The preference of European students to remain in Europe can no doubt be attributed to the Bologna Process and to the new Erasmus Programme promoting this type of mobility (though the introduction of Erasmus Mundus has since expanded the new Erasmus Programme to cover the whole world). For their part, African students have a clear preference for Europe – France alone receives 55 per cent of all African students in Europe and 42 per cent of all international African students enrolled in the OECD area. In turn, students from the Americas most often choose to stay in the region, though almost 40 per cent also opt to study in Europe. Asian students aim mainly for North America (40%) and, though 28 per cent also go to study in the Asia-Pacific region, in particular in Australia, 32 per cent also choose to go to Europe. Here again, the averages conceal major variations, as the United Kingdom (43%) and Germany (29%) together host 72 per cent of Asian students studying in Europe.

Table 4.1:

Destinations of Foreign Students Studying in OECD Countries by Origin, 2004 (%)

Origin	Destination			
	North America	Europe	Asia-Pacific	OECD
Africa	20	77	3	100
North America	44	43	13	100
South America	56	41	2	100
Asia	40	32	28	100
Europe	16	81	3	100
Oceania	27	19	54	100
World	31	52	17	100

Source: *OECD.*

Table 4.2:

Composition of Foreign Student Bodies in the OECD Area, 2004 (%)

Origin	OECD area			Total OECD
	North America	Europe	Asia-Pacific	
Africa	8	18	2	12
North America	5	3	3	4
South America	12	5	1	7
Asia	61	29	85	48
Europe	14	44	5	29
Oceania	1	0	3	1
Total	100	100	100	100

Note:
The percentages do not always add up to 100 per cent because of rounding.

Source: *OECD.*

At the country level, China (including Hong Kong SAR) ranks first as the country with the largest share of its nationals studying abroad, i.e. 17 per cent of all foreign students in the OECD area, followed by India (5%), South Korea (4%), Germany, Japan, Morocco and France (3% each). Two-thirds (66%) of all Asian students abroad are concentrated in four English-speaking countries, namely Australia, Canada, the United Kingdom and the United States. Whereas Asians generally turn to cross-border education to follow full courses, bearing the real cost of their studies themselves, American and European students prefer short stays, mainly to attend courses subsidized by European institutions (OECD, 2004a).

In relative terms, the situation again differs (Figure 4.2). The small countries are often those with the largest numbers of nationals studying abroad relative to the size of their higher education system. Frequently their offer, both quantitatively and in terms of the range of disciplines available is limited, and, consequently, their nationals most often study in neighbouring countries under more or less tacit agreements. A case in point is Luxembourg, which, in 2004, had twice as many students enrolled abroad than at home. For many larger African countries, the high degree of student mobility is no doubt attributable to limited capacity at home. In absolute terms, the number of students from the major source countries studying abroad is, in fact, relatively low considering the size of their system of higher education.

Figure 4.2:

Countries with over 20 per cent of all Tertiary-level Students Studying Abroad, 2004

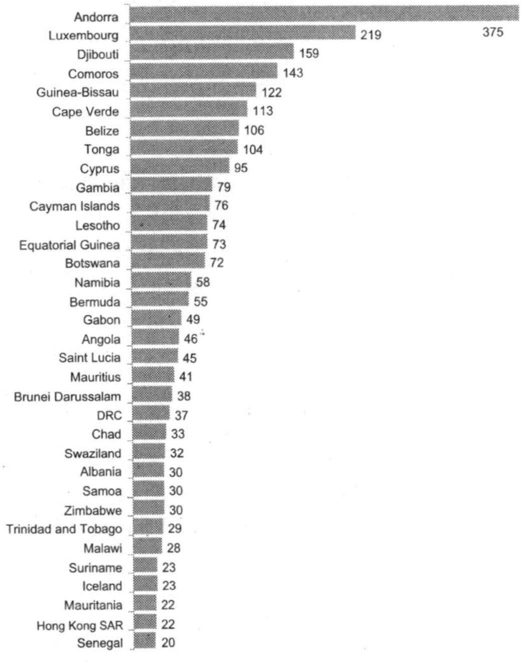

Source: *UNESCO.*

While some migration flows often display marked gender differences, these are less significant in student mobility, though not entirely absent. Thus, female students accounted on average for 50 per cent of foreign students in OECD countries in 2004, against a (national) average of 49 per cent male students in higher education (Table 4.3). The share of female students has steadily increased since 1998. While the share of European female students in international mobility reflects their share in higher education, female students from the United States are more willing to go abroad than their male counterparts, the reverse being true in Asia. In the case of the United States, this over-representation of women in international student mobility is no doubt related to the preponderance of female students in the humanities, which is the main discipline pursued by mobile U.S. students. Concerning Asia, apart from reasons related to the favoured disciplines pursued (many Asian students study science and technology), the under-representation of women in international student mobility is perhaps due to the fact that families are more willing to invest in males rather than females (OECD, 2004a). Hence, countries hosting many Asian students often have a smaller number of female students among their overall foreign student contingents.

Table 4.3:

Percentage of Women among Foreign Students in OECD Countries

	1998	2004
Australia	49	46
Austria	48	52
Canada	43	47
Czech Republic	37	50
Denmark	59	54
Finland	40	45
France	n.a.	49
Germany	45	50
Hungary	41	53
Iceland	66	66
Ireland	60	n.a.
Italy	50	57
Japan	46	48
South Korea	38	46
Netherlands	n.a.	54
New Zealand	52	52
Norway	52	56
Poland	47	55
Portugal	n.a.	49
Slovak Republic	n.a.	41
Spain	49	51
Sweden	56	54
Switzerland	45	45
Turkey	27	32
U.K.	46	50
U.S.	42	44
Country mean	**47**	**50**

Notes:
France - 2003 instead of 2004; United States - 2002 instead of 2004.
n.a. = not available

Source: *OECD.*

In countries for which numbers are available for 2004, an average of 32 per cent of international students were enrolled in the social sciences, 24 per cent in sciences and engineering (13% and 11%, respectively[2]), 16 per cent in the human sciences and art, 16 per cent in medicine, with agriculture, education and services making up the remaining ten per cent. Yet, the choice of disciplines by international students varies appreciably from one country to another. For example, in Australia, Germany, Norway, Switzerland and the United States, the proportion of foreign students enrolled in the sciences in 2004 was clearly higher than the average for all the countries for which data were available; this was the case for the social sciences in Australia, the Netherlands and New Zealand; the human sciences in Iceland, Japan, Austria and Germany; the medical sciences in Belgium, the Slovak Republic, Italy, Hungary, the Czech Republic, Denmark and Poland; engineering in Finland and Portugal; and agriculture in Hungary, Belgium and the Slovak Republic (OECD, 2006a: Table C3.5). Thus, different disciplines in

[2] In line with the ISCED classification (1997) this includes personal services, transport services, environmental protection, security services and other similar fields, some of which may be offered in a vocational tertiary education establishment and not a university.

different countries attract either more or fewer foreign students than the international average. Yet, while these disciplines are undoubtedly centres of attraction for foreign students in a given system of higher education, there is nothing to support the conclusion that they are centres of attraction (or excellence) at the international level. Indeed, some countries actually receive very few foreign students in their most attractive disciplines.

Generally speaking, almost 90 per cent of international students are enrolled in higher education. In 2004, the only countries where a significant percentage of international students had chosen vocational training (ISCED 5b) were Canada (30% of international students in a vocational education programme), Greece (29%), Belgium (26%), Japan (24%) and New Zealand (24%). Although cross-border students enrol mainly in undergraduate courses, relative to local students a proportionally greater number follow postgraduate courses. Compared to the student body as a whole, a higher proportion of foreign students is enrolled in advanced research programmes (i.e. doctorate level). In 2001, foreigners enrolled in such courses represented on average 10.2 per cent of all students in higher education, but a mere 3.8 per cent of the total number of students (foreign and national) in the countries for which statistics were available. Although this varies significantly depending on the country, international (or foreign) students in 2004 made up a significant portion of graduates from advanced research programmes (ISCED 6) in Switzerland (41.1%), the United Kingdom (36.8%), Canada (27.3%), the United States (26.4%), Belgium (23.4%) and France (23.5%). In these countries, international students represent a genuine contribution to the country's scientific output, as well as to its output of scientists (OECD, 2004a and 2006a). In 2003, more than half the recipients of doctoral degrees in the United States were born abroad (versus 27% in 1973), with 50 per cent in the physical sciences, engineering (67%) and economic sciences (68%) (Bound et al., 2006).

2.2 The Causes of Mobility

The decision to study abroad and where depends on a broad spectrum of cultural, educational, economic and social factors. The factors determining the choice of a foreign destination include:

- The destination country's immigration (or visa) policy for foreign students: Potential determinants are the ease of obtaining a visa, the possibility to work while studying or to remain in the country upon completion of studies.
- Employment possibilities in the host country and the country of origin: A host country will be more attractive if students can work there after completing their studies, or if their qualifications are highly regarded on the local job market when they return home.
- Recognition of skills and foreign qualifications in the country of origin and the host country: The frequent absence of any formal framework for such recognition partly explains the success of student mobility under joint university programmes or partnerships between establishments - leading to double degrees or automatic recognition of credits obtained in the partner establishment. On the one hand, the lack of recognition of degrees and professional qualifications obtained at home can induce mobility. Students may choose to pursue studies in another country because they may have decided to establish themselves and work there and have no choice but to obtain the local qualifications and degrees that would allow them to do so. Moreover, the degrees and qualifications obtained in the host country may enjoy greater international recognition. On the other hand, the lack of recognition of foreign qualifications inhibits mobility as it may oblige students to take up their studies again from scratch abroad or limit their job prospects on return to their country of origin. UNESCO and OECD jointly drew up the Guidelines for Quality Provision in Cross-border Higher Education, calling for greater transparency

and international cooperation as a means of facilitating the international recognition of skills (OECD, 2005b).

- The cost of studies abroad (tuition fees, living expenses, taking financial assistance into account) compared with the country of origin: The smaller the cost differential, the more mobile students are likely to be. In addition to geographical and cultural proximity, one of the reasons why students from the European Union (EU) prefer the United Kingdom as an English-speaking country in which to study is undoubtedly the fact that they pay the same tuition fees as local students.
- The reputation and supposed quality of the institutions of learning and educational system in the host country compared to the country of origin: A destination country perceived as having an advantage in this field is an inducement to mobility. Even if they are open to challenge, international classifications are making it increasingly possible to compare institutions of higher learning throughout the world (Salmi and Saroyan, 2007).
- The choice of post-secondary education offered in the country of origin and the possibilities of access: The limitation of admissions to higher education and the *numerus clausus* for some courses could prompt students to go abroad.
- The existence of networks of students or former students from the country of origin: When information about institutions abroad is relatively scant, the recommendations of other students will play an important role, as will the prospect of becoming integrated into one's own (student) community abroad. While academic standards undoubtedly become more stringent at the higher levels of education, studies show that the presumed quality of higher education in the destination country is more decisive than that of the programme being followed or the establishment where students enrol (OECD, 2004a).
- The language of the destination country and the language of instruction: Knowing that English currently ranks first as the main international language and second as the most widely spoken language in the world, the English-speaking countries have a comparative edge in this regard, that some universities in non-English-speaking countries are attempting to offset by also offering programmes in English.
- The perceived quality of life in the host country: As with all forms of travel, the activities offered by the host city and country, climate, cultural and tourist attractions, culture and religion, in short, the desired quality of life, are decisive factors.
- The geographical and cultural proximity of the host country and the country of origin, as well as historical ties: This, for example, is what accounts for the substantial student flows between the Nordic countries, between the Commonwealth countries and the United Kingdom, between the countries of French-speaking Africa and France, and between the former republics of the Soviet Union and the Russian Federation.
- The infrastructure and social benefits available to foreign students in the host country (i.e. medical coverage, university accommodation, language learning centres, etc.).

The choice of a host establishment by foreign students (and their families) may be viewed as the outcome of an assessment of the monetary and non-monetary costs of studying abroad, and the monetary and non-monetary benefits that the students (and their families) hope to reap from it. The tuition fees and cost of living in the host country are thus far from being the only important determinants. Asian students are often accustomed to paying (relatively) high tuition fees and hence do not necessarily consider the lack of subsidies as an obstacle to mobility. In contrast, students originating from the EU, who benefit from sizeable subsidies in their countries, are less willing to study in countries where tuition fees are significantly higher. Even so, low tuition fees do not determine student mobility: flows of foreign students are relatively negligible in some countries where tuition fees are relatively low, or even non-existent, such as the Nordic countries. The cost factor is undoubtedly more important for educational programmes in English-speaking countries. Similarly, there is no evidence to suggest that the wish to emigrate to a country is necessarily a deciding factor in the choice of a country in which to study. A student may well choose to study in one country and then emigrate to another or indeed return home.

2.3 What are the New Forms of Cross-border Higher Education?

Student mobility is but one form of cross-border higher education. A growing number of students are gaining access and benefiting from the new possibility of pursuing higher or post-secondary distance education offered by a foreign university without having to leave their own country. The international virtual mobility of programmes and establishments and the possibility of distance learning, initially as correspondence courses and, more recently, via the internet, has increased over the past decade, especially towards Asia and the Middle East. The link between such new forms of cross-border higher education and physical mobility of people, whether immediate or subsequent, is uncertain.

The mobility of educational programmes is the second most common form of cross-border higher education after international student mobility. Although it encompasses distance learning - including cyber-education (or e-learning) (OECD, 2005a; Larsen and Vincent-Lancrin, 2006) generally complemented by onsite courses at local partner establishments – it mostly takes the form of traditional face-to-face learning, made possible through a partner establishment abroad. Relations between foreign and local establishments have given rise to a variety of contractual arrangements, ranging from development aid to commercial contracts. Commercial cross-border education is now prevalent in the Asia-Pacific region, chiefly in the form of franchises or twinning, though many other forms also exist. Under a franchise, a local provider is generally authorized by a foreign establishment to offer all or some of its academic courses under very precise contractual arrangements. In most cases, such courses lead to a foreign qualification. Franchises may take numerous other forms, however. Under a twinning programme, students pursue studies with a foreign provider and follow a foreign programme; they undergo some of their training in their country of origin and complete it in the country of the foreign establishment. This type of cross-border education usually involves mobility of both students and programmes.

It is difficult to put a number on cross-border educational programmes or students registered in foreign programmes offered in their own country. The two countries most active in this field - the United Kingdom and Australia - have some 300,000 students registered in their cross-border programmes, mainly in Asia (McBurnie and Ziguras, 2007). Today, all of Australia's 38 public universities offer courses abroad, and their numbers have risen from a mere 25 in 1991 to 1,600 in 2003. Over 85 per cent of these courses are located in China (including Hong Kong SAR), Singapore and Malaysia, while the others are scattered throughout the rest of the world, from India to Canada, including Indonesia and South Africa. The number of students following Australian programmes in their countries represented 33 per cent of all international students registered in Australian establishments in 2004, a nine per cent increase since 1996. Hence, educational services represented Australia's third most important services export item in 2003, worth AUD 5.03 billion (IDP Australia, 2007).

Perhaps on account of the greater entrepreneurial risks entailed, the mobility of establishments is still limited, but has nonetheless become a significant dimension of cross-border higher education. It represents the foreign direct investments made by institutions of higher learning or educational enterprises. The most typical form of such mobility is the opening of campuses abroad by universities and of training centres by other educational service providers. According to the *Observatory on Borderless Higher Education*, there were about a hundred of these worldwide in 2005 (OBHE *Breaking News*, 27 June 2005). One can point to the examples of Nottingham University (U.K.) with campuses in China and Malaysia; Liverpool University (U.K.) set to open a campus in China; and Monash University (Australia), which has opened campuses in Malaysia and South Africa, while Australia's Royal Melbourne Institute of Technology (RMIT) University has a campus in Viet Nam. Mobility of establishments also includes creating entirely new educational establishments (not affiliated to any establishment of origin), as well as the partial or total acquisition of an establishment abroad. This latter form, for example, is preferred by the stock-listed U.S. group Laureate International Universities, which owns universities in the Americas (Brazil, Chile, Costa Rica, Ecuador, Honduras, Mexico, Panama, Peru), in China and in Europe (France, The Netherlands, Spain, Switzerland).

The relationship between these new forms of cross-border higher education on the one hand, and student mobility and skilled migration on the other, is somewhat unclear. For one thing, these are alternatives to student mobility that do not afford the same cultural and linguistic experience as a stay abroad, but which are less costly. It is conceivable that, apart from their potentially beneficial developmental spin-offs for their host countries (Vincent-Lancrin, 2006), these new forms are limiting the exodus of skills that could otherwise possibly result from student mobility. Moreover, these study courses sometimes entail brief stays abroad and often, though not invariably, lead to degrees and qualifications recognized in the country of the foreign partner university, and could pave the way for subsequent migration to countries where such qualifications are recognized. Subsequent migration could therefore be an underlying motive. In the Philippines, for example, the number of nursing students has increased dramatically in recent years, often driven by the hope of emigrating to an industrialized, generally English-speaking country. Obtaining a nursing qualification from these countries in the Philippines can only facilitate out-migration. Besides, the British Council encourages British tertiary institutions wishing to engage in cross-border activities in the Philippines to give preference to the medical disciplines. Nevertheless, these new forms of cross-border higher education are still in their early stages, and it would be premature to undertake an assessment of their impact on migration.

3. Today's Major Strategies for the Internationalization of Higher Education

By no means do all countries have an express policy aimed at the internationalization of higher education. Yet, based on current practice, it is possible to identify four major strategies that reflect the range of motivations and policy tools at work in this field. These strategies are not always coordinated and even less directly decided at government level, and their outcomes vary considerably from one country to another. They nevertheless make it possible to paint a picture of the current policy landscape. Each strategy takes a different approach to migration, but the objectives they pursue are not mutually exclusive. The traditional strategy in this field is based on mutual understanding, while the three others - those based on skilled migration, income generation and capacity building - which emerged during the 1990s, are quite clearly dictated by economic considerations. Migration is sometimes an integral part of these considerations.

The goals pursued by the strategy based on **mutual understanding** are primarily related to political, cultural, academic and development aid considerations. The strategy authorizes and encourages international mobility of students and staff, both national and foreign, through scholarship and university exchange programmes, as well as partnerships between institutions of higher learning. This strategy does not generally recruit foreign students through intensive campaigns, but instead targets a tiny elite of national and foreign students. The coordination aspect is mainly addressed under development aid and geo-strategic choices. Under this approach, it is not rare for scholarship programmes to fall within the purview of the Ministry of Foreign Affairs. As for the migration aspect, foreign students are expected to return to their country of origin and are not infrequently barred from remaining in their host country for more or less extended periods after completing their studies. This traditional strategy of internationalization is still the main approach pursued by countries like Japan, Republic of Korea, Mexico, Spain and, in fact, most developing countries. In the United States, the Fulbright Commission programmes are typical examples of this and associated with J-1 visas (which oblige the students concerned to leave the territory for at least two years before being able to apply for a residence permit allowing them to work in the country). The EU has also launched the Socrates-Erasmus programme in keeping with the same philosophy: student and teacher exchanges, the networking of university departments and establishments throughout Europe, and the joint design of study programmes were intended to foster a feeling of "European citizenship" among European youth, thanks to better mutual understanding and knowledge of several European languages. Although their knowledge of languages and of neighbouring countries could pave the way for subsequent migration by students and contribute to the emergence of a common labour market, stays abroad still tend to be short and part of the educational institution's study programme in the country of origin. Therefore, the principle that students should return to their country of origin is central to the concept of the programme.

The strategy based on **skilled migration** pursues the same goals as the preceding one, but in addition entails the more deliberate and targeted recruitment of foreign students. It is in line with the philosophy of the knowledge-based economy, but also aims to attract talented students (and university personnel) who could become knowledge workers at the service of the host country's economy or boost the competitiveness of research and higher education in that country. The internationalization of higher education enables national systems to compare themselves to foreign systems of higher education and often leads establishments and universities to come up with innovative ideas to adapt themselves to the requirements of foreign students (or of their own students returning from abroad). It also paves the way to attract foreign talent to the host country. Though scholarship programmes could remain an important part of this strategy, they are also complemented by other measures, such as actively promoting a country's higher education system abroad while simultaneously relaxing the visa or immigration regulations for the target groups. Dedicated entities are sometimes created to assist foreigners in relation to their studies and their stay in the host country. Instruction in English might be developed and encouraged in non-English-speaking countries. As such, studies pursued by international students are subsidized by the host country in the same way as for local students. They may target students from certain regions, postgraduate students or future researchers, rather than undergraduate students or students specializing in a particular field. This strategy generally leads to an increase in the number of foreign students received in the country, but has no real impact in terms of the mobility of courses and institutions. It can also prove difficult or impossible to implement, and generally remains embedded in development aid policy or in conventional university partnerships. The countries that have adopted this approach include. Canada (some provinces), France,

Germany, the United Kingdom (for students from the EU) and the United States (for postgraduate students).

The Bologna Process, launched in 1992, marked a reorientation of the policy of internationalization adopted throughout Europe. In particular, it moved the EU Socrates-Erasmus programme closer to the skilled migration strategy. Today, the mobility of students and university personnel is helping to create a European area of higher education and research designed to boost the attractiveness (outside Europe and, more specifically, in Asia) of higher education in Europe and to transform Europe's economies into knowledge-based ones (Huismans and van der Wende, 2004). The harmonization of European systems is not only aimed at promoting intra-European mobility, but also at enhancing the international appeal of tertiary education in Europe, especially vis-à-vis the United States. In 1998, the United States was host to 47 per cent of foreign students from Asia, a figure that had fallen to 40 per cent by 2004. Still, competition is as intense as cooperation among the countries of Europe.

The strategy based on **income generation** pursues the same goals as those based on mutual understanding and skilled migration but, in addition, it directly pursues commercial ends. One specific feature of that approach is that higher education services are invoiced at their real cost to international students, who, by and large, do not benefit from any public subsidies. By comparison with local students, therefore, international students often represent extra income for tertiary institutions, a factor that encourages them to be enterprising on the international education market. For the purposes of this strategy, government authorities allow institutions a high degree of autonomy with a view to creating a solid reputation for their higher education sector and protecting foreign students by means of quality assurance mechanisms. This strategy generally leads to a sizeable increase in the number of international students paying for their tuition at cost and to the development of profit-oriented mobility programmes and establishments. This sometimes goes hand-in-hand with a reduction of the relative share of public funding in university resources or even with a cut in government funding per student. It may also entail an active policy of commercial negotiations aimed at reducing the obstacles to cross-border educational activities. That may be undertaken via bilateral agreements or through negotiations on trade in educational services in the framework of the World Trade Organization's General Agreement on Trade in Services (GATS).[3] Generally speaking, the terms and conditions governing paid work by students are relaxed during the course of their studies but, as under the strategy based on mutual understanding, there are often different policies in place both to limit subsequent permanent immigration by students in general and to facilitate subsequent settlement for some. Public authorities and educational establishments must therefore come to grips with the issue of geographical balance among international students, not only in commercial terms (diversifying the countries of origin to ensure financial stability), but also in terms of immigration. The countries having opted for this approach include Australia, Canada (some provinces), New Zealand, the United States (for undergraduate students), but also Denmark, Ireland, the Netherlands and the United Kingdom (for non-EU students, as EU rules require countries to apply the same registration fees to nationals and to students from elsewhere in the Union).

Finally, the strategy based on **capacity building** involves encouraging the importation of higher education, regardless of how it is supplied, in order to quickly strengthen the human and productive capacities of a developing country. When a country lacks the capabilities to fully respond to its higher education requirements, or when its national system is still weak, cross-border education can help build local capacities both as regards courses available and

[3] See OECD (2004a) for a presentation of the GATS and its implications for education.

the human capital needed for the local economy and system of higher education (Vincent-Lancrin, 2005; Middlehurst and Woodfield, 2004; Larsen and Vincent-Lancrin, 2002). While the two preceding strategies are oriented primarily towards the export of education services, the strategy based on capacity building is predominantly import-oriented. In that connection, the scholarship programmes available to support the international mobility of civil servants, teachers, university personnel and students are crucial tools, as are the steps taken to encourage establishments, programmes and foreign universities to come forward and provide their teaching services on a commercial basis. Countries could use the GATS negotiations to signal their interest in transnational services of this kind, though they may also use other less formal means. By and large, the mobility of programmes and institutions falls under government regulations designed to ensure that these activities are in line with the country's academic and economic development strategy. Twinning arrangements and partnerships with local providers are encouraged (and sometimes imposed) so as to open the way for the transfer of know-how between foreign and local academic institutions. The short-term impact of this approach is a considerable increase in the number of national students going abroad, as well as of the number of profit-oriented foreign programmes and educational institutions entering the country to meet local demand. In principle, once the country's capacities are strengthened, there is no further justification for this approach, and its success should in theory lead to a change of the underlying strategy. It attaches capital importance to coordinating educational policy with economic and commercial policy. In particular, countries must ensure that their quality assurance systems cover foreign courses and institutions and that the latter do, indeed, contribute to the achievement of the country's objectives. Their migration policy must favour temporary mobility for professionals, and they often incorporate measures to encourage the return of their nationals going abroad to study or to complete their training so as to avoid a substantial outflow of needed skills. This strategy is being followed mainly in Southeast and East Asia and the Middle East — China, Hong Kong SAR, Indonesia, Malaysia, Singapore, Viet Nam and Dubai (as well as in other states part of the United Arab Emirates).

4. What are the Links Between the Internationalization of Higher Education, Student Mobility and Skilled Migration?

The internationalization of higher education raises new challenges for policymakers with respect to education policy (OECD, 2004a and b), as well as the coordination of their economic, social, migration and development policies (OECD, 2006b). The links between migration and the internationalization of higher education are reciprocal in that migration strategies and policies encourage and facilitate the internationalization of higher education while, at the same time, they are becoming increasingly influenced by, and dependent on, that process. The two major issues therefore pertain to reconciling the aims of migration with the internationalization of higher education and to the brain drain. To what extent are student mobility and the internationalization of higher education giving rise to skilled migration? In the absence of figures in reply to that question, this section will attempt to illustrate the current scale of the issues involved.

Visa policy for students and university personnel and, more generally, immigration policy are an important part of the machinery for the internationalization of higher education. Attracting international students to a country will make sense only if they are able to enter to pursue their studies and, ideally, to do so without undue difficulties. If international students are to be attracted while they are also being expected to pay market-driven tuition fees, authorization to work in the host country will go a long way to persuading them to come. Similarly, attracting foreign teaching establishments and educational programmes often entails facilitating temporary migration for professionals (university personnel, etc.). Many countries now attach growing importance to attracting foreign students and have therefore simplified or reviewed their application procedures for visas and residence permits for foreign students, not least by improving the available information concerning these procedures.

Yet, a country's migration policy can also hamper its strategy for the internationalization of higher education, above all when that strategy is decentralized. Migration authorities are sometimes fearful that any relaxation of the procedures to obtain student visas may lead to abuses or fraud. Moreover, other political priorities may conflict with these policies. After the events of September 11, 2001, the United States, for example, clamped down on the conditions governing the admission of foreigners to the country. This meant tightening the procedures to obtain student visas and introducing longer verification periods (each applicant for a student visa must be interviewed face-to-face by a representative of the U.S. authorities). Perhaps this policy acted in combination with stronger competition from other countries to reduce the number of candidates and to slow the rate of foreign student enrolment in the United States. The number of foreign students increased by a mere 0.6 per cent between 2002 and 2003, as against 6.4 per cent during the two preceding years. It contracted by a further 2.4 per cent between 2003 and 2004, and by 1.3 per cent between 2004 and 2005 - the first decline in the number of foreign students in the past 32 years (Institute for International Education (IIE), 2005). The geographical composition of the foreign student body also changed, with fewer students arriving from Arab countries and the Middle East, offset by an increase in the number of Indian and Chinese students. Academic institutions raised their concerns with the U.S. authorities, who have somewhat relaxed and improved the efficiency of their visa policy for foreign students and university personnel since 2003. The result was a nine per cent increase in the amount of student visa applications during the first half of 2004 (U.S. Department of State, 2005). That was the first increase since the 9/11 attacks, and student visa applications again reached pre-9/11 levels in 2006.

Furthermore, migration policies and strategies are themselves becoming increasingly dependent on the internationalization of higher education, although the available data are not sufficient to gauge the true impact of cross-border higher education on migration and, more specifically, on the migration of qualified individuals. In some instances, the pursuit of studies abroad is part of a deliberate migration strategy on the part of individuals, since obtaining a foreign qualification is sometimes indispensable to working in their particular field of specialization in the host country and an asset that often weighs favourably in the balance when applying for a residence permit. The free movement of persons in the EU no doubt partly explains the scale of student mobility in Europe relative to the more limited student mobility between North American countries. The North American Free Trade Agreement (NAFTA) does not provide for the free movement of labour across a common labour market. In some cases, the permanent establishment of students abroad after completing their studies is unintentional. Whether internationally mobile or not, students are often of an age to start families and may marry and stay in the country where they are studying. Moreover, the competition among countries to attract highly qualified individuals has intensified in recent years, as reflected in recent migration policy trends (Tremblay, 2005; OECD, 2006c; see also Chapter 2). As observed above, migration is becoming an increasingly important component of the internationalization strategies being pursued by source countries. Moreover, migrants who also hold a degree obtained in the host country frequently find it easier and are more ready to integrate. Therefore, migration policies are increasingly factoring in the authorization or facilitation of permanent residence for international students in the host country after their studies. Australia, Canada, New Zealand and the United Kingdom, for example, facilitate the settlement of foreign citizens with qualifications from their universities by granting them extra points in their immigration application file. Although they have no points system, France, Germany and some other countries have introduced more flexible immigration policies for qualified migrants and for foreign students wishing to work there after their studies.

Given these developments, the potential brain drain from developing countries encouraged by cross-border higher education is becoming a major concern and a topic of extensive discussion. While it may assist developing countries in their efforts to strengthen their own human resource capacities (Vincent-Lancrin, 2005), cross-border education can indeed favour brain drain rather than the circulation of skills between host and home country. There is no record of systematic data on the relationship between the mobility of students and researchers, and subsequent variations in immigration patterns. What little exists, however, confirms that there is a link. Some 75 per cent of Chinese students who studied abroad between 1978 and 1999 have not returned to China (Iguchi, 2003). In 1999, around 25 per cent of temporary migrants to the United States under the H1-B visa programme had been previously enrolled in U.S. universities (Cervantes and Guellec, 2002). For some years now, almost half of the candidates admitted under Australia's skilled migration programme hold an Australian degree (OECD, 2006c). A recent study of migration policies intended for international students sets out other estimates (Suter and Jandl, 2006) (see Textbox 4.2). In Canada, it is estimated that between 15 and 20 per cent of foreign students have stayed on and are working in the country; in New Zealand, 13 per cent of the foreign students who entered the country between 1998 and 2005 to study obtained a residence permit by 2006; in Norway, 18 per cent of the foreign students studying there between 1991 and 2005 and originating from outside the European Economic Area (EEA) remained in the country, as against nine per cent of foreign students from within the EEA; lastly, in the United Kingdom, a recent study showed that, in 2005, 27 per cent of international students from within the EU were employed in the U.K. six months after obtaining their degrees. However, statistics on the incidence of foreign students remaining in their host country following the completion of their studies are still insufficient.

Textbox 4.2

National and Regional Retention Policies for Foreign Graduates in Industrialized Countries

Today's labour markets in industrialized countries face two main challenges: the demographic decline of the native population and the transformation of the global economy into a knowledge-based and increasingly interdependent economy. For politicians as well as policymakers in the field of immigration and labour, both phenomena have given rise to significant new questions, particularly in the case of economies that must now depart from their traditional reliance on mostly low-skilled employment in heavy industrial production based on available local natural resources.

Many countries are responding to this development by seeking to attract and retain highly skilled migrants to fill particular labour shortages. Australia and Canada have long pursued proactive migration policies targeting highly skilled migrants through their points-based selection systems for permanent immigration. Other countries are following this example as offering an ideal response to the current labour shortages in specific sectors and to attract and retain highly skilled migrants.

In view of the growing competition for human capital, it is not surprising that policymakers are targeting international students to satisfy the growing demand for highly skilled human resources. Foreign graduates are seen to possess characteristics that facilitate integration both professionally and socially, which makes them particularly attractive for recruitment and retention. They are usually young, have a high propensity for acculturation and possess widely recognized professional and academic credentials and appropriate professional training in relevant fields of activity. This last point is especially important as many migrants encounter difficulties in having their foreign academic and professional credentials recognized and gaining access to the labour market.

The retention policies applied by a number of countries facilitate access to employment and, directly or indirectly, lead to permanent settlement. Some national immigration schemes have special provisions for the highly skilled and grant extra points under the points selection system for one or two years of studies in the country, while others have designed labour schemes specially targeting foreign graduates. In France, Germany and New Zealand, for example, foreign students are permitted to stay in the country for up to one year after graduation to look for a job.

The impact of such retention policies is difficult to evaluate as only few countries are currently able to produce statistics concerning the settlement of foreign students. Yet, some indicators are available. Thus, in Canada, between 15 and 20 per cent of foreign students can be expected to eventually settle and work; however, this estimate includes residence permits issued on all possible grounds, including family reunion. In 2001, Australia introduced the possibility of permanent settlement for overseas students and in 2002-03, nearly 8,500 permanent residence permits were granted to former students, representing about five per cent of all foreign students enrolled in 2001-02. In 2004-05, this number almost doubled to 16,700, accounting for eight per cent of all overseas students enrolled in 2003-04. In the United Kingdom, 19 per cent of EU-domiciled graduates had found employment in the country in 2000-01, rising to nearly 27 per cent in 2004-05. While such figures do not reflect the full story, they nevertheless indicate a trend in the interest among foreign students to settle and work in the country where they studied as well as the willingness on the part of the countries concerned to facilitate these processes.

Some constituent units of federal countries or regions[1] which have, or felt that they had been neglected or unable to fully participate in national immigration schemes, have started to pursue their own labour schemes either of a general nature or specifically aimed at foreign graduates to meet their labour market and demographic needs. Regional programmes aiming to attract and retain international students usually offer favourable conditions for admission, such as either allocating more points if a job offer is secured, lowering the minimum points threshold for admission or extending the validity of a temporary work and residence permit.

There is evidence to show that universities exert a strong and direct impact on the economic, social and political development in the regions where they are located and that they play an increasingly important role in national migration management schemes aimed at attracting and retaining foreign graduates. Their influence now extends well beyond the provision of quality education and community-building facilities such as theatre, museums and coffee shops where students can meet and mingle to include migration-oriented endeavours. Universities are increasingly seen as a source of highly skilled human capital for the national and regional labour markets while, from the perspective of migrants, they have come to be seen as stepping-stones to permanent immigration.

Note:

[1] E.g. some Canadian provinces and territories, Australian federal states, and Scotland in the U.K.

***Source:** Brigitte Suter, Malmö Institute for Studies of Migration, Diversity and Welfare (MIM), Sweden.*

The United States remains the only country to systematically compile data on the stay rates of foreign students after receiving their degree (Finn, 2003). There is no doubt that receiving international students is one way of attracting skills to the United States, and this attraction has increased steadily since the early 1990s as a result of the combined effect of the larger number of doctorates being delivered by American universities to foreign nationals and the increasing share of doctorate holders born abroad who remain in the United States. The average stay rate[4] for foreign recipients of science and engineering doctorates in the United States four to five years after earning their degrees rose from 41 to 56 per cent between 1992 and 2001.

[4] What the stay rate shows is not whether foreign students have remained permanently in the United States, but how many foreign doctorate recipients from a specific year were still in the United States some years later. Some of these degree holders may have left the country and returned again later. For example, the stay rate for 1991 graduates was 58 per cent in 2001, but would be 81.5 per cent if the rate were to reflect the proportion of persons who had worked in the United States for at least one year during the 1992-2001 period (Finn, 2003).

The figures leapt from 65 to 96 per cent for Chinese and from 72 to 86 per cent for Indian nationals. Stay rates in countries following the completion of studies vary considerably depending on the country of origin and the academic discipline pursued. But in most cases stay rates do not decline significantly over time and partly depend on the level of economic development of the country of origin, though there seems to be no systematic pattern in that regard. Concerning students from Argentina, China, Greece, India, Iran, Israel, eastern European countries as well as New Zealand and the United Kingdom, about 50 per cent are still in the United States five years after receiving their doctorate (Finn, 2003).

In this context, there are grounds to fear that cross-border education could reinforce brain drain as much as it builds capacities in developing countries. As noted earlier, 85 per cent of foreign students throughout the world were in the OECD area in 2004, but most of them (61%) arrived from non-OECD countries. The highly sensitive topic of skilled migration can represent a cost, while it also yields advantages for the countries of origin. On the one hand, countries of origin lose the human capital (and productivity) represented by their skilled people and, if they were educated at public expense, the investment made in their primary, secondary and higher education. On the other hand, this highly qualified diaspora could contribute to the home economy through investments, remittances and the links they establish between countries of origin and destination in terms of trade, innovation and know-how. Naturally, a clear distinction must be made between temporary and permanent out-migration. If they return to the country of origin with their acquired international expertise and experience and are able to employ their skills productively, this would represent a positive contribution to local capacity building and the sharing of expertise in the country of origin (see also Chapter 12).

The OECD's migration database yields unprecedented information regarding the scale of the brain drain (OECD, 2005c). Countries in Africa and the Caribbean are most affected: over 80 per cent of Jamaican and Guyanese graduates have migrated to an OECD country. In contrast, despite the high stay rates for Indian or Chinese students in the United States following their studies, they account for less than three per cent in OECD countries. The picture is similar for Brazil, Indonesia and Thailand, where an average of 17 per cent of skilled nationals migrated to an OECD country.[5] Figure 4.3 shows that the countries of Africa, as well as small countries, mainly in the Caribbean, are those most affected by high rates of skilled migration. One may be tempted to see a correlation between these findings and the data in Figure 4.2, which show that, in relative terms (i.e. relative to the country's overall student body), African students have the highest stay rates abroad. Conceptual and methodological problems aside, the countries for which data are available on these two indicators do not provide a sufficiently solid basis on which to establish a correlation. There is no way of determining whether these individuals received their degrees outside their country.

Figure 4.3:

Countries with over 20 per cent of their Graduates Living in an OECD Country

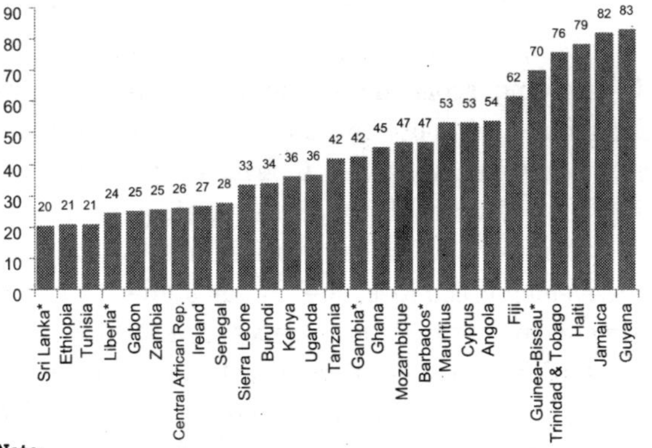

Note:

* Calculations using the Barro and Lee database on the human capital stock. The Cohen and Soto database is otherwise used for all countries for which data are available. The findings from the two databases are not perfectly comparable. It should be noted that the data reflect (accumulated) stocks, not flows.

Source: *OECD, migration database.*

[5] Not to be confused with 17 per cent of the world's skilled population, as this per-country average takes no account of population size.

Even for countries affected by brain drain, turning in upon themselves is no solution. Taking part in international higher education exchanges is their best option in their attempts to minimize the cost of the brain drain. Countries have been coming up with new initiatives designed to offset these movements which, it should be recalled, reflect individual desires and decisions. When foreign students are funded by their home authorities, the United Kingdom sometimes makes their admission contingent on prior authorization from their country of origin. Supported mainly by international organizations, including the International Organization for Migration (IOM), many developing countries are now attempting to harness the resources of their diasporas to develop the needed expertise at home by providing funds to enable their expatriates to undertake temporary but regular work in the country. Even in better-off countries, many programmes have been introduced to encourage renowned scientists to return and resettle in their country of origin.

5. Conclusion

Student flows grew rapidly over the past decade and show no signs of diminishing in the decades ahead. However, the proliferation of other forms of cross-border higher learning and capacity building in emerging economies could well transform this dynamic - without, for all that, reducing flows in the medium term. Globalization, increased migration flows of all types, the strategies followed by institutions of higher learning and the policies of developing countries are all combining to create a more competitive, homogeneous and globalized arena of higher education, which, in turn, makes for continuing student mobility. The growing worldwide movements of professionals, in particular, are generating pressures for greater harmonization and comparability of qualifications and degrees throughout the world. Undoubtedly, international cooperation between professional bodies and academic disciplines will thus go some considerable way towards increasing comparability and the recognition of studies abroad. This will make it less useful or necessary for skilled persons to go abroad to study, while at the same time, making it easier to do so.

Within the European Union, a certain convergence of quality assurance and accreditation systems can be observed for both vocational training and higher education. One of the aims of the Bologna Process is to implement European quality assurance mechanisms using comparable yardsticks and methods. The UNESCO/Council of Europe Convention on the Recognition of Qualifications concerning Higher Education in the European Region, adopted in 1997 in Lisbon, is yet another significant initiative. No longer does it simply take the approach of "equivalence" of degrees and diplomas based on the concepts of "recognition" and "accreditation". It is based more on **cooperation** and **trust** between national systems. When a country ratifies this Convention, it is required to recognize the degrees and diplomas delivered by the other signatories as similar and corresponding to the qualifications granted under its own system, unless a substantial difference between the respective degrees and diplomas issued by the respective parties can be shown to exist.

Of the international agreements on the mutual recognition of professional diplomas, the one that goes farthest is the 1989 Washington Accord concerning engineers and associations representing their profession in Australia, China, Hong Kong SAR, Ireland, New Zealand, South Africa, the United Kingdom and the United States have also recently signed and Japan has acceded to it provisionally. The Accord recognizes "the substantial equivalence" of engineering academic programmes in satisfying the academic requirements for the practice of engineering at the professional level, but does not yet envisage official mutual recognition of professional degrees and diplomas. The Accord also stipulates the rules and procedures for accrediting engineering academic programmes. The signatories mutually accept the respective accreditation decisions and therefore recognize the equivalence of each country's national accreditation mechanisms.

Is student mobility a major source of skilled migration? While there is no doubt that some countries are facing an exodus of skills (i.e. human capital with diplomas from higher education), especially in Africa and the Caribbean, there is still very scant evidence linking it to student mobility and cross-border higher education. In numerical terms, international students do not represent a very significant source of skilled migration. Assuming that one-quarter of the stock of international students complete their studies each year and that 25 per cent of this group stay in the country where they studied, that would represent no more than 20 per cent of the current level of skilled migration (and less than five per cent of migration flows) (OECD, 2006c). Although it is known that in some countries former students may account for a much larger proportion of skilled migrants, it is probable that most skilled migrants emigrate with diplomas received in their country of origin. In the future, however, it will be increasingly difficult to tell whether a skilled migrant holding a diploma from the host country actually studied and received it there, or whether it was obtained from the external branch of a foreign academic institution established in the country, or through distance learning, e.g. via the internet. Nor will it be evident whether diplomas not earned directly by studying in the host country were obtained in a country other than the home country. In short, the linkages between the internationalization of higher education, student mobility and skilled migration are growing more complex, and it will be increasingly difficult to view them strictly in terms of stay rates of international students in countries where they have studied. The internationalization of higher education will continue to be one of the driving forces behind skilled migration. This type of migration should continue to prompt countries to harmonize their systems of higher education and to implement mechanisms for the international recognition of professional diplomas and qualifications, thereby facilitating and further strengthening migration flows of students and graduates of higher education.

REFERENCES

Böhm, A., D. Davis, D. Meares and D. Pearce
2002 *Global student mobility 2025: Forecasts of the Global Demand for International Higher Education,* IDP Education, Sydney.

Bound, J., S. Turner and P. Walsh
2006 "Internationalization of U.S. Doctorate Education", National Bureau of Economic Research (NBER), mimeo.

Cervantes, M. and D. Guellec
2002 "Fuite des cerveaux: Mythes anciens, réalités nouvelles", *L'observateur OCDE*, March, Paris.

European Association for International Education (EAIE)
2005, *I gotta use words when I talk to you: English and international education,* Edited by M. Woolf, EAIE Occasional Paper No. 17, Amsterdam.

Finn, M.G.
2003 "Stay Rates of Foreign Doctorate Recipients from U.S. Universities, 2001", November, Oak Ridge Institute for Science and Education, TN, http://orise.orau.gov/sep/files/stayrate03.pdf.

Huisman, J. and M.C. van der Wende (Eds.)
2004 *On Cooperation and Competition, National and European Policies for the Internationalisation of Higher Education*, Lemmens Verlag, Bonn.

IDP Australia
2007 The independent guide to Australian study opportunities, http://www.idp.com/.

Iguchi, Y.
2003 "The Movement of the Highly Skilled in Asia: Present Situation and Future Prospect" in *Migration and the Labour Market in Asia: Recent Trends and Policies*, OECD, Paris, 29-50.

Institute for International Education (IIE)
2005 *Open Doors 2005: Report on International Educational Exchange*, Sewickley, PA.

Knight, J.
2004 "Internationalization remodeled: Definition, Approaches, and Rationales", *Journal of Studies in International Education*, 8(1): 5-31.

Larsen, K. and S. Vincent-Lancrin
2002 "Le commerce des services d'éducation: est-il bon? est-il méchant?", *Politiques et gestion de l'enseignement supérieur*, OECD, Paris, 14(3): 9-45.

McBurnie, G. and C. Ziguras
2007 *Transnational Education: issues and trends in offshore education*, Routledge Falmer, London.

Middlehurst, R. and S. Woodfield
2004 "The Role of Transnational, Private and For-Profit Provision in Meeting Global Demand for Tertiary Education: Mapping, Regulation and Impact", Summary Report for UNESCO and the Commonwealth of Learning, Commonwealth of Learning, Vancouver, BC, http://www.col.org/colweb/site/pid/3108.

Organisation for Economic Co-operation and Development (OECD)
2004a *Internationalisation and Trade in Higher Education: The Cross-border Challenge*, OECD, Paris.

2004b *Quality and Recognition in Higher Education: The Cross-border Challenge*, OECD, Paris.

2005a *E-learning in Tertiary Education. Where do we stand?*, OECD, Paris.

2005b *Guidelines for Quality Provision in Cross-border Higher Education*, OECD, Paris, http://www.oecd.org/dataoecd/27/51/35779480.pdf.

2005c *Trends in International Migration,* SOPEMI 2004, OECD, Paris.

2006a *Education at a Glance 2006*, OECD, Paris.

2006b "The internationalisation of higher education: towards an explicit policy", in OECD, *Education Policy Analysis 2005-2006*, OECD, Paris.

2006c *International Migration Outlook,* SOPEMI 2006, OECD, Paris.

Salmi, J. and A. Saroyan
2007 "League tables as policy instruments: uses and misuses", *Higher Education Management and Policy*, 19:2, 31-68.

Suter B. and M. Jandl
2006 *Comparative Study on Policies towards Foreign Graduates. Study on Admission and Retention Policies towards Foreign Students in Industrialised Countries*, International Centre for Migration Policy Development (ICMPD), Vienna, http://www.icmpd.org/774.html?&F=2&tx_icmpd_pi2%5Bdocument%5D=548&cHash=10fde5b0ec.

Tremblay, K.
2005 "Academic Mobility and Immigration", *Journal of Studies in International Education*, 9(3): 1-34.

United Nations Educational, Scientific and Cultural Organization (UNESCO)
2006 *Recueil de données mondiales sur l'éducation 2006: Statistiques comparées sur l'éducation dans le monde*, L'Institut de statistique de l'UNESCO, Montréal, http://www.uis.unesco.org/TEMPLATE/pdf/ged/2006/GED2006_FR.pdf.

United States Department of State
2005 "We Don't Want to Lose Even One International Student", U.S. Department of State, http://travel.state.gov/news/info/press/press_1511.html.

Vincent-Lancrin, S.
2005 "Building capacity through cross-border higher education", *Observatory on Borderless Higher Education*, London.

Textbox 4.2 - National and Regional Retention Policies for Foreign Graduates in Industrialized Countries

Australian Education International
2006 International Student Data, Australian Education International, http://aei.dest.gov.au/AEI/MIP/Statistics/StudentEnrolmentAndVisaStatistics/Default.htm.

Birrell, B., L. Hawthorne and S. Richardson
2006 *Evaluation of the General Skilled Migration Categories Report*, Australian Government, Department of Immigration and Citizenship (DIAC), http://www.immi.gov.au/media/publications/research/gsm-report/index.htm.

Dolin, B. and M. Young
2004 "Canada's Immigration Program", Parliamentary Information and Research Service, Library of Parliament, Background Paper BP-190E, Ottawa, http://www.parl.gc.ca/information/library/PRBpubs/bp190-e.htm.

Lebrun, D. and S. Rebelo
2006 "The Role of Universities in the Economic Development of Atlantic Canada: A Focus on Immigration", January, Atlantic Canada Opportunities Agency (ACOA), Moncton, NB, http://www.acoa.ca/e/library/reports/univ_econ_dev.pdf.

Martin, P.
2004 "Universities as Immigration Gatekeepers", Mimeographed draft paper.

Organisation for Economic Co-operation and Development (OECD)
2007 Project on supporting the contribution of higher education institutions to regional development, OECD, Paris, http://www.oecd.org/document/48/0,3343,en_2649_35961291_39872432_1_1_1_1,00.html.

Suter, B. and M. Jandl
2006 *Comparative Study on Policies towards Foreign Graduates. Study on Admission and Retention Policies towards Foreign Students in Industrialised Countries*, ICMPD, Vienna, http://www.icmpd.org/774.html?&F=2&tx_icmpd_pi2%5Bdocument%5D=548&cHash=10fde5b0ec.

2008 "Train and Retain: National and Regional Policies to Promote the Settlement of Foreign Graduates in Knowledge Economies", *Journal of International Migration and Integration*, forthcoming.

TOURISM AND SHORT-TERM BUSINESS TRAVEL*

CHAPTER 5

1. Introduction

This chapter reviews statistics, trends and policy issues in the areas of tourism and short-term business travel, that are typically under-researched and where the lack of data is an even greater problem than for most migration research. Normally, these areas would not be included in a discussion of labour mobility, but they constitute important and growing fields of mobility. Even though the implications for labour movements may not be immediately obvious, they do exist and are identified in this chapter.

The problems of definition and data are extreme in these areas. Definitions are typically diverse and incomplete, with only a limited number of countries collecting data on tourists who provide services or on the many classes of business people who move for limited periods. Some countries have no serviceable data to offer. In most instances, movements for tourism, visiting friends and relatives (VFR), short-term "business" trips and other such temporary movements are grouped together. The United Nations World Tourist Organization (UNWTO), the worldwide monitoring agency on tourism, measures flows in terms of numbers and receipts. Its data define one category only: combined business and leisure travel. Nevertheless, this chapter attempts to treat the two major flows of tourists and business travellers separately, where possible.

In 2006, the Organisation for Economic Co-operation and Development (OECD) produced a paper entitled "Harmonised statistics on immigrant inflows – preliminary results, sources and methods" by Lemaître et al. (2006). Although the paper focuses on permanent movements only, it concludes with the stated intention of extending the work to shorter-term movements (students, seasonal workers, service providers, and the like). This will be a welcome addition for OECD countries; in the meantime, this chapter presents such information as is available on major flows and implications.

2. Tourism: An Overview

Business and leisure travel is, by some measures, one of the world's largest industries: tourism receipts in 2003 represented approximately six per cent of global exports of goods and services (UNWTO, 2006).

* This chapter was written by Robyn Iredale, Adjunct Associate Professor, Australian Demographic and Social Research Institute, the Australian National University, Canberra, Australia. The author wishes to acknowledge the research assistance provided by Dr Richard Woolley in the preparation of this chapter.

Worldwide, international tourism receipts were estimated at USD 680 billion (EUR 547 billion) in 2005 (UNWTO, 2006), with all regions and subregions sharing in the increase from 2004. Europe gained an additional USD 20 billion, raising receipts to over USD 348 billion (51% of the world total); the Americas added USD 13 billion to USD 145 billion (21%) and Asia and the Pacific increased their total by USD 11 billion to USD 139 billion (20%). Estimates based on still limited available data point to an increase of USD 2 billion to USD 21 billion for Africa and of USD 2 billion to USD 28 billion for the Middle East, representing three per cent and four per cent of the world total, respectively.

For many destinations visitor expenditure on accommodation, food and drink, local transport, entertainment, shopping, etc. is an important pillar of their economy, creating much needed employment and opportunities for development. Some 70 countries earned more than USD 1 billion from international tourism in 2005. (...) Total receipts from international tourism, including international passenger transport, exceed USD 800 billion. (...) [F]or many destination countries, in particular developing countries and islands, tourism counts as the most important category of export earnings (UNWTO, 2006).

The number of international tourist arrivals worldwide exceeded 800 million in 2005, an increase of 42 million (5.5%) over 2004, representing an all time high. The majority of international tourist arrivals concerned leisure, recreation and holidays (50% of the total, or 402 million), while business travel accounted for some 16 per cent or 125 million, and visiting friends and relatives (VFR), religious purposes/pilgrimages, health treatment and the like for 26 per cent or 212 million. For the remaining eight per cent of arrivals, the purpose of the visit was not specified (UNWTO, 2006).

Between 1950 and 1990, Europe and the Americas received the largest numbers of tourists, representing a joint market share of over 95 per cent in 1950 and 82 per cent forty years later. However, by 2000 their combined share had declined to 76 per cent. This points to a greater diversification of destinations, as also of origins of tourism. Between 2004 and 2005, Africa recorded the highest relative growth (+ 9%) in arrivals, followed by Asia and the Pacific (+ 8%), the Middle East (+ 8%), the Americas (+ 6%) and Europe (+ 4%).

Table 5.1 lists the origins of international tourists from 1990 to 2005. It shows that international tourists still originate mainly from industrialized European countries (55.7%), the Americas (17%) and Asia and the Pacific (19.1%). However, over the last decades and with rising levels of disposable incomes, many emerging economies have shown rapid growth as sources of tourism, in particular in Northeast and Southeast Asia, central and eastern Europe, the Middle East and Southern Africa. By region, Africa recorded the largest increase in relative terms (+ 8.2%), followed by Asia and the Pacific (+ 6.9%) and the Middle East (+ 6.9%). The penultimate row in Table 5.1 shows that 78.6 per cent of international travel takes place within the same region.

Table 5.1:

International Tourist Arrivals, 1990-2005

	International Tourist Arrivals (millions)			Change (%)		Share (%)
	1990	2000	2005	2003/02	2005/04	2005
World	439.4	686.8	806.3	-1.8	5.5	100
Europe	252.6	396.7	449.0	1.0	4.1	55.7
Asia and the Pacific	59.1	115.5	154.3	-8.2	6.9	19.1
Americas	100.3	116.1	137.1	-4.8	5.3	17.0
Middle East	8.3	17.0	21.9	-2.1	6.9	2.7
Africa	10.0	17.7	20.3	1.1	8.2	2.5
Origin not specified*	9.2	13.3	23.6	-	-	2.9
Same region	350.8	540.9	634.1	-1.4	-	78.6
Other regions	79.4	133.0	148.6	-3.5	-	18.4

Note:
* Countries for which a specific region of origin could not be allocated.

Source: *UNWTO, 2006.*

Many countries now see tourism, especially international tourism, as a large potential source of revenue and are diversifying their production and marketing strategies to attract increasing numbers of tourists. There are clear economic and social benefits of tourism, but there are also social as well as environmental costs (see Textbox 5.1). The two countries experiencing the fastest growth in international tourist receipts between 2004 and 2005 were China and Turkey. In terms of numbers of arrivals, three out of the top ten countries are developing countries: China (ranking 4th), Mexico (7) and Turkey (9). Some countries experienced remarkable growth in 2005: Laos (65.1%), Cambodia (34.7%), Papua New Guinea (17%), Fiji (10%), Honduras (25.9%), Venezuela (45.2%), Swaziland (82.8%) and Senegal (15.3%). However, the figures are volatile and often start from a low base.

Textbox 5.1

Economic and Social Benefits and Costs of Tourism

Tourism can have both positive and negative impacts, but the main focus is on the gains to be made. Seen in this light, many countries are investing heavily in infrastructure projects and upgrading their human resources and facilities to become attractive destinations for more tourists. For example, the Greater Mekong Sub-region (GMS) attracted around 18.7 million international arrivals and more than 24 million border-pass tourists in 2004. This number is expected to rise to 30.6 million by 2010 and to 46.1 million by 2015 (International TravelDailyNews.com, 2006). Many initiatives are being launched to foster this development; however, the difficult part will be to manage such growth.

The potential benefits from tourism in terms of alleviating poverty, generating employment and stimulating various sectors of the economy are well known in many countries, and are being touted in others. In the GMS, for example, the impact of tourism on poverty alleviation is considered to potentially outweigh that of other productive sectors, since tourists are often attracted to poor areas. The tourism industry is also labour intensive and more easily accessible to local workers at the lower segments of this growing service sector and, if properly managed, can build and strengthen poor people's access to and control over their cultural and natural assets (Asian Development Bank, 2005).

On the other hand, tourism can also place enormous pressure on the fragile balance of natural environments at major tourist sites, especially World Heritage sites, and the development of tourism will have to be managed so as to ensure that natural resources are not depleted nor the absorption capacity exceeded (International TravelDailyNews.com, 2006).

The potential social impacts of tourism are also of major concern, including the proliferation of sex tourism and the trafficking of human beings, especially women and children.

A "Northern bias" often "pervades much national tourism planning across the developing world" (Rogerson, 2006: 2). According to Ghimire (2001: 2), "the dominant official concept of tourism in developing countries focuses on wealthy foreign visitors from the industrialized North" and neglects "the potentials - as well as the problems - related to mass tourism involving domestic and regional tourists." In the view of Rogerson (2004), the concern over the neglect of regional tourism is also shared by the World Bank and other international development agencies.

In that regard, South Africa is unique in the developing world in paying attention to its own and the rising global level of "South-South" tourism. Regional tourists are identified separately (in contrast to the statistics of the UNWTO) and their massive contribution to the South African economy is measured and acknowledged. In 2003, they accounted for approximately 4.5 million out of a total of 6.5 million tourists (Rogerson, 2004). There is a concerted strategy to encourage regional tourism not only for economic reasons, but also as a means of driving transformation and black economic empowerment (South African Tourism, 2002). The rise of regional tourism in the South is predicated on a number of factors. The strong desire to travel among urban populations, growing national economies, rapid developments in transport and increased workers' benefits are some of the most important (Rogerson, 2004). Motivations include pilgrimages, VFR, business and leisure travel. Upper-income travellers are joined by middle-income and lower-income persons.

The discussion below considers a number of different forms of tourist movement (beyond the specific context of leisure travel), including medical tourism. It then addresses the interrelationship between tourism and migration, the challenges involved in managing the entry and stay of tourists, and the place of Working Holiday schemes in tourist management policies.

2.1 Medical Tourism

Medical tourism accounts for a growing share in regional tourist flows, but it is seldom identified as such and, if data are collected, they are not necessarily retained and therefore scarce. Australia is an exception and the data collected on various forms of short-term movements (Textbox 5.2) show that 3,982 visas for medical treatment were issued at its consular offices overseas and 911 onshore in 2001-02.

Textbox 5.2

Short-term Movements to Australia

Australia collects some of the most comprehensive data on short-term movements that involve an element of business activity or the provision/use of services. The data available can thus offer interesting insights into the scope and diversity of contemporary movements of a temporary nature. The two main visa categories, temporary residents and visitors, contain statistical groupings of temporary entrants based on types of visa. These are broken down as follows:

Temporary Residents – These include working holidaymakers, long-term temporary business entrants and other persons intending to work or temporarily reside in Australia. These types of temporary resident visas are granted on the basis of there being an economic, social, cultural or sporting benefit to Australia. Initial stay in Australia is generally for at least three months but not exceeding four years.

Visitors – Non-permanent entrants to Australia with a visa for tourism, short business stays, visiting relatives or medical treatment.

Long-term Visitors – Visitors or temporary entrants intending to stay in Australia for 12 months or more before leaving again.

Short-term Visitors – Visitors or temporary entrants intending to stay in Australia for less than 12 months before leaving again. Arrival and departure data are collected through the issuance of visas and boarding and departure card information. Table 5.2 below shows stocks of the two major categories, temporary residents and visitors, at five reporting dates in 2004-05. The stock of temporary residents varied between 138,446 and 159,544, while the stock of visitors ranged more widely from 182,420 to 347,319 (probably due to seasonal factors). New Zealand nationals are counted separately, but their stock was consistently around 440,000 to 450,000 (including students). Free movement between Australia and New Zealand means that no distinction is made between short and long-term entrants.

Note:

1 Information is collected for temporary entrants on the following: date of movement; country of citizenship; country of birth; date of birth; age; sex; length of stay; arrival visa class and subclass; current visa class and subclass; current visa status; allowed length of stay; and intended duration of stay.

Source: *Department of Immigration and Citizenship (DIAC), 2006.*

Table 5.2:

Stocks of Temporary Entrants in Australia, Various Dates, 2004 and 2005

Category of Temporary Entrant	Quarterly Report Date				
	30/06/04	30/09/04	31/12/04	31/03/05	30/06/05
Stock of temporary residents*	138,446	142,545	148,516	159,544	149.852
Stock of visitors*	185,904	189,867	347,319	244,135	182,420
N.Z. citizens**	444,954	442,372	434,544	439,082	448,774

Note:

* Figures exclude New Zealand citizens. ** N.Z. figures include students.

Source: *DIAC, 2006.*

In his study on medical tourism in Southeast Asia, Leng (2007: 3) points out that travelling overseas for healthcare

> [is] not a new phenomenon for the elites of developing countries. ... In recent times, the privilege of travelling to another country has come within the reach of the middle classes. Destination countries are not necessarily only developed countries, but also developing countries that have positioned themselves to take advantage of this new market. In addition, a fairly new phenomenon may be observed, which is that of people from developed countries travelling to developing countries to seek medical care.

Long waiting lists, high costs, lack of or inadequate insurance coverage are some of the reasons. Governments and/or hospitals with inbound medical tourists have deliberately marketed their services.

Leng (2007) explains that Malaysia, Singapore and Thailand developed this strategy in response to the 1997 Asian financial crisis. Private hospitals were struggling to survive in the face of lower numbers of private patients and the high costs of drugs, and they "turned to foreign countries to attract patients, a move that had the full support, if not the active leadership, of the government" (Leng, 2007: 10). Hospitals and hotels have since teamed up to offer packages, while some preliminary diagnostic tests are conducted and the cost of the treatment is assessed in the country of origin before the patient travels abroad. Leng points out that although statistics on medical tourism are poor in Malaysia, the revenues generated by medical tourism provide some estimates of the trend: Malaysian Ringgit (MYR) 90-150 million in 2002 and projected to reach MYR 400 million in 2005, and MYR 2.2 billion by 2010 (Wong, 2003). In future, there may be an increased focus in Malaysia on healthcare for the elderly, linked to retirement tourism.

Medical tourism also accounts for a significant share of international tourist travel, for example to China for traditional Chinese herbal treatment and acupuncture; India for various western, ayurvedic and yogic treatments; Thailand for treatment in world-class hospitals; Cuba for advanced medical care (including bone-marrow transplants and other treatments following the Chernobyl disaster) and Singapore for heart, eye and cancer treatment. Singapore's aim is to increase the number of international patients from 200,000 in 2006 to one million by 2012 (yielding about USD 1.8 billion in revenue) (Leng, 2007). The economic gains are obvious, but there will also be additional demand for nurses, nursing aides, doctors, ancillary workers and others to staff the growing number of private medical facilities. This demand could, in turn, lead to further international labour mobility. Singapore is already bringing in significant numbers of nurses and nursing assistants from the Philippines, Myanmar and Indonesia. Many of these private medical service suppliers are not only regionally but also internationally integrated. As a result, they can refer patients and transfer staff from a hospital in one country to a medical facility in another (Leng, 2007).

At the same time, home country governments may be promoting or organizing patient outflows or "medical tourists" as a means of cutting their own costs, or to alleviate pressure on their own systems when necessary health services are not immediately or locally available, or to reduce long waiting periods. The U.K. is at the forefront of this development and is sending patients overseas for treatment under the National Health Service (NHS). The Department of Health website states:

> Treatment in the EEA (European Economic Area) is one of the options open to NHS Primary Care Trusts wishing to manage their waiting lists and reduce waiting times, and offer greater patient choice where this represents good value for money and increased convenience. Since January 2002, almost 600 patients have received treatment in the EEA in France, Belgium and Germany. The majority of these referrals have been for orthopaedic and some cardiac procedures. An independent evaluation of the overseas treatment pilot scheme found patients' reactions to be very positive. Feedback has remained positive in the "live" project and patient take-up rates have exceeded expectation (U.K. Department of Health, 2007).

This form of medical tourism from the U.K. is known as the E112 referral system, which covers maternity care and referral for specific medical treatment. Treatment is provided on the terms of the particular scheme in the country concerned, and the NHS pays the provider directly. Alternatively, some patients may go directly to hospitals in the EEA or Switzerland, rather than through the NHS, and claim some of their costs from the NHS. Recent decisions handed down by the European Court of Justice and domestic courts have confirmed this right to "direct purchase" (U.K. Department of Health, 2007).

Medical tourism, as tourism generally, falls under the designation of trade in services — the WTO's General Agreement of Trade in Services (GATS) Mode 2, namely, services that are supplied and consumed abroad. GATS Mode 3, commercial presence, covers the establishment of an affiliate, subsidiary or representation for the purpose of providing a particular service in a third country. Hence, the establishment of, for example, tour companies, hotels and hospitals and the corresponding placement of staff in a foreign country is classed as trade in services, though the distinction between this and labour mobility in general is clearly not always easy. Maurer et al. (2006: 7) estimate that "commercial presence as a mode for supplying services has become more important than conventional trade across borders".

2.2 Tourism for Other Specific Purposes

The importance of tourism for the purpose of religious pilgrimages (e.g. trips to Mecca), special events (e.g. World Youth Forum in Sydney, 2008, which attracted half a million visitors from overseas), sporting events (Olympic Games, Football World Cup) and many similar occasions needs to be acknowledged. While many of the flows are short-term, they may have long-term consequences if visitors subsequently decide to migrate to live or to do business in the country concerned.

2.3 Interrelationships between Tourism and Migration

The complex mutual interrelationships of tourism and migration have been explored since the early 1990s. Many flows for leisure and business are unrelated to earlier migration movements, but others spring from, or are related to, former migration patterns. Increasing disposable incomes in many parts of the world are enabling more people to explore, experience and appreciate different cultures, histories, environments and societies. However, many such movements do not arise spontaneously and are linked to earlier migration flows. In turn, tourist movements can generate new or additional forms of migration as people decide to move to what were originally their holiday destinations (viz. Australia, the Caribbean, New Zealand, Portugal, Spain) or to other parts of their own country (e.g. Florida, U.S. and Queensland, Australia).

Various researchers have examined the manner in which migration can generate tourist flows, in particular through the geographical expansion of friendship and kinship networks. Such tourist flows are significantly shaped by the particular characteristics of migrant populations, such as composition, duration and direction, with each round of migration generating new spatial patterns of friendship and kinship networks, which potentially represent VFR tourism flows (Feng and Page, 2000). Feng and Page's survey of Chinese permanent migrants to New Zealand and the ensuing tourist flows provides an interesting example of how migration and tourism can be related. The study found that 92 per cent of outbound tourism, mostly to China, was for VFR and the remainder for business and holidays.

On the other hand, tourism may also generate other types of mobility, including labour migration flows. First, tourists often prefer guides, cooking and food from their homeland; thus, over time, tourism and the preferences of tourists contribute to labour migration from their home countries, including of entrepreneurs. Other permanent and temporary migrants may also be needed for the construction of tourist resorts, hotels and restaurants in new locations catering to the growing tourist trade, and to fill job vacancies there. Second, tourism may eventually lead to the acquisition of new or second homes by regular tourists, and their relocation there following retirement or even earlier. Many people visit a country several times as tourists before they eventually decide to move there permanently or on a long-term basis. Such patterns can be clearly identified among migrants from Taiwan Province of China and Hong Kong SAR to Australia, as well as among a number of other migrant groups. These movements are particularly pronounced to the sunbelts of Europe, North America and Australia, and other attractive destinations (Pe-Pua et al., 1996). All of this has implications concerning the necessary resources in terms of workforce and qualified staff to construct and manage facilities. Third, as observed earlier, the growing phenomenon of medical tourism has specific implications for the number of health professionals needed at the destination, and the workforce required to build and manage hospitals and other facilities. Some of these health workers may relocate from the same country as the tourists they will be caring for, as is already the case, for example, of Norwegians moving to Spain to provide care for the elderly. Finally, a holiday to visit family, combined perhaps with a business trip (see Section 3 below), may act as a catalyst for temporary or permanent migration for employment to another part of the world (see Portrait 5.1).

Portrait 5.1

Canada Calling: From Tourist to Business Visitor to Immigrant

In the early 1990s, Andrew was working for a bioscience company in Oxford, U.K., a few years after completing his PhD in biochemistry. In 1992, he and his family took a holiday to visit his brother who was studying in Canada.

Andrew combined his holiday with his participation in an international biosciences conference. At the conference he met a business contact who owned and ran a small image analysis company in southern Ontario, Canada, with whom he had been corresponding but had never personally met before.

On returning to the U.K., Andrew remained in contact with the owner of the company in Ontario and, one year later, he was offered a job and invited to come and work there. On the basis of that job offer, Andrew and his wife decided to apply for permanent residence at the Canadian Consulate in London. The holiday they had spent in Canada the previous year had convinced them that they would like to live there. Their immigration application was processed and approved within two months.

The family left for Canada in June 2003 and settled in the Niagara region, close to the shores of Lake Ontario. They obtained Canadian citizenship a few years later. Andrew is no longer with the same company. Currently, he works for a biomedical company in Ontario piloting new laser scanning technology for use in the medical field.

***Source:** IOM Geneva.*

2.4 Migration Management Issues regarding the Entry and Stay of Tourists

As travel and communication costs decline, "visa requirements and border formalities have the potential to become the most significant impediments to the growth of travel and tourism" (Muqbil, 2005: 2). However, a 1996 Asia-Pacific Economic Cooperation (APEC) Tourism Impact study emphasizes that visa requirements per se are not obstructive; rather, the problems encountered concern the availability of information concerning visa requirements, the time involved in visa issuance and the processing of visas at entry points.

The realization of the value of inbound tourism has often led to increased national and regional marketing and promotion strategies, and a relaxation of regulations and visa requirements to make travel and entry procedures relatively straightforward and not too costly. Many new visa arrangements have been introduced to facilitate speedy and multiple tourist/ business movement clearances. These include visa-free schemes, visa waiver schemes and mechanisms for speeding up the issuance of visas.

(a) Visa-free schemes

Visa-free schemes are clearly the most liberal arrangement and enable unrestricted travel between certain countries or within particular regions (e.g. European Union (EU) concerning the list of countries whose nationals do not require a visa for short-term visits for up to a maximum period of three months; the Commonwealth of Independent States (CIS); and the Economic Community of West African States (ECOWAS)). In the ASEAN, an agreement providing for visa-free travel for nationals of member countries is also expected to be in place by 2010.

(b) Visa waiver schemes

The U.S. and Canada have introduced visa waiver programmes to enable tourists and business travellers from particular countries to travel without a visa, subject to certain conditions (Greico, 2006). Visa waiver schemes rely on relationships of trust between the countries to ensure that visitors return home.

Developing countries or countries in economic transition also unilaterally lift, or substantially ease, visitor visa requirements for tourists from developed countries (i.e. without the need for reciprocity) with a view to facilitating tourism to the country and generating revenue. For example, some Commonwealth countries (e.g. Sri Lanka) do not require visas for tourists from the U.K., even though the U.K. maintains visa restrictions on their nationals.

(c) Issues of facilitation and control

The management of visitor movements requires a delicate balance between facilitation and control as, on the one hand, governments seek to streamline and speed up the issuance of visas for bona fide arrivals while, on the other, they need control mechanisms to prevent abuse.

Australia has an Electronic Travel Authority (ETA) scheme available to passport holders from 34 countries, locations and regions. Since its introduction in 1996, more than 21 million travellers have been granted ETAs to come to Australia. ETAs now account for almost 83 per cent of all Australian tourist and short-term business visas granted worldwide. The ETA system can be accessed by more than 300,000 travel agents worldwide, over 75 airlines and through the Internet. ETA arrangements offer significant benefits in terms of speed, convenience and security to travellers, as well as airlines and the Australian authorities.

More recently, the fear of terrorism has led many governments to tighten their visa requirements. For example, students have had to satisfy much more stringent language tests to ensure that they are legitimate students prior to obtaining a visa (Iredale, 2006). In the U.S. the more onerous visa requirements have deterred some travellers, while Japan fingerprints all incoming foreign nationals aged 16 and above and has introduced a new passenger information system and posted crisis management officials at major ports and airports.

A further reason why some countries continue to maintain strict visa regulations is their concern over the potential cultural, social and environmental impact of large numbers of tourists. This is particularly important in some developing countries that do not have sufficient airline capacity or hotel or tour operating facilities and therefore only cater to a limited volume of tourists as, for instance, in Laos and Bhutan. Limiting access through visa restrictions sets a ceiling on inbound movements.

(d) Problem of overstay

The overstaying of tourist visas, or using tourist visas for purposes other than legitimate tourist activities, is very common. The relative ease of obtaining tourist visas relative to other visas has led to their being used as a means of entry for ulterior motives, such as overstaying the visa entitlement or to transit to other countries, and to live and work there without being authorized to do so. Many countries, including those with tight immigration controls (e.g. Australia, Japan, New Zealand, U.S. and EU countries) face this situation, but few make public the actual numbers of tourists overstaying or irregularly present within their borders. The visa requirements for nationals of countries perceived to be at a higher risk of generating irregular migration, such as overstaying visa entitlements and transit to a third country, have been tightened. For example, within the EU, the "Schengen visa", which allows third-country nationals to enter countries included in the Schengen area[1] for up to three months within a six-month period, is required of most African country nationals as well as those from Bolivia and Ecuador (EU Council, 2001). However, in the absence of relatively accessible and enforceable regular migration channels, such additional controls are also viewed by some as ineffective to dissuade and mostly failing to curtail further irregular migration from the countries concerned and thus to reduce irregular entries. Clearly, a viable solution to and the proper management of this issue calls for closer cooperation and coordination by the parties concerned regarding the control of such movements, and of the respective employment and immigration policies in effect.

2.5 The Place of Working Holiday Schemes in Tourist Management Policies

Many countries and regions have introduced working holiday schemes over the last few decades.[2] Such programmes are usually reciprocal and enable young people to travel and work in countries parties to bilateral arrangements, subject to certain conditions. The schemes vary as to the degree to which they are explicitly aimed at filling sectoral or seasonal gaps in the labour market concerned. Although they are not usually targeted at particular sectors, experience reveals various employment patterns among young persons participating in such schemes, making it possible to target groups known to accept work in particular hard-to-fill positions. A growing tendency to attract young and highly skilled people, who could potentially become permanent or long-term immigrants, can also be observed. The following three case studies illustrate the various schemes and trends.

(a) United Kingdom

In the U.K., the Working Holidaymaker Scheme entitles young citizens of any Commonwealth country, aged 17 to 30, to work for any employer in any type of work for up to two years. According to Salt (2005), annual numbers have risen from around 23,000 in 1990 to 45,800 in 1999, to fall again to 35,775 in 2001 before rising steeply to 62,400 in 2004. The dominant source countries are the "Old Commonwealth" — Australia, Canada, New Zealand and South Africa, which together accounted for the bulk of working holidaymakers (81.5%) in 2004. However, this was a drop from 88.3 per cent of the total in 2003, suggesting that the scheme is now attracting people from a wider constituency; for example, the number of participants from Ghana, India, Malaysia and Zimbabwe has risen substantially.

Though "little is known about the characteristics of working holidaymakers (including a breakdown of figures by sex) in the U.K., it may reasonably be assumed that they are generally well educated and adaptable" (Salt, 2005: 86). It is not possible to know how many of them will be working at any one time, nor what their total contribution to the labour market is. However, given the numbers it is likely to be substantial. "There is no regional breakdown in the statistics for working holidaymakers, nor is it known what jobs they take" (Salt, 2005: 86). Nevertheless, they provide a supply of young, mobile, largely English-speaking workers who may eventually become permanent residents. According

1 The 1985 Schengen Agreement was originally an agreement among the Benelux countries, France and Germany providing for the abolition of systematic controls at their internal borders. The 1985 treaty was implemented by the 1990 Schengen Implementing Agreement and participation has since expanded to include most EU countries and three non-EU members Iceland, Norway and, in the near future, Switzerland. By way of the 1997 Treaty of Amsterdam, which amended the Treaty Establishing the European Community, most of the Schengen measures were incorporated into the body of EU law. While the Republic of Ireland and the United Kingdom are not parties to Schengen, they participate in the EU measures relating to police cooperation and the prevention of irregular migration, but not the common border control and visa provisions.

2 Australia, Belgium, Canada, Cyprus, Denmark, Estonia, Finland, France, Germany, Hong Kong SAR, Ireland, Italy, Japan, the Republic of Korea (South Korea), Malta, the Netherlands, Norway, New Zealand, Sweden, Taiwan Province of China and the United Kingdom.

to the website of Y-AXIS, a large overseas career and immigration consultancy in India, the scheme now specifically targets students, young professionals, students who have returned home after having studied in the U.K., nurses and allied health professionals, doctors interested in locum work, teachers and IT professionals.

(b) Australia

The Australian Working Holiday and Work and Holiday Programmes "provide opportunities for people aged between 18 and 30 to holiday in Australia and to supplement their travel funds through incidental employment" (DIAC, 2007). Table 5.3 shows a significant increase in the number of one-year visas issued from 2001-02 to 2005-06. There are no numerical caps or quotas.

Table 5.3:

Australian Working Holiday and Work and Holiday Visa Approvals, 2001 2006

Visa Category	2001 - 2002	2002 - 2003	2003 - 2004	2004 - 2005	2005 - 2006
Working Holiday (subclass 417)	85,207	88,758	93,759	104,352	113,936
Work and Holiday (subclass 462)[1]	n.a.	0	85	254	751
Total Visa Approvals	85,207	88,758	93,845	104,606	114,582

Note:

[1] Visa subclass 462 was introduced in March 2003 and is only available to applicants from outside Australia. However, from 1 January 2004, Subclass 462 visa holders became eligible to apply for a further Subclass 462 visa while in Australia.

n.a. = not applicable

Source: *DIAC, 2007.*

For 2005-06, agreements were concluded with 20 countries, with the largest cohorts of Working Holidaymakers (WHMs) coming from the U.K. (28,821), followed by Republic of Korea (South Korea) (24,077), Ireland (12,554) and Germany (12,089). In recent years, there has been a notable diversification of source countries and regions with the addition of Belgium, Estonia and Taiwan Province of China. A 1997 survey conducted by Harding and Webster (2002), at a time when eight WHM agreements were in effect, found that 85 per cent of WHMs were in paid employment during their visit, averaging 2.9 jobs each during that period.

Around three-quarters of WHM jobs were low-skilled, covering basic or intermediate office duties, production and transport and general manual activities, relative to 46 per cent across the whole workforce. The main occupations were as waiters, harvesting fruits, providing basic services, secretarial work, labourer and similar manual and construction work. There were some differences among countries: Canadians were more likely to be employed as waiters, and a higher proportion of Dutch nationals were employed as fruit pickers, while Irish nationals were more likely to be active at both ends of the skills ladder as construction labourers and also in more professional occupations.

A positive effect of the Working Holiday and Work and Holiday Programmes was the creation of an additional 8,000 full-time jobs in Australia for every 80,000 WHMs through the employment generation effects of WHMs (Harding and Webster, 2002). Though WHMs were active in a range of low-skilled jobs, they were not shown to displace Australians who had not been interested in taking up these positions. The under-utilization of the skills offered by WHMs was not seen as a negative for Australia, as benefits are seen to outweigh any negative effects and rural, hospitality and other labour shortages have led to recent adjustments to the programme. The Migration Regulations 1994 were amended in July 2006 to increase the length of time holders of both Subclass 417 (Working Holiday) and Subclass 462 (Work and Holiday) visas were permitted to work and study. The limitation on working for any one employer was extended from three to six months, and the study or training limitation from three to four months. These "changes were based on representations made by various stakeholders, including Australian tourism and education bodies, and provide greater flexibility for visa holders and their employers" (DIAC, 2006).

(c) New Zealand

The N.Z. Working Holiday Schemes (WHS) allow persons of 18 to 30 years of age from partner countries to spend 12 months in New Zealand and accept work of a temporary nature, and foresee reciprocal arrangements for young New Zealanders to work abroad. New Zealand has concluded WHS with 23 countries, providing for a total of 31,000 WHS visas in 2004-05, though only 21,025 work permits were actually issued. There is an annual cap for each participating country. While in general slightly more women (54%) than men were issued work permits, under some WHS the gender differential is more pronounced with considerably more women than men participating from China, Hong Kong SAR, Japan and Taiwan Province of China. For the U.K. and most other European countries, the ratio of men to women was about equal. In contrast, among WHMs from Chile, Italy and Uruguay men outnumbered women, although total numbers in these schemes were also relatively low. A high proportion of WHMs were in their early twenties, with 40 per cent aged between 22 and 25 (N.Z. Department of Labour, 2005).

A number of adjustments were introduced in mid-2005 to enhance the attractiveness of the N.Z. WHS and turn them more into an employment programme. For example, it is now possible to convert from a WHS permit to permanent residence status and, in 2004-05, 182 individuals present in the country under the WHS obtained permanent residence status (N.Z. Department of Labour, 2005). Although numbers are low, this is an indication of the use of these schemes to fill labour market gaps on a more ongoing basis.

These developments point to a general trend towards the provision of longer-term employment opportunities for WHMs. They concern a self-selected group of young, often well educated tourists who are now being "tapped" as possible workers or permanent residents. The delineation between tourism management and the management of migration for short and long-term employment and even permanent migration is becoming increasingly blurred for countries such as Australia, New Zealand and the U.K. Other countries, however, seem to be keeping WHM schemes as a form of "work and pay for your holiday" tourist scheme, as, in fact, originally intended.

3. Short-term Movements for Business and Entrepreneurial Purposes

As with tourism, short-term movements for business and entrepreneurial purposes have greatly increased in all parts of the world in recent years. The interrelationship between this type of mobility and migration is more readily apparent than that of migration and tourism, although its nature and scope escape precise definition and analysis. A number of countries, however, do attempt to regulate short-term business movements and to gauge their extent, while others adopt more of a "laissez-faire approach". The growth of business travel and its diversity, particularly in the developing world, give rise to a number of economic and social benefits in developing countries, but also pose challenges that are not that dissimilar from migration management concerns.

3.1 Issues of Definition

The first issue is to consider the various terminologies and definitions used in some countries concerning the issuance of visas to control or manage entry. While permanent or long-term migration is characterized by the use of a large variety of terms and definitions, this is even more the case for short-term movements, though the concept is not well defined, recorded or researched by policymakers or others (see also Chapters 3 and 11 and the Migration Terminology section).

Globalization has generated a large increase in the volume and type of temporary business movements as not only multinationals but also the international expansion of many small and medium-sized enterprises has led to the rapid increase in the mobility of business people. According to Tani (2006: 323):

> With better communication and transportation technologies, firms can concentrate key managerial and technical skills in a single location and deploy them to peripheral geographic areas through short-term business trips in lieu of relocations and assignments. These developments, along with skill-based technological change, have benefited the highly skilled. International business travellers are almost entirely composed of entrepreneurs, professionals, senior government officials and managers and enjoy a wage premium over similarly skilled but not travelling workers.

International movements within transnational corporations (TNCs) are significant, but not always easy to identify as they concern a select group moving within specific channels and not subject to the same constraints as other business travellers. Nor is it possible to gauge the extent to which their physical moves may be and are being replaced by virtual travel, teleconferencing and other modern means of communication.

This group does not include the "suitcase traders" or small, self-employed entrepreneurs, who repeatedly move between different parts of the world. Though their numbers and individual trajectories are difficult to quantify on account of their erratic, circular and self-determined movements, they represent a growing group of merchants who move to trade or to set up small businesses as and where opportunities arise.

The international mobility of service providers gives rise to another potentially large group of short-term business travellers, as defined under the WTO's GATS Mode 4 (see Textbox Int. 1). There is some overlap and confusion as to how to differentiate between labour movements and GATS Mode 4 movements for services, but business persons and intra-company transferees could potentially refer to GATS Mode 4 to provide services on a short-term basis in another country. They would, however, be subject to various conditions, such as quotas and restrictions, educational qualification requirements and economic needs tests, stipulated by countries of destination in their GATS Schedule of commitments. At the moment, there is no specific GATS Mode 4 visa and people are admitted under the existing visa regulations of destination countries.

As each country treats business and entrepreneurial movement differently, a number of case studies are discussed below to illustrate the definitions, visas and provisions adopted for short-term business entries. Various regional groupings have also developed ways of facilitating business mobility, one of which is referred to below.

3.2 Management of Short-term Business Visits

Countries are increasingly developing various types of short-term business visas to facilitate the entry of business people. However, there is significant diversity and attempts at harmonization have been slow and difficult.

(a) Asia-Pacific Economic Cooperation (APEC)[3]

The APEC Business Travel Card (BTC) was introduced to lower trade transaction costs. This is a national visa waiver or three-year multiple entry visa valid for all participating economies for persons who satisfy the requisite visa conditions. Other provisions may eventually be attached to the APEC Business Travel Card, namely, an agreed 30-day service standard for intra-company transferees (executives, managers and specialists, the latter as defined by each economy), and an agreement to consider the streamlining of access to employment for spouses of intra-company transferees.

The aim is to move towards common agreed standards for the short and long-term entry of business people; to date, however, most countries, including a number of APEC participating economies, impose additional visa requirements on business people wishing to visit. Some of these are outlined below.

(b) Australia

Australia defines short-term business visits as covering (a) attendance at a conference or training session; (b) the conduct of business with an Australia-based company; (c) the conduct of business negotiations, or (d) an exploratory business visit. A choice of five business visitor visa options is available:

1. Short Stay Business Visitor (subclass 456): 3 months — for business people to make a short business visit to attend a conference, conduct negotiations or make an exploratory business visit.
2. Sponsored Business Visitor (subclass 459): 3 months — for business people who have an approved sponsor in Australia and may not be eligible to apply for an Electronic Travel Authority (ETA).
3. ETA (Short Validity) (subclass 977): 3 months — an electronically stored authority available to passport holders from a number of countries and regions. Applications must be made from outside Australia.
4. ETA (Long Validity) (subclass 956): 3 months, repeat visits — for business people to make regular short business visits, granted for the length of the validity of the passport.
5. APEC Business Travel Card (see above): 2 months, repeat trips — to streamline travel for business people from 16 participating economies in the APEC region. Nationals of all APEC members, besides New Zealand, must still apply for a subclass 456 or 977 visa (DIAC, 2007).

Table 5.4 shows the number of visas issued in four of these categories from 2001 to 2006. The short stay (subclass 456 and 977) visas are by far the most numerous. The persons in the sponsored 459 subclass are most probably intra-company transfers.

[3] Australia, Brunei Darussalam, Canada, Chile, China, Hong Kong SAR, Indonesia, Japan, Republic of Korea, Malaysia, Mexico, New Zealand, Papua New Guinea, Peru, the Philippines, Russia, Singapore, Taiwan Province of China, Thailand, United States, Viet Nam. For a description of APEC and its labour mobility-related activities, including a fuller discussion of the Business Travel Card, see Textbox 13.5.

Table 5.4:

Business Visitor Visas Granted Outside of Australia, 1 July 2001 to 30 June 2006

Visa Category	2001-02	2002-03	2003-04	2004-05	2005-06
Business Visitor Visas					
Short Stay Business Visitor (Subclass 456)	133,726	126,767	147,701	174,617	185,656
Sponsored Business Visitor (Subclass 459)	18	11	4	107	634
Electronic Travel Authority - Business Entrant - Long Validity (Subclass 956)	33,420	28,057	24,721	18,417	15,410
Electronic Travel Authority - Business Entrant - Short Validity (Subclass 977)	90,874	99,356	126,413	146,283	166,633
Total Business Visitor Visa Approvals	258,038	254,191	298,839	339,424	368,333

Source: *DIAC, 2007.*

It is interesting to note that a number of temporary entrants and visa categories, including the Class 457 Temporary Business (Long Stay) visa and the Working Holiday and Work and Holiday programmes, are linked to business migration. Class 457 entrants are actually sponsored employees. Their visas are valid for a stay of up to four years whereupon they may be converted to permanent resident status.

According to Khoo et al. (2005), the majority of 457 visa holders had applied for long-term temporary residence in Australia after a previous stay there under the Working Holiday and Work and Holiday programmes or as students. This was particularly true of Europeans, and their prior exposure to the country is considered to have facilitated their integration and adaptation to local living and working conditions. Conversely, 457 visa holders from India are least likely to have visited the country prior to their present stay.

Drawing on the findings of Coleman and Rowthorn (2004), Khoo et al. (2005) suggest that temporary skilled migration is the source of many economic benefits to Australia because it brings in young, well qualified and highly skilled people. Given that 457 visa holders are more likely to come from higher-income countries in North America and Europe, they note that the current temporary skilled migration policies link the Australian economy to other advanced economies.

(c) Canada

Canada receives a very large number of short-term visitors every year, with around 20 million annual crossings of the Canada/U.S. border alone. There is no statistical breakdown of the particular motives for a visitor's stay in Canada. A large majority of the many millions of business visitors entering Canada every year would not need visas as they are from visa-exempt countries, particularly the U.S. and Europe.

Around one million visas are issued annually to visitors who do require them and, although a global breakdown is not available, Table 5.5 demonstrates that regarding the Beijing issuing office, the business caseload accounts for a substantial proportion of the total number of visas issued to visitors.

Table 5.5:

Canada – Business Visitor Visas issued in Beijing

Business Visitor Applications	2005	2006	2007 (to 27 Nov.)
Total Number	36,835	43,701	37,721
% of all visitor visas issued in Beijing	60%	60.5%	54.9%
Official passport	25,281 (68.6%)	30,019 (68.7%)	24,316 (64.5%)
Private passport	11,554 (31.4%)	13,682 (31.3%)	13,405 (35.5%)

Source: *Canadian Permanent Mission, Geneva.*

In contrast to Australia and New Zealand (see below), however, Canada does not participate in the APEC BTC scheme (Citizenship and Immigration Canada, 2006).

(d) Japan and Republic of Korea

Both Japan and South Korea require short-term business visas for visits of up to three months for most business entrants. However, Japan and South Korea also waive visa requirements for nationals of certain APEC economies (APEC, 2007). South Korea offers multiple-entry visas for nationals from Australia, Canada, China, Japan and the U.S., in accordance with relevant bilateral agreements.

(e) New Zealand

The possibilities for short-term business visits to New Zealand are limited. The Long-term Business Visa (permit) requires the prior submission of a business plan. After nine months, the permit is subject to review and, if the business is deemed to be developing satisfactorily, it is extended for a further period of three years, following which a permanent residence permit may be applied for. N.Z. participates in the APEC BTC scheme and certain APEC economies benefit from the visa-waiver arrangements (N.Z. Department of Labour, 2005).

(f) United Kingdom

The U.K. has a new business visa for entries of up to six months. It makes a distinction between a business visitor and an employee, and the conditions for admission are clearly stated, as are the eligible occupations (advisers, consultants, trainers and trouble-shooters), the nature of the direct or contractual working relationship with the sending company and the type of work (including training) that can be undertaken (workpermit.com, 2007). The visa conditions provide for considerable flexibility concerning the corporate activities to be undertaken.

The same flexibility is foreseen under the generally long-term visas issued for the purpose of business creation, such as, for instance, the Sole Representative Visas for Employers, valid for two years for the establishment of a branch office of an overseas business in the U.K., or the U.K. Innovator Visa, also valid for two years for persons intending to realize a highly innovative business idea in the U.K. (workpermit.com, 2007).

(g) United States

The U.S. Office of Immigration Statistics (OIS) produces an *Annual Flow Report* that includes data on temporary flows. It examines the temporary non-immigrant admissions to the U.S., mainly tourists and business travellers on short-term trips. The bulk of the 175.1 million non-immigrant admissions in 2006 were from Canada and Mexico,[4] and the remaining 33.7 million from all other countries (using I-94 Forms). Canadians and Mexicans who hold a non-resident Border Crossing Card, commonly known as a laser visa or a multiple-entry non-immigrant visa, are not required to complete an I-94 Form (U.S. Office of Immigration Statistics, 2007).

Of the 33.7 million I-94 admissions, 73.9 per cent were for tourist purposes and 15 per cent for business travel, granted to 25.8 million individuals of whom 4.4 million were entitled to multiple entries (U.S. Office of Immigration Statistics, 2007: Table 2). The U.S. data provide a good breakdown, as shown in Table 5.6. Temporary business visitors can be separated from intra-company transferees and their families and from exchange visitors and their families.

Almost half (45.8%) of non-immigrant (I-94) admissions concerned nationals from Mexico, U.K. and Japan, followed by Germany, France, Republic of Korea, India, Italy, Australia, Brazil and the Netherlands. Men accounted for 52.9 per cent of all I-94 admissions, and 56.3 per cent were aged 15 to 44 (U.S. Office of Immigration Statistics, 2007: Tables 5 and 6).

The U.S. also has a visa category for "treaty traders and treaty investors". These E1, E2 or E3 visas are intended for nationals of countries with which the U.S. has concluded treaties of commerce and navigation, who wish to come to the United States to carry on substantial trade, including trade in services, or to develop and direct the operations of an enterprise in which they have invested or are in the process of investing, and who are not required to fill out an I-94 Form (U.S. Department of State, 2007).

Although the U.S. does not participate in the APEC BTC, nationals of Australia, Brunei Darussalam, Japan, New Zealand and Singapore are granted a visa waiver for up to 90 days.

[4] No estimate is provided for 2006, but in 2005 it was estimated that 148 million non-immigrant admissions out of a total of 175 million were from Canada and Mexico (Grieco, 2006).

Table 5.6:

U.S. Non-immigrant Admissions (I-94 only) by Class of Admission (excluding laser visa holders): 2004-2006 (in millions)

Class of Admission	2006		2005		2004	
	No.	%	No.	%	No.	%
Temporary visitors	**29.93**	**88.9**	**28.51**	**89.1**	**27.40**	**89.0**
For pleasure	24.89	73.9	23.81	74.4	22.80	74.1
For business	5.04	15.0	4.70	14.7	4.60	14.9
Temporary workers and families	**1.71**	**5.1**	**1.57**	**4.9**	**1.51**	**4.9**
Intra-company transferees and families	0.46	1.4	0.46	1.4	0.46	1.5
Intra-company transferees	0.32	1.0	0.31	1.0	0.31	1.0
Students, exchange visitors, and families	**1.17**	**3.5**	**1.05**	**3.3**	**1.02**	**3.3**
Exchange visitors[1] and families	0.42	1.2	0.38	1.2	0.36	1.1
Exchange visitors	0.38	1.1	0.34	1.1	0.32	1.0
Transit aliens[2]	**0.38**	**1.1**	**0.36**	**1.1**	**0.34**	**1.1**
All other classes[3]	**0.37**	**1.1**	**0.37**	**1.2**	**0.39**	**1.3**
Unknown	**0.11**	**0.3**	**0.14**	**0.4**	**0.13**	**0.4**
Total	**33.67**	**100**	**32.00**	**100**	**30.78**	**100**

Notes:

1 Exchange visitors are young people who take part in educational or cultural exchange programmes.

2 Transit aliens include C-1, C-2 and C-3 visas.

3 Other classes of admission include: A-1 to A-3, BE, G-1 to G-5, K-1 to K-4, N-1 to N-9, Q2 and Q-3, T-1 to T-5, U-1 to U-4, and V-1 to V-3.

Figures in the "Total" row have been rounded up.

Source: *Compiled from U.S. Office of Immigration Statistics (2007: Table 3).*

3.3 Intra-company Transfers

Of all business travels, intra-company transfers are among the most difficult to document. Table 5.7 lists intra-company transferees in seven OECD countries between 1996 and 2002, with the U.S. registering by far the greatest mobility of this type, followed by the U.K. and the Netherlands. Although no easily accessible data on such short-term business movements are available for Australia, a recent survey conducted by Khoo et al. (2005) showed that 30 per cent of 457 visa arrivals to Australia were intra-company transferees.

Table 5.7:

Intra-corporate Transferees in Selected OECD Countries, 1996-2002 (thousands)

	1996	1997	1998	1999	2000	2001	2002	1999 Relative frequency (US=100)[1]
Austria[2]			0.2	1.0	1.2	1.9	1.9	40
Canada[3]		2.1	2.8	2.5	3.0	3.2	2.8	26
France[4]	0.8	1.0	1.1	1.8	2.2	2.3	1.8	12
Japan	2.8	3.4	3.5	3.8	3.9	3.5	2.9	9
Netherlands[4]	1.6	2.3	2.7	2.5	--	--	--	50
U.K.[5]	13.0	18.0	22.0	15.0	16.0	17.0	19.0	84
U.S.[6]	69.7	80.1	82.5	88.0	112.0	--	--	100

Notes:

1 Transferees as a proportion of total employment relative to the same statistics for the United States, times one hundred.

2 Stock of non-EU intra-company transferees who hold a residence permit on 1 July of the given year.

3 Temporary business persons with employment authorization entering Canada under NAFTA, Canada-Chile Free Trade Agreement (CCFTA) or GATS.

4 Figures do not include transfers from other EU countries.

5 Results are derived from the Labour Force Survey and include intra-European transfers.

6 Issuance of L1 visas.

Sources: **Austria**: *Federal Ministry of the Interior;* **Canada**: *Citizenship and Immigration Canada;* **France**: *Office des migrations internationals;* **Japan**: *Ministry of Justice, Immigration Service;* **Netherlands**: *Employment Office;* **U.K.**: *Labour Force Survey;* **United States**: *U.S. Department of State, Bureau of Consular Affairs.*

3.4 Business Travel in the Developing World

(a) Developed to developing countries

Globalization and deregulation have opened up many developing countries where conditions are seen to be economically, socially and politically conducive to significant inflows of short-term business travellers or visiting nationals from more developed countries. In the 1960s and 1970s, the Asian "Tigers" were probably the best example of emerging economies that attracted much investment and technical input from more developed countries.

In recent years, temporary business visits from countries in Asia, Europe, North America and Oceania to many of the world's global cities and other major sites have become very prevalent. The expansion of multinationals and the establishment of offshore branches or client offices in mining, manufacturing and the services sector have given rise to countless and repeat visits by managers, technicians, engineers and supervisors.

Similarly, most non-resident Indians (NRIs) who have set up businesses in the IT sector in India (see Textbox 2.2) return home to attend to their business interests but do not go back permanently.

(b) Developing to developing countries

Disparities in economic development between neighbouring countries frequently give rise to short-term and often irregular movements for the purpose of trade.[5] For example, in 2003, over 300,000 individuals crossed the border from Mongolia into China, mostly for trading purposes. People come from Russia and eastern European countries, as well as from Mongolia, to buy cheap goods and to sell them elsewhere. The building of a free-trade zone and a new Trading Hall in Erlianhaut in Inner Mongolia led to an increase in cross-border activities (Zheng and Ren, 2004).

The dismantling of the apartheid regime in South Africa led to a more liberal migration regime and, since the early 1990s, many people from other parts of Africa have been able to enter on a 30-day visitor's permit issued at the border. The declining contract labour migration to the mines has led to the growth of informal migration for work or to conduct business (Andersson, 2006). Economic growth has also acted as a magnet for petty traders from other parts of sub-Saharan Africa.

For years, cross-border shoppers from Southern Africa have flocked to Johannesburg, South Africa's financial centre, to buy cheap goods that can be taken home and sold at a profit. Officials have quickly become aware of the profitability of such trading practices, after a study showed that the influx of African "tourism traders" added R 20 billion annually to the local economy. The shoppers' spending bonanza includes cash-register sales and expenditure on overnight accommodation, meals and transportation. In 2004 – the latest year for which data are available – the major points of attraction for more than half a million African visitors were South Africa's array of shops, mainly wholesalers. "These are typically low to middle-income people who come because there is a wide variety of goods and good quality. And these stores may just be popping up in their own country", says urban consultant Neil Fraser of the newly formed Joburg Cross-Border Shopping Association. Most visitors are from Lesotho, Swaziland, Botswana, Zimbabwe, Mozambique, Namibia, Zambia and Malawi, where many people live on less than a dollar a day (Star and Reuters, 2006).

(c) Developing to developed countries

Many irregular migration flows from China and other parts of Asia (India, Pakistan, the Philippines), Latin

[5] Cross-border migration is discussed in more detail in Chapter 7.

America and Africa (Morocco, Senegal), as well as from eastern Europe (especially Albania and Romania) to the more developed countries in Europe have been associated with the establishment and operation of small businesses. In recent years, southern Europe has attracted many new irregular migrants (see also Chapter 8), including Chinese nationals, to take up job opportunities in the informal sector.

> [An] important reason is that these new destinations provide fresh business niches for the Chinese. Communities of Chinese in western Europe have usually been concentrated in the catering business. The catering business has become increasingly saturated since the 1990s, however, and there is not much evidence that the communities are entering new industries. By contrast, the Chinese in eastern and southern Europe are often engaged in the import/export trade between China and Europe, and even manufacturing (e.g. the leather and garment industries in Italy), partly encouraged by the economic structures particular to these countries (Laczko, 2003).

New types of flows have often emerged in response to tighter regulatory systems in developed countries. Peraldi (2004) documents the rise of Algerian suitcase traders throughout the Mediterranean region, replacing traditional labour migration to France. "Often serving tourist markets, their moves take place within family networks which allow them to seize trading opportunities in whichever city they are present" (Salt, 2006: 18). Such business movements are generally unrecorded or included in tourist figures.

3.5 Economic and Social Benefits of Short-term Business Movements, Especially in the Developing World

The circulation of people as part of international business activities, aid programmes and projects and for other reasons is significant, but difficult to quantify. However, both countries of origin and of destination stand to gain from short-term business migrants. Host countries can sell more goods and provide accommodation and other services for business clients, and are themselves introduced to new products, technologies and business and management practices. It is with these benefits in mind that the city of Johannesburg is seeking to develop a visitor-friendly approach, for instance by setting up a welcome booth for cross-border traders, and building a new passenger boarding area. The private sector is considering to contribute to the effort through the construction of basic lodgings with cheap overnight rates.

At an early stage of its industrial development, Taiwan Province of China realized the value of the contribution its citizens abroad, particularly in the U.S., could make to its economy and society. Beginning in the 1950s, it implemented a series of policies and programmes to encourage the return of highly educated expatriates. Such return was to be preferably permanent, but short-term exchange and business trips were also promoted. The major incentives included a travel subsidy for returnees and their family, helping them to find jobs, providing business investment assistance, facilitating visits of academics and experts, setting up recruitment programmes by offering competitive salaries and improving working conditions (Tsay and Lin, 2000).

The contribution of short trips to economic growth is evident, but the means to measure such contributions are mostly lacking. One exception is research by Tani (2006), who surveyed business travellers at Sydney Airport and found that most Australian business persons going abroad were male, aged 35 to 54, highly skilled, had a university degree (83%) and were born abroad (64%). His survey reported that 38 per cent of these business travellers go to attend a conference or trade fair or to look for international alliances (37%), that is, to seek out information or to share knowledge. Only 31 per cent travelled for reasons related to production and administration. Incoming business travellers were more likely to be intra-company movers (44%) followed by 32 per cent attending conferences. He argues that the data for true business arrivals, as defined earlier in this chapter for Australia, should not be analysed in terms of net flows but as gross flows. The combination of inflows and outflows, or gross flows, is a better measure of the importance of such mobility per se in the "formation and diffusion of knowledge". He makes a distinction between "embodied" and "disembodied" knowledge, and argues that business movements generate "disembodied" knowledge. The more trips, the more knowledge is generated that benefits both the source and destination countries. Thus, from this point of view, it pays for countries to encourage, rather than discourage, such flows.

3.6 The Challenges Posed by these Different Types of Movements

The rapid growth of large trading and business locations and the difficulties in providing them with adequate housing, health, education and other facilities can be a major issue. For example, a study on the spread of HIV/AIDS in Northeast Asia found that the growth of major trading posts/towns on the borders between China and the neighbouring countries of Mongolia, Russia and North Korea, posed major infrastructure problems. At the same time, the emergence of an underground sex industry added another, very volatile factor. Together they have the potential to create a major health issue (Iredale et al., 2004).

Zheng and Ren (2004) emphasize that, in order to stop the spread of HIV/AIDS in the general population, relevant services or projects should not only focus on the high-risk populations, but also the "bridge populations", i.e. those who may have sexual contact with the high-risk population. Urgent programmes and research are needed to focus on two broad areas:

1. Groups vulnerable to HIV infection and their "bridge populations", such as overseas contract workers and their partners, commercial sex workers and their clients, transport workers/traders and their partners/families.
2. "Hot spots" where there is a volatile mix of highly mobile people (traders, visitors) or temporary workers (industrial workers, miners, sailors, etc.) and commercial sex workers.

On the other hand, the tendency for short-term business migrants to seek to become permanent residents is met with different responses. It is encouraged in some developed countries, viz. Australia, New Zealand and the U.K., while others have provisions that enable some "desirable" short-stay business migrants to apply for permanent residence status. The situation is less clearcut when small traders, who have entered a country irregularly or as tourists perhaps, decide to stay permanently. They frequently meet with a different response. Their situation is often regarded as being identical to that of many other irregular migrant workers who stay on after their working visas have expired and who are subject to mandatory return provisions.

4. Conclusion

This chapter has sought to make the recent massive growth in tourism and short-term business travel evident. The scale of these movements is much larger than for any other form of mobility, but they are not usually covered in migration reports. They have been included in this report because, although their links with labour migration are not immediately evident, such movements are nonetheless of major importance. The movement of tourists can have ramifications for labour mobility and affect the employment opportunities and practices of destination countries.

The chapter has shown how such flows can give rise to labour mobility to service tourist needs, how they may metamorphose into labour movements or so resemble labour movements (viz. Working Holiday Schemes) that it is difficult to separate them. Short-term travel for the purpose of business is often not differentiated from tourism in some national statistics, while in others (e.g. Australia) there is an array of visas covering various types of business visits. Many small business people are engaging in trade and other activities a long way from home, while other business people are moving as part of intra-company transfers or related arrangements.

Countries are endeavouring to find the best ways to handle these mushrooming flows that, on balance, are perceived to be beneficial to their economies and societies. Short-term business travel is productive for source and destination countries, as well as for the individuals themselves, and therefore warrants good management rather than limitation. However, issues of overstay, irregular entry and engagement in activities not covered by the visa entitlement must be addressed.

Innovative ways of encouraging skilled migrants (such as through the use of dual citizenship or special travel cards), in particular, to invest in or manage businesses at home are being found and such information needs to be disseminated so that developing and not only developed countries, can benefit from their skilled diasporas. Mahroum et al. (2007) stress the important role for governments in source countries in connecting with their diasporas, establishing networks, recognizing the potential contribution diasporas can make and creating opportunities that would allow them to contribute to local development through short-term visits to their home countries (see also Chapter 12).

REFERENCES

Andersson, J.A.

2006 "Informal Moves, Informal Markets: International Migrants and Traders from Mzimba District, Malawi", *African Affairs*, 105(420): 375-397.

American Association for the Advancement of Science (AAAS) Atlas

2000 "Migration and Tourism", AAAS Atlas, www.ourplanet.com/aaas/pages/population05.html.

Asia-Pacific Economic Cooperation (APEC)

2007 "Short-Term Business Visits to APEC Economies", www.businessmobility.org/travel/Short%20Business%20Stay%20Visa.pdf.

Australia, Department of Immigration and Citizenship (DIAC)

2006/07 Statistical Information, DIAC, www.immi.gov.au/media/statistics/statistical-info. www.immigration.gov.au/media/publications.

Canada, Citizenship and Immigration (CIC)

2006 *Annual Report to Parliament on Immigration 2006*, Minister of Public Works and Government Services Canada, Ottawa, http://www.cic.gc.ca/ENGLISH/pdf/pub/immigration2006_e.pdf.

Council of the European Union

2001 Regulation (EC) No. 539/2001 of 15 March 2001 listing the third countries whose nationals must be in possession of visas when crossing the external borders and those whose nationals are exempt from that requirement, OJ 2001 L 81/1 (as amended by Regulations (EC) 453/2003 of 6 March 2003 and 1932/2006 (EC) of 21 December 2006).

Feng, K. and S. Page

2000 "An Exploratory Study of the Tourism, Migration-Immigration Nexus: Travel Experiences of Chinese Residents in New Zealand", *Current Issues in Tourism*, 3(3): 246-281.

Ghimire, K.B.

2001 "The Growth of National and Regional Tourism in Developing Countries: An Overview" in K.B. Ghimire, (Ed.), *The Native Tourist: Mass Tourism Within Developing Countries*, Earthscan, London, 1-29.

Greico, E.M.

2006 "Temporary Admission of Nonimmigrants to the United States: 2005", *Annual Flow Report*, July, Office of Immigration Statistics, U.S. Department of Homeland Security, Washington, D.C., http://www.dhs.gov/xlibrary/assets/statistics/publications/2005_NI_rpt.pdf.

Harding, G. and E. Webster

2002 *The Working Holiday Maker Scheme and the Australian Labour Market*, September, Melbourne Institute of Applied Economic and Social Research, University of Melbourne, http://www.immi.gov.au/media/publications/research/whm/index.htm.

Iredale, R.

2006 Personal communication from overseas students, Sydney.

Iredale, R., T. Siddiqui, Z. Zheng, Q. Ren, S. Ghosh, H.K. Sung, J. Lee and J. Weeramunda

2004 *No Safety Signs Here*, United Nations Development Programme (UNDP), Delhi.

Japan, Ministry of Foreign Affairs

2007 "MULTIPLE Entry Visa for temporary visitors", The Ministry of Foreign Affairs of Japan, www.mofa.go.jp/j_info/visit/visa/05-c.html.

Khoo, S.-E., P. McDonald and G. Hugo

2005 *Temporary Skilled Migrants in Australia: Employment Circumstances and Migration Outcomes*, DIAC, Canberra, www.immi.gov.au/media/publications/pdf/457s_survey_report.pdf.

Laczko, F.

2003 "Europe Attracts More Migrants from China", *Migration Information Source*, July, Migration Policy Institute (MPI), Washington, D.C. www.migrationinformation.org/Feature/display.cfm?id=144.

Lemaître, G., T. Liebig and C. Thoreau

2006 "Harmonised statistics on immigrant inflows – preliminary results, sources and methods", Organisation for Economic Co-operation and Development (OECD), Paris.

Leng, C.H.

2007 "Medical Tourism in Malaysia: International Movement of Healthcare Consumers and the Commodification of Healthcare", Asia Research Institute, Working Paper Series, No. 83, National University of Singapore.

Mahroum, S., C. Eldridge and A.S. Daar
2007 "Transnational Diaspora Options: How Developing Countries Could Benefit from their Emigrant Populations", *International Journal on Multicultural Societies*, 8(1): 25-42, http://unesdoc.unesco.org/images/0014/001490/149086E.pdf#page=27.

Maurer, A., J. Magdeleine and B. d'Andrea
2006 "International Trade in Services – GATS, statistical concepts and future challenges", paper presented at the International Association for Official Statistics (IAOS) Conference on People on the Move: Measuring Environmental, Social and Economic Impacts Within and Between Nations, 6-8 September, Ottawa, http://www.iaos2006conf.ca/pdf/Andreas%20Mauer.pdf.

Muqbil, I.
2005 "B. Facilitation of Travel", United Nations Economic and Social Commission for Asia and the Pacific (UN ESCAP), http://www.unescap.org/ttdw/publications/tpts_pubs/pub_1748/pub_1748_tp-b.pdf.

New Zealand, Department of Labour
2005 *Migration Trends 2004/2005*, Department of Labour, December, Wellington, http://www.immigration.govt.nz/NR/rdonlyres/E05EABDB-9F88-4B68-9104-20D6D86C07EC/0/MigrationTrends200405.pdf.

Pe-Pua, R., C. Mitchell, R. Iredale and S. Castles
1996 *Astronaut Families and Parachute Children: The Cycle of Migration between Hong Kong and Australia*, Australian Government Publishing Service (AGPS), Canberra.

Rogerson, C.M.
2004 "The Rise of African Tourism to South Africa", Migration Policy Brief No. 13, Southern African Migration Project (SAMP), http://www.queensu.ca/samp/sampresources/samppublications.

Salt, J.
2005 *Report of the United Kingdom SOPEMI Correspondent to the OECD, 2005*, Migration Research Unit (MRU), University College London.

2006 *Current Trends in International Migration in Europe*, Consultant's Report to the Council of Europe, European Committee on Migration (CDMG), 15 March, Doc. CDMG (2006) 22e, Strasbourg, http://www.coe.int/t/dg3/migration/Documentation/Migration%20management/2005_Salt_report_en.pdf.

Saxenian, A.
2001 "Silicon Valley's New Immigrant Entrepreneurs" in W.A. Cornelius, T.J. Espenshade and I. Salehyan, (Eds.), *The International Migration of the Highly Skilled*, Center for Comparative Immigration Studies, University of California, San Diego, 197-234.

South African Tourism
2002 *Tourism Growth Strategy*, South African Tourism, Johannesburg.

Star and Reuters
2006 "SA shopping malls luring Africa's traders", 10 October, Star and Reuters, *SAMP Migration News*, http://www.queensu.ca/samp/migrationnews/article.php?Mig_News_ID=3992&Mig_News_Issue=22&Mig_News_Cat=8.

Tani, M.
2006 "International Business Visits", *Agenda*, 13(4): 323-337, http://epress.anu.edu.au/agenda/013/04/13-4-A-3.pdf.

Tsay, C. and J. Lin
2000 "Return Migration and Reversal of Brain Drain in Taiwan: an analysis of the 1990 Census", unpublished paper, The Institute of Economics, Academia Sinica, Taipei.

United Kingdom, Department of Health
2007 "Access to healthcare abroad", National Health Service (NHS), www.nhs.un/healthcareabroad/pages/healthcareabroad.aspx.

United Nations World Tourism Organization (UNWTO)
2006 *Tourism Highlights 2006 Edition*, UNWTO.

United States, Department of State
2007 "Treaty Traders and Treaty Investors", Bureau of Consular Affairs, U.S. Department of State, http://travel.state.gov/visa/temp/types/types_1273.html.

United States, Department of Homeland Security, Office of Immigration Statistics

2007 "Temporary Admissions of Nonimmigrants to the United States: 2006", *Annual Flow Report*, July, Office of Immigration Statistics, U.S. Department of Homeland Security, Washington, D.C., http://www.dhs.gov/xlibrary/assets/statistics/publications/NI_FR_2006_508_final.pdf.

Wong, C.

2003 "Health tourism, to drive earnings", Malaysian Institute of Economic Research paper, published in *The New Straits Times*, 19 April.

Workpermit.com

2007 "Business Visas", workpermit.com, http://www.workpermit.com/uk/business.htm.

Y-Axis

2007 "The United Kingdom Working Holiday Makers Scheme, Who is this visa for?", Y-AXIS, http://www.y-axis.com/emigrate/whmswho.shtml.

Zheng, Z. and Q. Ren

2004 "People's Republic of China" in R.R. Iredale, T. Siddiqui, Z. Zheng, Q. Ren, S. Ghosh, H.K. Sung, J. Lee and J. Weeramunda, *No Safety Signs Here*, United Nations Development Programme (UNDP), Delhi, 43-68.

Textbox 5.1 - Economic and Social Benefits and Costs of Tourist-related Migration for the Countries Concerned

Asian Development Bank (ADB)

2005 The Greater Mekong Subregion Tourism Sector Strategy, ADB, Manila, http://www.adb.org/GMS/tourism-study.asp.

International TravelDailyNews.com

2006 "Several ongoing challenges face GMS tourism ten years after they joined forces", International TravelDailyNews.com, 26 January, http://www.traveldailynews.com/pages/show_page/12155.

FAMILY MIGRATION*

CHAPTER 6

1. Introduction

> Immigrants migrate for various reasons. For some, the motivation is primarily economic, with the prospect of better wages or working conditions or more simply, of employment. Some come with their families with the aim of permanent settlement, others bring them in when they are themselves settled and are able to satisfy host country requirements for family reunion. ... Other reasons may include movement for marriage, adoption, retirement, or by aged parents of adult children (OECD, 2006: 34).

Family-related migration has been the main channel of legal entry into the European Union (EU) as well as to traditional immigration countries, such as Australia, Canada and the United States. It accounts for two-thirds of immigration into the U.S. and between one-third and a quarter in Canada and Australia (OECD, 2006). Even in countries where worker entries are now more common than in the past, for example in Portugal, Denmark, Switzerland and the United Kingdom (Martin, 2007), family migration remains significant. In contrast, family migration remains less significant in countries that hinder or prevent long-term settlement, as in the Middle East and Southeast and East Asia. In these regions family reunification is, as a general rule, unavailable, although cross-border marriages between citizens and foreigners have become more common, especially in Southeast Asia (Constable, 2005). Contract workers have married nationals, as is the case in Taiwan Province of China (but this is not permitted in Singapore nor in Malaysia); brides are sponsored in Japan; and male tourists marry Thai women (Piper, 2004).

Family migrations remain under-theorized (Bailey and Boyle, 2004) and have been relatively neglected by academics and policymakers. In part, this has been due to their conceptualization as a feminized and dependent form of movement with little relevance for labour force participation. Family migration is not only the largest single category in developed countries; it is also generally dominated by females, the extent of which depends on the type of family migration. The majority of women migrating to Australia, New Zealand, Europe and North America do so for family reunification, followed by labour and

* This chapter was written by Eleonore Kofman (Social Policy Research Centre, Middlesex University, United Kingdom) and Veena Meetoo (Institute of Education, United Kingdom).

asylum (UNFPA, 2006). In the United States, female family migration constituted 58.5 per cent of the total intake in 2000 and in Canada 61.6 per cent (UNRISD, 2005). It is necessary, however, to move beyond the narrow economic approaches adopted in previous work on family migration (Bailey and Boyle, 2004) and to examine the changing forms and (re)composition of the family, the diverse strategies deployed in the course of migration, the gendered composition of family migration, the position of specific members of the family, such as children and the elderly, and the implications of policy measures for men and women (Kofman, 2004). Furthermore, as women migrating as heads of household now make up almost half of global flows, they are themselves becoming major initiators of family reunification.

This chapter first considers the reasons why family migration has traditionally been marginal to studies of international migration and recent developments that have generated interest in the role of families in migration. Second, it outlines the trends and types of family migration and difficulties of comparing situations in different countries. Third, it examines international conventions concerning the right to family life and policy developments within the context of managed migration. This includes recent restrictions on entry, especially the control of marriage, and integration measures required for long-term settlement as well as debates on the relationship between family migration, skills and employment. The chapter focuses on policies in destination countries and the impact of family migration on host societies, although it is important to underline that mobility for the purpose of employment also has important economic and social consequences on societies of countries of origin as well as on those family members left behind (see Textbox 6.1).

Textbox 6.1

Social and Economic Costs of Migration on Family Members Left Behind - Bangladesh

International migration has profound impacts on family members left behind. The nature and importance of such impacts will depend on whether the migrant is a female or a male member of the household. In particular, the gender dynamics within households will be affected differently depending on whether it is women who migrate or are left behind. The different impacts are explored below and illustrated by drawing on the example of Bangladesh. In this particular instance it is important to note that typical rural Bangladeshi households often require the wife who is left behind to move in with her in-laws where she and her children live with her husband's extended family, including his father, mother, brothers and sisters.

A recent study conducted in Bangladesh examined the impacts of male migration on family members, specifically on wives left behind. In the majority of the observed cases, women, along with their children, experienced an increase in their standard of living as a result of the remittances sent by their migrant husbands. However, this increase varied significantly from one household to another. It was also noted that women who lived with their in-laws and did not receive the remittance directly in their names benefited less than women whose husbands sent the remittances to them directly. In other words, control over remittance earnings significantly dictated the degree of their financial independence and, consequently, their decision-making power. In almost all cases, women assumed many of the responsibilities previously held by their husbands, such as going to the market, dealing with household repairs and supervising the education of children. Hence, empowerment often also meant an increased workload. The research also sought to establish whether this empowerment was of a temporary or permanent nature and found that a majority of women resumed their traditional roles once their husbands returned.

The absence of migrant husbands also affected the women's sense of personal security. Women reported that they felt more vulnerable to harassment and indecent advances by other men, including members of their husbands' families. This feeling of insecurity, along with restrictions imposed on the women by the in-laws, also led to the increased use of *purdah*. Many women also admitted to being worried about the possibility that their husbands might be attracted to other women and abandon them and their family. In general, therefore, the study revealed that the social impacts on women resulting from the migration of their husbands are mixed and varied from case to case, depending on personal circumstances.

On the other hand, the migration of women appeared to have a particularly strong impact on the children left behind. In some cases, the mother's absence was felt to contribute to the decline in her children's school attendance while, in others, the remittances sent by the mother enabled her children to benefit from better schooling. There was also some evidence that the migration of mothers often led to the early marriage of the children, especially of adolescent girls, as fathers and other household members considered it too much of a burden to look after their daughters. However, the remittance earnings of the mothers also made it easier for the families to bear the costs of marriage. There was also evidence that some children suffered emotionally from the absence of their mothers, particularly when the fathers were unable to give them sufficient attention.

While women often assumed the roles and responsibilities traditionally assigned to men during the husbands' absence, husbands who stayed behind were usually more reluctant to perform housekeeping duties, although some of them did become more attentive towards their children during the mothers' absence.

The study concluded that, although both female and male migration brings financial benefits for the families left behind, it also incurs significant and gender-differentiated social costs.

Source: *Priyanka Debnath, formerly IOM Geneva.*

2. The Neglect of the Family

For a long time the family has constituted the forgotten form of migration (Bouamama and Sad Saoud, 1996). As Sriskandarajah (2005) notes:

> Scan the UK's current immigration policies and you are likely to get the impression that "families" do not migrate. Rather, there are measures to deal with 'principal applicants' who seek permission to work or claim asylum or want to become a British national. Sometimes there are separate regulations to deal with an associated and residual category of people called "spouses and dependents" (sic). The word "family" is rarely mentioned.

Zlotnik (1995) has argued that two factors have militated against the use of the family unit in the analysis of migration. The first is that economic theory neglects the family because the activities that take place within it cannot be measured in monetary terms. The second factor is the view that transactions occur between the individual and the state, and this is reinforced by the emphasis on the principal or primary applicant, assumed to be the male head of the household. However, two other elements should be added: (1) the dichotomy between the economic and the social spheres in which the economic motivation initiates migration and the family represents the social dimension, often associated with tradition; and (2), especially in Europe, the treatment of family migration in policy terms as a secondary type of migration, viewed initially as an unintended consequence of the stoppage of mass labour migration in the 1970s, and consisting of female dependants joining the male breadwinner as the primary migrant.

This gendered view can also be fostered by immigration legislation. One of the major consequences has been to treat family migration as having few repercussions on the labour market, which is widely regarded as the essential driving force of international migration. There is a dearth of studies on the labour market outcomes of family migrants, except for recent analyses of longitudinal surveys in settler societies such as Australia (Liebig, 2007b) and Canada, which have begun disaggregating data according to visa categories. There is also an unwarranted view that women migrants are uninterested in, or do not seek, employment. This issue is taken up in the discussion on family migration, skills and employment.

Nonetheless, since the late 1980s, theoretical, methodological and empirical aspects of family migration have become the subject of scholarly research (Boyd, 1989; Dumon, 1989). Dumon points out that the role of the family in migration was recognized as far back as the nineteenth century by Le Play (1871), writing on the organization of the family. Boyd and Dumon ascribe the interest in the role of the family in migration first to the growing significance of family migration both in North America and in Europe after the stoppage of mass labour migration, and second to the changing theorization of migration as a system connecting societies of origin and of destination through various personal and familial networks. Families are seen as socializing agents; they support a geographically dispersed social group and constitute networks of assistance, information and obligations (Boyd, 1989). Boyd identified a number of issues as being of relevance for the 1990s, including the refinement of the concept and dynamics of networks and the role of gender in their development and persistence across space and time. Lopes et al. (1994), writing about the failure to recognize the significance of the family in European Community migration policy, argued forcefully that family mobility represents the interface between the individual and the social, in other words, of public and private spaces. As a social unit, the family offers support for its members in accessing resources and services and in migrating.

Nauck and Settles (2001) argue that the decision to migrate is seldom the product of individual decisions; its timing is closely related to the family life cycle and major events over the course of the lives of first and second generations of immigrants, and not necessarily understood as a direct response to labour market opportunities. A different way of understanding migrant families is to see them as fluid and as being constantly reconstituted and negotiated, adapting across spaces and through time (Baldassar and Baldock, 2000; Bryceson and Vuorela, 2002; Creese et al., 1999; Foner, 1997; Vatz Laaroussi, 2001).

Moreover, family migration is now beginning to capture more academic and policy attention. North American and Asian-Pacific (Creese et al., 1999; Parr et al., 2000; Waters, 2001; Yeoh et al., 2002; 2005) and, more recently, European research has been stimulated by a growing interest in transnational families (Bryceson and Vuorela, 2002; Lauth Bacas 2002) and transnationalism (Faist, 2000; Vertovec, 1999; Vertovec, 2004). This refers to migrations across international borders in which persons establish and maintain activities and connections in both the polity from which they originated and the new state in which they live, and includes actors that are not states (Glick Schiller et al., 1995; Guarnizo and Smith, 1998; Levitt and Glick Schiller, 2003; Portes et al., 1999). Many of these writers pay due regard to gendered aspects of transnationalism (Fouron and Glick Schiller, 2001; Pessar and Mahler, 2003), drawing attention to migration and its impact on family forms, relations and strategies that are pursued in maximizing the benefits of migratory opportunities (Yeoh et al., 2002).

Transnational families have been defined as those "that live some or most of the time separated from each other, yet hold together and create something that can be seen as a feeling of collective welfare and unity, namely 'familyhood', even across national borders" (Bryceson and Vuorela, 2002: 3). Some women are increasingly migrating without their children, particularly to countries that do not permit family reunification, or where the nature of their work, such as in households, makes it difficult for them to have their children with them. They therefore leave their children in the care of female members of the extended family, while they work abroad (UNFPA, 2006), while in some societies, for instance in the Philippines, large numbers of children live in separated families and have to cope with intimacy at a distance (Parrenas, 2005). A national study of the consequences of separation on young children in the Philippines found that children of migrants were significantly better off in socio-economic terms than children of non-migrants (e.g. home ownership, durable goods) and more likely to attend private schools and engage in extra-curricular activities (Scalabrini Migration Center, 2003-04). Where one or both parents were absent, children experience a reconfiguration of gender roles and maintain a close family relationship through constant communication (Scalabrini Migration Center, 2003-04).

In policy terms, too, there is increasing interest in family migration, while there is a simultaneous shift away from seeing it as a positive force for integration to one which maintains traditional divisions of gender roles and responsibility, and fosters community separations and social divisions (Kofman and Kraler, 2006). This has resulted, especially in European countries, in a tightening of conditions of entry and settlement for family members. Another policy debate, for example in relation to the new immigration policy in France and the discussions in the United States (Malanga, 2006), has raised the issue of whether high rates of family migration bring in too many low-skilled migrants (see Section 5 below). Before family migration policy issues are discussed, however, the next section sets out trends and types of family migrations.

3. Trends and Types of Family Migration

Family migration is complex, variable in its significance (see Table 6.1 and Figure 6.1) and raises problems of comparison across countries (OECD, 2006; Salt, 2005). Firstly, for those moving under free-movement regimes, i.e. within the EU, or between Australia and New Zealand (see also Chapter 13), visas or permits may not be required and, even when they are, the reason for migration may not always be explicitly identified in the permit system. Secondly, in some countries it has not been possible to distinguish between accompanying family members and those arriving to join a worker, a distinction which the Organisation for Economic Co-operation and Development (OECD) has presented for the first time, but is not available for all countries. In some countries, such as Australia and Canada, the educational characteristics and work intentions of spouses are known. In contrast, there are many other countries for which data on family migration could be greatly improved. Thirdly, statistics do not include unauthorized worker movements.

Several types of family migration need to be distinguished. The first category is **family reunification**, which refers to the process of bringing in immediate family members (children, spouses and parents and others, where permitted) by the primary migrant. Although Geneva Convention refugees normally have the right to bring in immediate family members straightaway, those with subsidiary statuses usually have to wait for a given period and then satisfy certain conditions (e.g. housing, income) for family reunification. In the U.K. (Home Office, 2000), for example, immigration figures recorded an increase in numbers of husbands, wives and fiancé(e)s (of citizens and non-citizens) accepted for settlement, due partly to the growing number of asylum seekers, who have now obtained indefinite leave to remain (permanent residence), as well as the clearance of backlogs in 1999, leading to larger numbers qualifying for family reunification and family formation (see Table 6.1).

The second category, in the past often statistically treated as an aspect of family reunification, should instead be classified as **family formation** or **marriage migration** (Piper and Roces, 2003). It can be broken down into two subgroups. The first consists of second and subsequent generations of children of migrant origin (both citizens and non-citizens) who bring in a fiancé(e)/spouse from their parents' homeland or diasporic space. This group has increased due to the growth of second and subsequent generations who continue to marry external partners, a particular characteristic of Turkish and North African immigrant populations (Lesthaeghe and Surkyn, 1995; Muñoz, 1999). The second variant of marriage migration involves permanent residents or citizens bringing in a partner they have met while abroad for work, study or holiday. In this case, the marriage is a secondary effect of the reason for going abroad. In terms of migration legislation, this category may be separated into categories of family reunification, especially where the partner does not have an immediate right of permanent residence, as with third-country (non-EU) nationals in the EU, particularly those from developing countries (de Hart, 1999). Increased international mobility and subsequent marriage do not only result from citizens travelling abroad, but also from the increasing presence of transient and long-term migrants in a society, leading to rising percentages of mixed marriages. Increasing cross-border marriages in Asia and Europe often involve men of wealthier countries marrying women from economically less-developed countries, and intermediated marriages. The majority of the couples are introduced with the prior intention of marriage and have either no or only a comparatively short period of courtship (International Institute for Asian Studies, 2006). The internet is increasingly replacing face to face contact (hence the rather derogatory "mail-order bride" label) as a means of introducing potential spouses. In Asia, the demand for foreign brides has sharply increased to the point where half the total foreign population in Taiwan Province of China are brides. Since 1990, nearly 100,000 Vietnamese women have married Taiwanese men (Wong and Chang, 2002; UNFPA, 2006). Similarly, in the Republic of Korea (South Korea) and Japan, foreign women are marrying local men. An estimated 10,000-15,000 Russian women migrate as fiancées each year, of whom 80,000 have entered the U.S. in the past decade (UNFPA, 2006).

There is a third category of family migration where the **entire family** migrates. In the absence of official permanent immigration, as in settler societies, which encouraged this form of migration on the assumption that it would facilitate integration and contribute to population growth, this category is less common in Europe. Many countries do not allow temporary permit holders to be accompanied by family members (OECD, 2000), except the very highly skilled. The U.K. is the most liberal of the EU Member States, in allowing spouses of students, work permit holders and those undertaking training to enter with the right to work. With the increased demand for skilled labour (especially in the information technology (IT) and welfare sectors, such as education and health) and acceptance of long-term migration for this group in countries such as Germany and the U.K., family migration is likely to become more prevalent. Some refugees, especially those entering on settlement schemes or quotas, also enter with their whole family.

A fourth category, largely restricted to settler societies, consists of **sponsored family members** who are not necessarily defined as being of the immediate family and, as discussed more fully below, constitute discretionary flows. In settler societies, a wider range of family members may be sponsored (Khoo, 2003), but stricter conditions and capping[1] of numbers are applied, as in the U.S., for categories such as unmarried children over 21 years, married children, and brothers and sisters.

Figure 6.1:

International Migration by Category of Entry in Selected OECD Countries as a Percentage of Total Inflows, Standardized data, 2005

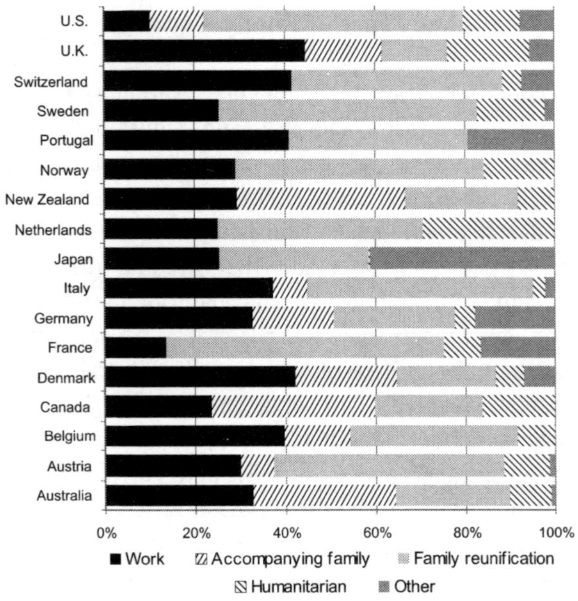

Source: OECD, 2007.

[1] This administrative procedure allows the government to set annual limits on the number of entries under a given migration category.

Table 6.1:

Proportion of Family Migrants among Long-term Migrants, 2005

Country	Family Migrants ('000)	Long-term Migrants ('000)	Family (%)
Australia	102.3	179.8	56.9
Austria	32.3	56.8	56.0
Canada	158.0	262.2	60.3
France	102.5	168.6	60.8
Germany	89.1	198.6	44.9
Italy	106.7	184.3	57.7
Japan	26.9	81.3	33.1
Netherlands	27.6	60.7	45.5
New Zealand	37.1	59.4	62.4
Norway	12.6	21.4	59.9
Portugal	5.3	13.3	39.6
Sweden	30.9	53.8	57.4
Switzerland	37.0	78.8	46.9
U.K.	113.8	362.4	31.4
U.S.	782.1	1,122.4	69.7

Note:
Family migrants in this table include family members of economic and work permit migrants, but not those entering either through humanitarian channels or through family streams.

Source: *OECD, 2006.*

Both Figure 6.1 and Table 6.1 show that in countries with low levels of permanent skilled migration, such as the U.S. or France, and with high levels of asylum seekers and refugees, such as Sweden, there are high levels of family migration, especially family reunification. In the U.S., the country with the largest proportion of family migration, family reunification has accounted for about two-thirds of lawful permanent migration since the mid-1980s, except for 1989-1994. If family members of other categories, such as migrants for employment and refugees, are also included, then family migration becomes even more significant, as indicated in Table 6.1. In some countries, such as Italy, the right to family reunification has been claimed by the growing number of foreign workers who have settled. In other countries, such as Australia, Canada and the U.K., the increasing emphasis on skilled migration has resulted in lower levels of family migration, though in certain instances the decrease may partly stem from reclassifications. In Australia, for example, the category of concessional family migration covering the sponsorship of relatives with skills has been relocated to the skilled migration stream as skilled sponsored migration. Changing skilled migration policies may lead to increasing numbers of family members entering as dependants, as has been the case in the U.K., where the proportion of dependants among work permit holders rose from 25.5 per cent in 2001 to 33.4 per cent in 2006 (Home Office, 2007).

What constitutes the family for the purpose of migration differs among states, as these apply different rules to members of a family, as discussed above. The 1990 International Convention on the Protection of the Rights of All Migrant Workers and Members of their Families (see Textbox 13.1) defines the family in terms of those who can benefit from its provisions. These are the migrant worker's spouse, persons in a relationship with the migrant worker that, according to applicable law, produces effects equivalent to marriage, and dependent minors and unmarried children. It largely corresponds to the distinction between non-discretionary and discretionary family migration (OECD, 2006 and Table 6.2).

Discretionary family migration, which accounts for a high percentage of migrant entries in settler societies, includes those members of the family not recognized by human rights conventions or free movement provisions (e.g. EU) for family reunification, for example adult children, siblings and, in many countries, non-dependent parents. In Australia, though the number of visas issued to parents is capped, they do not have to prove economic dependence on their child(ren). In addition, there is a separate category for aged dependent relatives, remaining relatives or carers. These are the family members whose numbers may be subject to capping or restricted interpretations of dependence on the sponsor. This is very much at the heart of the

Table 6.2:

Inflows of Permanent Family Migrants in Selected OECD Countries, 2003

	Non-discretionary %		Discretionary %		
Selected OECD countries	Total (including non-family migrants)	Spouses, children, fiancé(e)s, recognized asylum seekers	Total (including non-family migrants)	Work or settlement with accompanying family	Family migration (non-immediate family)
Australia	39	25	61	48	5
Canada	28	28	72	55	10
France	83	61	17	4	6
Italy	74	64	26	19	n.a.
New Zealand	28	18	72	49	12
Sweden	95	73	5	1	-
Switzerland	94	31	6	4	-
U.K.	49	23	51	34	2
U.S.	39	39	61	12	32

Note:
n.a. = not applicable

***Source:** OECD (2006).*

criteria laying down who belongs to the immediate family and therefore permitted to enter as a family member. One of the major differences between the EU and settler societies is that, in the former, only those deemed dependent, whether as children or parents, may enter as family members. Those who are considered to be independent, such as children over a certain age and/or married, or independent parents, are generally excluded from entering as family members.

However, it should be noted that, over time, many countries have recognized the changing ways in which familial relationships have been forged. For example, an increasing number of states recognize social units akin to the family, such as same-sex relationships (Cooke, 2005), cohabitation, single parents and adopted children. However, major cultural differences remain concerning divorce, cohabitation, single parent families, reproductive technologies and same-sex partnerships and will have direct impacts on migration (Bailey and Boyle, 2004).

4. International and Regional Instruments

A number of international instruments recognize the right to family reunification and to found a family, and call on states parties to respect the right to family life (Lahav, 1997). The right to family reunification has been included in two human rights conventions: the 1989 UN Convention on the Rights of the Child, in particular in Article 9, and the 1990 International Convention on the Protection of the Rights of All Migrant Workers and Members of their Families, in particular in Article 44. The latter only came into force in 2003, but it still has to be ratified by any major industrialized country of destination.

EU law also foresees that spouses, and children under the age of 21, or who are dependants, have the right to join EU citizens employed in other EU Member States. More recently the EU Council Directive on the right to family reunification for third-country nationals lawfully resident in the EU[2] has been transposed into the laws of EU Member States, except in Denmark, Ireland and the U.K.; however, it

[2] Council Directive 2003/86/EC of 22 September 2003 on the right to family reunification, OJ 2003 L 251/12.

allows a large measure of discretion in its application under national law (European Migration Network, 2008; Oliynik, 2004). A number of points should be noted in this connection. The Directive specifically recognizes unmarried partners and family members dependent on the sponsor or the spouse. In the case of family reunification, unmarried couples will be treated as married couples depending on the laws in the Member State in question where the sponsor is in a "duly attested stable long-term relationship" or bound by a "registered partnership", which vary according to the particular national laws concerning the treatment of such categories for the purpose of family reunification. Under the Directive, family members are, in the same way as the sponsor, inter alia, entitled to work in a dependent or independent (self-employed) capacity, although local laws may restrict such access for up to one year depending on the labour market situation. For a lawfully resident third-country national seeking to bring in a spouse, Member States may determine a minimum age of up to 21 years for both parties to ensure better integration and prevent forced marriages (Oezcan, 2003).

5. National Policy Changes and Management of Family Migration

At the national level, family migration policies generally have evolved in very different directions. Some OECD countries have introduced new measures to grant migrants the right to family reunification, simplified procedures and facilitated the integration of their relatives (OECD, 2006). This has been the case in Italy and Spain. Spain's family migration policies have undergone numerous changes making them less restrictive (Ortega Perez, 2003). The 1996 amendment to the 1985 immigration law established a permanent residence category and for the first time formally included family reunification. The 2000 Plan Greco was designed to address key areas, one of which was the integration of foreign residents and their families as active contributors to the economic growth of Spain. A special regularization procedure on grounds of family reunification was organized in 1994 (Arango, 2005). However, frequent regularization programmes generally lead to larger pools of family migrants entering in anticipation of future regularization programmes.

In Europe, family reunion policies are used as a means to facilitate integration (e.g. in Spain and Italy), but many northern European countries have also increasingly come to perceive family migrants as hampering the integration of the migrant population (Denmark, France, Netherlands, U.K.) and maintaining different family norms (Kofman and Kraler 2006; Van Walsum, 2004). As a result they have tended to tighten their policies regarding certain preconditions to be fulfilled by the sponsor, such as sufficient financial resources and minimum standards of accommodation, and for the family member, passing a prior language test and the obligation to participate in integration measures. There has also been an increase in controls on transnational marriages, especially between citizens and residents of migrant origin and persons from their homeland.

By imposing stricter conditions to qualify for permanent residence, such countries have sought to substantially reduce the numbers of family migrants. In France, for example, in response to a rise in the number of persons entering for family reasons, legislative changes have been introduced marking a shift away from family migration to a selective policy to attract more skilled migrants.[3]

[3] This increase was mainly due to persons joining or marrying a French citizen, and is more related to the granting of a personal and family permit rather than to classic family reunification with a primary migrant (Régnard, 2006). Unlike many other European countries, France created a **personal and family life** category in 1998, incorporating into French law Article 8 of the European Convention of Human Rights protecting the right to respect of private and family life. Its remit is wide, seeking to encompass a variety of family members, the initial stages of marriage with a French citizen, and diverse reasons for residence, e.g. the need for medical attention and legalization of the irregular status of long-term residents and children.

In contrast to migrants, French and EU citizens are not required to satisfy any resources conditions in order to bring in existing or future family members. Thus, renewed debates about immigration have led to further legislative changes marking a shift away from family migration to a selective policy to attract more skilled migrants. The immigration and integration law (No. 2006-911 of 24 July 2006) pursued four main objectives: recruiting skilled workers; facilitating entry and stay for foreign students; tightening the rules for family reunification; and limiting access to residence and citizenship (Murphy, 2006). It has tightened the conditions for the sponsor, for example by extending the period of residence from one year to 18 months, and requiring for non-EU migrants a probationary or conditional period of marriage of two to three years. The subsequent Bill No. 2007-1631 of 20 November 2007 aimed specifically at further reducing family migration, proved highly controversial in its introduction of DNA testing for children joining their mother in France. The test will be in place for an 18-month trial period, voluntary and paid by the French government (BBC News, 24 October 2007). In addition, the level of resources required to be eligible to bring in family members will depend on the size of the family. Parents will have to sign a parental contract vouching for the good behaviour of their children. The effects of these legislative changes in radically altering the migratory regime will depend not only on their capacity to reduce levels of family migration but also on an expansion of labour migration.

A number of countries, apart from France, have imposed mandatory integration conditions. In Austria, the Settlement and Residence Act foresees a mandatory integration agreement (Carrera, 2006). The Netherlands also foresees integration as a condition for family reunification to be legally sanctioned. Recent developments have meant that both newcomers and settled migrants will have to pass an integration test to demonstrate their actual integration into Dutch society. These rules are primarily aimed at non-EU migrant family reunifications, where migrants have to complete a basic integration test in their home country before arriving in the Netherlands, to be followed by another test at a higher level five years after admission.[4] This was the first European country in recent times to require permanent immigrants to complete a pre-arrival integration course (Expatica, 2004). Other countries, such as France, Germany, Netherlands and the U.K., require family members to pass language tests as a precondition for obtaining a long-term residence permit (UKREN, 2007), as the inadequate knowledge of the language has been identified as a major barrier to integration.

Denmark has introduced restrictions on family migration, reducing numbers in this category since 2001. The 2001 elections saw the Danish People's Party introduce new provisions in force since 2003. The provisions foresee that Danish citizens cannot bring a foreign spouse into the country unless both are at least 24 years old and provide evidence that the sponsor is able to support the nominee (in most cases, this requirement will be met if the spouse/partner has not received public assistance for at least 12 months prior to the application being processed by the Immigration Service). More importantly, Danish citizens who are themselves first or second-generation migrants have to provide evidence that their ties with Denmark are stronger than with any other country (Denmark, Ministry of Refugee, Immigration and Integration Affairs, 2006). The effects of such changes can be seen in the drop of family reunification permits from 13,000 in 2001 to under 5,000 in 2003 (BBC News, 2005) and a substantial reduction in non-western immigrants (Hedetoft, 2006). In addition to the tightening of family reunification rules in recent years, since July 2005 applicants for family reunification and their

[4] See, respectively, the Act on Preliminary Integration Abroad (*Wet inburgering in het buitenland*) of 22 December 2005, and the Act on Integration (*Wet inburgering*) of 7 December 2006. EU citizens, EEA nationals, Swiss citizens and non-EU nationals who are family members of EU citizens are exempt from these rules.

spouses have to sign a declaration of integration which obliges the applicant to actively participate with his/her children in Danish language courses and integration into Danish society.

Sham marriages have been in the spotlight in countries such as Denmark, France and the U.K. A sham marriage is characterized as a marriage that is contracted purely to procure the right of residence for one of the partners. In Denmark, prima facie or pro forma marriages, as they are also known, are assessed by the Immigration services to determine, inter alia, whether the parties are able to communicate in the same language, whether there is a large age difference between them, and how well they knew each other before the marriage (Ministry of Refugee, Immigration and Integration Affairs, 2006). In the U.K., as of February 2005, any non-EU migrant with a short-term visa had to seek permission to marry from the Home Office. However, in April 2006, a High Court judgment found this to be in breach of human rights (Article 12 of the European Convention on Human Rights concerning the right to marry) and discriminatory on grounds of religion (i.e. those marrying in the Church of England were regarded more favourably) and nationality. The challenge was brought by a male Muslim Algerian irregular migrant and a female Polish Roman Catholic migrant, who had entered the U.K. following EU enlargement (Daily Telegraph, 2006) and who had been refused permission to marry in February 2005 under the U.K. regulations.

A further means of testing whether a marriage is bona fide or not is to impose what is known as a **probationary or conditional period**, during which the marriage must continue for the spouse to acquire a permanent right of residence. Recently, several EU Member States have extended the probationary period; for example, from two to three years in France as of 2007 and from one to two years in the U.K. in 2003. Many European countries have introduced exemptions for domestic violence. In the U.K., for instance, after continuous lobbying from women activists, a concession was introduced in 2002 to allow a woman indefinite leave to remain if she can prove that she left a relationship because of domestic violence (Southall Black Sisters, 2001; 2004). The U.S. also has a two-year conditional period, but differs from the U.K. in that it takes into account the duration of the marriage. In the U.S. the conditional residency provision applies only if the marriage is of less than two years' duration (workpermit.com 2006). In the U.K. all spouses are subject to the two-year conditional period.

In the EU, the sponsor generally has to meet minimum standards of income and accommodation when bringing in a third-country national spouse.[5] The Directive on family reunification, discussed in Section 4 above, enables Member States to impose similar conditions on sponsors who are third-country nationals lawfully resident in the country in question. In Denmark, which does not apply this Directive, further criteria have been introduced under which the person in Denmark is required to provide evidence that no financial assistance has been requested or received for one year prior to the application for the residence permit, and that there has been no conviction for a violent act against a former spouse or companion for a period of 10 years prior to the processing of the application (New to Denmark, 2006). Furthermore, it is often the case that during the initial years family migrants are not entitled to income-related public funds or welfare benefits. For example, in the U.K. there is no recourse to income-related public funds for two years for British citizens and settled residents.

The **arranged marriage** stands out as one of the forms of marriage migration that needs to be scrutinized, contained and managed (Gedalof, 2007).

---

5 However, if the sponsor is an EU citizen who has taken up employment in another EU Member State, the more liberal EU rules on family reunion apply.

> The White Paper and the 2002 Act continue a long-standing theme in the history of British immigration policy that takes the family (or at least some kinds of family) as a potential danger to border integrity by providing an entry point for difference (Gedalof, 2007: 84).

The White Paper (Home Office, 2001) focuses in particular on two issues: arranged marriages and family visits for events such as weddings and funerals, which the White Paper presents as serious problems that need to be managed (Gedalof, 2007). It focuses in particular on "those communities that continue the practice of forced marriage" (Home Office, 2001: 18). "Those communities" means the Asian communities, although this is never explicitly mentioned. This has been used as a reason to raise the marriage age to 21 years, as in the Netherlands. Similarly, in Denmark, arranged marriages are also seen as a form of marriage to be managed and scrutinized. This has led to the raising of the minimum age at which marriage with a foreign spouse can take place from 18 to 24 years.

In settler societies, the capping of family members permitted under discretionary rules is applied in the management of family migration. In the U.S., each category of family migrant is numerically limited, including unmarried adult children of U.S. citizens, spouses and unmarried children of permanent residents (i.e. Green Card holders), married children of U.S. citizens, and siblings of adult U.S. citizens. In these numerically limited categories, no single country can account for more than seven per cent of total admissions. But if immediate family quotas are not filled, these can be transferred to family sponsored categories (McKay, 2003).

6. Family Migration, Skills and Employment

Although family migration continues to occupy an important place in the immigration programmes of established immigration countries, there has been a general tendency to adjust their composition and reorient their intake towards skilled labour migration. In large part, this stemmed from a concern to maximize labour market outcomes and enhance integration prospects, although Baringhorst (2004) sees it as a response to conservative requests for stricter policies. This strategy has been pursued most noticeably in Australia, where the family stream of the migration programme fell in relative terms from 47 to 35 per cent between 1997-98 and 2004-05.[6] Family migration entries have remained stable in Canada (Richardson and Lester, 2004) and remain dominant in the U.S. Textbox 6.2 examines the relationship between family and skilled migration policies in the established countries of immigration.

[6] Over the same period, the actual number of visas issued rose from 31,310 in 1997-98 to 41,740 in 2004-05.

Textbox 6.2

Family and Skilled Migration Policies in Australia, Canada, New Zealand and the United States

Immigration policy discussions often fail to distinguish between administrative mechanisms and individual motives. Policymakers tend to see their programmes in terms of sets of rules and regulations that are meant to allow right of entry to very specific groups of migrants. On the other hand, potential migrants see these same rules and regulations as a means (or opportunities) to achieve personal goals that may or may not coincide with programme objectives. This produces a situation where immigrants admitted under family reunion programmes and as partners are, in many instances, actually strongly motivated by economic factors while, conversely, significant proportions of skilled workers migrate to join their families abroad. This blurring of the distinction between family and skilled labour flows raises policy questions about the labour market performance and impact of family migration, and how it measures up against skilled workers who are admitted on the basis of labour market screening criteria. Australia, Canada, New Zealand and the United States all operate elaborate programmes for managing family and skilled migration. What do the results show?

Given the dichotomy in the debate over family versus skilled migration, perhaps the most surprising observation is how little is actually known about the economic performance of either group. The reason is that most surveys do not identify the programmes under which immigrants gained entry. Newly introduced longitudinal surveys in all four countries will start to shed more light on this topic in the next few years. In the meantime, the discussion below reveals some of the preliminary evidence that has emerged from the research in the four countries cited.

Family-related flows are not uniform in their labour market behaviour. Partner flows exhibit different behaviours from parents and other relations, and accompanying family members differ from sponsored family. These differences are recognized by authorities and the component flows are managed differently. All four countries prioritize the entry of partners and dependent children. These flows are not subject to any volumetric controls, while parents and other relatives are managed more tightly. Except for the United States, same-sex relationships are recognized and same-sex sponsorships are permitted.

Though none of the countries (except in very limited ways) manages the labour market characteristics of family migrants, the overall "quality" of family flows is nonetheless linked by virtue of social and cultural factors to the "qualities" of their sponsors – which are managed. This suggests that the economic performance and impact of family migration is functionally related to the overall structure and totality of a country's admission programmes. Supporting evidence from Australia finds that, following the reform of the skilled worker selection process, partner admissions show a higher proportion in skilled jobs, rising employment and participation, and falling unemployment. Trends in other countries corroborate this.

Limited measures aimed at influencing partner characteristics appear in the skilled worker selection systems of Australia, Canada and New Zealand. Additional points are awarded to the principal applicant if the spouse or partner possesses characteristics deemed favourable. Opinion is divided, however, as to whether the additional partner points create a stronger overall family unit or (since points are generally fungible in relation to an overall pass mark) or permit entry for candidates with weaker labour market skills.

Australia, Canada and New Zealand confine family reunion migration to roughly 30 per cent of total intake. In contrast, the U.S. system focuses predominantly on family migration. On the face of it, this would suggest huge differences in labour "quality" and economic performance between the three countries that screen immigrants and the United States, which does so only in a minority of cases. In practice, however, the differences appear small. This suggests that either the labour market impacts of family migration are larger, and more benign, than many analysts believe, or that the returns to foreign skills and education are smaller than is generally acknowledged. There is probably some truth to both. Other possible explanations are that authorities screen only a small percentage of skilled applicants (accompanying dependants are not tested), and sponsors are likely to "screen" relatives to ensure they will not be a permanent burden. An additional factor that may "explain" performance differences between migrants selected on the basis of family as opposed to economic criteria may lie in the different sources of these flows. Weaker economic outcomes ascribed to family migration may, in fact, be concealing differential (and, possibly, discriminatory) treatment by host country labour markets.

Notwithstanding overall inter-country comparisons, preliminary evidence from longitudinal surveys suggests that family migrants generally show weaker labour force attachment than migrants selected for the labour market. This manifests itself as follows: weaker labour market skills and a greater likelihood of ending up in low-skilled jobs (in services, light assembly or primary occupations, depending on the country); lower incomes (though how much lower and whether this persists is open to debate); weaker English language skills; and a greater propensity to rely on social assistance. This last point needs to be nuanced. Canadian data suggest that while both family reunion spouses and the accompanying spouses of skilled applicants report low earnings, the latter show higher rates of labour market participation and a lower incidence of dependency on employment insurance and social assistance. This reinforces the earlier point about programme structure and labour market impact.

Five important qualifiers need to be kept in mind with respect to the points made above concerning the economic and labour market impact of family migration:

- Notwithstanding overall trends, significant proportions of family migrants possess excellent qualifications and skills.
- The earnings of all groups, regardless of entry mode, improve with time spent in the country.
- There is uncertainty about the "catching-up" rates of family migrants as compared with skilled workers. Some American analysts argue that family migrants benefit from social capital in the form of greater investments in training, which produces favourable results in the long term.
- The labour market performance of all migrants is affected by the state of the macro economy. Higher propensities by skilled workers in Canada to suffer low income (i.e. below poverty levels) during economic downturns may be attributable to a lack of social capital.
- According to some analysts, family migration tends to be complementary, while skilled migration competes with the domestic workforce. This conclusion is based, in part, on the fact that forecasts of labour shortages have tended to be unsuccessful, leading to labour "imports" in areas of robust domestic supply.

Source: *Meyer Burstein, Consultant and former Chair of the Metropolis Project.*

In Australia, until the mid-1990s, family-linked migration accounted for the largest proportion of permanent visas issued, but this was gradually changed through increased emphasis on skilled migration. Of the migrants who arrived between 1996 and 2004, 56 per cent were highly skilled (diploma or above) compared with 32 per cent for the period 1981-1985 (Liebig, 2007b). Another reason for the "decline" in family migrants is the reclassification of elements of family migration. What had previously been a family concessional category with points for skills was moved to the skilled stream in 1997 and eventually renamed Skilled Australia-Sponsored in 1999, in which the migrant has to accumulate points in the same way as skilled independent migrants, but in addition is sponsored by a relative. The immediate family members of humanitarian migrants were also taken out of the family category and relocated into the humanitarian stream where they are able to tap a wide range of services (Liebig, 2007b).

Many of those attributed to the skilled worker category in Australia and Canada are in fact educated dependants who, if possible, will be entering the labour market. In Canada, for example, 77,976 out of 130,242 in the skilled worker class were spouses and dependants (Citizenship and Immigration Canada, 2005). Only 30 per cent of Australian immigrants are directly selected on the basis of their skills, i.e. principal applicants in labour migration flows. As has been pointed out, skilled migrants are often married to other skilled migrants, and their children are also skilled (Liebig, 2007b). Thus, as the skill levels of principal labour applicants increase, so do those of their accompanying family members. Both Australia and Canada include points for the skill level of the spouse.

While there is consequently little doubt that many if not most of those entering in the family stream are skilled, it is also clear from Table 6.3 that there are, in Australia at least, very different employment outcomes for men and women in every visa category and especially in the family stream. Gender differences within each category would merit further investigation.

Table 6.3:

Employment-population Ratios of the Native and Foreign-born Population in Australia by Visa Category, 15-64 years old, 2004

	Men (%)	Women (%)
By place of birth		
Native-born	81	66
Foreign-born	76	57
By visa category*		
Skilled-main applicant	86	79
Skilled-other than main applicant	89	71
Family	78	43
Humanitarian	68	40

Note:
* Only immigrants after 1984 aged 15 and above at arrival.

Sources: *"Data by visa category", Labour Force Status and Other Characteristics of Migrants Survey; Liebig (2007b: 27).*

There has been a noticeable improvement in the employment outcomes for parents and other preferential relatives between the first and second cohorts of the Longitudinal Survey of Immigrants in Australia, most likely owing to the restrictions placed on this category. Overall, the employment rates for skilled and family categories in Australia are higher than for similar Canadian surveys (Richardson and Lester, 2004).

In the U.S., debates have been conducted on the declining skill levels of the immigrant (permanent) population (Borjas, 1995) and the extent to which family migration is able to compensate for deficiencies in labour migration. While some argue there are too few opportunities for the entry of the less skilled (Paral, 2005), others criticize the excessive number of the less skilled and the dominance of family migration (Malanga, 2006).

There is evidence that source countries may be an important determinant of the skills mix in family streams. Antecol et al. (2002) argue that whilst skill levels of migrant women in Australia and Canada are much higher than in the U.S., this is due in the latter case to the high proportion of migrants originating in Central and South America (whose skill and English-language levels are low) compared to, for instance, Australia, where the level of migration from English-speaking countries remains high. Differences in female skill levels between these three countries are evened out once adjustments are made for the Central and South American migrants in the U.S. flows.

Family migration within a state varies quite considerably according to nationality. Particularly in states with family sponsorship (Khoo, 2003) where a broader notion of the family applies, family migration in effect substitutes for labour migration, as has happened with Mexicans and other nationals from Central and South American countries who have not been able to use the skilled routes for entry (Paral, 2005). Migrants looking for employment in the U.S. may therefore seek sponsorship by family members who have previously migrated and can be seen in the high percentage of discretionary non-immediate family members (see Table 6.4). Hence, they rely heavily on family migration as a pathway to labour migration. In contrast, Indian nationals, who are well represented in temporary skilled migration, have a relatively low proportion of family migrants.

Table 6.4:

Family Migrations in the U.S. – Top Ten Countries of Immigration through Family Reunification (FR), 2001

Country of origin	Total	FR	FR (%)
All countries	1,064,318	675,178	63.44
Mexico	206,426	196,234	95.06
Philippines	53,154	40,863	76.88
China	56,426	33,202	58.84
India	70,290	30,157	42.90
Viet Nam	35,531	24,112	67.86
Dominican Republic	21,313	20,969	98.39
Haiti	27,120	16,356	60.31
Colombia	16,730	14,884	88.97
Jamaica	15,393	14,536	94.43
El Salvador	31,272	13,932	44.55

Source: *Immigration and Naturalization Service (INS) Statistical Yearbook (2001).*

In many European countries, access to the labour market for family members has been at times denied or restricted. Already at the beginning of the 1980s, the Council of Europe (1981) expressed concern at the obstacles facing family members accessing the labour force and its consequences for irregular work. There is evidence of its negative effects on migrant women's employment. Until the new immigration law came into force in Germany in January 2005, spouses could only enter the labour market after a one-year waiting period and were subject to the labour market test, i.e. confirmation that they were not taking away work from a German or EU citizen. The difficulties of access to employment confronting female family migrants, especially among Turkish women, who have very low labour market participation (40%), are thought to be in part due to the restrictions imposed on labour market entry for family reunification spouses (Liebig, 2007a).

The recent trend has been to remove existing restrictions. Spouses, especially of skilled migrants, are generally able to enter the labour market immediately (e.g. U.K.), though they may encounter obstacles and deskilling. This is the legal requirement under EU law concerning spouses (irrespective of their nationality) of EU citizens employed in other EU Member States. Furthermore, in the Directive on Family Reunification discussed earlier, Article 14 grants the admitted spouse the same access to employment as the third-country national sponsor, although Member States retain the discretion to preclude family members from accessing the labour market for up to a maximum of one year after entry. However, Spain remains an exception in Europe where spouses and dependants are not granted immediate authorization to work based on the principal migrant's status. For work permit migrants, accompanying spouses and children will only be granted leave to enter, and they must obtain their own work visas to secure employment (workpermit.com, 2006).

Nonetheless, whether they are accompanying spouses, or entering through marriage migration or family reunification channels, aside from anecdotal evidence (see Portrait 6.1), little is known about their labour market outcomes. There is simply no statistical evidence to hand of the kind available in settler societies, such as the longitudinal surveys disaggregated by visa category or route of entry.

Portrait 6.1

The Story of a Software Specialist Family

Nothing in Helen and Alex Lis' name indicates that they are from Belarus. Two years ago, Elena Liseitchikau, which is her full name, came to Prague with her daughter to join her husband, Alexey, on the basis of a family reunification visa. Alexey had already been running a successful business in the Czech Republic for several years. Together with a friend, also from Belarus, they had established a successful software company and even managed to penetrate other markets in Europe.

"Of course, Alex could also have set himself up in business in our homeland", observes Elen, "but there are more opportunities for him here in the Czech Republic."

As their original Belarusian surname is not easy to pronounce or retain for most people, and could make communication difficult, they decided to abbreviate it to Lis, which is easier to say and remember.

Elen had learned about the Pilot Project on the Selection of Qualified Workers (see Portrait 2.1) from the Czech Ministry of Labour and Social Affairs while still in Minsk. Together with her husband, they decided to apply for participation in the project. They were accepted and have now completed the two-and-a-half year qualifying period required for permanent residence in the Czech Republic.

Elen works as a promotion manager for a Russian newspaper published in Prague. There are tens of thousands of foreigners living in Prague, many of whom speak Russian. "My customers are mostly Russians", Elen confirms.

Elen likes living in Prague, even though the cost of living there is higher than in other parts of the country. Obtaining permanent residence status will allow her family to resolve the problem of accommodation in a more acceptable way than through an expensive lease, and also give them the opportunity of taking up better or different employment.

"We also like to visit other parts of the country", Elen remarks. "I like southern Bohemia very much. It reminds me of Belarus, although the countryside is more rugged there. There are many ponds. The Czech countryside is nice, and I like living here, though I do not forget my homeland."

She says all this in Czech, although she has not fully mastered the language. She has the possibility to attend Czech language courses, but there is simply not enough time for everything. By contrast, her six-year old daughter, Alina, is as fluent as only a six-year old can be. She has a good teacher, who helps her cope in her new environment, and classmates who have accepted her without any problems. No doubt, she will soon start to help her mother to speak Czech better, as will the contacts and conversations with customers and friends and the steadily growing familiarity with the country and its people.

Source: *Adapted from Pilot Project Selection of Qualified Workers (Reporter: Milan Daniel, 15 October 2006), http://www.imigrace.mpsv.cz/?lang=en&article=media2&mm=4017.*

7. Conclusion

This chapter has argued for much more information about different types of family migrations in different parts of the world and, in particular, for research into the relationship between family migration and employment. Family migration, in its very diverse forms, has been with few exceptions (the position of overseas contract workers in the Middle East comes to mind) a major component of migration intakes. In policy formulation and debate it has often been placed in contradistinction to labour migration: in substance, family migration has been ascribed social significance, whereas labour migration has been attributed economic value.

In reality, these two concepts are more closely intertwined than appears at first glance. Historically, family migration has tended to be seen as an instrument of integration, but work concerns and interests have never been entirely absent from the scene. The fact that family migrants, and women especially, may not be selected on the basis of skills does not support the assertion that they do not contribute to the labour supply. Many, if not most, family migrants had work experience prior to entering a country of destination, including in skilled occupations, and many again use family reunion provisions to obtain access to employment abroad. There is a clear need to acknowledge the labour force participation of family migrants and to rethink the outdated image of the female and dependent family migrant with little interest in working. There are family members who may be engaged in "low visibility" occupations, such as older women, who may be carers enabling their children to enter the workforce.

More recently, policy objectives have been shifting away from family migration as an adjunct to social integration towards the recruitment of (often extended) family members to meet specific skilled labour market needs. Given the importance governments place on economic outcomes, this trend was perhaps inevitable, but there is more at stake here than just a re-orientation of policies towards skilled migration and a downsizing of the family component. A devaluation of family relationships is unlikely to be of assistance in the management of the complex human process that is international migration.

A great deal more research obviously needs to be done, first to define in more realistic and precise terms the issues at stake and to offer appropriate policy options to provide policymakers as well as the community at large with effective choices.

REFERENCES

Antecol, H., D. Cobb-Clark. and S. Trejo

2002 "Human Capital and Earnings of Female Immigrants to Australia, Canada, and the US", (IZA) Discussion Paper No. 575, September, Institute for the Study of Labour, Bonn, http://ftp.iza.org/dp575.pdf.

Arango, J. and M. Jachimowicz

2005 "Regularizing Immigrants in Spain: A New Approach", *Migration Information Source*, September, Migration Policy Institute (MPI), Washington D.C., www.migrationinformation.org/Feature/print.cfm?ID=331.

Australia, Department of Immigration and Citizenship (DIAC)

2006 *Immigration Update Financial Year 2005-2006*, November, Research and Statistics Section, DIAC, Canberra, http://www.immi.gov.au/media/publications/pdf/Update_June06.pdf.

Bailey, A. and P. Boyle

2004 "Untying and retying family migration in the new Europe markets", *Journal of Ethnic and Migration Studies*, 30(2): 229-241.

Baldassar, L. and C. Baldock

2000 "Linking migration and family studies: transnational migrants and the care of aging parents" in B. Agozino (Ed.), *Theoretical and Methodological Issues in Migration Research*, Ashgate, Aldershot, U.K., 61–89.

Baringhorst, S.

2004 "Policies of Backlash: Recent Shifts in Australian Migration Policy", *Journal of Comparative Policy Analysis*, 6(2): 131-157.

BBC News

2005 "Denmark's immigration issue", BBC News, 19 February, http://newsvote.bbc.co.uk/mpapps/pagetools/print/news.bbc.co.uk/1/hi/world/europe/4276963.stm.

2007 "French parliament adopts DNA bill", BBC News, 24 October, http://news.bbc.co.uk/2/hi/europe/7059186.stm.

Bouamama, S. and H. Sad Saoud

1996 *Familles maghrébines en France*, Desclée de Brouwer, Paris.

Borjas, G.

1995 "The economic benefits from immigration", *Journal of Economic Perspectives*, 9(2): 3-22.

Boyd, M.

1989 "Family and personal networks in international migration", *International Migration Review*, 23(3): 638-670.

Boyd, M. and E. Grieco

2003 "Women and Migration: Incorporating Gender into International Migration Theory", *Migration Information Source*, March, MPI, Washington, D.C., www.migrationinformation.org/feature/print.cfm?ID=106.

Bryceson, D. and U. Vuorela

2002 "Transnational Families in the Twenty-first Century" in D. Bryceson and U. Vuorela (Eds.), *The Transnational Family. New European Frontiers and Global Networks*, Berg, Oxford, 3-30.

Carrera, S.

2006 "Legal Migration Law and Policy Trends in a Selection of EU Member States", 4 December, Challenge: Liberty and Security, http://www.libertysecurity.org/article1190.html.

Citizenship and Immigration Canada (CIC)

2005 *Facts and Figures: Immigration Overview – Permanent and Temporary Residents*, CIC Canada, http://www.cic.gc.ca/ENGLISH/resources/statistics/menu-fact.asp.

Constable, N.

2005 "Introduction: Cross-Border Marriages" in N. Constable (Ed.), *Gender and Mobility in Transnational Asia*, University of Pennsylvania Press, Philadelphia, 1-16.

Cooke, T.J.

2005 "Migration of same-sex couples", *Population, Space and Place*, 11: 401-409.

Council of Europe

1981 *European Migration in the 1980s. Trends and Policies*, Council of Europe, Strasbourg.

Creese, G., I. Dyck and A. McLaren

1999 "Reconstituting the Family: Negotiating Immigration and Settlement", March, Research on Immigration and Integration in the Metropolis (RIIM), Paper 99-10, Vancouver Centre of Excellence, http://riim.metropolis.net/Virtual%20Library/1999/wp9910.pdf.

Daily Telegraph
2006 "High court overturns laws to combat sham marriages", *Daily Telegraph*, 11 April.

Denmark, Ministry of Refugee, Immigration and Integration Affairs
2006 New to Denmark 2006, Ministry of Refugee, Immigration and Integration Affairs, http://www.nyidanmark.dk/en-us/frontpage.htm.

Dumon, R.
1989 "Family and migration", *International Migration*, 27(2): 251–270.

European Migration Network (EMN)
2008 *Synthesis Report: Family Reunification*, January, EMN, http://ec.europa.eu/justice_home/doc_centre/immigration/studies/docs/emn_family_reunification_synthesis_report_jan08.pdf.

Expatica
2004 "Tracking the Dutch immigration policy", 19 May, Expatica, www.expatica.com/actual/article.asp?subchannel_id=10&story_id=7692.

Faist, T.
2000 "Transnationalism in international migration: implications for the study of citizenship and culture", *Ethnic and Racial Studies*, 23(2): 189–222.

Foner, N.
1997 "The immigrant family: cultural legacies and cultural changes", *International Migration Review*, 31(4): 961–974.

Fouron, G. and N. Glick Schiller
2001 "All in the family: gender, transnational migration and the nation-state", *Identities*, 7(4): 539–582.

Gedalof, I.
2007 "Unhomely homes: women, family and belonging in UK discourses of migration and asylum", *Journal of Ethnic and Migration Studies*, 33(1): 77-94.

Glick Schiller, N., L. Basch and C. Szanton Blanc
1995 "From immigrant to transmigrant: theorizing transnational migration", *Anthropological Quarterly*, 68(1): 48–63.

Guarnizo, L. and M.P. Smith (Eds.)
1998 *Transnationalism From Below*, Transaction Publications, New Brunswick.

Hedetoft, U.
2006 "Denmark: Integrating Migrants into a Homogenous Welfare State", *Migration Information Source*, November, MPI, Washington D.C., www.migrationinformation.org/Profiles/display.cfm?ID=485.

International Institute for Asian Studies/National Science Council
2006 Conference on Intermediated Cross-Border Marriage Migration in Asia and Europe, 18-20 September, Taipei.

Khoo, S-E.
2003 "Sponsorship of relatives for migration and immigrant settlement intention", *International Migration*, 41(5): 177-199.

Kofman, E.
2004 "Family-related migration: a critical review of European studies", *Journal of Ethnic and Migration Studies*, 30(2): 243-262.

Kofman, E. and A. Kraler
2006 "Civic stratification, gender and family migration policies in Europe", paper presented at the International Migration, Integration and Social Cohesion (IMISCOE) Cluster B3 Conference, 31 May - 1 June, Budapest.

Lahav, G.
1997 "International versus national constraints in family-reunification migration policy", *Global Governance*, 3: 349–372.

Lauth Bacas, J.
2002 *Cross-Border Marriages and the Formation of Transnational Families: A Case Study of Greek-German Couples in Athens*, Transnational Communities Programme WPTC-02-10, University of Oxford.

Le Play, F.
1871 *L'organisation de la famille selon le vrai modèle signalé par l'histoire de toutes les races et de tous les temps*, Paris.

Lethaeghe, R. and J. Surkyn
1995 "Heterogeneity in social change: Turkish and Moroccan women in Belgium", *European Journal of Population*, 11(1): 1-29.

Levitt, P. and N. Glick Schilller

2004 "Conceptualizing simultaneity: a transnational social field perspective on society", *International Migration Review*, 38(3): 1002-1039.

Liebig, T.

2007a "The Labour Market Integration of Immigrants in Germany", OECD Social, Employment and Migration Working Paper No. 47, OECD, Paris, http://www.oecd.org/dataoecd/28/5/38163889.pdf.

2007b "The Labour Market Integration of Immigrants in Australia", OECD Social, Employment and Migration Working Paper No. 49, OECD, Paris, http://www.oecd.org/dataoecd/28/12/38164878.pdf.

Lopes, P., C. Perelou and C. Balsa (Eds.)

1994 *Actes de la Conférence Européenne "Famille et mobilité humaine dans l'éspace de l'Union Européenne"*, 17-20 March. Lisbon, Commission of the European Communities D.G.V., University of Lisbon.

Malanga, S.

2006 "The Right Immigration Policy", *City Journal*, Autumn, Manhattan Institute for Policy Research, New York, http://www.city-journal.org/html/16_4_immigration_policy.html.

Martin, J.P.

2007 *Eurasylum's Monthly Policy Interviews,* with John P. Martin, Director for Employment, Labour and Social Affairs, OECD, March, www.eurasylum.org/Portal/DesktopDefault.aspx?tabindex=2&tabid=19.

McKay, R.

2003 "Family Reunification", *Migration Information Source*, May, MPI, Washington, D.C., www.migrationinformation.org/Feature/print.cfm?ID=122.

Muñoz, M-C.

1999 "Epouser au pays. Vivre en France", *Revue Européenne des Migrations Internationales*, 15(3): 101-123.

Murphy, K.

2006 "France's New Law: Control immigration Flows, Court the Highly Skilled", *Migration Information Source*, November, MPI, Washington D.C., www.migrationinformation.org/Feature/display.cfm?id=486.

Nauck, B. and B.H. Settles

2001 "Immigrant and ethnic minority families: An introduction", *Journal of Comparative Family Studies*, 32(4): 461-464.

Oezcan, V.

2003 "EU States Reach Landmark Agreement on Family Reunification Rules", *Migration Information Source*, April, MPI, Washington D.C., www.migrationinformation.org/feature/print.cfm?ID=112.

Oliynik, N.

2004 "Recent Developments in EU Immigration Law - Family Reunification Directive: Achievement or Failure of the EU Immigration Policy", EU Monitoring and Advocacy Program (EUMAP), Open Society Institute, Budapest, http://www.eumap.org/journal/features/2004/migration/pt2/eulaw.

Organisation for Economic Co-operation and Development (OECD)

2000 *Trends in International Migration: SOPEMI 2000*, OECD, Paris.

2006 *International Migration Outlook: SOPEMI 2006*, OECD, Paris.

2007 *International Migration Outlook: SOPEMI 2007*, OECD, Paris.

Ortega Pérez, N.

2003 "Spain: Forging an Immigration Policy", *Migration Information Source*, February, MPI, Washington D.C., www.migrationinformation.org/feature/print.cfm?ID=97.

Paral, R.

2005 "No Way In: U.S. Immigration Policy Leaves Few Legal Options for Mexican Workers", *Immigration Policy in Focus*, 4(5) (July), The American Immigration Law Foundation, Washington, D.C., http://www.robparal.com/downloads/nowayin.htm.

Parr, N. D. Lucas and M. Mok

2000 "Branch migration and the international dispersal of families", *International Journal of Population Geography*, 6(3): 213-227.

Parrenas, R.

2005 *Children of Global Migration. Transnational families and gendered woes*, Stanford University Press, Stanford, CA.

Pessar, P. and S. Mahler
2003 "Transnational migration: bringing gender in", *International Migration Review*, 37(3): 812-846.

Piper, N.
2004 "Rights of foreign workers and the politics of migration in South-East and East Asia", *International Migration*, 42(5): 71-97.

2006 "Gendering the politics of migration", *International Migration Review*, 40(1): 133-164.

Piper, N. and M. Roces
2003 "Introduction: Marriage and Migration in an Age of Globalization" in N. Piper and M. Roces (Eds.), *Wife or Worker: Asian Women and Migration*, Rowman and Littlefield, Lanham, Maryland, 1-21.

Portes, A., L. Guarnizo and P. Landolt
1989 "The study of transnationalism: pitfalls and promises of an emergent research field", *Ethnic and Racial Studies* 22(2): 217-237.

Regnard, C.
2006 *Immigration et présence étrangère en France en 2004*, La Documentation Française, Paris.

Richardson, S. and L. Lester
2004 *A Comparison of Australian and Canadian Migration Policies and Labour Market Outcomes*, September, DIAC, http://www.immi.gov.au/media/publications/pdf/comparison_immigration_policies.pdf.

Salt, J.
2005 "Types of migration in Europe: implications and policy concerns", European Population Conference: Demographic Challenges for Social Cohesion, Session 3 - Impact of migration on society and policies, 7-8 April, Council of Europe, Strasbourg, http://www.coe.int/t/e/social_cohesion/population/EPC_2005_S3.1%20Salt%20report.pdf.

Scalabrini Migration Center
2003-04 *Hearts Apart – Migration in the Eyes of Filipino Children*, Manila.

Sriskandarajah, D.
2005 "Dependent Variables: how migration policies treat families", Family Today, 10 March, Institute of Public Policy Research (IPPR), London, http://www.ippr.org/articles/archive.asp?id=1255&fID=55.

Southall Black Sisters (SBS)
2001 *Forced marriage: an abuse of human rights. An interim report one year after A Choice by Right*, July, SBS, Southall, Middlesex, U.K.

2004 Research and briefings: "Domestic Violence, Immigration and No Recourse to Public Funds", A briefing to amend the Domestic Violence, Crime and Victims Bill, April, Southall, Middlesex, U.K., http://www.southallblacksisters.org.uk/research.html.

United Kingdom Home Office
2000 *Control of Immigration Statistics 1999*, Home Office, London.

2001 *Secure Borders, Safe Haven: Integration with Diversity in Modern Britain*, CM 5387, Her Majesty's Stationery Office (HMSO), London, http://www.archive2.official-documents.co.uk/document/cm53/5387/cm5387.pdf.

2007 *Control of Immigration Statistics 2006*, Home Office, London.

United Kingdom Race and Europe Network (UKREN)
2007 "What is the impact of the European Integration Agenda on UK Policy", European Programme for Integration and Migration Consultation, UKREN Briefing paper, UKREN, http://www.runnymedetrust.org/uploads/projects/europe/13%20March%20UKREN.pdf.

United Nations Population Fund (UNFPA)
2006 *State of the World Population 2006 – A Passage to Hope: Women and International Migration*, UNFPA, http://www.unfpa.org/upload/lib_pub_file/650_filename_sowp06-en.pdf.

United Nations Research Institute for Social Development (UNRISD)
2005 *Gender Equality: Striving for Justice in an Unequal World*, February, UNRISD, Geneva, http://www.unrisd.org/80256B3C005BCCF9/(httpPublications)/1FF4AC64C1894EAAC1256FA3005E7201.

Van Walsum, S.
2004 "The dynamics of emancipation and exclusion: changing family norms and Dutch family migration policies", *IMIS Beiträge*, 24: 119-128.

Vatz Laaroussi, M.

2001 *Le Familial au Cœur de l'Immigration. Les Stratégies de Citoyenneté des Familles Immigrantes au Québec et en France*, L'Harmattan, Paris.

Vertovec, S.

1999 "Conceiving and studying transnationalism", *Ethnic and Racial Studies*, 22(2): 447-462.

2004 "Migrant transnationalism and modes of transformation", *International Migration Review*, 38(3): 970-1001.

Wang, H. and S. Chang

2002 "The Commodification of International Marriages: Cross-border Marriage Business in Taiwan and Viet Nam", *International Migration*, 40(6): 93-114.

Waters, J.

2001 "The Flexible Family? Recent Immigration and 'Astronaut' Households in Vancouver, British Columbia", January, RIIM Working Paper 01-02, Vancouver Centre of Excellence, http://www.riim.metropolis.net/Virtual%20Library/2001/wp0102.pdf.

workpermit.com

2006 http://www.workpermit.com (accessed 20 November 2006).

Yeoh, B., S. Huang and T. Lam

2005 "Transnationalizing the Asian family: imaginaries, intimacies and strategic intents", *Global Networks*, 5(4): 307-315.

Zlotnik, H.

1995 "Migration and the family: the female perspective", *Asia and Pacific Migration Journal*, 4(2-3): 253-271.

Textbox 6.1 - Social and Economic Costs of Migration on Family Members Left Behind - Bangladesh

Debnath, P. and N. Selim

2007 "Impact of Short Term Male Migration on Their Wives Left Behind: A Case Study of Bangladesh", September, Draft Study, IOM Dhaka.

UN-INSTRAW (United Nations International Research and Training Institute for the Advancement of Women) and International Organization for Migration (IOM)

2000 *Temporary Labour Migration of Women: Case Studies of Bangladesh and Sri Lanka*, IOM/UN-INSTRAW, Santo Domingo, Dominican Republic, http://www.un-instraw.org/en/docs/publications/tlmw.pdf.

UN-INSTRAW

2007 "Feminization of Migration 2007", Working Paper 1, Gender, Remittances and Development, UN-INSTRAW, Santo Domingo, Dominican Republic, http://www.un-instraw.org/en/downloads/gender-remittances-and-development/working-paper-1-feminization-of-migration/view.html.

INTERNAL MIGRATION*

CHAPTER 7

1. Introduction

Discussions on migration and globalization often tend to involve international migration; so much so, that the term **migration** has become synonymous with international migration. Yet, in many countries, **internal migration,** i.e. that which occurs inside the borders of a country, is actually far more important both in terms of the numbers of people involved and the resulting flow of remittances. This is especially true of countries with marked regional inequalities, but is not limited to the developing world.[1]

This chapter deals essentially with internal migration. In a slight departure from tradition, it also covers some types of cross-border migration, even though these are theoretically international movements. This is done to move away from simplistic typologies of migration that may lead to the impression that "internal" and "international" migrants are totally distinct. The borders in question are often highly porous, and the journeys undertaken are not very different from those within the country of origin. In the case of West Africa, as Adepoju (1998) notes, seasonal and short-term migrant workers regard their movements as simply an extension across national boundaries of internal movements and of rural-rural migration. In addition, in some cases it can be difficult to establish when, in fact, a traveller crosses international borders. Finally, borders often cut through the habitations of ethnic groups where their free movements across the region predates the drawing of colonial frontiers or the emergence of independent nation states and the creation of international borders and concomitant regulations governing immigration.

The chapter begins with a brief overview of the major patterns of internal migration. Rather than dwelling on what is already well known, the discussion focuses on five broad issues that have been highlighted recently in the international research and policy community and which have immediate implications for donor and government programming, namely:

- the growing incidence of temporary movements;
- internal remittance flows and their impact on development and poverty reduction;

* This chapter was written by Priya Deshingkar (Research Fellow, Rural Policy and Environment Group, Overseas Development Institute (ODI), London) and Claudia Natali (Associate Expert, Migration Policy, Research and Communications, IOM, Geneva).

1 A new study by the Centre for the Study of Living Standards has found that even a developed country like Canada received a huge boost in 2006 due to high migration from low-productivity eastern provinces to high-productivity western provinces; the study provided evidence that migration to western Canada offers jobs to unemployed people from eastern Canada (Sharpe et al., 2007). While it is worth underlining that internal migration is also making a difference in richer countries, this chapter will analyse more closely the impact on the less-developed regions of the world.

- the migration of women, children and ethnic minorities and the associated segmentation of migrant labour markets;
- the links between international and internal migration focusing on three types of movement: step migration, replacement migration and return migration; and
- undocumented or irregular cross-border migration.

It should be stressed at the outset that this chapter is concerned with voluntary migration for employment. It does not include displacement caused by development projects, conflict and civil unrest. Nor does it attempt to provide a comprehensive view on trafficking in human beings, which has become a subject in its own right. However, the divisions between migration for work and other kinds of migration are not watertight, and several forms of migration for work are akin to trafficking in human beings, especially in migration involving vulnerable and often marginalized groups, such as women, children and ethnic minorities. Some aspects of migration that overlap with trafficking will therefore be touched upon.

In the spirit of this volume, efforts have been made, where possible, to link movements with processes that have arisen as a consequence of globalization. And, finally, although this chapter is meant to be global in scope, it draws conclusions on the basis of a review of material pertaining to several, but not all, major economic and geographical regions of the world, namely East, South and Southeast Asia, Latin America, sub-Saharan Africa and the Middle East and North Africa. Gaps reflect the availability of information rather than any kind of bias.

The chapter concludes with remarks about the need for further policy development and research, recognizing the difficulties faced by internal and cross-border migrants and the need to improve their situation in order to increase the benefits of migration.

2. Broad Patterns of Internal Migration

It is well known that internal migratory flows are diverse and complex in terms of their direction (rural-rural, rural-urban, urban-urban and urban-rural); composition (men only, women only, entire families, children only, and ethnic minorities) as well as duration (seasonal, circular and permanent). Many of these exist side by side, and it is not uncommon to find in a single village several different kinds of migration streams that have evolved separately according to historical patterns of employment, social networks between source and destination areas, and the demand for specific skills.

Any discussion on internal migration patterns and trends is severely hampered by the paucity of data. Even where national data on demographics, occupations and incomes exist, short-term movements for work are not captured adequately. This creates an enormous gap in understanding migration and partly explains the lack of interest and political commitment to address it. For this reason, many of the important trends discussed below are highlighted through case studies (often undeservedly relegated to the category of anecdotal evidence) rather than large-scale surveys.

The following discussion shows that mobility has increased, especially short-term movements for work, despite the fact that regional economic trajectories are very different. Rural-urban migration appears to be the fastest growing type of internal migration in many parts of Asia, and a typical representation of such movement is illustrated in Portrait 7.1, On the other hand, Latin America and Egypt show high levels of urban-urban migration. Return migration is also significant as demonstrated by studies from West Africa and China.

Portrait 7.1

Seeking a Better Living in Ho Chi Minh City

Trung is part of a growing group of Vietnamese migrants who have left their rural home communities in search of better opportunities in the city. Born in 1979, just four years after the reunification of North and South Viet Nam, in the southern border province of Tay Ninh, life during Trung's childhood was never easy. "I was the youngest of four brothers. My parents worked in the field growing vegetables and rice. Sometimes they would also work on the rubber plantations or on government public works projects to earn additional income", Trung recalls.

His parents' hard work allowed him and his brothers to attend primary school, but, in time, educating all four children became too expensive. "When I was ten, my brothers and I began selling lottery tickets in the streets after school to support our education. However, even this was not always enough, and sometimes my parents had to borrow money to pay our tuition fees." Not wanting to accumulate debt, and realizing that of the four brothers Trung was the best student, his parents decided to concentrate their efforts on funding his education, while his older brothers took up jobs as labourers.

"Despite having been chosen by my parents to continue my education, I never felt any pressure, because I knew that my family loved and supported me," Trung says. "But it was not easy for my brothers, and when my eldest brother was sixteen, he went on foot to Cambodia to try and find work in the construction industry; but, after working there only for some weeks, he came back as he had been beaten by his employers."

In 1990, Trung's father migrated to Ho Chi Minh City, about 150 kilometres from Tay Ninh Province, to work as a security guard for a foreign company. Every month, he sent money home to support Trung's schooling, and in 1998 Trung completed secondary school. Trung soon went to join his father in the city, and they worked together for a short time at the same company.

"Having been educated in rural Tay Ninh put me at a disadvantage compared to students from Ho Chi Minh City. Still, I was able to enrol in the open university, where I studied accounting and finance. At that time, I also met some Australians in a café near my university. They wanted to learn Vietnamese, so I began teaching them for 50,000 dong per hour (about 3 US dollars). I was happy to have the extra income to buy the necessary books for my studies."

Around the same time, Trung met his wife, another migrant student from the central highlands city of Buon Me Thuot. They soon married, and the following year had a son.

"The money I earn is used to support my family. I spend about 500,000 dong (about USD 30) per month to rent a small room for my wife and son. I also send 300,000 dong (about USD 20) home to my mother who is now old, so that she can buy food and pay her bills. The rest of my income I try to save so that I can support my son's education in the future."

Trung says that it was not easy migrating to the big city. "People often looked at me strangely when they heard me speak with my rural accent. When I went to buy something, they assumed that I couldn't afford to buy certain things, as I am from the countryside. Sometimes my landlords raised my rent and my family and I had to change rooms frequently – we do not have much bargaining power, as we are not registered with the local authorities. But one day, maybe in ten years' time, my wife and I hope to buy some land and a house of our own and set up a small pharmacy. Once we have some property, we will no longer be considered as migrants."

Source: *IOM Hanoi.*

2.1 Asia: Temporary and Circular Movements for Work in Economies in Transition

There is persuasive evidence from several locations across Asia that population mobility has increased at an unprecedented rate in the last two decades. Internal regional inequalities and uneven development that characterize many Asian countries today (Balisacan et al., 2005; Kanbur and Venables, 2005) are important drivers of migration. Foreign direct investment and export-oriented industries have benefited some regions more than others and attract cheap labour from underdeveloped rural areas. The service and construction sectors are also magnets for workers.

What is especially striking is the increase in temporary and circular movements, which include a range of diverse movements from trips that last several months to daily commuting for work.[2] At the same time, there has been a dramatic improvement in communication and transport facilities, which has created the conditions for the large-scale internal movement of people at unprecedented levels.

(a) China: A life cycle strategy for people from poorer regions in a rapidly growing economy

In 2005, China had the fastest growing economy in the world and also the highest level of economic inequality in East Asia (Balisacan et al., 2005). Such internal regional differences have been an important cause of migration, especially since the mid-1990s (Song, 2004). The number of internal migrants has increased dramatically over the past two decades from about 26 million in 1988 to 126 million in 2004, a majority of whom are circular rural-urban migrants who retain strong links with their rural family. Current projections suggest that between 12 and 13 million migrants will move to urban areas each year over the next two decades, and the actual numbers will depend on the extent to which the household registration *(hukou)* system is relaxed. Around 70 per cent of migrants are aged between 16 and 35, and they generally view migration as an intermediary period in their life between leaving middle school and settling down to marry and having children (Murphy, 2006). Roughly a third of Chinese migrants return to their native homes as it is extremely difficult for them to find permanent white-collar jobs on which they would be able to retire (Murphy, 2006).

(b) South Asia: Low-skilled migrants dominate seasonal labour flows

Most South Asian economies have experienced growing inequality, mainly because of unequal access to land and education. Migrants typically come from agriculturally backward and poor areas, such as Bihar, to move to towns and cities, industrial zones and coastal areas to work in fish processing and salt panning, such as in Gujarat. High productivity agricultural areas ("green revolution areas") continue to be important, but more migrants are opting for non-farm activities because of greater returns. Moreover, they are increasingly becoming major sending areas of both skilled and less-skilled migrants to Australia, Canada and New Zealand. Migration rates are high among both the most and least educated and, unlike in East and Southeast Asia, people with little or no education appear to dominate seasonal labour flows. National statistics have underestimated the extent of mobility in the sub-region with the result that there is still some disagreement over whether it is actually increasing or decreasing. An International Monetary Fund (IMF) report states of India, for example:

> The anaemic response of cross-state migration to income differentials in India is most likely due to a combination of barriers to the mobility of labour: strong local workers' unions, which act to keep out competing potential employees; rigidities in nominal wages; lack of housing in fast-growing urban areas and, most important, social, cultural and linguistic barriers to the cross-regional substitutability of labour (Cashin and Sahay, 1996: 49).

Munshi and Rosenzweig (2005), based on panel data collected by the National Centre for Applied Economic Research, argue that India's relatively low spatial and marital mobility, despite increased growth rates and rising inequality in recent years, is due to the existence of sub-caste networks that provide mutual insurance to their members. On the other hand, a very large number of village studies show very high levels of short-term seasonal and circular internal

[2] Daily and weekly commuting are usually excluded from the category of temporary/circular migration, and this approach is followed in this chapter.

migration (for an overview, see Deshingkar, 2005). A vast majority of low-skilled workers are employed in the informal sector and are largely untouched by applicable labour laws.

In Bangladesh, too, migration is an integral part of the livelihood strategies of poor people. A three-year study on the livelihoods of the extremely poor in 16 villages by Proshika – one of the largest NGOs in Bangladesh, funded by the U.K. Department for International Development (DFID) – found that 110 of the 294 respondents had migrated. While 51 respondents said that they had benefited in some way, others spoke of theft, difficulties for those left behind and tough living conditions at the destination (Khan and Seeley, 2005). On the whole, migration to urban areas has been rising for some time, first to the urban informal sector and, more recently, to garment manufacturing units. A study of internal migration in Bangladesh (Afsar, 2003), based on the analysis of data sets generated by the United Nations, the International Labour Organization (ILO) and the Bangladesh Bureau of Statistics, showed that all types of migration had increased significantly. Rural-urban migration was found to account for nearly two-thirds of out-migration from rural areas, while rural-to-rural migration accounted for ten per cent of out-migration from rural areas, compared with 24 per cent migrating abroad.[3] The latest estimates by the Coalition for the Urban Poor of migration into the capital of Dhaka indicate a 6.3 per cent annual increase in migration. Dhaka is the most common destination because it offers greater work opportunities. Most people look for work in the garment industry, rickshaw transport and the domestic sector.

(c) Southeast Asia: Export-led growth and better infrastructure facilitates circular migration

Many Southeast Asian economies saw increases in population mobility long before the countries in South, West and Central Asia, as they opened up their economies earlier. Thailand was the earliest to implement an export-led growth strategy, and rural-urban migration, especially to the expanding service sector in Bangkok, increased during the period 1985-1990; net immigration to Bangkok more than doubled between 1975-1980 and 1985-1990 (Anh, 2003; Guest, 2003). Although the economic crisis of 1997 radically altered the economic context and migration patterns in Southeast Asia, especially for seasonal and short-term workers to the informal sector, it did not curtail or reverse the long-term growth in labour migration. Seasonal migration from the northeast of Thailand has continued on a large scale. Indeed, north-eastern households depend on remittances from their family members who migrated to Bangkok. Such seasonal movements are facilitated by extensive networks of friends and relatives spread all over the country.

Although poorer and less urbanized than Viet Nam and Thailand, Cambodia has also recently witnessed a sharp increase in rural-urban migration as more young girls and women migrate to urban centres to work in garment factories, as domestic helpers, or as bar girls and sex workers (Acharya, 2003). The Ministry of Planning estimates internal migrants at 35 per cent of the total population, and most of these internal movements are intra-provincial and very short-range (Maltoni, 2006). The garment sector was a major employer of rural-urban migrants, absorbing some 250,000 workers, but this avenue of employment may have suffered setbacks after the termination of the Multi-Fibre Agreement in early 2005.[4]

Circular migration and commuting from rural to urban areas in Indonesia has been documented since the 1970s (see e.g. Hugo, 2003). While Indonesia had relatively low levels of inequality due to more equal access to land and education, differentials

[3] On the basis of panel data generated from 62 randomly sampled villages in Bangladesh (Rahman et al., 1996).

[4] The Multi-Fibre Arrangements (MFA) (a.k.a. Agreement on Textile and Clothing (ATC)) governed the world trade in textiles and garments from 1974 through 2004, imposing quotas on the amount developing countries could export to developed countries. It expired on 1 January 2005.

have increased in the 1990s and appear to be driving internal migration to some extent.

The Viet Nam Living Standards Surveys show a rapid increase in seasonal migration over the course of the 1990s (de Brauw and Harigaya, 2004). According to Anh (2005), spontaneous inter-provincial migration occurred in three major directions during the 1990s: north to north, south to south, and north to south, while migration from the south to the north was not significant. This reflects the pull effect of the south-eastern areas and central highlands of Viet Nam in terms of economic development and natural endowments. A migration survey was carried out by the government of Viet Nam in 2004 in eleven major migrant-receiving cities and provinces covering 5,000 migrant households and an equal number of non-migrant households. The survey showed that nearly 63 per cent of those who moved for work had KT4 registration,[5] and 50 per cent of those who moved to improve their living conditions had KT4 registration (Deshingkar et al., 2006b).

Internal migration in the Philippines is a fundamental part of rural livelihood strategies and rural transformation, and not only to escape poor rural areas (Quisumbing, A.R. and S. McNiven, 2005). Research undertaken by the International Food Policy Research Institute (IFPRI) and the Research Institute for the Mindanao Culture, Xavier University (RIMCU) in the mid-1980s and repeated in 2003-2004, found that *poblaciones*[6] and cities attract better educated individuals to either find a job or further their education. The study also found that an exception to this trend was the significant migration of less educated men to nearby urban areas to engage in construction and other low-paid manual labour. However, rural-rural migration is significant, especially for first-time male migrants.

2.2 Latin America: Urbanizing Countries

Latin America as a whole has seen a rise in population movements fuelled by increasing disparities in the distribution of wealth due to globalization, restructuring of national economies and a succession of financial crises since the mid-1990s (Serageldin et al., 2004). While during the import-substitution era rural-urban migration constituted the major part of internal movements, this has recently levelled off or even decreased with urbanization. With a dwindling rural population, urban-urban migration has increased steadily since the 1980s. In Mexico, for example, between 1987 and 1992, 50 per cent of interstate movements (excluding intra-metropolitan movements) originated in and were directed at urban areas and, between 1995 and 2000, 70 per cent of all inter-municipal (*intermunicipio*)[7] movements took place between urban areas. In Brazil, 61 per cent of all inter-municipal movements between 1981 and 1991 were between cities (Cerruti and Bertoncello, 2003). In a study of internal migration in Argentina, Brazil and Chile, Busso (2006) concludes that population mobility is characterized by urban-urban movements, although, in some parts of Brazil, rural-urban migration is still high. Cities are often areas of both origin and destination in the three countries studied. In fact, a large proportion of migration on the South American continent takes place between small administrative divisions within the city and from the centre to the periphery. Intra-metropolitan movements are attracting the attention of academics and policymakers alike as they have many important consequences for urban policies (Pellegrino, 2006).

---

[5] There is a complex household registration system in Viet Nam. The system is applied in both urban and rural areas. There are four categories of residents: KT1, KT2, KT3 and KT4. The 2004 Migration Survey defines these categories as follows:
- KT1 – Person registered in the district of residence;
- KT2 – Person not registered in the district of residence, but registered at another district of the same province;
- KT3 – Person who has temporary registration for a period of six months and more;
- KT4 – Person who has temporary registration for a period of less than six months.

There is also a category of "no registration" at the destination.

[6] Primary administrative seats of rural districts in the Philippines.

[7] A *municipio* is an administrative entity corresponding roughly to a county.

Their link with issues of territorial segregation is high on the political agenda given that migrants tend to concentrate in poor areas separate from those where better-off people live. At the same time, there has been an increase in international migration, often to the United States, a theme explored in more detail later. Migrants are predominantly young, female and with an educational level higher than their non-migrant counterparts.

2.3 Sub-Saharan Africa: High Mobility, Much of it Temporary and Driven by the Need to Seek Alternatives to Farming

Results of the surveys carried out by the Network of Surveys on Migration and Urbanization in West Africa (NESMUWA) in seven countries (Burkina Faso, Côte d'Ivoire, Guinea, Mali, Mauritania, Niger and Senegal), summarized by Konseiga (2005), show very high rates of internal migration. Côte d'Ivoire and Senegal had the highest figures (62% of total migration flows) followed by Mauritania (54%), Mali and Guinea (51%) and Niger (47%). Burkina Faso had the lowest internal migration incidence (30%), probably due to the limited work opportunities available locally and the exodus of migrants to Côte d'Ivoire.

East Africa is not different. The 1999 Labour Force Survey (LFS) in Ethiopia shows high rates of internal mobility with rural–rural flows (as opposed to stocks) dominating and involving nearly a million people. Urban-urban migration accounted for a further million people and rural-urban flows are also significant and account for over half a million people (Casacchia et al., 2001). Reverse migration, i.e. urban-rural migration, was also recorded, involving around 370,000 people even though counter-urbanization is not yet the dominant process in Ethiopia. The LFS analysis found that the change of residence for employment purposes (looking for a job or job transfer) accounts for about a quarter (23%)[8] of all migration, and the majority of these movements are towards urban centres.

The importance of temporary migration for work is evident in many areas. Research conducted under the International Network for the Demographic Evaluation of Populations and their Health (INDEPTH) migration and urbanization project in eight countries (Burkina Faso, Ethiopia, Ghana, Kenya, Mozambique, South Africa, Tanzania and Uganda) between 1996 and 2001 by a consortium of researchers from Brown University, the University of Pennsylvania and the University of Witwatersrand among others, found that internal migration accounted for 15 to 25 per cent of the sample population and that much of it was temporary (Choi, 2003).

Recent studies indicate that mobility has been affected by economic crises and structural adjustments. Country studies conducted under the De-agrarianization and Rural Employment project (DARE) and the Sustainable Livelihoods, Access and Mobility (SLAM) project by Bryceson and others (2003) found increased mobility resulting from structural adjustment programmes, which, in turn, led to occupational diversification and increased travel. There are also examples of reduced mobility, as seen in Zimbabwe, where the fear of contracting AIDS and a rise in oil prices has curtailed travel (Bryceson and Mbara, 2003).

On the whole, although rural-urban and rural-rural migrations are still significant, the incidence of return migration, i.e. urban-rural, is rising in some countries. In Nigeria, retrenchment of workers in both the public and private sectors in the 1980s is thought to have increased return migration. Indeed, a study of Aba and its surrounding area in south-

8 It is noteworthy that some of the movements classified as "along with family" may be included in the categories of migration for work reasons, since they derive from the decision of the head of the household to migrate for work (Casacchia et al., 2001). See Chapter 6 for a more detailed analysis of the link between employment and family mobility.

eastern Nigeria by Okali and others (2001) found that nearly half the households in rural areas are headed by return migrants, who average about 50 years of age. In Ghana, about 35 per cent of migratory movements were urban-rural, 32 per cent rural-rural and almost one quarter (23%) urban-urban (Ghana Living Standards Survey, 2000).

2.4 Middle East and North Africa: Internal Movements are often more Significant than International Movements with Public Sector Downsizing an Important Cause

In the Middle East and North Africa (MENA), internal migration has increased with public sector downsizing (Al-Ali, 2004) and the resulting occupational diversification. Nonetheless, long-distance rural–urban migration to Cairo from Upper Egypt is a long-standing phenomenon that has existed for at least a hundred years. Greater Cairo, which includes Cairo, Giza, and Qualyoubyya governorates, attracted the bulk of internal migrants as shown by a number of studies mentioned in Zohry (2005). But successive censuses show only a slight increase in rural-urban migration. In contrast, return migration, i.e. urban-rural, has increased steadily and accounted for nearly a quarter (23%) of all movements in 1996. Urban-urban migration represented the bulk of movements (60.4% in 1996) between the large governorates of Cairo, Guiza, Qualyoubyya and Alexandria. Rural-rural migration was the least important type of movement, remaining at around four per cent at each census.

Internal migration in Morocco continues to be more important than international movements in numerical terms, notwithstanding the high number of international migrants originating from this country (De Haas, 2005). Interestingly, De Haas (2005) notes that patterns of rural-to-urban migration have changed lately, which is particularly the case in the provinces of the interior, as the policies of decentralization and improved road and electricity infrastructure favoured the growth of urban centres in rural areas. Therefore, urbanization and partial "de-agrarianization" are general processes that occur also within rural Morocco, as so-called rural populations increasingly earn additional income outside the traditional agricultural sector.

3. Cross-border Migration

The issue of cross-border migration needs to be viewed together with internal migration, especially for countries that are separated by porous borders and populated by people who are historically very similar in language and culture.

Ratha and Shaw (2007) assert, on the basis of datasets constructed by the University of Sussex,[9] that almost 80 per cent of South-South migration takes place across the land borders of adjacent countries and appears to occur between countries with relatively small differences in income. However, official statistics cannot capture the vast numbers of undocumented cross-border migrants.

An analysis of examples of cross-border migration in Africa and Southeast Asia will serve to illustrate the similarities with internal migration and the rationale for considering both types of movements within the same framework.

The NESMUWA surveys in Burkina Faso, Côte d'Ivoire, Guinea, Mali, Mauritania, Niger and Senegal recorded more than 6.4 million migratory movements between 1988 and 1992, of which 2.3 million were international, with flows between Côte d'Ivoire and Burkina Faso dominating. However, migration from Burkina Faso to Côte d'Ivoire has since dropped significantly due to the economic recession in the latter country. This has also been accompanied by return flows of migrants from urban areas of Côte

9 The bilateral migration matrix was created for the Global Trade Analysis Project using national censuses, population registers, national statistical bureaux and a number of secondary sources (OECD, ILO, Migration Policy Institute (MPI), DFID, UNDP) to compile bilateral migrant stocks for 162 countries.

d'Ivoire. Most of the return migrants are active (93.8%) and are entrepreneurs.

The circular migration[10] by West Africans dates back to the pre-colonial period. This process has received a boost with the increasing liberalization of economies. New communication technologies are helping to consolidate historical social networks between peoples who are ethnically and linguistically similar, but artificially separated by political borders. This has led to unprecedented levels of flows of information, ideas, people, goods and money (Balbo and Marconi, 2005). The circularity of the movements allows migrants, a large proportion of whom are women, to maximize the returns from seasonal agricultural production.

The other major area of cross-border migration in Africa is to South Africa from countries in the sub-region, especially Lesotho, Mozambique and Zimbabwe. South Africa is home to an estimated three to eight million migrants, most of whom are employed in the mining industry (Stalker, 2000, cited in Sanders and Maimbo, 2003).

In Southeast Asia, Thailand has emerged as the major destination for migrants in the entire Greater Mekong Sub-region (GMS). As Thailand's own population has aged and the economy has grown, the demand for foreign labour has increased, especially for low-skilled labour. Thailand currently hosts an estimated 2.5 million migrants from Cambodia, Laos and Myanmar (Maltoni, 2006) with nearly 90 per cent in an irregular status (World Bank, 2005). Thousands of border crossers from Myanmar flow into the Thai border town of Mae Sot every year. Most of them are looking for economic opportunities and are not eligible for refugee status. An estimated 50 per cent of Mae Sot's 80,000 migrant workers from Myanmar do not have proper work permits, which leaves them open to abuse from unscrupulous bosses, most of whom run garment factories (BBC News, 26 February 2007). Many others, especially women, commute on a daily basis from Cambodia to Thailand for petty trade, domestic work or agriculture, as the two countries share a very long and porous border. Men tend to migrate farther afield and for longer durations (Godfrey et al., 2001). Finally, in South Asia, India has a long history of migration from Bangladesh. Poorly demarcated borders between the two countries, cultural affinities (language and lifestyle) with certain Indian provinces such as West Bengal, physical proximity and the presence of earlier migrants contribute to the acceptance of these migrants as de facto members of local communities. These factors also explain why the largest numbers of migrants are believed to be concentrated in north-eastern India, close to the Bangladesh border, even though this region is not as economically robust as other areas in India that are now witnessing increased inflows from Bangladesh (Ramachandran, 2005).

4. Internal and International Labour Migration

The links between internal and international labour migration have recently begun to attract attention at the international policy level, especially in response to concerns by developed countries over migrant flows. Important questions are whether today's internal migrants are tomorrow's international migrants; whether international migration and internal migration are substitutes for each other; and whether internal and international migrants share the same profile. Needless to say, the answers depend very much on the local context and thus can only be arrived at through location-specific case studies. In very broad terms, the links between internal and international migration are of three types: step migration, where people move to one or more locations within their country before emigrating to

[10] Circular migration here refers to the livelihood strategy that has been traditional in West Africa for over 1,000 years as people followed livestock and crops on a seasonal basis; this concept therefore differs slightly from what is currently put forward in the European Union (EU) as a temporary labour migration policy (see Chapter 11): "Circular migration is a form of mobility that most closely ties migrants to their countries of origin, and allows them to build bridges between it and other (usually more developed) countries, thereby creating opportunity for the migrant's country of origin to make the most of its comparative advantages" (MPI, 2007: 3).

another country; replacement migration,[11] where the "vacuum" created by workers departing for another country is filled by workers from other parts within the country; and return migration, where people who had migrated return to their place/region of origin. These processes are illustrated through examples from different parts of the world.

The occurrence of replacement migration, whereby migrants of rural origin move to towns to fill jobs left vacant by nationals who have emigrated to other countries, can be observed in several sub-Saharan African countries (Adepoju, 2006). In Burkina Faso, Gabon, Côte d'Ivoire, Mali and Senegal, replacement migration has occurred where urban workers migrated to France. It has also been noted in Egypt (Zohry, 2005) where people have migrated to the Gulf. Replacement migration has also been documented in the Indian state of Kerala where the gaps in the workforce left by skilled workers leaving for the Gulf are filled by migrants from the neighbouring states (Zacharia and Rajan, 2005).

Step migration, i.e. rural-to-urban movement followed by international migration, has also been observed in Mexico by Fussel (2004), using the Mexican Migration Project dataset. She finds that, while the movement from the central-western rural area of Mexico to the United States still predominates and is reinforced by well-established social networks, there is a newer stream of migrants from interior urban communities. Using econometric analysis, she identifies within this group a sub-stream of migrants who first settle in the northern region (border urban community of Tijuana) and then, in a second phase, emigrate to the United States. Step migration to the border is a way to gain migration-related information and to improve one's chance to make it to the U.S., with or without authorization (Fussel, 2004). Fussel also finds that some returnees relocate to border regions to facilitate their next documented or undocumented trips to the U.S.

Morocco is another country where rural-urban migration often is a precursor of international migration (Laghout, 1989, cited in De Haas, 2005). But in this Maghreb country, the link between internal and international migration is not limited to only international out-migration from small towns within rural provinces, as the concomitant counter flow of remittances contributes to employment and entrepreneurial opportunities, creating an opposite movement of internal migration (i.e. from urban provinces to towns in rural provinces) (De Haas, 2005).

But not all cases are as clear-cut. A recent study in Egypt by Zohry (2005) found that people migrate internally and externally without any logical order or common pattern. In fact, buying a bus ticket to Libya is not much different from internal migration to Cairo or Alexandria. Pieke's (2004) work on migrants from Fujian Province shows that Chinese emigration has become much more intertwined with socio-economic changes and migratory flows within China itself. Many of the migrants they studied had spent considerable time elsewhere in China, or had worked for a few years in Singapore, or in the Macao SAR or Hong Kong SAR on fixed-term contracts before returning to Fujian and subsequent emigration to Europe. They also found that international migration in Fuqing in coastal Fuzhou prefecture was often supported financially by wives or other female family members circulating or commuting into nearby Putian county to work in factories producing shoes and other consumer items. Conversely, areas of emigration in Fujian attract in-migrants from elsewhere in Fujian or farther afield to undertake agricultural work that the local population either does not want or cannot do because of their absence.

What these examples illustrate is that even those who live in rural areas may be indirectly benefiting

[11] While the UN refers to replacement migration as the "international migration that a country would need to offset population decline and population ageing resulting from low fertility and mortality rates" (UN, 2001), it is defined here as the internal movement of workers in response to international migration.

from international migration by filling jobs that international migrants have left behind. They also respond to the demand created by the flow of remittances from abroad. However, it is not clear how these patterns will change in the longer term and more empirical research is needed. Moreover, there are no clear-cut policy implications, and governments in Europe and North America endeavouring to regulate immigration through interventions aimed at interrupting these migratory chains and steps find that there are no easy solutions. However, creating more attractive employment opportunities in countries of origin by facilitating the flow of remittances (among other strategies) is something that governments in both source and destination areas need to heed.

5. Labour Market Segmentation and the Migration of Ethnic Minorities

Circular migration is largely driven by labour market segmentation, as populations in prosperous destination areas are, or become, reluctant to perform low-wage, low-status, seasonal or physically demanding work. More often than not, the dirtiest, most dangerous and most difficult jobs ("3D" jobs) are performed by migrants who belong to the lowest segments of society; lower castes and tribes in the case of India, and ethnic minorities elsewhere. Segmentation is best captured through in-depth case studies that gather detailed information on ethnicity, occupations and seasonal movements.

5.1 Castes

Several case studies from India show that the lower castes and tribes have a greater propensity to migrate, and many of them migrate for short-term, low-skilled and low-paid work with the highest levels of vulnerability and lowest levels of social protection.[12] There are sharp sub-divisions even within caste categories with particular sub-castes doing particular kinds of work. In Bihar, for example, a recent study (Deshingkar et al., 2006a) found that the *Musahars*, who were traditionally landless rat-catchers and have largely remained on the fringes of society, almost always migrate for work in brick kilns, as casual construction labourers, farm workers and rickshaw pullers. Their earnings are too low to result in any savings and working conditions are difficult and degrading. Another study found that tribal girls from Jharkhand are employed as domestic maids in Delhi. All of these occupations involve strong elements of exploitation and bondage. Migration offers Scheduled Castes (SCs) and Scheduled Tribes (STs)[13] an escape from traditional structures of caste-based oppression in villages and gives poor labourers some bargaining power vis-à-vis their traditional employers. However, some analysts maintain that structures of oppression are reproduced through labour contracting arrangements at the destination and may even be more exploitative (Mosse, 2002; Olsen and Ramanamurthy, 2000).

5.2 Ethnic Minorities

In Viet Nam, ethnic minorities accounted for over four per cent of total recorded movements in 2001 (Anh, 2005). Detailed information on employment patterns collected under the 2004 migration survey conducted by the Government of Viet Nam shows that migrants belonging to minority groups earn half

[12] Deshingkar and Start (2003), for example, found that the scheduled tribes had higher migration rates in the Indian states of Andhra Pradesh and Madhya Pradesh. Similar observations have been made by Dayal and Karan (2003) regarding Jharkhand: whereas 15 per cent of scheduled castes and tribes migrated, only eight per cent of upper castes and three per cent of "other backward castes" migrated. A study by Jagori (2001), an NGO on migration in Rajasthan, found that 95 per cent of the migrants congregating at recruiting centres are *dalits* (*dalits*, often called untouchables or outcasts, have historically been prevented from doing any but the most menial jobs) coming from Bhilwara, Ajmer, Tonk and Kota. The latest Human Development Report for the State of Punjab notes that many migrants coming into the State from Bihar and Uttar Pradesh are *dalits* and tribals.

[13] SCs and STs are the lowest castes and most vulnerable persons in the Indian Caste System.

as much as those from the Kinh majority, are far less likely to have a work contract, or to receive help to find a job, and are far less likely to find work in a government organization (Deshingkar et al., 2006b). In Indonesia, too, minorities have faced difficulties in integrating into mainstream labour markets due to language differences. There are more than 200 distinctive ethno-linguistic groups in Indonesia, and although universal education has helped to some extent, difficulties in integrating in the mainstream remain.

6. The Internal and Cross-border Migration of Women and Children

6.1 Children

The independent migration of children (i.e. without their parents) appears to be very prevalent in certain regions such as West Africa and South Asia. Child migration has received much attention recently because of its similarities to trafficking, given the involvement of intermediaries, exploitation and infringements of rights. According to one estimate, approximately one to 1.2 million children are trafficked globally each year, and most of those in or from Africa originate from the West African region (Beyrer, 2004, quoted in Kiell and Sanogo, 2002). Burkina Faso has a high incidence of child migration. For example, a World Bank study by Kielland and Sanogo (2002) estimated that around 330,000, or 9.5 per cent of children aged between six and 17 years, lived away from their parents. Of these, 165,000 migrated for work, with poverty being the main reason for migrating. However, as case studies have shown, there are more sides to this phenomenon than blatant exploitation. For example, Hashim's (2005) study of the extremely poor Bawku East District of the Upper East Region in the very north-eastern corner of Ghana found that children viewed migration as a positive opportunity. Moreover, case studies on child migration in West Africa, published by the Development Research Centre on Migration, Globalisation and Poverty at the University of Sussex, point to the negative, but also the positive aspects of this labour mobility. On the one hand, they confirm that young migrants are vulnerable – as shown by their efforts to obtain work, to remain in work, to receive their wages and to avoid being cheated or manipulated. On the other hand, these studies also give a strong sense that such children are not just passive victims of circumstances and that motivation for migrating often involves the child's own desire to earn an income (Anarfi et al., 2007).

Kiell and Sanogo (2002) also found that poor rural families see it as desirable, or even a good investment, to send a child to the city or abroad to work. This is probably why NGO and government initiatives to return trafficked children to their villages have sometimes been met with an unhappy response from children, incredulity from parents and teasing and humiliation from the children's peer group (Black et al., 2004). A much more differentiated and sensitive approach is needed, one that understands the aspirations of the poor and creates the conditions to enable them to better look after their children at home.

6.2 Women

There is no doubt that migration is becoming increasingly feminized, and this development has been driven by two main factors. On the one hand, the improved access of females to education and training opportunities has enhanced their employability in the organized labour market, locally and across national boundaries (Adepoju, 2006), but, on the other, women have also been obliged to seek additional income-generating activities to support the family due to the loss of male employment following structural adjustment policies. Adepoju (2006) notes, for example, that the traditional pattern of migration in sub-Saharan Africa – male-dominated, long-term and long-distance – is rapidly changing as more women migrate. Women in West Africa work mainly in the informal sector, which is less affected by economic recession compared to the wage sector, where most male migrants work. As the formal job market becomes tighter many families are relying on women to earn money. Bah et al. (2003) draw on research in six case studies in Mali, Nigeria and Tanzania and point out that the great increase in female migration in Africa in recent years is linked to employment opportunities as domestic workers in urban centres or in new international tourist resorts. They also highlight that women's migration is increasingly acceptable socially in as much as it contributes to their family's household income through remittances

The INDEPTH surveys between 1996 and 2001 found that female migrants outnumbered male migrants in five sites and were equal at the other two. Female migrants are on average younger than male migrants. In particular, those aged between 15 and 35 years have the highest propensity to migrate. The 1999 Labour Force Survey in Ethiopia showed that roughly 55 per cent of migrants are women.

South African internal migration has also become more feminized as a recent study has shown (Posel, 2004). Overall, the migration of women has risen steadily between 1960 and 2000.

Bryceson et al. (2003) argue that the migration of women and children increased with the diversification of household livelihood strategies in response to the growing pressure on land and the deterioration of the international terms of trade for African small producers. Households increasingly abandoned the traditional pattern of growing food crops and relying on male migrant earnings in favour of one where everyone earns and non-farm activities are becoming central.

In Southeast Asia and Latin America the feminization of migration streams exceeds that of many other regions of the world. In Thailand, women are employed in five major export-oriented, labour-intensive industries, namely: the manufacture of small electrical appliances, electronics and computer parts; textiles and garments; chilled, frozen and canned food; precious stones and jewellery; and footwear. Work in the sex trade is also significant; however, while it provides more disposable income to women and their families at home, it also puts them at great personal risk. Cambodia experienced a sharp increase in female migration as more young girls and women migrated to urban areas to work in garment factories, as domestic helpers, beer girls and sex workers (Acharya, 2003). A similar trend can be observed in Viet Nam as female labour migration to Ha Noi and Ho Chi Minh City is increasing (Anh, 2005), reflecting a large demand for female workers in labour-intensive manufacturing (textiles, garments, footwear and food processing), commerce and service jobs (shopkeepers, housemaids, street vendors, café/restaurant workers, entertainers and trash collectors).

On the one hand, segmented labour markets reduce competition among migrants because different groups of migrants occupy different niches; but, on the other, there are also negative aspects that require urgent policy attention because the niches occupied by the most vulnerable and historically subjugated are often unregulated and authorities may turn a blind eye to exploitation.

7. Remittances, Poverty and Development

Remittances are an important additional or even principal economic resource for poor rural households worldwide, helping them to smooth income flows and to invest in assets and human capital. Yet, internal remittance flows are seriously under-reported, especially flows through informal channels.

Although generalizations are risky, there is some evidence to support the view that internal circular migrants often bring back more money than the remittances sent home by permanent migrants. For example, Van der Geest's study in Ghana (2003) found that seasonal migrant earnings amounted to about seven per cent of total household income and 14 per cent of the total cash income (while remittances from permanent migrants abroad accounted for 3% and 5%, respectively). Other contributions included food, clothes and payment of school fees. Rural-urban migrants usually send money, and rural-rural migrants are more likely to send food. As a cash earner, seasonal labour migration was more important than livestock production and the sale of food crops.

In Bangladesh, the Coalition for the Urban Poor (CUP) estimates that migrants in Dhaka remit up to 60 per cent of their income to relatives. For the receiving households, remittances provide up to 80 per cent of the household budget. A recent study in the poor Indian state of Bihar, from where very large numbers of migrants leave to work in small industries all over India, also found very high levels of remittances among circular migrants. These migrants, who are away for eight to nine months in a year leave mainly to earn and send money back home, and migration is part of the life-cycle planning of extended families. When the sons reach an age where they can begin to migrate, the fathers stay at home to look after the family farm (Deshingkar et al., 2006a).

7.1 Impacts at the Household Level

Earlier analyses questioned the significance of remittances in the household budget as well as their impact on poverty reduction (see, for example, Lipton, 1980), and many scholars still maintain that migration is mainly a distress phenomenon that perpetuates poverty (cf. Breman (1985, 1996)) and Reddy (1990) on India, and Blessing (2005) on Ethiopia). However, they rarely examine the counter-factual proposition, i.e. what these people would have done in the absence of the opportunity to migrate, and what their life prospects would have been in their villages.

Recent case studies show that even small migration earnings can contribute to household well-being (see for example, Deshingkar and Start (2003) on Andhra Pradesh and Madhya Pradesh; Deshingkar et al., (2006) on Bihar; Haberfeld et al. (1999) on Rajasthan and Dayal, and Karan (2003) on Jharkhand).

7.2 Impacts on the Source Economy

The development and poverty reduction impact of remittances remains disputed, but there is ample evidence to support the argument that remittances can lead to overall economic development.

On the one hand, remittances have often been seen as "disequalizing" because receivers are typically better off than their fellow villagers. It is known that migrants usually come from poor regions, although not necessarily the poorest regions, and that they are often poor but not the poorest of the poor since the poorest lack even the most basic resources (e.g. labour, information, social networks) needed to migrate (de Haan, 2005). Moreover, there is evidence that the degree of inequality in remittances-receiving villages will depend on the actual use of remittances. An empirical study by Barham and Boucher (1998) in Nicaragua adopts a "counter-factual approach" (i.e. the observed income distribution is compared to a counter-factual scenario without migration and remittances) to determine the impact of remittances on inequality. The study highlights that conclusions depend on the way remittances are treated in the analysis: when they are used as a substitute for home earnings, they tend to increase income inequality in the receiving community, while, when treated as an exogenous factor, they decrease inequality.

On the other hand, on the basis of research in Bangladesh, Afsar (2003) argues that remittances help to expand business in agricultural products and construction materials. Remittances also help to generate savings, the major source of capital in the absence of institutional credit on easy terms. She believes that migration and remittances have invigorated the land tenancy market in rural areas: the proportion of tenant farmers increased from 42 per cent to 57 per cent between 1988 and 2000, and the land under tenancy cultivation rose to 33 per cent, which was 11 per cent more than in 1988. Studies conducted in Thailand by Guest (1998) show that remittances are an important supplement to household income and have a multiplier effect on the economy, with many major items of expenditure, such as construction materials and labour, procured locally. Anh (2003) draws similar conclusions based on data from Bangladesh, China, Viet Nam and the Philippines. Cai Fang (2001) writes that migration contributed 16 per cent annually to the growth in China's GDP in recent years (Cai Fang, 2001, quoted in De Wind and Holdaway, 2005). Similarly, the ILO study on internal migration in Indonesia (2004) concludes that migration to urban areas can be associated with macroeconomic growth.

Any positive impacts notwithstanding, internal and cross-border migration is full of risks and costs that can reduce the benefits, especially for poor families (Textbox 7.1).

Textbox 7.1

The Hazards of Internal and Cross-Border Migration

Internal and cross-border migrants often face difficulties on account of their poverty and powerlessness. Among the many hardships are:

- debt bondage – many borrow to migrate;
- long working hours;
- living in the open or in very poor accommodation with inadequate water and sanitation;
- vulnerability to sexual abuse;
- restriction of freedom and movement because of fear of arrest and/or deportation on account of migrants' irregular status;
- lack of safety and vulnerability to criminals;
- dangerous, dirty and difficult working conditions;
- lack of access to health services and vulnerability to HIV/AIDS;
- unreliable and unsafe remittance systems;
- difficulties in registering with the local authorities;
- discrimination;
- language barriers;
- difficulty in contacting the family in the village of origin (although this is improving rapidly with the spread of mobile telephone networks);
- lack of information about rights, entitlements and the applicable law in general;
- inability of children to gain access to schooling;
- inability to access assistance and government services.

8. The Future and Directions for Policy

Internal migration will continue as long as regional inequalities persist. Circular migration will continue as long as land and other rural ties have a significant economic and cultural value and urban conditions are not secure enough to enable more permanent settlement. However, cross-border migration trajectories also depend on a range of other factors, including relations between the countries in question, demographic and economic trends, and levels of skills and education.

The Delphi Consultations,[14] conducted by the Italian organization CeSPI (Centro Studi Politica

[14] CeSPI and SID used the Delphi methodology to bring together international experts and researchers in an online discussion to analyze migration and development from various viewpoints. Delphi is a formal and iterative process of survey and discussion often used in the private sector to bring large groups of experts to a consensus estimate on the underlying drivers and assumptions.

Internazionale) and SID (Society for International Development) with the assistance of the Director General for Cooperation of the Italian Ministry of Foreign Affairs, were undertaken to forecast the pattern of migratory movements likely to emerge in Africa. Mazzali et al. (2006) assess the outcomes of a series of interviews with experts in the field of migration and development representing varying viewpoints and come to the conclusion that the largest migrations are likely to take place within continental boundaries. Similarly, the West Africa Long-Term Perspective Study (WALTPS), conducted by the Club du Sahel and the OECD (Cour and Snrech, 1998), warns that West Africa must come to terms with particularly high rates of intra-regional migration flows and rapid urbanization. Migration will continue from landlocked countries to the rest of Africa under the increasing constraints of climatic changes and environmental limits, as well as the demand for migrant labour in coastal countries. Such mobility is expected to reduce inequalities and foster growth.

Forecasts of labour mobility and migration trends in Asia, prepared by the Economist Intelligence Unit (2006), indicate that in all major Asian countries, especially the Philippines, Malaysia and India, but not Japan, working-age populations will increase. A positive outlook for economic growth of the region as a whole will drive demand for labour up to 2015. China will have one of the lowest growth rates because of its rapidly ageing population and as its working-age population is expected to peak by the early 2020s and decline thereafter.

In absolute terms, China and India will see the largest increases in working-age populations by 2015 (88 million and 148 million, respectively), followed by Indonesia and the Philippines. However, HIV/AIDS could impact on changes to the size of the working-age population.

9. Policy Developments

9.1 Policies Aimed at Labour Supply and Demand

Few countries have taken a progressive attitude towards rural-urban migration. In sub-Saharan Africa, for instance, current policies do not suggest that such is the case concerning either internal or cross-border migration. Adebusoye (2006) considers that in most African governments there is as yet insufficient awareness of the poverty reduction effects of internal migration. This view is supported by the UN (2002) review of policies affecting migration in sub-Saharan Africa, which shows that governments are averse or at best neutral to migration, especially rural-urban migration. This is based on the concern that movements from rural to urban areas burden urban services, and that housing, education, health and various welfare provisions will be strained because of a sudden influx of migrants, which is indeed the case as urban authorities are ill prepared to receive migrants. The focus of African governments has been on underdevelopment, poverty, socio-economic instability, population pressure on limited natural resources, and conflict as drivers of migration. Their main goal is to reduce migration and limit the formation of urban slums.

Similarly, internal migration was until very recently viewed negatively by many policymakers in Asia. Most governments have tried to control rural-urban movements through a combination of rural employment creation programmes, anti-slum drives and restricting entry to urban areas. However, this limited approach is changing for a variety of reasons, including: a) ineffectiveness of controls; b) the value of migration to poor households and growing industries becoming more visible; and c) the growing strength of the political voice of migrant workers. China is at the forefront of efforts to recognize the importance of internal migration, and the government is testing labour migration agreements between provinces of origin and destination.[15] The Ministry of Labour and Social Security has announced several measures aimed at improving conditions for millions of farmer-workers currently working in cities. The measures include approaching companies to abolish all limitations and unreasonable fees on workers seeking employment, and for charges for information and consultations provided by public agencies to migrants looking for work to be dropped. Local governments have been asked to establish professional training and education plans for workers. However, while controls on population movements have been relaxed, the right to settle still remains restricted under the household registration (*hukou*) system, which excludes rural migrant workers from claiming state benefits in urban areas as long as they remain registered in their place of origin.

A number of events in India have also signalled a change of attitude to internal migration in the country. There have been two high-level policy dialogues on internal migration and its potentially positive impact since 2005, and consultations at state level have been organized with the help of U.K. (DFID) funding by the Gramin Vikas Trust. Two state governments, Madhya Pradesh and Rajasthan, are actively engaged in developing policies to reduce the hardships faced by migrants. Rajasthan is piloting mobile ration cards[16] for 5,000 migrants, while Madhya Pradesh is introducing a comprehensive migrant support programme (see the next section on migrant support). At this point, it is difficult to say whether other states are likely to follow.

Viet Nam has an elaborate and complex KT registration system[17] for residents in urban and rural areas, which restricts access to government services outside the authorized location of residence/work. The fact that the government conducted a special survey on internal migration, among other key issues, to understand the difficulties faced by migrants, is in itself an indication of their concern to make migration less costly and risky.

In the case of cross-border migration, bilateral and multilateral agreements in such areas as trade, migration, financial channels, labour standards and information have a particularly important role to play in regulating migration and maximizing the potential returns for both areas of origin and destination (see also Chapter 13). Adepoju (2006) welcomes the determination of the Economic Community of West African States (ECOWAS)[18] to abolish rigid residence permits and introduce modern border procedures, information sharing and staff exchange programmes. The adoption of an ECOWAS passport as a symbol of unity to progressively replace national passports over a period of ten years is intended to advance the concept of a borderless sub-region (Adepoju, 2002; see also Textbox 13.2). The Common Market for East and Southern Africa's (COMESA) Protocol on Free Movement of Persons has been established, but has not made much progress so far on the free movement of workers owing to the reservations of some of its member states,[19] notably South Africa, which is the major recipient of migrant workers. Peberdy and Crush (1998) point out that within the Southern African Development Community (SADC)[20], agreements on free trade have been much more successful than

[15] Personal communication with Hans van de Glind, Manager/Chief Technical Advisor, ILO Programme on the Elimination of Child Labour (ILO-IPEC) project to prevent trafficking in girls and young women for labour exploitation in China (CP-TING project).

[16] Ration cards are issued to poor families in India to enable them to access subsidized foodgrains and other essentials. But entitlements through ordinary ration cards are based on proof of residence and cannot be transferred to another location.

[17] See n. 5 above.

[18] ECOWAS members are Benin, Burkina Faso, Cape Verde, Côte d'Ivoire, Gambia, Ghana, Guinea, Guinea Bissau, Liberia, Mali, Niger, Nigeria, Senegal, Sierra Leone and Togo.

[19] COMESA members are Angola, Burundi, Comoros, Democratic Republic of the Congo (DRC), Djibouti, Egypt, Eritrea, Ethiopia, Kenya, Libya, Madagascar, Malawi, Mauritius, Rwanda, Seychelles, Sudan, Swaziland, Uganda, Zambia and Zimbabwe. The Protocol on Free Movement of Persons has not yet entered into force. Members need to ratify the Protocol for it to come into force, and only four have done so to date.

[20] SADC Members are Angola, Botswana, DRC, Lesotho, Madagascar, Malawi, Mauritius, Mozambique, Namibia, South Africa, Swaziland, Tanzania, Zambia, and Zimbabwe.

those on free movement. In South Asia, the main focus of the South Asian Association for Regional Co-operation (SAARC) is on trade and transport rather than migration. The SAARC is working towards a South Asian Customs Union by 2015 and a South Asian Economic Union by 2020, which will have a bearing on the intra-regional mobility of the people of South Asia. However, progress has been slow so far.

Similarly, in Latin America a proposal within the Common Market of the South (MERCOSUR) for the gradual implementation of free movement of persons in the Southern Cone for Latin America was not followed up due to the subsequent redefinition of MERCOSUR,[21] and the current focus is mostly on the free movement of goods and capital (Maguid, 2007).

In Southeast Asia, efforts are being undertaken to match labour supply and demand across the borders of adjacent countries in a regular and orderly manner with a view to countering trafficking in human beings. For example, a Memorandum of Understanding has been drawn up between the Thai and Cambodian governments to create a bilateral administrative process for structured employment procedures regarding inter alia recruitment, a mechanism for the return of migrant workers at the end of their contract, labour protection guidelines and prevention and intervention mechanisms to combat irregular migration and human trafficking. However, the rules and procedures have been criticized for their complexity and lack of user-friendliness. In the meantime, people continue to move and face unnecessary hardship because they are often perceived as engaging in unauthorized activities (Maltoni, 2006).

Efforts are being made to reduce the costs and risks of migration in some countries, for instance in China, and by civil society organizations in others, such as in India and Viet Nam, often with donor support.

9.2 Migrant Support

(a) China

The Chinese Ministry of Labour and Social Security has rescinded the working card requirement for migrant farmer-workers in urban locations. Previously, farmers needed such permits to work outside their place of birth. The ministry has also asked local labour and social security departments to reform policies and cancel illegal charges targeting migrant workers. In addition, it is working on a draft law on household registration management to create conditions for free movement and settlement.

The All-China Federation of Trade Unions has submitted a proposal to the Legal Committee of the Chinese People's Political Consultative Conference, suggesting the ministry concerned issue a law concerning rural migrant employees to safeguard their legal rights, and advising the State Council to establish a special working committee on the protection of migrants.

The ILO CP-TING project in China, which aims to prevent the trafficking of young women and girls for labour, has succeeded in raising the level of understanding of migration and trafficking among policymakers. Hans van de Glind, project manager, believes that migration will continue and many will use irregular channels if regular channels are not made available.[22] This puts migrants at risk of trafficking and exploitation, as it is very difficult to protect the rights of migrant workers if their movement is not through safe channels. The project is trying to develop cheap, fast and transparent labour migration channels on a larger scale, geared especially towards those with low education and skills.

[21] MERCOSUR members are Argentina, Brazil, Paraguay and Uruguay

[22] See n. 15 above.

(b) India

In India, a large number of migrant support initiatives have emerged over the last two years, which can be broadly classified into five categories:

(i) The social protection model

This model provides a range of subsidized support services. Social protection aims to reduce poverty and vulnerability by promoting efficient labour markets, limiting risk exposure and enhancing the capacity of migrants to protect themselves against hazards and the interruption or loss of income. A well-known example is the DFID-funded Migrant Labour Support Programme implemented by the Gramin Vikas Trust. The project provides a range of services to migrants moving to the states of Gujarat and Rajasthan from poor tribal districts of Madhya Pradesh. These include identity cards issued through local government bodies, job information, creating awareness on rights, assistance with negotiating wages, communication facilities and help in accessing government programmes. The rationale of the social protection model is that poor migrants cannot fend for themselves in a job market that is dominated by labour market intermediaries and employers who are stronger, better informed and connected than they are. They are in need of support to reduce their vulnerability, but are unlikely to be in a position to pay for such services on a full-cost recovery basis immediately. The services provided will enable them to access better jobs and reduce the level of uncertainty and harassment that they face in the job market.

(ii) The market-based approach

This model works with existing labour market patterns and offers services on a cost recovery basis. An example of such an approach is the initiative launched by the NGO Samarthan and the District Poverty Initiatives Project (DPIP) in Madhya Pradesh, called Mazdoor.org, funded by the World Bank. This initiative will provide skills enhancement and certification programmes, advice and information on jobs, and help workers to link up with government schemes on insurance and workers' funds. The project implementers intend to work within the existing industry and labour market structures, i.e. recognizing that capital and labour are highly mobile and that capital/industry relocate where cheap labour is available. They also recognize that a majority of industrial workers are not listed on the employment registers of industries and are recruited by intermediaries who are not accountable to anyone under the existing law. Mazdoor.org will take on responsibility for the welfare of workers, even though by law it would be the responsibility of the industry and employers. For this, they plan to make industry pay service charges.

(iii) The labour union model

This is a rights-based approach for better implementation of labour laws and the regulation of labour flows. Some NGOs, such as Sudrak in Rajasthan and Disha in Gujarat, believe that unionizing migrant workers will go a long way towards realizing their rights, strengthening their bargaining power in the market and preventing exploitation. The Aajeevika Bureau, established by Sudrak, for example, has set up a union of migrant workers who work in cotton fields. One of its main objectives is to regulate the supply of labour as an oversupply of labour lowers the bargaining power of migrants. So far some 1,500 "mates" have enrolled, and the union has created a charter of demands and also set up around 16 manned check points at all the border crossings between Gujarat and Rajasthan. As a result, employers have offered partial wage rate increases and negotiations are continuing. A similar approach has been adopted by the Bandhkam Majoor Sangathan (BMS) established by Disha in Ahmedabad.

(iv) The rehabilitation model

The best example of this model is the work by Action Aid with brick kiln workers in Orissa and Andhra Pradesh. This NGO believes that migration of this kind amounts to a form of trafficking where workers are lured with false promises and often borrow money from recruitment agents whom they must then repay through punishing work schedules. Their movement is restricted at the work site, and wages are well below the legal minimum. In addition, women and children are also exploited in various ways, and living conditions are appalling. Action Aid conducts raids on brick kilns together with the police to release and rehabilitate bonded migrant workers.

(v) Providing migrant-friendly financial services

Poor migrants carry money themselves and at great risk. Some private banks have now started to recognize the need for financial services for migrants. For example, the Industrial Credit and Investment Corporation of India (ICICI) Bank has recently launched an initiative for Tamil migrants from Thirunelveli living in the slums of Dharavi in Mumbai. Some NGOs have also entered this area. Adhikar, an NGO in Orissa, has been helping migrants in Gujarat to send money back to Orissa. This service was started following the 2001 earthquake, when they found more than 10,000 migrants from Khurda district working in and around Gandhidham: at the Kandla port, in the free-trade zone, at the Indian Farmers Fertilisers Cooperative (IFFCO) and for the railways. Adhikar was supported by the research and innovation fund of CARE India's Credit and Savings for Household Enterprises (CASHE) project.

Possibilities for cross-learning on migrant support between different countries should be further explored. This is an area where donor organizations can effectively add value to efforts being made by government and civil society organizations.

10. Research Needs

Data on internal and cross-border migration need to be improved, and this has to be integrated into large-scale data collection efforts such as censuses, living standard surveys and other panel datasets. The Indian Government has planned to focus on migration as its theme for the 2008 National Sample Survey.[23] The Government of Viet Nam has already conducted a special survey on migration. It is heartening to note that there are now several academic institutions engaged in research and data collection, such as those involved in the Africa Migration Alliance in South Africa, the South Asia Migration Research Network in Bangladesh and the Asia Pacific Migration Research Network (APMRN) in Australia. A large number of NGOs are also conducting their own surveys and could use technical support and help with methodology. The importance of researchers' networks and lesson-sharing cannot be overstated. Finally, a greater understanding of the segmentation of migrant labour markets is essential for the development of effective and appropriate support systems able to reach different groups of people with different needs.

11. Conclusion

Assuming that labour migration can benefit areas of origin and destination, as well as migrants and their families, there is a strong argument for facilitating internal and cross-border migration, while limiting their negative aspects. However. until recently, policy attitudes towards such movements have been, for the most part, reserved if not entirely negative. As Harris (2002) points out, such attitudes are hardly justified, given that globalization has created markets in which some locations specialize

[23] Personal communication by Professor Amitabh Kundu, Jawaharlal Nehru University, New Delhi, a recognized authority on rural-urban links and migration.

in making particular types of workers available to other locations, thus creating a circulation of labour. There is a need for greater recognition of this at all policy levels, and the policy discourse needs to be informed by solid research of internal and cross-border migration and accompanying patterns and impacts of remittance flows.

REFERENCES

Acharya, S.
2003 "Migration Patterns in Cambodia – Causes and Consequences", Ad Hoc Expert Group Meeting on Migration and Development, 27-29 August, Bangkok.

Adebusoye, P.M.
2006 "Geographic Labour Mobility in Sub-Saharan Africa", International Development Research Centre (IDRC) Working Paper No. 1 on Globalization, Growth and Poverty, March, Ottawa, http://www.idrc.ca/uploads/user-S/11438237051GGPWP1-migration.pdf.

Adepoju, A.
1998 "Linkages between Internal and International Migration: the African Situation", *International Social Science Journal*, 50(157): 387-395.

2006 "Leading Issues in International Migration in Sub-Saharan Africa" in C. Cross, D. Gelderblom, N. Roux and J. Mafukidze (Eds.), *Views On Migration in Sub-Saharan Africa,* Proceedings of an African Migration Alliance Workshop, Human Sciences Research Council (HSRC) and Department of Social Development, HSRC Press, Cape Town, 25-47.

Afsar, R.
2003 "Dynamics of Poverty, Development and Population Mobility: the Bangladesh Case", Ad Hoc Expert Group Meeting on Migration and Development, Economic and Social Commission for Asia and the Pacific, 27–29 August, Bangkok.

Al-Ali, N.
2004 "The Relationship between Migration within and from the Middle East and North-Africa and Pro-Poor Policies", Report by the Institute of Arab and Islamic Studies, University of Exeter, U.K. for the U.K. Department of International Development (DFID) (obtained from the author).

Anarfi, J. S. Gent, I. Hashim, V. Iversen, S. Khair, S. Kwankye, C.A. Tagoe, D. Thorsen and A. Whitehead.
2007 *Voices of Child Migrants. "A Better Understanding of How Life Is"*, Development Research Centre on Migration, Globalisation and Poverty, University of Sussex, Brighton, U.K , http://www.migrationdrc.org/publications/other_publications/Voices_of_Children.pdf.

Anh, D.
2003 "Migration and Poverty in Asia: with Reference to Bangladesh, China, the Philippines and Viet Nam", Ad Hoc Expert Group Meeting on Migration and Development, United Nations Economic and Social Commission for Asia and the Pacific (UN ESCAP), 27–29 August, Bangkok.

2005 "Viet Nam Country Paper on Internal Migration: Regional Conference on Migration and Development in Asia", 14-16 March, Lanzhou, China.

Bah, M., S. Cissé, B. Diyamett, G. Diallo, F. Lerise, D. Okali, E. Okpara, J. Olawoye and C. Tacoli
2003 "Changing Rural-Urban Linkages in Mali, Nigeria and Tanzania", *Environment and Urbanization*, 15(1) (April): 13-23.

Balbo, M. and M. Marconi
2005 "Governing international migration in the city of the south", Global Migration Perspectives No. 38, September, Global Commission on International Migration (GCIM), Geneva, http://www.gcim.org/attachements/GMP%20No%2038.pdf.

Balisacan, A.M. and G.M. Ducanes
2005 "Inequality in Asia: A Synthesis of Recent Research on the Levels, Trends, Effects and Determinants of Inequality in its Different Dimensions", The Inter-Regional Inequality Facility, Overseas Development Institute (ODI), London.

Barham, B. and S. Boucher
1998 "Migration, Remittances and Inequality: Estimating the Net Effect of Migration on Income Distribution", *Journal of Development Economics*, 55(2): 307-331.

BBC News
2007 "Life on the Burma-Thai border", BBC News, 26 February, http://news.bbc.co.uk/2/hi/asia-pacific/6397243.stm.

Beyrer, C.

2004 "Global Child Trafficking", *The Lancet*, 364 (Supplement 1): 16–17.

Black, R., S. Ammassari, S. Mouillesseaux and R. Rajkotia

2004 "Migration and Pro-Poor Policy in West Africa", Working Paper C8, November, Development Research Centre on Migration, Globalisation and Poverty, University of Sussex, Brighton, U.K., http://www.migrationdrc.org/publications/working_papers/WP-C8.pdf.

Blessing, M.

2005 "Relationship between Migration Status and Household Living Conditions in Ethiopia?", African Population and Health Research Centre (APHRC), Nairobi.

Breman, J.

1985 *Of Peasants, Migrants, and Paupers: Rural Labour Circulation and Capitalist Production in West India*, Oxford University Press, Delhi/New York.

1996 *Footloose Labour: Working in the Indian Informal Economy*, Cambridge University Press, Cambridge.

Bryceson, D.F.

1999 "Sub-Saharan Africa Betwixt and Between: Rural Livelihood Practices and Policies, ASC Working Paper 43/1999, De-Agrarianisation and Rural Employment Network, Afrika-Studiecentrum, University of Leiden, The Netherlands.

Bryceson, D.F. and T.C. Mbara

2003 "Petrol Pumps and Economic Slumps: Rural-Urban Linkages in Zimbabwe's Globalisation Process", *Tijdschrift voor Economische en Sociale Geografie*, 94(3): 335–349.

Bryceson, D.F., D.A.C. Maunder and T.C. Mbara

2003 *Sustainable livelihoods, mobility and access needs*, TRL Report, TRL544. DFID, London, http://www.transport-links.org/transport_links/filearea/publications/1_788_TRL544.pdf.

Busso, G.

2006 "Migración interna y Proceso de Desarrollo en el Cono Sur. Análisis Comparativo e Implicaciones de Política en el Proceso 1985-2005 en el Caso de Argentina, Brasil y Chile", Ponencia presentada en el II Congreso de la Asociación Latinoamericana de Población, Guadalajara, México en Septiembre. ["Internal Migration and the Development Process in the Southern Cone. Comparative Analysis and Political Implications in the Process 1985-2005 in Argentina, Brazil and Chile", presentation prepared for the II Congress of the Latin American Population Association, Guadalajara, Mexico, September].

Cai Fang (Ed.)

2001 "Zhongguo renkou: liudong fangshi yu tujing [China's Population: Ways and Means of Migration]", Beijing Sheke Wenxuan Chubanshe [Beijing Social Sciences Document Publishing House].

Casacchia, O., M. Crisci and C. Reynaud

2001 "Internal Migration in Ethiopia", in *Migration and Urbanization in Ethiopia, with Special Reference to Addis Ababa*, Central Statistical Authority (CSA)/Institute for Population Research – National Research Council (Irp-Cnr), October, Addis Ababa/Rome, 53-92, http://www.irpps.cnr.it/etiopia/pdf/MigrationChap3.PDF.

Cashin, P. and R. Sahay

1996 "Regional Economic Growth and Convergence in India", *Finance and Development*, 33(1) (March): 49-52, http://www.imf.org/external/pubs/ft/fandd/1996/03/pdf/cashin.pdf.

Cerrutti, M. and R. Bertoncello

2003 "Urbanization and Internal Migration Patterns in Latin America", paper prepared for the Conference on African Migration in Comparative Perspective, 4–7 June, Johannesburg.

Choi, S.Y.P.

2003 *Report of the INDEPTH Migration and Urbanisation Workshop 21-24 January 2003*, Gauteng, South Africa, Centre for Health Policy, Witswaterand.

Cour, J.-M. and S. Snrech (Eds.)

1998 *Preparing for the Future. A Vision of West Africa in the Year 2020*, West Africa Long-Term Perspective Study, Organisation for Economic Development and Co-operation (OECD) - Club du Sahel, Paris.

Cross, C., D. Gelderblom, N. Roux and J. Mafukidze (Eds.)
2006 *Views on Migration in Sub-Saharan Africa*, Proceedings of an African Migration Alliance Workshop, HSRC and Department of Social Development, HSRC Press, Cape Town.

Dayal, H. and A.K. Karan
2003 *Labour Migration from Jharkhand*, Institute for Human Development, New Delhi.

de Brauw, A. and T. Harigaya
2004 "Seasonal Migration and Improving Living Standards in Vietnam", mimeo, Williams College, Williamstown, MA.

de Haan, A.
2005 "Migration in the Development Studies Literature: Has it come out of its Marginality?", paper for the United Nations University World Institute for Development Economics Research (UNU-WIDER) Jubilee Conference on WIDER Thinking Ahead: The Future of Development Economics, 17-18 June, Helsinki, http://www.wider.unu.edu/publications/working-papers/research-papers/2006/en_GB/rp2006-19/.

de Haas, H.
2005 "Morocco's migration transition: trends, determinants and future scenarios", Global Migration Perspectives No. 28, April, GCIM, Geneva, http://www.gcim.org/attachements/GMP%20No%2028.pdf.

Deshingkar, P.
2005 "Maximising the Benefits of Internal Migration for Development" in International Organization for Migration (IOM), (Ed.), *Migration, Development and Poverty Reduction in Asia*, IOM, Geneva, 23-53.

Deshingkar, P. and D. Start
2003 "Seasonal Migration for Livelihoods, Coping, Accumulation and Exclusion", Working Paper No. 220, ODI, London.

Deshingkar, P., S. Kumar, H.K. Chobey and D. Kumar
2006a *The Role of Migration and Remittances in Promoting Livelihoods in Bihar*, Report of the study commissioned by the World Bank-funded Bihar Rural Livelihoods Project (BRLP) and the International Fund for Agricultural Development (IFAD) funded Women's Empowerment and Livelihoods Project in the mid-Gangetic Plain (WELPMGP), India.

Deshingkar, P., A. Winkels, S. Akter and T.C. Thang
2006b *The 2004 Vietnam Migration Survey: The Quality of Life of Migrants in Vietnam*, United Nations Population Fund (UNFPA), General Statistics Office, Viet Nam, http://vietnam.unfpa.org/documents/TheQualityofLifeofMigrantsinVN_GSO1206_e.pdf.

DeWind, J. and J. Holdaway
2005 "Internal and International Migration in Economic Development", paper presented at the Fourth Coordination Meeting on International Migration, United Nations Department of Economic and Social Affairs (UN DESA), Population Division, 26-27 October, New York.

Economist Intelligence Unit (EIU)
2006 "Labour Mobility and Migration Trends in the Asia Region", EIU research paper prepared for Asia-New Zealand Foundation, http://www.asianz.org.nz/files/labour_mobility.pdf.

Fussel, E.
2004 "Sources of Mexico's Migration Stream: Rural, Urban, and Border Migrants to the United States", *Social Forces*, 82(3): 937-967.

Ghana Statistical Service
2000 "Report of Fourth Round", Ghana Living Standards Survey, (GLSS 4).

Godfrey, M., S. Sovannarith, T. Saravy, P. Dorina, C. Katz, S. Acharya, S.D. Chanto and H. Thoraxy
2001 "A Study of the Cambodian Labour Market: Reference to Poverty Reduction, Growth and Adjustment to Crisis" in Development Analysis Network, Phnom Penh, Cambodia.

Guest, P.
1998 "Assessing the Consequences of Internal Migration: Methodological Issues and a Case Study on Thailand Based on Longitudinal Survey Data" in R. Bilsborrow (Ed.), *Migration, Urbanization and Development: New Directions and Issues*, UNFPA, New York, 275-318.

2003 "Bridging the Gap: Internal Migration in Asia", paper prepared for the Conference on African Migration in Comparative Perspective, 4-7 June, Johannesburg, http://pum.princeton.edu/pumconference/papers/1-Guest.pdf.

Haberfeld, Y., R.K. Menaria, B.B. Sahoo and R.N. Vyas
1999 "Seasonal Migration of Rural Labour in India", *Population Research and Policy Review*, 18(6): 471–487.

Harris, N.

2002 *Thinking the Unthinkable. The Immigration Myth Exposed*, I.B. Tauris Publishers, London.

Hashim, I.M.

2005 *Research Report on Children's Independent Migration from Northeastern to Central Ghana*, Development Research Centre on Migration, Globalisation and Poverty, June, University of Sussex, Brighton, U.K., http://www.migrationdrc.org/publications/research_reports/ImanReport.pdf .

Hugo, G.

2003 "Urbanisation in Asia: An Overview", paper prepared for the Conference on African Migration in Comparative Perspective, June 4-7, Johannesburg, http://pum.princeton.edu/pumconference/papers/2-Hugo.pdf.

Kanbur, R. and A.J. Venables

2005 "Spatial Inequality and Development – Overview of UNU-WIDER Project", Working Paper 23, Department of Applied Economics and Management, Cornell University, Ithaca, NY.

Khan, I.A. and J. Seeley (Eds.)

2005 *Making a Living: the livelihoods of the rural poor in Bangladesh*, University Press, Dhaka.

Kielland, A. and I. Sanogo

2002 "Burkina Faso: Child Labor Migration from Rural Areas", The World Bank, Washington, D.C.

Konseiga, A.

2005 "New Patterns in the Human Migration in West Africa", Center for Development Research (ZEF), University of Bonn, http://www.zef.de/module/register/media/a127_New%20patterns%20in%20the%20Human%20migration%20in%20West%20Africa.pdf.

Mafukidze, A.

2006 "Discussion of Migration and Migration Patterns and Flows in Africa" in C. Cross, D. Gelderblom, N. Roux and J. Mafukidze (Eds.), *Views On Migration in Sub-Saharan Africa*, Proceedings of an African Migration Alliance Workshop, HSRC and Department of Social Development, HSRC Press, Cape Town, 25-47.

Maguid, A.

2007 "Migration Policies and Socioeconomic Boundaries in the South American Cone" in A. Pécoud and P. de Guchteneire (Eds.), *Migration without Borders. Essays on the Free Movement of People*, United Nations Educational, Scientific and Cultural Organization (UNESCO) and Berghahn Books, Paris/New York, 259-280.

Maltoni, B.

2006 *Review of Labor Migration Dynamics in Cambodia*, September, IOM, Phnom Penh, Cambodia, http://www.iom-seasia.org/resource/pdf/LMReport26OCT.pdf.

Mazzali, A., A. Muliro, A. Zarro and M. Zupi

2006 "It's our Problem too: Views on African Migration and Development", Major outcomes of an International Workshop, a Multidisciplinary Delphi Consultation and Interviews, CeSPI-SID Project.

Mosse, D.

2002 "Brokered Livelihoods: Debt, Labour Migration and Development in Tribal Western India", *Journal of Development Studies*, 38(5): 59–88.

Migration Policy Institute (MPI)

2007 "How can circular migration and sustainable return serve as development tools?", Background Paper for Roundtable 1 of the Global Forum on Migration and Development, 9-11 July, Brussels, http://www.migrationpolicy.org/research/MPI-GlobalForum_circularmigration.pdf.

Munshi, K. and M. Rosenzweig

2005 "Why is Mobility in India so Low? Social Insurance, Inequality, and Growth", July, Bureau for Research and Economic Analysis of Development (BREAD) Working Paper No. 97, http://ipl.econ.duke.edu/bread/papers/working/097.pdf.

Murphy, R.

2004 "Migration in China", Background Note prepared for the Asia 2015 Migration Conference, 6-7 March, London.

Narasimha Reddy, D.

1990 *Rural Migrant Labour in Andhra Pradesh*, Report submitted to the National Commission on Rural Labour, Government of India.

Okali, D., O. Enoch and J. Olawoye

2001 "The Case of Aba and its Region, South-Eastern Nigeria", Working Paper No. 4, Rural-Urban Interactions and Livelihood Strategies Series, International Institute for Environment and Development (IIED), London.

Olsen, W.K. and R.V. Ramanamurthy

2000 "Contract Labour and Bondage in Andhra Pradesh (India)", *Journal of Social and Political Thought*, 1(2) (June), http://www.yorku.ca/jspot/2/wkolsenrvramana.htm.

Peberdy, S. and J. Crush

1998 "Trading Places: Cross-border traders and the South African informal sector", Migration Series No. 6, Southern African Migration Project (SAMP), Cape Town, South Africa and Kingston, Canada.

2001 "Invisible Trade, Invisible Travellers: The Maputo Corridor Spatial Development Initiative and Informal Cross-border Trading", *South African Geographical Journal*, 83(2): 115-123.

Pécoud, A. and P. de Guchteneire

2005 "Migration without borders: an investigation into the free movement of people", Global Migration Perspectives No. 27, April, GCIM, Geneva, http://www.gcim.org/attachements/GMP%20No%2027.pdf.

Pellegrino, A.

2006 "La Migracion en America del Sur", Programa de Población, Facultad de Ciencias Sociales, Universidad de la República Uruguay. ["Migration in South America", Population Programme, Faculty of Social Sciences, University of the Republic of Uruguay].

Pieke, F.N.

2004 "Chinese Globalization and Migration to Europe", paper presented at the Research Seminar, Center for Comparative Immigration Studies (CCIS), 9 March, University of California at San Diego, http://www.ccis-ucsd.org/publications/wrkg94.pdf.

Posel, R.

2004 "Have Migration Patterns in Post-Apartheid South Africa Changed?", *Journal of Interdisciplinary Economics*, 15 (September): 277-292.

Quisumbing, A.R. and S. McNiven

2005 "Migration and the Rural-Urban Continuum: Evidence from the Rural Philippines", International Food Policy Research Institute (IFPRI), Food Consumption and Nutrition Division (FCND), Discussion Paper 197, October, Washington, D.C., http://www.ifpri.org/divs/fcnd/dp/papers/fcndp197.pdf.

Ramachandran, S.

2005 "Indifference, impotence and intolerance: transnational Bangladeshis in India", Global Migration Perspectives No. 42, September, GCIM, Geneva, http://www.gcim.org/attachements/GMP%20No%2042.pdf.

Ratha, D. and W. Shaw

2007 "South-South Migration and Remittances", 19 January, Development Prospects Group, The World Bank, Washington, D.C., http://siteresources.worldbank.org/INTPROSPECTS/Resources/South-SouthmigrationJan192006.pdf.

Sander, C. and S.M. Maimbo

2003 "Migrant Labor Remittances in Africa: Reducing Obstacles to Developmental Contributions", Africa Region Working Paper Series No. 64, November, The World Bank, http://www.worldbank.org/afr/wps/wp64.htm.

Serageldin, M., Y. Cabbanes, E. Solloso and L. Valenzuela

2004 "Migratory Flows, Poverty and Social Inclusion in Latin America", World Bank Urban Research Symposium, February, Center for Urban Development Studies, Harvard University, Cambridge, MA, http://www.worldbank.org/urban/symposium2003/docs/papers/serageldin.pdf.

Sharpe, A., J-F. Arsenault and D. Ershow

2007 *The Impact of Interprovincial Migration on Aggregate Output and Labour Productivity in Canada, 1987-2006*, November, Centre for the Study of Living Standards (CSLS), Ottawa, http://www.csls.ca/reports/csls2007-02.pdf.

Song, L.

2004 "East Asian Experience: China", Mimeo, Australian National University, Canberra.

United Nations Department of Economic and Social Affairs (UN DESA), Population Division

2001 *Replacement Migration: Is It a Solution to Declining and Ageing Populations?*, UN DESA, Population Division, New York, http://www.un.org/esa/population/publications/migration/migration.htm.

2002 *International Migration Report 2002*, Doc. ST/ESA/SER.A/220, UN DESA, Population Division, New York, http://www.un.org/esa/population/publications/ittmig2002/2002ITTMIGTEXT22-11.pdf.

Van der Geest, K.

2003 "Rural migration and livelihood security in Ghana", International Workshop on Migration and Poverty in West Africa, 13-14 March, University of Sussex, Brighton, U.K., http://users.fmg.uva.nl/kgeest/phd/brighton_workshop.pdf.

World Bank

2006 *Labor Migration in the Greater Mekong Sub-region. Synthesis Report: Phase I*, November, World Bank, http://siteresources.worldbank.org/EXTEAPREGTOPLABSOCPRO/Resources/GMSMigrationReportCompleteVersion.pdf?resourceurlname=GMSMigrationReportCompleteVersion.pdf.

Zachariah, K.C. and S. Irudaya Rajan

2005 "Unemployment in Kerala at the turn of the century: Insights from CDS Gulf migration studies", Working Paper 374, August, Centre for Development Studies (CDS), Tiruvanthapuram, Kerala, India, http://www.cds.edu/download_files/374.pdf.

Zohry, A.

2005 "Interrelationships between Internal and International Migration in Egypt: A Pilot Study", July, Development Research Centre on Globalisation, Migration and Poverty, University of Sussex, Brighton, U.K., http://www.migrationdrc.org/publications/research_reports/AymanReport.pdf.

IRREGULAR MIGRATION*

CHAPTER 8

1. Introduction

Irregular migration is undoubtedly one of the most discussed issues in migration management, whether in political debate, in conferences on migration management or on the front page of news dailies. It is by no means a recent phenomenon, although there is reason to believe that it has increased in magnitude and complexity since migration started to attract concerted attention from governments and international organizations in the early 1970s. It was largely in response to concerns about the problems faced by irregular migrants that the International Labour Conference of the International Labour Organization (ILO) adopted the Convention concerning Migrations in Abusive Conditions and the Promotion of Equality of Opportunity and Treatment of Migrant Workers, 1975 (No. 143).[1] Those same concerns featured strongly in the discussions that led to the finalization of the International Convention for the Protection of the Rights of All Migrant Workers and Members of their Families in 1990.[2] Governments, for their part, expend considerable energy on the formulation of legislation and policies to deter irregular migration, including through regularization of status programmes, which some regard as appropriate solutions, while others consider that they do little more than invite further influxes of unauthorized arrivals.[3]

Almost 40 years of attention to irregular migration have therefore produced a great deal of analysis and experimentation, but there are no indications that the phenomenon is on the wane or that the living and working conditions of irregular migrants have improved significantly.

This chapter begins with a brief discussion of terminology and methods of measurement of irregular migration. It then goes on to identify some basic determinants of irregular migration. Following an overview of current patterns of movement across different regions of the world, the chapter concludes

* This chapter was written by Graziano Battistella, Director, Scalabrini International Migration Institute (SIMI), Rome, Italy.

1 Known also by its shorter title, Migrant Workers (Supplementary Provisions) Convention, 1975 (No. 143). The text of the Convention is available from ILOLEX, the ILO database of international labour standards, at http://www.ilo.org/ilolex/english/convdisp1.htm.

2 UN General Assembly Resolution of 18 December 1990. The text of the Convention is available from the web site of the Office of the UN High Commissioner for Human Rights at http://www2.ohchr.org/english/law/cmw.htm. See also Textbox 13.1.

3 For some examples of recent regularization programmes, see the discussion in Section 6.6 below and Chapter 11.

with a brief survey of policy strategies commonly utilized against irregular migration.[4]

2. Irregular Migration: Towards Terminology Convergence

A word about terminology is necessary to establish the scope of the phenomenon under consideration in this chapter. Many descriptive labels have been proposed and discussed, often heatedly, over the years. They include "illegal" migration, "undocumented" migration and "unauthorized" migration, each of which has its proponents and detractors in migration literature. Some convergence seems to be emerging on the use of **irregular** migration as the most appropriate word to refer to migrants whose status does not conform, for one reason or another, to the norms of the country in which they reside.[5] The term "irregular" may refer variously to conditions of entry, stay and employment, including possession of appropriate documentation. Most commonly, irregularity is determined by reference to the norms of the country of destination or transit, although recent research has shown that irregularity is a multifaceted concept that is often not reflected in policy responses (see Textbox 8.1). Countries of origin with specific legislation governing employment of their citizens abroad may also consider the latter to be irregular when they do not comply with its provisions.

[4] See also Chapter 11 for a fuller discussion of some of these policy strategies.

[5] For a discussion on the definition of irregular migrant, see Guild (2004). The term was officially endorsed by the UN General Assembly Resolution 3349 (XXX) of 9 December 1975.

Textbox 8.1

Contested Spaces of (Il)Legality

Policy debates on illegality in the immigration and employment of migrants are typically based on simple conceptual dichotomies, for instance "legal/illegal", "regular/irregular", "authorized/unauthorized" or "documented/undocumented". However, the legal frameworks that govern the immigration, residence and employment of migrants in most destination countries are typically quite intricate. This means that, in practice, rather than a clearly defined dichotomy, it is "spaces of (il)legality" that are created. The spaces of (il)legality are contested, particularly where complex immigration laws collide with flexible labour markets.

In the United Kingdom, where flexibility is at the core of the government's labour market policies, there are currently more than eighty different types of entry and immigration statuses. Each type of immigration status is associated with specific conditions. For example, arrivals on student visas – the largest category of non-European Union (EU) entrants in recent years – are legally allowed to work 20 hours during term time, but full time during vacations. Migrants on self-employed permits (a type of "business visa") cannot work as employees. Au pairs must not work outside their host families, and so on.

The complexity of these rules and conditions means that there are a potentially significant number of migrants who are legally resident (i.e. with "leave to remain in the U.K."), but working beyond the employment restrictions attached to their immigration status. To account for this contested space of (il)legality, the notion of "semi-compliance" is introduced.

It is useful to distinguish between three levels of compliance. **Compliant** migrants are legally resident and working in full compliance with the employment restrictions attached to their immigration status. **Non-compliant** migrants are those without the right to reside in the host country (i.e. those "illegally resident"). **Semi-compliance** indicates a situation where migrants are legally resident but working in violation of some or all of the employment restrictions attached to their immigration status.

The category of semi-compliance – the "space between" strict legality and (il)legality – is extremely broad and captures a wide range of violations of the conditions of employment attached to a migrant's immigration status, with varying degrees of severity. Consider the case of four student visa holders working 20, 21, 25 and 40 hours per week, respectively, in the U.K. Clearly, there is a substantial difference – in terms of the degree to which the employment restrictions attached to immigration status are violated – between a student who works 21 hours per week and a student who works 40 hours per week. The discussion of where and how the line should be drawn between semi-compliance and non-compliance – or indeed between compliance and semi-compliance – can be highly politicized or rest on a personal judgment. Different actors may draw the line in different places, an example of how illegality is "socially constructed".

National laws – and the popular legal/illegal dichotomy in policy debates – usually make no distinction between semi-compliance and non-compliance. In the U.K., any action that violates the conditions attached to a migrant's immigration status makes the migrant subject to removal and employers subject to sanctions. However, a study based on survey and in-depth interviews with over 600 east European migrants and over 300 employers carried out in April 2004[1] showed that both migrants and employers perceive semi-compliance as different from non-compliance. Many interviewees felt that they were "bending" rather than "breaking" the rules. ("There are times when you do twist it a bit ... you work for an extra couple of hours, you know, nudge, nudge and so on," as an employer of a student visa holder in the hospitality sector put it). Although some migrants in this situation faced difficulties similar to those of the illegally resident, others perceived semi-compliance as a way of accessing the U.K. labour market that was preferable to illegal entry or overstaying. From the employers' point of view, semi-compliance was often perceived as a way of circumventing the complex U.K. immigration laws to suit the needs of the flexible labour market.

If governments are serious about wanting to understand and address what is typically described as "illegal migration", they need to go beyond the simple "legal/illegal" dichotomy and instead recognize the spaces of (il)legality in the migrant labour market. Otherwise, policies and public debates risk being increasingly distanced from the actual practices of employers and migrants. A more nuanced approach to the study of various types of illegality may also help to switch the debate away from viewing illegality as a social "problem" that needs to be eliminated, to analyses and policies that view illegality as a multifaceted phenomenon that can have complex consequences, not all of which are as problematic and undesirable as typically assumed.

Note:

[1] The interviews were part of a research project on *Changing status, changing lives? The socio-economic impact of EU enlargement of low wage migrant labour in the UK*, by Bridget Anderson, Martin Ruhs, Sarah Spencer and Ben Rogaly.

Source: *Martin Ruhs and Bridget Anderson, Centre on Migration, Policy and Society (COMPAS), University of Oxford, United Kingdom.*

In view of the central topic of *World Migration 2008*, namely labour mobility, an attempt to identify in accurate statistical terms those migrants whose irregularity is demonstrably linked to active participation in employment might be expected. However, the scarcity of data in this field and the absence of reliable databases thwart any such intention. Irregular migrants do not have a single prime motivation. Some of them seek family reunion, others move in search of asylum and protection. There is nonetheless good reason to believe that a preoccupation with gainful employment is common to virtually all of them. If explanatory distinctions must be established, there may be value instead in laying out the conceptual linkages and differences between irregular migration, on the one hand, and the smuggling and trafficking of human beings, on the other.

According to the Protocol Against the Smuggling of Migrants by Land, Sea and Air, which supplements the International Convention Against Transnational Organized Crime 2000,[6] "smuggling of migrants" is defined as

> the procurement, in order to obtain, directly or indirectly, a financial or other material benefit, of the illegal entry of a person into a State Party of

[6] UN General Assembly Resolution A/RES/55/25 of 15 November 2000. The text of the Convention and its Protocols is available on the web site of the UN Office on Drugs and Crime at http://www.unodc.org/pdf/crime/a_res_55/res5525e.pdf.

which the person is not a national or a permanent resident (Article 3(a)).

Trafficking is another process that feeds irregular migration flows, most frequently for work purposes, and is characterized by its exploitative nature and a disregard for the migrant's human rights. The Protocol to Prevent, Suppress and Punish Trafficking in Persons, Especially Women and Children, supplementing the United Nations Convention against Transnational Organized Crime (2000), defines trafficking as:

> (t)he recruitment, transportation, transfer, harbouring or receipt of persons, by means of the threat or use of force or other forms of coercion, of abduction, of fraud, of deception, of the abuse of power or of a position of vulnerability or of the giving or receiving of payments or benefits to achieve the consent of a person having control over another person, for the purpose of exploitation. Exploitation shall include, at a minimum, the exploitation of the prostitution of others or other forms of sexual exploitation, forced labour or services, slavery or practices similar to slavery, servitude or the removal of organs (Article 3(a)).

For the purpose of this definition, the consent of the victim is irrelevant if any of the identified means are used, and "the recruitment, transportation, transfer, harbouring or receipt of a child for the purpose of exploitation" is considered "trafficking in persons" even if such means are not used (Article 3(b), (c) and (d)). As this definition and indeed the very title of the Protocol indicate, many forms of trafficking affect mainly women and children, who are most frequently trafficked for sexual abuse or labour exploitation, although they may also be trafficked into forced marriages or delinquency. Victims of trafficking are exposed to physical and psychological abuse, denied human and labour rights and often found in a forced and unwanted dependency relationship with their traffickers, originating in the financial debt incurred for migration and placement services. A perspective on the extent of trafficking for forced labour of men, women and children, extrapolated from the data in the International Organization for Migration's Global Human Trafficking Database, is described in Textbox 8.2.

Textbox 8.2

Trafficking for Forced Labour

No discussion of the place of labour migration in an evolving global economy is complete without reflection upon the phenomenon of trafficking in persons.[1]

Traditionally, national and international counter-trafficking activity and policy have sought to combat the phenomenon by addressing the supply side, or what can be referred to as the root causes of trafficking in countries of origin, including economic inequality, gender discrimination, violence and corruption, and the lack of safe and regular migration opportunities. However, there has been increasing international recognition that serious attention must also be given to the root causes in countries of destination, and above all the demand for cheap and unprotected labour.

Irregular migration, and particularly the trafficking in persons for all forms of exploitation, cannot be separated from the process of globalization in general and the move towards a more global economy. New labour markets emerge, creating new employment opportunities across the globe for skilled and less-skilled workers, both men and women. But such economic growth has not been matched with the evolution of safe, humane and orderly migration channels to facilitate and satisfy this demand for labour. This tension between the growing need for labour and services on one side, and too few regular migration opportunities on the other, creates a niche for intermediaries to intervene and make profit. These intermediaries are the human traffickers, who exploit, abuse and victimize the migrant workers, especially those in an irregular, and hence more vulnerable, situation.

Only recently has the necessary attention been afforded to trafficking for non-sexual forms of exploitation as well as to men and boy victims. The exploitation of individuals by human traffickers exists in a number of employment sectors, often informal ones that are less subject to official labour inspections, including construction work, agriculture and food processing, the fisheries sector, domestic and care work, hospitality and entertainment. Women, men, boys and girls are also trafficked for the purposes of begging and low-level criminal activities.

While accurate figures on the number of persons trafficked each year are difficult to obtain given the clandestine nature of the phenomenon, one estimate states that, globally, there are at least 2.45 million people in forced labour as a result of internal or international trafficking in persons (Belser et al., 2005).[2] It is clear that significant numbers of male and female migrants are being exploited and their human rights abused by human traffickers. Child trafficking for sexual and labour exploitation also continues to exist to an alarming degree.

If human trafficking for all forms of labour exploitation is to be combated, it is necessary to tackle also the demand for cheap, unprotected and often irregular labour. Informal and unregulated work activities need to be brought within the protection of labour laws so that the rights of all workers are protected. And lastly, though by no means least, the demand for migrant workers needs to be matched with safe, humane and orderly migration channels, and with migration management policies between source and destination countries that fully stand to protect the rights of all migrants.

Information from the IOM Global Human Trafficking Database

The International Organization for Migration (IOM)'s Global Human Trafficking Database is a unique tool, which is used to collect information and monitor IOM's return and reintegration assistance to victims of (human) trafficking (VoTs). The database is the world's largest of primary data on registered VoTs, containing only primary data on registered victims of more than 80 different nationalities trafficked to more than 90 destination countries. At the end of December 2007, the database contained data on 12,681 registered cases of VoTs assisted by IOM, with a breakdown of 10,510 females (83%) and 2,169 males (17%) (Table 8.1).[3] Individuals assisted by IOM encompass all age groups, with just under half the caseload aged between 18 and 24 at the time of interview, and approximately one-fifth aged below the age of 18.

While the majority of individuals assisted by IOM are females trafficked for prostitution and other forms of sexual exploitation (8,326 cases to date), IOM's return and reintegration assistance programmes do not focus solely on trafficking for sexual exploitation; assistance is also provided to individuals who have been trafficked, both internally and internationally, for exploitation in such sectors as agriculture, construction work, food processing, domestic employment and childcare work, fisheries, and for the purposes of begging to name but a few.

Table 8.1:

Victims of Trafficking Assisted by IOM, by Gender and Type of Exploitation, 1999-2007

Type of Exploitation	Sex	1999	2000	2001	2002	2003	2004	2005	2006	2007*	Total
Labour exploitation	Female	0	17	50	78	172	161	392	367	303	1540
	Male	0	0	6	120	219	251	514	453	290	1853
Labour exploitation and low-level criminal activity	Female	0	0	0	0	1	0	1	0	1	3
	Male	0	0	0	0	1	1	0	0	1	3
Low-level criminal activity	Female	0	0	0	9	13	22	32	8	5	89
	Male	0	0	0	0	4	7	3	1	2	17
Other exploitation	Female	0	8	24	13	9	43	61	87	61	306
	Male	0	0	2	21	3	0	1	5	3	35
Sexual exploitation	Female	28	566	725	957	639	1,224	1,584	1,567	1,036	8,326
	Male	0	0	11	19	45	21	24	78	57	255
	Not known	0	0	0	0	1	0	0	0	1	2
Sexual exploitation and labour exploitation	Female	0	0	0	7	27	48	69	52	43	246
	Male	0	0	0	1	0	2	0	1	2	6
Total		28	591	818	1,225	1,134	1,780	2,681	2,619	1,805	12,681

Note:

*Based on cases registered in the database up to and inclusive of 31 December 2007.

***Source:** IOM Global Human Trafficking Database.*

Although not readily citable as a trend per se, given that IOM counter-trafficking activities are project-specific,[4] it can be noted that IOM field missions are increasingly assisting individuals trafficked for labour exploitation (3,393 cases), and also an increasing number of male VoTs (2,169 cases). For example, IOM has provided return and reintegration assistance to Ukrainian males trafficked to Russia for labour exploitation. Within the IOM global human trafficking dataset, the most significant number of individuals trafficked for forced labour are indeed trafficked to the Russian Federation, with Ukrainian and Belarusian nationals appearing as the most represented nationalities of individuals trafficked for forced labour.

IOM has further assisted 2,046 VoTs under the age of 18 at the time of interview. The majority consisted of girls trafficked for sexual exploitation; however, it can be noted that IOM has a regional counter-trafficking project in Ghana, which, at the time of publication, had assisted more than 500 children (boys) internally trafficked for exploitation in the fishing industry.

Notes:

1 See Section 2 above for the definition of trafficking under the Protocol to Prevent, Suppress and Punish Trafficking in Persons, Especially Women and Children, supplementing the United Nations Convention Against Transnational Organized Crime.

2 The *Trafficking in Persons Report 2006* of the U.S. Department of State estimates that 600,000 to 800,000 persons are trafficked across international borders each year. Other organizations have stated similarly higher and lower figures.

3 There are missing data for two cases.

4 Further, as stated, policy and practice have predominantly focused on the trafficking of women and girls for sexual exploitation and thus there has arguably been a bias towards the number of VoTs identified as having been trafficked for sexual exploitation compared to the number of VoTs identified as having been trafficked for labour exploitation. Such a bias in turn impacts upon data collection.

3. Determinants of Irregular Migration

In very broad terms, the determinants of irregular migration are not different from those of regular migration. It can be argued that both movements are outcomes of the various and interconnected social and economic dynamics operating in our globalized world. However, while, by definition, regular migration proceeds along open and established channels, irregular migration seeks to circumvent them. In this regard, the Global Commission on International Migration (GCIM) draws attention to limitations of the meaning of a "global labour market":[7] highly skilled professionals such as information technology specialists or health professionals and world class athletes may be able to pursue their careers across the world, but "for the majority of people and in most regions of the world, national labour markets prevail and the opportunities for them to seek work in other countries remain limited" (GCIM, 2005: 15, para. 22). This mismatch between supply and demand is one of the factors underlying the so-called "nexus" between asylum and migration: the propensity of significant numbers of irregular migrants to make use of asylum procedures not because of a genuine need for protection, but to gain entry to new countries and access to their labour markets. This pattern is particularly evident when asylum systems are perceived as the primary or only official mechanism sanctioning the entry and stay of foreigners in the absence of an alternative means of access to the labour market.

Channels for regular migration, in particular labour migration, are defined by the policies of countries of destination, sometimes, but not always, in consultation with and the assistance of countries of origin (see also Chapter 13). They are, to a large extent, a response to the demand for foreign workers coming from domestic labour markets. When the supply through established channels does not match the demand, irregular migration dynamics come into their own. For instance, in Italy, 520,000 requests from employers for foreign workers contended with 170,000 available places offered in 2006 by government decree (see Section 5.1 below).

Another way of gauging the magnitude of opportunity, if not demand for irregular migration, is to examine the operation of informal economies,

7 See Chapter 1 for a discussion of "global labour market".

their underlying social networks and, ultimately, the migrant-recruiting industry that services them. The informal economy is the natural point of insertion into the labour force for migrants who cannot find regular employment because of their lack of appropriate documentation. According to Schneider (2004), the informal economy as a percentage of official GDP accounted for 28.2 per cent in Greece, 25.7 per cent in Italy, 22.0 per cent in Spain and 21.9 per cent in Portugal in 2003 – all of them countries that have repeatedly implemented regularization programmes. However, the informal economy is not evenly developed throughout all sectors of the economy. According to conservative estimates by the Italian National Institute on Statistics (ISTAT, 2006), 11.5 per cent (2.7 million) of employed workers were in an irregular situation in Italy in 2004; the figures were much higher in the service (18.4%) and agricultural sectors (18.3%). It is important to note, however, that migrants accounted only for a very modest proportion (4.5%) of the informal labour market, with nationals actually making up the vast majority of those working in an irregular situation.

Social networks are constantly linked to irregular labour migration, as they provide the necessary information and contacts to migrants for both unauthorized entry into the country and subsequent insertion into the workforce. Some studies contend that the impact of social networks is limited compared to that of employers (Krissman, 2005), but there is much evidence that little irregular movement can occur without the information, advice, encouragement and support of family and friends, although it is by no means unknown for the latter to seek to exploit those who rely on them.

Beyond family and friends, there are more structured systems of recruitment, sufficiently developed to bear the collective name of a recruitment industry. The industry has a pervasive role in the phenomenon of irregular migration, from advertising and recruiting in the country of origin, to connections with migration officials and transportation employees, to linkages with migration brokers, employers and social networks abroad. This, however, does not imply that there is one monolithic system overseeing irregular migration around the world. Rather there is a multiplicity of profit-making concerns that change their configurations at will, setting up and dismantling business fronts, initiating and reacting to market needs and opening or closing routes in response to enforcement patterns (Salt and Stein, 1997; Battistella and Asis, 2003).

4. Measurements of Irregular Migration

Virtually every research paper on irregular migration deplores the lack of reliable data on the subject since, by its very nature, it eludes established data collecting systems. Accurate statistics are rarely available and, at best, one generally has to make do with estimates, and at worst with wild guesswork. The data are often influenced by the methodology utilized and sometimes by the agenda of those reporting on the subject.

Jandl (2004) and Massey and Capoferro (2004) explore the limitations of both commonly exercised and less frequently utilized methods of measurement. Census data provide very sound and comprehensive information on immigrant populations as a whole since they identify the place of birth and citizenship of respondents, but they do not distinguish between regular and irregular migrants. Highly sophisticated residual techniques must then be applied to arrive at estimates of the irregular migrant contingent, but the results require careful interpretation (Costanzo et al., 2004).[8] Intercensal surveys are more focused and more frequently conducted than statutory censuses, but they are not based on sufficiently large samples for safe conclusions to be drawn about the size and composition of the irregular migrant

8 According to these calculations, the estimated "residual" foreign-born population in the U.S. was 3.77 million in 1990 and 8.71 million in 2000. These figures include irregular migrants, arrivals residing lawfully, but not yet included in official figures, and arrivals awaiting finalization of their requests for regularization.

population. Some, but by no means all, countries have registration systems that require individuals to notify authorities of their arrival, departure or change in status, but irregular migrants are unlikely to bring themselves to notice, at least not until they can apply for regularization.[9] Matching arrival and departure records would appear to be a relatively simple and reliable way of determining the number of overstayers in a country. However, in addition to errors in reporting such information, there are many countries that do not require exit controls (for instance, the U.S. abolished them in 1957) and record matching can be costly in terms of both time and money.[10] Massey and Capoferro (2004) suggest the use of ethnosurveys, which combine quantitative and qualitative methods with ethnographic and survey techniques. The resulting databases are certainly rich in information, but the question remains whether they can really lead to a better approximation of the number of irregular migrants in a particular country.[11]

The European Union (EU) has established the Centre for Information, Discussion and Exchange on the Crossing of Frontiers and Immigration (CIREFI), which began its work in 1995. It gathers data on irregular migrants derived from different administrative operations, but the results are subject to numerous limitations, including the important issue of comparability of the figures among participating countries (Mitsilegas, 2004).[12] Officials are relying more on data from removals of non-nationals, although such data do not specify whether removal was forced or voluntary, nor whether the same person might have been involved and counted more than once.

Estimates of the number of irregular migrants based on those remaining after regularizations have been used in particular in southern Europe. One advantage of such data is that they concern the stock of irregular migrants present in the territory and that they contain a host of qualitative data. Obviously, this measurement does not capture those migrants ineligible for regularization or who decided for some reason not to take advantage of it. A similar data set results from mass registration exercises, which have often been conducted in Asia. In the case of registrations, however, as persons are invited to return to their country either immediately or after a short time, the danger of missing people who would prefer to remain in an irregular status is higher, and the possibility that the same person might be counted in a subsequent registration very real.

Given this rather bleak picture, it is hardly surprising that specialists in this field are reluctant to provide anything more specific than orders of magnitude or scales of possibility. On the basis of a national survey of employers, Piguet and Losa (2001) concluded, for instance, that there were between 70,000 and 180,000 foreign-born persons employed without authorization in Switzerland. Similarly, the estimated number of unauthorized migrants in France in the late 1990s was between 140,000 and 500,000 (Delaunay and Tapinos, 1998).

[9] An exception might be Spain, where even irregular migrants are registered at local municipalities.

[10] In the "Schengen zone", applicable for the time being to 25 of the 27 EU Member States as well as Iceland and Norway, the passports of all third-country nationals have to be stamped on entry and exit, which should make it easier to detect overstayers as well as the extent of the problem. See Regulation 562/2006/EC of the European Parliament and of the Council of 15 March 2006 establishing a Community Code governing the movement of persons across borders (Schengen Borders Code), OJ 2006 L 105/1.

[11] See also Chapter 9 for a discussion of the various sources of data on irregular migration.

[12] However, on 11 July 2007, the EU Council of Ministers and the European Parliament adopted Regulation (EC) No. 862/2007 on Community statistics on migration and international protection (OJ 2007 L 199/23), which establishes common rules for the collection and compilation of EU statistics on inter alia immigration to and emigration from the territories of Member States, including on third-country nationals refused entry, those found to be present without authorization and the number of undocumented third-country nationals who are obliged to leave (or who have in fact left) the territory of the Member State concerned (Articles 1, 5 and 7).

At the global level, ILO estimates refer to irregular migrants as representing 10 to 15 per cent of total migrant stocks and flows (ILO, 2004),[13] although this average obviously masks large regional or national variations.

5. Irregular Migration Flows and Trends

Any ambition to identify clear routes and patterns involved in irregular migration flows is quickly dispelled when one is confronted with the diversity of possibilities offered in an increasingly mobile world. Maps that try to depict such routes often appear as intricate webs of arrows and dots, with limited explanatory power. However, it is true, particularly for irregular migrants, that the migration process depends on information and that mediators play a crucial role. If clear routes might not always be identifiable, some cities and border-crossings have emerged as hubs, offering a high density of information sources on how to proceed with the journey. At these staging posts, smugglers set up their operations to offer travel packages, often proposing the guarantee of one or several repeat attempts should the first one fail.

Considering the difficulties and limitations of reporting on irregular migration flows by routes and hubs - and bearing in mind that a large proportion of regular migrants lapse into this status after entry through a legal point of entry - this section attempts to provide a broad overview of patterns of movement discernible across geographical areas that do not correspond to strictly defined migratory systems, but represent zones of more or less intense activity.

5.1 Southern Europe – Irregular Access by Sea

Countries in southern Europe were the source of large migratory outflows for almost two centuries during the industrial development phase in Europe and North America. Then, when the economies of these countries progressed to the post-industrial stage at the beginning of the 1970s, they became the main destination of new migrations, first from Africa, then from eastern Europe and Latin America. In the years following the fall of the Berlin Wall, Germany was the major net destination of migrants in Europe (almost 70% of the total) as it experienced the arrival of *Aussiedler*[14] as well as asylum seekers. Since 1998, Spain has become the leading net immigration country in the EU, accounting for 35 per cent in 2003, followed by Italy with 28 per cent, while Germany ranks fourth, after the United Kingdom (European Commission, 2005). Portugal's conversion to being a net destination of migrants occurred as recently as 1998.

As irregular migration is a component of migration flows, it is hardly surprising that Europe has also become a major destination of irregular migration. The major entry points are in the south and southeast of the continent. North Africa, for a long time an important region of origin, is now also a main region of transit. The short distance to the mainland or to islands that are constituent parts of European countries and the increasingly organized smuggling industry override the potential dangers of a journey at sea. Based on apprehension data, the UN Office on Drugs and Crime (2006) estimates that at least 200,000 irregular migrants enter Europe from Africa annually. However, although most prominent in terms of media exposure and numbers of tragedies, irregular migration from Africa is not the most important source of irregular migrants, as many irregular migrants enter over eastern land borders with a valid visa and subsequently, owing to intervening circumstances, such as overstaying and working without authorization, shift into irregular status (see Section 5.6 below).

[13] "Information obtained from regularization programmes and other sources suggests that 10 to 15 per cent of migrants are irregular" (ILO, 2004: 11, para. 37, citing Hatton and Williamson (2002)).

[14] Persons of German ancestry mainly from central and eastern Europe and the former Soviet Union.

The two main destinations for irregular migration in southern Europe are Spain and Italy, where the phenomenon has been resistant to both regularization programmes and reinforced interdiction efforts at sea.[15]

On the basis of the difference between the number of foreigners registered on the census lists and the number of residence permits issued, it was estimated that there were over one million unauthorized migrants in Spain in 2003 (SOPEMI, 2004). Two years later, nearly 700,000 applied under a major regularization programme. The overwhelming majority of irregular migrants in Spain come from Latin America (at 20%, Ecuadorians were the largest group, followed by Colombians (8%) and Bolivians (7%)). Eastern Europeans, especially Romanians (17%), were also present in significant numbers, as were Moroccans (12%). Information derived from the 2005 regularization exercise reveals that 59 per cent of migrants were male and 41 per cent female. Most of the applicants held low-skilled jobs: 32 per cent were domestic workers (83% women), 21 per cent construction workers (95% men), 15 per cent working in agriculture, 10 per cent in catering and 5 per cent in commerce (Karaboytcheva, 2006).

According to the Italian Ministry of Interior, the number of unauthorized arrivals by sea has increased by almost 50 per cent since 2003, reaching a total of 22,016 people in 2006 (Caritas/Migrantes, 2007). The corresponding figures for 2005 show that 96 per cent of the arrivals were male, while a disconcerting 7 per cent were minors (Caritas/Migrantes, 2006). To have a more realistic picture of the dimension of irregular migration in Italy, one can turn to the 2006 amendment to the decree establishing the number of residence permits to be granted to third-country nationals with a work contract in Italy. The number was limited to 170,000, but 517,000 who were already present and working in Italy, filed an application. The approval of an additional 350,000 residence permits[16] puts the size of the irregular migration contingent living in Italy at that point in time at around 500,000. About 90 per cent of arrivals consist of 10 nationalities, among which migrants from North Africa and the Middle East are the most numerous, underlining that geographic proximity is still one of the main factors influencing the decision to migrate irregularly; Egyptians account for the largest group (45%), followed by Moroccans (15%), Eritreans and Tunisians.

Portugal and Greece rank after Spain and Italy as the two major recipients of irregular migrants in southern Europe. According to government estimates, Portugal would have had 500,000 irregular migrants at the end of 2004, with about 30,000 from Brazil. Results of the regularization process in Greece indicate that the total number of irregular migrants in April 2006 could have reached about 550,000, although fewer than 200,000 applied for regularization around that time, possibly because of the high application fees (EUR 1,176 per person) and the complexity of the application process.

Crossing the Mediterranean has always been, and still is, the main route for migrants to irregularly access southern Europe from Africa. This pattern seems to persist notwithstanding the recently increased controls. However, in response to this reinforcement of surveillance and interdiction activities, alternative routes have been developed. While the traffic was once concentrated in the Gibraltar Strait, through the two enclave cities of Ceuta and Melilla, the route via the Canary Islands has now become the preferred staging post into Spain from various departure points along the West African coastline. However, in the first seven months of 2007, the number of migrants intercepted on or off the Canary Islands dropped by

[15] It has been reported that EU patrols have substantially reduced arrivals since the beginning of 2007, although the European Commission has also called for improvements in EU cooperation (EU business.com, 2007a, 2007b).

[16] *Gazzetta Ufficiale della Repubblica Italiana* [*Official Journal of the Republic of Italy*], Anno 147, No. 285, 7 December 2006, p. 13.

55 per cent to 5,700 from 13,700 during the same period in 2006. This drop has been attributed inter alia to greater vigilance on the part of countries of departure and surveillance missions conducted by Spain alone or within the framework of the EU border agency FRONTEX (*Migration News Sheet*, September 2007).

Substantial patrolling operations have also been undertaken along the short route which connects the Libyan and Tunisian coasts to the island of Lampedusa, the main entry point for irregular migrants heading to Italy from Africa. While traffic along this route decreased by 4.5 per cent in 2006 (*Corriere della Sera*, 5 January 2007), it is very likely that migrants have opted to enter Europe through the alternative Canary route. In addition, patrolling operations have not been really effective in limiting the presence and power of organized gangs, who still handle the whole operation and charge between EUR 1,000 to 2,000 per person for the sea crossing from Libya to Italy (Moscarelli, 2008).

In both routes towards Spain and Italy, countless migrants perish along the way. If the numbers of irregular migrants can only be estimated, the number of migrants dying en route to their destination is even more uncertain. According to the NGO Andalusian Association for Human Rights [*Asociacion Pro Derechos Humanos de Andalucia*], 289 irregular migrants were confirmed dead or lost at sea in 2004, but some estimates suggest that the real number of deaths might have been closer to 500. Yet, approximately 1,200 to 1,700 migrants who left Mauritania in February and March 2006 never reached Spain and might have died. Finally, the then EU Commissioner Franco Frattini's conjecture was that during the summer of 2006 perhaps 3,000 people died while crossing the Mediterranean to reach Europe (Palidda and Cuttitta, 2007).

5.2 Western Europe – In and Out of Irregularity

Compared to the southern borders of Europe, western European countries appear less exposed to the large-scale entry of irregular migrants, particularly those entering without documents in a clandestine manner. In the past, intermediate central European countries operated as a buffer zone. Since the EU enlargement, to 15 and now to 27 countries, the former buffer role played by central European countries has become rather more complex. They are now the frontline states on the external EU border and are major suppliers of migrant workers to western Europe.

All western European countries are host to a number of irregular migrants, many of whom entered with a regular visa but then overstayed and worked without authorization. Figures on irregular migration are not published regularly, but at the political level there are frequent acknowledgements of both the magnitude and persistence of the problem. In France, the then Minister of Interior, Nicolas Sarkozy, estimated in June 2006 that there were between 200,000 and 400,000 irregular migrants (PICUM, 2006). In April 2005, a report on *"sans-papiers"* in Switzerland revealed that there were some 90,000 persons living in the country without authorization (Swiss Federal Office for Migration, 2005). In the United Kingdom, a report for the Home Office estimated the number of irregular migrants in 2001 at 430,000, suggesting that the actual number could be as low as 310,000 and as high as 570,000 (Woodbridge, 2005).

The participation of irregular migrants in the economy, especially the informal one, is a subject of much conjecture, but it is generally acknowledged that it is high, especially in agriculture and in the construction and service industries.

5.3 North America – The Focus on the U.S.-Mexican Border

Irregular migration is an issue affecting, in particular, the United States, where the number of irregular migrants has continued to increase, irrespective of countervailing legislative measures, beginning with the Immigration Reform and Control Act (IRCA) in 1986 and all control measures thereafter. The consistent demand for labour in the U.S. economy, the still hefty, though now reduced to a 1:6 ratio income differential between the U.S. and Mexico, the long border between the two countries, the increasing trade and industrial relations, the large Mexican community residing in the U.S. (about 12 million, approximately 10% of the Mexican population, perhaps half in an irregular status[17]) with large social networks, are among the determinants of a social phenomenon which remains a major concern of policymakers and public opinion.

Estimates of the number of irregular migrants in the U.S. are for the most part convergent. A report of the U.S. Department of Homeland Security estimated the number of irregular migrants at 11 million as of January 2006, an increase of 500,000 compared to January the previous year, while a report by the Pew Hispanic Center (Passel, 2006) put the estimate at between 11.5 and 12 million as of March 2006, two-thirds of whom would have been in the country for ten years or less. A breakdown by nationality indicates that six million are from Mexico, 470,000 from El Salvador, 370,000 from Guatemala, 280,000 from India, 230,000 from China, 210,000 from South Korea, 210,000 from the Philippines, 180,000 from Honduras, 170,000 from Brazil and 160,000 from Viet Nam. In terms of occupations, 7.2 million, almost five per cent of all workers in the U.S., were employed, with a significant presence in some occupations, such as farm work (24%), cleaning (17%), construction (14%) and food preparation (12%).

As to the mode of entry, the Pew Hispanic Center estimated that up to half of irregular migrants might have entered the country legally and overstayed their visa, while the rest entered by evading border inspection in many ways (hiding in vehicles, trekking through the desert, wading across the Rio Grande). Perhaps between 250,000 and 350,000 annually overstay their visa, a tiny fraction of the 179 million non-immigrant admissions, but a significant contribution to the stock of irregular migrants. A specific group of overstayers consists of holders of a Border Crossing Card (Mexicans and Canadians), who are authorized to stay for a maximum of 30 days within 25 miles of the border (75 miles at the border with Arizona) but fail to observe these conditions.

Mexico is not only the major country of origin of irregular migration to the U.S. (over 450,000 a year), but also a transit country for irregular migration from Central and South America. This flow has become more pronounced since the 1990s. At the same time, under pressure from the U.S., Mexico has increased the number of apprehensions and deportations of irregular migrants. In 2004, 215,695 Central Americans, half of them arrested in the border region of Chiapas, were deported. According to the Mexican Government's National Migration Institute (*Instituto Nacional de Migración*), deportations increased to 240,269 in 2005, to decrease again to 167,437 in the first 10 months of 2006. The decline could be a sign of a more general decline in migration from Central to North America, but some experts point instead to the development of alternative routes and the use of more effective methods to evade detection. The Central American region and the Caribbean are not only points of origin of irregular migration, but also transit areas, even for people coming from other continents, for example, the Chinese.

The 5,500 mile border between the U.S. and Canada (a third of which is with Alaska) is subject to increasing levels of border security. The U.S. is adding Border Patrol agents, and Canada plans to provide its agents with arms. The number of irregular migrants in Canada was estimated at approximately 200,000

[17] When not indicated otherwise, figures concerning irregular migration to North America are taken from the Internet quarterly *Migration News*: http://migration.ucdavis.edu/mn/index.php.

in 2006, employed particularly in construction and other blue-collar jobs. The government is not considering granting them amnesty as demanded by some employers. However, employer demands for more workers are being met to a certain degree through the recent expansion of Canada's temporary migrant worker programme (see Chapters 3 and 11).

5.4 Central America and the Caribbean – Mainly Labour Movements

Significant irregular migration flows also occur within the Central American sub-region.[18] Approximately half of the 500,000 migrant workers in Costa Rica have irregular status. Many of these irregular migrants come from neighbouring countries, particularly Nicaragua (somewhere between 65,000 to 100,000)[19] and are concentrated mainly in agriculture[20] but also in other forms of lower-skilled employment, such as construction, tourism and domestic work.

In the case of Haitian migration, the enhanced U.S. policies to protect its coastal areas and territorial waters from incursions over the past decade have reduced the number of attempts by irregular migrants to reach the State of Florida, with the result that the migration route has switched towards other Caribbean islands, especially the Bahamas and the Dominican Republic. Estimates of the number of Haitian migrants in the Dominican Republic vary from 500,000 to 1.5 million. However, reliable sources suggest there are between 500,000 and 700,000 Haitians living in the Dominican Republic, the majority of whom do not have valid visas or work permits (Achieng, 2006).[21] An estimated 40,000 to 50,000 Haitians or Haitian descendants reside in the Bahamas, most of whom work in low-paid, lower-skilled jobs in agriculture/landscaping, construction, domestic service and informal trading (Fernández-Alfaro and Pascua, 2006). Smuggling rings take advantage of the demand for labour by bringing in irregular migrants from Haiti.

5.5 South America – Fluctuating Policies and Fluctuating Flows

Migration in South America has traditionally been organized around two sub-systems: one involving the countries of the Andean region with Venezuela as the major destination; the other concerning the countries of the south, with Argentina as the main destination.

Migration in these two regions, as on the continent as a whole, has changed considerably in recent times. Both the Andean region and the countries of the south have become characterized by intensive out-migration, particularly from Ecuador and Peru, but also from traditional countries of destination like Argentina and Brazil. Increasingly, these migrants head towards North America and Europe as intra-regional movements have declined, especially in the years of economic crisis in Argentina. During the crisis, perhaps as many as 300,000 migrants left Argentina, by far the largest immigration country in South America with 1.5 million immigrants in 2001. This movement has already subsided, and Argentina once again attracts low-skilled foreign workers, particularly from Paraguay and Bolivia, who arrive to find seasonal employment and feed the informal economy.

Regularization mechanisms have certainly been one of the major policy strategies pursued by South American countries in an effort to tackle the phenomenon of irregular migration. Overall, changes in migration trends and policies have resulted in a drop in the numbers of irregular migrants in the southern part of South America. Chile, Bolivia and Peru regularized about 700,000 migrants in 2004 (O'Neil et al., 2005) within the Common Market of the South (MERCOSUR) cooperation

---

18 Some of these movements are also described in Chapter 3 on low and semi-skilled workers.

19 Most of this migration responds nevertheless to the demand for seasonal jobs (IOM, 2001).

20 According to the Costa Rican Ministry of Labour and Social Security, in 2002-03 there were 50,400 seasonal migrants working in agriculture, of whom 40,900 (or 81%) were undocumented.

21 Only some five per cent of these Haitian migrants are said to have identification (Achieng, 2006).

framework. Following its migration policy reform of 2003, Argentina suspended the repatriation of Peruvian citizens in 2004 and, beginning in July 2004, immigrants coming from non-MERCOSUR countries were given 180 days to regularize their status (Jachimowicz, 2006). These opportunities for regularizations did not attract a large response (although about 200,000 migrants regularized their status), mostly because the benefits only partially offset the costs of regular status, including payment of social security contributions. The regularization launched in Argentina in April 2006, called *"Patria Grande"*, is having more success and, in November 2006, the Minister of Interior estimated that 332,000 people were eligible for regularization, 80 per cent of them from Paraguay and Bolivia, and the remainder from Brazil, Peru and Uruguay. Textbox 8.3 presents a fuller account of some of the recent regularization programmes in this region as well as other countries in Latin America.

Textbox 8.3

Regularization Programmes: The Latin-American Case

The issue of migrant regularization is of importance for both the migrants concerned and their host societies.

While countries of destination can rely for guidance on general international instruments addressing the fundamental rights of migrants, their specific attitudes and approaches to regularization will be influenced by a wide range of factors, such as their available human and material resources, their perceived need for foreign talent and their capacity for the integration of newcomers.

Regularization processes grant legal status to non-authorized immigrants in countries of destination on the basis of certain criteria and vary considerably in both format and content. They may, for instance, be established unilaterally by a country of destination or may be part of a bilateral agreement between a country of origin and a country of destination. They can be ongoing or limited in time, individual or collective.

The Latin American region has a long tradition of implementing regularization programmes, some of which are referred to below:

Argentina

In December 2005, the Argentine Government launched the National Programme for the Regularization of Migrants *"Patria Grande"*, which seeks to facilitate the insertion and integration of the migrant population through the granting of residence status. The programme is in keeping with the government's ideal of South American integration and intended to eradicate exploitation of irregular migrants by the business sector.

In its first phase, the programme was aimed at migrants from outside the MERCOSUR, the Common Market of the South consisting of Argentina, Brazil, Paraguay and Uruguay. According to the Interior Ministry, a total of 13,000 people, mainly from Asia and eastern Europe, were granted residence during this phase. The second phase, which started on the 17 April 2006, has facilitated the regularization of 552,909 migrants from MERCOSUR and associated countries, including Bolivia, Colombia, Ecuador and Peru (Ministry of the Interior, Argentina, 2008).

In this regard, a new settlement criterion is to be implemented, based on the possession of the nationality of one of the countries of the region and the principle of good faith, as a guiding principle for further regularization programmes.

Ecuador

In Ecuador, a decree has been issued to coordinate administrative processes enabling the regularization of undocumented Peruvians in the southern part of the country.

Through dialogue, Ecuador seeks to create legal options to introduce a regularization process for third-country nationals present in Ecuador and to establish a database for authorities to know how many foreigners are living in Ecuador, where they are living and their occupations.

Mexico

Mexico implemented a large regularization programme which benefited 15,000 migrants in the period 2002-2006, most of whom were from countries in Central America (National Institute of Migration, 2007).

Venezuela

The *"Mision Identidad"* (Identity Mission) implemented by Venezuela provided documentation to migrants who had been living in the country for many years and who did not possess identity cards, thereby formally incorporating them into the country's national development plans. The government regularized over 615,000 migrants during 1998-2006 (Ministry of Foreign Relations, Venezuela, 2006).

Source: *José-Angel Oropeza, IOM Bogotá.*

5.6 Africa

Africa is a vast continent characterized by many different migratory sub-systems besides two clearly defined poles of attraction. On the one hand, North Africa attracts people heading for Europe as their final destination (but who increasingly diversify their points of departure in West and East Africa) and, on the other, there is South Africa, which receives migrants from a large catchment area in the southern part of the continent. The Sahara desert used to serve as a separation boundary, but it has increasingly become a transit area, often a deadly one.

(a) North Africa – the African gate to Europe: from transit to settlement

The presence of North African migrants in Europe, particularly in southern Europe, is, at least in part, the result of irregular movements eventually normalized through regularization processes. This experience has generated the knowledge and logistics to sustain well established routes for migrants from East and West Africa. The most utilized one originates from the Gulf of Guinea (Benin, Cameroon, Ghana, Nigeria, Togo), crosses Mali and Niger, and leads north, through Algeria, where it bifurcates east towards Libya and west towards Morocco. Agadez in Niger, Gao and Kidal in Mali, and Tamanrasset in Algeria are transit nodes. A different route cuts southwest towards Senegal and Mauritania to cross over to the Canary Islands. The route that originates from East Africa cuts across Sudan, with Selima as the nodal point, and enters Libya at Kufra, the major port of entry, where migrants stay a short time before reaching the coast. Tripoli and Benghazi are the main departure points, with Lampedusa as the preferred destination.

Finally, it is worth noting the partial transformation the Maghreb countries are undergoing. They are now both transit and destination countries for sub-Saharan migrants. The countless tragedies that have occurred during the passage across the Mediterranean have certainly played a role in prompting some potential irregular migrants to delay their departure and in discouraging others from undertaking the crossing altogether. Some studies concerning Morocco have estimated the average time a migrant will stay between entry and embarkation for Europe at approximately 15 months (Collyer, 2006). The total number of such migrants has not been very high (between 7,000 and 13,000), but their condition as irregular migrants puts them under severe stress, as Morocco is under pressure from European countries to act to control irregular migration from its shores. The same can be said of Libya, where migrants break their journey to collect money for the crossing, and where they also end up if their attempts to proceed fail. In Libya, an economy for transit migration has flourished, both in Kufra, where people of many nationalities have settled to provide information to arriving new migrants, and the coastal cities where they prepare for departure (Hamood, 2006).

(b) Sub-Saharan Africa – diversity of movements

Sub-Saharan irregular migration is characterized by significant cross-border movements (see also Chapter 7) as well as flows to Europe and South Africa.

As opposed to migrants from North Africa, sub-Saharan communities are much less numerous in Europe and tend to gather by nationality. Irregular migrants from Senegal are found mostly in France and Italy, Nigerians are more numerous in the U.K. and Ireland. In the U.K., there are also irregular migrants from Zimbabwe and South Africa, while irregular migrants from Cape Verde, Angola and Guinea are found mainly in Portugal.

South Africa is the most prominent, although certainly not the only African destination of irregular sub-Saharan migrants (see also Chapter 3). Categories of irregular migrants include, among others, retrenched miners who remain in the country, tourists and students who work without permits, overstayers and migrants who entered evading border controls. A study estimated their numbers at anywhere between 390,000 and 470,000 (Crush and Williams, 2005).

5.7 East Asia – The Lure of Strong Economies

A region with diversified migration policies, East Asia experiences irregular migration mostly in the form of overstayers or persons engaging in work without proper documentation. In the Republic of Korea (South Korea), the phenomenon was connected in a very specific way to the presence of foreign trainees, employed in the textile, rubber and plastic industries (Ja-young, 2006), who turned into irregular workers in response to the ample employment opportunities provided by medium and small-sized companies but also to move away from stringent working conditions in their designated workplaces (UN Human Rights Council, 2007). The adoption of the Employment Permit System (EPS) in 2004, which was subsequently expanded to replace the industrial trainee system in January 2007, offered the opportunity to many irregular migrants to obtain regular status.[22] However, irregular migration – mainly in the form of overstaying – continues to be significant, but the number seems to be stabilizing: by mid-2006, about 190,000 individuals – half of all the migrant workers – lived and worked irregularly in South Korea (OECD, 2007). Similarly, in Japan, irregular migrants are mostly overstayers, and the Ministry of Justice estimated that at the beginning of 2005 they numbered approximately 207,000, while another estimated 30,000 persons were smuggled in by boat. Taiwan Province of China, is reported to be experiencing some irregular migration in the form of regular migrant workers who become clandestine residents because of problems with employers or as a result of lay-offs.

A new trend in East Asian irregular migration is the decrease of some intra-regional flows, while other less traditional destinations are becoming more attractive. On the one hand, "irregular migration" from mainland China to Hong Kong SAR and Taiwan Province of China has decreased, particularly because of the rapid development of the inland provinces (Hong Kong SAR is planning to attract skilled

[22] In 2003, the number of irregular migrant workers registered by the Ministry of Labour exceeded 227,000, and 80 per cent of them were afforded regular status under the Employment Permit System (UN Human Rights Council, 2007).

workers from mainland China under its Quality Migrant Admission Scheme). On the other hand, it is estimated that up to 200,000 irregular migrants from China are taking advantage of work opportunities created by the declining population in the Russian Far East (Akaha, 2004).

5.8 Southeast Asia – Cross-border Irregular Migration

Southeast Asia is a region of origin, transit and destination of migrants, where the most prevalent mode of entry is over land borders (see Chapter 7). Irregular migration in this region, however, takes many forms as illustrated in Portrait 8.1.

Portrait 8.1

Sailing to Nowhere – A Cambodian Migrant's Tale

Nang, aged 25, is a Cambodian fisherman from Banteay Meanchey province. He has very little formal education and, following the advice of some friends, decided to leave Cambodia in early 2004 to work in neighbouring Thailand to support his family.

He was recruited by a Cambodian broker (*mekhal*) who came to his village and promised him a job in the construction industry in Thailand paying up to THB 4,500 (USD 128) per month. The broker's fee, payable in advance, was THB 3,000 (USD 85).

Nang borrowed the money for the broker's fee from relatives, and he was then taken to the Malay district in Banteay Meanchey, where the broker helped him cross the border into Thailand unlawfully for an additional fee of THB 200 (USD 6).

Once in Thailand, he was taken to Patnam in Samut Prakan province, where he was kept in a guesthouse for several days before being told that there was no job in construction and that he would have to work on a fishing boat.

When he complained that he had been promised a job in construction, the broker threatened him that he could easily find himself in the custody of the Thai police as an irregular migrant. In fact, Nang believes that the broker sold him to the captain of the fishing boat for THB 5,000 (USD 150).

According to Nang, the conditions onboard his boat, which sailed towards Indonesian waters and remained there for six months, were extremely harsh. The crew had to work day and night for three days before having a day to rest, and was continually harassed and threatened by the captain.

Nang was never allowed to leave the boat, and even if the captain had allowed him ashore, he would have not gone for fear of being arrested by local police as an irregular migrant.

Eventually the boat docked in Ranong on the Thai-Myanmar border, where the Cambodian crew was replaced by a crew from Myanmar prior to moving on into that country's waters. Nang was paid a total of THB 2,000 (USD 57) for six months of work.

With no travel documents and unable to afford transport back to Cambodia, let alone the sum of THB 6,000 (USD 171) demanded by a broker to help him return home, Nang realized that it was only a matter of time before he would be picked up by the Thai police as an irregular migrant.

On the advice of other Cambodian fishermen stranded in Ranong, he signed up with another Thai fishing boat and was given forged papers identifying him as Thai.

In August 2004, while fishing illegally in Indian waters, the boat was intercepted by the Indian navy and escorted to Port Blair in the Andaman and Nicobar islands.

Before they arrived, Nang and the other Cambodian crew members were threatened by the crew that unless they stuck by their story that they were Thai, they would never be allowed to return home.

The entire crew was jailed, but after six weeks the Thai owner of the vessel arrived to stand bail and obtain their release. The Thai crew immediately left India, leaving Nang and the other Cambodians to fend for themselves.

Nang was then taken to the Port Blair Immigration Police Centre and held there for three months. When the case was finally heard in court, he pleaded guilty to entering India unlawfully and was sent to an internment camp, where he remained for two years.

In March 2007, working with the Cambodian and Indian governments, IOM was able to at last repatriate Nang from Port Blair to his home province of Banteay Meanchey.

Source: *IOM Bangkok.*

Both Malaysia and Thailand have large numbers of irregular migrants. In July 2006, some 1.8 million regular foreign workers, 65 per cent from Indonesia, were known to be employed in Malaysia, particularly in manufacturing, construction, service and plantation industries, though actual numbers are thought to be much higher, and the Malaysian Interior Ministry estimates that at least a further 600,000 irregular migrants were present, notwithstanding periodic repatriations (Hugo, 2007).

In Thailand in 2004, approximately 1.28 million migrants from Myanmar, Cambodia and Laos registered with the Ministry of Interior. Registration is a process by which such migrants are still considered to be present without authorization but which enables them to stay in the country and to apply to the Ministry of Labour for a work permit, which, if granted, can be renewed on an annual basis. Out of those irregular migrants who registered in 2004, nearly 850,000 received work permits. In the subsequent registration process conducted in 2006, a further 220,892 irregular migrants registered with the Ministry of Interior, and 208,262 of these obtained work permits.[23]

Although figures for irregular migration are not available for Singapore, the government is particularly watchful over the domestic services sector, and has introduced numerous regulations to ensure that workers respect their conditions of entry and employers abide by the terms of work contracts (Yeoh, 2007).

Irregular migration is also of concern in the Philippines, an important country of origin, where illegal recruiters make use of various schemes, including internet advertising, to lure workers to work abroad, including deployment to prohibited destinations such as Iraq,[24] or impose working conditions inconsistent with the minimum conditions laid out in the standard employment contract, in violation of the regulatory framework established by the government.

5.9 South Asia – The Close Line Between Trafficking in Human Beings and Labour Migration

While irregular migration in South Asia is mostly discussed in connection with human trafficking cases (Textbox 8.4), irregular labour migration is also a focus of attention. This is particularly the case from Bangladesh to India, where the phenomenon has been going on for more than a century and does not seem to be decreasing (Joseph, 2006). On the contrary, the flows of migrants irregularly crossing the border have intensified lately, prompting the installation of a fence at the border to stem entries

[23] Information provided by the Ministry of Labour to IOM Bangkok.

[24] The Philippines, along with Bangladesh, India and Nepal, expressly outlaws travel to Iraq for its nationals, while in Sri Lanka employment agencies are prohibited from offering jobs in Iraq (Brothers, 2007).

into the State of Assam. Bangladeshis in India have now begun to move away from the border into more prosperous areas in northern and northwestern India as well as into cities such as Delhi and Mumbai (Joseph, 2006; Ramachandran, 2005). Once at destination, these migrants are mainly employed in daily work wage labour, or as seasonal agricultural workers, construction or domestic workers. However, some of them become part of settled communities and acquire land or engage in business.

Reliable statistics about the number of Bangladeshis irregularly living and working in India are very difficult to obtain, but one source, drawing on both official and unofficial estimates, reports a figure as high as 10 million (Joseph, 2006). Deportation data collected by the different states provide additional information on trends, but they can be contradictory. For instance, statistics provided by the Delhi authorities state that a total of 2,957 migrants were deported between 1995 and 2002, with the number increasing to 5,028 in 2003. However, another source claims that from 2001 to 2004 the Delhi police sent back some 12,200 individuals to Bangladesh (Ramachandran, 2005).

Irregular migration from Bangladesh does not affect India only but also farther destinations such as the Gulf States. Research conducted on 200 Bangladeshi returnees from the Gulf (Siddiqui, 2006) found that, while 80 per cent migrated with valid documents, 70 per cent of them fell into irregularity at some stage of their migration process. While some of the migrants became irregular simply by switching to better paid jobs without authorization, the study identified unscrupulous recruiters, intermediaries and travel agents in the country of origin, as well as some employers, recruiters and members of law enforcement agencies in the country of destination as contributors to the problem (Siddiqui, 2006). Irregular migrants from Bangladesh, India and Pakistan have also begun to make their way to Europe, either by flying to West African capitals (sometimes via the Gulf States) and taking the common Saharan route to Morocco, or by entering North Africa through Egypt and moving on to Libya and Tunisia. From these three Maghreb countries they then attempt the sea crossing to Italy and Malta (de Haas, 2007).

Sri Lanka is another country affected by irregular migration, although the government has recently introduced several measures, such as bilateral discussion with countries of destination and pre-departure orientation for potential migrants to promote their regular migration. Among the destinations of irregular migrants from Sri Lanka are Canada, Italy, Japan, and South Korea. A study carried out on 200 irregular migrants sheds some light on the many different and circuitous routes used by irregular migrants to reach Italy. For example, sometimes they were taken to Karachi by small and very unseaworthy boats and from there to central or eastern European countries such as Bulgaria, Hungary, Romania or the Russian Federation. The last leg of the journey was undertaken by land to Italy. The study also found that a majority of the study sample did not have any vocational training and would engage in low-skilled jobs (Siddiqui, 2006).

Irregular movements for work in South Asia also include flows from Afghanistan, Bangladesh and Myanmar to Pakistan. Many irregular Afghani migrants, for instance, manage to enter and work in Pakistan with the help of networks established during the conflict period.

Textbox 8.4

Out-of-reach and Out-of-danger: Keeping Girls Safe from Traffickers in Nepal

Every year an estimated 12,000 Nepalese women and girls are trafficked into India. The Asian Development Bank estimates that 100,000 to 200,000 Nepalese women and girls are held against their will in Indian brothels, with roughly 25 per cent under the age of 18 years. Traffickers typically lure impoverished girls with promises of jobs in urban areas or abroad. Some families knowingly send their daughters to brothels because they consider them a burden. Many of the women and girls are illiterate and are not even aware that they have been taken across the border. The Government of Nepal has identified 26 districts from which women and girls have disappeared.

In response, the Reproductive Health Initiative for Youth in Asia (RHIYA), a partnership of the European Union and the United Nations Population Fund (UNFPA) working in collaboration with NGOs, is focusing on 19 "high-risk" impoverished districts. The programme educates parents, community leaders, district health officials and young people about the dangers of trafficking. It also provides girls and young women with training and empowerment opportunities. Trafficking survivors are reintegrated into their communities through efforts designed to reduce stigmatization and are referred to social and legal services for additional assistance.

The initiative is proving effective. In the district of Prasauni VDC, a RHIYA peer educator was able to rescue three adolescent girls the very same day they were scheduled to depart. She had learned that the young men who had promised the girls work were, in fact, traffickers. After the peer educator raised the alarm, villagers caught the traffickers and handed them over to the police. They soon admitted their guilt. In Rupandehi District, a young woman was asked by her brother-in-law to accompany him on a one-day shopping trip to Gorakhpur, just across the border. But when she arrived at the crossing, her brother-in-law introduced her to two other girls and asked her to accompany them into India, claiming that he would join them later after taking care of some personal business. She became alarmed, recalling the RHIYA educational sessions on trafficking, and realized that her brother-in-law must be a trafficker. She immediately sought help from the border NGO Maaiti Nepal, and all the girls were returned safely to their homes.

Source: *UNFPA (2006: 50).*

5.10 Middle East

Irregular movement for work is also an issue in the labour markets of Gulf Cooperation Council (GCC) States. As restrictions on work permits are progressively tightened, more migrant workers are prepared to enter without authorization or to stay beyond the expiration of their permits. In Kuwait, for instance, the Department of Immigration in the Ministry of Internal Affairs estimates the number of irregular migrants at up to 60,000 (UN DESA 2006, citing Shah, 2005). Two mechanisms working in favour of irregular migration are to be found in the employment sponsorship system, on the one hand, and the annual pilgrimage to Mecca (the *Hajj*), on the other.[25] Another striking characteristic of the region, which to a certain extent nurtures irregular flows, is the high dependence on foreign workers (remittances sent home from the Gulf States in 2005 represent nearly 9% of GDP). According to United Nations figures, 12.8 million foreigners lived and worked in the GCC States in 2005. The proportion of non-nationals within the local population is as high as 62.1 per cent for Kuwait and 71.4 per cent for the United Arab Emirates (UAE) (UN DESA, 2006). The Gulf States are committed to reducing the number of irregular contract workers: for instance, in Saudi Arabia and the UAE by making the sponsorship system more flexible and allowing workers to change employer before the traditional one-year period,

[25] Approximately 700,000 persons are deported from Saudi Arabia annually. Many come for the *Hajj* and then stay and work in the country (Shah, 2005).

and in Saudi Arabia by discouraging nationals from harbouring overstayers by imposing a maximum fee of SAR 5,000 (i.e. USD 1,335) and imprisonment of up to two years. However, the effectiveness of these measures has yet to be determined. Other important patterns of irregular movements in the region include arrivals from Somalia, Ethiopia and other African countries in Yemen, and irregular Afghan workers (perhaps 800,000) in Iran, where the authorities have announced their intention to proceed with repatriations.

5.11 Summary Points

Following this broad, though cursory, overview of irregular migration in various regions some summary points may be offered:

- Irregular migration is present in all major regions; therefore, it is of general interest to the international community.
- The magnitude of irregular migrant populations differs significantly across the various regions. Irregular migration seems to be a function of the overall volume of migration in a given region, the proximity of places of origin and destination, the permeability of borders and the strength of migration networks.
- The existence of work opportunities for lower-wage, low-skilled migrant workers is an important incentive for irregular migrants.
- Although irregular migration is a complex phenomenon and resistant to analysis, it is a global industry with connections to both legitimate migration agencies and to criminal networks.
- The choice of regular or irregular migration channels depends on a variety of factors: availability of regular channels; time necessary for the migration process to be completed; bureaucratic difficulties in the process; excessive conditions and requirements; preference for immediate profit over long-term benefits; and lack of or difficult access to available alternatives.
- Although irregular crossings attract the highest attention, most irregular migration occurs through the lawful entry of persons who then drift into irregularity by violating the terms of their admission through overstaying and/or working without authorization to do so. It may, therefore, be argued that the possibility of finding work is the ultimate determinant of irregular migration.

6. Policies

Policies to address irregular migration have coalesced around a number of well-established policy objectives: the fight against organized smuggling in migrants; control of external borders to reduce irregular entries; inspection of labour sites to reduce irregular employment; and cooperation towards development to ease migration pressure from countries of origin; and repatriation and return programmes, and agreements between countries of destination, origin and transit. Another policy option, the regularization of migrants to lower the number of irregular migrants present in the country, does not attract general consensus. While some countries have implemented it repeatedly, others have remained sceptical.

6.1 Efforts against Organized Smuggling

There is international consensus on the need to combat the organized crime of smuggling in migrants and this is one of the few areas where a multilateral approach to migration management is pursued. The 1990 International Convention on the Protection of the Rights of All Migrant Workers and Members of their Families specifically calls for such cooperation (Article 68). The 2000 Protocol against the Smuggling of Migrants by Land, Sea and Air has attracted 114 ratifications. There are numerous declarations and statements of governments committing or re-committing themselves to action (among the most recent ones are the 11 July 2006 Rabat Plan of Action, adopted by the Euro-African Ministerial

Conference on Migration and Development,[26] and the 13 January 2007 Association of Southeast Asian Nations (ASEAN) Declaration on the Protection and Promotion of the Rights of Migrant Workers).[27] Many Regional Consultative Processes have the topic as a standing item on their agenda.[28] However, the constant reiteration of the need for common efforts against organized smuggling is in itself an indication of how difficult it is to translate intentions into practice.

6.2 Control of Borders

In recent years, and particularly after September 11, 2001, much attention was given to the link between migration and security and the control of borders. At times, this has resulted in the reinforcement of border controls as best exemplified perhaps by the U.S. decision to build a 700-mile long fence along the U.S.-Mexican border, under the terms of the 2006 Secure Fence Act. The construction of a wall at the border between Thailand and Malaysia, the fence between Bangladesh and India, and the fences around Ceuta and Melilla reflect the pressures governments are facing from people wishing to move irregularly in search of better life opportunities.

Increasing use is also being made of high technology, including movement and heat sensor devices, sophisticated radar systems and automated identification systems incorporating biometric components (Redpath, 2007).

6.3 Internal Controls and Labour Inspections

All countries of destination are faced with the problem of establishing the identity of irregular migrants. A major challenge is the prevalence of forged documents; hence the ongoing attempts to introduce tamper-proof travel documents through the inclusion of high-technology security features. Another is the fact that irregular migrants are routinely advised by smugglers to conceal or destroy their travel documents to delay identification and make repatriation more difficult.

As employment opportunities play a key role in encouraging irregular migration despite the administrative obstacles, inspections of labour sites constitute an important deterrent, and indeed there are indications that many governments are moving in that direction. In 2006, for instance, the U.K. Border Agency (2008a) carried out over 5,200 operations to detect unauthorized employment and removed more than 22,000 people from the country. At the end of February 2008, new rules have been brought into effect, whereby employers could be fined up to £10,000 for every unauthorized worker they negligently hire or, if they knowingly hire such a worker, an unlimited fine and/or a maximum two years prison sentence (U.K. Border Agency, 2008b). However, there are challenges in conducting such operations in a planned and systematic way over time rather than relying on highly publicized one-off interventions. Human resource limitations and differences in enforcement priorities among the relevant agencies are hurdles that have to be overcome. In addition, such inspections are very difficult in areas of employment where migrants are scattered, for instance in the agricultural sector, or where controls can be carried out only indirectly, as in domestic employment.

6.4 Prevention through Development

The idea that prevention should begin with the stemming of migration pressures at source has been much debated over the years without leading to the development of concrete and sustainable intervention strategies. Put simply, the argument is that prevention of irregular migration should begin

[26] The text of the Action Plan is available from the website of the Government of Morocco's Ministry of Foreign Affairs and Cooperation at http://www.maec.gov.ma/migration/Doc/PA%20final%20EN.pdf.

[27] See the ASEAN website at http://www.aseansec.org/19264.htm.

[28] E.g. the Regional Ministerial Process on People Smuggling, Trafficking in Persons and Related Transnational Crime, known simply as the Bali Process, is devoted largely to this issue. See http://www.baliprocess.net/.

with socio-economic development in countries of origin, although a reduction in flows in the short term is not to be expected, as theorists of the "migration hump" have articulated (Martin and Taylor, 1996). In more recent times, the linkage between migration and development has taken on renewed significance, but from a different perspective, as demonstrated at the UN General Assembly's High-Level Dialogue on International Migration and Development in September 2006, and the Global Forum on Migration and Development in July 2007.[29] The switch in international thinking is that migration, while not a panacea for economic distress, can itself be a development factor, contributing in the shorter term to the reduction of poverty levels in the longer term, to sustainable growth. The spectacular increase in the recorded levels of remittances transferred to developing countries has played a large part in ensuring broad acceptance of that shift of perception in the international community. Research and international consultations have yielded a wide range of recommended actions, some of which are being implemented, although a comprehensive global effort has yet to be attempted.[30]

[29] For the GFMD, see also Textbox Int. 2.

[30] Chapter 12 offers a fuller discussion of the labour migration and development relationship.

6.5 Repatriation and Return Programmes and Agreements

Enforcement measures against irregular migration are often intended to lead to the repatriation of those identified as irregular migrants. Large-scale repatriations have been conducted in specific circumstances, for instance between Thailand and Myanmar or Malaysia and Indonesia. They appear to work best when coupled with offers of legitimate re-entry for the purpose of employment. In industrialized countries of destination, the acceptance rate is generally modest, even when return assistance is provided (see Portrait 8.2). Deportations are also practised, but are expensive to conduct on a large scale. It has been estimated, for instance, that the expulsion of one person from Spain to Romania costs USD 2,300, to Senegal USD 2,500, to Ecuador USD 4,900 and to China USD 8,600 (Caritas/Migrantes, 2005). Consequently, EU interior ministers decided in April 2004 to cooperate on organizing joint flights for the expulsion of third-country nationals to reduce costs.[31]

[31] Council Decision of 29 April 2004 on the organization of joint flights for removals from the territory of two or more Member States of third-country nationals who are subjects of individual removal orders, OJ 2004 L 261/28.

Portrait 8.2

From Kayes to Tripoli and back

Diakite was born in Kayes, Mali, on 1 January 1943. The name Kayes comes from the Soninke word *karre*, meaning a low, humid place prone to floods in the rainy season. Kayes is also referred to as the "pressure cooker of Africa" because of its extreme heat, to which the iron ore found in the surrounding mountains is said to contribute.

Diakite has always been a farmer, working the five hectares of land he inherited from his father. A drought in 2004 made it difficult to eke out enough from the arid soil to live on, and his son decided to search for a better life by heading towards North Africa and later, perhaps, Europe. Then, one year later, Diakite also left to search for his son, who had disappeared. At the time of their last phone call, he had been working as an employee in Ghatt, south-western Libya.

Diakite travelled across his large country by any means he could find; he entered Algeria with the "assistance" of a smuggler, and then Libya. "Unfortunately, I did all this just to find my son's name written on a gravestone in a Ghatt cemetery. I never did find out how and why my son died", Diakite said. When he found himself a stranger and irregular migrant in a new country, without a job or money, he decided to go to Tripoli to find work that would allow him to earn the money needed to get back home. "Like many others from sub-Saharan Africa, I was sitting on the sidewalk of a street near a big market in Tripoli, with a brush and a tin of paint in front of me to indicate to passers-by the service I could offer for a few dinars. Sometimes I was lucky, and I found work for a few days or weeks decorating Libyan houses. At other times, I would wait in vain sitting under the sun the whole day", relates Diakite. For one year, he managed to survive by doing occasional jobs, but was unable to save enough money to return home. At the beginning of 2007, the Malian Embassy in Tripoli referred him to IOM as a possible candidate to benefit under an Assisted Voluntary Return and Reintegration (AVRR) programme. Diakite was able to return to Kayes, where he will buy a water pump to make his land prosper again. "This water pump will be beneficial to my family and the whole community, and I am glad to be back and able to tell the young people in my town how the dreams of emigrating can turn into nightmares."

Source: *IOM Tripoli.*

Another crucial aspect of repatriation is the willingness of countries of origin to accept expelled migrants. In December 2005, in response to a Parliamentary question, the Spanish Government announced that between 1 January 2001 and 31 May 2005 a total of 122,238 expulsion orders were not carried out (*Migration News Sheet*, December 2005). Most consulates of sub-Saharan countries refused to recognize the migrants to be returned as their citizens. Consequently, countries of destination have been eager to sign readmission agreements with countries of origin. Italy has signed more than 20 such agreements (IGC, 2002), but not all of them are yet operative. Spain has succeeded in signing agreements with some sub-Saharan countries (Cape Verde, Gambia, Guinea Conakry, Guinea Bissau, Mauritania, Nigeria, Ghana) (Embassy of Spain (London, U.K.), 2007), but others are resisting entering into readmission agreements. However, there are no indications of a close correlation between numbers of agreements signed and numbers of irregular migrants sent home.

Some lessons learnt from return programmes are described in Textbox 8.5 below.

Textbox 8.5

Return Programmes – Lessons Learnt

- Return programmes are best implemented as one important element within a comprehensive approach to migration management.
- To be successful, return interventions must not be a policy afterthought. Return interventions begin at the point of entry through the provision of timely and accurate information about options and consequences, not when weeks or months later a decision on return is eventually taken.
- Counselling by authoritative and credible interlocutors can create an appropriate context for return decisions.
- Protection of the dignity and integrity of the individual is essential.
- Both mandatory and voluntary programmes have their place in a properly designed approach to return, although there is a real challenge in ensuring that they are complementary and mutually supportive.
- Return programmes are best developed in partnership between countries of origin and destination. A prerequisite to this is the establishment of effective communication lines between the two parties, and the creation of mutual confidence.
- Carefully designed reintegration programmes that take account, where appropriate, of the needs of local residents as well as of returnees can contribute significantly to the sustainability of return.

- The range of available options is practically unlimited, ranging from preparation for return to return visits, on-the-job training, setting up of small businesses and community development activities.

Among the most successful return programmes are those that operate on a small scale and are tailored to the particular circumstances of particular returnees and countries of origin.

Source: *Nicoletta Giordano, Former Head, Return Migration Management, IOM.*

6.6 Regularizations

Beginning in the 1980s, regularizations have become a frequent means of addressing the presence of a large number of irregular migrants, especially those with a stable record of employment and other claims to local integration, for whom any other outcome would be politically or socially unacceptable or too difficult to implement. There are wide differences in both terminology and actual administrative measures: amnesties, regularizations, and registration have all been decreed from time to time (Levinson, 2005). In southern Europe, since the early 1990s, regularization campaigns have been conducted more often than anywhere else in the world (three in Greece, three in Portugal, four in Italy, five in Spain, involving more than three million migrants in total), to the point of being a major instrument of migration management. The last regularizations by Spain and Italy were directed only at migrants in employment with applications submitted on their behalf by their respective employers. While regularizations may represent a highly favourable outcome for irregular migrants (particularly if they do not fall back into irregular status) who can thus accede to legitimate employment and services, they are also criticized for creating the perception that irregular entry and stay is a calculated risk, and one worth taking as it pays off eventually. This reasoning explains the policy stance of countries, such as Germany, which have remained steadily opposed to the idea of regularization programmes.[32]

[32] But see the decision of the German Länder in November 2006 to legalize the situation of migrants with the precarious temporary *Duldung* status (referred to in Chapter 11), which may represent a turning point in the traditional line taken on regularization in Germany.

In the Gulf Cooperation Council (GCC) States and Southeast and East Asia, irregular migrants are not regularized as permanent residents. Rather, they are invited to register for the right to reside and work on a temporary basis (see Sections 5.7 and 5.8 above and Map 7b). The frequency of registrations is even higher than that of regularizations, indicating that this policy is not necessarily more effective in discouraging irregular migration.

In the U.S. there has been a vigorous ongoing debate about the policies that should be introduced to address the problem of the estimated 11 to 12 million irregular migrants present in the country. Since 2004, the government has tried repeatedly to put into place a plan to address the issue of undocumented workers within the context of a comprehensive temporary worker programme that would be accessible to both irregular migrants within the U.S. and applicants from abroad. The issue remains unresolved (Levinson, 2005).

7. Conclusion

Irregular migration is undoubtedly one of the most complex, sensitive and intractable migration management problems confronting the international community. Most of the responses to the problem have been and continue to be implemented essentially at the national level, but there is a clearly discernible evolution towards the development of cooperative approaches on either a bilateral or multilateral basis (for example, see Textbox 8.6).

One form of cooperation has focused increasingly on measures of control between countries of destination and transit. Such cooperation typically covers joint interdiction operations and capacity building – including the training of personnel and procurement of equipment. One unintended consequence of this approach is that irregular migrants become more inclined to seek to gain access to informal economies and settle in the country of transit (Collyer, 2006), thus giving rise in the medium to longer term to problems of social exclusion and petty criminality.

Another avenue of cooperation leads to migration and development initiatives, to lower the costs of remittance transfers, create savings schemes for migrants, apply the remittances to sustainable development enterprises and to mobilize the resources of diasporas.

In parallel with this, there is good reason to be optimistic about the part that managed labour migration programmes can play. While there is no evidence that labour migration programmes spell the end of irregular flows, they do offer an important, more manageable and more predictable alternative. And crucially, they provide better protection for the rights and dignity of migrants, which is what all policies should aim to do.

Textbox 8.6

Cooperation on Preventing Unauthorized Employment of Migrant Workers with a view to Promoting Regular Employment

In 2006, IOM Helsinki carried out a project called "Cooperation on preventing illegal employment of labour migrants with a view to promoting legal employment opportunities" (PIELAMI), involving partners from Finland, Latvia and North-West Russia. The project was funded under the European Commission's ARGO programme,[1] with co-funding from the Finnish Ministry of Labour, and largely focused on the service and construction sectors.

The impetus for the project came from IOM Helsinki's interest in exploring the interplay between unauthorized employment of migrant workers and labour market demand.

The project involved three main activities:

1. The drafting of working papers on the scope of unauthorized employment as well as regular employment opportunities for third-country nationals in Finland, Latvia and North-West Russia.[2]

2. A seminar in Helsinki in November 2006 attended by representatives from the Baltic Sea states.

3. A project report including the material and findings of the project (available from http://iom.fi/content/view/159/8/).

The working papers concluded that it was not possible to either generalize or simplify the causes or, indeed, the outcomes of unauthorized employment of migrant workers, as they reflected the very different migration contexts and labour market conditions of each country. Furthermore, different countries use different methods to combat unauthorized employment, often with little coordination between relevant authorities such as the police, tax authorities and migration officials. Officials who participated in the PIELAMI seminar pointed to the need for intensified administrative cooperation and exchange of information not only on methods to prevent unauthorized employment of migrant workers, but also to promote lawful employment opportunities.

Based on the papers and seminar discussions as a source of inspiration, IOM formulated a number of recommendations on the subject, which focused on the questions at issue from various angles. Some of the key recommendations are listed below:

- The encouragement of cooperative action among all stakeholders, including employers' associations and unions.

- Wide dissemination of information about employment opportunities and working conditions abroad.

- The creation of regular channels to enable workers to obtain access to the labour market in countries of destination.
- The protection of the rights of migrant workers, including through the signing and ratifying of relevant international conventions, the setting of minimum wages and the provision of access to justice and health care systems.
- The adoption of measures to combat intolerance, discrimination and xenophobia to facilitate the integration of migrant workers in host societies.

Notes:

[1] Action programme for administrative cooperation in the fields of external borders, visas, asylum and immigration (2002-2006).

[2] For North-West Russia, the term "foreign national" was used because in Finland and Latvia "third-country national" refers to a citizen from outside the European Economic Area (EEA).

Source: *IOM Helsinki.*

REFERENCES

Achieng, M.

2006 "Managing Haitian Migratory Flows to the Dominican Republic: The Challenges and Opportunities" in T. Lesser, B. Fernández-Alfaro, L. Cowie and N. Bruni (Eds.), *Intra-Caribbean Migration and the Conflict Nexus*, Human Rights Internet in collaboration with the International Organization for Migration (IOM), the Association of Caribbean States, and The University of the West Indies (Center for Latin America and the Caribbean), Ottawa, 343-367.

Akaha, T.

2004 "Cross-Border Human Flows in Northeast Asia", *Migration Information Source,* October, Migration Policy Institute (MPI), Washington, D.C., http://www.migrationinformation.org/Feature/display.cfm?ID=257.

Battistella, G. and M.M.B. Asis (Eds.)

2003 *Unauthorized Migration in Southeast Asia*, Scalabrini Migration Center, Quezon City, Philippines.

Brothers, C.

2007 "Migrants fall into hardship in Iraq", *International Herald Tribune*, 11 May, http://www.iht.com/articles/2007/05/11/news/refugees.php.

Caritas/Migrantes

2005 *Immigrazione. Dossier statistico 2005. XV Rapporto [Statistical Dossier on Immigration, 2005; 15th Report]*, Idos, Rome.

2006 *Immigrazione. Dossier statistico 2006. XVI Rapporto [Statistical Dossier on Immigration, 2006; 16th Report]*, Idos, Rome.

2007 *Immigrazione. Dossier statistico 2007. XVII Rapporto [Statistical Dossier on Immigration, 2007; 17th Report]*, Idos, Rome.

Collyer, M.

2006 "States of insecurity: Consequences of Saharan transit migration", Working Paper No. 31, Centre on Migration Policy and Society (COMPAS), University of Oxford, http://www.compas.ox.ac.uk/publications/Working%20papers/WP0631-Collyer.pdf.

Costanzo, J., C. Davis, C. Irazi, D. Goodkind and R. Ramirez

2001 "Evaluating Components of International Migration: The Residual Foreign Born", Unauthorized Migration Evaluation Team (UMET), Working Paper Series No. 61, December, Population Division, U.S. Census Bureau, Washington, D.C., http://www.census.gov/population/www/documentation/twps0061/twps0061.html.

Crush, J. and V. Williams

2005 "International Migration and Development: Dynamics and Challenges in South and Southern Africa", Doc. UN/POP/MIG/2005/05 (30 June), United Nations Expert Group Meeting on International Migration and Development, 6-8 July, Population Division, UN Department of Economic and Social Affairs (UN DESA), New York, http://www.un.org/esa/population/meetings/ittmigdev2005/P05_Crush&Williams.pdf.

de Haas, H.

2007 "The myth of invasion – Irregular migration from West Africa to the Maghreb and the European Union", International Migration Institute (IMI) Research Report, October, University of Oxford, http://www.imi.ox.ac.uk/pdfs/Irregular%20migration%20from%20West%20Africa%20-%20Hein%20de%20Haas.pdf.

Delaunay, D. and G. Tapinos

1998 "La mesure de la migration clandestine en Europe", Vol. 1 - Rapport de synthèse, Vol. 2 - Rapport des experts, Eurostat Working Papers, Series "Population et conditions sociales", 3/1998/E/No.7 (March), Luxembourg, http://horizon.documentation.ird.fr/exl-doc/pleins_textes/pleins_textes_6/griseli1/010016012.pdf.

Embassy of Spain (London, U.K.)

2007 "Spain in the Fight against Illegal Immigration", Doc. E/06-07/F166 FRO, Memorandum submitted to the Inquiry of the U.K. House of Lords Select Committee on the European Union on "FRONTEX: the EU external borders agency", http://www.parliament.uk/documents/upload/FRO%20166%20Spanish%20Embassy%2019.10.07.doc.

EUbusiness.com

2007a "EU patrols cut migrant arrivals: border agency", EUbusiness.com, 13 April.

2007b "EU says cooperation on immigrants at sea wanting", EUbusiness.com, 29 May, http://www.eubusiness.com/Living_in_EU/1180443610.71.

European Commission

2005 *Policy Plan on Legal Migration,* COM (2005) 669, 21 December.

Fernández-Alfaro, B. and G. Pascua

2006 "Migration Management Challenges in the Caribbean" in T. Lesser, B. Fernández-Alfaro, L. Cowie and N. Bruni (Eds.), *Intra-Caribbean Migration and the Conflict Nexus*, Human Rights Internet in collaboration with the IOM, the Association of Caribbean States, and The University of the West Indies (Center for Latin America and the Caribbean), Ottawa, 70-87.

Guild, E.

2004 "Who is an irregular migrant?" in B. Bogusz, R. Cholewinski, A. Cygan and E. Szyszczak (Eds.), *Irregular Migration and Human Rights: Theoretical, European and International Perspectives*, Martinus Nijhoff, Leiden/Boston, 3-28.

Hamood, S.

2006 *African Transit Migration through Libya to Europe: The Human Cost*, January, The American University in Cairo, http://www.migreurop.org/IMG/pdf/hamood-libya.pdf.

Hatton, T.J. and J.G. Williamson

2002 "What Fundamentals Drive World Migration?", National Bureau of Research (NBER) Working Paper 9159, September, Cambridge, MA, http://www.nber.org/papers/w9159.

Hugo, G.

2007 "Indonesia's Labor Looks Abroad", *Migration Information Source*, April, MPI, Washington, D.C., http://www.migrationinformation.org/Profiles/display.cfm?ID=594.

Huguet, J.W. and S. Punpuing

2005 *International Migration in Thailand*, IOM, International Labour Organization (ILO), United Nation's Children Fund (UNICEF), United Nations Development Programme (UNDP), United Nations Economic and Social Commission for Asia and Pacific (UN ESCAP), The World Bank, World Health Organization (WHO), Bangkok, http://www.iom-seasia.org/resource/pdf/SituationReport.PDF.

Intergovernmental Consultations on Migration, Asylum and Refugees (IGC)

2002 *IGC Report on Readmission Agreements*, January, IGC Secretariat, Geneva.

International Labour Organization (ILO)

2004 *Towards a Fair Deal for Migrant Workers in the Global Economy*, Report VI, International Labour Conference, 92nd Session, International Labour Office, Geneva, http://www.ilo.org/global/Themes/Labour_migration/lang--en/docName--KD00096/index.htm.

International Organization for Migration (IOM)

2001 *Binational Study: the State of Migration Flows between Costa Rica and Nicaragua - Analysis of the Economic and Social Implications for Both Countries*, prepared for IOM by The State of the Nation Project, December.

Istituto Nazionale di Statistica (ISTAT)

2006 "La misura dell'economia sommersa secondo le statistiche ufficiali. Anni 2000-2004" ["Assessment of the underground economy according to official statistics. Years 2000-2004"], 14 December, ISTAT.

Jachimowicz, M.

2006 "Argentina: A New Era of Migration and Migration Policy", *Migration Information Source*, February, MPI, Washington, D.C., http://www.migrationinformation.org/Profiles/display.cfm?ID=374.

Jandl, M.

2004 "The Estimation of Illegal Migration in Europe", *Studi Emigrazione/Migration Studies*, XLI(153) (March): 141-155.

Ja-young, Y.

2006 "Foreigners replace Koreans in labor-intensive sectors", *The Korea Times*, 26 July.

Joseph, J.

2006 "Securitization of Illegal Migration of Bangladeshis to India", Non-Traditional Security in Southeast Asia, Working Paper Series on Non-Traditional Security in Southeast Asia, No. 100, January, The Institute of Defense and Strategic Studies (IDSS), Singapore, http://www.ntu.edu.sg/RSIS/publications/WorkingPapers/WP100.pdf.

Karaboytcheva, M.K.

2006 "Una Evaluación del Último Proceso de Regularización de Trabajadores Extranjeros en España (Febrero-Mayo de 2005). Un Año Después (DT)". ["An Evaluation of the Last Regularization Process of Foreign Workers in Spain (February-May 2005). One Year On"], DT No. 15, Real Instituto Elcano de Estudios Internacionales y Estratégicos [The Elcano Royal Institute for International and Strategic Studies], Madrid.

Krissman, F.

2005 "Sin Coyote Ni Patrón: Why the 'Migrant Network' Fails to Explain International Migration", *International Migration Review*, 39(1): 4-44.

Levinson, A.

2005 "The Regularisation of Unauthorized Migrants: Literature Survey and Country Case Studies", COMPAS, University of Oxford, http://www.compas.ox.ac.uk/publications/papers/Regularisation%20Report.pdf.

Martin, P.L. and J.E. Taylor

1996 "The anatomy of a migration hump" in J.E. Taylor (Ed.), *Development Strategy, Employment and Migration: Insights from models*, Organization for Economic Cooperation and Development (OECD), Paris.

Massey, D.S. and C. Capoferro

2004 "Measuring Undocumented Migration", *International Migration Review*, 38(3): 1075-1102.

Mexico, National Institute of Migration

2007 *Estadísticas Migratorias [Migration Statistics 2007]*, Instituto Nacional de Migración [National Institute of Migration].

Migration News Sheet

2005 "Spain: 122,238 expulsion orders not carried out in five years", *Migration News Sheet*, December, Migration Policy Group (MPG), Brussels, 6.

2005-2006 Various issues, MPG, Brussels.

2007 "Spain: 55% drop in number of irregular migrants to the Canary Islands", *Migration News Sheet*, September, MPG, Brussels, 10-11.

Mitsilegas, V.

2004 "Measuring Irregular Migration: Implications for Law, Policy and Human Rights" in B. Bogusz, R. Cholewinski, A. Cygan and E. Szyszczak (Eds.), *Irregular Migration and Human Rights: Theoretical, European and International Perspectives*, Martinus Nijhoff, Leiden/Boston, 29-39.

Moscarelli, S.

2008 "Consolidating reception capacities in respect of migration flows reaching the island of Lampedusa and other strategic border points on the Sicilian coasts", presentation at the IOM's International Dialogue on Migration Workshop (IDM) on Managing Return Migration, 21-22 April, Geneva, http://www.iom.int/jahia/Jahia/policy-research/pid/1964.

O'Neil, K., K. Hamilton and D. Papademetriou

2005 "Migration in the Americas", paper prepared for the Policy Analysis and Research Programme of the Global Commission on International Migration (GCIM), September, Geneva, http://www.gcim.org/attachements/RS1.pdf.

Organisation for Economic Co-operation and Development (OECD)

2004 *International Migration Outlook*, SOPEMI, OECD, Paris.

2007 *International Migration Outlook*, SOPEMI, OECD, Paris.

Palidda, S. and P. Cuttitta

2007 "Europe's Mediterranean Border: of boats and men", *Shift Mag* No. 5, 16 May, 10-11, http://www.shiftmag.eu/index.php/?2007/05/16/23-europes-mediterranean.

Passel, J.S.

2006 "The Size and Characteristics of the Unauthorized Migration Population in the U.S.", 7 March Research Report, Pew Hispanic Center, Washington, D.C., http://pewhispanic.org/files/reports/61.pdf.

Piguet, E. and S. Losa

2001 *Travailleurs de l'ombre? Demande de main-d'oeuvre du domaine de l'asile et ampleur de l'emploi d'étrangers non déclarés en Suisse*, Rapport de recherché, Swiss Forum for Migration Studies, Etude mandatée par l'Office fédéral des réfugiés, 19/20.

Platform for International Cooperation on Undocumented Migrants (PICUM)

2006 "France", *PICUM Newsletter*, 9 June, Brussels, http://www.picum.org/HOMEPAGE/NewsletterJune2006/NEWS%20ENGL%2006-06.doc.

Ramachandran, S.

2005 "Indifference, impotence, and intolerance: transnational Bangladeshis in India", Global Migration Perspectives No. 42, September, GCIM, Geneva, http://www.gcim.org/attachements/GMP%20No%2042.pdf.

Redpath, J.

2007 "Biometrics and International Migration" in R. Cholewinski, R. Perruchoud and E. MacDonald (Eds.), *International Migration Law: Developing Paradigms and Key Challenges*, Asser Press, The Hague, 427-445.

Ruhs, M.

2005 "The potential of temporary migration programmes in future international migration policy", paper prepared for the Policy Analysis and Research Programme of the GCIM, September, Geneva, http://www.gcim.org/attachements/TP3.pdf.

Salt, J. and J. Stein

1997 "Migration as a Business: The Case of Trafficking", *International Migration*, 35(4): 467-494.

Sarzanini, F.

2007 "Controlli su chi finanzia le moschee. Il Viminale studia il modello francese" [Controls on those who finance the mosques. The Ministry of Interior studies the French model], *Corriere della Sera*, 5 January.

Schneider, F.

2004, "The Size of the Shadow Economies of 145 Countries all over the World: First Results over the Period 1999 to 2003", IZA DP No. 1431, December, Institute for the Study of Labour, Bonn, http://ftp.iza.org/dp1431.pdf.

Scott, P.

2004 "Undocumented Migrants in Germany and Britain: The Human 'Rights' and 'Wrongs' Regarding Access to Health Care", *Electronic Journal of Sociology*, http://www.sociology.org/content/2004/tier2/scott.html.

Shah, N.M.

2005 "Restrictive Labor Immigration Policies in the Oil-Rich Gulf: Implications for sending Asian Countries", paper presented at the XXV International Union for the Scientific Study of Population (IUSSP) International Population Conference, Session No. 141: Impact of International Migration Policies, 18-23 July, Tours, France, http://iussp2005.princeton.edu/download.aspx?submissionId=50842.

Siddiqui, T.

2006 "Securitization of Irregular Migration: The South Asian Case" in R. Emmers, M. Caballero-Anthony and A. Acharya (Eds.), *Studying Non Traditional Security in Asia: Trends and Issues*, Marshall Cavendish Academic, Singapore, 143-167.

Switzerland, Federal Migration Office

2005 "Sans-papiers en Suisse: c'est le marché de l'emploi qui est déterminant, non pas la politique d'asile", Rapport final sur mandat de L'Office fédéral des migrations, 6 April, Berne, http://www.bfm.admin.ch/etc/medialib/data/migration/illegale_migration/sans_papiers.Par.0006.File.tmp/sans_papiers_studie.pdf.

United Kingdom, Home Office, Border Agency

2008a "New Advertising Campaign Launched To Stop Businesses Employing Illegal Workers", 14 January, Home Office Press Release, http://press.homeoffice.gov.uk/press-releases/Campaign-To-Stop-Illegal-Workers?version=1.

2008b "For employers and sponsors: Preventing illegal working - Complying with the law", U.K. Border Agency, http://www.ind.homeoffice.gov.uk/employers/preventingillegalworking/.

United Nations, General Assembly, Human Rights Council

2007 *Report of the Special Rapporteur on the human rights of migrants. Mission to the Republic of Korea (5-12 December 2006)*, Doc. A/HRC/4/24/Add.2 (14 March).

United Nations, Department of Economic and Social Affairs (UN DESA), Population Division
2006 *International Migration in the Arab Region*, UN Doc. UN/POP/EGM/2006/14 (11 May), UN Expert Group Meeting on International Migration and Development in the Arab Region: Challenges and Opportunities, Beirut, 15-17 May, UN DESA, Population Division, http://www.un.org/esa/population/meetings/EGM_Ittmig_Arab/P14_PopDiv.pdf.

United Nations, Offices on Drugs and Crime (UNODC)
2006 *Organized Crime and Irregular Migration from Africa to Europe*, July, UNODC, Regional Office of West and Central Africa and the Research and Analysis Section.

Woodbridge, J.
2005 *Sizing the unauthorised (illegal) migrant population in the United Kingdom in 2001*, Home Office Online Report 29/05, http://www.homeoffice.gov.uk/rds/pdfs05/rdsolr2905.pdf.

Yeoh, B.S.A.
2007 "Singapore: Hungry for Foreign Workers at All Skill Levels", *Migration Information Source*, January, MPI, Washington, D.C., http://www.migrationinformation.org/Profiles/display.cfm?ID=570.

Textbox 8.1 - Contested Spaces of (Il)Legality

Ruhs, M. and B. Anderson
2007 "The origins and functions of illegality in migrant labour markets: An analysis of migrants, employers and the state in the UK", 1 December, COMPAS, University of Oxford, http://www.compas.ox.ac.uk/publications/Working%20papers/wp-06-30a.shtml.

Textbox 8.2 - Trafficking for Forced Labour

Belser, P., M. de Cock and F. Mehran
2005 *ILO Minimum Estimate of Forced Labour in the World*, April, International Labour Office, Geneva, http://www.ilo.org/sapfl/Informationresources/ILOPublications/lang--en/docName--WCMS_081913/index.htm.

United States Department of State
2006 *Trafficking in Persons Report 2006*, June, U.S. Department of State, Washington, D.C., http://www.state.gov/g/tip/rls/tiprpt/2006/.

Textbox 8.3 - Regularization Programmes: The Latin-American Case

Arango, J. and M. Jachimowicz
2005 "Regularizing Immigrants in Spain: A New Approach", *Migration Information Source*, September, MPI, Washington, D.C., http://www.migrationinformation.org/Feature/display.cfm?id=331.

Argentina, Ministry of the Interior
2008 "Programa Patria Grande", Ana Alfonso, Jefa de la Oficina de Temas Internacionales, Dirección Nacional de Migraciones, Ministerio del Interior, Argentina, presentación realizada en la primera Sesión Especial sobre Temas de Actualidad del Derecho Internacional de los Refugiados de la CAJP. 29 de enero, Organización de Estados Americanos (OEA), http://www.oas.org/dil/esp/refugiados_sesion_especial_2008_presentacion_adriana_alfonso_anexo_III.pdf.

Geronimi, E.
2004 *Admisión, contratación y protección de trabajadores migrantes: Panorama de la legislación y la práctica nacionales de Argentina, Bolivia, Brasil, Chile, Colombia, Ecuador, España, Perú, Portugal y Uruguay*, International Migration Papers No. 70, International Labour Office, Geneva, http://www.ilo.org/public/english/protection/migrant/download/imp/imp70s.pdf.

Mexico, National Institute of Migration
2007 Estadísticas Migratorias [*Migration Statistics 2007*], Instituto Nacional de Migración [National Institute of Migration].

Turner, E. and M.R. Rosenblum
2005 "Solving the Unauthorized Migrant Problem: Proposed Legislation in the US", *Migration Information Source*, September, MPI, Washington, D.C., http://www.migrationinformation.org/Feature/display.cfm?id=333.

Organisation for Economic Co-operation and Development (OECD)
2001 *Trends in International Migration*, SOPEMI, OECD, Paris.

Venezuela, Ministry of Foreign Relations
2006 *"Sistema de identificación nacional es uno de los cinco mejores y más seguros del mundo (II)"*, 27 November, Ministry of Foreign Relations, http://www.minci.gob.ve/entrevistas/3/11048/sistema_de_identificacion.html.

Textbox 8.4 - Out-of-reach and Out-of-danger: Keeping Girls Safe from Traffickers in Nepal

United Nations Population Fund (UNPFA)
2006 *The State of World Population 2006. A Passage to Hope: Women and International Migration*, UNFPA, http://www.unfpa.org/upload/lib_pub_file/650_filename_sowp06-en.pdf.

PART B

MANAGING LABOUR MOBILITY IN THE EVOLVING GLOBAL ECONOMY

ENHANCING THE KNOWLEDGE BASE*

CHAPTER 9

1. Introduction

Migration management is a sensitive public policy domain where every policy proposal is the subject of close scrutiny by political parties, the media, interest groups and the community at large. Migration is increasingly recognized by countries of origin and destination as having the potential to provide appropriate solutions to problems of labour supply and demand, but public opinion is sharply divided over this issue. Some may see migration as the answer to demographic problems, such as low birth rates, population ageing and contracting labour forces. Others view migrants as competing for scarce resources. Policymakers therefore confront various challenges as they seek to develop balanced and effective migration policies. They are conscious of the risks they incur in generating unintended dynamics that can be detrimental to the labour market in particular, and economic growth in general (Boswell et al., 2004).

Governments considering the introduction of labour migration programmes as a means of addressing labour market concerns need to base their decisions on reliable information and migration data.

This chapter discusses the ways in which governments can and do enhance their knowledge base and their capacity to devise timely and effective labour migration policies. As discussed in greater detail in Chapter 11, the governments of destination countries often rely on the available knowledge base in the labour market provided by, for example, employers and trade unions, to formulate, implement and evaluate their labour migration policies. Governments may, however, also develop their own knowledge base by collecting and analysing appropriate data and sponsoring/conducting their own research on migration, including labour migration. This chapter deals primarily with the knowledge base at the disposal of governments and the means to enhance it. Since labour migration is an integral part of international migration, some of the initiatives discussed in this chapter are of relevance to the management of international migration in general, but the main focus is on labour migration. Three areas of activities are emphasized.

The first addresses the nature and quality of existing data collection mechanisms. Official government statistics may suffer from a lack of reliability and

* This chapter was written by Jobst Köhler, Research Officer (Statistics and Survey Analyst), IOM, Geneva. The author would like to thank Christine Aghazarm for her research assistance and Marina Peunova for her comments.

comparability, in part owing to different definitions used, concepts of measurement and data collecting methods. Governments and international bodies are therefore looking for ways and means to improve the reliability and comparability of their official data.

Second, governments sometimes need to adjust their statistical systems in order to respond to new labour migration challenges for which only limited or no data are available. The chapter discusses different strategies and initiatives to collect data on emerging or rapidly evolving policy issues such as transnational communities or diasporas, circular migration, remittances, highly skilled migration, irregular migration and the impacts or outcomes of various migration programmes.

Lastly, a range of measures exists to improve the availability and policy relevance of data and information on migration. Though many and diverse sources are engaged in the collection and generation of migration data, such sources are not necessarily always known to policymakers, or may not be perceived to be of relevance to their decision-making processes or, indeed, such data as exist may not always reach or be available to them. The chapter discusses different approaches and mechanisms to make data more widely accessible and policy-relevant.

2. Enhancing the Knowledge Base on Labour Migration: A Comprehensive Approach to Data Collection

The collection of pertinent data is fundamental to appropriate and timely policymaking. As in other policy areas, data collection systems in the field of migration, especially concerning labour migration, face the challenge of having to serve and reconcile different, and at times conflicting, information needs at various levels of government.

Thus, to formulate and enact legal and policy frameworks, the legislative and executive branches of governments require reliable aggregate and analytical information from which to draw the necessary insights and understandings concerning the different trends and impacts of migration in various areas of interest to the public domain.

In the middle, there are those officials who run the agency offices that deal directly with migrants, in either service or law enforcement roles; they are largely involved in the effective day-to-day management of services offered and activities performed. At this level, the need is also for aggregated information, but of a somewhat different nature. Generally limited in detail or characteristics, the data consist of summaries – of the number of clients processed at a particular time or similar measures used to measure productivity and outcomes of a particular programme.

Finally, the various categories of staff involved in frequent and individual contact with migrants, such as case workers, require detailed and individual information and access to records of migrants to be in a position to align and conduct their programmes and activities in accordance with the particular characteristics, experiences and needs of individual or groups of individual migrants on a predominantly personal and individual basis (Pember and Djerma, 2005).

Although policymakers, programme managers and case workers have different interests in the data collected, they typically have to rely on the same data collection system. In fact, much of the data used for policy or programme management purposes and/or on which expert reports may be based, are initially generated by the programme staff who often have little stake in, or understanding of, how the aggregate records of their individual transactions are used by agency heads and policymakers. In order to generate accurate and timely data on labour migration for policy purposes, a data collection system needs to recognize the different information needs at the various levels of government and find ways to balance them.

3. Improving the Reliability of Existing Data Sources

The compilation of statistics on international migration, including labour migration will also depend on how "international migration" is defined. There are no universally agreed definitions. Although there are international recommendations on "international migration statistics", differing national definitions still persist, especially regarding subsets of international migration such as labour migration (UN DESA, 1998). Indeed, varying definitions and the methods used to assess labour migration can lead to very different results. The broadest definition includes all international migrants who are currently in the labour force (both employed and unemployed, regular and irregular) as migrant workers. A more restrictive definition counts as migrant workers only those who entered a country for the explicit purpose of employment.

Compared to data on demographic variables, such as fertility and mortality, international migration data are inherently difficult to obtain. For instance, while birth and death occur only once in an individual's life cycle, migration may occur repeatedly, and it is at times hard to determine with precision when it begins and when it ends. Furthermore, many official sources for migration data are frequently intended to achieve particular administrative objectives rather than to yield reliable measurements of migrant stocks and flows. For that reason, statistics compiled from such sources may often be unsatisfactory in terms of coverage and accuracy.

3.1 Main Data Sources and Their Limitations

To obtain quantitative information about migration, including labour migration, multiple sources are typically used to measure flows and stocks.

(a) Administrative records

Official international migration statistics are often a by-product of administrative processes and record-keeping related to the activities of institutions and agencies dealing with various aspects of migration or migration-related areas, such as, for instance, population management. Each country has its own data collection methods and traditions. This is one of the main reasons why the sources from which official statistics on international migration are compiled tend to differ from country to country.

A number of European countries (e.g. Austria, Estonia, Lithuania, the Netherlands) have comprehensive **population registers** and/or **registers of foreigners**, which are accounts of persons residing lawfully in a country. These registers can be used to measure the total stocks of international migrants in a country, as well as inflows when new migrants are recorded (usually after one year in the case of population registers) and outflows when people de-register and leave the country (Hoffmann, 1995; IOM/OSCE/ILO, 2006, 2007).[1]

Countries that do not have a population register often use **residence and work permits** to measure migration flows. These administrative sources generated from operations designed to regulate international migration are particularly suitable to produce information about specific subsets of international migrants. Records covering the grant of residence and work permits, for example, are popular sources for the measurement of labour migration statistics (IOM/OSCE/ILO, 2006, 2007).

Data on visa issuance are another administrative source that allows greater disaggregation of migration flows into specific subsets of international migrants. Such data are typically collected at the point of issue (usually an embassy or consulate) and allow

[1] A problem with emigration statistics from registries, however, may occur when people leave the country and fail to de-register.

visa holders to be grouped into specific categories according to the purpose of entry (e.g. to study, for family unification or for employment). Such data can be cross-checked against information captured at the point of entry through passenger cards. Visa and border collection data are a popular source of international migration statistics, particularly for island states that have a small number of well-controlled ports of entry and departures, such as the U.K. and the Philippines (Bilsborrow et al., 1997).

An important statistical source of information on labour migration for countries of origin, especially in South and Southeast Asia, are **emigration clearances.** Such information on the number of workers departing each year, disaggregated by destination, gender, age, education and occupation is available from the Philippines, Sri Lanka and Thailand, for instance (Bilsborrow et al., 1997).

(b) Population censuses and other household surveys

Administrative records are not the only source of information on labour migration stocks and flows. Population censuses are a major statistical source for measuring stocks of international migrants. Depending on population coverage and definitions of usual residence, census returns that include "place of birth" or "citizenship" provide a good estimate of international migrant stocks. If the census collects labour force data, these can also be used to identify migrant workers. International migration inflows can also be estimated from previous residence questions, while questions about household members or family members living abroad can capture international migration outflows.

Annual labour force surveys (see Section 3.2(a)(ii), below) provide the richest source of labour force information related to migration. These surveys ask questions on place of birth, citizenship and previous residence, as well as other dimensions of international migration, such as reasons for moving. They are able to measure socio-economic conditions of migrant workers that are not captured elsewhere and allow the use of statistical methods to estimate degree of accuracy.

(c) Limitations of existing sources

The strengths and limitations of various sources vary. Administrative records can be reliable sources of statistics in cases where the administrative system is well organized, the quality of reporting is sound and coverage is reasonably complete (owing to incentives for registration or correct reporting, major penalties for not reporting or registering, or a combination of both incentives and penalties). This is often not the case, especially in countries that lack the appropriate resources to ensure complete coverage. The collection costs for administrative statistics are low, but there may be high processing costs to convert administrative records into useable forms. The concepts, definitions and classifications used in the legislation and or procedures within the administrative system are often different from those required to meet statistical user needs. Furthermore, administrative records may miss certain elements of information, given the greater mobility of workers across borders with the liberalization of travel and cheaper transport, especially within regional integration areas. In addition, the data are not always entered into the administrative database in accordance with the normal statistical standards of quality (Pember and Djerma 2005). Thus, the data content of administrative records, although rich in detail, often remains insufficiently exploited.

Among the limitations of official statistics from administrative sources is that they fail to capture irregular migration, or pay insufficient attention to qualitative elements of information, such as working conditions or respect for the rights of migrant workers.

The particular strength of population censuses and surveys is that they yield information that is used only for the production of statistics. This means that information provided through surveys does not have direct consequences for the responding person or organization who are thus able to reply without constraint or apprehension. The reliability of the information derived from statistical sources is therefore relatively high compared to administrative records (Hoffmann and Lawrence, 1995).

A drawback of population censuses is that the collection costs for survey data are relatively high and the information obtained is not always timely. Population censuses are normally only conducted once every ten years.

Special household surveys, such as annual labour force surveys, also have limitations. They tend to suffer from small sample sizes, particularly for small groups such as migrant workers. This reduces the comprehensiveness of data, particularly with regard to stocks and flows, even if detailed labour force information is collected from them. Another drawback to household surveys is that they often do not collect information from collective housing or group quarters, where many migrant workers often live.

3.2 Improving the Reliability and Accuracy of Existing Data Sources?

(a) Using complementary sources to improve data reliability

No single data source can meet all needs, and governments must carefully choose the source(s) of statistics concerning their strengths and limitations to develop a system of labour migration statistics that is both comprehensive and as statistically sound as possible. Users will need to relate statistics from different sources in order to make statistics more coherent and consistent in regard to concepts, definitions and units of measurement.

(i) Centralizing data collection

Some of the countries that rely on population registers as a source of their international migration statistics, including on labour migration, have sought to link these registers with other registration systems that are more directly concerned with the employment situation, such as social security and tax registrations (Hoffmann and Lawrence, 1995). A good example of centralized data collection can be found in Scandinavian countries where different data sets are linked. All vital events (births, deaths, marriages, etc.) and demographic characteristics, such as age, marital status, citizenship and number of children, among others, are registered against a Personal Identification Number (PIN), which is assigned to any migrant included in the central population register. In addition, a number of registers in the private and governmental sectors that are relevant for the labour market, including employment, educational attainment and activity records, use the same PIN. From this information it is possible to reconstruct the individual demographic and labour market biographies of a migrant (Aalandslid, 2006). Other countries with centralized registers, such as Belgium and the Netherlands, have followed the example of Scandinavian countries of improving links between diverse sets of administrative records (Poulain and Perrin, 2003).

Similar initiatives to move away from statistics based on documents to those based on the person have also been introduced in countries that do not rely on population registers. For example, Australia has sought to improve its border registration statistics by introducing a unique person identifier for each arrival/departure passenger card record to match it to other passport movement transactions within the immigration system. This measure is intended to avoid double counting and to provide more accurate data on movements to and from Australia (Corr et al., 2005).

Some countries operate centralized statistical systems with a single agency being responsible for the coordination and operation of the national statistical system. Other countries have decentralized systems in which sectoral ministries are responsible for a range of statistical services. In decentralized systems there may be a need for greater coordination to improve the coherence and consistency of the data collected and to ensure that statistical services of sectoral ministries receive the necessary technical and political support. These considerations may have prompted countries like the Philippines to set up a specialized body coordinating the compilation of migration related statistics. To obtain a more accurate estimate of overseas Filipino emigration, the Philippines set up a Commission on Filipinos Overseas (CFO). As the Secretariat of the Inter-Agency Working Group on the Shared Government Information System on Migration, the Commission compiles annual estimates of the number of Filipino citizens abroad from a range of sources, including the emigrant registration system of CFO and statistics on departing overseas Filipino workers (Castro, 2006).

(ii) Greater use of statistical sources of information such as household surveys

A major drawback in using migration information from administrative records is that the administrative rationale for their collection may be quite different from their intended ultimate use as migration statistics. For this purpose, population censuses and surveys are often preferable methods of data collection, as illustrated by evolving practice in the U.S. For many years, the U.S. Census Bureau relied on administrative records from the former Immigration and Naturalization Service (INS) in its annual estimates of international migration. The concern for comparability when using administrative (flow) data to measure a stock population has led the Census Bureau to turn to census data to improve the estimates of international migration, especially after the development of new nationally representative household surveys.

Timeliness remains an important issue nonetheless. Population censuses are normally conducted once every ten years. National statistical authorities have therefore tried to reduce the interval between population censuses. For example, the new American Community Survey can provide quality data on an annual basis through new sampling and outreach techniques. The more frequent collection of census data now enables the U.S. Census Bureau to provide more timely data on the year-to-year change in the foreign population (Norris and Costanzo, 2005).

While population censuses provide broadly aggregated information on labour migration, annual labour force surveys enable closer analysis of the situation. Labour force surveys are standard household-based surveys of work-related statistics, but may also include questions on place of birth, citizenship and previous residence, as well as other aspects of migration, such as reasons for moving. The samples of these surveys are quite large and representative of the country's working-age population. The International Labour Organization (ILO) is currently testing a number of migration-related questions for inclusion in international labour surveys, Armenia being one of the test countries (Schachter, 2006).

(b) Improving comparability of data sources

Greater reliability of data collection systems does not necessarily guarantee comparability of data between countries. This is becoming an important concern because the comparability of national and regional migration flows and stocks of migrants is an essential prerequisite for the proper study and understanding of the functioning of international labour market dynamics. International bodies, such as the United Nations and the Statistical Office of the European Communities (Eurostat), are prominently involved in coordinating efforts to harmonize data on migration, including labour migration. The approaches to improving comparability of migration data may take different forms: (i) top-down approaches where data harmonization is the result of national data collection systems adjusting to internationally recognized definitions and recommendations on international migration statistics; and (ii) bottom-up approaches where data harmonization is a by-product of enhanced data-sharing mechanisms among states.

(i) Top-down approaches to data harmonization

Top-down approaches are particularly associated with the UN system. Outside the UN framework, Eurostat and the Organisation for Economic Co-operation and Development (OECD) are actively involved in data harmonization.

A basic working method adopted by the UN system is the development of recommendations on international migration statistics, such as the definitions and sources to be used to measure international migration stocks and flows (Bilsborrow, 1997). The UN Recommendations on Statistics of International Migration were adopted by the UN Statistical Commission in 1976. Much of UN activity in the field of international migration statistics is aimed at encouraging states to adopt and collect data on the basis of the UN Recommendations. Given both the changes in international migration and continuing lack of uniformity among countries in the collection of data, the Recommendations were subject to expert review and a revised set was published in 1998 (UN DESA, Statistics Division, 1998).

One way in which international bodies promote data harmonization is through standardized data collection programmes in which countries are requested to provide data not only on the basis of existing practices, but also adjusted to correspond as far as possible to the UN recommendations. Since the latter half of the 1990s, Eurostat, the UN Economic Commission for Europe (UNECE), the UN Statistics Division (UNSD), the ILO and the Council of Europe have set up a joint data collection programme in order to reduce the response burden on governments caused by the duplication of data collection efforts. A joint questionnaire has been developed and agreed to. Governments are requested to present data matching as closely as possible the internationally recommended definitions of long-term and short-term migrants. The joint questionnaire includes a range of questions related to migrant workers and the labour force. In order to understand problems of international comparability in the data, it is requested that countries should highlight, for each of the data items, any differences in definition between the national data supplied and the standard definitions published in the UN recommendations (Herm, 2006).

Greater regional economic and political integration can also trigger efforts to harmonize data at the regional level. In Europe, for example, the gradual extension of EU decisions in the field of migration has prompted demands for reliable and timely Community statistics. The 2007 Regulation on Community statistics on migration and international protection[2] constitutes a milestone in the harmonization of migration statistics. Until the adoption of this measure, harmonization of statistics was mainly governed by informal agreements (Poulain et al., 2006) among Member States, but now, for the first time, there is a legally binding regulation concerning migration statistics across the whole of the European Union. The Regulation establishes common standards for the collection of statistics relating to international migration flows, foreign population stocks, acquisition of citizenship, asylum applications and decisions, measures taken against unauthorized entry and stay, returns of irregular migrants, and residence permits issued to third-country nationals. The focus of this Regulation is on harmonized statistical outputs, with common definitions based on existing and forthcoming EU measures relating to immigration, border management

[2] Regulation (EC) No. 9862/2007 of the European Parliament and the Council of 11 July 2007 on Community statistics on migration and international protection and repealing Council Regulation (EEC) No. 311/76 on the compilation of statistics on foreign workers, OJ 2007 L 199/3.

and asylum issues, and on established international standards (EUROPA, 2007).

An important criticism of the UN recommendations is that they approach international migration from a demographic rather than labour market perspective. The OECD has started to redress this international bias towards a demographic perspective on international migration by encouraging harmonization of international migration statistics on the basis of residence permit statistics. The OECD has no authority to impose changes in national data collection procedures. It mainly collects statistics through its continuous reporting system (Herm, 2006). However, in the 2006 and 2007 editions of the SOPEMI report, *International Migration Outlook*, the OECD changed its approach and used residence permit statistics rather than traditional sources[3] to harmonize statistics on flows of long-term migrants. This enables the OECD to provide more information on the composition of migration flows, including the inflows of migrants for the purpose of work (OECD, 2006; Lemaître, 2006). Residence permits are used to regulate the duration of stay and economic activities of migrants and therefore provide a good basis for statistics on labour migration.

(ii) Bottom-up approaches: harmonization as the result of data sharing

While initiatives to improve the quality of data on migration have been particularly stimulated by international organizations, pairs or groups of countries have also collaborated bilaterally by establishing inventories of data sources and definitions, proposing data comparisons and developing other efforts towards data comparability. All this work has helped to illuminate and explain the inconsistencies in the data and show the way to possible solutions.

For example, under the umbrella of Eurostat, bilateral migration flows between Belgium, on the one hand, and Denmark, Sweden and Italy, on the other, were compared on the basis of anonymous individual records (Herm, 2006; Perrin and Poulain, 2003). Individual events were matched using age, sex and citizenship, date of migration and code of municipality of arrival and departure, as a result of which it was possible to estimate the impact of missing records of immigrants.

There are also data collection projects where the sharing of relevant migration data between states is the primary aim rather than harmonization of migration data. However, greater harmonization of data collection among participating states may often be a positive additional consequence of such data sharing (IOM, 2003; Folden et al., 2007).

Some of these data-sharing mechanisms are the concrete outcomes of Regional Consultative Processes (RCPs) (see Chapter 13). For example, the oldest RCP in the field of migration, the Inter-Governmental Consultations on Migration, Asylum and Refugees (IGC), has had experience in the collection of data on asylum and refugees from participating states since 1992. The data submitted are operational rather than statistical and follow a national rather than a pre-designed format. Participating states may nevertheless adjust their national practices in the light of the practices and data submitted by other states (Folden et al., 2007). The end result is a de facto harmonization process over a period of time.

Broader in focus than the IGC's data-sharing mechanism is the Statistical Information System on Migration in Mesoamerica (SIEMMES), which includes information on migrant workers. SIEMMES is also a product of an RCP, the Regional Consultation on Migration, also known as the Puebla Process. The data shared are from statistical sources, such as population censuses, household surveys and entry and departure records, and are standardized according to five variables: type of movement, age,

[3] Most of the OECD Member States base their official statistics on other sources than residence-based statistics, such as population registers, border collection statistics and similar data. Therefore, there may be discrepancies between the country's official data and OECD statistics.

border point crossing, sex and nationality (Folden et al., 2007).

Some of the data-sharing projects also focus specifically on capacity-building assistance, especially in cases where some of the participating states lack adequate capacity to collect data. A good example of this approach is the "General Model" for the Collection, Application and Sharing of Migration-related Data, developed by IOM and the Organization for Security and Co-operation in Europe's Office for Democratic Institutions and Human Rights (OSCE/ODIHR) upon the request of participating OSCE countries in eastern Europe and Central Asia. The "Model" combines data sharing with targeted capacity building through the mapping of the national infrastructure and holding of specific training modules and workshops at national and regional level. The "Model" was first pilot tested in Moldova, Kazakhstan, Tajikistan and Ukraine (Folden et al., 2007; see also Textbox 9.1).

Textbox 9.1

The "General Model" for the Collection, Application and Sharing of Migration-related Data – An Emerging Approach

Introduction

At the workshop on Organizational Structures, Collection and Sharing of Migration-related Data, held in Prague in July 2002, hosted by the OSCE's Office for Democratic Institutions and Human Rights (OSCE/ODIHR), IOM and the Government of the Czech Republic, and representatives from eastern Europe and Central Asia (EECA) called for the establishment of a mechanism to facilitate the systematic, timely and reliable exchange of migration-related data, both at the national and regional level. In response, IOM, OSCE/ODIHR – with inputs from the Inter-Governmental Consultations on Migration, Asylum and Refugees (IGC), and the Danish Immigration Service – initiated the Programme for the Creation of a General Model for the Collection, Application and Sharing of Migration-related Data in early 2003 (hereinafter "The Model").

All countries in EECA were invited to take part in the Programme – at the regional level or nationally (pilot countries are Kazakhstan, Moldova and Ukraine, with initial introductory activities being carried out in Belarus, the Russian Federation, Kyrgyzstan and Tajikistan).

The Model

For those countries interested in and committed to developing and enhancing their statistical infrastructure, the "Model" offers a flexible, proactive approach to data management. The Model can be used for all types of migration data. Its elements can be applied at different times and in a different order and are therefore not mutually exclusive, nor do they represent an "all or nothing" approach. The Model recognizes that the reality of migratory trends is based on **timely, consistent** and **objective** data which already exist – though not necessary shared – in the country. The approach also includes an important principle of connecting **producers** and **users** of migration-related data.

The "Model" includes the following elements:

- Establishment of a national network, including core institutions, which handle migration data with well-defined focal points (national institutions) coordinating activities at the national level and facilitating regional exchange of agreed-upon data.
- Mapping out existing statistical infrastructures, including the definition of data governments wish to collect and share (where, when, why, how and by whom).
- Identification of the national demand for migration data at different levels and of a minimum set of 5-10 aggregated, overall data indicators recognized and recognizable for the country concerned, e.g. asylum data, labour migration, data on cross-border flows and some demographic variables. Documentation for the data is essential.

- Establishment of a data-sharing mechanism with data that are not necessarily comparable (i.e. minimum format), yet will enable the sharing of information and data in an informal, transparent and effective manner. Data sharing occurs electronically on the basis of agreed principles. It is driven by the network and, depending on user needs, can be gradually expanded by adding new data indicators, increasing the frequency of data collection (from annual to semi-annual and quarterly data submission) and introducing new data categories (i.e. gender, age, occupation).
- A homepage on the web for the exchange of information on statistical, policy and legal issues of relevance for understanding and using the data.
- Regional workshops for countries with a view to exchanging effective practices, discussing new issues and approaches, and identifying common trends of interest in the region.
- Training modules which satisfy regional and national demand for basic training on different issues related to data collection, sharing and management. Study tours are also envisaged.
- National projects developed in response to national needs and priorities.

Source: Folden et al. (2007: Annex 1).

4. New Challenges in Collecting Labour Migration Data

As discussed in Part A of the Report, employment-related mobility across and within borders is becoming increasingly more complex and diverse. The geographic origin, direction and the nature of flows continue to change and new migratory patterns emerge. Established categories of data collection are therefore no longer sufficient to capture the complexity of labour-related migratory movements (Hovy, 2006) or to promote understanding of attendant policy issues. New data collection strategies are therefore required to explore these emerging realities, including:

- Transnational communities/diasporas
- Return and circular migration
- Migration of the highly skilled
- Remittances
- Irregular migration
- Outcomes/impacts of migration

4.1 Transnational Communities/Diasporas

There is growing awareness in countries of origin of the potential benefits of migration for economic and social development (see Chapter 12). Consequently, their governments have become interested to obtain more reliable information on the size and characteristics of their expatriate communities. As discussed earlier, their statistics on emigration often cannot meet these needs. Most governments are reluctant or unable to closely monitor the exit of their own nationals and emigrants often do not have much incentive to notify the authorities of their departure. Departures, therefore, tend to be less well recorded than arrivals. This applies to both stocks and flows. Once these persons have left the country, they are difficult to seize statistically. Censuses and sample surveys, which collect information on the resident population, are not designed to yield statistical returns on absent persons and have difficulty in trying to do so, especially when no family member is present in the country of origin (UNECE/Eurostat Taskforce, 2006).

One possible way of compensating for the weakness of emigration data is to use existing immigration data in countries of destination. Some international bodies have pioneered the use of immigration data of countries of destination to estimate the size of diaspora communities. An example of such practice is the Database on Foreign-born and Expatriates developed by the OECD. Using data mainly from the 2000 census and national statistical offices, the OECD obtained statistics on the foreign-born population for each OECD Member State by country of birth and educational attainment (Dumont and Lemaître, 2004). A more comprehensive version of the OECD database, the Bilateral Migration Matrix, was recently developed by the World Bank and the University of Sussex in the U.K. (Parson et al., 2005). The Matrix covers more countries than the OECD database and provides time-series data on the stock of emigrants.

There are also activities that focus on developing guidelines to improve emigration data. On the basis of a data exchange exercise in which 19 countries participated, a UNECE/Eurostat Taskforce proposed a set of guidelines for measuring emigration through the use of immigration statistics of countries of destination (UNECE/Eurostat Taskforce, 2006).

4.2 Return and Circular Migration

Return and circular migration hold considerable benefits for countries of origin (see also Chapters 11 and 12). For instance, it is widely acknowledged that circular migration and, in some cases, the return migration of highly skilled nationals have benefited China and India by promoting skills transfer and creating social and economic linkages to important export markets (Kapur and McHale, 2005). Short-term return migration is difficult to capture statistically as this type of migration does not necessarily involve a change of usual residence. Furthermore, to measure the flow of nationals poses an even greater challenge, as data collection on inflows and outflows of nationals is usually poorer than for non-nationals.

Movement-based data collection systems, such as the one used in Australia, are more likely to capture this type of migration flow than those that focus primarily on stock data. Australia is able to gather useful information on departures because of the high quality of its border controls, which allow close measurement of border movements. However, the Australian Bureau of Statistics (ABS) identifies the increasing frequency and complexity of international travel as one of the key challenges to measuring migration (see also Chapter 5). Many of the legally defined long-term travellers interrupt their 12-month stay, and there is discrepancy between the intended and actual length of stay. The ABS is responding to this particular challenge by matching movement records of individual travellers to build up movement histories (ABS, 2006).

Few initiatives to measure circular/short-term movements are as systematic as the one used in Australia. Evidence of circular migration is often acquired incidentally through related data collection activities. For example, the National Agricultural Workers Survey, conducted by the U.S. Department of Labor, specifically targets the nature of agricultural work through an employment-based, random survey of the demographic and employment characteristics of crop workers hired in the U.S. The Employment and Migration Profile components of the survey cover the profile and history of all farm workers including occupation, type of non-agricultural work if employed off-farm, periods of unemployment and time spent outside the U.S., and the respondent's whereabouts for every week of the year preceding the interview. Thus, the survey provides detailed information on circular migration among foreign farm workers.[4]

4.3 Migration of the Highly Skilled

Detailed information about the emigration and flow of highly skilled individuals (see Chapter 2) is in high demand, especially in countries experiencing a rapid loss of human capital owing to this type of migration (Diallo, 2004).

As in the case of data on emigration more generally, several international organizations have launched initiatives to improve the availability of data on the movements of highly skilled persons. As discussed earlier, the OECD database includes statistics on

[4] See the U.S. Department of Labor website at http://www.doleta.gov/agworker/naws.cfm (Employment and Training Administration).

the foreign-born population for each OECD country by educational attainment. The World Bank has developed a similar database with greater coverage of countries and drawing on a wider range of data sources. The World Bank has also conducted a series of econometric studies on the impact of highly skilled migration on the economy of the country of origin (World Bank, 2006; Özden and Schiff, 2005).

These databases rely on statistics collected by host countries of highly skilled migrants. Few attempts have been made to assess the actual or potential level of highly skilled emigration from countries of origin. Although they are often the most affected in social or economic terms by the emigration of their highly skilled nationals, developing countries lack the resources to set up appropriate data collection mechanisms. Most initiatives in this field remain based on specialized surveys conducted by academic research institutions, such as the Potential Skills Base Survey of the Southern African Migration Project (SAMP), to assess the propensity to emigrate of final-year students at training institutions across the region. It is nonetheless encouraging to note that many developing countries are now calling for more importance to be accorded to the collection of reliable data on highly skilled emigration, as illustrated by the recent decision of the National Statistics Offices in India and Sri Lanka to identify the development of improved tools for the measurement of highly skilled migration as a priority for future work (Castro, 2006; Gunasekera, 2006).

4.4 Remittances

In recent years, remittances have received increased attention because of their visible and positive impacts on the economies of countries of origin. Relevant data for measuring remittances are collated by the International Monetary Fund (IMF) from national data compiled and reported by appropriate statistical authorities in IMF member countries, and reported as part of the IMF's Global Balance of Payments (BOP) statistics (Bilsborrow, 1997).

Useful as they are, however, official remittance data derived from BOP suffer from certain limitations. These include the inability of banks to distinguish between short and long-term migrants; lack of information about "informal" (e.g. hand-carried) or "in kind" remittances; the exclusion of transactions made at money transfer centres (which comprise a large percentage of remittances); the inability to identify flows (i.e. the origin and destination of remittances); and different recording and reporting practices of BOP across and even within countries over time (UN DESA, 2005; Schachter, 2006).

Detailed data on remittances are usually obtained from surveys. When they are conducted, nationally representative household surveys of income usually include questions on remittances, although they are not always identified separately. Specialized surveys on remittances and migration are also conducted on an ad hoc basis, for example to study remittance "corridors" and sending and receiving practices. There are also a number of surveys sponsored by the World Bank that include questions on migrant remittances, such as Living Standard Measurement Surveys (LSMS). The LSMS multi-topic questionnaires are designed to study multiple aspects of household welfare and behaviour, including remittances, and have been used for remittance corridor studies. IOM has also developed specialized surveys to explore the relationship between migration patterns and remittances (IOM, 2005, 2006; Petree and Baruah, 2007). Rather than conducting specialized surveys, ILO has developed a project that uses standard labour force surveys to measure remittances on the assumption that adding a migration module to pre-existing surveys reduces costs while ensuring a large sample size (Schachter, 2006).

4.5 Irregular Migration

As measures to prevent or reduce irregular employment and migration gain increasing prominence, reliable information on the size, structure and dynamics of irregular migration becomes more important. By its very definition, irregular migration is difficult to capture statistically as it concerns (mainly) undocumented and covert events. There are no official statistics on irregular migration. Statements about the magnitude of this phenomenon tend to draw on statistics of observed events that are usually collected for law enforcement purposes (e.g. by the police and border guards). Given the sensitivity surrounding this type of information, such data are rarely shared and generally not released for public use.

An exception is the data flowing from the Centre for Information, Discussion and Exchange on the Crossing of Frontiers and Immigration (CIREFI) developed by the European Commission and Eurostat. CIREFI is the only available Europe-wide source of data on law enforcement measures taken in the field of irregular migration. Three types of published data from the CIREFI database are linked to irregular migration: refusal of entry, apprehension of non-citizens present without authorization and foreigners removed.

Different assessments of the data show that all three types are inadequate to capture the various levels and trends in irregular migration. For example, the data on apprehensions submitted to CIREFI's database by EU Member States may not distinguish between stocks and flows, while data on refusal of entry often do not distinguish between the reasons for such refusals. Similarly, the data on removals do not specify the type and category of removals in question. The EU Regulation to govern national statistics, referred to earlier in Section 3.2(b)(i), may present an opportunity to improve the quality of the CIREFI data (Poulain and Singleton, 2006).

Another rich source of data on irregular migration is the annual survey and analysis of border management and border apprehensions carried out by the International Centre for Migration Policy Development (ICMPD) in central and eastern Europe. Besides data on border apprehensions, removal of non-citizens and refusal of entry, the survey yields data on the demographic breakdown of irregular migrants and information on their particular routes. ICMPD, the European Police Office (EUROPOL) and FRONTEX, the European agency for coordination of cooperation between EU Member States in the field of border management, have also sought to improve the data exchange and information on irregular migration from the Mediterranean basin and Africa to Europe by developing a map on African and Mediterranean Irregular Migration Routes[5] in the framework of the ongoing Dialogue on Mediterranean Transit Migration (MTM).

A more reliable official source of data on irregular migration can be derived from regularization exercises, if and when they occur (see Chapters 8 and 11). Regularization data can provide an estimate of the stock of irregular migrants, although not all irregular migrants may decide to seek or be eligible for regularization. Explanatory notes on the specific conditions of regularization programmes are, therefore, important to interpret the estimate of irregular migrants derived from regularization figures (Jandl and Kraler, 2006).

There are also databases that contain data on special categories of irregular migrants, such as trafficked persons. One such database, the Global Human Trafficking Database (see Textbox 8.2), has been developed by IOM to gather data from the counter-trafficking programmes it conducts. A unique feature of this database is that the information is collected directly from the victims of trafficking and therefore

5 For this map, see the FRONTEX web site at http://www.frontex.eu.int/gfx/frontex/files/mtmmapen.pdf.

provides a rich source of qualitative and quantitative data on this type of migration (see Textbox 8.2).

4.6 Evaluating the Outcomes or Impacts of Migration

As migration acquires increasing prominence on the socio-economic agendas of many countries of origin and of destination, it spurs demand for information on outcomes and/or the impacts of migration on the economy and society. All public implementing agencies of migration programmes resort to some form of evaluation to accompany a number or all stages of the policy cycle, i.e. ex ante to assess the anticipated impact and viability of planned policies and programmes; at mid-term to assess the ongoing outputs of policies and programmes; and ex post to measure the final outcome and impact of policies, and their sustainability. Countries with long experience of employment-based migration are particularly advanced in developing the appropriate tools to gather data for ex post evaluations of labour migration programmes and policies. As the integration of immigrants is essential to ensure social cohesion and public support for particular programmes, the efforts in these countries are particularly focused on gathering data on the labour market outcomes of immigrants.

An example of good practice in obtaining outcome data is the Longitudinal Survey of Immigrants to Australia, which interviews cohorts of immigrants at regular intervals during three years after their arrival. Data are collected on labour market outcomes and a range of other settlement indicators, including housing, health and settlement services. Plans are also under way to link this database with census data to provide more detailed information on how migrants fare after longer intervals following their arrival (ABS, 2006).

The impact of the emigration of health workers on the health sector is a particularly significant concern in many African countries. There is a great need for the accurate projection of human resource development needs in this area, as well as means of measuring losses of skilled personnel through emigration. The World Health Organization (WHO) assists developing countries in their efforts to meet these needs through special survey work and research, and its World Health Survey aims to provide a range of quantitative information that can be used to assess population health and health systems. This survey, conducted in more than 70 countries, includes follow-up questions on migration (Diallo et al., 2003).

5. Linking Data and Research with Policymaking

The collection and processing of appropriate data is a necessary, but not a sufficient condition to provide a government with adequate information to guide and support the decisions to be made. Data providers often face the challenge of how to present the information collected for use by policymakers. The latter work in a fast-paced environment and do not have the time to engage in the intricacies of statistical analysis. They demand timely information that addresses directly the issues at hand. A "filter" is therefore needed to convert the analytical information into a format more readily usable by policymakers, while respecting the complexities of the issues.

One filter some governments have adopted is the creation of inter-ministerial working groups composed of both data users and providers. The dialogue between data users and providers sensitizes data providers to the needs of users when designing new, or adjusting existing, data-collection methods. For example, in Denmark, an ongoing data user and provider dialogue has made it easier to publish commonly defined statistics and to agree on common principles underlying the definition and compilation of statistical indicators (Folden et al., 2007).

Research networks are another mechanism for the improvement of the dissemination of migration statistics and research that has recently received considerable attention from donors. Research networks have, potentially at least, the dual advantage of ensuring broader dissemination of migration data and research, while building local capacity for conducting policy-relevant research. They are also flexible structures that can easily be extended to incorporate other existing networks. Research networks are therefore often regarded as the appropriate tool to overcome the divide between developed and developing countries in terms of research capacity and technological resources (Costello and Alimuddin, 2000; Wickramasekara, 2006).

Two models of research networks prevail: (a) academic-based networks, which focus on capacity building, primarily among scholars, and promote academic research on migration; and (b) the electronic web networks that focus primarily on cataloguing information, networking institutions and other research communities, and disseminating policy-relevant information (Laczko and Long, 2006).

Each type has its specific strengths and weaknesses in the dissemination of policy-relevant information. Academic-based networks[6] may not produce the kind of research that policymakers require. Policymakers need rapidly available results in order to make timely decisions, and cannot wait for the kind of long-term, in-depth research preferred by academics. However, through research training, seminars and research competitions, these networks can stimulate new research initiatives and disseminate new tools to analyse data of use to policymakers.

In contrast, the issues of timeliness and accessibility do not arise with electronic web networks because information can be accessed instantly and shared publicly. They can be useful mechanisms in regional integration processes, such as the European Union, to ensure synergies and avoid overlaps among existing networks. For instance, the purpose of the EU-sponsored European Migration Network (EMN) is to: (a) provide a clearing house to filter and synthesize information; (b) develop comparable up-to-date information on legal and policy developments related to migration and asylum in EU Member States; and (c) provide accurate, up-to-date and comparable statistical data on migration and asylum (Laczko and Long, 2006; Folden et al., 2007; Kraler and Jandl, 2006). The EMN relies largely on a web of national focal points to keep track of developments in their respective countries and transmit and exchange timely information. On the other hand, electronic web networks such as this may not be conducive to generating the kind of network opportunities that arise from face-to-face encounters in research seminars or training workshops. To ensure maximum productivity and results, electronic web networks need to rely not only on virtual but also face-to-face exchanges between users and producers through training and capacity-building workshops (Laczko and Long, 2006). The EMN has, therefore, introduced regular meetings for national focal points to maximize the exchange between EU Member States.

The coordination of activities at the national level related to data harmonization may become a more important activity for regional research networks as it is included on the agendas of regional integration and trade regimes in different parts of the world. One recent illustration of this trend was a study on the prospects of migration data harmonization in the Southern African Development Community (SADC) region (Williams and Tsang, 2007) by the Southern African Migration Project (SAMP), an international network of organizations founded in 1996 to promote awareness of migration-development linkages in SADC, with the help of IOM.

[6] One of the first academic networks set up in the field of migration is the Asia Pacific Migration Research Network (APMRN), funded primarily by UNESCO and based at Wollongong University in Australia. APMRN has a network of partner institutions in Australia, China, Fiji, Hong Kong SAR, Indonesia, Japan, New Zealand, Philippines, Singapore and Thailand, and implements projects related to the "social and political aspects of international migration and growing ethno-cultural diversity as major factors in the social transformation of the societies of the Asia-Pacific region" (APMRN, 2002).

6. Conclusion

As labour migration becomes more prevalent at the global level, the demand for reliable and comparable statistics on migration for employment becomes more insistent. The changing nature of current labour mobility makes the task of harmonizing statistics on international migration more complex. As new categories of labour migration flows are emerging, their origins and destinations also diversify. How these particular challenges are addressed will depend partly on the development of new concepts of measurement and data collection techniques, but also on improved quality of the administrative data collected for different labour migration programmes.

It is commonly recognized that governments require an appropriate knowledge base to effectively manage migration. It is also acknowledged that this is particularly so in the area of labour migration. Three types of initiatives to enhance the national knowledge base were discussed in this chapter, concerning: (i) the improvement of the reliability and comparability of existing data sources; (ii) the gathering of new data on emerging issues, especially regarding labour migration; and (iii) the dissemination and utilization of data and research on labour migration.

The chapter has also emphasized the importance of recognizing and catering to different data needs at the policy, programme and case management level. Success in this endeavour will depend on the development of a comprehensive approach to the collection, analysis and dissemination of data through the mobilization and coordination of all national bodies and instrumentalities involved, both generally in international migration management and specifically in the management of labour flows.

However, to be fully productive and meaningful, these national efforts need to be complemented by broader regional and global endeavours with the support of appropriate international bodies to promote the adoption of a new culture of measurement, record keeping and exchange of information in this field.

REFERENCES

Aalandslid, V.
2006 "Using Register Data to Monitor the Immigration and Emigration of Immigrants", presentation prepared for the UN Expert Group Meeting on Measuring international migration: Concepts and methods, 4-7 December, UN, New York, http://unstats.un.org/unsd/demographic/meetings/egm/migrationegm06/DOC%207%20Norway.ppt.

Asia Pacific Migration Research Network (APMRN)
2002 "Migration Research and Policy Landscape: Case studies of Australia, the Philippines and Thailand", APMRN Working Paper No. 9, Migration and Multicultural Program, Centre for Asia Pacific Social Transformation Studies, University of Wollongong, Australia, http://www.unesco.org/most/apmrpap9.htm.

Australian Bureau of Statistics (ABS)
2006 "Country Paper: International Migration Statistics in Australia", paper prepared for the Expert Group Meeting on the United Nations Economic and Social Commission for Asia and the Pacific (UN ESCAP) Regional Census Programme, 27-28 November, Bangkok, http://www.unescap.org/stat/meet/egm2006/ses.4_Australia_1.pdf.

Bilsborrow, R.E., G. Hugo, A.S. Oberai and H. Zlotnik
1997 *International Migration Statistics: Guidelines for Improving Data Collection Systems*, International Labour Office, Geneva.

Boswell, C., S. Stiller and T. Straubhaar
2004 "Forecasting Labour and Skills Shortages: How can Projections Better Inform Labour Migration Policies?", Migration Research Group, Hamburg Institute of International Economics, July, paper prepared for the European Commission, DG Employment and Social Affairs, http://ec.europa.eu/employment_social/employment_analysis/docs/forecast_short3.pdf.

Castro, L.V.
2006 "Measuring international migration in the Philippines", paper prepared for the UN Expert Group Meeting on Measuring international migration: Concepts and methods (Doc. ESA/STAT/AC.119/18), 4-7 December, UN, New York, http://unstats.un.org/UNSD/demographic/meetings/egm/migrationegm06/DOC%2018%20Philippines.pdf.

Corr, P., A. Hakim and J. Farrow
2005 "Measuring International Migration with Traveller-completed Passenger Cards: The Conceptual, Administrative and Statistical Challenges Experienced by Australia", paper prepared for the XXV International Union for the Scientific Study of Population (IUSSP) International Population Conference, 18-23 July, Tours, France.

Costello, A. and Z. Alimuddin
2000 "Moving to research partnerships in developing countries", *British Medical Journal*, 321, 30 September: 827-829.

Diallo, K.
2004 "Data on the migration of health-care workers: sources, uses and challenges", *Bulletin of the World Health Organization*, 82(8) (August): 601-607, http://www.scielosp.org/pdf/bwho/v82n8/v82n8a10.pdf.

Diallo, K., P. Zurn, N. Gupta and M. Dal Poz
2003 "Monitoring and evaluation of human resources for health: an international perspective", *Human Resources for Health*, 1(3), http://www.human-resources-health.com/content/1/1/3.

Dumont, J.-C. and G. Lemaître
2004 "Counting Immigrants and Expatriates in OECD Countries: A New Perspective", Directorate for Employment Labour and Social Affairs, OECD, Paris, http://www.oecd.org/dataoecd/27/5/33868740.pdf.

EUROPA
2007 "The European Union improves the framework for the collection of migration and asylum statistics", Press Release IP/07/804, 12 June, Brussels, http://europa.eu/rapid/pressReleasesAction.do?reference=IP/07/804

Folden, C., M. Manke and T. Mortensen
2007 *Sharing Data - Where to Start: An Emerging Approach to Migration Data Management*, Technical Cooperation Centre, IOM, Vienna, http://www.iom.int/jahia/Jahia/cache/offonce/pid/1674?entryId=15669

Gunasekera, H.R.

2006 "Development of international migration statistics in Sri Lanka", paper prepared for the UN Expert Group Meeting on Measuring international migration: Concepts and methods (Doc. ESA/STAT/AC.119/11), 4-7 December, UN, New York, http://unstats.un.org/unsd/demographic/meetings/egm/migrationegm06/DOC%2011%20Sri%20Lanka.pdf.

Herm, A.

2006 "Recommendations on International Migration Statistics and Development of Collection at an International Level" in M. Poulain, P. Perrin and A. Singleton (Eds.), *Towards Harmonised European Statistics on International Migration*, Presses universitaires de Louvain, 77-106.

Hoffmann, E. and S. Lawrence

1995 *Statistics on International Labour Migration: A Review of Sources and Methodological Issues*, Bureau of Statistics, Interdepartmental Project on Migrant Workers 1994-95, International Labour Office, Geneva, http://staging2.ilo.org/public/english/bureau/stat/download/migr.pdf.

Hovy, B.

2006 "Emerging Issues in Migration Policies: Implications for Data Requirements", presentation prepared for the UN Expert Group Meeting on Measuring international migration: Concepts and methods, 4-7 December, UN, New York, http://unstats.un.org/unsd/demographic/meetings/egm/migrationegm06/DOC%201%20UNPD.ppt.

India

2006 "Country Paper on International Migration Statistics – India", paper prepared for the Expert Group Meeting on the UN ESCAP Regional Census Programme, 27-28 November, Bangkok, http://www.unescap.org/stat/meet/egm2006/ses.4_India_1.pdf.

International Organization for Migration (IOM)

2003 "Challenges and effective approaches to national, regional and international migration data collection, sharing and management: Focusing on short term and practical solutions", Concept Paper, Programme for the Creation of a General Model for the Collection, Application and Sharing of Migration-Related Data, Data Sharing Mechanism in Eastern Europe and Central Asia, 26 August, https://www.dsm-migration.net/dsm-uploads/concept_paper_eng_050816091110.pdf.

2005 *Survey on Remittances 2005 and Microenterprises*, Working Notebooks on Migration 21, September, Guatemala, http://www.oim.org.gt/Cuaderno%20de%20Trabajo%20No.%2021%20(English).pdf.

IOM/Organization for Security and Co-operation in Europe (OSCE)/International Labour Organization (ILO)

2006 *Handbook on Establishing Effective Labour Migration Policies in Countries of Origin and Destination*, 23 May, IOM/OSCE/ILO, Vienna, http://www.osce.org/item/19187.html.

2007 *Handbook on Establishing Effective Labour Migration Policies*, Mediterranean edition, 6 December, IOM/OSCE/ILO, Vienna, http://www.osce.org/item/28725.html.

Jandl, M. and A. Kraler

2006 "Links Between Legal and Illegal Migration" in M. Poulain, P. Perrin and A. Singleton (Eds.), *Towards Harmonised European Statistics on International Migration*, Presses universitaires de Louvain, 337-372.

Kapur, D. and J. McHale

2005 *Give Us Your Best and Brightest: The Global Hunt for Talent and Its Impact on the Developing World*, Center for Global Development, Washington, D.C., http://www.cgdev.org/content/publications/detail/4415.

Kraler, A., M. Jandl and M. Hofmann

2006 "The Evolution of EU Migration Policy and Implications for Data Collection", in M. Poulain, N. Perrin and A. Singleton (Eds.), *Towards Harmonised European Statistics on International Migration*, Presses universitaires de Louvain, 35-76.

Laczko, F. and L. Long

2006 "Building capacity for policy-relevant research on migration and development" in K. Tamas and J. Palme (Eds.), *How Migration Can Benefit Development*, Institute for Futures Studies, Stockholm, 203-215.

Lemaître, G.

2005 "The Comparability of International Migration Statistics. Problems and Prospects", July, OECD Statistics Brief No. 9, Paris, http://www.oecd.org/dataoecd/4/41/35082073.pdf.

Lemaître, G., T. Liebig and C. Thoreau

2006 "Harmonised statistics on immigrant inflows - preliminary results, sources and methods", June, OECD, Paris, http://www.oecd.org/dataoecd/61/7/37035672.pdf.

Levine, D.B., K. Hill and R. Warren

1985 *Immigration Statistics: The Story of Neglect,* June, National Academy Press, Washington, D.C.

Lücke, M., T.O. Mahmoud and P. Pinger

2007 *Patterns and Trends of Migration and Remittances in Moldova*, June, IOM, Chisinau, Moldova, http://www.iom.md/materials/5_patterns_eng.pdf.

Martin, P.L.

2003 "Highly Skilled Labor Migration: Sharing the Benefits", May, International Institute for Labour Studies, ILO, Geneva, http://www.ilo.org/public/english/bureau/inst/download/migration2.pdf.

Norris, D. and J. Costanzo

2005 "Measuring Migration Across U.S. Borders: A comparison and evaluation of migration data and data sources in Canada and the United States", paper prepared for the XV IUSSP International Population, Conference, 18-23 July, Tours, France.

Organisation for Economic Co-operation and Development (OECD)

2006 *International Migration Outlook,* SOPEMI 2006, OECD, Paris.

Özden, C. and M. Schiff (Eds.)

2005 *International Migration, Remittances, and the Brain Drain*, The World Bank and Palgrave Macmillan, Washington, D.C.

Parsons, C.R., R. Skeldon, T.L. Walmsley and L.A. Winters

2005 "Quantifying the International Bilateral Movements of Migrants", Working Paper T13, September, Development Research Centre on Migration, Globalisation and Poverty, University of Sussex, U.K., http://www.migrationdrc.org/publications/working_papers/WP-T13.pdf.

Pember, R.J. and H. Djerma

2005 "Development of labour statistics systems", Working Paper (June), Bureau of Statistics, ILO, Geneva, http://www.ilo.org/public/english/bureau/stat/download/articles/2005-1.pdf.

Petree, J. and N. Baruah

2007 *A Study of Migrant-Sending Households in Serbia Receiving Remittances from Switzerland*, IOM Migration Research Series No. 28, Geneva, http://www.iom.int/jahia/Jahia/cache/offonce/pid/1674?entryId=13943.

Phillips, H.

2006 "Measurement, concepts and definitions of international migration: The case of South Africa", paper prepared for the UN Expert Group Meeting on Measuring international migration: Concepts and methods (Doc. ESA/STAT/AC.119/12), 4-7 December, UN, New York, http://unstats.un.org/unsd/Demographic/meetings/egm/migrationegm06/DOC%2012%20South%20Africa.pdf.

Poulain, M.

2006 "Registration of the Resident Population" in M. Poulain, N. Perrin and A. Singleton, (Eds.), *Towards Harmonised European Statistics on International Migration*, Presses universitaires de Louvain, 109-132.

Poulain, M. and N. Perrin

2003 "Can UN Migration Recommendations be Met in Europe?", *Migration Information Source*, July, Migration Policy Institute (MPI), Washington, D.C., http://www.migrationinformation.org/Feature/display.cfm?id=139.

Poulain, M. and A. Singleton

2006 "Conclusion: Improving the Quality of Measurement of Migration and International Protection in the European Union" in M. Poulain, N. Perrin and A. Singleton (Eds.), *Towards Harmonised European Statistics on International Migration*, Presses universitaires de Louvain, 373-378.

Poulain, M., N. Perrin and A. Singleton (Eds.)

2006 *Towards Harmonised European Statistics on International Migration*, Presses universitaires de Louvain.

Schachter, J.P.
2006 "The Potential of Using Household Surveys to Improve the Measurement of International Migrant Remittance Data", Working paper 8, Joint UN Commission for Europe (UNECE)/ Eurostat Work Session on Migration Statistics, 20-22 November, Edinburgh, http://www.unece.org/stats/documents/ece/ces/ge.10/2006/wp.8.e.doc.

Tamas, K. and J. Palme (Eds.)
2006 *How Migration Can Benefit Development?*, Institute for Futures Studies, Stockholm.

United Nations, Department of Economic and Social Affairs (DESA), Statistics Division
1998 "Recommendations on Statistics of International Migration, Revision 1", Statistical Paper Series M, No. 58, Rev. 1, UN DESA, Statistics Division, New York, http://unstats.un.org/unsd/publication/SeriesM/SeriesM_58rev1E.pdf.

2005 *International Working Group on Improving Data on Remittances: Interim Report, November 2005*, Meeting of the UN Technical Subgroup on Movement of Persons – Mode 4, 22-24 February 2006, UN DESA, Statistics Division, New York, http://unstats.un.org/unsd/tradeserv/TSG3-Feb06/tsg0602-5.pdf.

United Nations Economic Commission for Europe (UNECE)/ Eurostat Taskforce on Measuring Emigration Using Data
2006 "Guidelines for measuring emigration through use of immigration statistics of receiving countries", Working paper 5 Add. 1, Joint UNECE/Eurostat Work Session on Migration Statistics, 20-22 November, Edinburgh, http://www.unece.org/stats/documents/ece/ces/ge.10/2006/wp.5.e.pdf.

Wickramasekara, P.
2006 "Migration and development: Reflections on research and policies" in K. Tamas and J. Palme (Eds.), *How Migration Can Benefit Development*, Institute for Futures Studies, Stockholm, 181-202.

Williams, V. and T. Tsang
2007 *The Prospects for Data Harmonisation in the SADC*, Migration Dialogue for Southern Africa (MIDSA) Report No. 2, Cape Town.

World Bank
2006 *Global Economic Prospects 2006: Economic Implications of Remittances and Migration*, The World Bank, Washington, D.C. , http://www-wds.worldbank.org/external/default/WDSContentServer/IW3P/IB/2005/11/14/000112742_20051114174928/Rendered/PDF/343200GEP02006.pdf.

HUMAN RESOURCE DEVELOPMENT AND FOREIGN EMPLOYMENT POLICIES IN COUNTRIES OF ORIGIN*

CHAPTER 10

1. Introduction

An increasing number of developing countries and countries with economies in transition have adopted or are seeking to adopt legislation and policies to take advantage of foreign employment opportunities for their citizens, while ensuring that safeguards are in place for the protection of their rights.[1] For these countries, job creation at home remains, in theory at least, the preferred option, but labour migration is seen as an important and reliable vector of economic development through the remittances that workers send back home. At the individual level, with or without facilitation of the state, many people seek overseas employment opportunities to augment their income, improve the living conditions and life prospects of their families and acquire new skills and experience. However, while regular, albeit selective entry channels are available to skilled workers, this is often not the case for low and semi-skilled workers, who may be tempted to resort to irregular modes of entry and employment.

This chapter discusses policy approaches to the management of international labour movements from the perspective of countries of origin. It opens with the argument that human resource development planning is a vital element in the management of international worker mobility. Section 2 looks closely at key constituent elements of the process of human resource development (HRD) planning, including the setting of appropriate goals and objectives, the identification of quality standards and indicators, and the financing and provision of appropriate education and training opportunities. The importance of maintaining coherence of purpose and action is underlined. Due attention is paid to the further aim of preventing the loss of local talent and the role to be played by the private sector.

---

* This chapter was written by Edita Tan, Professor Emeritus, Department of Economics, University of Philippines, and Nilim Baruah, Chief Technical Adviser, Regional Migration Programme, Subregional Office for Eastern Europe and Central Asia, ILO Moscow (Formerly Head of the Labour Migration Division at IOM).

1 In keeping with the standard terminology used in this report, such countries are referred to as "countries of origin" in this chapter, although it is acknowledged that the labels "labour-sending countries" or simply "sending countries" are often used, particularly to describe those countries that have designed and implemented explicit policy frameworks aimed at sending their citizens for work abroad. It is recognized, however, that such frameworks may differ significantly in terms of purpose, content and degree with the result that not all governments are prepared to consider themselves as promoting overseas employment. Use of the neutral term "countries of origin" is therefore preferred throughout. For similar reasons, "countries of destination" has been used instead of "receiving countries". "Foreign employment policies" is used in this and the next chapter as a generic term covering the international labour mobility policies of both countries of origin and destination.

Section 3 acknowledges the diverse characteristics of countries of origin, and considers those with long-established labour migration programmes; those in the process of economic and socio-political transition; and still others that are relative newcomers to organized labour migration. Such diversity notwithstanding, most countries face similar policy challenges. The first part of this section focuses on the actual management of international worker mobility through policy measures aimed at protecting migrant workers from exploitative recruitment and employment practices, and at ensuring worker welfare and productivity through pre-departure and on-site support services. The second part of the section proposes policy options for the optimization of the benefits of organized labour migration through the development of new markets; the facilitation of remittance flows and the enhancement of their impact on development (see also Chapter 12); the strengthening of local institutional capacity; and, finally, the promotion of international cooperation (see also Chapter 13). While the issues covered in this chapter are of broad international relevance, its research base is grounded in contemporary developments in Asia.

2. Human Resource Development

Although world demand for foreign workers is very diverse, for ease of exposition, when discussing labour mobility, foreign workers fall into three broad categories. First, there are the highly skilled or those who hold at least a first degree from a reputable university, college or other institution of higher learning. The second group consists of skilled blue-collar workers such as, for example, aviation technicians, heavy equipment operators, automotive mechanics, welders, metal workers and pipe setters. They make up a large group of migrant workers. The third group of low-skilled workers includes housemaids, janitors and waiters in hotels and restaurants, and manual labourers, for instance on construction sites. All workers would have acquired their skills through a combination of formal education and experience. As a general rule, and depending on the particular educational system in question, professions, including those in the modern creative sectors, require higher formal qualifications, such as a first postgraduate degree for a career in computer science or genetics, and a higher post-graduate degree up to doctoral level for the medical and legal professions. For most other professions, including nursing and engineering, the requirement is normally a first degree. Blue-collar occupations have less stringent formal education requirements. Generally, a high school background is sufficient to ensure that the worker is able to be trained and to perform his or her duties. The skills are acquired mainly through experience, loosely referred to as on-the-job-training (OJT). The low-skilled category has the lowest requirements in formal education or training.

Though job applicants are carefully screened by prospective employers to ascertain how much schooling they have had and what job skills they have, the wide diversity of standards and requirements in the educational systems worldwide make it difficult to evaluate and compare the level of competence of highly skilled workers. The value of a degree programme depends on such diverse factors as the curriculum and the quality of the instructors, the library, laboratory and other instructional facilities. Globally, there are many thousands of higher educational institutions from which a professional/scientific degree may be obtained, but no universally recognized benchmarks exist by which to rate the quality of the instruction offered or the educational attainment of graduates. Although highly selective quality ratings of universities/colleges have been conducted, they cover only a relatively small number of institutions. This poses a serious problem in relation to the employment of highly skilled foreign workers, since employers have to develop their own measures to evaluate the quality of the institutions from which applicants have graduated.

By comparison, the evaluation of the competence of blue-collar workers appears less difficult, as it is based more on experience than on the quality of formal schooling, and skills are assessed through trade or skill testing and quality and length of experience. The quality of experience is reflected by the scale of production, the technology embodied in the machinery and equipment used as well as Information Communications Technology (ICT) applications and other physical operational features. Some overseas employers require experience in the use of particular brands of machinery and equipment.

A recently completed survey conducted by the International Organization for Migration (IOM) of placement agencies in the Philippines indicates that foreign employers require very specific qualifications (Tan, 2007). A variety of quality indicators are used for highly skilled workers, that differ according to the particular professions or occupations. The minimum requirement for doctors is to have completed the corresponding degree course, passed the professional licensure examination and gained relevant experience in a large general hospital. In addition to their studies, teachers are required to have gained relevant experience in a reputable teaching institution. On completion of their degree, engineers must obtain experience in selected fields such as the petrochemical industry and industrial design, while blue-collar workers are expected to have the appropriate experience in the use of modern production equipment and techniques.

Faced with the complexities of the global market for skilled labour, how should a country of origin go about designing its human resource development policy? At the outset, of course, it will be necessary to have clearly defined objectives and the necessary means to achieve them. Such an undertaking may be hampered by the scarce or incomplete information concerning the demand and supply of the numerous skills. Moreover, the financial constraints most families and individuals face in deciding which skills they should invest in will have to be taken into consideration. Successful HRD planning in open labour markets characterized by significant and continuing migration, such as the Philippines, for example, will have to take due account of the particular skills requirements of foreign labour markets.

2.1 Human Resource Development Planning

Human capital theory may be applied to HRD planning in an education labour market (ELM).[2] When factoring migration into their computations, the aim of HRD planners should be to maximize social and economic returns from the outflow of migrants for the purpose of employment (see Textbox 10.1). This means guiding would-be migrants and assisting them financially and in other ways to enable them to invest in the acquisition of skills that promise the highest returns. Planners should also ensure that they have access to reliable information on skills that are in strong demand abroad, the respective qualifications required and how and where the requisite standard of qualifications and skills is best acquired. Moreover, improving quality requires financial resources. For a country to be able to take advantage of skilled employment opportunities abroad, human resource planners will have to develop a financing system to support the aim of raising quality standards in major skill areas in demand abroad.

[2] The ELM is characterized by three interacting parties: the employers who need and hire human resources, the suppliers of human resources and the education/training institutions. The government is an employer and policymaker and influences both demand and supply. The employers consist of domestic and foreign entities who require appropriate human resources and whose demand for labour of a particular skill level is relayed to human resource suppliers and education/training institutions. The response to this demand can be twofold: if available, to either offer the requisite skills; alternatively, to acquire them through formal or information channels with a view to offering them in due course and joining the active labour force.

Textbox 10.1

HRD Planning and Maximizing Economic Gains from Labour Migration

What may be the objective of HRD planning for the whole education labour market (ELM) market, including foreign employment, albeit of selective skills? In theory, the government would wish to maximize the social returns to investment in human capital of the population as a whole. There are private (both economic and non-economic) and social returns to the investment. Most visible are the private returns that consist of monetary and non-monetary gains from the investment. There is enjoyment to be gained from the possession of knowledge, and there are benefits to be derived from the ability it offers for making life choices and to further develop the knowledge acquired. The calculations below focus on the more tangible monetary gains, i.e. the incremental income gain minus the cost of investing in a category of human capital formation, for instance nursing education. Theoretically, it is possible to think of maximizing private returns to individuals pursuing the best investment options/skills. The returns to a skill *i* relative to skill *j* are estimated as follows.

Returns to a skill *i* is estimated as:

$$R_{i,t} = \sum_{t=D}^{T} D_t W_{i,t} - C_i - \left(\sum D_t W_j - C_j \right)$$

Where: R = returns to investment in skill formation
W = nominal wage rate
C = cost of investment
D = discount rate $1/(1+r)^t$
r = interest rate (cost)
i, j = skill categories
t = time period in years

Note the returns to investment in skill *i* takes account of its opportunity cost, or returns to investment in alternative skill *j*. Skill *i* is preferred to skill *j* if its (net) return R is positive. Another way of assessing skills is to array the skills according to their own returns:

$$\left(\sum_{t=0}^{T} D_{t_r} W_t - C_t \right)$$

It is assumed that the skills with the higher returns will attract more workers or labour units. In the short term, labour supply would originate from the current stock of available workers with the required skill. In the long term, the increased supply would come from the existing stock of workers with the skill and from new entrants, i.e. the students who would pursue the skill and those workers who might switch from other skills by retraining. In the equation, the reservation wage is the total cost of investing in skill *i*, comprising the cost of investment in that skill and the opportunity cost in forgoing skill *j*, or

$$\left(C_i + \sum_{t=0}^{T} D_t W_j - C_j \right)$$

When there is migration, the return takes account of the foreign wage and the probability of finding a job abroad. Return to a skill is estimated as follows:

$$R_i = \left\{ P_d \sum_{t=0}^{T} D_t W_{i,d,t} + P_f \sum_{t=0}^{T} D_t W_{i,d,t} \right\} - C_i - \left\{ P_d \sum_{t=0}^{T} D_t W_{j,d,t} + P_f \sum_{t=0}^{T} D_t W_{j,d,t} - C_j \right\}$$

The gross returns are averages of expected domestic and foreign wages. Gross returns to a skill rise as the probability of obtaining a foreign job, P_f, rises, given that foreign wage rates are significantly higher than the domestic wage rate.

It is possible to view an efficient ELM as one where information about demand for various skill categories and their specific job qualifications exists and where persons can acquire skills without significant financial constraints. Foreign job openings are taken for skill *i*. These jobs pay much more than the domestic wage. Consequently, the youth and some workers already in the labour force will be drawn to invest in skill *i*. The supply in other skills will fall and raise their wage rate. Skill *i* will continue to attract people until its return equalizes the returns to the other skills. This adjustment leads to maximum private returns on the investment. An efficient market needs no government intervention. However, if the ELM is inefficient because information about demand, the required job qualifications and where to obtain the skill is unavailable, or if the youth are prevented by poverty from acquiring the skill, there will be supply rigidity.

Market imperfections are known to be serious in the ELM. There are millions of youth preparing for entry into the labour market and millions of employers in the domestic and foreign labour markets. Information is generally poor and unevenly distributed; it is usually concentrated among the more educated in the cities. Financial resources for education are notoriously lacking for the great majority of families who may wish to invest in their children's education/training. Additionally, there are some highly skilled professionals, such as research scientists, innovative business executives, historians or creative artists, whose outputs are in the nature of public goods or have large positive social impacts or externalities. Governments would be well advised to invest in their education/training in order to increase the number of persons pursuing them. Producing and disseminating information on employment opportunities, required job qualifications and where to acquire the necessary skills is essential so that members of the labour force, and young people especially, can make optimal choices. HRD planners should also identify where financial constraints on education or training choices arise. Which are the employment categories with significant positive externalities or that are public goods by nature and hence require government subsidies? What subsidy strategy ought to be developed to address critical financial constraints? The task is so daunting in scale and complexity that, in many cases, governments tend to be very selective when choosing areas of intervention. The U.S. Government, for instance, poured resources in science education and research in response to the Soviet launch of Sputnik in the 1950s. The Kennedy administration established the Equal Opportunity Program to mitigate inequality of access to higher education. In a similar way, scholarship programmes have been instituted by many governments to address the inequality problem and/or to increase enrolment numbers and research in science and technology (S&T) so as to promote technological progress.

2.2 Defining Requirements (Quantity and Quality)

To define requirements at the national level, both a profile of current human resources and a forecast of future requirements are necessary, as well as reliable and up-to-date information about employment opportunities and skill requirements in relation to both the domestic and foreign labour markets. Although international demand for major skills categories, such as engineering, computer science, natural science, management and finance, education and medicine is high, detailed information, for instance, on the specific skills and levels of competence required is lacking. Such information is necessary to allow for realistic and timely national HRD policy planning and implementation, as well as to guide and support individuals in their choices regarding education, work and migration.

2.3 Quality Standards and Indicators

Quality standards used by foreign employers evolve through different means. Through observed performance of their workforce, foreign employers arrive at standards by which to gauge the competence of applicants from countries of origin and use these yardsticks to identify reliable sources of qualified professionals. As a result, universities and colleges acquire a reputation based on employers' experience with their graduates, consultations with other employers and academic ratings based on periodic assessments through independent evaluators of higher education. ICT companies in the U.S. and Europe, for instance, compete for graduates from the highly acclaimed Indian Institutes of Technology. Similarly, hospitals in other countries recognize the licensure examinations administered by the Philippine Professional Regulatory Commission. The Japan-Philippines Economic Partnership Agreement[3] provides for the employment of Filipino nurses on condition that they undergo two to three years' language and practical training in Japan before being recognized as professional nurses. The adoption in 1984 of the International Standard for Training, Certification and Watchkeeping of Seafarers has contributed greatly to the establishment of high quality standards of education/training for Filipino seafarers and to their recognition by international shipping companies.

For blue-collar occupations, the quality of experience is critical. The recently completed survey of placement agencies in the Philippines for the IOM by one of the authors (Tan, 2007) demonstrates that experience in operating modern equipment is essential for tool and die makers, welders, pipe setters, heavy equipment operators and other construction workers. However, the country's industrial base has only a limited capacity to produce experienced workers with these skills, as the pool of heavy equipment and machinery operators is too small and only a few workers are able to become proficient at operating them. Less stringent qualifications may be required of other blue-collar workers, especially when employers are willing to provide the necessary training, as in the case of household workers. The Government of the Philippines has undertaken skill certification – accepted in most countries of destination – based on occupational tests for low-skill categories such as household employment, popular entertainment, hotel and restaurant services, and general welding. However, this initiative does not yet amount to a fully developed strategy for the training of skilled blue-collar workers.

As yet, no information system has been developed in countries of origin concerning the prospective demand for specific skill categories and the qualifications they call for and there is no known programme for collecting this information on a systematic and continuous basis and relaying it to the public and to education/training institutions in order to adjust their course offerings to coincide with world market requirements. It is difficult for potential migrants to obtain information about specific job opportunities and required levels of proficiency. Any available information on the qualifications required by foreign employers is generally disseminated by recruitment agencies to job applicants, and by job applicants to their friends and relatives. The reach of such informal channels is necessarily limited. Most, if not all, overseas employment initiatives of countries of origin have been concerned mainly with the protection of workers in their workplace and the fight against fraudulent recruitment agencies. They have not yet taken on the responsibility of guiding would-be migrants to acquire the skills and competencies that would maximize the returns on their investment in training and migration. The next section considers whether the education/training system can be relied upon to produce these skills.

[3] The text of this agreement is available from the website of the Ministry of Foreign Affairs of Japan at http://www.mofa.go.jp/region/asia-paci/philippine/epa0609/.

2.4 The Education/Training System

The quality of formal education, especially at university/college level, is a serious issue in most developing countries. For example, only a small proportion of the numerous universities and institutions in South and Southeast Asia are of world standard. Asian countries have established large numbers of higher educational institutions. India has 10,403; China 4,102; Bangladesh 2,711; Indonesia 1,891; the Philippines 1,314; Pakistan 1,108; and Thailand 750 (Tan, 2006). Sri Lanka is the only country to have strictly limited the number of its universities or institutes, currently at 13. Each country also maintains a small number of prestigious universities and colleges. Graduates from the good universities account for only a small fraction of individuals with tertiary education. Many of the professionals who qualify for highly skilled jobs in destination countries are likely to have graduated from the elite institutions. The Indian ICT specialists in the U.S. are most likely to have graduated from the Indian Institutes of Technology and other well-known Indian schools (Murali, 2003). In the Philippines, placement agencies actively recruit nurses for American hospitals from reputable nursing schools, such as the Medical College of the University of the Philippines (Tan, 2006).

Two sources of data serve to indicate the scarcity of high-quality higher educational institutions: the McKinsey study, *The Emerging Global Labor Market* (2005), and the *Asiaweek* Rating of the best universities and Science and Technology Institutes in the Asia-Pacific region in 2000. The McKinsey study looked into demand and supply of high-level human resources by conducting a survey of transnational corporations (TNCs) from Australia, Canada, Ireland, Republic of Korea (South Korea), the U.K. and the U.S., to "quantify the supply of talent in 28 low-wage countries (including China, India, Malaysia and the Philippines) and eight mid and high-wage ones". The study points to the very large number of young university-educated persons in low-wage countries, but states that the surveyed TNCs found that only a fraction qualified for employment in professional jobs in their firms. Of Philippine graduates, only 20 per cent qualified in engineering, 30 per cent in finance/accounting and 25 per cent in general occupations. The corresponding figures for Indian graduates are 25 per cent, 15 and ten per cent. The respective shares for Chinese graduates are even lower – ten, 15 per cent and three per cent. Ratings for Malaysia are similar to those of the Philippines. The Asian sample countries have higher proportions of qualified graduates than the other low-wage sample countries. The differences in ratings between India and the Philippines in engineering and finance/accounting reflect the relative strength of India's science and technology institutes and the accounting schools in the Philippines.

When *Asiaweek* magazine undertook to assess the "best" multi-disciplinary universities and Science and Technology (S&T) centres in the Asia-Pacific region in 1999 and 2000, it focused on a small but representative sample of the region's more than 20,000 institutions. The institutions were rated according to several criteria: academic reputation, student selectivity, faculty reputation, research, financial resources, student/academic staff ratio, citations in international journals and internet bandwidth per student. The schools were ranked from the highest to the lowest according to the scores obtained overall. Among the 77 participating universities, five were in Thailand, four in China, four in the Philippines, four in Indonesia and two in India; all ranked below the median. Pakistan did not rate in the multi-disciplinary group of universities, but three of its science and technology institutes ranked, respectively, 20th, 23rd and 32nd. Three institutions in China participated in the science and technology rating and eight in India, all above the median ranking. According to the *Asiaweek* survey, the institutions with the highest ranking in the Asia-Pacific region were all located in the advanced economies – Australia, Hong Kong SAR, Japan, New Zealand, Singapore and Taiwan Province of China.

2.5 Experience as an Important Source of Training

On-the-job training is the most common form of training for most skilled workers in either the highly skilled or blue-collar category. While medical doctors and nurses have to complete their respective degree programmes and pass their respective licensure examinations, the quality of their experience matters as a gauge of their competence. The capacity to produce high-quality experience depends to a large extent on the size of the economic sector and the technology it uses. The more advanced and industrialized an economy, the larger the workforce with experience in high-tech skills. Consequently, a well-developed sector is required in this field to be able to produce a large number of high-tech experienced workers. Nurses and doctors need to be familiar with state of the art medical interventions. Engineers must work in industries that use modern machinery and equipment, as too must electricians, welders, pipe-setters and metal workers. The less developed countries of origin of the Asia-Pacific region face the challenge of a high demand for such workers while having only a small industrial base to train workers in modern and high-tech skills. There is said to be a large demand for a variety of aviation skills, but countries with a relatively small airline industry will not have the capacity to produce large numbers of specialists in this field. Similarly, most countries in the region have no petrochemical industry and their universities and technical institutes do not produce engineers and technicians in this field; neither do they produce design engineers when their firms are generally of small size. Faced with these industrial realities, what HRD strategy can the region adopt? Formal education and training could provide workers with technical knowledge that would pave the way for on-the-job training. But such formal courses need to be carefully identified and developed. Another option is for foreign recruitment companies to establish training institutions in countries of origin to meet their employment needs. Several such institutions now operate in countries like the Philippines. Placement agencies for U.S. nurses provide instruction to nurses applying for U.S. visas to improve their chances of passing the U.S. nursing examinations (National Council for Graduates of Foreign Schools and the National Council for Licensure Examination). It is informally reported in the Philippines that U.S. hospitals face such a shortage of nurses that they are willing to pay recruitment agents USD 10,000 to USD 12,000 per nurse placed.[4]

2.6 Role of the Private Sector

Wherever there is the opportunity, the private sector will respond to demand for education, as indeed demonstrated in several Asian countries. Private colleges and universities have assumed a relatively large responsibility in higher education in Indonesia, Japan, the Philippines and South Korea. Thailand has begun to authorize private institutions to offer tertiary education. The participation of private schools naturally increases access to education. However, the challenge is to ensure quality. Moreover, as discussed in Chapter 4, the Asia-Pacific region is also a popular testing ground for the adoption by foreign universities of contractual arrangements with private or public institutions in the form of franchises or twinning programmes with the objective of offering their academic courses to local students.

2.7 Emigration of Skilled Human Resources

Skilled migration is a controversial issue (see also Chapter 2). From one perspective, the movement of highly skilled workers may be seen as equally benefiting developed and developing countries by reducing the supply-demand mismatch in the former

[4] Information obtained from interviews with recruitment agencies in the preparation of Tan (2007).

and reallocating unused human resources from the latter. Seen from a different perspective, however, this movement is seen as detrimental to both by creating an unhelpful reliance on the "import" of talent from abroad (as opposed to the development of home-grown skills) in developed countries, and by depriving developing countries of their scarce professional and technical resources. There is also an ethical dimension to be considered, as the poorer countries of origin bear the cost of educating their nationals and potential migrants (including through private funding of students), while the countries of destination reap the benefits.

Clearly, when there is a skills shortage or when skills are difficult to replace, the cost is high for the country of origin. This is the case in much of Africa as well as in the Caribbean. Two-thirds of Jamaica's nurses emigrated over the period 1980-2000 and only few return (Lowell and Findlay, 2001). According to Docquier and Bhargava (2006), Grenada and Dominica have lost more than 90 per cent of their physicians, while the small island nations of Saint Lucia and Cape Verde have lost more than 50 per cent (Ratha and Xu, 2008). The problem has not been as acute in other parts of the world, but it exists nonetheless. The shortage of high-quality professionals and high-tech experienced blue-collar workers can be symptomatic of brain or skill drain. The number of nurses leaving the Philippines has exceeded the number of those who pass the licensure examination over the past five years. Foreign employers usually select nurses who already have experience, leaving hospitals and clinics with new graduates or those who may not have passed the licensure examination (Tan, 2007).

The following steps can be taken to mitigate the adverse impact of brain drain, although they should not prevent migrants from exercising the right to leave their country:

- promotion of ethical recruitment to prevent indiscriminate international recruitment in sensitive sectors such as health, particularly in small and fragile economies, through managed recruitment under bilateral labour agreements (see also Chapter 13);
- creation of a system to recoup some of the loss of investment in countries of origin by requiring the inclusion of practical training as part of some higher education programmes; investment by destination countries in training and education, proportional to the loss in investment suffered by the country of origin; and retention of skilled workers through voluntary means; and
- better targeting of subsidies in higher education by, for example, concentrating such subsidies in priority programmes of instruction and research.

2.8 Achieving Policy Coherence

Given the complexities of developing education and training policies to meet the prospective demand for skilled human resources, countries of origin cannot rely on one-dimensional modes of intervention, however important they may be. The concept of HRD planning needs to be mainstreamed to give purpose and coherence to efforts aimed at matching labour demand with supply while at the same time providing the necessary means to mitigate the loss of skilled workers.

3. Foreign Employment Policies[5]

Countries of origin have different profiles. Some have long-established labour migration programmes, while others are experiencing a migration transition characterized by both labour inflows and outflows, and finally there are those that are relative newcomers to organized labour migration. Nevertheless, as countries of origin, they all face some common challenges, such as:

- Protecting migrant workers from exploitative recruitment and employment practices, and providing appropriate assistance to migrant

[5] This section has been updated and distilled from the OSCE/IOM/ILO Handbook on Labour Migration (2006, 2007).

workers in terms of pre-departure, welfare and on-site services.

- Optimizing the benefits of organized labour migration, particularly regarding the development of new markets and directing remittance flows through formal channels, as well as enhancing the development impact of remittances.
- Mitigating the adverse impacts of the emigration of skilled human resources.
- Building institutional capacity and inter-ministerial coordination to be able to respond to new issues and challenges arising in relation to labour migration.
- Increasing cooperation with destination countries for the protection of migrant workers, access to labour markets and the prevention of irregular migration.[6]

These challenges call for very specific responses in terms of policies, structures and procedures.

3.1 Protection of Migrant Workers and Support Services

Given that the supply of lower skilled workers far exceeds demand and that many more workers wish to work abroad to than there are jobs, migrant workers can be vulnerable to abuse during recruitment, travel and employment abroad. A problem many migrant workers face is high migration costs as a result of excessive, and mostly illegal, intermediation fees. In addition, problems occur in the country of employment. Those most commonly cited by migrant workers are contract substitution and violations; the late, insufficient or total lack of payment of agreed wages; non-fulfilment of return airfare obligations; and harassment and actual abuse of women workers by employers (IOM, 2003). Other problems encountered include poor working conditions, the lack of social protection, denial of freedom of association and other human and labour rights, discrimination and xenophobia and social exclusion (OSCE/IOM/ILO Handbook on Labour Migration, 2006, 2007).

These abuses erode the potential benefits of migration for all parties concerned, and seriously undermine the expected development impact. Migrant workers are best able to realize their potential and make the best contribution when their working conditions are correct and their fundamental human and labour rights respected.

Although there is no single perfect labour migration regulation system, countries of origin do have a range of policy strategies at their disposal with which to expand the scope and improve the efficiency of their regulatory mechanisms and support services. Key policy strategies include:

- Conducting pre-employment orientation seminars (PEOS) and intensified information campaigns to provide applicants with sufficient information on which to base their decisions.
- Empowering migrant workers, especially through the formation of community-based organizations, to make their voices heard and taken account of in policy formulation and development.
- Streamlining and simplifying regulations and procedures for the protection of workers, and preventing the regulatory framework from becoming too unwieldy and complex, which may itself act as an unintended inducement to irregular migration.
- Close supervision and monitoring of recruitment activities undertaken by overseas employment promoters/agencies, to minimize malpractice and abuse against those seeking overseas jobs.
- Foreseeing criminal proceedings against serious offenders, in addition to cancellation of agencies' licences.
- Paying special attention to the supervision of recruitment and deployment of categories of workers especially vulnerable to malpractice and abuse, such as women domestic workers and low-skilled workers.

[6] For cooperation with destination countries, see also Chapter 13.

- Raising workers' skill levels to improve their employment opportunities and promote their deployment abroad, with due attention to concerns relating to brain drain (see Section 2.7 above).
- Introducing effective measures to ensure observance of the employment contract at the worksite, in particular through bilateral arrangements and agreements between home and host governments (see also Chapter 13).
- Providing support services such as pre-departure orientation to ease adaptation to a new life and work environment abroad, and inform on the availability of and access to welfare funds and services.
- Establishing mutual cooperation on common areas of concern between home and host countries.

Some of these key policy strategies are discussed in more detail below.

A number of international instruments have also been negotiated and concluded under the auspices of the International Labour Organization (ILO) and the United Nations concerning the protection of migrant workers and their families (see Chapter 13). If widely ratified and implemented by countries of origin and destination, they would provide a comprehensive normative framework for the protection of this group.

(a) Regulation of private employment agencies

Many migrant workers lack information about job opportunities, particularly when they leave their country for the first time in search of employment abroad. Likewise, employers in destination countries who wish to fill particular vacancies with migrant workers require information about suitable candidates. In a global environment characterized by the rapid expansion of new migration routes and increasingly diversified migration flows, the role of private recruiters is gaining in importance.

The evolving migration industry has opened opportunities for a wide range of private recruiters, from small and specialized private employment agencies to multinational companies. Apart from such legally operating businesses, there are "the parallel operations" of semi-legal or outright unlawful recruiters, with some often linked to smuggling or trafficking networks. Research has shown that where regular migration channels are limited, migrant workers will largely turn to illegitimate recruiters or their own social networks (OSCE/IOM/ILO Handbook on Labour Migration, 2006, 2007). Government intervention is therefore required to regulate private employment agencies, to curb unfair and unethical recruitment methods and thus to protect migrant workers against abuse.

There are different approaches to regulating and monitoring the activities of recruiters, while trying to ensure that migrant workers are protected from abuse. The most suitable approach will best be identified through an analysis of the recruitment industry, its main type of activities and possible problems. The scope of regulation may differ according to the type of private employment agency (PEA) concerned; however, it is important that the legal status of PEAs be properly defined and determined in all cases. Since it is relatively straightforward for recruiters to pursue their activities covertly, it is essential to combine regulatory measures with promotional campaigns to ensure compliance with the law.

(i) Registration and licensing

The most common approaches to regulating the activities of PEAs are registration and licensing. Registration requires the agency to register with the Ministry of Labour or other relevant authority and pay a fee. A registered agency is then subject to routine checks by tax authorities and labour inspectors like any other business. However, given the level of concern about unfair recruitment practices, many countries have opted for a licensing system.

Unlike registration, requirements to obtain a license are more rigorous to fulfil.

The Philippines and Pakistan are two countries with an active private recruitment sector. In 2003, there were 1,327 licensed recruitment agencies in the Philippines. Table 10.1 illustrates licensing requirements in Pakistan and the Philippines.

Table 10.1:

Licensing Requirements in Pakistan and the Philippines

Requirements	Pakistan	Philippines
National	Yes	Yes
Application fee	USD 16	USD 200
Registration	Company	Company (with paid up capital of USD 40,000)
Character Certificate	Certificate of good conduct	Clean criminal record
Refundable Deposit	USD 5,000	USD 20,000
Other	Licence fee – USD 500	Licence fee – USD 1,000 Surety bond – USD 2,000 Minimum capital – USD 40,000
Validity of Licence	3 years	4 years

Note:
Original sums were in national currencies and converted to U.S. dollars by the authors.

Source: *Mughal and Padilla, 2005.*

(ii) Fees

ILO Convention No. 181 on Private Employment Agencies (1997), ratified by 20 countries and in force since 10 May 2000, stipulates that recruitment fees and costs should not be charged to workers other than in exceptional circumstances. While it is clearly preferable for all the costs to be borne by the employers, in practice this is often not the case, and many governments do allow fees and costs to be charged to migrant workers. Supply and demand factors underpinning migration also require attention when regulating fees. In India, fees vary according to the worker's level of qualification (Table 10.2).

Table 10.2:

Fees Charged to Migrant Workers by PEAs in India

Type of worker	Fee (in USD)
Low-skilled	45
Semi-skilled	65
Skilled	110
Highly skilled	220

Source: *Adapted from India, Office of the Protector General of Emigrants (2004).*

In the Philippines, the recruitment fee must not exceed one month's salary, although charging fees is not permissible when the prevailing system in the destination country where the worker is to be deployed, either by law, policy or practice, does not allow the charging or collection of placement and recruitment fees.[7] Responding to problems of overcharging by recruitment intermediaries and exorbitant migration costs, some countries of destination have placed legal limits to such fees. In Israel, for example, the maximum fee the migrant worker can be charged is approximately USD 950, which includes the sums paid to recruitment agents abroad as well as the sum paid to the Israeli agency but which excludes the airfare (MOITAL, 2008).

(iii) Involvement of public employment agencies

While in most countries of origin the role of public recruitment agencies has been taken over by the private sector, there are arguments in favour of the deployment through state-run agencies of categories of workers that are especially vulnerable to malpractice and abuse, such as women domestic workers.

[7] See 2002 Revised POEA Rules and Regulations Governing the Recruitment and Employment of Land-based Overseas Workers (http://www.poea.gov.ph/rules/POEA%20Rules.pdf), Rule 5, Section 3.

International organizations like IOM with wide-ranging experience in migrant application processing and services can also be called upon to facilitate recruitment and are indeed taking up this role within the framework of bilateral arrangements (e.g. IOM, 2008) concerning labour migration to Canada, Italy and Spain. A particularly interesting example is the Seasonal Agricultural Workers Project: Guatemala-Canada (see Textbox 10.2 and Portrait 10.1).

Textbox 10.2

Seasonal Agricultural Workers Project - Guatemala-Canada

The Guatemala-Canada Seasonal Agricultural Workers Project is the result of joint efforts by the Ministry of Foreign Affairs and the Ministry of Labour and Social Welfare, and IOM cooperation.

The project was established in 2003 through an agreement with La Fondation des entreprises en recrutement de la main d'oeuvre agricole étrangère (FERME) of the Province of Québec under the supervision of the Department of Human Resources and Skills Development Canada (HRSDC).

The Government of Guatemala and FERME agreed to promote the migration of seasonal agricultural workers with the objective of benefiting the country of origin and the host country, while reducing irregular migration and the associated risks. The Government of Guatemala requested technical cooperation and implementation of the agreement by IOM as follows:

- Assistance in the selection of candidates to meet the Canadian needs for seasonal agricultural workers.
- Coordination with the Ministry of Labour to assure that the rights of Guatemalan seasonal workers are protected and compliance with other requirements of the Ministry in addition to immigration requirements.
- Travel arrangements for seasonal migrant workers.

IOM signed a Memorandum of Understanding with FERME regarding the project.

Guatemalan workers are also protected under Canadian labour laws and have access to life and medical insurance. The project is monitored by Guatemalan consular staff in Canada who supervise the farms where Guatemalans work, with the aim of supporting Guatemalan workers as well as Canadian employers.

Main Procedures

Demand: Associated farms in Canada submit requests for seasonal workers to FERME, which are then processed and assessed for approval. Once approved, they are sent by FERME to IOM Guatemala with copies to the Guatemalan Embassy in Canada. Each request includes the number of workers, expected date of arrival in Canada, duration of the work contract and type of farm crop.

Recruitment: Recruitment is carried out in different communities and municipalities in various departments in Guatemala. During that process, candidates are interviewed and assessed to ascertain that they meet the requirements under the project, and fill in a form with general information for their possible selection. Some Canadian entrepreneurs also participate in the recruitment process. Workers then visit the IOM office and submit the documents required for inclusion in the project. Once these documents have been received, a visa application is made and the respective file created.

Visa Application: The visa application and all the appropriate documents are forwarded to the Canadian Embassy for the relevant Medical Examination Forms to be issued. Depending on the test results workers are deemed to be fit to undertake seasonal agricultural work in Canada.

Work Permit Application: Workers who have passed the medical test are registered for seasonal agricultural work and a work permit from HRSDC is requested through FERME. Once the Canadian Embassy has the HRSDC work permits, the visas are issued.

The Journey: Workers are invited to visit the IOM office a few days before leaving to receive information regarding their journey, the expected conduct and discipline to be observed during their work in Canada, and their relations with other people on the farms. Each worker receives a folder with all travel documents on the first day of the journey. These documents are classified to facilitate emigration and immigration clearance in Guatemala and in Canada, respectively, and include the documents the worker will be handing over to the employer.

Main Results

The number of beneficiaries is increasing and the institutional coordination mechanisms between national institutions (e.g. foreign ministries and labour ministries) are being supported and reinforced through technical cooperation from IOM. Project evaluations carried out with the participation of national authorities and Canadian employers confirm these positive results.

The project was launched in 2003 with an initial group of 215 workers: 180 men and 35 women. Since then the number of workers included in this programme has increased substantially: 2,075 as of 2 November 2007, including 1,948 men and 127 women.

Source: *IOM Guatemala (November 2007), http://www.oim.org.gt/SeasonalAgriculturalWorkersProject.pdf.*

Portrait 10.1

Temporary Migration of Agricultural Workers to Canada

Ernesto is from the Guatemalan indigenous community of El Llano, Patzún, Chimaltenango. He has already travelled twice with the Guatemala/Canada Seasonal Agricultural Workers Project to work on a farm tying onions, cutting lettuce and washing carrots. As instructions on the Canadian farm are given in Spanish, it is not difficult for him to follow them and to carry out his work efficiently. Also, he gets along well with his co-workers and generally feels that his stays in Canada have been positive.

"When I travel to Canada, I am usually sad saying goodbye to my wife and six children," he recalls, "but I am happy for this opportunity to improve my family's living conditions. Work in Canada is hard, but it's worth the effort as I am able to send money to my family every two weeks. In Guatemala, it is so much more difficult to earn money!"

Moreover, any new skills he acquires in Canada help him to improve his own land and farming methods in Guatemala. "However," explains Ernesto, "it will not be easy as the farm machines used in Canada are expensive." Then he adds, "I thank God and the Project as in the first year I was able to build a home for my family, and with my earnings from the second year I bought another piece of land to grow peas. Also, I have bought a TV set and a CD player. In Canada, I usually buy presents for my wife, and clothes and toys for my children."

During the last years, Ernesto and his family have been able to improve their diet and to occasionally add meat. "At first, my wife was sad when I left to work in Canada. But now she is grateful and happy as this allows us to live a better life." "I tell my children that I have to work in Canada to earn enough money in order to buy their food and to send them to school."

When working in Canada, Ernesto sends his wife money for food and basic expenses, and she knows that the extra money they are saving could be used in case of any emergency.

"The Project is a great help for poor people like me, as it gives us the chance of working and earning enough money to improve our life and future prospects for our children. I am thankful to have been given this opportunity which allows me to look ahead and gain hope and confidence, and to leave poverty behind us."

Source: *IOM Guatemala.*

(b) Minimum standards in employment contracts

Ensuring that employment contracts guarantee fair wages and basic provisions has been an important concern for countries of origin in protecting their nationals abroad. For that reason, countries of origin have developed model employment contracts which establish minimum requirements for their workers in the countries where they will be working.

Such provisions take into account the existing labour and social laws of the host country, as well as national customs, traditions and practices, and local labour market conditions. They should also be in conformity with applicable international standards and bilateral labour migration agreements adopted between countries of origin and destination.

The Philippine Government, for example, has set minimum wages for certain occupations, such as household employees, seafarers and production workers, which must not be lower than the standards fixed under bilateral agreements or international conventions to which the host country is a party. In no case may a migrant worker be paid a salary lower that the prevailing minimum wage in the Philippines. Recently, the Philippine Government imposed a minimum wage of USD 400 per month for out-bound domestic workers.[8]

Standards set by the local administration and included in model employment contracts may form the basis for permitting the employment of nationals abroad. However, in the absence of a bilateral agreement between countries of origin and destination to ensure the observance of minimum wages, it is relatively easy for contract substitution to occur or for workers from one country to be replaced by those of another. It is incumbent on the host country authorities to ensure the availability of legal recourse if labour contracts are violated, for instance such as provided for by the Department of Labour in Hong Kong SAR (Abella, 2000).

In Jordan, the government has endorsed a legally enforceable Special Unified Working Contract for foreign domestic workers, developed with the assistance of the United Nations Development Fund for Women (UNIFEM) and national stakeholders. The contract is the first of its kind in the Middle East and is required for the issuance of visas and permits. The government is also amending national labour laws to provide domestic workers with legally recognized and enforceable rights protection (UNIFEM, 2004).

Implementation of regulatory measures, whether by controlling recruitment or by using emigration clearance to check the validity of overseas employment contracts, becomes more challenging for countries of origin when movement is facilitated through the introduction of visa-free regimes (e.g. such as in the Commonwealth of Independent States) or by proximity (e.g. Indonesians and Filipinos working in Malaysia). The easing of movement, whether deliberate or due to physical factors, enables potential migrant workers to travel to the country of destination without necessarily first obtaining a job (and employment contract). In such cases, while regulatory measures remain important, countries of origin will need to rely more on support services and interstate cooperation to ensure the protection and welfare of their citizens working abroad.

(c) Support services

The provision of support services to migrant workers may include access to information, the establishment of a contributory welfare fund to meet emergency needs in the country of destination, the provision of insurance coverage and posting of labour attachés to advise and assist workers abroad.

8 See Guidelines on the Implementation of the Reform Package Affecting Household Service Workers, http://www.poea.gov.ph/hsw/Guidelines%20on%20the%20Implementation%20of%20the%20Reform%20Package%20Affecting%20Household%20Service%20Workers.pdf.

(i) Information dissemination

Pre-employment

As millions of people move across borders each year, the need for information has become fundamental to all migration decisions. Distorted perceptions and insufficient knowledge about the realities in the countries they are intending to go to only serve to increase the importance of ensuring that migrants have access to information. Most migrants are unaware of the practical, legal, social and economic consequences of moving to another country. This lack of awareness heightens the risk migrants may be exposed to, while also undermining orderly migration. The dissemination of relevant information reduces such risk and provides migrants with a sound basis on which to make informed decisions.

In recent years, countries of origin have recognized the need to provide their citizens intending to go abroad for purposes of employment with sufficient information to make informed choices about regular travel options, means of recruitment and travel and employment arrangements. Such information can be conveyed in two ways: through preparatory pre-employment sessions for particular contingents of workers or through broader mass information campaigns. The latter can be especially useful in drawing attention to the risks and dangers of irregular labour migration. Information resource centres for actual and intending migrant workers have also been established in some countries with the assistance of international organizations (see Textbox 10.3 and Portrait 10.2).

A variety of communication activities using various media can be used. Mass media ensure that information reaches large audiences quickly, while direct grassroots contacts provide the informal setting required for more in-depth and frank discussions.

Textbox 10.3

Information Resource Centre for Migrant Workers in Tajikistan

An Information Resource Centre for Migrant Workers was established in Dushanbe, Tajikistan, in 2004 by IOM and the Government of Tajikistan with the support of the Organization for Security and Co-operation in Europe (OSCE) to provide intending and actual migrant workers with reliable information on living and working abroad. Tajikistan's limited employment opportunities and mountainous terrain make it difficult for its inhabitants to make a living. As a result, to escape poverty, almost every Tajik family has at least one member who is a migrant worker. Tajiks seasonally migrate to neighbouring Kazakhstan, Kyrgyzstan and Uzbekistan, though most go to the Russian Federation. An IOM study on labour migration in the region revealed that some 600,000 Tajiks are migrants (Olimova and Bosc, 2003). Unfortunately, however, Tajik migrants are not well informed about the realities of life abroad.

Most Tajiks work in informal and low-skilled sectors in Russia and, even when they have regular status, labour exploitation is common. Many migrants do not know where to go to seek advice and information on travel and work abroad and are an easy prey for unofficial recruiters and traffickers.

The Government of Tajikistan, IOM and OSCE agreed to create a public resource centre with qualified counsellors to provide information relevant to the needs of migrants. The Resource Centre informs potential migrants about employment conditions, travel and documentation requirements, registration, the rights of migrants, press reports, maps and contacts, the risks of trafficking and smuggling in human beings, health risks and other useful tips. Through this project, information is also provided on community organizations and resources, social services and longer-term integration facilities.

Particular attention is paid to collecting, preparing and disseminating up-to-date information in the field of labour migration to intending migrant workers.

1. Travel and documentation:

- documents required for travel (passport and other documents);
- entry and exit (rights and responsibilities of border guards and citizens);
- customs (customs procedures, rights and responsibilities on both sides of the border);
- police (how to prevent abuse);
- transport means and ticketing (air and road transport);
- visa information and embassy addresses;
- information on the dangers of trafficking.

2. Admission and post-admission:

- regularization in destination country (registration);
- regularization of employment (work permit);
- health (first aid, HIV/AIDS prevention);
- education (admission);
- overseas representations of the Republic of Tajikistan and other contact addresses;
- relationship with employer (employment contract and possible risks);
- housing (rental and leases, and risks);
- employment in foreign countries (realities and possible risks for Tajik citizens).

The information is disseminated via booklets, posters, counselling services, tours, mass media, meetings, workshops and seminars.

Source: *IOM Dushanbe.*

Portrait 10.2

The Importance of Pre-departure Consultation

In June 2006, Oleg saw an advertisement in a local newspaper offering a well-paid job in the United States. Until then, he had only been able to find some temporary jobs and the money he earned was quite insufficient to pay for his family's daily needs and the education of his children. Working in the U.S. for a monthly wage of USD 2,500, as stated in the advertisement, seemed to offer a solution to his problems. Oleg called the agency and, when he got through, was told to prepay USD 1,200 for the agency to prepare the necessary documents and obtain a work visa from the U.S. Embassy. As this was much more than Oleg could afford, he borrowed USD 1,000.

Oleg went to Kiev, located the agency and met the manager. The staff seemed friendly and accommodating. Oleg spoke of his financial problems and the manager reassured him that the prospective job would not be difficult, and provide high wages, accommodation and meals. Oleg signed the contract without even reading it, trusting what he had heard, and deposited his passport and the requested sum of money with the agency, and returned home expecting to be contacted one week before his departure for the U.S. as agreed.

However, nothing happened, and when he again called the agency, there was no reply. Becoming suspicious, Oleg continued to call and eventually left again for Kiev to see what was happening. However, there was nobody at the address, only empty offices. The cleaner informed him that the agency had rented the room only for a few days before leaving again, but she did not know where to.

Oleg needed some time before he realized what had happened. Only now did it occur to him as strange that the office was so small, that there was no official sign or name, that only a laptop had been placed on the table, and that the "manager" had been far too friendly. He did not know what to do now.

Oleg returned home and found a temporary job. He handed all the money he earned to the creditor to repay his debt. Although working abroad to earn some money became more of a necessity each day, his experience had made him suspicious and he was not ready to take any more risks.

One day, Oleg saw a banner at a railway station, with a hotline number. He called and was advised to apply to a Centre of Migrant Advice (CMA). When Oleg went there for a personal consultation, he was informed of the possibilities available to work abroad lawfully. Based on this information, Oleg chose to apply for work in the Czech Republic. The Centre assisted him to access the employment websites in the Czech Republic and offered him the use of free Internet access. The CMA consultants helped him to prepare his personal history form in English and to post it on the employment websites. He was then able to contact some of the potential employers and, in time, received an answer from a construction company in Brno. This time, Oleg prepared and collected all necessary documents himself and obtained a working visa. Before he left for his new job in the Czech Republic, Oleg was provided with all useful and necessary contact information concerning the Ukraine Consulate in Prague as well as non-governmental aid agencies able to assist migrants in the Czech Republic.

Oleg has since departed for Brno where he is satisfied with his new job. He has also referred his neighbours to the CMA.

***Source:** IOM Kiev.*

Pre-departure orientation

Pre-departure orientation courses are intended to prepare the departing migrants for life and work abroad, including their protection from abusive employment practices. Such short courses are often seen as a useful way of providing basic, introductory information relating to future living and working environments such as cultural adaptation issues, language skills and financial services, including advice on the gains that can be made; health counselling and human rights awareness; and eventual return and reintegration arrangements.

With this objective in mind, the Governments of the Philippines and Sri Lanka have developed two-day pre-departure orientation programmes for domestic workers leaving for Hong Kong SAR and the Middle East, covering the following areas:

- rights of a domestic worker based on the standard employment contract;
- obligations of a domestic worker according to relevant regulations;
- "do's and don'ts" in relation to the employer and living conditions in the destination country;
- destination country profile;
- services and benefits offered by government bodies and non-governmental organizations (NGOs);
- options and procedures for sending remittances;
- travel documents, airport procedures and travel tips;
- initial reception arrangements in the destination country;
- return and reintegration;
- savings options.

For similar reasons, the Italian Ministry of Labour provided funds for IOM to develop five orientation modules covering legal aspects of migration; the management of the migrant labour market; socio-cultural aspects; psycho-cultural aspects; and language learning. Those modules have been used as resources for pre-departure orientation courses in a number of countries, including Moldova and Sri Lanka.

(ii) Migrant welfare funds

Migrant welfare funds (MWFs) are an innovative and financially sustainable means of providing support services to vulnerable migrants and to migrants in distress. Although so far only implemented in Asia, they have the potential to be of value to all countries of origin by providing a solid resource base for action against the abuse of migrant workers and ensuring decent working and living conditions. They have proved to be particularly useful in assisting migrants who encounter problems on worksites.

Three major Asian countries of origin have established MWFs: Pakistan, the Philippines and Sri Lanka. The principal objectives of the funds are to provide protection to migrant workers on the job site. The funds also provide for a number of other services for workers and their families.

MWFs are administered by public or semi-public agencies: the Overseas Pakistani Foundation (OPF), the Philippine Overseas Workers Welfare Administration (OWWA) and the Sri Lanka Overseas Workers Welfare Fund (OWWF). All three involve representatives of migrant workers and the national government office in charge of labour migration. They are financed by contributions from departing migrant workers fixed at about USD 25 per person. OWWA, together with the Philippine Overseas Employment Administration (POEA), were created by Presidential decree in 1977, just two years after the first group of 35,000 construction workers left for the Middle East. The Pakistani Emigration Ordinance, adopted in 1979, provided for the establishment of OPF, while Sri Lanka created its welfare fund in 1985. Apparently, both funds were adapted from the Philippine model, since there are great similarities in their objectives, organization and funding sources.

The operations of MWFs in the Philippines, Pakistan and Sri Lanka have been assessed in an IOM study (Tan, 2005) focusing on their effectiveness in achieving their objectives. Financial reports published by the welfare funds reveal the scope of their activities. Pakistan allocated 13 per cent of its welfare services budget to job sites, covering consultations, legal services, the return of migrants and repatriation of remains. Sri Lanka allocated a higher proportion, 35 per cent of its budget, for the same purposes. The Philippine MWF runs 28 migrant worker centres in countries with large concentrations of Filipino migrant workers. It pays for legal services to defend migrant workers in foreign courts. All three funds pay for the fares of migrant workers whose employment has been terminated because of physical abuse, contract violations or other reasons, and for the cost of repatriating remains.

The three MWFs, but especially OPF, have tried to establish other services such as scholarships, vocational training and business loans to migrant workers and their families to the point where they risk intruding on services already offered by specialized government agencies. In general terms, however, demand for these extra services has not been particularly strong (Tan, 2005).

(iii) Government assistance in destination countries through labour attachés

The role of embassies and consulates in providing support and assistance to migrant workers is most developed in established Asian countries of origin and Mexico. The labour attaché is a member of the diplomatic mission, appointed from the ministry or department of labour, and charged with functions relating to labour relations between the home and the host country. For example, a labour attaché from the Philippines has the following duties:

- protection of workers abroad falling within the diplomatic mission's jurisdiction;
- undertaking marketing and identification of job opportunities;
- assistance in the development of labour migration policies;
- promotion of good relations with the host country on labour matters.

In the Philippines, labour attachés are supported by Philippine Overseas Labour Officers (POLOs), whose work is described in Textbox 10.4.

Textbox 10.4

Philippine Overseas Labour Officers: Serving Overseas Filipino Workers Abroad

The Philippine Administrative Code and Labour Code provide the legal basis for a service delivery programme in countries of destination through the Philippine Overseas Labour Officers or POLOs. The Department of Labour and Employment (DOLE) is responsible for the development of policy and programme guidelines, while the International Labour Affairs Service (ILAS) of the DOLE provides ongoing administrative support. The Philippine Overseas Employment Administration (POEA) and the Overseas Workers Welfare Administration (OWWA) are the POLOs' key institutional partners within the DOLE for the implementation of their programmes and day-to-day operations. From a personnel management perspective, the POLOs are attached to the Philippine diplomatic missions abroad and subject to the relevant regulations of the Department of Foreign Affairs for service attachés. The POLOs' activities are therefore supervised by their respective heads of mission at the posting station.

To ensure organized legal entry of Filipino workers to the place of work, POLOs verify whether foreign employers, foreign recruiters, worksites, project sites, job vacancies and terms and conditions of employment meet the standards set by bilateral agreements or Philippine Government policy. They also negotiate with host governments and employers to secure improvements of the terms and conditions of employment and to facilitate worker recruitment and documentation.

Post-arrival orientation activities, worksite inspections, the social mobilization of workers and consultative dialogues are undertaken to address adjustment needs by promoting a sense of belonging in their temporary work setting, the fostering of cultural unity among Filipino workers and the maintenance of communication with the Philippine Mission. When problems and crises arise, Filipino migrant workers are given access to counselling, mediation, conciliation, medical services, legal assistance and court representation, as required. Visits to workers in detention can also be arranged, temporary shelter offered and evacuation or repatriation effected in case of civil conflict or unrest, or for health reasons. Where permissible under host country policy, referrals for employment transfer may be organized. In addition, POLOs help update and implement crisis response programmes with the Consular Division of the Philippine Mission, whenever necessary. In preparation for their post-employment options in the Philippines, Filipino workers are provided access to skills training, reintegration counselling and service referral.

POLOs are counted upon to establish cooperative linkages with a wide range of partners and stakeholders, including host governments, employers' associations, worker organizations, Filipino communities, NGOs, faith-based organizations and the media. They have the responsibility to provide regular situational analyses, identify new market opportunities or make a recommendation when they are of the view that a ban on the deployment of workers to a company or country is warranted. They can also make recommendations towards the imposition of administrative penalties against or blacklisting of abusive foreign employers and recruiters.

POLOs have been deployed in 34 countries around the world and are led by 42 labour attachés. In most posts, the complete staff establishment of a POLO team includes a welfare officer, an administrative assistant, an interpreter and a driver. The POLO team works in partnership with Philippine consular officers and, depending on specific issues of concern, with other members of the diplomatic service. For example, the POLO works closely with trade attachés whenever bilateral discussions on economic cooperation agreements involve labour and employment issues. While police matters relating to nationals, including those concerning irregular work, are handled by consular officials, the POLOs maintain an open system of informal cooperation to assist in such cases. At other times, the POLOs work hand-in-hand with social workers and medical attachés deployed by the Department of Social Welfare and Development and the Department of Health.

The Migrant Workers and Overseas Filipinos Act of 1995 reinforced the role of the POLOs and provided impetus for further experimentation in team management and mainstreaming of services within the Philippine diplomatic service to provide overseas Filipino workers with the services they need wherever they may be.

***Source:** Ricardo Casco, National Programme Officer, Labour Migration Services, IOM Manila.*

3.2 Optimizing the Benefits of Organized Labour Migration

For countries seeking to promote foreign employment, labour migration policy must also address the broader question of the promotion and facilitation of managed external labour flows. Countries of origin have an interest in discouraging irregular migration (while advocating an increase in regular channels for labour migration, including through circular migration initiatives). The benefits of organized labour migration can be optimized through the promotion of foreign employment by way of marketing strategies, cooperation with the private sector, human resource development (see Section 2 above) and leveraging the funds migrant workers send home (remittances). The importance of marketing is considered below, while circular migration and the question of enhancing the development impact of remittances are discussed in Chapter 12.

3.3. Importance of Marketing

Since labour migration is primarily determined by demand, countries wishing to deploy their workers abroad must be able to seek out prospective employers and compete with other countries of origin. Thus, it can be argued, a "marketing strategy" is the lifeblood of any overseas employment programme.

Marketing is a necessary first step in the effort to "promote" a country's labour. It also points to a country's deliberate purpose in using labour mobility as a means to attain certain specific economic goals, such as easing unemployment or the generation of flows of remittances to augment its foreign exchange earnings. Countries intending to deploy their nationals abroad need to identify opportunities beyond their national boundaries in a highly competitive international market. In this case, market research becomes essential.

In the Philippines, the market research group maintains a "desk officer" system that allocates work responsibilities according to regions of interest (e.g. the Gulf Cooperation Council (GCC) states, Europe, Asia, Oceania/Australia) or to occupational sectors (e.g. seafarers, nurses/health workers, domestic workers).[9] A monthly Market Situation Report (MSR) is provided to private sector associations, which in turn distribute it to their members. The MSR is a consolidated report on current international labour market developments and relevant economic trends and events that have a bearing on the Philippine overseas employment programme. In addition, comprehensive destination country reports are prepared, covering the labour, political and socio-economic conditions as well as prospects and problems in each country of interest. Information on immigration policies and labour laws of different countries are continuously gathered, analyzed and disseminated. This type of research is essentially based on analytical reading of secondary sources such as trade journals, regional economic magazines and national development plans of countries of destination. This is complemented by feedback derived from consultations and close liaison work with the marketing staff of private sector groups. Inputs are also derived from reports of labour attachés and whatever information can be culled from Philippine embassy reports.

In addition to disseminating market research information to the private sector, marketing missions are undertaken by the Philippine Government to negotiate bilateral agreements or arrangements for the deployment of Filipino workers.[10]

As part of an inter-regional project for legal and managed labour migration,[11] financed by the European Commission, IOM is helping to create or strengthen existing marketing activities in ten Asian countries of origin. Market research units, or MRUs, are to be located in the ministries of overseas employment/

---

9 Information provided by Ricardo Casco, National Programme Officer, Labour Migration Services, IOM Manila and former POEA official.

10 Information provided by Ricardo Casco, National Programme Officer, Labour Migration Services, IOM Manila.

11 AENEAS: Regional Dialogue and Programme on Facilitating Legal Migration between Asia and the European Union. A brochure describing the programme can be downloaded from the Colombo Process website (see Textbox 10.5) at http://www.colomboprocess.org/.

labour to collect labour market information on selected European Union Member States and disseminate it to recruitment agencies.

3.4 Administration of Labour Migration - Sample Policy and Procedural Interventions

Ultimately, labour migration programmes are most effective when they are supported by comprehensive sets of policies and procedures. An analysis of those already in place in four Asian countries is shown in Table 10.3 below. While there are undoubtedly similarities in these countries' policies, there are also significant differences in their content and application.

Table 10.3:

Government Functions and Services Provided by Overseas Employment Programmes, Selected Countries of Origin

	Bangladesh	India	Sri Lanka	Philippines
Supervision of Recruitment				
Registration and licensing of private recruiters	*****	*****	*****	*****
Ban/restriction of direct hiring	*****	*****	*****	*****
Periodic inspection of recruitment agencies	*****	*****	*****	*****
Limit to recruitment fee charged to worker	*****	*****	*****	*****
Cash/security bond requirement	*****	*****	*****	*****
Regulation of job advertising	*****	*****	*****	*****
Joint liability			*****	*****
Complaints mechanism and adjudication	*****	*****	*****	*****
Performance-based incentives				*****
State recruitment agency	*****	*****	*****	*****
Departure Procedures for Migrant Workers (MWs)				
Minimum standards for employment contracts	*****	*****	*****	*****
Emigration clearance	*****	*****	*****	*****
Trade test		*****	*****	*****
Support Services to Migrant Workers				
State subsidized skills training	*****	*****	*****	*****
Pre-departure orientation	*****	*****	*****	*****
Migrant welfare fund	*****		*****	*****
Labour attaché assistance	*****	*****	*****	*****
Overseas Workers Welfare Centres			*****	*****
Insurance	*****	*****	*****	*****
Conciliation on-site	*****	*****	*****	*****
Legal aid on-site	*****	*****	*****	*****
Return assistance			*****	*****
Reintegration assistance			*****	*****
Marketing Support to Recruitment Agencies				
Client referral system				*****
Market research units			*****	*****
Labour attaché reports				*****
Interstate Cooperation				
Social security arrangements		*****	*****	*****
MoUs/agreements on deployment/protection of MWs	*****	*****	*****	*****

Notes:
A migrant welfare fund is currently being established in India.
Policies by governments have also been formulated in the area of remittances.
***** In operation.

Source: *Achacoso, 2002; updated in 2007 by IOM and author.*

4. International Cooperation

There are clear limits to what a country of origin can do to protect its migrant workers without the active cooperation of destination countries. Interstate cooperation and, more broadly, international cooperation, can play an essential part, not only in the protection and welfare of migrant workers, but also in the expansion of organized labour migration and the curbing of irregular movements. Cooperation may take many forms. For instance, it may be conducted at the bilateral level, or regionally, between a number of like-minded countries, or even at the global level.[12] Nor should such cooperation be restricted to government actors; the participation of other stakeholders, such as employers' or workers' organizations, is of crucial importance.

Formal mechanisms of interstate cooperation are essentially binding treaty commitments relating to cooperation on labour migration, which have been concluded either on a global level as in multilateral agreements and conventions protecting the rights of migrant workers under the auspices of the ILO and the UN, on a regional level as in the treaties establishing regional integration mechanisms, or on a bilateral level as in the case of bilateral labour agreements (see Chapter 13). The various forms of formal cooperation, such as mandated in bilateral agreements, regional integration and international conventions, often operate simultaneously.

Where it is not desirable or feasible to work on the basis of formal commitments, other forms of cooperation are available. These include non-binding consultative mechanisms, such as regional consultative processes (RCPs), joint commissions on labour, working groups and non-binding multilateral frameworks, such as the Berne Initiative which culminated in the elaboration of the International Agenda for Migration Management (IAMM) (Swiss Federal Office for Migration and IOM, 2005) (see also Chapters 11 and 13).

One of the most active RCPs in operation is provided by the Ministerial Consultations on Overseas Employment and Contractual Labour for Countries of Origin in Asia, commonly referred to as the "Colombo Process" (see Textbox 10.5).

[12] See Chapter 13 for a more detailed discussion of formal and less formal mechanisms of interstate cooperation on migration, including bilateral labour migration agreements, international agreements protecting the rights of migrant workers and their families and regional consultative processes (RCPs), as well as global means of cooperation. In the latter regard, see also Textbox Int. 2 on the Global Forum on Migration and Development (GFMD). Given its importance and cross-cutting nature, interstate and international cooperation is also discussed in other chapters in Part B of the Report (viz. on the exchange of migration data in Chapter 9; from the perspective of destination countries in Chapter 11; and between countries of origin and destination as well as with and among other pertinent stakeholders, with a view to harnessing the development potential of migration in Chapter 12).

Textbox 10.5

Ministerial Consultations on Overseas Employment and Contractual Labour for Countries of Origin in Asia: The Colombo Process

In response to a request from several Asian countries of origin, IOM organized Ministerial Consultations in 2003, 2004 and 2005. The ten original participating States (Bangladesh, China, India, Indonesia, Nepal, Pakistan, the Philippines, Sri Lanka, Thailand and Viet Nam) made recommendations for the effective management of overseas employment programmes and agreed to the implementation of a range of follow-up activities.

The aim of the Ministerial Consultations is to provide a forum for Asian countries of origin to:

- share experiences, lessons learned and best practices on overseas employment policies and practices;
- consult on issues faced by overseas workers, countries of origin and destination;
- propose practical solutions for the well-being of vulnerable overseas workers;

- optimize development benefits and
- enhance dialogue with countries of destination.

Achievements so far include:

- identification at ministerial and senior official level of policy challenges and needs, and exploration of the range of possible responses and exchange of experiences in programme development;
- development of training curricula for labour attachés and administrators and implementing joint training courses;
- establishment of Market Research Units (MRUs) and creation of more channels for regular labour migration; and
- implementation of specific recommendations at the national level.

The third Ministerial Consultations in Bali, Indonesia, were greatly enriched by the participation of countries of destination, with delegations from Bahrain, Italy, Kuwait, Malaysia, Qatar, Saudi Arabia, South Korea and the United Arab Emirates. Afghanistan was welcomed as a new member to the group after participating as an Observer in 2004. International and regional organizations participating in the Consultations included the Asian Development Bank, the Association of Southeast Asian Nations (ASEAN), the European Community, the Gulf Cooperation Council (GCC) countries, the U.K. Department for International Development (DFID), ILO, UNIFEM and the World Bank.

On 21 and 22 January 2008, Colombo Process countries met in Abu Dhabi with GCC countries and Malaysia, Singapore and Yemen. The Abu Dhabi Dialogue resulted in the adoption of the Abu Dhabi Declaration which provides a basis for cooperative action to be undertaken with the support of IOM. Four specific areas of partnership were identified:

- **Partnership 1**: Enhancing knowledge in the areas of: labour market trends, skills profiles, temporary contractual workers and remittance policies and flows, and their interplay with development in the region.
- **Partnership 2**: Building capacity for the effective matching of labour demand and supply.
- **Partnership 3**: Preventing illegal recruitment practices and promoting welfare and protection measures for contractual workers that are supportive of their well-being and preventing their exploitation at origin and destination.
- **Partnership 4**: Developing a framework for a comprehensive approach to managing the entire cycle of temporary contractual mobility to the mutual benefit of countries of origin and destination.

Sources: *IOM and http://www.colomboprocess.org/.*

At the global level, the constituents of the ILO have developed a non-binding Multilateral Framework on Labour Migration (see Textbox 10.6). The Framework aims to provide a rights-based approach to labour migration that takes into account labour market needs, proposing guidelines and principles based on best practices and international standards. The Framework also underlines the importance of international cooperation in dealing with labour migration. It is composed of 15 broad principles, each with corresponding guidelines and a follow-up mechanism.

Textbox 10.6

The ILO Multilateral Framework on Labour Migration

The *ILO Multilateral Framework on Labour Migration: Non-binding principles and guidelines for a rights-based approach to labour migration* forms the centrepiece of the ILO Plan of Action for Migrant Workers, adopted by the tripartite constituents (governments, and employers' and workers' organizations) at the 92nd Session of the International Labour Conference in June 2004. The Framework was the negotiated outcome of an ILO tripartite meeting of experts (31 October-2 November 2006), subsequently endorsed by the ILO Governing Body in March 2006.

The objective of the Framework is to provide practical guidance to its tripartite constituents and other stakeholders (civil society, international and regional agencies) on the development, improvement or strengthening, implementation and evaluation of national and international labour migration policies. The Framework supplements existing ILO and UN migrant worker instruments, and takes into account new global challenges and developments such as the growth of temporary labour migration programmes; the feminization of migration; the greater role of the private sector in arranging migration across borders; high incidence of irregular migration, including trafficking and smuggling of human beings; and the growing interest of the international community in migration and development linkages.

The ILO Multilateral Framework on Labour Migration is the most comprehensive international collection of principles, guidelines and best practices on labour migration policy. It is "rights-based" in the sense of bringing together the principles and rights that apply to labour migration and treatment of migrant workers already contained in various international instruments. The Framework consists of 15 principles and corresponding guidelines organized under nine broad themes, and a collection of 132 best practices worldwide. The five major themes that underlie the Framework are: decent work for all; international cooperation; governance and management of migration; promotion and protection of migrant rights; and migration and development. The Framework recognizes the important role to be played by social partners, social dialogue and tripartism in migration policy. It advocates gender-sensitive migration policies that address the special problems faced by women migrant workers. It is important to highlight that most of these principles and guidelines are already present in varying degrees in many parts of the world, as shown by the extensive compilation of examples of best practices.

At the same time, the Framework acknowledges the sovereign right of all nations to determine their own migration policies. Since it is a non-binding Framework, constituents can draw upon its extensive compilation of principles, guidelines and practices – in full or in part – in formulating, improving, implementing and evaluating their own legislative and regulatory frameworks on labour migration. Global trade union federations, such as the International Trade Union Confederation (ITUC) and international and regional NGOs (e.g. Migrant Forum in Asia), have incorporated the ILO Multilateral Framework on Labour Migration into their policy agendas.

The ILO will continue to promote and support implementation of the Framework principles and guidelines by Member States through its regular advisory services, advocacy work and technical cooperation programmes in active collaboration with its tripartite partners, the Global Migration Group (GMG), and other concerned international, regional and national organizations.

Source: *International Migration Programme, ILO, Geneva.*

International cooperation is vital to an orderly and managed labour migration system. In the absence of a widely accepted international migration system for labour migration – for instance, the expansion of the General Agreement on Trade in Services (GATS) to encompass broader categories of service providers thus increasing the mobility of temporary workers (see Textbox Int. 1) and considerably more ratifications of the International Convention on the Protection of the Rights of All Migrant Workers and Members of their Families, and of relevant ILO instruments (see Chapter 13) – there is a need to expand and develop concurrently bilateral, regional and international cooperation through formal and informal mechanisms on the basis of existing effective practices. Cooperation has to take into account the interests of countries of origin and of destination, of governments at all levels (central, regional and local), migrant workers and their representatives, social partners (employers and trade unions) and civil society.

5. Conclusion

An increasing number of developing countries and countries with economies in transition seek to adopt policies, legislation and administrative structures that promote foreign employment for their workforce and generate remittances, while providing safeguards to protect migrants. While job creation at home is their preferred option, these countries see overseas employment as part of a national development strategy to take advantage of global employment opportunities and as a source of foreign exchange. Countries of origin that are keen to facilitate labour migration must grapple with the challenge of formulating policies and priorities that both satisfy the needs of their domestic markets and produce talent able to compete for job opportunities abroad. This chapter has argued that this challenge is best addressed within a comprehensive HRD framework that emphasizes good information on job opportunities and requirements, and quality education and training.

At the core of such a framework is a properly resourced educational system that offers formal learning complemented, where necessary, by practical work experience and training, with both leading to assessment and certification by recognized authorities. Of necessity, however, HRD planning starts well upstream of educational processes, with the identification and forecast of labour market needs and employment opportunities in relation to both domestic and international spheres.

HRD planning then connects with policies required for the specific management of labour mobility. Foremost among these is a wide range of measures that are collectively intended to protect migrant workers from different forms of abuse and to enhance their personal welfare. Access to authoritative, accurate and up-to-date information is of great importance in this respect. A well-informed worker is better able to make choices – whether they concern the destination, type of employment or duration of contract – and better equipped to adapt to a new social and working environment in the country of destination. In addition, processes of selection, recruitment and employment, while, by their very nature, subject to market movements, can and indeed do benefit from careful regulation and monitoring to ensure that workers are shielded from exploitative practices. Support services, for instance through the operation of migrant welfare funds, or consular assistance, can further contribute to both the migrant's well-being and productivity as a worker.

Finally, two important interconnected policy undertakings concern the establishment of an effective administrative infrastructure to bring overall coherence and purposefulness to labour mobility policies, and the pursuit of partnerships among governments and with other stakeholders.

REFERENCES

Abella, M.

2000 "Policies and Institutions for the Orderly Movement of Labour Abroad", ILO Briefing Paper, Geneva.

Achacoso, T.D.

2002 "International Labour Migration Institutions of Bangladesh, India, Sri Lanka in Ferment: The Philippines as a Catalyst", paper prepared for the IOM Regional Office for South Asia, November, Dhaka, http://www.un-bd.org/pub/unpubs/IOM International%20Labour%20Migration%20Institutions%20of%20Bangladesh,%20I.pdf.

Asiaweek

2000 Asia's Best Universities 2000, *Asiaweek*, Special Report, http://cgi.cnn.com/ASIANOW/asiaweek/features/universities2000/index.html

Docquier, F. and A. Bhargava

2006 "The Medical Brain Drain. A New Panel Data Set on Physicians' Emigration Rates (1991-2004)", September, The World Bank, Washington, D.C., http://siteresources.worldbank.org/INTRES/Resources/DataSetDocquierBhargava_Medical_BD100306.xls.

India, Office of the Protector General of Emigrants

2004 *Emigration and You: An Information Booklet*, New Delhi.

International Labour Organization (ILO)

2006 *ILO Multilateral Framework on Labour Migration: Non-binding principles and guidelines for a rights-based approach to labour migration*, International Labour Office, Geneva, http://www.ilo.org/public/english/protection/migrant/download/multilat_fwk_en.pdf

International Organization for Migration (IOM)

2003 *Labour Migration in Asia – Trends, challenges and policy responses in countries of origin*, IOM, Geneva, http://www.iom.org.bd/images/publications/Labour_Migration_in_Asia-Trends,challenges_and_policy_respo.pdf.

2008 "Facilitation of the Recruitment of Foreign Workers", IOM Position Paper, March, Labour and Facilitated Migration Division, IOM, Geneva.

Israel, Ministry of Industry, Trade and Labour (MOITAL)

2008 *Foreign Workers' Rights Handbook*, updated as of January 2008, MOITAL, http://www.moital.gov.il/NR/exeres/702AE5C9-4AD2-4F96-9BBB-DCCE264A94EE.htm?wbc_purpose=ba

Lowell, B.L. and A. Findlay

2001 *Migration of Highly Skilled Persons from Developing Countries: Impact and Policy Responses - Synthesis Report*, International Migration Papers 44, International Labour Office, Geneva, http://www.ilo.org/public/english/protection/migrant/download/imp/imp44.pdf

McKinsey Global Institute

2005 *The Emerging Global Labor Market*, June, McKinsey Global Institute, http://www.mckinsey.com/mgi/publications/emerginggloballabormarket/.

Mughal, R. and L. Padilla

2005 "Regulatory Frameworks for Recruitment of Migrant Workers and Minimum Standards in Employment Contracts: A Comparative Study of Pakistan, the Philippines and Sri Lanka" in IOM, *Labour Migration in Asia: Protection of Migrant Workers, Support Services and Enhancing Development Benefits*, IOM, Geneva, 13-83, http://www.iom.int/jahia/Jahia/cache/offonce/pid/1674?entryId=7993.

Murali, K.

2003 "The IIT Story: Issues and Concerns", *Frontline* 20:3 (1-14 February), http://www.hinduonnet.com/thehindu/fline/fl2003/stories/20030214007506500.htm.

Organization for Security and Cooperation in Europe (OSCE), IOM and ILO

2006 *Handbook on Establishing Effective Labour Migration Policies in Countries of Origin and Destination*, Vienna, OSCE/IOM/ILO, http://www.osce.org/item/19187.html.

2007 *Handbook on Establishing Effective Labour Migration Policies*, Mediterranean edition, Vienna, OSCE/IOM/ILO, http://www.osce.org/item/28725.html.

Pritchett, L.
2006 *Let their People Come: Breaking the Gridlock on Global Labor Mobility*, Center for Global Development, Washington, D.C., http://www.cgdev.org/content/publications/detail/10174.

Ratha, D. and Z. Xu
2008 "Migration and Remittances: Top 10" in *Migration and Remittances Factbook 2008*, Migration and Remittances Team, Development Prospects Group, The World Bank, Washington, D.C., http://siteresources.worldbank.org/INTPROSPECTS/Resources/334934-1199807908806/Top10.pdf.

Swiss Federal Office for Migration and IOM
2005 *International Agenda for Migration Management*, 16-17 December, IOM/Swiss Federal Office for Migration, Geneva/Berne, http://www.iom.int/jahia/Jahia/cache/bypass/pid/1674?entryId=8005.

Tan, E.A.
2005 "Welfare Funds for Migrant Workers – A Comparative Study of Pakistan, the Philippines and Sri Lanka" in IOM, *Labour Migration in Asia: Protection of Migrant Workers, Support Services and Enhancing Development Benefits*, IOM, Geneva, 153-218, http://www.iom.int/jahia/Jahia/cache/offonce/pid/1674?entryId=7993.

2006 "Capacity of the Developing East Asian Region to Supply Skilled Manpower to Foreign Labour Markets", working paper submitted to ILO.

2007 "Supply Response to Foreign Demand for Skilled Manpower, the Philippine Case", draft paper prepared for IOM.

United Nations Development Fund for Women (UNIFEM)
2004 *The UNIFEM Asia-Pacific Arab States Regional Program on Empowering Women Migrant Workers in Asia*, Phase I: 2001-2004 (Report), UNIFEM, Bangkok.

Textbox 10.3 - Information Resource Centre for Migrant Workers in Tajikistan

Olimova, S. and I. Bosc
2003 *Labour Migration from Tajikistan*, IOM in cooperation with the Sharq Scientific Research Center, Dushanbe, http://www.iom.tj/publications/labour_migration_2003.pdf.

Textbox 10.6 - The ILO Multilateral Framework on Labour Migration

International Labour Organization (ILO)
2006 *ILO Multilateral Framework on Labour Migration: Non-binding principles and guidelines for a rights-based approach to labour migration*, International Labour Office, Geneva, http://www.ilo.org/public/english/protection/migrant/download/multilat_fwk_en.pdf.

FORMULATION AND MANAGEMENT OF FOREIGN EMPLOYMENT POLICIES IN COUNTRIES OF DESTINATION*

CHAPTER 11

1. Introduction

Foreign workers are employed in many countries at all skill levels, even though some of them may originally have arrived as students, tourists or family members (see Chapters 4, 5 and 6, respectively), and then remained in the country to work. There are significant numbers of foreign workers in the European Union (EU); established countries of immigration such as Australia, Canada, New Zealand and the United States; the Gulf Cooperation Council (GCC) states; new immigration countries such as the Russian Federation; as well as a number of middle-income countries in the developing world, viz. Malaysia, South Africa and Thailand. As described earlier in Chapters 7 and 8, cross-border labour mobility between neighbouring developing countries is common, while considerable irregular labour migration also occurs not only from developing to developed industrialized countries, but also among developing countries themselves.

The preparation of nationals in countries of origin for their temporary employment abroad, discussed in Chapter 10, cannot be wholly successful without the development of partnerships between these countries and countries of destination, either on a bilateral basis or in the context of regional economic integration or trade agreements (see Chapter 13), and the adoption of transparent, flexible and complementary regulations and policies in countries of destination. But, a "one-size-fits-all approach" to policymaking in this field is not feasible because countries of destination have to address their own sovereign concerns regarding the employment of foreign workers.[1]

This chapter presents the principal policy options to be considered by countries of destination in their admission policies for both permanent and temporary migrant workers. It begins by underlining the increasing importance of labour mobility in the context of migration management and the need for an explicit official statement to guide public policy in this field and the appropriate administrative

* This chapter was written by Ryszard Cholewinski, Labour Migration Specialist, Migration Policy, Research and Communications, IOM, Geneva. The author is particularly grateful to Elizabeth Warn (Labour Migration Specialist, Labour and Facilitated Migration Division, IOM, Geneva), who provided material and assisted in drafting Sections 4 and 7.

[1] A country-specific approach to policymaking is inevitable because, as Ruhs (2005: 203) observes, "the design and implementation of immigration policy remain principally the domain of **domestic** policymaking of sovereign and self-determining states" (original emphasis) and because of significant contextual differences between countries (e.g. levels of economic development, regulation of labour markets, degree of democratic institutions).

structure to put such policies into effect. Regarding the design of temporary labour migration programmes, in particular, the chapter builds on the policy discussions presented in Chapter 3 and appraises some of the challenges involved in the effective implementation of such schemes. The chapter goes on to assess the main elements of a comprehensive post-admission policy, taking account of the concerns of destination countries regarding the protection of their labour markets, the economic and social integration of newcomers and maintenance of social cohesion. It also considers the principal tools at the disposal of policymakers in destination countries to comprehensively address irregular labour migration and the related issue of an informal labour market. Finally, the chapter provides an overview of the types of cooperation and partnerships destination countries might enter into with countries of origin and transit as well as other pertinent stakeholders, to formulate and manage their foreign employment policies more effectively and equitably.

While state sovereignty is the prevailing order in international relations, it is not absolute. Global economic interdependence, exemplified in the globalization process (Chapter 1), has a strong bearing on national policymaking in this field. States have also entered into agreements that foresee a certain balance of interest among the parties regarding their respective regulation of international labour mobility or the treatment of migrant workers. Such concerns have become an important subject of international negotiations and are reflected in bilateral or regional trade and/or economic integration agreements (Chapter 13), and regional and international human rights and labour standards.

2. Labour Mobility at the Core of Migration Management

An important line of argument in this Report is that labour mobility lies at the heart of migration management today against a background of economic globalization and labour shortages at all skills levels in such key sectors as health care, construction and agriculture; significant demographic decline in industrialized countries, and a decrease in asylum applications in these countries (see Textbox 11.1). Consequently, more attention to, and resources for, migration management in these and more recent countries of destination (e.g. the Russian Federation) (see Textbox Reg. 2 in the Europe Migration Overview) might be devoted to the development of a greater choice of regular labour migration channels, facilitated by explicit policy statements in support of appropriate policies and regulations involving the whole government structure and administration. Appropriate instruments to monitor and evaluate the efficacy of foreign employment policies are also integral to taking labour migration more seriously (Ardittis and Laczko, 2008). However, to do so requires the existence of appropriate mechanisms to allow the collection of accurate and reliable data (see Chapter 9).

Textbox 11.1

The Evolution of Asylum Applications in IGC Participating States, 1983-2007*

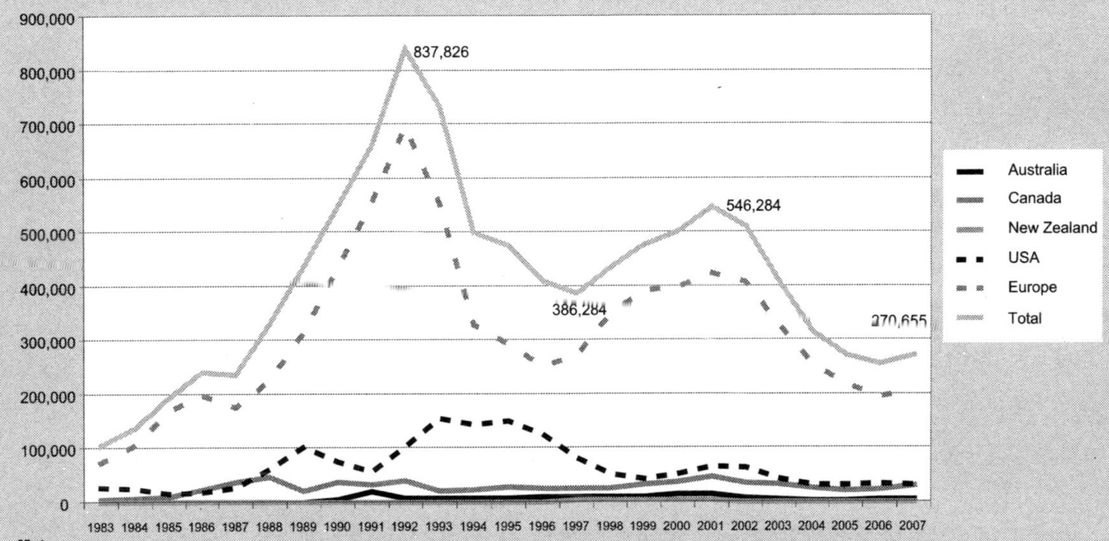

Note:

* The Intergovernmental Consultations on Migration, Asylum and Refugees (IGC) is an informal, non-decision making forum for inter-governmental information exchange and policy debate on the management of international migratory flows. The IGC brings together 16 Participating States, UNHCR, IOM and the European Commission. The IGC maintains databases on, among others, the number of asylum applications received in present and former IGC Participating States.

Present IGC Participating States are Australia, Belgium, Canada, Denmark, Finland, Germany, Greece, Ireland, the Netherlands, New Zealand, Norway, Spain, Sweden, Switzerland, the United Kingdom, and the United States. Former IGC Participating States from where IGC continues to collect data on asylum applications are Austria, France and Italy.

During the period 1983-2007, over 10 million asylum applications were filed in countries participating in the Intergovernmental Consultations (IGC; see above for a list of countries).

In 1985, some 100,000 asylum applications were received by IGC participating states. By 1989, annual applications had increased fourfold to 435,000. From 1983 to 1992, the major countries of origin were Sri Lanka, Iran, Turkey, Poland, the Czech Republic and former Zaire (today the Democratic Republic of the Congo).

In 1992, asylum applications reached a new peak of 840,000, with 85,000 applications received in July 1992, with most of the increase attributable to the rise in claims filed by persons from the former Federal Republic of Yugoslavia.

From 1993 onwards, numbers again dropped to a low of 390,000 applications in 1997; this was followed by a slight increase between 1998 and 2001, again owing to a rise in claims by persons from the former Federal Republic of Yugoslavia.

Since 2001, applications have continued to fall to stand at 240,000 in 2006, which corresponds to the number of annual applications in 1987.

In 2007, numbers increased for the first time since 2001 due to an increase in asylum applications by persons from Iraq.

Destination Countries

Throughout the period under review, Germany received the largest number of claims among all IGC participating states, with a peak of 440,000 in 1992, or 52 per cent of total claims filed in the IGC states for that year.

Distribution of Asylum Claims Among all IGC States, 1983-2007[1]

Germany	27%	**Belgium**	4%
United States	16%	**Norway**	2%
United Kingdom	10%	**Spain**	2%
France	9%	**Denmark**	1%
Canada	7%	**Australia**	1%
Sweden	6%	**Italy**[2]	1%
Netherlands	5%	**Ireland**	1%
Switzerland	5%	**Finland**	<1%
Austria	4%	**New Zealand**	<1%

Notes:

[1] Greece is not included in this chart because data is only available for 2006 and 2007

[2] Data for Italy are included only up to 2001.

France, the United States, the United Kingdom and Sweden receive most asylum applications, with Sweden, Austria, Switzerland and Norway receiving the largest number of claims in relation to their populations.

Source: *The Intergovernmental Consultations (IGC) Secretariat, Geneva.*

2.1 The Case for an Explicit Policy Statement to Guide and Inform the Elaboration of Transparent Regulations and Policies

Ideally, the immigration and labour migration policies and objectives[2] in destination countries should be clearly stated, and based on broad political and popular support, not only to enjoy wide legitimacy, but also to obviate the risk of subsequent policy inconsistencies espoused and pursued by different political formations, which often become apparent in the period leading up to general elections. For example, the importance of immigration to Canada's economic growth generally, and of labour migration in particular, to countervail the prevailing demographic profile and labour shortages together with the importance of integrating newcomers, is clearly articulated in the Citizenship and Immigration Canada (CIC) Minister's *Annual Report to Parliament on Immigration*:

> Immigration will play an increasingly important role in supporting Canada's economic prosperity and competitiveness. In a few short years, given our aging population, Canadians who leave school for the workplace will only offset the number of retirements. Immigration will therefore be a key source of labour force growth in the future. Moreover, the country is currently facing significant labour market shortages in some sectors and regions. Immigration can contribute to addressing both short- and long-term labour market needs by attracting people with the right mix of skills and talents to support economic growth today and in the future. With other industrialized countries confronting similar challenges with respect to sustaining population and economic growth, Canada will be operating in an increasingly competitive worldwide market for higher skilled workers.
>
> ...
>
> Bringing immigrants to Canada is only part of the challenge. Just as important is ensuring that they

[2] For a list of the different types of impacts that policymakers should give regard to in defining policy objectives, see Ruhs (2005). High-level policy objectives (which may however also be conflicting) include: realization of labour market objectives, protecting national security, minimizing public expenditure, promoting social cohesion, compliance with human rights obligations, and promoting international development and cooperation (Spencer, 2003).

> settle successfully upon arrival and integrate fully over the longer term. The challenges newcomers face are many: acquisition of English and/or French; recognition of their credentials, skills and work experience acquired abroad; and familiarity with the norms of the Canadian workplace and society, to name just a few. It will be important to look at ways in which the current range of settlement programs and services – including those provided by provincial and community partners – can be improved to better help immigrants in the early settlement period. (CIC, 2007a: 6).

The importance of migration for the economy of the United Kingdom and the contribution being made to the cultural and social fabric of the country are underlined in the proposal made by the government in 2006 concerning the introduction of a points-based system for migration management:

> All the main political parties, employers' organisations, trade unions and educational institutions agree that migration is vital for our economy. Migration makes a substantial contribution to economic growth, helps fill gaps in the labour market, including key public services such as health and education, and increases investment, innovation and entrepreneurship in the U.K. Culturally we are enriched by people with diverse backgrounds from other countries (U.K. Home Office, 2006: 1).

Clear policy statements serve to guide and inform the elaboration and the adoption of comprehensible and coherent regulations and policies on foreign employment;[3] and this for two reasons. First, they are an important part of the knowledge base on labour mobility, discussed in Chapter 9. Clear and coherent rules concerning migration and admission for employment, together with information about labour migration opportunities, would encourage regular labour migration and access to destination countries, with migrants either travelling individually and by their own means, or with the assistance of legitimate public or private employment agencies. Second, transparent rules also send a signal to host populations that the government has its labour migration policy "under control", provided that the rules themselves reflect a realistic policy response to the prevailing labour migration situation in the destination country concerned. For example, an otherwise clearly defined admissions policy that however fails to devote sufficient attention to an obvious demand for domestic[4] or agricultural workers (many of whom are often found in an irregular situation) will not be conducive to the development of a coherent and realistic response to the actual labour market situation in the country concerned.

2.2 Identifying an Appropriate Administrative Structure and the Need for a Coherent "Whole of Government" Approach

In many countries of destination, migration management falls within the responsibility of the ministry of the interior[5] or a government department set up specifically for this purpose.[6] Often, these ministries are also primarily responsible for the design and implementation of managed labour migration policies, which may result in the collision of two philosophies: an enforcement approach on the one hand, focusing on the control of borders and the prevention of irregular migration, particularly the eradication of its worst forms, i.e. human trafficking and smuggling, including trafficking for

[3] In the South African context, for example, it has been argued that "[p]erhaps, as the current Minister has pointed out on more than one occasion, the biggest problem with the [2004 Immigration] Act is that its provisions are not informed by any substantively agreed on set of policy outcomes, given that the process of developing policy (in the form of a White Paper) was not completed before the process to draft legislation was put in place. As a consequence, amendments to immigration legislation since 2002 have been ad hoc and by default rather than by design" (Williams, 2007).

[4] Also referred to as "household service providers".

[5] E.g. the newly established Border Agency of the U.K. Home Office.

[6] E.g. CIC Canada, the Department of Immigration and Citizenship in Australia, or the Singapore Immigration and Checkpoints Authority.

forced labour; and on the other hand, an approach which seeks to facilitate the planned admission of foreign workers (on a permanent or temporary basis) to fill gaps in the labour market, whether in highly skilled, semi-skilled or low-skilled positions. Given that the two approaches are hardly compatible, some commentators take the view that the economic and social considerations linked with the latter type of movement are better handled by officials in economic or labour ministries in collaboration with officials in other relevant departments, such as finance, education and health. Indeed, this is often the case in countries of origin, where labour emigration is the concern of specialized overseas employment departments in labour ministries (e.g. the Philippine Overseas Employment Administration (POEA) or the Pakistani Bureau of Emigration and Overseas Employment).

Irrespective of whether a destination country has opted for a centralized or decentralized administrative structure, migration, and labour migration in particular, call for a "whole of government" approach, in collaboration with agencies active outside of government, to ensure that all aspects of such migratory movements are sufficiently taken into account in the policy response (NESC/IOM, 2006). Needless to say, both centralized and decentralized systems have their strengths and weaknesses. For example, centralized systems as in Canada and Australia may find it a challenge to maintain the balance between enforcement and facilitation but they do provide responsive programme delivery across the board. On the other hand, while decentralized systems avoid potential internal lines of tension through the split of facilitation and enforcement functions, "whole of government" coherence can be harder to achieve when several ministries are involved in migration management. In those countries with decentralized systems, the formulation, implementation and management of successful foreign employment policies require responsive internal coordination mechanisms between and within government ministries (e.g. foreign and home affairs/interior, labour, economy, finance, development) to ensure policy cohesion and coherence. These mechanisms may take the form of statutory immigration advisory boards, such as the one established in South Africa under the Immigration Act 2004 comprising representatives of a wide range of government departments and other stakeholders, namely the private sector, trade unions and the academic community (Williams, 2007). In federal countries, policymakers will need to consider whether internal coordination should extend to the constituent regional or state units, which, although they may not have primary and direct immigration-related powers, often have responsibilities regarding the settlement, integration and welfare of migrants.

3. Key Policy Considerations

Although certain policy elements concerning the employment of foreigners will differ according to the labour and demographic profile of the country concerned, three important general considerations will remain valid.

One such consideration concerns employment-based immigration and whether this is to form part of a country's foreign labour admissions policy in accordance with national interests.[7] As discussed in Section 5(1)(a) below, the established countries of immigration show a clear preference for this type of migration to boost their population and labour force and sustain economic growth, although they also support temporary foreign worker programmes to fill urgent labour market shortages (see Chapter 3). On the other hand, European countries have only recently begun to seriously consider the permanent admission of foreign workers, although labour shortages in a number of key sectors, in particular in health care, information communication technology (ICT), science and technology, and engineering,

7 However, as discussed in Section 8 below, a balanced national labour migration policy will also take account of the legitimate interests of countries of origin.

together with demographic decline, have meant that, even if not granted upon entry, permanent residence is increasingly facilitated for these categories of foreign workers.[8]

Second, clear, transparent and flexible foreign labour policies matched by efficient and streamlined administrative procedures are essential to successful labour migration management. The most appropriate way to address labour shortages, while also taking demographic issues into consideration, is through a combination of permanent and temporary foreign worker admissions. To be able to respond to increased local demands for foreign labour, the processing of entry applications should not be unduly lengthy. For example, the processing of employment-based permanent residence applications to Canada can now take up to four years or more in certain countries (Mason and Preston, 2007). In order to reduce this backlog, in March 2008 Canada proposed changes to its immigration laws that would enable applications from needed skilled workers to be processed more quickly.[9] In the U.S., a backlog in labour certifications for the issue of immigrant visas (*Migration News*, July 2006; Abella 2006) means that it continues to be easier for employers to meet rapidly changing labour needs by hiring foreigners in the "temporary" skilled visa category (H-1B) and to subsequently sponsor them for immigrant visas, since H-1B visa holders are allowed to remain in the U.S. for a total of six years (i.e. three years in the first instance, renewable for a further three years). The Russian Federation introduced new legislation in January 2007 to partly ease the excessively bureaucratic features of the previous labour migration system (see Textbox Reg. 2 in the Europe Migration Overview). These examples confirm the importance of the need to devote sufficient administrative resources to remove cumbersome bureaucratic procedures in the management of employment-based immigration and to avoid the conflation with existing temporary labour migration programmes. If this is not heeded, the inevitable result will be continued inefficiency and delays in the functioning of the migration system and policy incoherence.

Third, while the main aim in many industrialized countries is to facilitate the settlement of highly skilled workers, shortages in low-skilled and semi-skilled labour market segments also need to be filled. While many of these shortages are addressed by the temporary admission of migrant workers and, in the absence of appropriate policies, by irregular migrants, policy consideration should also be given to filling such vacancies with workers admitted on a permanent basis, particularly where the demand is of a structural nature, such as in the domestic services employment sector. The extent of demand in low-skilled sectors is perhaps best illustrated by the 2002 regularization programme in Italy, which was originally designed for migrant domestic workers. While the programme was eventually extended to include other categories of workers, just under half of the over 700,000 applications received were submitted by migrant women domestic workers (OECD, 2004, 2005). In such instances, therefore, the main policy challenge for governments is to openly acknowledge the existence of such specific demands and, in the absence of a local labour force able and willing to undertake the work in question, to convince the local population of the need and general benefit of admitting foreign workers through regular channels to fill such jobs.

---

8 This does not mean that it had previously not been possible for migrant workers to settle in European host countries. For a historical overview of how migrant workers became permanent settlers in western Europe following the halt to immigration after the 1974 oil shock, see Castles (2006). In March 2001, in proposing the Directive on the status of third-country nationals who are long-term residents, the European Commission observed that EU Member States granted secure residence status to such workers after two to 15 years of legal residence, as the case may be (with eight of the then 15 EU Member States requiring five years of continuous regular residence in the country), subject to such considerations as whether the person concerned constitutes an actual threat to public order or public security, possession of sufficient means and employment (European Commission, 2001). For example, in the U.K., migrant workers can apply for indefinite leave to remain (i.e. settlement) after a period of five years of employment under the ordinary work permit scheme, subject to **sufficient knowledge of the English language and life in the U.K.** See U.K. Immigration Rules (U.K. Home Office 2008: para. 134(iv)).

9 CIC, 2008: http://www.cic.gc.ca/english/department/laws-policy/irpa.asp.

In addition to these general considerations, a number of specific policy elements can be identified that, in broad terms, are relevant to destination countries seeking to manage foreign employment: (i) assessment of the demand for foreign workers in the light of current and projected shortages on the national labour market, and demographic considerations; (ii) design of a foreign labour admission policy; (iii) the protection of migrant workers in the workplace and the host country generally, with particular attention to be paid to ensuring social cohesion (through integration and fighting discrimination and xenophobia); (iv) prevention or reduction of irregular labour migration; and (v) consultation and cooperation with countries of origin at the bilateral, regional and international level, as well as development of partnerships with other key stakeholders with an interest in labour mobility, i.e. the private sector, trade unions and civil society at large (NGOs, diaspora and migrant associations). These specific policy elements are discussed in the remainder of this chapter.

4. Assessing the Need for Foreign Labour

Regardless of the type of labour migration system in place in any particular country, one of its objectives is to address labour shortages. However, the mere existence of a labour shortage does not necessarily also express a need for foreign workers. For this to be the case, the causes of actual and potential labour and skills shortages and their potential scale have to be analyzed and the effectiveness of various possible policy responses to address them, including migration policy, evaluated (Boswell et al., 2004). Even where labour shortages are generally recognized to exist, political factors and the need to manage conflicting and competing migration policy concerns will determine whether, and to what degree, shortages call for the admission of foreign workers.

4.1 Detecting and Projecting Labour Shortages

There is no clear consensus as to what constitutes a labour shortage,[10] and much depends on how and where such a shortage is perceived. Shortages may occur not because there is an overall lack of workers to fill the jobs in question, but because of mismatches in the labour market:

> In most cases, such shortages are not caused by an aggregate shortage of labour, but can be attributable to problems of mismatch between labour demand and supply. Jobs remain unfilled despite high unemployment rates, because workers lack the relevant qualifications or skills, are reluctant to take up work in particular occupations or geographical areas, or have insufficient information about job opportunities. Alternatively (or in addition), employers are unwilling or unable to offer sufficiently attractive salaries or conditions to encourage occupational or geographical mobility (Boswell et al., 2004: 3).

In Ireland, the Expert Group on Future Skills Need in a report in 2005 also drew a distinction between skill shortages and labour shortages. The Expert Group found that foreign workers with specific skills would probably be needed in certain sectors in Ireland with skills shortages (e.g. foreign chefs received most of the work permits in the first half of 2005) for a period during which national workers are acquiring the necessary skills; while labour shortages (i.e. insufficient workers at prevailing wages and conditions) were identified generally in low-skilled employment (i.e. agriculture, food processing and jobs in services such as the security industry and catering) (NESC/IOM, 2006).

Further, labour shortages are difficult to predict as there may be limits to the accuracy of the available

[10] Boswell et al. (2004: 5) provide a working definition: "[I]n the most basic sense, labour shortages occur where the demand for workers in a particular occupation exceeds the supply of workers who are qualified, available and willing to do that job". They then proceed to make the further distinction between aggregate labour shortages and shortages resulting from mismatches in the labour market.

information sources (Chapter 9), while the types of labour shortage (e.g. long or short-term, absolute or relative) may vary considerably among destination countries. A key feature of labour shortages is that they may be prevalent in only some employment sectors and at certain skill levels; for example, in the EU labour shortages have been identified in the ICT, engineering, health and education sectors, as well as among low and semi-skilled workers generally (e.g. agriculture, construction, food production and hospitality). The causes of labour shortages are various and influenced by a number of trends in labour demand and supply (Boswell et al., 2004) that are also linked to national and global economic patterns and demographic factors (discussed in Section 4.2 below).

One trend affecting labour supply is emigration: "outflows of nationals (...) can have an important impact on skills composition where high-skilled workers leave because of more attractive business or research conditions in third countries" (Boswell et al., 2004: 14). For example, emigration from the U.K. has become quite significant in the last few decades, with the country experiencing a total net loss of approximately 2.7 million nationals between 1966 and 2005. More than 198,000 nationals left the country in 2005, while only 91,000 returned. Moreover, two-thirds of those who left the country did so to take up or seek employment opportunities abroad (Sriskandarajah and Drew, 2006). A similar net exodus, though to a lesser extent, was experienced in Germany (Landler, 2007).[11] However, not all countries quantify the emigration of their nationals and this question is rarely discussed in the context of designing foreign labour admission policies.

Conventional estimates of current labour shortages include, in particular, surveys and employers' reports on labour requirements in specific sectors.[12] However, such sources should be interpreted with some caution as they concern recruitment difficulties rather than labour shortages per se, and because employers may have unrealistic or overly ambitious expectations concerning growth in their sector. Governments can also conduct research into labour sectors and occupations. While such research may yield a more precise evaluation of the prevailing situation, it is less effective in predicting economic contraction or expansion and related changes in labour demand. More sophisticated econometric models are used to project future labour shortages, and these are considered essential for mid and long-term policy planning, especially for countries characterized by population ageing and decline, although theoretical and methodological shortcomings affecting their ability to produce accurate projections have also been identified.[13] Indeed, there is always the risk of error as when governments subsidize the training of teachers, nurses or engineers to meet projected labour shortages only to find that ultimately students graduate in a period of unemployment (NESC/IOM, 2006). Regardless of the difficulties, government interventions play a critical role in developing labour migration policies, particularly as concerns the different approaches needed depending on whether the problem to be addressed is one of labour shortage or rather tightness in a particular sector, and to provide the wider macroeconomic overview. As noted by one commentator:

> [I]t is necessary to recognize that, regardless of economic conditions and the number of vacancies advertised in a given economy, there is always the need for host countries to **manage the demand for migrant labour** [original emphasis]. This is

[11] In 2005, 144,800 Germans emigrated and only 128,100 returned – the first time in nearly four decades that more Germans left the country than returned (Landler, 2007, citing figures from the German Federal Statistics Office).

[12] E.g. the U.K. annual Employer Skills Survey (ESS) of approximately 4,000 employers, which inquires into the nature, extent, causes and implications of skills deficits, and the monthly Job Openings and Labor Turnover Survey (JOLTS) undertaken by the U.S. Bureau of Labor Statistics measuring labour market tightness and efficiency (matching) (Boswell et al., 2004; Abella, 2006).

[13] For an overview of such models in Australia, Canada, Germany, the Netherlands, the U.K. and the U.S., see Boswell et al. (2004).

because the level of labour immigration that is in the interest of individual employers is unlikely to coincide with that in the best interest of the economy as a whole (Ruhs, 2006: 14).[14]

4.2 Taking Demographic Issues into Consideration

As discussed above, it is more complex to predict labour shortages in the long term owing to demographic factors, as well as national, regional and global economic changes. For example, in the EU, which mainly comprises labour destination countries, the ageing of the population is the result of a number of interactive demographic trends: a decline in birth rates; the post-war "baby boom" resulting in a large population now approaching retirement age; and rising life expectancy. Though the EU receives 1.8 million immigrants annually and will continue to do so, with 40 million people estimated to emigrate to the EU between now and 2050 thus boosting the labour force and bringing down the average age of the population, the longer-term demographic impact remains uncertain. There is general consensus, however, that immigration can only partially offset the negative effects of the ageing of the population and the labour force (European Commission, 2006a; Bijak et al., 2007).[15] Based on current forecasts, the EU is likely to experience significant labour shortages over the next 50 years according to projections that the share of the working age population (aged between 15 and 64) will decrease significantly from 67.2 per cent in 2004 to 56.7 per cent in 2050, or by 52 million inhabitants of working age (European Commission, 2005a).

4.3 Tools for the Assessment and Designation of Levels of Need

Once labour market shortages have been identified, different policy tools are used to assess and designate the levels of need for foreign workers taking account of the possible impact of their admission on the local labour force. These policies include immigration quotas, labour market tests, occupational shortage lists and employer fees, with no country allowing an unlimited number of foreign workers to enter, irrespective of the potential economic gains such labour migration might be presumed to bring.

(a) Quotas

Quotas are common means of regulating the number of workers entering the labour market by establishing numerical programme targets or ceilings, and are seen as important tools by some destination countries. They can be used in various ways. National quotas and ceilings set fixed limits (either expressed as percentages of the labour force – e.g. Austria, Kazakhstan – or as absolute numbers – e.g. Italy, Spain) for the admission of foreign workers to a country. Quotas are usually established on a periodic basis, in most cases annually, often at a high governmental level (e.g. Republic of Korea - South Korea), based on such criteria as economic forecasts, employer reports or regional unemployment rates (e.g. Italy), and negotiated and administered in consultation with employers and trade unions, regional governments (e.g. Spain) and civil society. Quotas normally distinguish between different regions, industries and employment sectors

[14] According to Ruhs (2006), assessment of the size of the required migrant labour force needs to take account of three considerations: (1) the expense to employers of recruiting migrant workers, which depends not only on employers' recruiting and wage costs but also the employment conditions at which migrant workers are available; (2) that the demand for migrant workers in most countries is residual in that employers are first required to make all reasonable efforts to recruit local workers (i.e. nationals or lawfully resident migrants, or, in the EU context, EU nationals); and (3) that the employment of migrant workers is often only one of a variety of means to respond to a perceived shortage of labour, such as relocating to countries where labour costs are lower, increasing the working time of workers already in employment, or recruiting inactive (in particular, women) or unemployed local workers. Abella (2006) observes that these forms of adjustment to labour shortages have been particularly notable in Japan, which from the beginning adopted a policy of not importing low-skilled foreign workers.

[15] Moreover, as far as meeting labour shortages in ageing societies is concerned, temporary labour migration (see Section 5.2 below) is viewed as a preferable solution because it boosts the national labour force while, assuming the migrants return home, not adding to the ageing population as permanent immigration would in the medium and long term (Abella, 2006).

and can also set a maximum ratio of foreign to local workers in individual enterprises.[16]

The disadvantage of quotas is that they can be overly rigid and thus unable to readily respond to shifting labour demands. It should be possible, however, to devise more flexible quotas that can be revised during the year in response to changing employer demand. For example, in 2007, Spain set a quota of 180,043, covering non-EU professionals, seasonal and other migrant workers, but that could be reviewed upwards to 200,000. This was a significant increase from the 2006 quota of 16,878 when the government found itself overwhelmed by requests from employers (*Migration News Sheet*, January 2007). Despite their potential inflexibility, quotas also provide advantages, offering a clearly defined benchmark for administrators and employers and allaying concerns about immigration in the national population.

(b) Labour market tests

Most European destination countries, as well as Canada and the United States, apply a labour market test to first-time applicants for a work permit, or to migrant workers already in the country who wish to change jobs. Though admission procedures are usually simplified, the existence of a quota does not necessarily mean that the labour market test is withdrawn. The test serves to ascertain whether there are local workers available, by either requiring employers to advertise the post for a set period of time (e.g. U.K.), or demonstrate that they have taken active steps towards recruiting local workers, or both (e.g. the Netherlands). A third option, sometimes also combined with the latter, is to require that foreign workers are paid the average or prevailing wage in the industry or sector concerned (e.g. Canada, U.S.). Where no local workers are either available or willing to accept the conditions offered, foreign workers can then be employed. In some countries, it is left to the employer to provide evidence of labour scarcity (e.g. Mauritius, U.K.), whereas in other countries this is incumbent on the competent authority. For example, in Canada, before a foreign worker can be hired, the Department of Human Resources and Social Development Canada (HRSDC) must normally provide a positive labour market opinion (LMO) to certify the impossibility of finding suitable local candidates to fill the job in question and that the admission of foreign workers would not negatively affect the Canadian labour market (Canada, 2006).[17] In the U.S., the need for certification by the U.S. Department of Labour in respect of specialty occupations (H-1B workers – see Chapter 3) has been replaced by a simpler system of legally binding employer attestations, whereby the employer undertakes to respect the terms and conditions under which the foreign worker will be engaged, such as the payment of an appropriate wage and that there will be no adverse effect on the working conditions of similarly employed workers (Abella, 2006). In the EU, the preference principle applies, requiring Member States to ensure that there are no suitable EU workers available prior to hiring a non-EU national lawfully resident within the EU or to newly admit a non-EU national for employment; however, more information is still needed to see how this principle operates in practice in different Member States. While a number of policy options exist in the application of labour market tests, it is also important for evaluation and enforcement measures to be built into their design to ensure they actually work in practice and serve the needs of employers, local workers and the economy (Ruhs, 2006).

Several countries (including Norway, Spain and the U.K.) have introduced exceptions to the labour market test in respect of certain professions with

[16] See Abella (2006) referring to the approach taken in Latin America and the Caribbean.

[17] When applying for a LMO, the employer has to demonstrate that: (1) all necessary efforts were made to recruit and/or train willing and available local candidates; (2) the wages offered are consistent with the prevailing wages paid to local workers in the same occupation in the region; (3) the working conditions for the occupation meet the current provincial labour market standards; and (4) potential benefits may result from the hiring of the foreign worker for the Canadian labour market (e.g. creation of new jobs, transfer of skills and knowledge, etc.) (Canada, 2006).

shortages, such as health professionals, engineers, teachers and ICT specialists, and either do not apply the test or relax the rules. This more flexible and less bureaucratic approach has considerable economic advantages, since it enables a speedier and more efficient admission of migrant workers to fill shortages in important employment sectors.

(c) Occupational shortage lists

Occupational shortage lists can be an efficient way to channel foreign workers into sectors of the economy suffering from a lack of workers with specific skills. In the U.K., the National Shortage Occupations List, modified in July 2008, indicates shortages for certain categories such as engineers, doctors, social workers, veterinary surgeons and teachers for compulsory schooling posts in England and Scotland.[18] No labour market test is required to fill these posts under the ordinary U.K. work permit scheme.

In Australia, a Migration Occupations in Demand List (MODL) has been drawn up containing, as at 17 May 2008, 53 professional occupations/specializations and 49 trades persons' categories in which shortages have been identified nationally. The list is reviewed twice a year. Points are assigned to each category which can then be used by migrants applying for skilled migration visas (Australia, 2007; Abella, 2006) (see also Section 5.1(a) below).[19]

(d) Employer fees

Levying fees on employers for every foreign worker hired may be used to ensure that migrant workers are in fact brought in to fill genuine gaps in the labour market rather than just as convenient – and perhaps cheaper – substitutes for local workers. In Singapore, such fees are charged to employers wishing to employ medium-level skilled, semi-skilled or low-skilled workers in certain sectors, such as manufacturing, construction and services, and which are increased if the worker is less skilled.[20] The official website refers to the foreign worker levy as "a pricing control mechanism to regulate the demand of foreign workers in Singapore" (Singapore Ministry of Manpower, 2008). Such policies serve to minimize distortions in certain sectors of the economy, for instance agriculture, that often depend on a foreign workforce, and make funds available to restructure these sectors to make them less dependent on migrants (Martin et al., 2006).[21] However, the effective implementation of such policies depends on the extent to which governments of destination countries are prepared to recognize the merits of setting fees when weighed against the additional costs generated through increased government intervention and the introduction of adequate enforcement mechanisms to ensure that fees are not deducted from the wages of migrant workers (Ruhs, 2006; Ruhs, 2005).

5. Designing Foreign Labour Admission Policies: Permanent or Temporary Labour Migration?

Once there is a policy consensus on the need to admit foreign workers, policymakers need to decide whether to opt for employment-based immigration

---

18 However, there is currently no longer a need for nurses generally in the U.K., with the exception of certain categories of registered nurses. The National Shortage Occupation List is available at http://www.ukba.homeoffice.gov.uk/sitecontent/applicationforms/workpermits/businessandcommercial/occupationshortagelist.pdf.

19 The MODL is available at http://www.migration.gov.au/skilled/general-skilled-migration/skilled-occupations/occupations-in-demand.htm. The May 2008 list also included two occupations in an Associate Professionals category (Chef and Dental Technician) and two occupations under the general heading Managers and Administrators.

20 Moreover, the levy for these categories of foreign workers in Singapore is combined with a Dependency Ceiling, which means the employer will have to pay higher fees in sectors such as manufacturing or services if the percentage of foreigners to nationals in the workplace is higher (Singapore Ministry of Manpower, 2008). A foreign workers' levy is also applied in Malaysia and Taiwan Province of China (Abella, 2006).

21 Ruhs (2005) adds that such fees can also be used for a variety of other purposes: to generate funds for enforcement activities and integration assistance; to reduce the opposition of local workers to temporary labour migration programmes by compensating any losses suffered by such workers in terms of wages and/or working conditions; or to mitigate any adverse impact on local workers by funding their retraining and skills development.

or temporary labour migration, or a combination of both. As a general rule, employment-based immigration channels have usually been available to more skilled migrants, while temporary labour migration programmes are normally aimed at low-skilled workers (Chapter 3), largely because of a profound reluctance of local or resident workers to take up these jobs even in times of high unemployment.[22]

In principle, there is nothing to stop destination countries from opening up employment-based immigration to low-skilled workers, and a few examples of such opportunities exist, particularly in Canada and the United States (see Section 5.1(a) below). Skilled workers continue to be preferred for permanent settlement because they are considered more likely to be able to adapt their skills in the event of an economic downturn. However, low-skilled temporary migration programmes are seen increasingly as affording a number of advantages to all stakeholders in the labour migration process (see Chapter 3), and some of these are also discussed below.

The issue of circular migration, relevant to both employment-based immigration and temporary labour migration as well as to the question of return to the country of origin, is discussed in a separate section from the standpoint of policy formulation in destination countries.

5.1 Employment-based Immigration

(a) Established countries of immigration

Today's established countries of immigration (e.g. Australia, Canada, New Zealand and the United States) have long implemented immigration programmes to admit foreigners for the purpose of employment on a permanent basis from the moment of their entry with a view to promoting economic growth and ensuring a stable population and labour force. In the period 2005-2007, over 400,000 immigrants in total in this category were admitted annually for permanent residence in the four countries concerned (Table 11.1). Both Australia and Canada registered an increase in this type of migration. Indeed, the Australian Government enlarged the Skilled Stream visa category by 20,000 in 2005-2006 (DIAC, 2006).

The figures for skilled immigration to the four countries are somewhat misleading because the number of persons admitted for employment is actually much higher when taking into account dependants in both the economic and family classes (see also Chapter 6), as well as refugees admitted for permanent residence who are all permitted to take up work. In Canada, in 2006, a total of 251,649 persons were admitted for permanent residence, and Canada's Immigration Plan for 2008 is to admit between 240,000 and 265,000 permanent residents (CIC Canada, 2007a). The United States foresees a fixed annual employment-based immigration quota of 140,000, defined in the Immigration Act 1990, although this can be adjusted by means of a complex formula. Moreover, the majority of persons (59%) granted permanent residence in 2007 were already living in the United States, with women accounting for 55 per cent of all new permanent residents (U.S. Office of Immigration Statistics, DHS, 2008).

[22] "One of the most significant factors generating labour market mismatches is the unwillingness of resident workers to do certain low-skilled, low-status and low-paid work. ... Many professions have now become associated with immigrant or ethnic minority workers, often implying a social stigma for native, or non-minority workers. Occupational preferences may generate serious mismatches in situations of high unemployment, especially where social benefit systems provide limited incentives to take up low-paid or seasonal work" (Boswell et al., 2004: 15).

Table 11.1:

Employment-based Immigration to Australia, Canada, New Zealand and the United States as compared with Family and Humanitarian Admissions, 2004-2007

	Skilled stream/class	Family	Refugees/Protected persons
Australia			
2004-05	77,880[1]	41,740	13,178
2005-06	97,340	45,290	14,144
2006-07	97,920	50,079	13,017
Canada			
2004	133,745[2]	62,260	32,686
2005	156,310	63,354	35,768
2006	138,257	70.506	32,492
2007 (January to June)	59,248	31,860	12,774
New Zealand			
2004-05	34,649[3]	15,560	5,316
2005-06	34,801	16,684	4,982
2006-07	30,902	16,579	5,284
2007-08 (1 July to 8 March)	19,820	10,689	3,195
United States*			
2005	246,877[4]	649,085	142,962
2006	159,081[5]	802,577	216,454
2007	162,176	689,829	136,125

Notes:

1 Includes the following categories: Employer Sponsored, Skilled Independent, State/Territory Sponsored, Skilled Australian Sponsored, Distinguished Talent, Business Skills.

2 Includes the following categories: Skilled Workers, Business Immigrants, Provincial/Territorial Nominees, Live-in Caregivers (and their dependants).

3 Includes the following categories: Employee of Business, Entrepreneur, General Skill, Investor, Skilled Migrant, Work to Residence.

4 This is the employment-based preferences category which encompasses: priority workers; professionals with advanced degrees; skilled workers, professionals without advanced degrees, and needed low-skilled workers; special immigrants; investors (and their spouses and children).

5 The large number of persons admitted for permanent residence in this category in 2005 is explained by the American Competitiveness in the 21st Century Act 2000, which recaptured approximately 130,000 unused employment-based visas from 1999 and 2000 (U.S. Office of Immigration Statistics, DHS, 2008).

* Another significant category of permanent residents in the United States comprises diversity immigrants who are nationals of countries with low rates of regular immigration to the U.S. Since 1999, this category has been limited to 50,000. In 2005, 2006 and 2007, 46,234, 44,471 and 42,127 diversity immigrants, respectively, were admitted to the U.S.

Sources: *(Australia DIAC, 2006; DIAC 2007), (CIC Canada, 2006, 2007b), (Immigration New Zealand, 2008a), (U.S. Office of Immigration Statistics, DHS, 2008).*

The established countries of destination provide for employment-based immigration in two ways. The first involves the use of a supply-based points system (Australia, Canada, New Zealand), grounded on the assumption that "an increased supply of skilled workers will have a generally positive impact on innovation, productivity and growth" (Boswell et al., 2004: 41). Under points systems, applicants are selected in accordance with a number of objective criteria.[23] For example, in Canada, the successful applicant must demonstrate (i) possession of minimum work experience in the chosen profession

[23] According to Abella (2006: 31), "the [points] system takes much of the discretion out of the selection process by specifying ... objective criteria, assigning points for each criterion, and requiring candidates to reach a certain minimum score. ... The points system today only applies to the process of screening potential entrants under skilled migrant schemes, especially professionals whose academic degrees and years of experience lend themselves to some kind of ordinal or cardinal ordering. ... The system aims at expanding the general supply of skilled workers, not at meeting the specific job offers of employers".

or a related field; (ii) proof of adequate funds for settlement; and (iii) earn a sufficient number of points in six selection criteria to meet the "pass mark" of 67 points. These selection criteria comprise: education, knowledge of English and French (Canada's official languages), experience, age, arranged employment in Canada, and adaptability (including previous work or study in Canada) (CIC Canada, 2008).[24] The second way is through a demand-based system as applied in the U.S., whereby the individual employer has to demonstrate that no national or resident foreigner is available for the job in question, which, broadly speaking, is usually satisfied by a labour market or resident worker test, discussed in Section 4.3(b) above, although recently these rules were relaxed in respect of H1-B visa workers. In the U.S., an employment-based preferences system is also in place for the admission of various categories of skilled workers, and no labour market test is required for the first category, Priority Workers, which comprises persons of extraordinary ability in the sciences, arts, education, business and athletics; outstanding professors and researchers seeking to enter in senior positions; and executives and managers of transnational companies with one year of prior service with the firm (OSCE/IOM/ILO, 2006, 2007). In countries applying mainly supply-based points systems (e.g. Australia, Canada, New Zealand), a demand-based component can also be discerned as additional points are awarded for the possession of a job offer from an employer in the country in question.

(b) European countries

Employment-based immigration to Europe also occurs, but in a less explicit manner. Under the revised German Immigration Law, which came into force on 1 January 2005, it is possible for a select group of highly skilled workers (i.e. senior academics and researchers and top-level managers in business and industry) to obtain permanent residence upon admission (German Federal Ministry of the Interior, 2008). However, there are certain admission criteria to be met by the person concerned, such as a minimum annual income of EUR 85,000.[25] In 2005, only 900 persons benefited from this scheme (*Migration News Sheet*, September 2006), which contrasts sharply with the figures for employment-based immigration in the established countries of immigration. In European destination countries, most foreign workers are admitted on a time-limited basis, although some categories of workers can obtain a more secure residence status. In a number of countries, highly-skilled migrants are put on a "fast track" to permanent residence (e.g. Czech Republic, Norway, U.K.) (OSCE/IOM/ILO, 2006, 2007).

Points systems are also increasingly adopted in certain European countries as the most efficient means of regulating skilled migration. For example, the new points tier system introduced in the U.K., which is being phased in as of the beginning of 2008, is intended to regulate all forms of employment-based migration, permanent and temporary, high-skilled and low-skilled, as well as admissions for the purpose of study. The first two tiers, however, are reserved for highly skilled and skilled migrants, who are viewed as candidates for permanent settlement (U.K. Home Office, 2006; 2007b). In the Czech Republic, a Pilot Project for Permanent Labour Migration (2003-2008), administered by the Ministry of Labour and Social Affairs with the assistance of IOM, aims to facilitate the permanent residence of skilled persons from specific countries on the basis of a points system (Czech Ministry of Labour and Social Affairs, 2008; see also Portrait 2.1). In Germany, the provisions proposed in the previous immigration law envisaged the admission of skilled migrants based on a points system (Germany, 2001), although this proposed

[24] See specifically http://www.cic.gc.ca/english/immigrate/skilled/apply-who.asp.

[25] Representatives of German industry take the view that this salary threshold should be lowered to EUR 35,000 (*Migration News Sheet*, September 2006), particularly given a chronic shortage of IT specialists (i.e. 45,000 vacancies) and the fact that this threshold is nearly three times the salary of EUR 30,000-35,000 paid to entry-level computer programmers (*Migration News Sheet*, January 2008).

scheme was abandoned in the new compromise legislation that came into force on 1 January 2005.

5.2 Temporary Labour Migration

Given the prevalence of more "flexible labour market" practices in today's globalizing world, temporary migrant worker programmes have been increased in many industrialized destination countries to fill the (mainly low and semi-skilled) jobs available and that cannot be filled by drawing on the domestic labour force (Martin, 2003; Chapter 3). In the European context, the view that temporary migration of low-skilled migrants should be avoided because it inevitably leads to settlement and unpredictable social impacts has given way to a more positive attitude as not all low-skilled activities can be delocalized to developing countries, and owing to the concern over demographic imbalances and ageing populations and the decline in the working age population (Castles, 2006).

This section focuses in more detail on the policy challenges in making temporary labour migration programmes work, and builds on the more general policy issues outlined in Chapter 3, which also provides an overview of the global and regional trends relating to temporary labour migration with particular reference to low and semi-skilled workers.

(a) The potentially positive impact of temporary labour migration

The potentially positive impact of temporary labour migration for all actors involved in, or affected by, that process (i.e. countries of destination and origin, and migrant workers, especially low-skilled workers, and their families) has been widely recognized by the international community in recent years (GFMD, 2008; UN, 2006; World Bank, 2006; GCIM, 2005; IOM, 2005; ILO, 2005; UN DESA, 2004) (see also Textbox 3.5), and there is a convergence of interests by countries of destination and origin regarding temporary labour migration (Ruhs, 2005). For countries of origin, such programmes provide authorized access to the labour markets of richer destination countries, particularly for their low-skilled workers, and the positive development impact on their economies (i.e. transfer of remittances and know-how and creation of business and trade networks) is arguably optimized if their citizens' stay abroad is temporary and they retain strong links with their home country. For destination countries,

> [t]emporary migration ... is viewed as contributing to greater flexibility in the labour market. For many countries this is of considerable importance given their ageing workforces, the demands of industry for new skills, and the tendency of people to become less mobile as societies become more prosperous. Secondly, compared to permanent immigration, liberalizing temporary admissions is politically easier to sell to electorates that have come to feel threatened by more immigration. And, thirdly, some societies have experienced increasing difficulties with integrating long-settled immigrant communities, hence they opt for solutions that would not compound their problems (Abella, 2006: 1).[26]

For migrant workers, such programmes provide access to authorized, albeit temporary, work abroad and the opportunity to earn higher wages (Ruhs, 2005).[27]

---

[26] With regard to the first reason, it has been observed that such persons will be less inclined to migrate for lower skilled employment abroad because they are more likely to be attracted by better opportunities at home. See also Nonnenmacher (2007a): "temporary labour migration is seen as a means to meet sectoral, seasonal and peak demands for labour **in a flexible manner.** Its temporary character ensures that **public opinion** is less negative towards it than towards permanent migration. It alleviates concerns relating to the social integration of migrants and their reliance on public services and welfare payments" (Original emphasis).

[27] But also at the risk of restricting some of their rights, a "trade-off" which temporary migrant workers might be willing to accept to improve their economic situation (Ruhs, 2005). For arguments relating to the trade-off between migrant numbers and rights, see the discussion below and Chapter 3.

(b) Policy challenges

Despite the opportunities offered by temporary labour migration, there are a number of difficult policy challenges for destination countries relating to the design of specific programmes (Martin, 2003; Ruhs, 2005). The principal challenge is to ensure the feasibility, equity and efficiency of such programmes on a reasonably large scale, given past policy failures,[28] which can be summarized as follows: (1) segmentation and distortions of national labour markets causing certain sectors, such as agriculture, food production, hospitality and low-skill domestic services to depend on foreign labour; (2) the failure of temporary migrants to return to their countries of origin on completion of their employment, which is also identified as a particular disincentive for destination countries to develop new programmes; and (3) the exploitation temporary migrants, especially the low-skilled among them, are prone to during the recruitment process and in the workplace, and the risk of social exclusion and discrimination and xenophobia in destination countries.

The policy challenges created by labour market distortions in certain sectors and the dependence on foreign workers this may generate have been discussed in Chapter 3. Levying realistic (monthly) fees on employers for the hiring of foreign workers in the sectors concerned, as discussed in Section 4.3(d) above, to ensure that they seek out local workers or consider other alternatives such as mechanization of production processes or outsourcing (Ruhs, 2005), has been advanced as one possible solution to addressing the segmentation of the labour market. However, the problem here runs deeper and also relates to systemic issues such as low pay or lack of decent work (exacerbated by intense global competition) in these sectors.

Second, a number of policy interventions are applied (or have been advanced) with the objective of encouraging the return of migrant workers admitted under temporary labour migration programmes, such as:

- issuing temporary but longer-term work permits to enable workers in low-skilled occupations to repay the expenses incurred in connection with their migration and to save enough money with which to return home;
- requesting migrants to announce their return at the embassy or consulate of their former destination country, which also serves to facilitate their subsequent return to that country for a further period of employment;
- enabling migrants with valid work permits to travel relatively freely between their countries of origin and destination for family and business visits;
- enabling the transfer of social security payments (for pension and health benefits) to the country of origin (see also Section 6.5 below);
- designing a sponsor system for employers whose record on return counts towards their future prospects to sponsor and hire foreign workers;
- the formulation and implementation of relevant procedures to ensure the return of migrant workers who overstay, and enforcement measures such as workplace inspections and employer sanctions;
- requiring workers to invest a portion of their wages in special high-interest bearing savings accounts, the funds from which may be accessed on their return to their home country; and
- subjecting employers to financial security bonds which may be retained by the authorities if the worker does not leave after his or her permit has expired (Agunias and Newland, 2007; Ruhs, 2006; Ruhs, 2005; U.K. Home Office, 2005).

Some of these measures, especially the last two, raise labour and human rights concerns on account of

[28] Two past temporary programmes frequently described in terms of failures are the Bracero programme involving Mexican migrant workers to the United States (1942-1964) and the *Gastarbeiter* ("guest worker") programme in Germany (1955-1973). See also Chapter 3 and Ruhs (2006).

their coercive nature.[29] No temporary foreign worker programmes or bilateral labour migration agreements include all or even most of these mechanisms. It has been suggested that the establishment of small pilot projects to test the impact of the various components of a temporary (and circular – see Section 5.3 below) labour migration programme, including the return components, is the best way forward and one most likely to achieve optimal policy results (Agunias and Newland, 2007). Further, attempting to ensure the strict observance of temporariness throughout all temporary labour migration programmes appears an unrealistic policy objective and one likely to fail in practice, given that some of the jobs filled by temporary migrant workers are actually permanent in nature. Therefore, and as discussed below, a better policy option may be to identify criteria that would allow a limited number of foreign workers to transfer to a more secure status in the destination country (Ruhs, 2005; Abella, 2006).[30]

Third, as observed in Chapter 3, the admission of larger numbers of temporary low-skilled foreign workers to high-income destination countries often involves a trade-off in the form of limited rights, to reduce the costs of low-skilled labour to employers and the economy as a whole.[31] While such a trade-off may also result in economic gains for foreign workers and their families, a general survey of international human rights and labour standards applicable to migrant workers reveals that few distinctions between the treatment of temporary foreign workers and nationals or more established foreigners employed in the country can be justified (Böhning, 2003) although, in practice, the situation may be very different. Beyond some restrictions regarding access to the labour market to safeguard the position of local workers and limits on family reunion, particularly in relation to short-term seasonal employment, the universal nature of human rights and labour standards precludes the imposition of unjustified limitations in respect of wages and working conditions. These issues are discussed further in Section 6.2 below.

5.3 Circular Migration

Temporary labour migration is often discussed by policymakers together with circular migration and return migration in view of the benefits to be gained by origin and destination countries and migrants themselves, in terms of transfer of skills and know-how and the business activities and investment that may result from the regular movement of migrants between the countries in question.

Circular migration has been broadly defined by the EU Commission as "a form of migration that is managed in a way allowing some degree of legal mobility back and forth between two countries" (European Commission, 2007: 8). The team that prepared Roundtable 1.4 on Circular Migration for the first meeting of the Global Forum on Migration and Development (GFMD), held in July 2007 (see Textbox Int. 2), proposed the following definition: "Circular migration is the fluid movement of people between countries, including temporary or more permanent movement which, when it occurs voluntarily and is linked to the labor needs of countries of origin and destination, can be beneficial to all involved" (GFMD, 2007: 4). While there is as yet no widely accepted definition of the concept, as underlined in the definition proposed at the GFMD, circular migration clearly goes beyond temporary labour

[29] E.g. Abella (2006) argues that withholding a part of wages to use them as savings which migrants can only release on return contravenes ILO's Protection of Wages Convention No. 95 (1949), ratified by 95 countries and in force since 1952. Moreover, such compulsory deductions may encourage the migrant worker to avoid them by taking up unauthorized employment in the informal labour market.

[30] In some countries it is possible for migrants working on a temporary work permit to obtain permanent status (e.g. Canada, U.K.) provided that the conditions for admission for employment-based immigration are met. In Spain, migrant workers holding seasonal work permits (a type "T" permit) with an initial validity of nine months, may secure a more stable status after four years of temporary employment, whether consecutively or not (Cholewinski, 2005). Elsewhere, however, such as in the Gulf Cooperation Council (GCC) states (e.g. Kuwait), switching between temporary and permanent status is not possible. This is so also in Singapore, where migrant workers on temporary permits cannot acquire permanent residence status (Ruhs, 2006).

[31] See also Ruhs and Martin (2006).

migration[32] and is also used in connection with the temporary or permanent return of members of the diaspora, many of whom are already settled in the host country (Agunias and Newland, 2007).[33]

Consequently, in order to harness the benefits from circular migration in line with a "development-friendly" approach (see Section 8 below), policymakers in destination countries may consider a number of options to facilitate circular movements, either in respect of temporary migrant workers, while they are working in the host country or to enable them to return to that country for successive periods of employment, or permanent foreign residents. As far as the latter are concerned, policymakers should be aware of disincentives that might preclude or hinder permanent foreign residents from conducting employment, business or investment activities beneficial to the development of their countries of origin and which also have positive trade and business impacts on the host countries. Thus, the adoption of flexible laws and policies in host countries is important for generating and supporting circular movements or to promote sustainable returns. Such dispositions would, for instance, enable migrants to travel outside the country without prejudice to qualifying periods in view of a more secure residence status or naturalization;[34] assure foreigners with long-term or permanent residence status of the possibility to return in the event of a temporary or medium-length return to their country of origin;[35] and facilitate the portability of pensions and other benefits (Agunias and Newland, 2007).[36] The EU Council Directive on the status of third-country nationals who are long-term residents, adopted in November 2003, is an important measure in this regard.[37] Article 9 of the Directive provides that third-country nationals who hold long-term resident status (for which they are eligible after five years of residence in a participating EU Member State) can leave their country of residence for a period of up to 12 consecutive months without losing their status.[38] The European Commission has suggested that this 12-month period might be extended for a 2-3-year period to promote circular migration of long-term residents.

With regard to temporary migrant workers, the Commission proposes that circularity be promoted within the development of the evolving EU law and policy framework for regular migration to the EU by enabling highly skilled migrants and remunerated trainees to return to work in the EU following a period of lawful employment, training or study

32 However, return for short stays is excluded from the concept. In this regard, the UN Secretary-General's 2006 *Report on International Migration and Development* observes: "Migrants who return for a period and leave again are said to be engaged in 'circulation'. Circulation, however, does not occur when migrants return only for short visits but essentially remain settled abroad" (UN, 2006: 68, para. 247). See also the section on Migration Terminology at the end of the Report, which contains an adapted version of the definition discussed at the GFMD.

33 In the EU context, the two main forms of circular migration that are most relevant concern third-country nationals settled in the EU, and persons residing in a third country who wish to come to the EU temporarily for employment, study, training or for a combination of these activities (European Commission, 2007).

34 E.g., in the U.S., migrants applying for permanent residence cannot travel abroad without prior special permission, which is a lengthy and cumbersome process, and an application for naturalization can only be submitted at the end of a continuous five-year period of residence (Agunias and Newland, 2007).

35 "It is thought that migrants who have rights to long-term residence in countries of destination may be more willing to try life back home if they can be assured of being able to emigrate again. Security of residence in countries of destination may thus promote either return or circulation. Similarly, allowing dual citizenship may be conducive to return" (UN, 2006: 70, para. 254).

36 Cooperation between host and home countries concerning information on jobs and business opportunities in the latter is also important to facilitate circulation among migrants who are permanent residents (Agunias and Newland, 2007). Other means of facilitating circular migration include policies relating to the recognition of qualifications acquired in the destination country and relaxed investment and tax regimes.

37 Council Directive 2003/109/EC of 25 November 2003 concerning the status of third-country nationals who are long-term residents, OJ 2003 L 16/44. The Directive should have been transposed into the laws of EU Member States by 23 January 2006. Three EU Member States are not participating in this measure, i.e. Denmark, Ireland and the U.K. because they negotiated opt-out provisions at the time the treaty amendments providing the EU with competence to legislate in the asylum and immigration field were adopted, although it is possible for Ireland and the U.K. to opt into the Directive at a later date.

38 Member States may also provide that absences exceeding this period or for specific or exceptional reasons shall not entail withdrawal or loss of the status.

there, and through the introduction of residence/work permits valid for several years for low-skilled seasonal migrants to permit them to return to the EU for a period of consecutive years for seasonal work (European Commission, 2007).

While the emphasis on the contribution circular migration could make to development normally concerns highly skilled migrants, who have most to offer in terms of the transfer of skills and know-how, this does not mean that the regular temporary migration for employment of low or semi-skilled migrants cannot, if managed properly, bring benefits to all parties concerned. This is well illustrated in the recent proposals by the European Commission discussed above, and the example of the temporary and circular migration of agricultural workers from Colombia to Spain (see Portrait 11.1).

Portrait 11.1

Circular Migration for Co-development

Amalia is a peasant woman from the municipality of Puerres (Nariño, southern Colombia) near the border with Ecuador and has been working in the fields since she was a small girl. She heads her own household and, until three years ago, Amalia and her four children lived on less than three U.S. dollars a day. In an effort to improve her life and future prospects for her children, she migrated to Spain under the Temporary and Circular Labour Migration Model (MLTC), together with other peasants from this region, to work in the vineyards and the fruit orchards around Barcelona during the harvesting season. A decision that changed her life.

The agricultural working experience of Colombian peasants, together with their facility to adapt to different people and cultures as they work alongside Moroccan and Romanian migrant workers, has meant that temporary migrant workers like Amalia are increasingly in demand by Spanish employers.

The MLTC, initially implemented by a group of Spanish farmers (Unió de Pagesos, UP) and currently supported by IOM Colombia and funded under the European Union's AENEAS programme, benefits approximately 1,200 Colombian temporary migrant workers.

Under this temporary labour migration scheme, Amalia has travelled to Lleida in Spain already three times for periods of less than six months to work for different agricultural companies during the harvest season. Her wages are far higher than what she could earn for the same kind of work in Colombia; in fact, her hourly earnings are equal to two days of work in her own country.

During her stays in Spain, Amalia has also been able to benefit from training to identify and formulate development projects to benefit her home community in Colombia. The community is being followed by UP and IOM throughout the entire process to help them carry out their projects.

For that reason, Amalia and other temporary migrants from Puerres have become development agents for the community after they returned home. With advice from Amalia and support from the Unió de Pagesos through its Fundación Agricultores Solidarios (FAS), the temporary migrants implement their development projects, in which they also invest part of their savings accumulated while working in Europe. This has enabled the peasants' association to which Amalia belongs to identify and implement projects such as growing quinua (a traditional local cereal) and breeding guinea pigs and trout, and so to contribute to the community's development.

The achievements of these temporary labour migration projects, as illustrated by this example from Puerres, go well beyond the possibility of earning more money for their work so as to be able to meet recurring expenditures such as for health care, education and housing. In fact, the possibility for migrants, such as Amalia, to migrate and work abroad temporarily is the more important and long-lasting contribution to the local economy and community, as it clearly demonstrates the benefits of leaving the country through regular migration channels and of actively participating in a temporary labour migration model for co-development that not only benefits the migrant workers themselves, but also the country of origin and the country of destination.

Thanks to the Temporary and Circular Labour Migration Model, every time Amalia returns from Spain, besides savings and gifts for her four children, she also brings back with her opportunities for socio-economic development and a better quality of life for herself, her family and the entire community.

Source: *IOM Bogotá.*

6. Post-admission Policies: Labour Market Regulation, Protection of Migrant Workers, Social Cohesion and Integration

Post-admission policies comprise a number of interrelated policy elements, namely: labour market regulation, including access to and mobility within the labour market, and recognition of qualifications; the protection of migrant workers in the employment context; facilitation of social cohesion; enhancement of social welfare, in particular through access to adequate healthcare, education and housing; and social security provision (OSCE/IOM/ILO, 2006, 2007). In many destination countries, the content of these policy elements are determined by the extent to which the governments concerned have accepted international standards, such as international human rights and labour norms. Even if conditions in these countries are such that it is not possible to formally comply with these standards, they may still serve as a model for the development of national legal frameworks. As observed in the Introduction, the protection of migrant workers (particularly those with temporary or irregular status) in a globalizing labour market is one of the most difficult and sensitive challenges facing policymakers. The content of post-admission policies is shaped further by participation in regional and bilateral agreements (see Chapter 13). In the EU, for example, full access to the labour market for most EU citizens is a reality,[39] which means that the focus of policy concerns regarding these nationals has shifted essentially towards recognition of their qualifications and the provision of adequate social protection, rather than regulating their access to the labour market per se. Irrespective of the policy directions agreed to at the multilateral, regional and bilateral level, however, these still have to be effectively implemented at the national level. Clearly, some policy elements, such as the adequate protection of workers in countries of destination, will also be determined to a certain extent by the existence of appropriate unilateral policies in countries of origin, which are discussed in Chapter 10, or through the adoption of bilateral arrangements between countries of origin and destination (see Section 8 below and Chapter 13).

6.1 Labour Market Regulation

Regulating the labour market in the context of migration for employment is largely concerned with the restrictions governments may legitimately impose on migrant workers regarding their access to the labour market, particularly during the first work authorization, and the mobility of migrant workers within this market with a view to protecting the local workforce.

While in many countries access to the labour market for migrants is regulated by a variety of administrative restrictions affecting both workers and employers, reductions in and streamlining of such bureaucracy as well as providing greater autonomy to workers over their employment status are emerging as effective practices, to ensure that available jobs in destination countries are filled quickly and efficiently without

[39] With the exception of nationals from the ten central and eastern European new EU Member States in five former EU-15 Member States, which continue to apply transitional arrangements (see Chapter 13 and Textbox 13.3).

resorting to irregular migrant workers, and also to provide more safeguards for the worker. For example, to enhance the protection of migrant workers in the labour market, the important recent reform introduced by the Irish Employment Permits Act 2006, which came into force on 1 February 2007, provides for the work permit to be granted to the worker rather than the employer. The permit also lists entitlements and the principal employment rights of the employee (Ireland, DETE, 2007(a), 2007(b)). For similar reasons,[40] it is advisable that migrant workers enjoy a degree of mobility, at least within the same employment sector and also in the context of temporary labour migration schemes, in order to reduce the risk of exploitation that may arise from being tied to one employer.[41] Such exploitation can be exacerbated by the illegal practice of retaining the passports of migrant workers and in those situations where employers provide accommodation to migrants only as long as they continue to work for the employer (i.e. "tied accommodation") (Ruhs, 2005). As noted earlier in connection with employment-based immigration, it is possible for certain groups of migrant workers who initially entered on a temporary basis to be granted free access to the labour market and eventually permanent residence. While this practice is prevalent in respect of the admission of skilled migrants in Canada and the U.S. and EU destination countries, where settlement is usually encouraged today, this is not the policy in the GCC and Asian countries of destination, where employment of foreign workers is perceived as strictly temporary.[42] Nonetheless, as discussed in Section 5.2(b) above, provided that the rules are transparent, a defensible argument may be made for allowing for some transition from temporary labour migration to employment-based permanent residence, particularly where migrants have resided and worked in a country for a number of years and are successfully integrated. There are also advantages to the employer in ensuring a readily available supply of workers into sectors where there is a structural demand for such labour and in not having to train new workers.

Eliminating discrimination against women migrant workers in respect of access to the labour market and the adoption of appropriate policies in this area are also important considerations. First, the demand for domestic workers, nurses and entertainers may appear neutral at first sight, but in practice recruitment to fill the available jobs is effectively aimed at women. Second, the majority of women migrant workers end up in low-skilled jobs and, in some countries, are also subject to intrusive questioning regarding possible pregnancy and even pregnancy tests before being permitted to take up employment, practices that amount to unlawful sex discrimination in international human rights law (OSCE/IOM/ILO, 2006, 2007).

Putting in place appropriate mechanisms to recognize the diplomas and qualifications of migrant workers acquired in their countries of origin or third countries would give them more opportunities to make an optimal contribution to the destination country, and to the country of origin in terms of remittances and the eventual transfer back home of additional skills and know-how. The phenomenon of "brain waste" is particularly pronounced in the case

[40] The Institute for Employment Rights in the U.K. reasons as follows: "The rules on the possibility of migrant workers to change employer are of fundamental importance within the labour market. The operation of the labour market in allocating labour to where it is most useful, and the individual's right to work, each point in the direction of allowing migrant workers to change employer where they consider it advantageous to them to do so. There are also basic issues as regards fairness. The narrower a worker's options as regards a change of employer, the greater the scope for an employer to impose unfair pressure as regards performance, conditions at work, or terms of employment. This is a matter of legitimate concern not just to the individual in question, but to interested third parties such as co-workers and trade unions" (Ryan, 2005: 40).

[41] Under the new Irish work permit rules, however, the worker issued with a first permit must stay with the same employer for a period of 12 months unless there are exceptional circumstances. With regard to the U.K., it has been proposed that migrants should be able to obtain an unlimited right to change employer and occupation after a short period, i.e. three months (Ryan, 2005).

[42] Concerning the GCC States, this is also connected to the fact that the foreign population greatly outnumbers citizens, thus giving rise to security concerns (Ruhs, 2005).

of unauthorized employment in which many migrants end up because of the absence of regular migration opportunities, and adversely affects women in the care and domestic work sectors, where demand, as noted above, frequently remains unrecognized (OSCE/IOM/ILO, 2006, 2007).

6.2 Protection in Employment

While equal treatment of local and migrant workers is an accepted principle of international human rights and labour law, such protection has to be assured in practice, which can be realized only in a framework of partnerships between governments and social partners. In this regard, a number of difficulties are identified and policy solutions proposed.

One difficulty concerns the need to ensure that national labour laws are applicable to employment sectors such as agriculture and domestic work or household employment, which, in some countries, have been excluded, either wholly or in part, from the legal protection foreseen under these laws,[43] a particularly important consideration when addressing discrimination against women migrant workers in the domestic service sector. Second, more careful attention deserves to be paid to the protection of a number of specific labour rights that are more likely to be neglected in the context of temporary labour migration, such as security of employment and access to vocational/ language training. Protection of the former requires that migrant workers are not dismissed first during downturns in the economy without good reason, while provision for the latter, particularly language training, ensures that migrant workers and their family members are able to adjust more quickly to their new environment and can upgrade their skills with the resulting benefits this may have in terms of their employment in the destination country and eventual return to their country of origin. Third, ensuring that migrant workers may join or form a trade union in the sector concerned would make it possible for them to exercise their rights in the workplace (OSCE/IOM/ ILO, 2006, 2007). Though the principles of freedom of association and collective bargaining are well established, in some countries obstacles continue to hamper the full exercise of trade union rights by irregular migrant workers (ILO Committee on Freedom of Association, 2001 and 2002). In addition to the important role of organizing migrant workers and protecting their labour rights, trade union activities may also include: conducting campaigns for ethical recruitment to counter the effects of the "brain drain"; making arrangements with local banks to reduce the cost of remittance transfers; entering into bilateral agreements with other trade unions in origin or destination countries; participation in government pre-departure orientation schemes in the country of origin (e.g. the Philippines); provision of assistance to migrant workers to enable them to keep in contact with their country of origin; and, particularly in Africa, collaboration with employers to fight the spread of HIV/AIDS (OSCE/IOM/ILO, 2006, 2007). Finally, the protection of labour rights of irregular migrant workers is especially problematic in practice and is discussed in more detail in Section 7.1 below.

6.3 Facilitating Social Cohesion

In a world characterized by high labour mobility, the nature of the relationship between the migrant and the host society is changing rapidly, where such concepts as assimilation, integration and multiculturalism are no longer entirely satisfactory either as explanatory or prescriptive terms. New approaches are needed to define a host society's core values and principles, while at the same time providing scope for diversity. There is no single formula for success: permanent resident migrants may require policies quite different from those that are required by temporary migrants. In general terms, however, the starting point is the recognition

[43] For example, in the Province of Ontario, Canada, agricultural workers are not covered by the legal minimum standards foreseen in the Employment Standards Act relating to maximum hours of work, daily and weekly rest periods, statutory holidays and overtime pay (Brem, 2006).

of the migrant as a legitimate participant in social and economic processes, and acknowledgement and definition of **mutual** rights and responsibilities.

The need to ensure social cohesion in host countries is a crucial determinant of policymaking. Large-scale migration for employment to address labour shortages and demographic deficits is not considered feasible in many parts of the world because of the perceived difficulties in integrating a significant number of foreigners into the host society and providing them with adequate social services. Canada, however, which in 2006 admitted over 250,000 migrants on a permanent basis and more than 110,000 temporary migrant workers, demonstrates that larger-scale admissions are possible with careful planning and where appropriate reception policies are in place (CIC Canada, 2007a). Moreover, in practice, the social fabric of the host country is more likely to be at risk when migrants are subject to various forms of discrimination, both in the workplace and in the general community, and where there are no proper integration mechanisms in place.

Discrimination against migrants is a serious barrier to the realization of social cohesion and integration:

> Discrimination produces differential treatment in labour markets, preventing equal opportunity, provoking conflict within the working population and undermining social cohesion. Discrimination reinforces attitudes that constrain certain identifiable groups to marginalized roles and poor conditions in the work force. The results of consistent denial of employment opportunities, relegation to ghettos, lack of education or training opportunities, absence of police protection, and multiple discriminations in community life are exclusion and ultimately, breakdown of social cohesion. Migrant workers face various forms of discrimination in employment and occupation, and discrimination suffered by migrants often begins at the recruitment stage. Difficulties in finding suitable employment often result in highly qualified men and women doing relatively menial jobs.
>
> Discrimination prevents integration. The consequences of past policies that neither anticipated nor prevented discrimination can be seen in ethnic ghettos, high unemployment, low school attainment, higher violence and crime rates in numerous countries. It is evident that the longer migrants and their offspring live and work in a host society under discriminatory provisions, the more likely it is that this prejudice and discrimination will prevent them from reaching similar economic and educational attainments as the majority population (Taran et al., 2006; OSCE/IOM/ILO, 2006, 2007: 144).

Though the principle of non-discrimination is at the core of international human rights and labour law, and its applicability to migrants has been reinforced by regional human rights tribunals (Cholewinski, 1997, 2007), effective implementation of this principle in policy and practice is lacking in many countries. For example, research conducted under ILO auspices in western Europe and North America revealed significant and persistent discrimination against migrants concerning the hiring process (ILO, 2006). Discrimination also has multiple impacts on women migrants, many of whom work in gender-segregated and unregulated sectors of the economy (e.g. domestic services and the commercial sex industry) (OSCE/IOM/ILO, 2006, 2007). Prevention of discrimination against migrants, therefore, calls for the development of a comprehensive and multifaceted agenda for action comprising a wide range of legislative, administrative, educational and cooperative measures.[44]

[44] Some of the key elements of this agenda identified by the ILO include: strengthening the rule of law by adopting relevant international standards: outlawing racist and xenophobic behaviour; elaborating administrative measures and procedures to fully implement legislation; setting up independent human rights/anti-discrimination bodies with powers to address discrimination against non-citizens; encouraging the communication media to emphasize positive images of diversity and migration; including diversity training in educational curricula; putting in place practical measures and procedures in the workplace, and cooperating with civil society and community groups (ILO, 2006; OSCE/IOM/ILO, 2006, 2007).

The link between social cohesion in host societies and the integration of migrants is commonly accepted, but there are different conceptions of integration (IOM, 2006), some of which, like assimilation, do not sit comfortably with modern understandings of social cohesion. There is growing consensus, however, that integration is a two-way process entailing responsibilities and obligations on the part of both the migrant and host society.

> While the term is used and understood differently in different countries and contexts, "integration" can be defined as the process by which migrants become accepted into society, both as individuals and as groups. It generally refers to a two-way process of adaptation by migrants and receiving societies, while the particular requirements for acceptance by a host society vary from country to country. Integration does not necessarily imply permanent settlement. It does, however, imply consideration of the rights and obligations of migrants and host societies, of access to different kinds of services and the labour market, and of identification and respect for a core set of values that bind migrants and host communities in a common purpose (IOM, 2006: 2).[45]

The resort to the use of voluntary or obligatory "integration contracts" in a number of EU Member States, such as in Denmark and France (European Commission, 2006c), and settlement strategies in the established countries of immigration[46] reflects this dual approach, and from the point of view of the destination country, the concern to ensure that new arrivals understand and adhere to the core social values of the host society.

Irrespective of whether migration for employment is permanent or temporary, an element of integration is important because it contributes to the health and safety of migrant workers and facilitates the exercise of their rights in the workplace and in the host community (i.e. social and cultural rights – see Section 6.4 below), and prepares migrants for eventual return to their home countries. Practical measures assisting integration include the establishment of migrant information and resource centres, such as the Information and Resource Centres for Migrants in Portugal and Slovakia (OSCE/IOM/ILO, 2006, 2007); facilitating learning of the local language, including during working hours; and access to vocational training, which, as discussed in Section 6.2 above, is rarely afforded to migrant workers in a temporary situation. Moreover, supporting private sector and civil society initiatives, such as those of NGOs and trade unions,[47] which interact with migrant workers on a daily basis at the grass roots level, is also key to successful integration.

Social cohesion and integration are also facilitated by the provision of opportunities for migrants to be reunited with their families in the host country. While international human rights standards proclaim the family as "the natural and fundamental group unit of society",[48] this principle has not been elaborated to provide for a right to family reunification for migrants. EU law constitutes an exception, however, because it affords a generous right to EU citizens who exercise their right to free movement to be joined by members of their families, and a more limited right to third-country nationals lawfully resident in the EU who hold a resident permit valid for one year or more and have reasonable prospects of obtaining

[45] See also Council of the EU (2004).

[46] E.g. the national Immigration Settlement Strategy of the New Zealand Immigration Service, which identifies the following six goals for migrants and refugees, namely that they are able to: (i) find employment appropriate to their qualifications and skills; (ii) be confident in using the English language in the local setting or access appropriate language support to bridge the gap; (iii) access appropriate information and responsive services available to the wider community (e.g. housing, education and services for children); (iv) form supportive networks and establish a sustainable community identity; (v) feel safe in expressing their ethnic identity and are accepted by, and are part of, the wider host community; and (vi) participate in civic, community and social activities (Spoonley et al., 2005).

[47] Trade unions play a key role in assisting the integration of migrants in many host societies by organizing language courses and establishing information centres (OSCE/IOM/ILO, 2006, 2007).

[48] E.g. International Covenant on Civil and Political Rights 1966, Article 23(1): "The family is the natural and fundamental group unit of society and is entitled to protection by society and the State".

the right to permanent residence.[49] In general, however, the established countries of immigration admitting migrants for permanent settlement and employment do not place any obstacles before those migrants wishing to bring in close family members. Similarly, European countries admitting migrant workers (usually in the higher skills categories) on a long to medium-term basis also admit spouses and children. However, the position is very different in the GCC States and Asian host countries, such as Malaysia and Singapore, where the admission of foreign workers is perceived as strictly temporary.[50] Similarly, low-skilled temporary or seasonal migrant workers in Europe and North America are often precluded from bringing their family with them (e.g. seasonal agriculture workers in the U.K. and Canada) or face time restrictions (e.g. a one-year waiting period in Spain). While it is legally possible to justify such restrictions for a limited period of time, the longer they are in force the greater the social and humanitarian costs are likely to be for migrant workers and their families, for their integration prospects and for both host and home societies. Consequently, the design of family reunion policies needs to be very carefully assessed and balanced to ensure that these costs are kept to a minimum and to preclude human rights violations.

6.4 Enhancing Social Welfare

The difficulties governments in industrialized countries are increasingly experiencing in ensuring social protection for their nationals in the context of ageing societies, particularly in those European countries which have traditionally supported robust social welfare systems, have adversely affected the access migrants may have to these diminishing resources.

The principal policy challenges therefore centre on the appropriateness of drawing distinctions between citizens and migrants in the social sphere, the extent to which differentiated access to such rights and services based on the specific category of migrant is permissible, and whether the rights concerned, if afforded, should be tailored in accordance with migrants' specific cultural needs.[51] While migrants who are permanent residents are normally treated on equal terms with citizens (e.g. Canada, U.K.), the position of migrant workers who are in a country on a temporary or time-limited basis, and of irregular migrants (see Section 7 below) is considerably less advantageous.

The challenge of according foreign workers equal treatment with nationals in the social sphere is reflected well in the gap that exists between the content of international human rights standards adopted in this field and their application in practice. For example, the International Convention on the Protection of the Rights of All Migrant Workers and Members of Their Families (1990) (see Textbox 13.1) (which, to date, has not been ratified by a single high-income destination country) stipulates that emergency medical care must be available to all migrant workers and their families, including those in an irregular situation,[52] and yet the more widely ratified International Covenant on Economic, Social and Cultural Rights (1966) guarantees the "right of everyone to the enjoyment of the highest attainable standard of physical and mental health",[53] which has been interpreted broadly by the Committee monitoring its application to include "preventive" health care (UN ECOSOC, 2000). In practice, many destination countries grant irregular migrants access to emergency health care, although these policies are

[49] See respectively Council Regulation 1612/68/EEC of 15 October 1968 on free movement for workers within the Community, OJ 1968 L 257, Article 10, and Council Directive 2003/86/EC of 22 September 2003 on the right to family reunification, OJ 2003 L 251/12, Article 3(1). See also Chapter 6.

[50] However, in Singapore, foreign professionals and executives can be accompanied or joined by spouses and dependent unmarried children under the age of 21 (Singapore Ministry of Manpower, 2008).

[51] E.g. tailoring the provision of health care and social services to the specific needs of migrant women.

[52] Article 28 in Part IV of the Convention, which applies only to migrant workers and their families in a regular situation, is broader in scope because it grants lawfully resident migrants equal treatment with nationals regarding "access to... health services" (Articles 43(1)(e) and 45(1)(c)).

[53] International Covenant on Economic, Social and Cultural Rights (1966), Article 12(1).

often not explicit and access for irregular migrants is difficult because of bureaucratic obstacles and the fear of expulsion if they make themselves known, exacerbated by the obligation on officials to denounce irregular migrants to immigration authorities (Cholewinski, 2005). Similar policy contradictions stem from the implementation of the right to education, which too is to be enjoyed by everyone and, at a minimum, to be provided free for all at the primary or elementary level.[54] In practice, however, the children of migrants often experience difficulties in gaining access to an appropriate level of education in the destination country, which are compounded by the lack or inadequate knowledge of the host country's language, and subsequent recognition of the education and the diplomas received there on return to their countries of origin. As with access to health care, these difficulties are exacerbated in respect of the children of irregular migrants. Giving proper effect to the right to "an adequate standard of living", including housing,[55] also to be enjoyed by everyone and defined more generously than the mere provision of basic shelter (UN ECOSOC, 1992), remains problematic in a context of scarce and expensive accommodation in large cities in destination countries where many migrant workers and their families tend to congregate.

With regard to schemes facilitating the temporary migration of low-skilled workers, policymakers in a number of destination countries have attempted to address the problem of the availability of adequate accommodation by imposing a legal obligation on employers to provide this accommodation in accordance with minimum standards. For example, as observed in Chapter 3, the Low Skill Pilot Project in Canada requires employers to assist temporary migrant workers to find suitable and affordable accommodation, and under the Seasonal Agricultural Workers Scheme (SAWS) in the U.K., employers must ensure clean and sanitary accommodation (OSCE/IOM/ILO, 2006, 2007).

6.5 Social Security

Social welfare, as referred to in the preceding section, and social security are closely interrelated; indeed, medical care is one branch of social security, and certain categories of persons (e.g. the unemployed, families with children, the elderly) may also be eligible for social benefits to assist them with their payments for accommodation. Regarding foreign workers, three specific interests concerning social security rights can be identified: (i) entitlement to social security and benefits on equal terms with national workers (which, however, may be denied to them on the basis of their nationality or because they have been unable to meet requirements of residence and/or payment of contributions): (ii) to maintain acquired rights on leaving the country (including the portability of benefits); and (iii) to benefit from the cumulative rights acquired in different countries (OSCE/IOM/ILO, 2006, 2007).

One of the best ways to ensure appropriate social security coverage for migrant workers is through bilateral or multilateral agreements that are particularly relevant with regard to the second interest (maintenance of acquired rights). Multilateral agreements have the advantage of setting common standards, thus avoiding the problem of different rights available under different bilateral agreements for migrant workers from different countries, and easing bureaucratic procedures by establishing common administrative rules in the implementation of the agreement (OSCE/IOM/ILO, 2006, 2007). EU rules on the portability of social security benefits are instructive in this regard. While initially applicable only to EU citizens moving and working within the EU, they have now been extended also to third-

[54] Ibid. Article 26; Convention on the Rights of the Child (1989), Articles 2 and 28(1)(a); Migrant Workers Convention (1990), Article 30.

[55] International Covenant on Economic, Social and Cultural Rights, above n. 53, Article 11(1).

country nationals moving within the EU.[56] These rules are also applicable to third-country nationals lawfully resident in the EU who are citizens of countries with which the EU has concluded Association Agreements (e.g. Algeria, Morocco and Tunisia, and Turkey). An example of a multilateral agreement on social security in a different part of the world is the Caribbean Community and Common Market (CARICOM) Agreement on Social Security (1996) in force since 1 April 1997, which has been ratified by 13 CARICOM members.[57] The agreement safeguards entitlements to long-term benefits by providing for the aggregation of all periods in which contributions were paid to social security systems in member states (Nonnenmacher, 2007b).

In the absence of bilateral and multilateral agreements, it is also possible to secure social security coverage for migrant workers on a unilateral basis. Examples of unilateral measures in host countries include equal treatment of local and migrant workers; waiving long qualifying periods in favour of migrant workers; crediting insurance periods completed in other countries; and reimbursement of medical expenses for migrant workers who, upon retirement, return to their country of origin and do not qualify for a pension and thus the statutory health scheme (OSCE/IOM/ILO, 2006, 2007).[58]

7. Preventing and Reducing Irregular Labour Migration and Unauthorized Employment

There is a general consensus in countries of destination that irregular labour migration needs to be prevented and reduced, and yet, at the same time, that perfection in this endeavour is not a realistic policy objective and that it is not possible to eliminate irregular flows altogether (Papademetriou, 2005). Moreover, as discussed in Chapters 8 and 9, there are still few credible estimates to verify the actual scale of the phenomenon, which, by its very nature, is statistically not quantifiable, although it is possible to point to a number of data sources (e.g. census results, registers of foreigners, border and in-country apprehensions of irregular migrants, demographic statistics – births, deaths and hospitalization rates – and regularization data) which can assist in arriving at more reliable estimates of irregular migration (Jandl, 2003). While policymakers may differ as to its impact, the fact is that irregular migration in most destination countries, including Europe and North America, remains prominent, if not foremost, in policy thinking on international migration and, since September 11, 2001, has also been increasingly linked to security concerns (Castles, 2006; Papademetriou, 2005).[59]

It is also important to make a clear distinction between unauthorized employment and irregular migration (IOM, 2008). In most countries of destination, resources and means to address unauthorized employment have so far been limited, and have instead focused mainly on the traditional forms of dealing with irregular migration, such as strengthening border controls, imposing restrictions on entry (e.g. visa requirements, including airport transit visas) and applying voluntary or, more commonly, forced return. At times, measures have been formulated with little consultation of countries of origin, and some of these strategies

[56] See, respectively, Council (of the European Union) Regulation 1408/71/EEC of 14 June 1971 on the application of social security schemes to employed persons, to self-employed persons and to members of their families moving within the Community, OJ 1971 L 149/2 (as amended) and Council Regulation 859/2003/EC of 14 May 2003 extending the provisions of Reg. (EEC) No 1408/71 to nationals of third countries who are not already covered by these provisions solely on the ground of their nationality, OJ 2003 L 124/1.

[57] CARICOM has 15 full members (Antigua and Barbuda, the Bahamas, Barbados, Belize, Dominica, Grenada, Guyana, Haiti, Jamaica, Montserrat, Saint Kitts and Nevis, Saint Lucia, Saint Vincent and Grenadines, Suriname, Trinidad and Tobago) and five associate members (Anguilla, Bermuda, British Virgin Islands, Cayman Islands, Turks and Caicos Islands).

[58] Unilateral measures can also be adopted in countries of origin, such as the imposition of requirements (liabilities) on recruitment agencies to pay social security contributions to the national security system for each worker recruited for employment abroad (e.g. Philippines, Indonesia); voluntary coverage for nationals working abroad (e.g. France, Jordan, Philippines); and the possibility for the payment of retroactive contributions to returning migrant workers for periods spent abroad (OSCE/IOM/ILO, 2006, 2007).

[59] For the irregular migration/terrorism nexus and for some words of caution about equating the two, see Papademetriou (2005).

have inevitably given rise to human rights concerns. Moreover, while coercive measures are generally deemed necessary,[60] they are unlikely in themselves to stop the movements of irregular migrants.

Consequently, coercive measures are best implemented in tandem with more constructive measures. For example, there is a need to reconcile security concerns with the protection of the human rights of migrants (Schoenholtz, 2007) and, in particular, of irregular migrants, who are most vulnerable to exploitation in the migration process as well as in the destination country.

Furthermore, it is acknowledged that a preventative approach is required and that an isolationist strategy is bound to fail, which means that destination countries need to collaborate and cooperate with transit and origin countries to develop coherent complementary approaches with the help of employers and civil society actors. As observed in Chapter 8, there is a clearly discernible trend towards the development of such cooperative approaches.

7.1 The Need for a Comprehensive Approach

The need to adopt a comprehensive approach to address irregular migration is advocated by EU institutions. In July 2006, the European Commission issued a Communication on policy priorities to address irregular migration, which includes cooperation with countries of origin, secure borders, the fight against human trafficking, secure travel and identity documents, regularizations, tackling unauthorized employment, an effective return policy, improving information exchange, and carriers' liability (European Commission, 2006b). A number of these policy priorities are described in Chapter 8 with reference to specific examples in various parts of the world, whereas for the purpose of underlining the need for a more balanced overall approach, this section will focus on a number of constructive measures to be envisaged by policymakers, such as the introduction of specific safeguards in the employment context for male and female irregular migrants; the opening up of more regular labour migration opportunities; consideration of a range of regularization options; and recent initiatives linking readmission arrangements to labour migration and visa facilitation.

One fundamental issue is that of minimal guarantees for **protection**[61] needed as part of a comprehensive and preventative approach, and without which a restrictive policy to prevent or reduce irregular migration would lack credibility. Irregular migrant workers require special protection from slavery-like practices, forced labour, and inhuman and degrading treatment, as well as safeguards for their personal security and rights in the workplace. Although a migrant's immigration status should not constitute an obstacle to accessing protection in the employment context (IACHR, 2003), in practice it is very difficult for irregular or undocumented migrants to claim their rights before employment tribunals or courts primarily because of the fear of expulsion. This difficulty arises also in relation to rights pertaining to past employment, such as payment of outstanding wages, which employers often refuse to pay to irregular migrants, and is exacerbated if the employment contract is rendered void because of the irregular immigration status of the worker (Ryan, 2005). Some innovative and practical ways of protecting irregular migrant workers have been advanced by the Brussels-based NGO, Platform for International Cooperation on Undocumented Migrants (PICUM) (see Textbox 11.2). One appropriate policy response is to separate the protection of employment rights from immigration

[60] E.g. Papademetriou (2005): "A strong "law-and-order" component to the overall approach to illegal [irregular] immigration is nonetheless necessary because illegal [irregular] immigration subverts a society's legal order and undermines or perverts a variety of foreign and domestic policy priorities."

[61] European Commission (2006b: 3): "Fundamental rights must be protected and promoted. Irregular migrants must be offered a humane and dignified treatment particularly as they are often victims of traffickers' networks and exploited by employers".

enforcement on the basis that exploitation in the workplace is to be avoided generally in respect of **all** workers. Complementary measures relate to adequate monitoring and inspection of the workplace, focusing on the detection of abuse rather than irregularity and particularly in those sectors where workers are most likely to be subject to exploitative conditions or forced labour (i.e. agriculture, domestic work, garment industry, the construction sector and sex work). There is also a significant gender dimension to be considered; women migrants are particularly vulnerable to becoming irregular, especially in the domestic services sector, which is often unregulated and not covered adequately, if at all, by national labour laws. Further efforts are therefore needed to regulate household employment, for instance by preventing the immediate return of victims of migrant smuggling and human trafficking and instead providing for a period for recovery and reflection, and possibly a residence permit, depending on the victim's circumstances.[62] The position of irregular migrants has been especially weakened in the social sphere because they are often perceived as "scrounging" on the state and thus not eligible to benefit from national welfare systems even though the vast majority of them are in employment. In contrast to such realities, and as observed in Section 6.4 above, are the strong assertions in international human rights treaties affording basic social rights, such as health care, education and housing to everyone regardless of their nationality or immigration status (OSCE/IOM/ILO, 2006, 2007; Cholewinski, 1997, 2005).

[62] Indeed, this kind of protection is applied at the national level in some countries and also by the EU Council Directive 2004/81/EC of 29 April 2004 on the residence permit issued to third-country nationals who are victims of trafficking in human beings, or who have been the subject of an action to facilitate illegal immigration, who cooperate with the competent authorities, OJ 2004 L 261/19, which had to be transposed into the laws of EU Member States by 6 August 2006.

Textbox 11.2

Ten Ways to Protect Undocumented Migrant Workers

Every day millions of undocumented migrant workers labour in different sectors of the economy in Europe, the United States and in many other countries worldwide. Undocumented migrant workers often work and live in inhumane conditions, with very little or no pay at all and insufficient legal protection. Facing exploitation and abuse, many undocumented migrant workers believe that they have no other option than to accept this situation. Fearing that they may be deported if they spoke out, an overwhelming number suffer in silence.

The following is a brief overview of ten methods used by NGOs, trade unions and activists in Europe and the United States to strengthen the position of undocumented migrant workers and to defend their rights (PICUM, 2005).

1. Engaging Public Support Through Events and Consumer Campaigns

Undocumented migrant workers are too often thought of as taking advantage of public benefits and as causing or aggravating unemployment for nationals. Changing the poor image of undocumented migrant workers and gaining the support of the public is of paramount importance in order to protect their rights. Without this support, undocumented migrant workers stand little chance of fighting the exploitation and abuse many face on a daily basis. Many organizations therefore endeavour to raise general awareness in the population of the fact that undocumented migrants have human rights and also contribute considerably to local economies.

2. Collecting Data

Policies on migration, employment and social inclusion are often developed in the absence of concrete data about undocumented migrants. As a result, many of these policies are ineffective. Collecting both qualitative and quantitative data on undocumented migrants is of utmost importance.

NGOs can play a crucial role by setting a relevant research agenda and in overcoming the many difficulties in gathering relevant information on undocumented migrants.

3. Informing Undocumented Migrant Workers of their Rights

Undocumented migrant workers do have rights, but many are unaware of this and put up with exploitation and abuse without challenging employers who violate their rights. Informing undocumented migrant workers about their rights is the first step towards ending the silent suffering of millions of undocumented migrant workers.

4. Building Capacities Through Empowerment

In order to stop the exploitation of undocumented migrant workers, they must be helped to acquire the ability to effectively exercise their rights. Empowering and building the leadership capacities of undocumented migrant workers allows them to defend themselves and even to engage in and influence the decision-making affecting their lives. This is essential in order for them to become agents of their own rights.

5. Unionizing Undocumented Migrant Workers

"What we've always said is that 'a worker is a worker is a worker; there is no such thing as an illegal worker'." Pauline Doyle of the Transport and General Workers' Union (T&G).

There are several obstacles preventing undocumented migrant workers from joining a trade union, and not all traditional union structures and working methods are directly applicable to undocumented migrant workers. Yet many trade unions in Europe and the U.S. have managed to overcome these difficulties, leading to a higher level of protection of undocumented migrant workers.

6. Working with Employers to Prevent Exploitation and Advocating for Laws to Hold them to Fair Labour Standards

Another means by which many organizations prevent abuse and exploitation of undocumented migrant workers is by working together with employers. Several successful examples exist of organizations inviting, and sometimes pressuring employers to respect well-defined minimum standards of employment.

Yet there is also a need for legal measures to hold abusive employers accountable for the exploitation of undocumented migrant workers. Such measures are indispensable to ensure effective protection of undocumented migrant workers' rights.

7. Challenging Exploitation and Abuse through Mediation and Collective Actions

Other ways to raise the enforcement and the effectiveness of the protection of undocumented migrant workers include mediation with those employers who wish to avoid going through the various administrative procedures involved in the official claims process, and collective actions such as public protests, demonstrations, strikes and campaigns, where mediation does not reach the desired solution and where filing a complaint in the legal system is not a solution.

"Nobody wants a bunch of angry workers on their doorstep or circling their car, making it hard for them to do their work...now, essentially all it takes is a call from our organization to the employer, telling him that so-and-so worked for him for x number of days, that he owes him x amount, and when can he get a check over to our office?", said Julia Perkins of the Coalition of Immokalee Workers.

8. Asserting Undocumented Migrant Workers' Rights in the Legal System

When conciliatory means of protecting workers' rights prove unproductive, undocumented migrant workers can resort to formal legal channels. But this can be difficult and strewn with many obstacles, such as the fear of being deported, high legal fees and having to prove the abuse.

"As undocumented migrant workers we do have rights, the trade unions and everyone else tell us that we do, but the problem is exercising them. It's like having a Porsche without knowing how to drive", said Henry Cardona of the Collectif des travailleurs et des travailleuses sans statut légal – Genève (CTSSL).

Nonetheless, the law protects undocumented migrant workers in many countries, and undocumented migrant workers in Europe and in the United States have won many cases.

9. Working with Government Agencies to Promote Undocumented Migrant Workers' Rights

Undocumented migrants tend to be reluctant to approach government agencies. Nevertheless, many government agencies and labour inspectors do not let the legal status of workers impede their main task of upholding fair working conditions and sanctioning employers who fail to observe labour requirements.

Liaising with these agencies can therefore be helpful, since they often can and will intervene to protect undocumented migrant workers.

10. Advocating for Legal Status of Undocumented Migrant Workers

A final means of preventing abuse and exploitation is regularizing the status of undocumented migrant workers.

There are many arguments for regularizing undocumented migrant workers: it leads to the increased visibility of this particular social group and thus to increased protection. It is strongly arguable that it is not only the workers who benefit, but society at a large. Regularizing undocumented migrant workers is a means to combat the informal economy and to stop the deterioration of general working conditions, which in the end affect all workers.

Source: *Michele LeVoy, PICUM – Platform for International Cooperation on Undocumented Migrants.*

Although there is no demonstrable evidence to sustain that the creation of **more opportunities for regular migration** will necessarily result in less irregular labour migration, the opening up of more channels for regular migration, that are equitable and sufficiently attractive in both scale and benefits to deter individuals from taking up irregular employment, has a place in any comprehensive approach.

Limited regular labour migration channels and the failure of some traditional preventive measures have drawn greater attention to **regularization policies** as a means of reducing irregular labour migration. While immigration rules in some destination countries contain limited regularization provisions applicable to individuals as apart of their overall immigration policy (e.g. U.K.) (Apap et al., 2000), the implementation of more visible and large-scale collective regularization exercises poses a dilemma. On the one hand, it has been argued that regularization rewards irregular migrants for entering without authorization or overstaying their entry entitlement and, indeed, encourages further irregular entries. On the other hand, it clearly provides a solution for individuals who, for legal, political, humanitarian or practical reasons, are unable to return to their country of origin. Proponents of regularization point out that there are also distinct economic and social advantages for destination countries in promoting regularization, including integration into the labour market of those irregular migrant workers who are unlikely to be paying taxes and social security contributions. For example, in November 2006, the Head of the Russian Federal Migration Service was reported as stating that the presence of approximately 10 million irregular migrant workers in the territory cost the economy more than USD 9.3 billion in unpaid taxes, which was equivalent to the Russian Federation's total budget on education and healthcare (Russian News and Information Agency, 2007). Moreover, regularization prevents the creation of a marginalized group of persons living and working in the midst of the host society. Consequently, policymakers have chosen to undertake both sporadic and periodic regularizations: the most recent examples being the collective decision of the German Länder in November 2006 to allow the regularization of persons holding the temporary and precarious "tolerated status" (*Duldung*) (Geyer, 2007); a pilot regularization of migrant workers in an unauthorized situation conducted in the Russian Federation in the last quarter of 2005 (OSCE/IOM/ILO, 2006, 2007); and the large-scale regularization of irregular migrant workers in Spain in 2005, which resulted in nearly 700,000 applications (Arango and Jachimowicz, 2005: see also Map 7a). Regularization and/or registration programmes have also been implemented recently in a number of Latin American and Southeast Asian countries (see Textbox 8.3 and Maps 7a and 7b). However, the downside is that regularizations may have limited application and thus not necessarily be of lasting effect as the individual in question may for a variety of reasons slip back into irregularity.[63] Some EU Member States, particularly in northern Europe, are negatively inclined towards large-scale regularizations as these may have adverse impacts on other Member States in view of the abolition of internal EU border controls.[64] ILO has argued in favour of an individual right to "earned adjustment" for irregular migrants who cannot be removed and have demonstrated good prospects of settling in the host country (ILO, 2004).

Return is often regarded as the counter measure to further regularization measures, and is sometimes seen as a means of guaranteeing the integrity of regulations concerning regular migration for employment. Return mechanisms are most effective when they include and promote an option for voluntary return (see Textbox 8.5). Readmission agreements, referred to in Chapter 8, are considered as a necessary deterrent by countries of destination, but are often viewed with reluctance and scepticism by countries of origin, in particular concerning commitments to take back irregular migrants without papers but who are deemed to be their citizens, or non-citizens who transited their territory on the way to the destination country. Within the context of international cooperation (see also Section 8 below and Chapter 13), return measures, such as readmission, have been increasingly connected to the opening up of further regular migration channels, such as labour market quotas for some foreign nationals (e.g. Italy) (OSCE/IOM/ILO, 2006, 2007). Similarly, at EU level, readmission agreements have been negotiated with the Russian Federation, Ukraine and a number of Western Balkan countries,[65] in conjunction with visa facilitation agreements, and the European Commission (2007) has proposed the development of mobility partnerships between interested groups of EU Member States and third countries.[66]

7.2 Addressing the Informal Labour Market

It is increasingly acknowledged that irregular migration is essentially a labour market and not only a legal or security issue; the fact that many irregular migrants are able to find work in the informal economy indicates that there is a clear link between irregular migration and the labour market (Awad, 2006). In EU Member States, the informal economy accounts for between seven and 16 per cent of GDP (Mormont, 2002), although the majority of workers who comprise it are nationals.

The use of irregular migrant labour in certain employment sectors in countries of destination, especially in low-skilled sectors (viz. agriculture, construction, hospitality and catering, cleaning and domestic services), creates a dependence relationship

[63] E.g. if continued regular status is tied to employment and the migrant loses his or her job.

[64] Indeed, this approach resulted in the adoption of the EU Council of Ministers Decision referred to in n. 70 below.

[65] Albania, Bosnia and Herzegovina, Former Yugoslav Republic of Macedonia (FYROM), Montenegro and Serbia.

[66] The EU and a number of its Member States recently signed mobility partnerships with Cape Verde and Moldova (see Chapter 13).

and distortions in the labour market that is somewhat similar to the criticism levelled at past temporary labour migration programmes (see Chapter 3 and Section 5.2(b) above). A common policy response in destination countries involves the imposition of legal sanctions against private employment agencies and employers, although in practice such measures have not yielded many successful prosecutions. Often, this ineffective outcome is tied to the absence of adequate workplace monitoring and inspections, identified in Section 7.1 as being particularly important in those sectors where migrants are most prone to be subject to exploitative conditions. However, as observed in Chapter 8, the viability of such monitoring and inspections also gives rise to particular difficulties in some sectors, such as domestic services, where conducting inspections in private households leads to concerns regarding infringements of privacy, and in agriculture, where irregular employment is not easily detected because the place of work covers a large area. One recent discernible policy trend has been to focus less on legal sanctions and instead to encourage and reward self-regulation and incentives for compliance. For example, the U.K. Gangmaster Licensing Authority, established in 2005 for the licensing of recruitment agencies providing workers for the agriculture and food-processing sectors,[67] will only inspect those agencies which in its view are at a medium to high risk of future non-compliance on the basis of a statistically sound risk profile mechanism (OSCE/IOM/ILO, 2007). In Australia, the recent law on employer sanctions focuses largely on education and the encouragement of voluntary compliance among employers, reserving criminal prosecution for persistent offenders or more serious offences such as forced labour or knowingly employing trafficked migrants.[68]

Other policy responses have targeted certain employment sectors in which significant numbers of irregular migrant workers are found, and involve partnerships between government ministries, the private sector and trade unions.[69]

8. Cooperation and Partnerships

The formulation and successful management of foreign employment policies in destination countries cannot be envisaged without cooperation and collaboration with other countries at the bilateral, regional and multilateral level, and the development of a network of partnerships between relevant ministries and interested stakeholders.

Chapter 13 discusses international cooperation in some detail, but, in summary, cooperation and collaboration with other countries occurs at various levels:

- **Bilateral** - between countries of destination and origin to develop equitable, temporary and circular labour migration programmes; and to facilitate the mobility of skilled, semi-skilled and low-skilled migrant workers under bilateral labour migration and trade agreements. Bilateral arrangements are also negotiated by destination countries to secure the readmission of irregular migrants by their country of origin or transit.
- **Regional** - in the framework of regional cooperation processes (RCPs) where information

[67] The Authority was established in the aftermath of a tragic incident in 2003 when 20 Chinese cockle pickers, recruited through such gangmasters (which at the time functioned essentially without regulation), drowned when working in the sea off the coast of northwest England.

[68] Migration Amendment (Employer Sanctions) Act 2007. See Commonwealth of Australia Law at http://www.comlaw.gov.au/ComLaw/Legislation/Act1.nsf/0/8CA4BABF172D6AECCA257352002244E5/$file/0072007.pdf.

[69] E.g. in October 2002, the Belgian Ministry of Employment and Labour, and the Construction Confederation employers' organization signed a partnership agreement to combat unauthorized employment in the Belgian construction sector. Under this agreement, the government undertook to develop monitoring activities on unauthorized work in construction; the employers committed themselves to mount a campaign aimed at providing information to their members and raising awareness with a view to promoting transparency and publicity about the situation on construction sites, which was to include the signing of a "charter of commitment"; and the establishment of a working group of government and employers' representatives was proposed for the prevention of unauthorized work and to improve standards of detection. However, while supporting the goal of preventing unauthorized work, trade unions were aggrieved that they had been excluded from the initiative (Mormont, 2002).

and effective practices on mobility for the purpose of employment and preventing/reducing irregular migration, including human trafficking and smuggling (especially trafficking for forced labour), can be shared and discussed, as well as more formal regional regimes that already provide for an element of labour mobility, such as regional economic integration regimes (e.g. EU, CARICOM and the Common Market of the South (MERCOSUR)) and Regional Trade Agreements (RTAs).

- **Multilateral** – in the context of global trade negotiations under the auspices of the World Trade Organization (WTO), particularly the temporary movement of service providers under Mode 4 of the GATS (see also Chapters 1, 2, 5 and 13) and such processes as the Global Forum on Migration and Development (GFMD) and the Berne Initiative, which produced the *International Agenda for Migration Management* (IAMM) (IOM/Swiss Federal Office for Migration, 2005); the ILO's *Multilateral Framework on Labour Migration* (ILO, 2006b) adopted by its tripartite membership; and the implementation of international agreements protecting the human and labour rights of all persons, including migrant workers and members of their families.

While the design of foreign employment policies is usually perceived as touching closely on matters of sovereignty in destination countries and rarely, if at all, discussed externally,[70] consideration should be given to the scope of such policies and their impact on countries of origin, particularly where there is a significant presence (regular or irregular) of migrant workers from the country concerned (Crush, 2007). Moreover, it is difficult to envisage the formulation and application of successful "development-friendly" policies in the absence of cooperation with countries of origin on at least some aspects of policy design and implementation.[71] Such collaboration is particularly crucial in the design and implementation of temporary labour migration programmes where, as noted above, there is a considerable convergence of interest between countries of destination and origin (Ruhs, 2005).

The involvement of other interested stakeholders in policy formulation and implementation is also important. It is difficult to contemplate the development of successful temporary migrant worker programmes to fill job shortages in certain sectors of the economy without the acquiescence of the private/business sector and trade unions concerned with the protection of the interest of local workers as well as incoming migrant workers. Civil society actors, such as diaspora organizations, migrant associations and NGOs, also play an essential role in the implementation of integration strategies given that such strategies can only be put into effect productively at the grass roots level. Civil society can also play a part in the establishment of cooperative mechanisms with countries of origin to promote circular migration or brain circulation.

9. Conclusion

The four terms or labels that probably best sum up the task of formulating and managing successful foreign employment policies in destination countries, able to produce benefits for all countries involved in labour mobility, as well as the migrants themselves, are transparency, comprehensiveness, flexibility and cooperation and/or partnerships: **transparency**, in the sense of drawing up a consensual statement on labour migration defining policy objectives and

[70] However, in the context of the development of an EU common law and migration policy framework, EU Member States have agreed to inform each other of any recently adopted or planned national immigration measures that are likely to have a significant impact on several Member States or the EU as a whole. Council Decision 2006/688/EC of 5 October 2006 on the establishment of a mutual information mechanism concerning Member States' measures in the areas of asylum and immigration, OJ 2006 L 283/40.

[71] According to Ruhs (2005), there is a certain obligation on destination countries to make their policies "development-friendly" largely because of the asymmetries in the regulation of international labour migration (i.e. relatively fewer opportunities for countries of origin to regulate emigration – because of the human right to leave one's own country – than for destination countries to regulate immigration).

outcomes, and in developing clear and workable rules and regulations that can be understood by those who apply them, by migrants affected by them and by the public at large; **comprehensiveness**, in the sense of recognizing that successful policies are not merely concerned with the admission of foreign workers to fill existing labour shortages, but that they need to relate more broadly to the economic and demographic situation in destination countries and to the whole migration process from departure to the treatment of migrant workers (and their families) in the workplace and the host society, including policies for their integration, to their return and reintegration at home, as well as the possibility of further circulation between their country of origin and host country; **flexibility**, in the sense of recognizing that policies may need to accommodate both temporary labour migration and long-term or permanent employment-based immigration and, in certain instances, to provide a bridge between these; and the development of **cooperation and/or partnerships** with countries at a bilateral, regional and global level, as well as with other interested stakeholders nationally and across borders.

Admittedly, many of the policy responses advanced in this chapter are hardly new in themselves; but, taken together, they offer a broad foundation for a coherent, albeit complex, policy framework, which, if implemented prudently, should contribute considerably to the appropriate formulation and management of foreign employment programmes in destination countries.

REFERENCES

Abella, M.

2006 "Policies and Best Practices for Management of Temporary Migration", paper presented at the International Symposium on International Migration and Development, United Nations Department of Economic and Social Affairs (UN DESA), Population Division, Doc. UN/POP/MIG/SYMP/2006/03, 28-30 June, Turin, http://www.un.org/esa/population/migration/turin/Symposium_Turin_files/P03_SYMP_Abella.pdf.

Agunias, D.A. and K. Newland

2007 "Circular Migration and Development: Trends, Policy Routes, and Ways Forward", Migration Policy Institute (MPI) Policy Brief, April, Washington, D.C., http://www.migrationpolicy.org/pubs/MigDevPB_041807.pdf.

Apap, J., P. De Bruycker and C. Schmitter

2000 "Regularisation of Illegal Aliens in the European Union. Summary Report of a Comparative Study", *European Journal of Migration and Law*, 2(3/4): 263-308.

Arango, J. and M. Jachimowicz

2005 "Regularizing Immigrants in Spain: A New Approach", *Migration Information Source*, MPI, September, Washington, D.C., http://www.migrationinformation.org/Feature/display.cfm?ID=331.

Ardittis, S. and F. Laczko (Eds.)

2008 *Assessing the Costs and Impacts of Migration Policy: An International Comparison*, International Organization for Migration (IOM), Euroasylum, Geneva and Stockport, U.K.

Australia, Department of Immigration and Citizenship (DIAC)

2006 *Annual Report 2005-06*, October, DIAC, http://www.immi.gov.au/about/reports/annual/2005-06/pdf.htm.

2007 *Annual Report 2006-07*, November, DIAC, http://www.immi.gov.au/about/reports/annual/2006-07/pdf.htm.

Awad, I.

2006 "Determinants of Irregular Labour Migration", paper presented at the Workshop on Labour Market Impacts of Temporary Foreign Workers: Issues and Considerations, 11th International Metropolis Conference on Paths and Crossroads: Moving People, Changing Places, 2-6 October, Lisbon, http://www.ceg.ul.pt/metropolis2006/WorkshopPresentations/HotelContinental/IbrahimAwad_metropolis2006.pdf.

Bijak J., D. Kupiszewska, M. Kupiszewski, K. Saczuk and A. Kicinger

2007 "Population and labour force projections for 27 European countries, 2002-2052: impact of international migration on population ageing", *European Journal of Population*, 23(1): 1-31.

Böhning, W.R.

2003 "The Protection of Temporary Migrants by Conventions of the ILO and the UN", paper presented to the International Institute for Labour Studies Workshop on Temporary Migration – Assessment and Practical Proposals for Overcoming Protection Gaps, 18-19 September, ILO, Geneva, http://www.ilo.org/public/english/bureau/inst/download/bohning.pdf.

Boswell, C., S. Stiller and T. Straubhaar

2004 "Forecasting Labour and Skills Shortages: How can Projections Better Inform Labour Migration Policies?", Hamburg Institute of International Economics (HWWA), paper prepared for the European Commission, DG Employment and Social Affairs, July, http://ec.europa.eu/employment_social/incentive_measures/studies/forecast_short3.pdf.

Brem, M.

2006 *Migrant Workers in Canada: A Review of the Canadian Seasonal Agricultural Workers Program*, The North-South Institute, Ottawa, http://www.nsi-ins.ca/english/pdf/MigrantWorkers_Eng_Web.pdf.

Canada

2006 *How to Hire A Temporary Foreign Worker (TFW): A Guidebook for Employers*, Minister of Public Works and Government Services Canada, http://www.cic.gc.ca/english/pdf/pub/TFWguide-e.pdf.

Canada, Citizenship and Immigration (CIC Canada)

2006 *Facts and Figures. Immigration Overview 2005: Permanent and Temporary Residents,* September, CIC Canada, Ottawa.

2007a *Annual Report to Parliament on Immigration 2007,* Minister of Public Works and Government Services Canada, Ottawa, http://www.cic.gc.ca/english/pdf/pub/immigration2007_e.pdf.

2007b *Facts and Figures. Immigration Overview 2006: Permanent and Temporary Residents*, Research and Evaluation Branch, CIC Canada, Ottawa, http://www.cic.gc.ca/english/pdf/pub/facts2006.pdf.

2008 CIC Canada website, http://www.cic.gc.ca/english/index.asp.

Castles, S.

2006 "Back to the Future? Can Europe meet its Labour Needs through Temporary Migration?", International Migration Institute (IMI) Working Paper No. 1 (2006), University of Oxford, http://www.imi.ox.ac.uk/pdfs/wp1-backtothefuture.pdf.

Cholewinski, R.

1997 *Migrant Workers in International Human Rights Law: Their Protection in Countries of Employment*, Clarendon Press, Oxford.

2005 *Study on Obstacles to Effective Access of Irregular Migrants to Minimum Social Rights,* Council of Europe, Strasbourg.

2007 "The Rights of Migrant Workers" in R. Cholewinski, R. Perruchoud and E. MacDonald (Eds.), *International Migration Law: Developing Paradigms and Key Challenges*, T.M.C. Asser Press, The Hague, 255-274.

Council of the European Union

2004 Common Basic Principles for Immigrant Integration Policy in the European Union, Press Release, Doc. 14615/04 (Presse 321), 2618th Council Meeting, Justice and Home Affairs, 19 November, Brussels.

Crush, J.

2007 "South African Immigration Reform", *Crossings*, Southern African Migration Project (SAMP), January, 8(1): 1, 3.

Czech Republic, Ministry of Labour and Social Affairs (MLSA)

2005 Pilot Project: Selection of Qualified Foreign Workers, http://www.imigrace.mpsv.cz/?lang=en&article=home.

European Commission

2001 *Proposal for a Council Directive concerning the status of third-country nationals who are long-term residents*, COM (2001) 137, 13 March.

2005a *Policy Plan on Legal Migration*, COM (2005) 669, 21 December.

2005b *Migration and Development: Some concrete orientations*, COM (2005) 390, 1 September.

2006a *The demographic future of Europe – from challenge to opportunity,* COM (2006), 12 October.

2006b *Communication on Policy priorities in the fight against illegal immigration of third-country nationals*, COM (2006) 402, 19 July.

2006c *Second Annual Report on Migration and Integration*, SEC (2006) 892, 30 June.

2007 *Communication on circular migration and mobility partnerships between the European Union and third countries,* COM (2007) 248, 16 May.

Germany

2001 *Structuring Immigration. Fostering Integration: A Report by the Independent Commission on Migration to Germany*, Chairperson: R. Süssmuth, 4 July, Berlin, http://www.bmi.bund.de/Internet/Content/Common/Anlagen/Broschueren/2001/Structuring__Immigation__-__Fostering__Id__14626__en,templateId=raw,property=publicationFile.pdf/Structuring_Immigation_-_Fostering_Id_14626_en.pdf.

Germany, Federal Ministry of Interior

2008 Highly skilled workers, Federal Ministry of Interior, http://www.zuwanderung.de/cln_108/nn_1120100/EN/ImmigrationToday/ImmigrationAZ/Functions/AZ__catalog,lv2=1123182,lv3=1085844.html.

Geyer, F.

2007 "Germany's regularisation of November 2006: Committed to an EU immigration policy?", *CEPS Commentary*, 9 February, Centre for European Policy Studies (CEPS), Brussels, http://www.libertysecurity.org/IMG/pdf_Germany_s_regularisation_of_November_2006.pdf.

Global Commission on International Migration (GCIM)

2005 *Migration in an Interconnected World: New directions for action*, October, SRO Kundig, GCIM, Geneva, http://www.gcim.org/attachements/gcim-complete-report-2005.pdf.

Global Forum on Migration and Development (GFMD)

2007 "Session 1.4. How can circular migration and sustainable return serve as development tools?", Roundtable 1: Human capital development and labor mobility: Maximizing opportunities and minimizing risks, GFMD Background Paper, 9-11 July, Brussels, http://www.migrationpolicy.org/research/MPI-GlobalForum_circularmigration.pdf.

2008 *Report of the first meeting of the Global Forum on Migration and Development*, Belgium, 9-11 July, Bruylant, Brussels.

Hönekopp, E. and H. Mattila

2008 *Permanent or Circular Migration? Policy Choices to Address Demographic Decline and Labour Shortages in Europe*, April, IOM, Budapest, http://www.iom.int/jahia/Jahia/cache/offonce/pid/1674?entryId=17844.

International Labour Organization (ILO)

2001 Committee on Freedom of Association, Case No. 2121 (23 March), Complaint presented by the General Union of Workers of Spain (UGT), *Report No. 327*, Vol. LXXXV, 2002, Series B, No. 1, http://webfusion.ilo.org/public/db/standards/normes/libsynd/index.cfm?hdroff=1.

2002 Committee on Freedom of Association, Case No. 227 (18 October), Complaint presented by the American Federation of Labor and Congress of Industrial Organizations (AFL-CIO) and the Confederation of Mexican Workers (CTM), *Report No. 332*, Vol. LXXXVI, 2003, Series B, No. 3, http://webfusion.ilo.org/public/db/standards/normes/libsynd/index.cfm?hdroff=1.

2004 *Towards a Fair Deal for Migrant Workers in the Global Economy*, Report VI, International Labour Conference, 92nd Session, International Labour Office, Geneva, http://www.ilo.org/public/english/standards/relm/ilc/ilc92/pdf/rep-vi.pdf.

2006a *Facts on Discrimination against migrants*, September, International Labour Office, Geneva, http://www.ilo.org/public/english/protection/migrant/equality/download/discrimination/factsheet.pdf.

2006b *ILO Multilateral Framework on Labour Migration: Non-binding principles and guidelines for a rights-based approach to labour migration*, International Labour Office, Geneva, http://www.ilo.org/public/english/protection/migrant/download/multilat_fwk_en.pdf.

International Organization for Migration (IOM)

2005 *World Migration 2005: Costs and Benefits of International Migration*, IOM, Geneva, http://www.iom.int/jahia/Jahia/cache/offonce/pid/1674?entryId=932.

2006 "Integration in Today's Mobile World", *IOM Policy Brief*, July, Geneva, http://www.iom.int/jahia/webdav/site/myjahiasite/shared/shared/mainsite/policy_and_research/policy_documents/policy_brief_1.pdf.

2008 *Addressing the Irregular Employment of Immigrants in the EU*, IOM (forthcoming).

IOM/Swiss Federal Office for Migration

2005 *International Agenda for Migration Management*, 16-17 December, IOM/Swiss Federal Office for Migration, Geneva/Berne, http://www.iom.int/jahia/Jahia/cache/offonce/pid/1674?entryId=8005.

Inter-American Court of Human Rights (IACHR)

2003 "Juridical Conditions and Rights of Undocumented Migrants", IACHR Advisory Opinion OC-18/2003 of 17 September, Requested by the United Mexican States, http://www.corteidh.or.cr/docs/opiniones/seriea_18_ing.pdf.

Ireland, Department of Enterprise, Trade and Employment (DETE)

2007a *New Economic Migration Arrangements: Main Features*, 24 January, DETE, Dublin, http://www.entemp.ie/labour/workpermits/employmentpermitslaunch.pdf.

2007b *Employment Permits Arrangements: Guide to Work Permits*, January, DETE, Dublin, http://www.entemp.ie/publications/labour/2007/guideworkpermits.pdf.

Jandl, M.

2003 "Estimates on the Numbers of Illegal and Smuggled Immigrants in Europe", presentation at Workshop 1.6, Eighth International Metropolis Conference on Gaining from Migration - A Global Perspective on Opportunities for Economic and Social Prosperity, 15-19 September, Vienna, http://www.net4you.com/jandl/Metropolis2003.pdf.

Landler, M.

2007 "Germans seek greener pastures abroad", *International Herald Tribune*, 5 February, http://www.iht.com/articles/2007/02/05/news/germany.php.

Martin, P.L.

2003 *Managing Labour Migration: Temporary Worker Programs for the 21st Century*, September, International Institute for Labour Studies, ILO, Geneva, http://www.ilo.org/public/english/bureau/inst/download/migration3.pdf.

Martin, P.L., M. Abella and C. Kuptsch

2006 *Managing Labor Migration in the Twenty-first Century*, Yale University Press, New Haven, CT/London.

Mason, C. and J. Preston

2007 "Points system for immigration causes problems of its own in Canada", *International Herald Tribune*, 27 June, http://www.iht.com/articles/2007/06/27/europe/canada.php.

Migration Dialogue for Southern Africa (MIDSA)

2007 MIDSA Workshop on Human Capital Mobility, Labour and the Millennium Development Goals in Southern Africa, 26-28 March, Victoria Falls, Zimbabwe (various presentations).

Migration News

2006 "Immigrants and Wages, H-1B, Nurses", *Migration News*, 12(3) July, University of California, Davis, http://ruralwelfare.ucdavis.edu/mn/more.php?id=3202_0_2_0.

Migration News Sheet

2006 "Germany: Plan to encourage skilled workers proves to be a failure", *Migration News Sheet* (September): 2, Migration Policy Group (MPG), Brussels.

2007 "Spain: Government has established a migrant worker quota of 180,000 and is prepared to increase this to 200,000 if necessary", (January): 7, MPG, Brussels.

2008 "Chancellor recognises chronic shortage of skilled computer specialists but calls on industry to recruit from German labour market", *Migration News Sheet* (January): 7-8, MPG, Brussels.

Mormont, M.

2002 "Agreement on combating illegal working in the construction sector [in Belgium]", *European Industrial Relations Observatory on-line* (EIROnline), http://www.eurofound.eu.int/eiro/2002/12/inbrief/be0212301n.html.

National Economic Social Council (NESC) and IOM

2006 *Managing Migration in Ireland: A Social and Economic Analysis*, September, NESC, Dublin, http://www.nesc.ie/dynamic/docs/Full%20IOM%20report.pdf.

New Zealand, Immigration Statistics

2008 *R1 – Residence decisions by financial year*, 10 March, http://www.immigration.govt.nz/NR/rdonlyres/4441CE54-1F96-4C87-B9E3-524BEE486050/0/R1.pdf.

Nonnenmacher, S.

2007a "Overview of Global Trends in Temporary Labour Mobility: A Policy Perspective", paper presented at the United Nations Development Programme (UNDP), Commonwealth Secretariat, and Pacific Islands Forum Secretariat Regional Workshop on Labour Mobility and Mode 4 (GATS), 9-11 May, Nadi, Fiji.

2007b "Free Movement of Persons in the Caribbean Community" in R. Cholewinski, R. Perruchoud and E. MacDonald (Eds.), *International Migration Law: Developing Paradigms and Key Challenges*, T.M.C. Asser Press, The Hague, 387-401.

Organisation for Economic Co-operation and Development (OECD)

2004 *Trends in International Migration*, SOPEMI 2003, OECD, Paris.

2005 *Trends in International Migration*, SOPEMI 2004, OECD, Paris.

Organization for Security and Cooperation in Europe (OSCE)/IOM/ILO

2006 *Handbook on Establishing Effective Labour Migration Policies in Countries of Origin and Destination*, 23 May, OSCE/IOM/ILO, Vienna, http://www.osce.org/item/19187.html.

2007 *Handbook on Establishing Effective Labour Migration Policies*, Mediterranean edition, 6 December, OSCE/IOM/ILO, Vienna, http://www.osce.org/item/28725.html.

Papademetriou, D.G.

2005 "The Global Struggle with Illegal Migration: No End in Sight", *Migration Information Source*, September, MPI, Washington, D.C., http://www.migrationinformation.org/Usfocus/display.cfm?ID=336.

Ruhs, M.

2005 "Designing Viable and Ethical Labour Immigration Policies", in IOM, *World Migration 2005: Costs and Benefits of International Migration*, IOM, Geneva, 203-220.

2006 "The potential of temporary migration programmes in future international migration policy", *International Labour Review*, ILO, 145 (1-2): 7-36.

Ruhs, M. and P.L. Martin

2006 "Numbers vs. Rights: Trade-offs and Guest Worker Programmes", The Centre on Migration Policy and Society (COMPAS) Working Paper No. 40, University of Oxford, http://www.compas.ox.ac.uk/publications/Working%20papers/WP0640-Ruhs-Martin.pdf.

Russian News and Information Agency (Novosti)

2006 "Russia loses over $9 bln/yr from illegal immigration – govt.", Novosti, 3 November, http://en.rian.ru/russia/20061103/55351198.html.

Ryan, B. (Ed.)

2005 *Labour Migration and Employment Rights*, Institute of Employment Rights, London.

Schoenholtz, A.I.

2007 "Anti-Terrorism Laws and the Legal Framework for International Migration" in R. Cholewinski, R. Perruchoud and E. MacDonald (Eds.), *International Migration Law: Developing Paradigms and Key Challenges*, T.M.C. Asser Press, The Hague, 3-27.

Singapore, Ministry of Manpower

2008 Ministry of Manpower website, http://www.mom.gov.sg/publish/momportal/en/home.html.

Spencer, S.

2003 "Introduction" in S. Spencer (Ed.), *The Politics of Migration*, Blackwell, Oxford, 1-24.

Spoonley, P., R. Peace, A. Butcher and D. O'Neill

2005 "Social Cohesion: A Policy and Indicator Framework for Assessing Immigrant and Host Outcomes", *Social Policy Journal of New Zealand* (March) (No. 24): 85-110.

Sriskandarajah, D. and C. Drew

2006 "Brits Abroad: Mapping the Scale and Nature of British Emigration", Institute for Public Policy Research (IPPR), 11 December, London.

Taran, P., I. McClure and R. Zegers de Beijl

2006 *Challenging Discrimination in Employment: A Summary of Research and a Typology of Measures*, ILO, Geneva.

United Kingdom, Home Office

2006 *A Points-Based System: Making Migration Work for Britain*, Cm 6741, March, Home Office, http://www.homeoffice.gov.uk/documents/command-points-based-migration?view=Binary.

2007 "New Points Based System To Start In The New Year", Press Release, 18 April, Home Office, http://press.homeoffice.gov.uk/press-releases/migration-syytem-points.

United Kingdom, Home Office, Border Agency

2008 Immigration Rules (consolidated version), U.K. Border Agency, http://www.ind.homeoffice.gov.uk/policyandlaw/immigrationlaw/immigrationrules/.

United Nations Department of Economic and Social Affairs (UN DESA)

2004 *World Economic and Social Survey 2004: International Migration*, Docs. E/2004/75/Rev.1/Add.1, ST/ESA/291/Add.1, UN DESA, New York, http://www.un.org/esa/policy/wess/wess2004files/part2web/part2web.pdf.

United Nations Economic and Social Council (ECOSOC)

1992 *General Comment 4, The Right to Adequate Housing (Art. 11(1) of the Covenant)*, Committee on Economic, Social and Cultural Rights, 6th Session, Doc. E/1992/23, http://www.unhchr.ch/tbs/doc.nsf/(symbol)/CESCR+General+comment+4.En?OpenDocument.

2000 *General Comment No. 14 (2000), The right to the highest attainable standard of health*, Committee on Economic, Social and Cultural Rights, 22nd Session, Geneva, 25 April – 12 May, Doc. E/C.12/2000/4, 11 August, http://www.unhchr.ch/tbs/doc.nsf/(symbol)/E.C.12.2000.4.En.

United Nations General Assembly (UNGA)

2006 *International Migration and Development*, Report of the Secretary-General, UNGA, 60th Session, Doc. A/60/871, 18 May.

United States, Department of Homeland Security (DHS), Office of Immigration Statistics

2008 "U.S. Legal Permanent Residents: 2007" (by K. Jefferys and R. Monger), *Annual Flow Report*, Office of Immigration Statistics, DHS, March, http://www.dhs.gov/xlibrary/assets/statistics/publications/LPR_FR_2007.pdf.

Williams, V.

2007 "Immigration Act 19 of 2004: A summary and review", *Crossings*, SAMP, January, 8(1): 1, 3.

World Bank

2006 *Global Economic Prospects 2006: Economic Implications of Remittances and Migration*, The International Bank for Reconstruction and Development/The World Bank, Washington, D.C., http://econ.worldbank.org/WBSITE/EXTERNAL/EXTDEC/EXTDECPROSPECTS/GEPEXT/EXTGEP2006/0,,menuPK:1026834~pagePK:64167702~piPK:64167676~theSitePK:1026804,00.html.

Textbox 11.2 - Ten Ways to Protect Undocumented Migrant Workers

LeVoy, M. and N. Verbruggen

2005 *Ten Ways to Protect Undocumented Migrant Workers*, PICUM, Brussels, http://www.picum.org.

MANAGING THE LABOUR MIGRATION AND DEVELOPMENT EQUATION*

CHAPTER 12

1. Introduction

Migration has profound economic consequences for countries of origin - many of them salutary, others more worrisome.[1] Exploring these consequences has become a major focus in the current debate surrounding globalization: the UN Secretary-General's High-Level Dialogue on International Migration and Development addressed the labour migration and development equation in September 2006 and the Global Forum on Migration and Development (GFMD) followed in 2007.[2]

This chapter reviews the evidence surrounding the labour migration and development equation, outlining the potential benefits and risks of labour migration for development, the roles and responsibilities of the governments of source and destination countries, and the prospects for more effective partnerships among the various stakeholders. Section 2 introduces the notion of the migration cycle, viz. a sequence of stages through which many migration source countries pass. During the cycle, the relative importance of the various channels through which migration affects development change. Section 3 proposes policy recommendations for the governments of destination countries, encouraging them to look at their migration policies through a development lens. This includes rethinking policies related to the recruitment of workers at all skill levels, and to remittances. Section 4 recommends policy innovations for source country governments; living with emigration calls upon the latter to rethink policies related to macroeconomic management, human resources, higher education, infrastructure and regional cooperation. Section 5 suggests that mobility partnerships between source and destination countries offer a vehicle to make the necessary policy changes in order to better manage the labour migration and development equation.

The links between international migration and development, which are the subject of this chapter, cannot exhaustively cover all aspects of the labour migration and development equation. Accordingly, it focuses on economic impacts, leaving aside

* This chapter was written by Louka T. Katseli (Professor of Economics, University of Athens) and Jeff Dayton-Johnson (Senior Economist, OECD Development Centre, Paris). The chapter is a product of the OECD Development Centre's *Gaining From Migration* project (see Dayton-Johnson et al., 2007) and has also benefited from Anna di Mattia's (formerly of the OECD Development Centre) comments. It was written while Professor Katseli was Director of the OECD Development Centre.

1 "Home countries", "source countries" and "countries of origin" are synonymous and used interchangeably in this chapter.

2 For a summary of the GFMD, see Textbox Int. 2

social and cultural dimensions of migration and development. Moreover, as the central focus of *World Migration 2008* is on labour mobility, this chapter has little to say on the development impact of other flows (e.g. refugees and asylum seekers, family reunification). Textbox 12.1 from the Office of the United Nations High Commissioner for Refugees (UNHCR) provides information on the contribution of refugees' employment to the development of host communities.

Textbox 12.1

Initiatives to Enhance the Contributions by Refugees to the Development of Host Communities

The Office of the United Nations High Commissioner for Refugees (UNHCR) estimates that there are some 15 million refugees worldwide, a fraction of the world's "migrants". However, refugees are not migrants in the traditional sense of that term, since they move out of compulsion, not choice. The refugee protection regime is premised on the international community's recognition of the specific rights and needs of refugees, as well as the obligation of states not to return them to countries where their life or liberty would be at risk.

In recent years, there has been intense interest in the "migration-development nexus", most of it focused on labour migration and on issues such as the developmental impact of remittances, brain drain, diaspora investments in countries of origin and circular labour migration between countries of origin and destination. Among these issues, remittances and brain drain are also gaining importance in the refugee context.

There is growing evidence to suggest that refugees and asylum seekers, especially those in industrialized countries, remit significant amounts of money to household and community members in countries of origin, and to refugees in other asylum countries. Such remittances have played an important role in cushioning the impact on some refugees of reductions and blockages in the provision of assistance, especially in Africa. Remittances may also enable family members to remain in their country of origin or in countries of first asylum, rather than feeling compelled to move abroad to make a living. UNHCR therefore supports the current efforts made by the Global Forum on Migration and Development, the World Bank and other actors to reduce the transaction costs of remittances and to reinforce their impact on poverty reduction and development.

With regard to the issue of brain drain, all refugee populations include people whose talents could and should be put to good use, both in countries of asylum and in countries of origin, if and when they choose to return. In this context, UNHCR has been encouraging states to ensure that refugees are not excluded from, or discriminated against, in national labour markets and for any qualifications and professional credentials they possess to be recognized in their country of asylum.

While there is growing recognition of the fact that migrants contribute to the prosperity of their host countries, this recognition does not always extend to refugees. Indeed, refugees are increasingly portrayed as a threat to national security, a drain on public resources and a constraint to local development. As a result, serious limitations are often imposed on their right to engage in wage-earning employment or other economic activities. Strict encampment policies in some countries effectively oblige refugees to become dependent on international humanitarian assistance.

UNHCR has endeavoured to counter such negative perceptions and policies, highlighting the fact that refugees have the potential to become "agents of development" in their countries of asylum by boosting production, filling gaps in the labour market and creating new trading and business opportunities. This will also enable them to contribute to rebuilding the economy upon their eventual return back home.

UNHCR and partners actively promote self-reliance and livelihood creation for refugees. This provides a chance for a meaningful and dignified life during exile, and prepares them for a better future once a durable solution is achieved. The promotion of self-reliance and livelihoods also helps to reduce any risks to the protection of refugees, in particular for certain groups such as women and youth as they will be less dependent on others for their living and therefore less vulnerable to exploitation and abuse.

The most effective initiatives aimed at promoting self-reliance and livelihoods have entailed full government ownership and strong partnerships with the development community, including agencies of the United Nations system, international financial institutions, NGOs and civil society groups, as well as donors. These partnerships are vital to ensure the integration of such initiatives into local development plans and, hence, their sustainability.

Under the broad heading of "Development Assistance to Refugees" (DAR), such initiatives have been coupled with community-based assistance, for example to improve local physical and social infrastructure, (e.g. building schools, clinics, roads and bridges, building wells and similar activities). This has contributed to the socio-economic development of often isolated and marginalized host communities, some examples of which are listed below.

Case 1: Benefits from apiculture in Uganda

The national agency promoting an increase in the local honey production in Uganda also developed markets in Europe; however, as the volume of honey produced was insufficient to meet demand, the agency sought to both increase national production and improve the quality to bring it into line with international standards. Together with UNHCR, the agency was able to involve a refugee-hosting area and include both refugees and the local population in this endeavour. These efforts led to improved bee-keeping skills and to the local production of beehives and of protective clothing for bee-keepers. In a few years time, the national agency had improved honey production and found a local partner through whom to expand its market reach. The higher production and improved quality of the honey resulted in more income being generated for both refugees and the local host community.

Case 2: Improved vegetable production in Tanzania

Prior to the influx of refugees from Rwanda, agriculture was not well developed in western Tanzania, but the incoming Rwandans were soon able to introduce some useful changes. As farmers who have had to make the most of small plots of land back home, they knew how to maximize production and productivity. Although they did not have plots of their own, many worked for local Tanzanian farmers. Within a few seasons, the volume, variety and quality of produce on the local markets had increased dramatically. Not only did the standard of living increase among both local Tanzanians and refugees, but the local economy also improved quite significantly. Grass-thatched roofs were increasingly replaced with iron roofing material. When it was time for the Rwandan refugees to return home, the District Commissioner admitted that it was a big blow to the local economy, but the improved agricultural skills they had been able to introduce remained and will help to bring about further improvements.

Case 3: Stimulating the local economy in Zambia

From 2003 to 2004, some 120,000 refugees and members of the local population benefited from loans for food production. This led to a significant increase in the area of cultivated land from an average of two hectares per household to 2.5 hectares. Thanks to the loans and their own hard work, the refugees and the host population were able to produce sufficient food for domestic consumption and a surplus to sell. Not only did the community become self-reliant, its income tripled. A total of 564 metric tons of maize was sold to the World Food Programme and the proceeds reinvested to boost maize production still further. For the first time, the local host community and refugees were **suppliers** of food rather than **recipients** of food aid.

Source: *UNHCR.*

2. The Migration Cycle[3]

Will migration foster economic growth in the migrants' home country? At the most basic macroeconomic level, the balance of the migration and development equation depends on the relative strength of three effects: (1) the impact of labour mobility on domestic labour supply and, in particular, the supply of specific types of labour; (2) the impact of migration on productivity in the domestic economy; and (3) the impact of remittance inflows. The net effect of labour migration on economic growth at a given moment in time is the sum of these effects, some of which are positive, some negative.

Finally, the balance of these effects for a given country – that is, their effect on the economic growth rate – at a given point in time will depend on where that country is situated within a "migration cycle", which is summarized in Table 12.1 below. The table sketches a kind of stylized generic history of a country's emigration experience, from the initial departure of workers to their eventual return.

Even if migration has a positive impact upon growth, this may not always be accompanied by poverty reduction. For example, if the benefits of migration flow to families placed in the middle of the income distribution spectrum rather than to the poorest members of society, which would be the case if the middle or upper classes have a higher propensity to emigrate, poverty reduction may be either modest or even zero.

[3] The migration cycle is explored in greater detail in OECD (2007); references to the relevant research literature are provided by Katseli, Lucas and Xenogiani (2006a).

The migration cycle can be briefly described as follows:

Table 12.1:

The Migration and Development Equation over the Migration Cycle

	Labour Supply	Productivity	Remittances	Growth	Poverty
Phase					
Exit	-	-	0/-	0/-	+
Adjustment	-/0	?	0/+	0/-	+/0
Consolidation	0	+	+	+	-
Networking	0	+	+/0	+	-
Return	+	?	-	?	?

Source: *OECD (2007: 54).*

When workers initially leave an economy during the **exit** stage, there may be a decline in the supply of labour in the domestic economy and therefore a drop in output. However, in many countries of origin there are high rates of unemployment, under-utilization of labour or internal migrants available as replacements, so that the risk of a significant drop in economic output is not always a serious one. In the case of skilled emigration, productivity may be expected to decline, unless the skills of such workers were in fact either not or only insufficiently used in their jobs at home.

As migration continues, more information becomes available regarding employment opportunities in destination countries, thus reducing the information and transaction costs related to migration. This encourages more households, perhaps with lower incomes than the initial wave of migrants, to employ emigration as a livelihood strategy. Furthermore, the possibility of migration might also encourage those left behind to invest in skills required to leave the country in their turn to seek improved prospects abroad (for instance, to train as a nurse). At this stage, the home economy starts **adjusting** to migration.

This may take the form of increased labour force participation, as women for example, enter the labour market. Adjustment often leads to the restructuring of the economy, including the mechanization of agriculture, or increased investment in other sectors, including human capital accumulation. However, massive emigration of skilled labour may turn out to be disastrous if it leaves the home country without a critical mass of human capital and with no prospects to replenish the stock.

Although reunification of emigrants' families in the destination country may continue during the **consolidation** stage, international labour flows at some point stabilize. That is, emigration flows continue to be large, but cease to grow year after year. At the same time, emigrants' improving economic fortunes in destination countries increases their ability to transfer money home. Economic activity in countries of origin improves as migrants' remittances increase and the benefits of economic restructuring and human capital accumulation undertaken during the adjustment stage are realized. The magnitude of remittance flows and the way they are used depend on financial market conditions and the characteristics of the migrants themselves. Remittances first increase consumption, especially of food and other basic needs. They are also frequently used to finance improvements in housing and living conditions as well as to cover education expenses for children.

Growth tends to increase and poverty to fall during this consolidation stage. In principle, economic growth is promoted through each of the channels identified in Table 12.1. Stabilizing emigration flows reduces pressure on the labour supply, while economic adjustments and investment of remittances in human and physical capital favour productivity increases. A continuing decline in the cost (information and administrative) of migration, meanwhile, leads to changes in the composition and characteristics of households whose members migrate. Poorer households can now afford to send a family member abroad and the remittances sent home can help to reduce absolute poverty and inequality.[4]

The consolidation phase may also witness a decline in the competitiveness of local exports. This so-called "Dutch Disease" occurs for at least two reasons. Massive infusion of foreign currency in the form of migrants' remittances could cause the local currency to appreciate or, if exchange rates are fixed, reduce the cost of imported goods.[5] Second, migrants' families often use their increased income to purchase more non-traded goods, such as many consumer items and housing improvements. Increased demand for such goods will lead to higher prices and further depress the local currency price of the exchange rate just as remittances are increasing its local supply. The other consequence of a rise in the exchange rate of the local currency is that exports become more expensive, which would penalize the country's export industry as foreign consumers have to pay more for the home country's exports.

During the **networking** stage, migrants become better integrated in the destination country and form networks across transnational communities; the process of family reunification is largely complete and a second generation of migrants appear in the destination country. The creation of hometown associations in the destination country improves the communication between the two countries and enhances economic links; other means of improving communication between destination and source countries develop as well. In time, migrants are

4 The empirical evidence is stronger for the impact of migration on poverty reduction than it is on growth; for the poverty reduction evidence, see the cross-country evidence by Adams and Page (2005), or the careful summary of Latin American evidence in Fajnzylber and López (2007). Growth effects will be difficult to detect, in part because the impacts of migration will be localized only in particular communities (where household-level survey data provide evidence of poverty reduction) and will not be large enough to affect GDP.

5 This is called the "Dutch Disease" because a similar phenomenon befell the Netherlands economy during the 1970s when surging prices of natural gas – a major Dutch export – increased the exchange rate, depressing the competitiveness of other exports.

able to exploit their knowledge of markets in both countries and thus may become good trade and investment intermediaries.

As remittances continue to flow into the local economy, they will fuel consumption and investment at home. Human capital accumulation is spurred in part by remittance flows and by the stronger incentives for personal advancement provided by the possibility of emigration. All of these phenomena boost productivity in countries of origin. Although growth may be accompanied by a reduction in absolute poverty, changes in the distribution of income and wealth depend in large measure on who migrates and how remittances are used. Growth alone does not guarantee that inequality will decline.

In most cases, by the time of the **return** stage, emigration will have contributed to skill formation for the migrant and to home country development and economic growth. As a result, the home country may begin to experience certain labour shortages, especially in some low-skill labour market segments, which may then be filled by internal migration or labour migration from neighbouring countries. The return of former emigrants may also coincide with such low-skilled labour migration and thus contribute to the local labour supply. As the number of returnees increases, the level of remittance transfers may decline. Irrespective of their original place of residence, returnees often choose to settle in cities on return, which increases pressure on urban labour markets, while new arrivals from neighbouring countries are more flexible and usually settle where there are labour shortages, finding employment as agricultural workers in rural areas or as household employees.

Whether growth is boosted or dampened at this stage depends upon the degree to which migrants either complement or "crowd out" native workers, upon the kind of skills introduced by return migrants and on labour market flexibility. Where regional markets are more integrated, flows of seasonal or contract migrant workers facilitate the creation of economic and social networks leading to positive externalities in trade and investment with neighbouring countries.

The impacts of the migration cycle on economies and societies in both home and host countries will differ depending on the characteristics and particular local socio-economic condition, and vary among countries. Some stages might be skipped or never reached in a given migration experience, and the duration of certain phases may differ significantly within the migration cycles themselves, as well as among countries. The critical lesson is that the net balance from migration for a country's development depends upon the particular stage in its migration history. Overall, the effect on growth can become more positive over time.

3. Managing the Labour Migration and Development Equation: The Role of Destination Countries

The joint consideration of migration and development cooperation policies, in a properly structured institutional setting, can form the basis of genuine migration and development partnerships between countries of origin and destination, as well as of transit countries, where applicable. Such partnerships should exploit the full range of benefits of cooperation – and the costs of non-cooperation – to pursue more effective management of labour mobility. This does not imply that migration policies do not need to take into consideration other major domestic policy concerns, including employment, social protection, security or social cohesion; nor does it imply that domestic policy priorities need to yield to development objectives of partner countries. Rather, the joint consideration of migration and development issues, including development assistance, could facilitate policy formulation and make difficult trade-offs (e.g. between development assistance for capacity building and recruitment of skilled workers) easier to handle.

Development assistance can help to resolve some of the challenges posed by international labour migration, particularly by enhancing the capacity of countries of origin to successfully adjust to emigration, for instance through support for infrastructure development, improvement of education and health systems, co-development projects, or support for appropriately designed fellowships and training schemes. However, it should also be pointed out what aid should **not** be expected to do: some observers suggest, for example, that aid be used by the OECD Development Assistance Committee (DAC) donors to stop or control immigration. This recommendation is misplaced for a number of reasons. First, the links from aid to growth are weak and, even if aid spurs growth, that does not mean that migration will necessarily diminish as a result.[6] In fact, the opposite might be true: as income rises in a developing country, households initially unable to afford the cost of migration now choose to move, a phenomenon referred to as the "migration hump".[7]

Second, using development assistance as a bargaining device to secure cooperation in controlling irregular migration, as is sometimes suggested, would be fraught with difficulties — not least because low and middle-income countries with limited resources, would be at least as hard pressed to enforce emigration border controls as destination countries are to enforce immigration border controls. Finally, the principal objective of development assistance is and should remain poverty eradication. Official development assistance (ODA) should not be intended to serve the double aim of poverty reduction and migration control. Given that very little of the low-skilled migration to the European Union (EU), for example, originates from the least developed countries, redirecting development assistance towards the high-migration middle-income countries in order to influence migration patterns there, would run counter to the objective of eradicating the most severe poverty.[8]

3.1 Looking at Migration Policies Through a Development Lens

To improve migration management and to maximize the positive impact of migration, destination countries need to address the development impacts of their recruitment and admission policies, as well as development cooperation policies and the degree of mobilization and the channelling of remittances towards productive uses.

(a) Tackling the brain drain

Many developed countries have programmes to facilitate the entry of **highly skilled migrants**. Indeed, the global competition to attract the best and the brightest is intensifying (see Chapter 2). The disruption from the loss of key personnel, such as healthcare workers and educators, and the public costs incurred to train potential emigrants can be very real.[9] Of course, a highly educated diaspora could, in principle, provide benefits to the home economy – but the evidence for this remains weak and pertains more to upper middle-income countries, which are better placed to take advantage of technologies transferred from abroad and any fresh skills of returning diaspora members. Meanwhile, the poorer the country, the more it is likely to feel the loss of highly educated persons migrating to industrialized countries. How can these trends be

6 The modern, largely pessimistic, empirical analysis of the effects of aid begins with the World Bank's report *Assessing Aid* (1998), which found that aid promotes growth, but only in good policy environments. Even this modest conclusion was called into question by subsequent research that suggested that it was not econometrically robust. The principal authors of the World Bank's research reviewed the criticism and responded in Burnside and Dollar (2004).

7 On the "migration hump", see Faini and Venturini (1993), Hatton and Williamson (1998, 2002), Stark and Taylor, (1991) and Vogler and Rotte, (2000), among others. The cover of the 2006-2007 *Human Development Report* for Mexico (UNDP, 2007) suggests a variation on the migration hump, plotting an index of migration intensity against the human development index for many hundreds of Mexican municipalities.

8 Cogneau and Gubert (2005) demonstrate that emigration rates are much higher for middle-income developing countries than they are for low-income countries. See also Dayton-Johnson and Katseli (2006b).

9 For a discussion on the evidence of losses and potential gains from skilled migration, see Katseli, Lucas and Xenogiani (2006a and 2006b).

influenced to enhance the benefits — the brain gain — while mitigating the costs?

Developed countries' efforts to attract highly skilled migrants are unlikely to abate. Policy innovations can nevertheless help to mitigate some of the risks for developing countries.

First, innovative circularity schemes - including resort to flexible, multi-use, multi-annual work permits - may allow countries of origin to manage migration flows more effectively and avoid critical shortages in the provision of public services, such as healthcare or education, in particular. They could be expanded to include multi-annual fixed-term contracts for professionals to train or work for a certain period in developed destination countries. Such schemes could furthermore be aimed at students and/or postgraduates from developing countries. Under the terms of such agreements, the country of origin could commit itself to upgrade and modernize its social service delivery system, such as education or health, supported, if need be, by the destination country. Measures to ensure appropriate training of personnel, and the deployment and replenishment of staff to maintain social service delivery at the desired level, could also be included. Moreover, the circular migration of the highly skilled also means that their skills will be made more widely accessible at home during the process and enhance local capacity through the transfer of technology and knowledge acquired by such migrants during their professional activities abroad.

Other steps might also be considered to limit negative impacts on the countries of origin. Countries of destination should continue to develop guidelines for the recruitment of highly skilled workers from developing countries. In that context, it should be borne in mind that self-imposed recruiting restraints by public-sector employers have not been effective in limiting the migration of healthcare workers. Exhorting private-sector employers to recruit ethically is likely to prove equally ineffective. However, there may be a role to play for internationally agreed upon guidelines;[10] these can serve as a benchmark against which civil society organizations and the nationals and governments of destination and origin countries can evaluate the practice of destination countries. Such peer pressure can help to avoid imminent crises, for example in developing countries' healthcare systems.

(b) Organizing recruitment of low and semi-skilled migrants

Developed countries are less likely to target **low and semi-skilled migrants**, despite the mutual benefits that can be derived from their mobility (see Chapter 3), and the significant advantages for many destination countries as they fill labour shortages in specific sectors such as agriculture, construction and domestic services, where natives are more reluctant to work. For countries of origin, low and semi-skilled migration has typically a greater impact on poverty reduction than the emigration of professionals.[11] There are three reasons for this. First, such workers come from lower-income families and communities, who therefore stand to benefit more directly from migration. Second, their withdrawal from the home labour market opens opportunities for other low or semi-skilled replacement workers. Finally, low and semi-skilled migrants tend to remit a larger proportion of their income than highly skilled professionals, especially if they have left their families behind.

Most countries of destination address low and semi-skilled migration through temporary/circular labour migration programmes. However, when workers do integrate into the host societies of destination countries, there are often sound reasons to offer them the opportunity to stay in the country (see also Chapter 11). Temporary workers, who demonstrate

[10] See e.g. Commonwealth Code of Practice for the International Recruitment of Health Workers, http://www.thecommonwealth.org/shared_asp_files/uploadedfiles/%7B7BDD970B-53AE-441D-81DB-1B64C37E992A%7D_CommonwealthCodeofPractice.pdf.

[11] See Katseli, Lucas and Xenogiani (2006a) for a review of the evidence.

their ability and willingness to remain in the labour market, to play by the rules, to learn the local language and to meet other reasonable requirements, may welcome the opportunity to "graduate" to "permanent" status. In this "gradual incentive scheme", temporary worker visas would formally become what they often already are in practice today for those who choose to treat them as such - "transitional" or provisional permanent immigration visas. While such graduation is generally more feasible today for highly skilled workers than for migrants in general, such gradual incentive schemes could, in principle, be introduced for migrants of all skill levels.

Bilateral schemes between countries of origin and destination to promote circular migration of low and semi-skilled workers can enhance the impact of migration on development in the countries of origin (see Textbox 12.2).[12] Effective recruitment of temporary or circular migrants in the context of such partnerships might also prove effective in tackling irregular migration. Seasonal or temporary work arrangements under multi-annual contracts for specific work (e.g. in agriculture) or service provision, and the establishment of clear criteria for return and subsequent re-entry, could significantly enhance the incentives of migrants to prefer regular admission channels and honour fixed-term contracts.

[12] See also Chapters 11 and 13.

Textbox 12.2

Mauritius: Heading Towards a Migration Miracle?

The economic success experienced by Mauritius since the 1970s has meant that it has not been known as a source country of organized labour migration. Instead, especially since the 1990s, Mauritius has been a country of destination for thousands of foreign workers employed in various sectors of the economy, including in the Export Processing Zones (EPZs). However, with the end of the Multi-Fibre Agreement, an agreement relying on a framework of bilateral agreements or unilateral actions that established a quota system designed to protect clothing and textile manufacturing in developed countries, while facilitating access for developing countries, Mauritius has recently witnessed the retrenchment of thousands of textile workers. In addition, in September 2009, the EU sugar protocol will come to an end and Mauritius will no longer enjoy preferential prices for sugar above the global market price and, in consequence, will have to reform its sugar industry leading, in turn, to massive job cuts. These two measures are estimated to lead to the loss of some 12,000, mainly low-skilled, jobs over the next three years.

Hence, the local authorities have been looking at alternatives to revive the economy and to reintegrate laid-off workers into the labour market, whether locally or abroad. In doing so, the government has to address a number of challenges: an unemployment rate which currently stands at 9.1 per cent; high female unemployment (currently 16.5%, three times the rate for men) and the fact that women, who constitute the bulk of the unemployed, are mainly low-skilled; as well as a mismatch of available skills.

A two-pronged approach to migration management is being pursued. Firstly, the government wishes to develop circular migration opportunities for the locally unemployed. In order to best match the profile and supply of local workers with demand, the Mauritian authorities are targeting a number of key economic sectors, in particular: carers and nurses (in response to the growing demand in relation to an ageing population in many destination countries); seasonal agricultural work, in particular in France, Greece, Portugal and Spain; and agro-processing and manufacturing for those retrenched from the textile sector. Secondly, the authorities are looking to mobilize the Mauritian diaspora through creative solutions to harness their intellectual and financial resources with a view to enabling them to return home to assist in the development of the country. One approach is to encourage the diaspora to contribute to the new growth sectors identified, which include information communications technology (ICT), a seafood hub and tourist villages, among a range of suggested options.

Encouraging the return of workers is no easy undertaking, especially of individuals who are already close to retirement age. However, Mauritius has been known to overcome obstacles and adversity: in 1961, James Meade, recipient of the Nobel Prize in Economics, reported that Mauritius faced a bleak future. Relying on a mono-crop culture of sugarcane, subject to weather and price shocks, facing the prospect of overpopulation, multi-ethnic and with wide income inequalities, it had, in addition, experienced political conflict. And yet, within a decade, the country was able to turn such dire predictions around by diversifying its economy and promoting external investment. Within Africa, this small island in the southwest Indian Ocean became the "Mauritian miracle".

As during the 1970s, when Mauritius turned its fate around, it again appears that it will once more be able to turn some of its current disadvantages into distinct advantages in the international labour market. Mauritius has a vibrant and multicultural population; speaking both French and English, and local Creole; a mix of religions including Hinduism, Christianity, Islam and Buddhism - all factors which can potentially facilitate integration into host communities. Mauritians also pride themselves on their adaptability, which is evident from the 200,000 members of the Mauritian diaspora.

Apart from such natural advantages, the Government of Mauritius is also keen to implement its own policy direction and has set up an "Empowerment Programme", which aims to rapidly reduce unemployment by identifying and supporting new employment possibilities, retraining and investment. The Empowerment Programme has been allocated five billion Rupees (approximately USD 180 million) for the first five years to initiate the various components of the programme.

Through an IOM 1035 facility project,[1] the Government of Mauritius has been assisted in the development of an overseas employment strategy, the outcome of which was the establishment of a subcommittee on circular migration within the Empowerment Programme. Since May 2007, with a view to primarily addressing the unemployment problem, this subcommittee has met to formulate the conditions necessary for short-term placement of Mauritian workers to take up temporary employment abroad and to acquire skills and save money before coming back to start a small business or invest in other economic activities. The pilot placement of the first migrant workers abroad began in 2008. Perhaps this is the start of a new "migration miracle"?

Note:

[1] IOM's 1035 facility provides special support to IOM developing Member States and Member States with economies in transition for the formulation and implementation of joint government-IOM projects addressing particular areas of migration management.

Source: *Elizabeth Warn, Labour Migration Specialist, Labour and Facilitated Migration, IOM Geneva.*

Regional schemes among developing countries also deserve attention. Policies to facilitate cross-border regional market integration through improved infrastructure and appropriate visa policies, including perhaps also the introduction of regional passports, should be considered. This is supported by the evidence that a large part of the migration of less-skilled workers (and even more so of refugees) is intra-regional, and that migration by the less-skilled has the greatest potential to alleviate poverty.

(c) Mobilizing and channelling remittances for development

Remittances sent by migrants to families and friends in home countries constitute an important driver of development, particularly as a country's migration cycle moves into the consolidation phase,[13] although assessing the economic impacts of migration and remittances gives rise to a number of challenges (see Textbox 12.3). The actual amounts remitted by migrants will depend on economic and financial conditions in both countries of origin and destination, on the composition of migration flows as well as the conditions on which the migrants are admitted into the host country, and are therefore in part determined by admission policies in developed countries. The pro-poor effects associated with remittances are much stronger in the case of low-skilled as opposed to highly skilled migration, especially if highly skilled migrants settle permanently abroad with their families. Low-skilled migrants tend to remit a larger proportion of their income and direct their savings to their low-income families, who often remain in the home country.

[13] See Katseli, Lucas and Xenogiani (2006a) for a review of the evidence on the development impact of remittances and multiplier effects.

Textbox 12.3

Challenges in Assessing the Economic Impacts of Migration and Remittances

The rapid growth in the transfer of remittances has increased the interest in the economic impacts of migration and remittances on recipient developing countries.

It is frequently assumed that receiving households tend to spend all or a large part of the remittances they receive on consumption and that, in the absence of increased spending to improve human capital, i.e. on education and training, or to launch entrepreneurial activities, this might generate or perpetuate a cycle of dependency rather than lead to self-reliance and economic growth.

However, to gain a more realistic and detailed picture of the impact of remittances on receiving communities, a number of factors need to be considered:

- ***The fungibility of money***: Remittances are an additional source of income for most households and, though they may be spent on consumption or traditional festivals and other celebrations, they nevertheless augment available household resources and enable the diversification of household expenditures, including on better nutrition which, in turn, improves health and well-being. Therefore, to concentrate only on "spending on consumption" falls short of the full picture and fails to measure the actual economic impact of remittances.

- ***Self-selection concerning the decision to migrate***: To simply contrast the respective outcomes for households with and without migrants, or with and without remittances, is misleading, since those who in fact migrate are not a random sample of the population, rather they "self-select" for both observable and unobservable reasons. Many reasons underlying a desire to work abroad are closely tied to the actual outcomes used to measure the impact of labour mobility. For example, poor parents who value education very highly might send a migrant abroad to earn money to pay for schooling and also encourage their children to stay in school. Then, if it is observed that children in households receiving remittances are more likely to stay in school, this could reflect differences among households in how much they value education, rather than just the effect of receiving remittances.

- ***Reverse causality***: Both migration and remittances may be driven by specific interests rather than be the cause of observed outcomes. For example, if remittances are sent in response to a household member's ill health, it may be observed in due course that households which receive remittances have poorer health than households which do not receive remittances. This does not in any way mean that receiving remittances is bad for one's health.

The consequence of these challenges is that estimation of the economic effect of migration requires comparing the situation of a household with a migrant to the unobserved situation in which the household would have been had a member not migrated. There are a variety of econometric methods available for approximating the latter. In a unique study, McKenzie, Gibson and Stillman (2006) are able to assess how well these different methods perform by taking advantage of a migration lottery used to select among Tongans applying to work in New Zealand. Comparing winners in this lottery (who migrate) to losers (who stay in Tonga) reveals an income gain from migration of NZ$274 per week, which is only half of what the difference in GDP per capita would suggest. Figure 12.1 below compares the performance of a number of non-experimental estimators against this mode of calculation. Using a good instrumental variable gives results close to the experimental estimates, whereas the other non-experimental methods overestimate the gains to migration by 20 per cent or more. This suggests that migrants in their study have higher unobserved ability than non-migrants.

With careful use of an instrumental variable, it is possible therefore to obtain reasonably accurate measures of the overall impact of migration on outcomes such as schooling, child health, poverty and inequality, and business ownership. However, most of these effects cannot be interpreted as being simply due to remittances. The main difference between remittances and other sources of household income is that the receipt of remittances is typically accompanied by the absence of a household member, which in turn will affect development outcomes. The absence of one or both parents may have a number of different direct impacts, on children, the single spouse left behind or grandparents (see also Textbox 6.1). Also, absent household members may transfer ideas and knowledge, as well as money; the migration of one family member may increase the propensity to migrate by other family members in the future, and may, by way of anticipation, already affect their decisions today.

Figure 12.1:

Comparison of Estimates of Income Gain from Labour Migration to New Zealand from Tonga by Different Estimation Methods

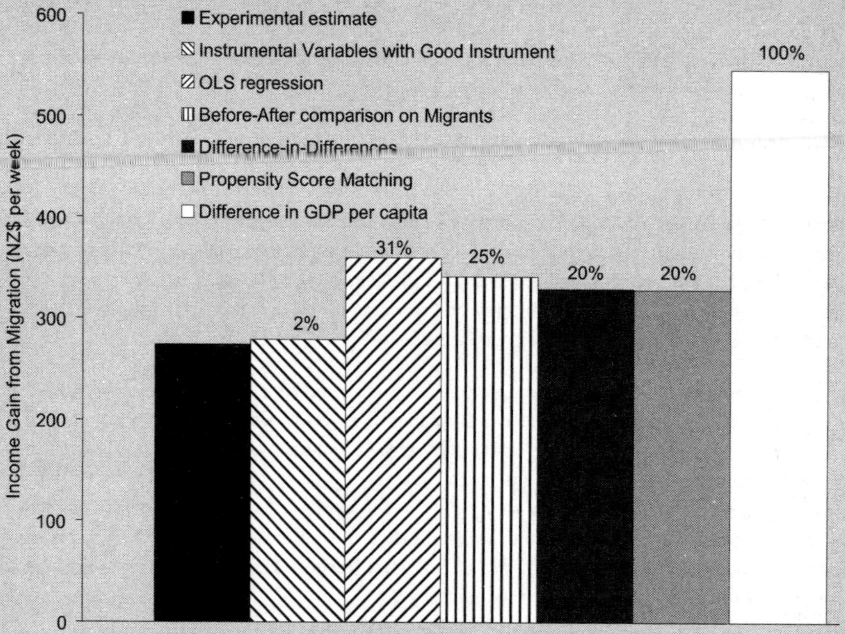

Estimations taken from McKenzie, Gibson and Stillman (2006). Percentages give the degree of overestimation of income gains compared to the experimental estimate.

Separating the impact of remittances from all other impacts of migration raises the double challenge of self-selection and endogeneity referred to above. There is a need to identify the exogenous reasons to explain not only why persons in one household migrate and others do not, but also why some migrants send more remittances than others. There are few, if any, studies in the literature able to do this. Moreover, from a policy perspective, it is not clear whether such an exercise is required. Remittances are a private resource that households should be free to spend as they wish. Policies aimed at reducing the cost of remittance transfers or encouraging investments in countries of origin should not be premised on how households choose to spend their income.

On the contrary, it is precisely in relation to some of the non-remittance effects of migration, such as the effects of absent parents or a spouse on children or the single spouse as sole head of household, where the design of appropriate policy interventions critically depends on the proper understanding of migration impacts and on overcoming the methodological obstacles to the measurement of such impacts.

***Source:** World Bank.*

The reported size of remittances (estimated in 2007 at USD 318 billion worldwide with 240 billion going to developing countries – Ratha et al., 2007) is most likely underestimated. Remittances are often transferred through informal channels rather than banks or other formal institutions. The cost of transferring money remains extremely high for migrants in many developed countries, varying between five and 15 per cent of the amount transferred, with significant differences across countries. For example, the cost of remittances between Europe and West Africa is ten times higher than that between the United States and the Philippines (Table 12.2).

Table 12.2:

Approximate Cost of Remitting USD 200 (Percentage of principal)

	Major MTOs[1]	Banks	Other MTOs	Hawala
Belgium to Nigeria[2]	12	6	9.8	—
Belgium to Senegal[2]	10	—	6.4	—
Hong Kong SAR to the Philippines	4.5	—	—	—
New Zealand to Tonga (USD 300)	12	3	8.8	—
Russia to Ukraine	4	3	2.5	1-2
South Africa to Mozambique	—	1	—	—
Saudi Arabia to Pakistan	3.6	0.4	—	—
United Arab Emirates to India	5.5	5.2	2.3	1-2
United Kingdom to India	11	6	—	—
United Kingdom to the Philippines	—	0.4-0.5	—	—
United States to Colombia	—	17	10	—
United States to Mexico	5	3	4.7	—
United States to Philippines	1.2-2.0	0.4-1.8	—	—

Notes:
Figures do not include currency-conversion charge.
1 Money transfer operators.
2 World Bank survey of African diasporas in Belgium.
— Data not available.

Source: *Adapted from World Bank (2006: Table 6.1, p. 137).*

Governments and banks in countries of origin and of destination might take concerted steps to lower the transfer costs through formal channels, and to expand financial services to poor rural communities. Such action would facilitate the channelling of remittances to poor communities. Involving migrants and migrant associations in such schemes would increase pressure for appropriate services and thus increase the volume of remittances transferred. Migrant networks play an important role in facilitating remittances and promoting their use as a development tool; they serve as lobby groups to improve access to financial services for migrants in both their country of destination and their country of origin. Moreover, they contribute to the collection and dissemination of information on the available channels to transfer their savings to their families back home.

Whether the positive impacts of remittances spread from the household level to the whole of the economy depends in large part on how well domestic markets function. If markets are well integrated, increases in local incomes can lead to increased economic exchanges with other communities, enhancing growth and employment creation. The availability of necessary infrastructure (e.g. transport infrastructure) is therefore a precondition for the diffusion of benefits across regions. Development assistance towards capacity building and infrastructure development in the context of national development strategies can substantially enhance the positive impact of remittances on development.

3.2 Coherence of Policies for More Effective Management

Many of the factors that affect the labour migration and development equation span two or more policy domains, including policies related to migration and development, but also agriculture, trade, environment and security. The potential for international migration to contribute to economic development is greater if migration, trade, investment and development assistance considerations are jointly addressed at the national, regional and global level (Dayton-Johnson and Katseli, 2006a; Katseli, Lucas and Xenogiani, 2006b).

The trade policies pursued by developed countries should be crafted with due regard to their impact upon labour mobility. Being able to export products that make intensive use of low-skilled labour is a critical strategy for accelerated growth in countries of origin and a principal rationale for opening to trade. Expansion of such export industries might even have the effect of easing migration pressure as some workers may choose to work in export industries rather than emigrate. However, such a growth strategy is complicated by the trade policies of developed countries. For instance, the use of agricultural subsidies by many of the industrialized countries that depress world prices for agricultural products[14] hurt living conditions in countries that are exporters of cash crops, possibly exacerbating migration pressures. While the effects of such policies on potential migrants vary within and across developing countries, this example illustrates that the impacts of trade, migration and development policies of developed countries on specific low and middle-income developing countries need to be considered alongside migration policymaking.

Meanwhile, a new agenda on security and development would provide an opportunity to explore the many interlinkages between development, migration and security – links that have been sidelined in the wake of the September 11, 2001 terrorist attacks on the United States (Katseli, 2006). Such a new agenda calls for a broad conception of security. "Security" certainly includes the security from terrorist attack, but also the security from a broader class of negative shocks that make poor people vulnerable. Policies and programmes could explicitly aim to address the various sources of insecurity[15] that often cause people to emigrate and also hamper development. Strategies for risk prevention, risk mitigation and coping with risk should be incorporated ex ante into the design of policies in countries of origin; and, here too, development assistance can help. Improving access to land and water, supporting agricultural extension programmes and irrigation infrastructure, and promoting institutional capacity building, as well as appropriate land titling and regulatory modernization, are only a few examples of policy priorities that could significantly enhance security in countries of origin and stem the desire for relocation.

Linking migration and development cooperation policies at the national, regional or international level will require substantial rethinking of existing institutional parameters to address the current segmentation of policy competencies across ministries and various agencies and organizations.[16]

At the national level, inter-ministerial initiatives can promote coordination of development and migration policies. Sweden's 2003 Government Bill, committing

[14] See Verdier and Suwa-Eisenmann (2006) and Xenogiani (2006) for more discussion of these issues.

[15] Four proximate sources of insecurity include inability to access strategic assets, access to food or other inputs, large market volatility or failed institutional set-ups (Katseli, 2006).

[16] The momentum towards more coherent development policy is gaining in the European Union. In December 2004, the EU Council called for the further strengthening of policy coherence for development: "making wider and more systematic use of existing mechanisms for consultation and impact assessment and procedures to screen all relevant policies for their impact on developing countries" (European Commission, 2005: 18). Particularly noteworthy is the EU's December 2005 "European Consensus on Development", which explicitly calls upon the Commission and the Member States to observe coherence among their policies that affect development (European Commission, 2006).

various ministries to greater policy coherence in relation to measures that affect development through annual reporting to Parliament, is probably the institutionally most ambitious initiative (Sweden, 2003).

4. Managing the Labour Migration and Development Equation: The Role of Countries of Origin

The development impact of international labour mobility depends not only on the policies pursued by host countries or the choices migrants make, but also on the capacity of home countries to adjust successfully to emigration. This capacity will, in turn, depend on the active engagement of migrants themselves – consultation, cooperation, coordination with migrants and their various organizations – as well as on the institutions and policies in their home countries, and can furthermore be strengthened with the support of countries of destination.

In countries where emigration is a prominent feature, national development strategies (in particular "Poverty Reduction Strategy Papers" (PRSPs)[17]) need to pay adequate attention to the migration dimension in their policy development processes, and include it in their macroeconomic policies, human resource management, education policies, infrastructure investments and regional (including "South-South") initiatives.

4.1 Macroeconomic Policies

The budgetary implications of large-scale emigration and remittances can be profound and therefore warrant explicit recognition in national poverty-reduction strategies. First, when migrants – particularly the highly skilled among them – leave, potential tax revenues decline. Consequently, alternative mechanisms of raising tax revenues so as to avoid a budget deficit need to be adequately addressed. Similarly, when remittances start flowing in, real exchange rate appreciation needs to be avoided through careful management of the exchange rate. Emigration may also shift expenditure priorities. Resources might need to be shifted towards public and social service delivery systems weakened by the loss of qualified staff (e.g. healthcare, education) or towards services for dependent children, spouses or elderly parents not effectively supported by absent migrant family members. However, any such scheme may have the undesired side-effect of weakening the personal responsibility and readiness of remittance-sending migrants to continue to offer support for their family back home, or to reduce such support over time. Thus, the design of transfer programmes (i.e. social assistance expenditures to support poor households) should be sensitive to the possibility that remittance receipts might level off where there are publicly funded alternatives. Some governments offer matching grants to encourage remittances.[18] However, such matching grants tend to go to communities already relatively well endowed through remittance receipts and may divert spending from other needier communities that do not benefit from migrant remittances.

4.2 Human Resource Management

Human resource management (see also Chapter 10), including employment policies, should also take into consideration current and projected effects of migration on domestic labour markets. The design of sufficient incentives for public sector posts (or for private sector companies hired to work for the public sector) is critical. Such incentives include not

[17] The PRSP, according to the World Bank's web site, is "a country-led, country-written document that provides the basis for assistance from the World Bank and the International Monetary Fund, as well as debt relief under the Heavily Indebted Poor Country initiative. A Poverty Reduction Strategy Paper describes a country's macroeconomic, structural, and social policies and programs to promote growth. It summarizes the country's objectives, policies, and measures for poverty reduction. A Poverty Reduction Strategy Paper should be country-driven, comprehensive in scope, partnership-oriented, and participatory."

[18] The *Tres por uno* [Three for one] programme in Zacatecas state, Mexico, is among the most celebrated examples; see Iskander (2005).

only acceptable pay but also appropriate facilities and working conditions. Where the concern is the loss of key personnel and the resultant lack of capacity to deliver basic services (such as healthcare or education), the effective deployment of available personnel becomes especially critical. Conscription of personnel to designated posts is rarely an effective or feasible option. Instead, incentives should be provided to ensure labour force participation among those with needed skills, employment in occupations that make use of these specific skills, and location in areas where the skills are most in demand. Examples exist of programmes that have been successful in placing students in rural communities, or incorporating poverty relief efforts as part of their training. For example, South Africa introduced compulsory community service for health workers in an attempt to address the problems of regional access to healthcare services (Lucas, 2006). Programmes in Australia, Canada and the United States ease restrictions for foreign health workers who are willing to work in rural areas (Clemens, 2007). Mexico's *Progresa* programme has tapped into graduating doctors to staff their rural clinics (Levy, 2006).

4.3 Financing Higher Education

If a given country's principal concern is the loss of public resources invested in the education of highly skilled emigrants, policymakers should consider restructuring the methods of financing higher education rather than continue subsidizing developed countries of destination. Programmes offering student loans, rather than outright grants to students, offer greater potential to recoup training costs. Such loan programmes could be combined with debt forgiveness for those undertaking predefined tasks at home, such as healthcare work, teaching in rural areas or public service more generally. It is important that the design of any such programmes does not have the effect of discouraging children from lower-income families from continuing their education; a means-tested grant element might have to be considered. In addition, mechanisms would need to be explored for repayment of interest and principal while the migrant is abroad. Possibilities include bilateral arrangements with the host countries and intermediation by the banking sectors of both countries. Policymakers need to attentive to the incentives provided by the subjects of study to be supported in public higher education and training. People trained in certain specializations (e.g. medicine) have relatively easy access to the global labour market; those trained in fields more closely related to the needs of the poor in a developing country (e.g. agronomists) might have fewer opportunities to visit and work abroad. Specialization and vocational training in areas in high demand in developing countries need to be encouraged through appropriate incentives, including, where appropriate, scholarships and temporary work programmes in developed countries. Temporary stays abroad for additional training or work can produce important incentives for others to do likewise and thereby raise the availability of experts in these specialized fields. Through fellowships or training schemes, universities and training institutions in developed countries can similarly support the specialization of international students in these areas.

A number of developing countries have programmes to encourage the return of their highly skilled diaspora and students studying abroad. Offering salary premiums, tax breaks and attractive research facilities can prove very costly, generate resentment among those who stayed at home, and increase the incentive to move abroad to take advantage of such packages upon return. It is nonetheless important to at least remove any disincentives for return. Prime examples of such disincentives include the lack or difficulty of possible advancement in public sector posts based on experience acquired abroad, or the inability to transfer pension and social security benefits to the country of origin upon return. Some returning international migrants choose to enjoy their savings from abroad and take early retirement. Others choose to re-enter the labour market or to become self-employed. Excessive regulatory requirements or poorly defined land property rights can inhibit commercial activities. Providing lines of credit for start-up enterprises can lower barriers to self-employment opportunities for returning workers. Access to information about the realities of such business ventures and existing credit lines may also be important; business failures among returned migrants with inadequate management experience are common. Not only can the dissemination of such information make return a more attractive option, it can also stimulate the home economy and hence diminish the pressure to emigrate.

4.4 Infrastructure

Optimal infrastructure policy might well change when emigration occurs on a large scale. Plans for investment in public infrastructure need to be drawn up in recognition of the demographic implications of migration flows. From which communities and regions are migrants leaving? Do these migration streams include families, or are children and others left behind? Where do returning migrants settle? The answers to these questions have implications for infrastructure development. If, for example, migrants leave rural areas on a large scale, but settle in urban locations upon return (perhaps with internal migration of family members to join the returning migrant) the balance of desired investments in rural versus urban contexts may have to be adjusted.

Since international migrants tend to originate from quite specific regions of their home country, encouraging internal replacement migration may have the effect of turning the negative impact of the loss of workers due to emigration into an opportunity for others to gain a place in the job market and secure a living for themselves. Removing obstacles to internal migration (see Chapter 7) can therefore help to spread the indirect benefits of emigration from specific areas. Improved infrastructure and abolition of barriers to internal migration, if adequately incorporated into domestic development strategies, can enhance the capacity of the country of origin to adjust to migration and benefit from ripple effects. Examples might include removing licensing requirements for entry to formal sector activities, or giving access to public works schemes in other regions of the country.

4.5 Regional and "South South" Initiatives

For many developing countries, the dominant destinations for their low or semi-skilled migrant workers are often other neighbouring developing countries or countries within the region.[19] Much of this migration is irregular, offering little or no protection of rights to foreign workers. In many countries, the institutional capacity required to manage migratory flows and for effective policy formulation and implementation is weak, and must be strengthened through training of officials. Another problem facing South-South migrant workers include high migration costs, in part driven by corruption.

At the national level, collaboration between and within government agencies dealing with migration matters, though essential, rarely exists. Bilateral and regional arrangements among developing countries exchanging workers are to be encouraged (see also Chapter 13). This might include an expansion of current efforts to introduce regional passports with automatic entry rights. Another example is the reciprocal extension of the right to work to nationals of all participating states, where this is not already the case, and more systematic enforcement of these rights where they exist but are not necessarily respected in practice. Technical cooperation in critical areas such as education and health can also play a role. Cuba, Brazil, India and other developing countries carry out such programmes.

[19] Ratha and Shaw (2007) document the quantitative importance of South-South remittances.

5. Effective Partnerships for Better Migration Management

Countries of origin and destination can use bilateral agreements and arrangements as a vehicle for maximizing the gains from international labour mobility by effectively linking recruitment with capacity building and development in countries of origin. Under such arrangements, developed destination countries offer to rethink their labour migration policies, including, notably, measures to promote circular mobility, accompanied by development assistance to increase adaptive capacity in countries of origin. In turn, developing countries could undertake to mainstream migration and remittances into their national development strategies.

For example, such a partnership approach could link migration policies in developed destination countries and human resource development policies in countries of origin. In the presence of emigration, countries of origin need to be encouraged to develop human resource development policies that take account of current and projected effects of migration on domestic labour markets as well as the potential loss of public resources invested in highly skilled emigrants (see also Chapter 10). This implies the provision of sufficient incentives for public sector posts, effective deployment of available personnel and possible restructuring of methods of financing higher education. The retention of highly skilled professionals in developing countries, especially in the health and education sectors, can be substantially improved through investments in public service delivery systems, continuous training of personnel and better working conditions. Development assistance can play an important role in such partnership arrangements by providing resources to the economies of countries of origin to strengthen their capacity to adjust. This capacity could include better transport and communication infrastructure to link up labour markets in different regions of the country of origin, and promotion of financial sector development to encourage greater use of formal channels to transfer remittances.

6. Engaging Diaspora Networks

Migration management partnerships can be made more effective still if they engage diaspora networks: such groups include migrants (whether they have retained their original citizenship or adopted that of their new country) and they can include second, third and subsequent generations as well.[20] As a country's migration experience moves into the networking phase, the activities of diaspora groups, which can range from informal social relationships to formally constituted associations, become more visible and significant.

In general, the contribution diaspora networks can offer stems from the information advantages and social mechanisms at their disposal. The first information advantage has to do with the flow of information among various parties. Network members know about business opportunities in their host countries that might interest counterparts in their home countries, and vice versa.

Diaspora networks are familiar with labour market conditions in the host country or how to access social services. that can be of help to newcomers to the network (that is, newly arrived migrants). For example, 60 per cent of Moldovan migrants claim to have had a job lined up before they emigrated, based on existing networks (Borodak, 2006). These information flows are not limited to transmitting labour market information. In the field of public health, researchers in the U.K. show that immigrants have low take-up rates of preventative measures such as screening and immunization, and that uncertain immigration status is one of the main reasons why migrants do not access primary health care (Spencer

[20] This broad definition of "diasporas" is also that used by the European Commission in recent policy statements on immigration (European Commission, 2005). For a discussion of diaspora definitions, see Ionescu (2006).

and Cooper, 2006). Often migrants' command of English is insufficient to navigate among service providers, while the foreign-language competency of medical workers is too weak to meet them halfway. For their part, medical practitioners are equally unclear as to who is entitled to which service, while those outside metropolitan areas may lack the cultural competency to provide appropriate care (Spencer and Cooper, 2006). Could intermediaries in diaspora networks help to better match up care providers and migrants in need of care? More generally, diaspora intermediaries can help provide better targeting of social services, including, but not limited to, health care.

The second sense in which diaspora networks provide informational value has to do with what economists call an "asymmetric informational advantage" over other actors. Network members know more about their members than outsiders, and this information would be genuinely valuable in a credit or insurance market. Thus, diaspora networks can judge who among them is in need of material assistance, even if their members do not have easy access to formal insurance contracts (or publicly provided social assistance). Similarly, networks can assess whether a given immigrant is a good credit risk, though he or she may have no collateral of any value to a formal bank in the host economy. Indeed, a frequently cited benefit of ethnic (social) networks is the access to the financial capital they provide. Rotating credit associations, for example, often perceived as divided along ethnic or national lines, allow members access to capital for businesses through informal channels; members pool the sums so that each can raise money for small business operations (Rindoks et al., 2006).

A third asset of diaspora networks is that they have access to means of contract enforcement that are presumably unavailable to those outside the network. These may range from social norms of cooperative behaviour within the network (i.e. a network member feels shame if he or she breaches a contract with another network member, but not if he or she does so in relation to an outsider) to social sanctions, namely, costly actions taken by network members to punish rule-breakers in their midst (the most draconian of which is expulsion). While these social norms are powerful, in diaspora groups, as in many social organizations, they might not be very democratic or fair; the negative aspects of such informal community powers must be acknowledged. Too often, for example, women's participation and voice in such organizations can be weak or non-existent.

These characteristics of diaspora networks allow them, in principle, to provide services more easily to their members that other members of society access directly from the public sector (e.g. information about the healthcare system) or from markets (e.g. a business loan). The promise of diasporas as a policy lever is that they can bridge gaps not filled by the public sector or markets; it remains an open question whether a more efficient solution would be to address market failures directly.

The role of diaspora networks may not be as productive or as positive as it appears at first glance. Experts voice some scepticism that the observed behaviour attributed to networks – loans, information-sharing, investment, cross-border trading, etc. – might often be more accurately ascribed to family contacts. Research on ethnic business networks shows that much of the putatively network-based financing available to ethnic entrepreneurs is, in fact, intra-family lending; moreover, family-based businesses of this type are at a competitive disadvantage when family objectives compete with profit maximization or other economic motives. Other observers point out that there are risks that while such organizations can effectively build social cohesion among migrants, they can also create barriers to broader participation, "filtering them out of mainstream politics into marginal spheres of political activity" (Spencer and Cooper, 2006). Indeed, this concern mirrors the distinction made between "bridging social capital" – institutions that create links between communities –

and "bonding social capital" – institutions that affirm fellow-feeling within communities. Some migrants' associations might be far more effective at providing the latter than the former. Additionally, the very fact that many migrant communities are marginalized reduces their capacity to be effective political or social intermediaries (Rindoks et al., 2006).

Keeping in mind these potential limitations, migrant networks can nevertheless help migrants find jobs and to integrate economically. Migrant organizations can often play a leadership role within social networks by providing guidance and services to migrants. While some organizations provide assistance in filing documentation for family reunification or citizenship, others offer second-language programmes (such as English as a Second Language in the U.K.) and vocational training to upgrade job skills. By partnering with local schools, community colleges, hospitals and vocational training centres, migrant organizations are able to provide meaningful services to their clients.

As the networking stage progresses and information flows through diaspora networks, migration increasingly promotes trade. Migrants may serve as trade intermediaries and facilitators because of their knowledge of opportunities and potential markets, their access to distribution channels, contacts and language. Membership in such networks (which may not be primarily economic in nature, as in the case of religious brotherhoods in North and West Africa, or village-based groups) may play a significant part in contract enforcement given the importance of reputation. Furthermore, access to information and knowledge not available outside the diaspora about market and trade opportunities among their members offer immigrants an advantage for setting up their own businesses (see Textbox 12.4). Thus migrants often create trading networks that increase trade flows between their host countries and their countries of origin (Xenogiani, 2006). This information channel implies that, for all these reasons, migration may actually have an impact both on exports and imports.

Textbox 12.4

Diaspora Linkage in Development: A Bangladesh Case

International migration from Bangladesh goes back to the 18th century and early colonization (de Bruyn and Kuddus, 2004), when sailors from the south-eastern part of Bangladesh, namely Chittagong and Noakhali, travelled from the port of Kolkata to different parts of the world in the British Merchant Navy (Siddiqui, 2005). In the 1940s and 1950s, Bangladeshi crews, especially Sylhetis, of British merchant ships used to land in British ports and settle in the U.K. to cater to the shortage of labour in low-skilled industries (de Bruyn and Kuddus, 2005). Over time, these migrants brought their wives and children and permanently settled there, creating Sylheti communities in different parts of the U.K. In the 1960s, mass migration occurred to the United States; however, it was mostly students and professionals who migrated (de Bruyn and Kuddus, 2005). During this period Bangladeshis also migrated to Australia, Canada, Greece and Japan (Siddiqui, 2004). In the late 1970s, educated Bangladeshis obtained political asylum in Germany and Switzerland and then students began travelling to different European countries in large numbers (Knights, 1996). These movements throughout Europe created small Bangladeshi communities in many European countries and such networks have facilitated chain migration of family and friends, for example in Italy and Spain (Zeitlyn, 2006). Although the long-term emigrant community of Bangladesh is spread throughout various countries, an overwhelming majority still resides in the U.K and the U.S. (Siddiqui, 2004).

Over the years, the diaspora linkages have evolved through the maintenance of social capital, family ties and assistance during natural disasters. However, the significant role of diasporas in the overall development of a country in areas such as business, trade links, investments, remittances, skill circulation and exchange of experiences (Ionescu, 2006) has been studied only in recent times. One such topic of study is the Nandan Group of Companies in Bangladesh.

The Nandan Group of Companies is a progressive initiative of a group of non-resident Bangladeshis (NRBs) living in the U.K. and the U.S. In 1999, Mr. Masrur Choudhury, now Chairman and Chief Executive Officer of the Nandan Group, encouraged 23 NRBs from the U.K. to pool resources and invest in a project in Bangladesh named "Nandan". This initiative led to the establishment of the Nandan Group of Companies, which has now expanded to over 800 employees and a customer base of over half a million (British-Bangladeshi Youth.net, 2007).

The initiative can be considered a success for two main reasons. Firstly, it delivered commercially viable and profitable projects from the funding of NRBs and, secondly, the initiative was an "eye opener" for all NRBs about the possibilities and benefits of investing profitably in their country of origin. The various projects undertaken by Nandan include the development of a theme park constructed in a 60-*bigha* (approximately 20 acres) property on the outskirts of Dhaka in collaboration with Nicco Park and Resorts, India (Amin, 2004). In addition, a major purpose-built supermarket chain, selling different items ranging from groceries to electronics to clothes to fresh fruits, was constructed in different parts of Dhaka.

Over the years, the Nandan Group has expanded further to include the Nandan Water Park – the largest water park in the country – and Nandan Tea and Fatehbagh Tea, which grows organic tea in Sylhet for export to the U.K. and the U.S. (British-Bangladeshi Youth.net, 2007).

The Nandan Group is now in its eighth year, and though the number of investors over the years has remained stable, as Mr. Choudhury observes, the amount invested by the diaspora group has increased substantially.

Future plans of the Nandan Group include the development of a resort behind the existing Nandan Park. In addition, as part of an attempt to establish a bridge between NRBs in the U.K. and Bangladesh, the Nandan Group has plans to take Bangladeshi investment to the U.K. through the creation of an amusement park in the U.K. built around an Eastern theme. Furthermore, the Nandan Group is considering opening a supermarket in the U.K. to sell Bangladeshi products, including foodstuffs and spices, predominantly for Indian and Bangladeshi restaurants based in the U.K.

The Nandan experience has been a revelation for many NRBs about the possibilities of having profitable links with their home countries. Such opportunities are excellent examples of how beneficial partnerships can be developed between the country of origin and its diaspora.

Source: *IOM Dhaka.*

Immigrants have a natural preference for home products, either because of habit or homesickness. If the products they used to consume at home are not available in the host country, then imports from the home country may increase to meet this demand. Several studies have demonstrated a strong link between trade and migration, in part based on such factors.[21] For migrants to act as trade intermediaries, the intention to return home is critical: their knowledge of trade and investment opportunities at home, ability to enforce contracts through personal contacts at home and specific knowledge about conditions at home deteriorate the longer they are away.

Finally, migrant and diaspora networks can be important partners in development cooperation. Traditionally, governments in developed countries and international organizations have engaged diaspora networks to facilitate the return of migrants by means of diaspora-focused return or circulation programmes,[22] and to assist them in their reintegration in home countries. Examples include the International Organization for Migration's Return of Qualified Nationals programme, which provided much of the inspiration for its Migration for Development in Africa (MIDA) capacity-building programme, or the Transfer of Knowledge Through Expatriate Nationals (TOKTEN) programme of the

[21] See the review of the literature in Xenogiani (2006).

[22] In general, however, voluntary return programmes have induced very few migrants to go home.

United Nations Development Programme (de Haas, 2006).

Recent initiatives have started engaging migrants' networks as development partners in more imaginative ways. That is, the diaspora is viewed as a reservoir not only of financial capital, but of human and social capital as well. In place of encouraging voluntary return (which has had mixed success), diaspora networks are being increasingly mobilized to foster a kind of "virtual return". The IOM's MIDA programme is a case in point. Initiatives of this kind focus on repatriation of skills and resources, but not necessarily of the migrants themselves (see Portrait 12.1). Remittances are among the most important of these resources. In addition to endorsing the idea of government matching funds (like the example of the *Tres por uno* programme in Zacatecas state, Mexico (Iskander, 2005), in which migrant remittances for community investment projects are matched by local, state and federal governments), the European Investment Bank (EIB), for example, recommends that banking systems offer banking services specifically targeted at migrants — including mortgage products, remittance-tailored bank accounts and investments funds — in order to channel remittances into productive investments (de Haas, 2006). Such innovative initiatives promise to promote both household and community investment of remittances in human development.

Portrait 12.1

Entrepreneurship for Development

Thomas was born in Ghana almost 41 years ago. Arriving in Naples in 1988, he soon moved to Modena in northern Italy where, friends had told him, it was easier to find a job. "At first, Italy was a big disappointment. In Ghana we thought that Italy was like paradise: a sunny, friendly place where you could become rich easily. This was not the case, of course. And for us, coming from Africa, the big shock was the fact that winter is cold, that people live indoors and are actually not as friendly as we had been told. But you know, life is not only relationships, nice people and fun, it is also work and commitment. We all need to survive and to carry on. In fact, even if it was not really what I expected, Italy was able to give me the chance to carry on with my own work."

For Thomas, commitment, seriousness and willpower are key to realizing almost everything. Within a few weeks of his arrival in Modena, he started to work for a company specialized in waterproofing. After that, he worked for six years in a metal workshop. In the meantime, he attended language courses and obtained his driving licence. He married in Ghana, and his wife joined him in Modena in 1991. In the years that followed, he changed jobs, and his attitudes to Italy gradually evolved.

"There comes a moment in life when you start to feel different: one day you wake up, you look out of your window and you feel at home. Now I can say that 80 per cent of me wants to stay in Italy and 20 per cent to return to Ghana for good. I have two daughters, they were born here but I have already taken them several times to Ghana. They feel like Italians, but they have not forgotten their African roots".

In 2005 came the big change: he decided to leave his job and become president of Ghanacoop – a challenging and also risky decision. Ghanacoop is a cooperative run by the Ghanaian migrant community in the Province of Modena, set up with the help of the IOM Rome Office's MIDA-Italia (Migration for Development in Africa) Pilot Project.

This initiative started by importing pineapples from small Ghanaian producers to Italy with the aim of enhancing sustainable trading flows of typical Ghanaian produce and consumer goods between Ghanaian migrant associations in Italy and the small producers in Ghana.

The Ghanaian community in Modena counts about 4,000 people, and the initiative of starting an entrepreneurial activity stemmed from the will to make a concrete contribution to the development of the home country and to build the basis for the creation of social enterprises in Ghana. So far, Ghanacoop has proven to be successful; the pineapples imported to Italy, called

Missghananas, are sold in many regions by three leading retailers and will very soon be distributed nationwide. "I work 12 hours a day, but I really believe that it is worthwhile: we are doing something huge for our community and for our homeland as well. The success of Ghanacoop will be of historic importance and significance for the coming generations."

In February 2004, Thomas obtained Italian citizenship. After 20 years, Thomas is now in the midst of a new challenge, but the first, that of integration, has already been won.

Source: *IOM Rome.*

Co-development projects, pioneered by France, while still relatively modest in numbers and scale, include projects in the home countries involving migrants living in developed countries (i.e. business people, academics, health personnel, engineers). Migrants are encouraged to promote commercial activities or implement social development projects (by building schools or health centres), or lend their expertise to their home country. Moreover, the concept of co-development also includes helping migrants to better direct their savings towards productive investments in their countries of origin. This concerns especially the transfer of monies as well as strengthening the capacities of microcredit institutions. As such, an increasing concern to co-development is how to catalyze and amplify the effects of social investments made with remittances (OECD, 2007).

7. Conclusion

Better management of labour migration promises greater gains for migrants, countries of origin and countries of destination. This chapter has explored the potential costs and benefits developing countries should take into account as they seek to gain more from the labour migration and development equation. The chapter has argued that the economic gains from migration depend upon three effects of emigration: changes in labour supply, induced changes in productivity and receipt of remittances. At different points in a country's migration cycle, the relative contribution – positive or negative – of each of these effects differs; so too, the appropriate policies differ at different points in the migration cycle.

The chapter advocates genuine partnerships between destination and origin countries for the latter to gain more from migration. Destination countries bring to such a partnership the commitment to look at their migration policies through a development lens: what is the impact of these policies on migrants' countries of origin? This does not mean subordinating migration policies to the objectives of development cooperation, but rather taking advantage of complementarities between both policy domains. Origin countries, conversely, commit themselves to take a fresh look at their development policies through a migration lens: how does the fact of large-scale emigration change optimal policy decisions in the macroeconomic, human resources, education, infrastructure and regional cooperation spheres? This does not invite origin countries to pursue emigration as a development strategy, but rather to adapt decision-making to the realities of labour mobility.

Destination and origin countries alike must commit themselves to more coherent policymaking, as the labour migration and development equation is affected by a broad range of policies, including trade, agriculture, investment, labour, social security and national security policies – as well as development and immigration/emigration policies. Policy coherence will require new institutional set-ups to facilitate greater information-sharing, negotiation and consensus building across ministries and agencies within governments and, indeed, between governments.

Finally, more effective partnerships for migration management are not just a job for governments. Diaspora networks, with anchors at each end of the migration corridor, can be uniquely effective partners for governments of countries of destination and of origin. They can serve as intermediaries in integration and labour market policies in destination countries, and as partners in development cooperation policies with both destination and origin countries. The private sector, too, has a role to play. Banks and other financial institutions can, if given appropriate incentives, reduce the costs of transferring money back home and increase access to financial services for migrants' families and communities in remote and rural parts of origin countries.

REFERENCES

Adams, R. and J. Page

2005 "Do International Migration and Remittances Reduce Poverty in Developing Countries?" *World Development*, 33: 1645-1669.

Borodak, D.

2006 "Migration et Développement Economique en Moldavie", Unpublished manuscript, Organisation for Economic Co-operation and Development (OECD) Development Centre, Paris.

Burnside, C. and D. Dollar

2004 "Aid, Policies, and Growth: Reply", *The American Economic Review*, 94(3): 781-784.

Clemens, M.

2007 "Do visas kill? Health effects of African health professional emigration", Working Paper No. 114, March, Center for Global Development, Washington, D.C., http://www.cgdev.org/content/publications/detail/13123.

Cogneau, D. and F. Gubert

2005 "Migrations du Sud, pauvreté et développement" in E.M. Mouhoud (Ed.), *Les nouvelles migrations, un enjeu Nord-Sud de la mondialisation*, Editions Universalis, Paris.

Dayton-Johnson, J. and L.T. Katseli

2006a "Migration, Aid and Trade: Policy Coherence for Development", Policy Brief No. 28, OECD Development Centre, Paris, http://www.oecd.org/dataoecd/55/26/37860544.pdf.

2006b "Plus d'aide, moins d'immigration? Une solution en trompe-l'oeil", *Le Monde*, 12 December.

Dayton-Johnson, J. and T. Xenogiani

2006 "Immigration, Development and Policy Trade-offs", paper presented at the Fourth Agence française de développement (AFD)/European Development Network (EUDN) Conference on Migrations and Development: Who benefits?, 8 November, Paris, http://www.eudnet.net/download/Dayton%20Johnson.pdf.

Dayton-Johnson, J., L.T. Katseli, G. Maniatis, R. Münz and D. Papademetriou

2007 *Gaining from Migration: Towards a New Mobility System*, September, OECD Development Centre, Paris.

de Haas, H.

2006 "Engaging Diasporas: How governments and development agencies can support diaspora involvement in the development of origin countries", June, study prepared for Oxfam Novib, The Hague, International Migration Institute (IMI), University of Oxford, http://www.imi.ox.ac.uk/pdfs/engaging-diasporas-hein-de-haas.pdf.

European Commission

2005 *Policy Coherence for Development - Accelerating progress towards attaining the Millennium Development Goals*, COM (2005) 134, 12 April, Brussels.

2006 Joint statement by the Council and the representatives of the governments of the Member States meeting within the Council, the European Parliament and the Commission on European Union Development Policy: "The European Consensus", OJ 2006 C46/1, Brussels.

Faini, R. and A. Venturini

1993 "Trade, Aid and Migrations: Some Basic Policy Issues", *European Economic Review*, 37: 435-442.

Fajnzylber, P. and J.H. López

2007 *Close to Home: The Development Impact of Remittances in Latin America*, The World Bank, Washington, D.C., http://siteresources.worldbank.org/INTLACOFFICEOFCE/Resources/ClosetoHome.pdf.

Hatton, T. and J. Williamson

1998 *The Age of Mass Migration: Causes and Impact*, Oxford University Press, New York.

2002 "What Fundamentals Drive World Migration?", paper presented at the Conference on Poverty, International Migration and Asylum, 27-28 September, Helsinki.

Ionescu, D.

2006 *Engaging Diasporas as Development Partners for Home and Destination Countries: Challenges for Policymakers*, IOM Migration Research Series No. 26, International Organization for Migration (IOM), Geneva, http://www.iom.int/jahia/webdav/site/myjahiasite/shared/shared/mainsite/published_docs/serial_publications/MRS26.pdf.

Iskander, N.

2005 "Social Learning as a Productive Project: The Tres por uno [Three for one] experience at Zacatecas, Mexico", in OECD, *Migration, Remittances and Development*, OECD, Paris, 249-264.

Katseli, L.

2006 "EU Policy Coherence on Security and Development: A New Agenda for Research and Policy Making" in H.G. Brauch (Ed.), *Institutional Security Concepts Revisited for the 21st Century*, ch. 60, Springer Verlag, Berlin.

Katseli, L.T., R.E.B. Lucas and T. Xenogiani

2006a "Effects of Migration on Sending Countries: What Do We Know?", OECD Development Centre Working Paper No. 250, Paris, http://www.oecd.org/dataoecd/24/54/37053726.pdf.

2006b "Policies for Migration and Development: A European Perspective", Policy Brief No. 30, OECD Development Centre, Paris, http://www.oecd.org/dataoecd/55/37/37862315.pdf.

Levy, S.

2006 *Progress against Poverty. Sustaining Mexico's Progresa-Oportunidades Program*, Brookings Institution Press, Washington, D.C.

Lucas, R.E.B.

2006 "Migration and Economic Development in Africa: A Review of Evidence", *Journal of African Economies*, 15(2): 337-395.

Organisation for Economic Co-operation and Development (OECD)

2005 *Migration, Remittances and Development*, OECD, Paris.

2007 *Policy Coherence for Development 2007: Migration and Developing Countries*, OECD Development Centre, Paris.

Ratha, D. and W. Shaw

2007 "South-South Migration and Remittances", Working Paper No. 102, The International Bank for Reconstruction and Development/ The World Bank, Washington, D.C., http://siteresources.worldbank.org/INTPROSPECTS/Resources/334934-1110315015165/SouthSouthMigrationandRemittances.pdf.

Ratha, D., S. Mohapatra, K.M. Vijayalakshmi and Z. Xu

2007 "Remittance Trends 2007", Migration and Development Brief 3, Migration and Remittances Team, Development Prospects Group, The World Bank, Washington, D.C., http://siteresources.worldbank.org/EXTDECPROSPECTS/Resources/476882-1157133580628/BriefingNote3.pdf.

Rindoks, A., R. Penninx and J. Rath

2006 "What works in networks? Examining economically related benefits accrued from greater economic linkages, migration processes and diasporas", Unpublished manuscript, Institute for Migration and Ethnic Studies (IMES), University of Amsterdam, OECD Development Centre, Paris.

Spencer, S. and B. Cooper

2006 "Social Integration of Migrants in Europe: A Review of the European Literature 2000 – 2006", 28 September, COMPAS, University of Oxford/OECD Development Centre, Paris, http://www.compas.ox.ac.uk/publications/papers/Spencer%20Literature%20Review.pdf.

Stark, O. and J.E. Taylor

1991 "Migration Incentives, Migration Types: The Role of Relative Deprivation", *The Economic Journal*, 101: 1163-1178.

Suwa-Eisenmann, A. and T. Verdier

2006 "The Coherence of Trade Flows and Trade Policies with Aid and Investment Flows: A Background Paper", OECD Development Centre Working Paper No. 254, August, Paris, http://www.oecd.org/dataoecd/9/63/37450734.pdf.

Sweden

2003 *Shared Responsibility: Sweden's Policy for Global Development*, Government Bill 2002/03:122, 15 May, http://www.regeringen.se/content/1/c6/02/45/20/c4527821.pdf.

United Nations Development Programme (UNDP)

2007 *Informe sobre desarrollo humano México 2006-2007, Programa de las Naciones Unidas para el Desarrollo*, UNDP, Mexico City.

Vogler, M. and R. Rotte

2000 "The Effects of Development on Migration: Theoretical Issues and New Empirical Evidence", *Journal of Population Economics*, 13: 485-508.

World Bank

1998 *Assessing Aid: What Works, What Doesn't, and Why*, November, Policy Research Report, Development Research Group, The World Bank, Washington, D.C., http://www-wds.worldbank.org/external/default/WDSContentServer/IW3P/IB/2000/02/23/000094946_99030406212262/Rendered/PDF/multi_page.pdf.

2006 *Global Economic Prospects 2006: Economic Implications of Remittances and Migration*, The World Bank, Washington, D.C., http://econ.worldbank.org/WBSITE/EXTERNAL/EXTDEC/EXTDECPROSPECTS/GEPEXT/EXTGEP2006/0,,menuPK:1026834~pagePK:64167702~piPK:64167676~theSitePK:1026804,00.html.

Xenogiani, T.

2006 "Migration Policy and its Interactions with Aid, Trade and Foreign Direct Investment Policies: A Background Paper", OECD Development Centre Working Paper No. 249, June, Paris, http://www.oecd.org/dataoecd/60/28/37036220.pdf.

Textbox 12.3 - Challenges in Assessing the Economic Impacts of Migration and Remittances

McKenzie, D. and M. Sasin

2007 "Migration, Remittances, Poverty and Human Capital: Conceptual and empirical challenges", MOVe Operational Notes 1, The World Bank, Washington, D.C.

McKenzie, D., J. Gibson and S. Stillman

2006 "How Important is Selection? Experimental versus Non-Experimental Measures of the Income Gains from Migration", World Bank Policy Research Working Paper 3906, May, Washington, D.C., http://www-wds.worldbank.org/external/default/WDSContentServer/IW3P/IB/2006/05/01/000016406_20060501143118/Rendered/PDF/wps3906.pdf.

Textbox 12.4 - Diaspora Linkage in Development: A Bangladesh Case

Amin, K.S.

2004 "Water World in Nandan Park Opens", Aviatour: Internet Edition, http://www.weeklyholiday.net/300504/aviatour.html#top.

British-Bangladeshi Youth.net

2007 "4th Dialogue on Transnationalism and Development Opportunities and Challenges of NRB Investment: Experiences of the Nandan Group", British-Bangladeshi Youth.net, http://www.bbyouth.net/dialogues4.php.

de Bruyn, T. and U. Kuddus

2005 *Dynamics of Remittance Utilization in Bangladesh*, IOM Migration Research Series No. 18, IOM, Geneva, http://www.iom.org.bd/images/publications/Dynamics_of_Remittance_Utilization_in_Bangladesh.pdf.

Ionescu, D.

2006 *Engaging Diasporas as Development Partners for Home and Destination Countries: Challenges for Policymakers*, IOM Migration Research Series No. 26, IOM, Geneva, http://www.iom.int/jahia/webdav/site/myjahiasite/shared/shared/mainsite/published_docs/serial_publications/MRS26.pdf.

Knights, M.

1996 "Bangladeshi immigrants in Italy: from geopolitics to micropolitics", *Transactions of the Institute of British Geographers*, 21(1) (March): 105-123.

Siddiqui, T.

2004 *Institutionalising Diaspora Linkage: The Emigrant Bangladeshis in UK and USA*, Ministry of Expatriates' Welfare and Overseas Employment/Government of Bangladesh and IOM, February, IOM, Dhaka, http://www.iom.org.bd/images/publications/Institutionalising_Diaspora_Linkage_The_Emigrant_Bangladesh.pdf.

2005a "Introduction" in T. Siddiqui (Ed.), *Migration and Development: Pro Poor Policy Choices*, The University Press Limited, Dhaka.

2005b "International Migration as a Livelihood Strategy of the Poor: The Bangladesh Case" in T. Siddiqui (Ed.), *Migration and Development: Pro Poor Policy Choices*, The University Press Limited, Dhaka.

Zeitlyn, B.

2006 "Migration from Bangladesh to Italy and Spain", Occasional Paper for the South Asia Migration Resource Network (SAMReN) and the Refugee and Migratory Movements Research Unit (RMMRU), June, Dhaka, http://www.samren.org/Fellowships/papers/Beji.pdf.

ACHIEVING BEST OUTCOMES FROM GLOBAL, REGIONAL AND BILATERAL COOPERATION*

CHAPTER 13

1. Introduction

Migration is by its very nature a transnational process. No country can claim to be in a position to respond to and manage these movements on its own, all the more so since the policies of other countries influence migration flows and the effectiveness of domestic policies. The awareness of the ineffectiveness of unilateral actions, increased diversity of migratory routes and patterns of flows (cutting across regions and continents; reacting to changes in external factors such as immigration policies, economic situations and employment opportunities), and interlinkages with other global issues such as trade, development and human rights have increasingly led states to acknowledge the need for international cooperation in migration management.

However, states have generally been reluctant to translate this growing awareness into concrete action by accepting trade-offs between sovereignty and international regulatory mechanisms. Progress has mainly occurred at the regional and bilateral levels, where common interests between countries of origin and destination are more easily identified and mutual benefits worked out. But even at these levels, the general tendency has been to engage in informal, as opposed to legal or more formal means of cooperation.

Among the main obstacles to entering into binding legal frameworks on migration are the divergences of opinion on the respective merits of liberalizing or restricting migration flows; administrative and financial burdens of adapting national frameworks; concerns about limiting the state's capacity to intervene because of the nature and extent of the rights to be granted to migrant workers and, especially, to irregular migrants; the diverging views between countries of origin and destination regarding the categories of workers to be given access to domestic labour markets, e.g. skilled, low-skilled or both; and, perhaps most importantly, the general preference for a high degree of flexibility in determining national migration policy.

This chapter provides an overview of the formal and less formal mechanisms in place for managing labour mobility at the multilateral, regional and bilateral levels, with a particular focus on temporary migration for employment, and considers their respective advantages and disadvantages in practice.

* This chapter has been written by Sophie Nonnenmacher, Migration Policy Specialist, Migration Policy, Research and Communications, IOM, Geneva.

2. Multilateral Approaches

Although a limited number of instruments cover specific aspects of cross-border mobility for economic purposes, there are no comprehensive global agreements or international conventions in place to manage temporary labour migration.

2.1 ILO and UN Conventions

The International Labour Organization (ILO) has adopted two conventions (Nos. 97 and 143) and two accompanying non-binding recommendations (Nos. 86 and 151) applying to persons moving from one country to another for the purpose of employment.[1] The first convention and its accompanying recommendation, adopted in 1949, focus on setting standards for the recruitment of migrant workers and their conditions of work, while the two other instruments, adopted in 1975 in the wake of the oil crisis, reflect a growing concern about the resulting increase in unemployment, and emphasize the need to prevent irregular migration and the unauthorized employment of migrants (ILO, 2004). Both conventions cover issues related to the entire migration process and provide for equal treatment between lawfully resident migrant workers and nationals. Convention No. 143 obliges states parties to respect the basic human rights of **all** migrant workers and also provides for equal treatment between irregular and regular workers in respect of rights arising out of past employment, such as remuneration, social security and other benefits.[2] Both conventions exclude certain categories of workers from their scope, such as the self-employed, seafarers, frontier workers, and artistes and members of liberal professions who have entered the country on a short-term basis. In addition, Convention No. 143 excludes students and trainees and temporary workers sent by their employer to perform specific duties or assignments in the destination country from its Part II on equality of opportunity and treatment.

In its 2004 report *Towards a fair deal for migrant workers in the global economy*, the ILO recognizes that international labour standards "were not drafted with the protection of temporary migrant workers in mind and the provisions applicable to other lawfully admitted migrant workers may not always be well suited to their situation" (ILO, 2004: 89). For example, while movements of temporary workers who are sent by their employers to perform a specific duty or assignment for a limited period of time are increasing and are the subject of discussion under Mode 4 of the World Trade Organization's General Agreement on Trade in Services (GATS),[3] as noted above, such workers are excluded from the provisions on equality of opportunity and treatment in Part II of Convention No. 143,[4] together with artistes and members of the liberal professions who have entered the country on a short-term basis.[5] In addition, these instruments do not adequately reflect the increasing role of private actors in the world of work and international mobility for employment, in particular of private employment agencies. This trend led to

[1] See respectively: Convention No. 97 concerning Migration for Employment (Revised 1949); Convention No. 143 concerning Migrations in Abusive Conditions and the Promotion of Equality of Opportunity and Treatment of Migrant Workers (1975); Recommendation No. 86 concerning Migration for Employment (Revised 1949); and Recommendation No. 151 concerning Migrant Workers (1975). These instruments can be accessed from the ILO website at http://www.ilo.org/global/What_we_do/InternationalLabourStandards/lang--en/index.htm.

[2] Articles 1 and 9(1) respectively.

[3] See Textbox Int. 1.

[4] Part II is also concerned with, inter alia, the obligation of a state to facilitate family reunion (Art 13), the right to free choice of employment and geographical mobility (Art 14(a)), as well as to recognition of qualifications (Art 14(b)).

[5] But "project-tied" (Article 2(2)(f)) and "specified-employment" workers (Article 2(2)(g)) are covered in the 1990 UN Migrant Workers Convention, discussed below, subject to some limitations (see Part V). The identification of gaps in international standards related to the protection of seasonal workers, project-tied workers, special purpose workers, cross-border service providers, students and trainees resulted in the adoption by the ILO of "Guidelines on special protective measures for migrant workers in time-bound activities" covering such issues as housing, tied employment, wages and other terms of employment, family migration and reunification, freedom of association, social security and return issues for regular migrants during its Tripartite Meeting of Experts on Future ILO Activities in the Field of Migration, 21-25 April 1997 (Doc. MEIM/1997/d.4, Annex I).

the adoption by the ILO in 1997 of Convention No. 181 concerning Private Employment Agencies.[6]

In 1990, the UN adopted the International Convention on the Protection of the Rights of All Migrant Workers and Members of Their Families, which represents an important step towards the more effective protection of the rights of migrant workers and their families by providing in a single instrument a comprehensive set of standards for the protection of all migrant workers, including migrants in an irregular situation (Part III), and more extensive safeguards for regular migrant workers (Parts IV and V) (see Textbox 13.1),[7] including categories of workers not covered by ILO Conventions Nos. 97 and 143 (i.e. seafarers, frontier workers and the self-employed). The UN Convention is more detailed and specific regarding the rights of **temporary** migrant workers than are the ILO Conventions.[8] Nonetheless, the UN Convention underlines in explicit terms that it does not interfere with the sovereign competence of states to design their own rules on the admission of foreigners. Article 79 stipulates that "nothing in the present convention shall affect the right of each state to establish the criteria governing admission of migrant workers and members of their families".

[6] Convention No. 181 contains provisions for preventing abuses of migrant workers in the placement and recruitment processes; e.g. Article 7 states: "Private employment agencies shall not charge directly or indirectly, in whole or in part, any fees or costs to workers." To date, the Convention has received 20 ratifications.

[7] Part IV provides for additional rights to all lawfully resident migrant workers, except as otherwise provided for in Part V (limitations can be applied to seasonal workers (Art. 59), itinerant migrant workers (Art. 60), project-tied migrant workers (Art. 61) and specified-employment workers (Art. 62)).

[8] However, ILO offers potentially better protection to seasonal migrant workers, itinerant migrant workers, technically unqualified project-tied migrant workers, whose rights can be limited according to Part V of the UN Convention, and to students and trainees not covered by the latter (Böhning, 2003).

Textbox 13.1

The International Convention on the Protection of the Rights of All Migrant Workers and Members of Their Families*

The Convention, which came into force on 1 July 2003, establishes minimum standards for migrant workers and members of their families. As of September 2008, 39 countries had ratified the Convention.

Article 2(1) of the Convention defines a migrant worker as "a person who is to be engaged, is engaged or has been engaged in a remunerated activity in a state of which he or she is not a national". It should be noted that the protection provided under the Convention can be invoked not only in the country of employment, but already before departure in the country of origin, during the travel in the country of transit and again upon return in the country of origin.

The Convention distinguishes between migrants who are either in a regular or in an irregular situation. All migrant workers enjoy basic human rights, including irregular migrants, while additional rights are foreseen for regular or documented migrant workers. Parties to the Convention are under an obligation not to discriminate against migrant workers on the grounds of sex, race, colour, language, religion or conviction, political or other opinion, national, ethnic or social origin, nationality, age, economic position, property, marital status, birth or other status (Part II, Article 7).

One of the more interesting features of the Convention is contained in Part VI, which calls for the promotion of humane conditions of migration.[1] States parties undertake to cooperate with each other and maintain appropriate services, such as the exchange of information and assistance, recruitment of migrant workers, orderly return of migrant workers and members of their families, prevention and elimination of illegal and clandestine movements, and employment of migrant workers in an irregular situation.

Concerning labour mobility, of most relevance are the rights of documented migrant workers set out in Part IV of the Convention.[2] Part IV includes not only the right of migrant workers and members of their families to be fully informed by the state of origin or of employment, as appropriate, of all conditions applicable to their admission (particularly concerning their stay and the remunerated activities in which they may engage), but they also have the right to be fully informed of the terms on which temporary absences from the state of employment are authorized and which the state is required to make every effort to provide to them without this adversely affecting their right to remain or work.[3] In addition, Part IV includes the obligation for the state to take measures to avoid double taxation of migrants' earnings and savings, as well as the right of migrant workers to equal (national) treatment in the host country in such fields as access to vocational training and placement services, exemption from import and export duties for household effects and professional equipment, and the transfer and repatriation of their earnings and savings.

Part III of the Convention concerns the rights of all migrant workers and members of their families, including those in an irregular situation, and establishes the right to equality with nationals of the country of employment regarding wages and working conditions (Article 25). The aim of this provision, as set out in the Preamble, is not only to ensure humane and decent working conditions for migrant workers, but also to discourage the employment of undocumented workers by removing any inducement for employers to hire such labour.

The Convention's monitoring body, the Committee on the Protection of the Rights of All Migrant Workers and Members of Their Families (Committee on Migrant Workers), commenced its work in 2004 and started to examine the reports submitted by states parties to the Convention at its 4th Session in April 2006. In its first observations on the reports, the Committee emphasized the need for cooperation to effectively combat illegal or clandestine movements of migrants, and paid special attention to the particular vulnerability of women and children, as well as domestic and agricultural migrant workers.

On the occasion of the High-Level Dialogue on International Migration and Development, held at the General Assembly of the United Nations in September 2006, the Committee organized a "Day of General Discussion on Protecting the Rights of all Migrant Workers as a Tool to Enhance Development".[4] It then adopted a written statement highlighting the human-rights based approach to migration and emphasized the shared responsibility of all states to guarantee the human rights of migrants, as well as the importance of international consultations and cooperation in order to promote and ensure humane conditions of migration.

Notes:

[*] Adopted by UN General Assembly Resolution 45/158 of 18 December 1990. The Convention entered into force on 1 July 2003.

[1] Part VI: Promotion of sound, equitable, humane and lawful conditions in connection with international migration of workers and members of their families.

[2] Part IV: Other rights of migrant workers and members of their families who are documented or in a regular situation.

[3] Articles 37 and 38, respectively.

[4] See http://www2.ohchr.org/english/bodies/cmw/mwdiscussion.htm.

Source: *Carla Edelenbos, Secretary, Migrant Workers Committee, Office of the United Nations High Commissioner for Human Rights, Geneva.*

All these instruments recognize the importance of interstate cooperation in addressing labour migration. ILO Conventions Nos. 97 and 143 contain provisions on the exchange of information on national policies, laws and regulations. The UN Convention (in Part VI) requests states parties to consult and cooperate with the competent authorities of other states parties on measures regarding the orderly return of migrants. Both the UN Convention and ILO Convention No. 143 also envisage interstate cooperation to suppress clandestine movements of migrants for employment and to act against organizers of irregular migration and the unauthorized employment of migrant workers.

The exact form of cooperation is not prescribed and it is for the states parties to determine. However the drafters were of the view that, while general principles or standards can be spelled out at the multilateral level, the differences in situations and legal frameworks between countries call for more specific, complementary modes of cooperation at other levels of operation. The ILO Conventions refer to bilateral agreements as an appropriate means of putting general principles into practice, and Recommendation No. 86 of 1949, provides, in an Annex, for a model bilateral agreement covering the different stages of the migration process which includes a model contract for employment (Article 22). The model agreement also recommends the conclusion of separate bilateral agreements with respect to social security.[9] The UN Convention acknowledges, in its Preamble, the progress made in bilateral and multilateral regional agreements towards the protection of the rights of migrant workers, and their importance and usefulness, and also specifies in Article 81(1)(b) that nothing in the Convention shall affect more favourable rights granted to migrant workers and members of their families by virtue of any bilateral or multilateral treaty in force for the state party concerned.

However, these instruments have been ratified by a limited number of states only[10] and, in so far as the UN Convention is concerned, by no major developed destination country.[11]

[9] Migrant workers can face difficulties in benefiting from social security provision as such systems are generally based on contributions and the period of employment or residence (see also Chapter 11). Social security provides another illustration of complementarity between multilateral and bilateral approaches. While ILO Convention No. 157 of 1982 on the Maintenance of Social Security Rights and its accompanying Recommendation No. 167 provide an international framework for the maintenance of acquired rights or rights in the course of acquisition by workers who change their country of residence, they recommend the conclusion of bilateral and multilateral agreements and the Recommendation contains model provisions for such agreements.

[10] ILO Convention Nos. 97 and 143 have been ratified by 48 and 23 states, including both countries of origin and destination, respectively, and the UN Convention has been ratified by 39 states (as of September 2008).

[11] Two destination countries, which have ratified the UN Convention, are Argentina and Libya. Important transit countries that have ratified include Libya, Mexico and Morocco. For obstacles cited by governments to ratification of the ILO Conventions on migrant workers, see ILO (1999). For obstacles relevant to the UN Convention, see the country and regional reports commissioned by UNESCO on the webpage of the UNESCO Project on the International Migrants' Rights Convention at http://portal.unesco.org/shs/en/ev.php-URL_ID=6554&URL_DO=DO_TOPIC&URL_SECTION=201.html.

2.2 General Agreement on Trade in Services (GATS)

The GATS provides for the liberalization of trade in services. Under Mode 4, the GATS offers a multilateral framework for negotiations,[12] with a set of principles (covering domestic regulations, transparency requirements and other issues) designed to facilitate the movement of service providers. However, the GATS does not create universal criteria for the admission of defined categories of service providers and their access to labour markets. Indeed, it does not provide a definition of service providers nor does it prescribe the range, depth or sectoral coverage of country commitments. Inclusion of individual sectors within the GATS schedules is at the discretion of WTO Member States, which must define the commitment they are prepared to make on market access and national treatment on a sector-by-sector basis. States can also make "horizontal commitments", i.e. cross-sectoral commitments given by Member States for market access (e.g. categories of stay, duration of stay, and conditions of entry and compliance by natural persons). Moreover, the GATS does not require its members to offer market access or conditions that are more liberal than those in national policy settings. Departures from market access and national treatment are not prohibited per se under the GATS, but must be identified in schedules as limitations.[13] Therefore, each party defines in its commitments the category of service providers to be granted freer access and, to date, these commitments reflect merely what is already permitted under existing immigration policies.[14]

[12] See the WTO's website at http://www.wto.org/english/tratop_e/serv_e/gatsqa_e.htm#14 (GATS: objectives, coverage and disciplines).

[13] Limitations to market access can take the form of quota restrictions and economic needs or labour market tests, including wage parity requirements (for a fuller description of these mechanisms, see Chapter 11).

[14] Current commitments focus mainly on the highly skilled, such as executive managers and professionals. These categories usually already enjoy quite liberal access in national immigration admission policies (see Chapter 2), while lower-skilled migrants have fewer or no possibilities to enter the country (see Chapter 3).

Each party also determines its own admission criteria. The only limitation to a member's competence to regulate the entry and temporary stay of natural persons within its borders is the obligation to ensure that such measures are not applied in such a way as to nullify or impair the benefits accruing to another.[15] However, some members would like to see the scope of the GATS expanded with the adoption of multilateral rules in the area of admission (such as a standard GATS visa) (Winters, 2005). Other commentators take this idea one step further and would like WTO to monitor and/or participate in the allocation of visas concerning the movement of natural persons.[16] The proposed inclusion of migration management issues within WTO competences is highly controversial and probably unlikely to secure the support of all WTO Member States as required for an amendment of its mandate.[17]

A further contentious aspect is that GATS Mode 4, as a trade agreement, focuses only on one aspect of the migration process, namely the entry and access of service providers, and does not refer to social and labour standards, such as the quality of working conditions for service providers. The argument usually advanced in this context is that the WTO is a trade body and therefore not the appropriate forum to set social or labour standards for the protection of workers worldwide. However, this question is present in the negotiations in an oblique fashion through the notification of limitations to market access in countries' schedules. Indeed, over 50 WTO members stipulate in their commitments that they require wage parity. In addition, 22 members have reserved the right to suspend Mode 4 commitments in the event of labour-management disputes with a view to precluding employers from hiring foreigners as "strike-breakers" (to replace national workers) (Dommen, 2005). A number of recent regional and bilateral trade agreements also contain explicit references to social issues or core labour standards, either in the text of the agreement or, indirectly, through side agreements on labour cooperation.[18] These provisions do not generally secure any particular labour protection for migrant workers and/or service providers, but they can benefit from broader requirements, such as the obligation to enforce domestic labour standards in a non-discriminatory manner.[19] From a legal point of view, however, these provisions and/or their enforcement mechanisms appear to remain generally weak.

Would it be possible to include a social clause in the GATS to ensure respect for core labour standards (such as non-discrimination in the payment of wages) at the multilateral level? Those in favour of such a clause argue that it will protect local workers from "social dumping", whereas those against express the view that it will reduce the advantage for a country in being involved in recruiting/sending workers abroad. However, to date, it seems that there are no strong voices to advance this issue apart from those of trade unions and some NGOs (GURN, 2007).

While multilateral trade negotiations stalled at Cancun in September 2003, and no significant progress was made in Hong Kong SAR in December 2006, the number of bilateral and regional trade agreements and negotiations has been growing, reigniting a debate about whether such regional

---

[15] GATS, Annex on movement of natural persons supplying services under the Agreement. See http://www.wto.org/english/tratop_e/serv_e/8-anmvnt_e.htm.

[16] See e.g. Ng and Whalley (2007), who envisage this possibility for the WTO or a new international body.

[17] However, some commentators argue that visas already fall within the GATS Mode 4 mandate as they can be part of "measures" referred to in the Annex on the movement of natural persons.

[18] The U.S.-CAFTA-D.R. (U.S.-Central America-Dominican Republic Free Trade Agreement) and the U.S.-Chile Free Trade Agreement (FTA) include commitments to core labour standards (except for the ILO core conventions on discrimination and equal remuneration). In parallel to the Canada–Costa Rica FTA, there is also an agreement on labour cooperation (Canada-Costa Rica Agreement on Labour Cooperation (CCRALC) signed in April 2001). In this agreement, the parties are obliged to embody in their labour legislation the principles enshrined in the 1998 ILO Declaration on Fundamental Principles and Rights at Work and to enforce this legislation effectively (ICFTU, 2004).

[19] E.g. the 11th Principle of the North American Agreement on Labour Cooperation under the North American Free Trade Agreement (NAFTA) provides migrant workers on a state party's territory with the same legal protection as that provided to the state party's nationals in respect of working conditions.

and/or bilateral agreements complement multilateral trade agreements, or undermine them (Brown et al., 2005; ICFTU, 2004; see also Textbox 13.7 at the end of this chapter).

2.3 Other International Instruments

There are a number of other binding international legal instruments of relevance to labour migration. They can be divided into two broad categories: instruments indirectly and directly related to migration. Under the first category are human rights treaties protecting the fundamental rights of all migrant workers as human beings (the two International Covenants on Civil and Political Rights, and Economic, Social and Cultural Rights, 1966), as women (International Convention on the Elimination of All Forms of Discrimination against Women, 1979), as children (Convention on the Rights of the Child, 1989) and as foreigners (Migrant Workers Convention, 1990).[20] Like any other workers, migrants are also covered by ILO international labour standards.[21] Under the second category, it is necessary to mention the 2000 UN Convention against Transnational Organized Crime and its two protocols addressing trafficking in human beings and smuggling of migrants.[22]

2.4 Non-binding Initiatives

In addition, a number of non-binding initiatives have been taken or are taking place at the multilateral level with a view to fostering dialogue and effective practices in managing labour migration, either by focusing exclusively on this objective or as part of a broader migration agenda. Focusing on the protection of the human and labour rights of migrants, in 1999 the UN Commission on Human Rights (now the Human Rights Council) established the mandate of the UN Special Rapporteur on the human rights of migrants,[23] who has since issued a number of reports focusing specifically on migrant workers and conducted several country visits. In 2006, the ILO Governing Body endorsed the non-binding Multilateral Framework on Labour Migration (ILO, 2006), which comprises principles and guidelines promoting a rights-based approach to labour migration, and provides guidance to governments, and employers' and workers' organizations on the formulation and implementation of national and international policies (see Textbox 10.6).[24] IOM's International Dialogue on Migration (IDM) offers a platform for its Membership to exchange information and effective practices in the formulation and implementation of migration policy.[25] An International Agenda for Migration Management (IAMM), published in December 2005, was the outcome of the Berne Initiative, a states-owned process sponsored by the Swiss Government and for which IOM provided the Secretariat (IOM/Swiss Federal Office for Migration, 2005a). More recently, and as discussed in the Introduction and Chapter 12, the international community has been preoccupied with the theme of international migration and development, which includes an important labour mobility component.[26]

20 See also here the Vienna Convention on Consular Relations, 1963.

21 The 1998 ILO Declaration on Fundamental Principles and Rights at Work requires ILO Member States to respect four categories of principles and rights at work, even if they are not signatories to the relevant conventions: freedom of association and rights of collective bargaining, equality of opportunity and treatment, abolition of forced labour, and the elimination of child labour.

22 Protocol to Prevent, Suppress and Punish Trafficking in Persons, Especially Women and Children, and Protocol Against the Smuggling of Migrants by Land, Sea and Air. These Protocols were adopted at Palermo on 15 November 2000 and, as of September 2008, have been ratified by 123 and 114 states, respectively. See also Chapter 8.

23 For more information on the Special Rapporteur's work, see the website of the Office of the UN High Commissioner for Human Rights at http://www2.ohchr.org/english/issues/migration/rapporteur/index.htm.

24 The Framework focuses on areas such as inter alia decent work, international cooperation, the effective management of migration and the protection of migrant workers.

25 See the IDM webpages at http://www.iom.int/jahia/Jahia/lang/en/pid/385 for the recent themes addressed. For example, in 2007 the overarching theme of the IDM, "Migration Management in the Evolving Global Economy", was closely tied to the subject matter of this Report and a workshop was convened on 8-9 October on Global Making Labour Mobility a Catalyst for Development. See http://www.iom.int/jahia/Jahia/pid/1826.

26 See the UN General Assembly's High-Level Dialogue on International Migration and Development (New York, September 2006) and the Global Forum on Migration and Development (GFMD) (Brussels, July 2007). For an overview of labour mobility in the context of the GFMD, see Textbox Int. 2.

Other elements for the management of labour migration are scattered throughout many legal instruments, and are at the heart of several non-binding initiatives of various international agencies. For this reason, in order to increase efficiency, policy consistency and to pool available expertise, the Global Commission on International Migration (GCIM)[27] considered in its October 2005 final report, as a longer-term option, the possible establishment of a global agency in charge of the portfolio of "economic migration" (GCIM, 2005), which is a concept that goes beyond labour migration per se and includes other movements for economic purposes, such as business travel and family migration, that are also discussed in Part A of this Report. Such an agency would have a leading role in developing linkages between the migration sphere and related domains, such as development, trade, security and human rights.

3. Regional Approaches

Although labour migration flows are becoming geographically more diverse, the largest share of labour movement is taking place within regions. It is therefore not surprising that regional initiatives to facilitate and manage these flows are flourishing. Regional processes tend to be more efficient than global ones because small groups of countries can more easily tackle emigration and immigration dynamics and reach a common understanding for cooperation, harmonization of policies and liberalization of labour movements. On regional agendas, labour migration is typically dealt with in conjunction with issues such as visa policies, return and readmission, border management and, increasingly, migration and development.

The achievements to date towards the liberalization of labour markets, the increase in the categories of workers eligible to move to another country to work, the streamlining of procedures, the granting of permanent migration opportunities and access to family reunion, nonetheless, vary tremendously. Some of the progress results from the drive towards economic integration, which has led to formal labour-migration related agreements being inscribed in the regulatory framework for common markets and free trade agreements. While the evaluation of regional consultative processes is difficult to conduct on account of their informal and non-binding character, they have undoubtedly been helpful in strengthening interstate cooperation in the management of international migration.

3.1 Regional Economic Integration and Worker Mobility

Based on current and past experiences of regional integration, the following four preliminary conclusions may be drawn with respect to labour mobility at the regional level:

- Labour migration policy agendas are generally more ambitious when drafted within the framework of the establishment or further development of common markets than under the auspices of free trade agreement initiatives, for example, the European Union (EU) as compared to the North American Free Trade Agreement (NAFTA).
- Positive results are more likely to be reached when progress on migration issues can advance projects in other policy areas of interest to countries in the region.
- Efforts to remove barriers to labour mobility are more likely to succeed when the process of economic integration is already well under way; they are less likely to succeed when presented as a potential engine for progress towards regional integration. For example, compare the difficulties in the implementation of the Common Market for Eastern and Southern Africa (COMESA) Protocol on Free Movement of Persons, Labour, Services and the Right of Establishment, and the delays in the

[27] The GCIM was created in 2003 as an ad hoc body with the approval of the UN Secretary-General and with the mandate to propose the framework for the formulation of a coherent, comprehensive and global response to international migration. For a fuller description of its mandate, see the GCIM's website at http://www.gcim.org/en/.

full implementation of the Economic Community of West African States (ECOWAS) Protocol on Free Movement of Persons, Establishment and Settlement (see Textbox 13.2) with the EU example where the liberalization of worker mobility was treated as a cornerstone of economic integration.

- Agreements between countries sharing geographical proximity, similar levels of development and limited (current and potential) labour migration flows are generally more liberal with respect to the movement of people (e.g. the Common Nordic Labour Market, which contains even more favourable free movement and residence provisions than those operating in the European Union. However, the Common Market of the South (MERCOSUR) and the Andean Community in South America present a different experience in that there have been limited initiatives among neighbouring countries to liberalize the movement of persons (Santestevan, 2007).

Textbox 13.2

Prospects for Greater Labour Mobility within ECOWAS/West Africa

Historically, migrants have always regarded West Africa as an economic unit within which trade in goods and services flowed and people moved freely. Colonial administrators recruited, attracted or coerced workers from the hinterlands to work on the infrastructure and development projects in coastal areas. Over time, labour migration became voluntary and institutionalized.

Independence changed all that as new national governments enacted laws and regulations governing conditions of entry, residence and employment of non-nationals. These regulations and indigenization laws restricted the participation of non-nationals in major economic activities and distinguished between regular and irregular movements.

The Economic Community of West African States (ECOWAS) Protocol on Free Movement of Persons, Establishment and Settlement is a pacesetter in Africa. The implementation of the initial phase over the first five years abolished requirements for visas and entry permits, enabling Community citizens in possession of valid travel documents to enter Member States without a visa for up to 90 days. However, the second and third phases have not yet been fully implemented.

The Meeting of Heads of State and Government, in Abuja, Nigeria, in March 2000, had as its major agenda item the creation of a borderless sub-region in a determined effort to invigorate the faltering implementation of various aspects of the Protocol. Henceforth, immigration officials are to accord the maximum 90-day period of stay to ECOWAS citizens at the entry point. Residence permit requirements for Community citizens were abolished. The ECOWAS travel certificate and subsequently the ECOWAS passport should progressively replace national passports in circulation over a transitional period of ten years. Rigid border formalities were to be eliminated and border procedures modernized through the use of passport scanning machines to facilitate the free and easier movement of persons across borders. ECOWAS travellers' cheques and a common currency – the West African Unit of Account – were proposed to harmonize monetary policy. All these and other measures helped facilitate ongoing and new patterns of labour migration, especially to Nigeria and Côte d'Ivoire, the sub-region's demographic and economic giants, as well as to Ghana and Senegal.

Yet, countries in West Africa have retained national laws and treaties and investment codes that are at variance with the ECOWAS Protocol and, in effect, restrict "foreigners", including nationals of Community states, from participating in certain kinds of economic activity. During periods of economic and political crises, non-nationals become scapegoats and have been expelled, as occurred in Nigeria in 1983 and 1985, and in Côte d'Ivoire in 2000, situations that shook the Community. Many citizens do not have access to national passports, and only very few have obtained ECOWAS travel certificates and passports, owing in large part to bureaucratic bottlenecks. Many also enter Member States, and then overstay or work without authorization.

The labour migration system in West Africa is quite complex. Countries that were once destinations for migrants have metamorphosed into countries of origin. Since the late 1980s, traditional countries of origin and attractive destinations for migrants have experienced endemic political and economic crises, as a consequence of which there have been outflows from both sets of countries.

ECOWAS Member States are searching for policies that would enhance the prospects for greater labour mobility in the sub-region, and priorities for action include:

- The establishment of a Permanent Observatory to provide up-to-date information on labour migration patterns and facilitate internal labour mobility within ECOWAS with limited travel documentation.
- The setting up and/or revamping of an Advisory Board on Migration as a forum for formulating and monitoring the status of implementation of national laws and ECOWAS decisions relating to labour migration.
- Raising migration discourse to the top of the political agenda, showcasing the potential contribution of migrant workers to development and underlining the positive outcomes of migration for migrants and countries of origin and destination.
- Harmonizing national laws and employment codes that regulate the types of economic activity that nationals of Community Member States can practice according to the terms of the ECOWAS Protocol on Free Movement of Persons, Establishment and Settlement.
- Concretely addressing the right of residence and establishment of migrants and obligations of the host countries, and ensuring that the rights of migrant workers in the host countries are protected.
- Enhancing capacity of immigration, customs, police and security officials to help transform their role into that of migration managers, assisting to facilitate rather than restrict regular migration within the sub-region. Officials have to be sensitized to the revised national laws and treaties and ECOWAS protocols.
- Mounting an intensive and sustained public education campaign to raise awareness of the ECOWAS passport and travel certificate and its benefits to Community citizens for travel within the sub-region and also to help halt hostility against migrant workers.
- Promoting student exchange and study programmes to help break language and colonial barriers among countries and peoples, and promoting labour migration and more effective utilization of human resources.
- Promoting access of Community nationals to employment and settlement, and easing remitting of earned income through formal banking channels.
- Harmonizing and implementing the policies of trade, investment, transport and movement of persons in a coherent and integrated manner.

Source: *Aderanti Adepoju, Coordinator, Network of Migration Research on Africa (NOMRA) and Chief Executive, Human Resources Development Centre (HRDC), Lagos, Nigeria.*

The European Union represents the most far-reaching form of regional economic integration, and its principal characteristics are discussed below. The right of free movement of workers within the region was introduced by the 1957 Treaty of Rome and expanded to include the free movement of all EU citizens in 1993.[28] The EU has succeeded in creating an area where **all** workers who are nationals of EU Member States are entitled to equal treatment regardless of their nationality with respect to employment, remuneration and other working conditions, access to accommodation and the right to be joined by family members.[29] This means, inter alia, that any national of a Member State is entitled to take up and engage in gainful employment on the territory of another Member State in conformity with the relevant regulations applicable to national workers. In order not to jeopardize this right through improper requirements concerning entry into and residence in Member States, workers must be admitted to their territory simply on the production of a valid identity card or passport and be granted the right of residence.[30] Spouses and, where applicable, registered partners, as well as their children up to the age of 21, are authorized to reside with them.

[28] Consolidated Version of the Treaty Establishing the European Community (EC Treaty), OJ 2006 C 321/E/37, Arts. 39 and 18, respectively.

[29] Arts. 12 and 39(2) of the EC Treaty and Council Regulation 1612/68/EEC of 15 October 1968 on freedom of movement for workers within the Community (OJ Sp. Ed. 1968-69, 475, JO 1968 L 257/2, as amended).

[30] For a stay of more than three months the requirement for a residence permit has been abolished, but Member States may require EU citizens to register with the relevant authorities (see Directive 2004/38/EC of the European Parliament and of the Council of 29 April 2004 on the right of citizens of the Union and their family members to move and reside freely within the territory of the Member States, OJ 2004 L 229/35, Article 8).

Under the system of mutual recognition of qualifications, EU citizens fully qualified in one Member State are entitled to exercise a regulated profession[31] in another Member State. Depending on the activity in question and the training completed, recognition will be either automatic or subject to a period of probation or an aptitude test. Self-employed persons and service providers can also exercise free movement rights by virtue of Articles 43-48 (Chapter 2 on the Right of Establishment) and 49-55 (Chapter 3 on Services) of Part Three, Title III of the EC Treaty. Moreover, national social security systems are coordinated at the EU level to prevent discrimination against persons who are exercising their right to free movement.[32]

With regard to service providers, the EC Treaty enables an economic operator providing services in one Member State to also offer services on a temporary basis in another Member State, without having to be established there. In particular, "services" covers activities of an industrial and commercial character; craftspersons' activities; and professional activities. In those instances where restrictions on the provision of specific services have not yet been abolished, the application of such restrictions must be applied without discrimination based on nationality.

The possibility of derogating from the general rules governing the mobility of EU workers has nonetheless been envisaged for workers from countries joining the EU after the 2004 and 2007 enlargements.[33] "Transitional arrangements", as this label suggests, permit the former EU-15 to derogate temporarily from the principle of free movement of workers in respect of workers coming from the new EU Member States for a maximum period of seven years. These arrangements only apply to workers and not service providers, with some limited exceptions for Austria and Germany (see Textbox 13.3).[34]

[31] Regulated professions imply de jure professional recognition, because either the education leading to a professional activity or the pursuit of the particular professional activity are regulated by legal acts (i.e. laws, regulations, administrative provisions), and the final decision on mandatory recognition is in the hands of professional or governmental bodies, or both. The professions regulated vary among countries, generally motivated by consumer protection and public interest concerns. Many countries regulate professions which can have an impact on health or life or result in material or moral loss, such as professions relating to medicine and pharmacy, veterinary medicine, architecture, law or transport.

[32] Article 42 of the EC Treaty and Council Regulation 1408/74/EEC of 14 June 1971 on the application of social security schemes to employed persons, to self-employed persons and to members of their families moving within the Community (JO Sp. Ed. 1971, 416, JO 1971 L 149/2, as amended).

[33] Over a three-year period (2004-2007) the EU has been transformed from a 15-country Union to one of 27 countries. In May 2004, 10 countries joined the 15 EU Member States: Cyprus, Czech Republic, Estonia, Hungary, Latvia, Lithuania, Malta, Poland, Slovakia and Slovenia. In January 2007, Bulgaria and Romania also became members.

[34] The transitional arrangements in the Accession Treaties of 16 April 2003 provide that for workers from the 8+2 new EU Member States in Central and Eastern Europe (the transitional arrangements do not apply to Cyprus and Malta), access to the labour markets of the former EU-15 will depend on the national laws and policies of those Member States. These arrangements only apply to the taking up of employment, with the exception of Austria and Germany, where the movement of service providers in a limited number of sectors, for example construction and industrial cleaning, may also be restricted in the event of serious disturbances in the service sectors in question.

Textbox 13.3

EU Enlargement – Free Movement of Workers

General Provisions

On 1 January 2007, Bulgaria and Romania joined the European Union, taking the total to 27 Member States. While nationals of all 27 Member States are also EU nationals, not all enjoy from the outset equal rights of free movement. All EU nationals are entitled to move freely among the Member States without visas or other pre-entry conditions. They are entitled to remain on the territory of any other Member State for a period of not more than three months without further formalities and longer if they are self-employed, service providers or recipients, or as students, retirees or economically inactive persons, provided they produce evidence of sufficient independent means and will not have to rely on the social security/welfare system of the respective EU host country.

For the nationals of eight of the ten 2004 accession states (i.e. the Czech Republic, Estonia, Hungary, Latvia, Lithuania, Poland, Slovakia and Slovenia, collectively referred to as "A8 states"), the right to employment and to remain in the country to work has been limited, though not for Cyprus and Malta. Thus, "A8" nationals are subject to a gradual labour market liberalization scheme under which pre-2004 Member States (the former EU-15) are entitled to restrict labour market access in their regard for an initial two-year period and, subject to notification, for a further three years. In the presence of serious disturbances in a Member State's labour market, these restrictions may be extended for a further two years. However, A8 workers who have completed twelve months or more of lawful employment in a Member State acquire full Treaty rights and are no longer subject to the transitional provisions.

Among the substantial issues that arise in restricting access to the labour market for workers only, and not for the self-employed and service providers, is the suspicion that the self-employed and service providers might be "abusing" the rules against labour market access by falsely presenting their economic activity as self-employment. Similarly, the fact that companies have the right to bring in workers to carry out service provision, though these workers have no right of access to the labour market, has lead to tensions regarding the working conditions applicable to such posted workers (who tend to be from the EU Member State of origin) and the effect on competition.

Free Movement of Workers: Current Situation of A8 Workers

At present, of the pre-2004 Member States, ten have opened their labour markets completely: Ireland, Sweden and the United Kingdom did so as of 1 May 2004; Finland, Greece Portugal and Spain (1 May 2006); Italy (27 July 2006); the Netherlands (1 May 2007); and France (1 July 2008). The U.K. is continuing its Worker Registration Scheme[1] and Finland is developing one.

While the remaining pre-2004 Member States (Austria, Belgium, Denmark, Germany and Luxembourg) extended the transitional arrangements for a further three years as of 1 May 2006, they have relaxed their labour market access rules for A8 workers, either generally or on a sectoral basis.

Concerning the new EU Member States, Hungary proceeds on a reciprocal basis, while Poland and Slovenia first applied and subsequently removed such reciprocity measures.

Free Movement of Workers: Bulgaria and Romania

Ten Member States (the Czech Republic, Cyprus, Estonia, Finland, Latvia, Lithuania, Poland, Slovakia, Slovenia and Sweden) have introduced no restrictions in regard to workers from Bulgaria and Romania, while Denmark, Hungary and Italy have relaxed their labour market access rules in their regard. However, concerns have been raised in some Member States over the application of general national regulations rather than EU rules to foreigners, particularly in the case of expulsions.

Note:

[1] In the U.K., an A8 worker is obliged to register under the Worker Registration Scheme (WRS) within one month of starting employment. A8 nationals who have been lawfully employed in the U.K. for a continuous 12-month period or who are self-employed or service providers are not required to register. The registration fee is GBP 90, to be paid by the worker who is then issued a registration card and certificate. Employers may face sanctions if they violate this obligation and a fine of up to GBP 5,000. For more information on the WRS, see the UK Border Agency website at http://www.ukba.homeoffice.gov.uk/workingintheuk/wrs/.

Source: *Elspeth Guild, Centre for European Policy Studies (CEPS), Brussels, Belgium.*

One of the unique EU features is a specific approach to the management of migration flows from regions outside the EU through the development of a common policy on asylum and immigration.[35] However, progress on the adoption of a common EU law and policy on regular or legal migration has been relatively slow. Member States have found it easier to adopt measures in the fields of visa policy; external border controls, including the establishment of the European External Border Agency (FRONTEX); prevention of irregular migration (e.g. through information exchange and measures to combat smuggling and trafficking in human beings);[36] and the establishment of an EU return policy involving the negotiation of EU-wide readmission agreements with third countries (agreements with Albania, Hong Kong SAR, Macao SAR and Sri Lanka have already come into force), and common measures on the return of third-country nationals who are resident without authorization within their territories.[37]

While Directives on the right to family reunification (see also Chapter 6), on the status of third-country nationals who are long-term residents and on the admission of students and researchers have been adopted,[38] Member States have demonstrated a reluctance to engage at the EU level with the issue of economic-related migration from third countries. In order to break this impasse, in January 2005 the European Commission (2005a) presented a Green Paper on an EU approach to managing economic migration, a consultative document which paved the way for the adoption in December 2005 of a Policy Plan on Legal Migration (European Commission, 2005c).[39] This plan led to two legislative initiatives presented in October 2007. The first is a proposed Directive on the conditions of entry and residence of highly skilled migrants from third countries (European Commission, 2007d), the so-called "Blue Card" proposal, and the second a proposed Directive on a single application procedure for a single permit for third-country nationals to reside and work in the territory of a Member State, as a well as a common set of rights for lawfully resident third-country workers (European Commission, 2007e).[40]

A further characteristic of EU migration policy is close cooperation with countries of origin on managing migration flows, which is supported by a special budget line (originally AENEAS, recently replaced by a new programme, the Thematic Cooperation Programme with Third Countries on the Development

[35] EC Treaty, Part Three, Title IV. Key elements of this policy were identified by the European Council in Tampere in 1999: the adoption of a comprehensive approach to the management of migratory flows so as to find a balance between admissions for humanitarian and those for economic purposes; fair treatment for third-country nationals; and forging partnerships with countries of origin, including policies of co-development. The Hague Programme (2004-2009) reinforced these elements and identified new ones. See also n. 39 below. It should be noted that one of the ultimate objectives of the Southern African Development Community (SADC) 2005 Protocol on the Facilitation of the Movement of Persons (which has not yet come into force) is also to eliminate obstacles to the **movement of persons into** the Community (Williams, 2008).

[36] One the most recent initiatives to address irregular migration is the proposed Directive on employer sanctions (European Commission, 2007c).

[37] In June 2008, the Council of Ministers and the European Parliament reached agreement on a Directive on Common standards and procedures in Member States for returning illegally staying third-country nationals. The Directive includes common measures on the voluntary return, detention and expulsion of irregular migrants, and Member States will be required to transpose these measures into their domestic legal and administrative systems within a period of two years from the Directive's formal adoption.

[38] See, respectively, Council Directive 2003/86/EC of 22 September 2003 on the right to family reunification, OJ 2003 L 251/12; Council Directive 2003/109/EC of 25 November 2003 concerning the status of third-country nationals who are long-term residents, OJ 2004 L 16/44; Council Directive 2004/114/EC of 13 December 2004 on the conditions of admission of third-country nationals for the purposes of studies, pupil exchange, non-remunerated training or voluntary service, OJ 2004 L 375/12; and Council Directive 2005/71/EC of 12 October 2005 on a specific procedure for admitting third-country nationals for the purpose of scientific research, OJ 2005 L 289/15.

[39] The Policy Plan defines a roadmap for the remaining period (2006-2009) of the European Council's Hague Programme, a five-year programme for the development of the Area of Freedom, Security and Justice adopted in November 2004. The Policy Plan was one of the priorities identified in the Hague Programme and lists the actions and legislative initiatives that the Commission intends to take to pursue the consistent development of an EU legal migration policy.

[40] Proposed directives on seasonal workers, intra-corporate transferees and remunerated trainees are in the process of formulation (European Commission, 2005c).

Aspects of Migration and Asylum).[41] This cooperation now encompasses the global approach to migration management adopted at the end of 2005.[42] It also builds on earlier initiatives, such as the support of a linkage between migration and non-related issues as a means to secure greater cooperation on migration issues,[43] and the inclusion of migration concerns in EU external and development policies and agreements (European Commission, 2005b).[44] The recent introduction of mobility partnerships to better manage migration flows between the EU and specific third countries is the latest development in the construction of a comprehensive cooperation framework.[45]

All these elements make the EU the most advanced regional entity in managing external and internal movements of persons, even though it took several decades to reach that level. However, the framework applicable to the movement and treatment of non-EU nationals is still incomplete and does not cover admission for employment, which remains within the competence of individual Member States.

Other regional economic integration processes (e.g. Andean Community, Caribbean Community and Common Market (CARICOM), COMESA, ECOWAS SADC and MERCOSUR), which support free movement to various extents,[46] are some distance from the progress made at the level of the European Union, although the EU experience also demonstrates that such an advanced degree of integration is the result of a lengthy and painstaking process and requires the support of an institutional infrastructure and a strong resource base. It should also be underscored that each region is unique on account of its history and level of economic and social development with the result that migration management objectives, whether they are to be applied in an internal or external context, or both, are often also quite different. Nevertheless, this does not mean that progress cannot be achieved through other less formal regional mechanisms, as discussed in the section below.

3.2 Regional Consultative Processes

The purpose of Regional Consultative Processes (RCPs) is to discuss migration-related issues in a cooperative manner with a view to reaching a common understanding of, and where possible, effective solutions for regional migration management (IOM/Swiss Federal Office for Migration, 2005b). A number of factors explain their emergence and breadth:

- RCPs offer a structure for dialogue, exchange of information and expertise without requiring a government to enter into formal commitments. This facilitates confidence building, the identification of like-minded partners and the search for common understandings and approaches. It also allows the discussion of sensitive issues in a non-confrontational manner.

[41] See the European Commission website at http://ec.europa.eu/europeaid/where/worldwide/migration-asylum/index_en.htm (External cooperation programmes - Migration and Asylum).

[42] In December 2005, the European Council adopted the "Global Approach to Migration", which brings together migration, external relations and development policy to address migration in an integrated, comprehensive and balanced way in partnership with third countries.

[43] Every cooperation and association agreement concluded by the EU must contain a clause on joint management of migration flows and on compulsory readmission in the event of irregular migration (see the Conclusions of the European Council in Seville in June 2002).

[44] See e.g. the Partnership Agreement between the Members of the African, Caribbean and Pacific (ACP) Group of States and the European Community and its Members States, Cotonou, 23 June 2000, and the European Neighbourhood Policy with countries to the South and East of the EU (European Commission, 2007a).

[45] In May 2007, the European Commission (2007b) presented a Communication on *Circular migration and mobility partnerships between the European Union and third countries*. The Communication proposes partnerships between the EU and third countries interested in working with the EU to address irregular migration, while facilitating regular migration and circular migration. In June 2008, two joint declarations on mobility partnerships were signed between the EU and Cape Verde (in cooperation with four EU Member States) and Moldova (in cooperation with 14 EU Member States).

[46] While free movement of persons has not been advanced in the context of the Association of Southeast Asian Nations (ASEAN), the protection of migrant workers is a particular concern, as reflected in the ASEAN Declaration on the Protection and Promotion of the Rights of Migrant Workers, adopted by the Heads of State/Government in Cebu, the Philippines on 13 January 2007. See the ASEAN website at http://www.aseansec.org/19264.htm.

- States are more willing to join RCPs since they can withdraw from them just as easily if they so desire.
- States interact on equal terms, which favours a broad sense of ownership of the process.
- Membership can be open to states sharing migratory routes (countries of origin, transit and destination). Unlike more formal entities based on economically or politically motivated membership, RCPs may select participants according to their potential contribution to the advancement of the migration agenda (e.g. the 5+5 Dialogue on Migration in the Western Mediterranean[47]).
- They can extend participation to non-state actors, such as intergovernmental organizations or NGOs, and bring together officials from different ministries (IOM/Swiss Federal Office for Migration FOM, 2005b).

RCPs' agendas are flexible and responsive to members' main concerns, hence the evolving nature of their work priorities. RCPs typically revolve around a key theme. In the past, many of them focused on issues linked to irregular migration, such as the return of irregular migrants and readmission agreements, visa policy, border management, and human smuggling and trafficking. They are now inclined to have a broader work programme and increasingly cover development issues, labour mobility (see Textbox 13.4), remittances, protection of the human rights of migrants, integration or visa facilitation.

[47] The 5+5 Dialogue involves Algeria, France, Italy, Libya, Malta, Mauritania, Morocco, Portugal, Spain and Tunisia. It is an informal process in which governments cooperate and exchange information and analyses on topics such as migration trends, irregular migration and trafficking in human beings, migration and co-development (e.g. the role of diasporas), human rights and duties of migrants, integration, movement of people and management of regular migration, labour migration and vocational training, migration and health, local cooperation and gender equality in the context of migration. For more information, see IOM's website at http://www.iom.int/jahia/Jahia/pid/860.

Textbox 13.4

Regional Consultative Processes and Labour Mobility

Regional Consultative Processes (RCPs) are informal, non-binding and regularly scheduled meetings attended by government representatives – generally at senior official, but sometimes at ministerial level – to discuss issues of mutual concern related to migration. In keeping with the non-institutional character of RCPs, their administrative structures are kept simple, often in the form of small secretariats hosted by an international organization.

RCP membership is wide and varied. The meetings may be attended by either both home and host countries or, alternatively, only countries of origin or destination. Some of the better known RCPs are:

- Intergovernmental Conference on Migration, Asylum and Refugees (IGC). Established in 1985, it involves destination countries in Europe, North America and Australia and New Zealand, and examines border control, asylum, immigration (regular and irregular) and security issues.
- Regional Conference on Migration (RCM) (Puebla Process). Established in 1996, it includes Canada, the United States, Mexico and Central American countries, and focuses on migration policy, rights of migrants and development.
- 5 + 5 Dialogue on Migration in the Western Mediterranean. Established in 2002, it includes five southern European and five North African countries and examines migration, trafficking in human beings, rights of migrants, health, gender equality and public awareness.
- Migration Dialogue for Southern Africa (MIDSA). Established in 2000, it includes Botswana, the Democratic Republic of the Congo (DRC), South Africa and 12 other Southern African countries. It focuses on migration/border management, health, development, rights of migrants, return and readmission, and trafficking in human beings.
- Intergovernmental Asia-Pacific Consultations on Refugees, Displaced Persons and Migrants (APC). Established in 1996, the APC brings together 29 countries from the Asia-Pacific region. It focuses on return, refugees, trafficking in human beings, remittances, public awareness, burden sharing and capacity building.

- Bali Process. Established in 2002, it includes a wide range of countries of origin, transit and destination from many different regions of the world. It focuses on trafficking and smuggling in human beings and related transnational criminal activities.
- Ministerial Consultations on Overseas Employment and Contractual Labour for Countries of Origin in Asia (Colombo Process). Established in 2003, its membership consists of Afghanistan, Bangladesh, China, India, Indonesia, Nepal, Pakistan, the Philippines, Sri Lanka, Thailand and Viet Nam. In addition, certain countries of destination, viz. Bahrain, Italy, Kuwait, Malaysia, Qatar, Republic of Korea (South Korea), Saudi Arabia and the United Arab Emirates (UAE) participated as observers in the Ministerial Consultations in September 2005. The Colombo Process focuses on three thematic clusters: protection of vulnerable migrants and provision of support services; optimization of the benefits of organized labour migration; and capacity building, data collection and interstate cooperation (see also Textbox 10.5).
- Abu Dhabi Dialogue. The Abu Dhabi Dialogue was launched in January 2008. It brings together Colombo Process countries and countries of destination in Asia for consultations focusing on the facilitation of labour mobility and the protection of temporary contractual workers (see also Textbox 10.5).

RCP agendas have evolved considerably over the years. The initial focus on individual topics of interest (such as asylum policies and procedures, trafficking in human beings or border control) has gradually given way to broader, comprehensive perspectives on migration management in which labour mobility now occupies an increasingly important place. Even issues that appear less directly related to labour mobility – trafficking and irregular migration, for instance – have implications for labour mobility, in the sense that the effective control of borders can contribute to the development of a climate of public confidence supportive of the facilitation of the movement of migrant workers. Two RCPs, the Colombo Process and the related Abu Dhabi Dialogue, have chosen labour mobility as their prime focus of interest and have developed a range of capacity-building activities to equip participating countries with the legislative and administrative tools needed to manage their labour flows effectively.

Source: *Randall Hansen, Canada Research Chair in Immigration and Governance, Department of Political Science, University of Toronto, Canada.*

Regional consultations often lead to the adoption of recommendations, action plans or regional strategies setting shared principles and goals. Financial mechanisms are sometimes devised to sustain a component of technical cooperation assistance (e.g. joint training). Past experiences have proven that the success of RCPs may result from the choice of a limited number of participants combined with the support of an ad hoc (e.g. IGC) or internationally-based (IOM, UNHCR, UN Institute for Training and Research - UNITAR) secretariat. A participating state or a regional intergovernmental organization (e.g. Association of Southeast Asian Nations – ASEAN) may also host the process.

RCPs dedicated to labour migration issues do not create openings within the regional labour market. Rather, they facilitate movements through the adoption of recommendations or guidelines on issues such as visa facilitation (e.g. Asia-Pacific Economic Cooperation - APEC), or the protection and training of the labour force (e.g. Colombo Process[48]), which in turn can create the impetus for the realization of projects in these fields (e.g. training of labour attachés or the establishment of migrant resource centres). Although APEC is not a typical RCP, its pro-mobility activities are a good illustration of the levels of progress that can be achieved in a regional forum on the basis of consensus and voluntary commitments (see Textbox 13.5).

[48] This is the short title for the RCP on overseas employment and contractual labour for countries of origin in Asia. See also Textbox 13.4.

Textbox 13.5

Asia-Pacific Economic Cooperation (APEC)

APEC,[1] which gathers members bordering the Pacific Ocean and often separated by large geographical distances (e.g. Australia, China, Peru), does not increase access to the labour markets of its members. Rather it is committed to facilitating labour mobility for certain categories of highly skilled persons through (1) exchanging information on regulatory regimes; (2) streamlining the processing of short-term business visitor visas and procedures for temporary residence of business people; and (3) maintaining a dialogue on these issues with the business community. This work is coordinated by the Informal Experts' Group on Business Mobility.

The APEC Business Travel Card (ABTC) is one of the key initiatives being pursued. This card provides pre-cleared short-term entry to the 17 APEC economies participating in the scheme. The card holders do not need to individually apply for visas or entry permits each time they travel, as the card provides for multiple entries into participating economies during its three-year period of validity. In addition, immigration processing on arrival is accelerated via fast-track entry and exit through special APEC lanes at major airports. APEC has also developed an electronic APEC Business Travel Handbook providing a quick reference guide to the visa and entry requirements of APEC participating economies.[2]

The introduction of the ABTC followed a pathfinder approach, allowing countries to join when ready (conditions include: sufficient resources, necessary legislative frameworks in place and capacity to be an equal partner) and providing technical assistance to developing economies. The principles and procedures of the programme are compiled in an ABTC Operating Framework (including card manufacturing standards, eligibility criteria and service standards), which should be followed on a "best endeavour basis", and are not legally binding.

> Applications for the ABTC card are made to the designated home country agency (each state determines which particular agency accepts applications). The home country then carries out necessary vetting procedures in order to select bona fide applicants: it was agreed that the country of origin is in the best position to implement the specific procedures to determine who is eligible for the ABTC, and thereby maintain the integrity of the scheme. Although the basic eligibility requirements are set out in the Operating Framework, economies may use additional criteria to ensure bona fide applicants. Applications approved by the country of origin are sent to the participating economies and, if accepted, are given a pre-clearance permission. Member states are not required to give reasons for refusing pre-clearance to any applicants. Finally, the home country can issue the ABTC card, which allows entry into all economies that have given a pre-clearance permission. The ABTC pre-clearance system ensures that states retain the control over the movement of people across their borders and over the eligibility of domestic applicants. The ABTC members also benefit from the increased integrity of the scheme, which results from the double-screening procedure by home and destination countries. The programme inspires a high degree of confidence in both government officials and the business community: in the history of the ABTC, no instances of fraud have been discovered (David Watt, Department of Immigration, Multicultural and Indigenous Affairs, Australia, speaking at the OECD/World Bank/IOM Seminar on Trade and Migration, Geneva, 12-14 November 2003).

One of the keys to the success of the scheme is that it is designed and supported by a major destination country, Australia, which has considerable experience in migration management and pre-entry clearance, thereby reassuring other destination countries of the efficiency of the entire system. Nonetheless, despite this and the good record of the scheme, it is important to note that Canada has not yet joined, while the U.S. only became a transitional member in September 2007 (with the aim of full participation within three years).

Other pro-mobility initiatives include a 30-day processing standard for applications for, and extensions of, temporary residence permits for APEC intra-company transferees, the development of standards in all major immigration areas,[3] assistance to regional economies to develop Advance Passenger Information (API) Systems (information about incoming airline passengers supplied to the destination government) and Advance Passenger Processing (using API provided by airlines to run checks against electronic immigration records for pre-arrival screening); as well as the creation of a Regional Movement Alert System (RMAS – provision of real-time access to a database of lost and stolen passports).[4] Since 2002, APEC has also paid more attention to remittances with a working group established by finance ministers to examine the economic, structural and regulatory factors that encourage the use of remittances in the APEC economies. The APEC initiative on remittances systems has helped launch research projects (undertaken by the World Bank and the Asian Development Bank, in particular) and led to the organization of two symposia.[5]

Notes:

[1] APEC's 21 member economies are: Australia, Brunei Darussalam, Canada, Chile, China, Hong Kong SAR, Indonesia, Japan, Republic of Korea (South Korea), Malaysia, Mexico, New Zealand, Papua New Guinea, Peru, Philippines, Russian Federation, Singapore, Taiwan Province of China, Thailand, United States and Viet Nam.

[2] The Business Travel Handbook is available at http://www.businessmobility.org/travel/index.asp. It lists the basic eligibility criteria and procedures for applying for visas and the terms and conditions that apply to business travellers. This information is provided for both short-term business visits and temporary residence for business purposes in APEC economies. The Handbook also provides contact details for the embassies, consulates and other visa-issuing agencies of each member economy.

[3] Including pre-arrival, entry, stay and departure. Standards and/or best practice guidelines have been agreed by the Business Mobility Group covering short-term and temporary residence arrangements, transparency, API implementation, e-commerce, immigration legislation, travel document examination, travel document security, professional immigration services and the APEC Business Travel Card scheme.

[4] See http://www.businessmobility.org/key/index.html.

[5] APEC Symposia on Alternative Remittances Systems, Tokyo, 3-4 June 2004 and The Role of the Private Sector in Shifting from Informal to Formal Remittance Systems, Bangkok, 26-27 May 2005.

RCPs' perceived success is based partly on the common interest of participants in the topical issues considered by the group of states concerned. RCPs are well positioned to add coherence to the broader regional agenda and complement formal regional processes by involving neighbouring or like-minded states in special or ad hoc discussions. They are particularly useful when progress in formal arrangements is lagging, as they allow continuation of dialogue. They are similarly well placed to enhance bilateral cooperation (see Section 4 below) by creating trust relationships between countries and generating opportunities for interactions in a broader setting. The number of RCPs specializing in international labour mobility is still rather limited and their impact on the development of national labour migration policies is difficult to assess owing to the non-normative approach adopted. The informality of these processes may therefore be regarded both as a strength (as this fosters broader participation) and as a weakness (as the concretization of identified goals is left to the discretion of each country).

4. Facilitating and Managing Temporary Labour Migration through Bilateral Cooperation

Bilateral labour migration agreements were first used extensively at the end of the Second World War, when large emerging economies in "New World" countries decided to meet their considerable labour market needs through large-scale immigration programmes.[49] They have regained currency more recently as a flexible policy instrument used by two countries in the management of migratory flows (OECD, 2004). Such agreements can target specific groups of migrants, contain provisions enabling policies to adapt to labour market fluctuations in countries of destination and equitably attribute responsibilities between countries of origin and destination for the monitoring and overall management of the labour migration process.

The scope of these agreements varies. Their provisions generally specify the purpose of the agreement; define the categories of labour concerned; and provide for admission criteria, the terms of migration, fair and equitable treatment and annual quotas, where applicable. However, some specific issues, such as social security and double taxation, recognition of qualifications and irregular migration, are often dealt with in separate agreements (e.g. the bilateral social security agreements signed by the U.S. with 20 countries, including Chile, France and South Korea, or

[49] For more information on the historical context of bilateral labour migration agreements, see the textbox written by the author for IOM (2005: Textbox 12.2: "Bilateral Labour Agreements: Effective Tools for Managing Labour Flows?"), from where the material in this section is mainly drawn.

the readmission agreements in force, signed or under negotiation between Switzerland and 33 countries[50]). The diversity of agreements and their provisions reflect the differences in the economic environment and the nature of labour market shortages, as well as a variety of broader economic, social and political objectives for entering into bilateral cooperative approaches for the management of these flows.

4.1 Objectives of Countries of Destination

When engaging in bilateral labour agreements, countries of destination follow mainly four broad types of objectives that are not mutually exclusive. The first of these is to satisfy their labour market needs and to better manage the labour migration process. Through such agreements, a country of destination can respond to its labour market needs by recruiting workers from other countries. Alternatively, where regular channels for migration are already in place, bilateral agreements may help to better match supply and demand, for instance by streamlining recruitment procedures or by stipulating the activities and responsibilities of public authorities and private partners. The most comprehensive agreements cover all phases of the migratory process and various issues related to movement (e.g. access to health care, pre-departure information on labour laws and the cultural and social environment of the destination country, and vocational and language training).

A second objective is to prevent or reduce irregular migration by affording regular migration opportunities. The motivations to offer such opportunities are twofold. First, the idea is to relieve the pressure to migrate from countries of origin and curb the number of irregular migrants by channelling such movements into regular avenues.[51] Second, the opening up of a regular channel is sometimes used as a negotiation tool to secure the willingness of countries of origin to cooperate on managing irregular migration, and especially on the readmission of their nationals who are in an irregular situation (e.g. rejected asylum seekers).

A third objective is the use of bilateral labour agreements to promote and support broader economic relations with countries of origin. The movement of workers in this case is aimed at facilitating regional economic integration and the development of countries of origin. The bilateral agreements signed by Germany with some central and eastern European countries (CEECs) are good examples (OECD, 2004). They establish several forms of temporary migration for work purposes (e.g. seasonal work, contract work and "guest worker" programmes). In that sense, their purpose goes beyond the satisfaction of German labour market needs to the strengthening of economic relations between Germany and CEECs.

A final specific objective is to preserve or strengthen ties between countries sharing historical (sometimes post-colonial) and cultural links. For example, the United Kingdom operates a "working holidaymaker" scheme with participating Commonwealth countries, allowing persons aged between 17 and 30 to come

[50] Information taken from the IGC Matrix on Countries of Origin/Transit Countries parties to IGC States' and the EC's Readmission Instruments (in force, signed or under negotiation).

[51] Some bilateral labour agreements are signed at the time of a regularization programme and target the principal countries of origin of irregular migrants. The idea behind this approach is to encourage irregular migrants to leave the destination country, return home and benefit from regular work opportunities set out in the agreements. Special clauses on the implementation of the regularization programme can figure in the agreement (with a limited period of validity), e.g. migration agreements between Argentina and Bolivia, and Argentina and Peru, signed in February 1998 and May 1999, respectively, and their additional Protocols. The agreement between Spain and Ecuador concerning the regulation and control of migratory flows (*Acuerdo entre España y Ecuador relative a la regulación y ordenación de los flujos migratorios*) (Madrid, 29 May 2001), stipulates in Article 14(3) that migrants returning home to regularize their situation will have their visa and work permit applications treated as a priority: "[T]he authorities of the requesting contracting party undertake to facilitate the departure and gradual and voluntary repatriation of undocumented persons in their territory, so that those who so request are guaranteed that the respective embassy will provide fast-track treatment for their residence and work visas, with the guarantee of a job in the requesting contracting party."

to the United Kingdom for an extended holiday of up to two years and to engage in part-time or casual work.[52] In the same vein, in 1998, Portugal concluded an agreement with Cape Verde on the temporary recruitment of workers (Fonseca et al., 2005).

4.2 Objectives of Countries of Origin

The objectives of countries of origin in entering into bilateral labour migration agreements are mainly economic and social. The first and obvious motivation is to offer their workers wider, facilitated access to the international labour market and, at the same time, to prevent criminal activities involving the smuggling and trafficking of human beings, and the exploitation, suffering and sometimes deaths of migrants, frequently associated with attempts to migrate in an irregular manner.

Nationals of countries of origin are provided preferential entry by destination countries under bilateral arrangements in three different ways:

- **Special categories**: Employment of certain categories of workers (especially the low or semi-skilled or for certain types of jobs not covered under the general immigration admission system is authorized for nationals of countries having signed bilateral arrangements (e.g. in Germany, seasonal employment in agriculture and other sectors can only be accessed through bilateral agreements). This provision is sometimes capped.
- **Preferential admission or employment**: When the categories covered by bilateral agreements are not different from those covered by the general migrant entry provisions, workers covered by these agreements can benefit from preferential admission or employment over other foreigners (e.g. in Spain nationals from countries with which Spain has signed bilateral agreements are given preference).
- **Preferential quota**: When countries regulate the number of foreign workers to be admitted under their general migration programmes through quotas, a special quota can be attributed to countries having signed a bilateral labour agreement (e.g. Italy has a preferential quota for for the employment of Albanian and Tunisian nationals in tourism and agriculture), or they can benefit from unrestricted entry.

Bilateral agreements can include guarantees on ensuring return to home countries[53] or cooperation in matters involving irregular migration, which can be key for securing the support of destination countries in opening their labour markets, in particular to more "sensitive" categories of workers, such as low-skilled workers (see Textbox 13.6).

In addition to relieving the strain on domestic labour markets, by providing opportunities abroad for unemployed or underemployed persons and broadening the tax base (mainly through family members' consumption and indirect taxes), bilateral agreements are also seen as a means to support the link between labour migration and development by (i) regulating outflows, including the reduction

[52] The details of the scheme are described in more detail on the U.K. Border Agency's website at http://www.ind.homeoffice.gov.uk/workingintheuk/tier5/workingholidaymakers/. See also Chapter 5.

[53] E.g. the employment agreement for Caribbean workers in Canadian agriculture stipulates a 25 per cent mandatory remittance from the worker's wages under a "Compulsory Savings Scheme". This deduction is remitted to the country of origin liaison officer and is handed back to the worker upon return. Another feature of this agreement is that it authorizes workers to re-enter the scheme year after year and thus acts as an incentive to return. In the agreement between Spain and Ecuador, above n. 51, a specific provision concerning return has been included. According to Article 12 of the agreement, prior to recruitment, temporary workers must sign a commitment to return to Ecuador when their permit expires, and within a month of their return they are obliged to present to the Spanish consular office from where they obtained their visa for temporary work in Spain their passport with the stamp of the original visa. The failure to do so will disqualify them from obtaining future contracts in Spain and will be taken into account when considering any future applications for work and residence permits they may lodge with Spanish authorities.

of brain drain;[54] (ii) setting up mechanisms to facilitate remittances and the transfer of know-how and technology; and, more generally, (iii) building confidence between communities of origin and destination, which in turn fosters forms of cooperation beyond labour migration management.

Bilateral agreements are also seen as a tool to promote and protect the welfare and rights of migrant workers. Some agreements are used to state the general working and wage conditions applicable to migrant workers, and may provide a standard employment contract (e.g. the Canada-Mexico Memorandum of Understanding (MoU) states that employment conditions should be equivalent to those of Canadian workers, and Annex 2 includes the employment contract which should be signed by the employer and the worker).[55] Bilateral labour agreements can provide for social security arrangements or refer to parallel bilateral social security agreements already concluded or to be signed (e.g. Article 5 of the Protocol for temporary migration from Cape Verde to Portugal) and may also cover issues such as health insurance or job safety measures (e.g. provision of training and adequate equipment). Some specific clauses for the protection of migrants regarding freedom of religion and trade union rights can be built into the agreement as well.

In many cases, clauses pertaining to working conditions and wages are simply a reminder that foreign workers are subject to the same laws and regulations applicable to nationals. However, they can also address gaps in sectors that are often not covered in national labour codes (which is mainly the case for agricultural and domestic workers[56]) and in countries where there is no minimum wage.

[54] With regard to highly skilled workers, bilateral agreements can provide safeguards to respond to the concerns of some countries of origin over potential brain drain effects. These may include specific measures relating to, e.g. the return of workers, joint training or the exchange of expertise. The United Kingdom developed a code of practice for the international recruitment of healthcare professionals that encourages the use of bilateral agreements in the prevention of adverse consequences on developing countries. The use of bilateral agreements to prevent brain drain is also part of the recommendations of the 2003 Commonwealth Code of Practice for the international recruitment of health workers and its companion document (http://www.thecommonwealth.org/Internal/34040/34042/human_resources_for_health/), and the 2004 Teacher Recruitment Protocol (http://www.thecommonwealth.org/shared_asp_files/uploadedfiles/%7B90CCBAE1-D475-47EC-BD52-02BE05EA0D27%7D_PROTOCOL.pdf).

[55] Another example concerns the Bilateral Labour Service Cooperation Agreement between the Government of the Republic of Mauritius and the Government of the People's Republic of China, signed in January 2005. The Agreement provides, inter alia, for (i) the establishment of a working group within the framework of the Sino-Mauritian Economic and Trade Joint Committee for the exchange of views on a regular basis and the review of the employment situation of Chinese workers in Mauritius; and (ii) the recruitment of workers from China through Chinese recruitment agencies approved by the Chinese Government.

[56] However, these types of instruments are limited in number. To address the problem of the rights of domestic workers, in 2001, Jordan instituted an MoU between the Ministry of Labour and the UN Development Fund for Women (UNIFEM) that also involves the following countries of origin: India, Indonesia, Nepal, the Philippines and Sri Lanka. In 2003, a standardized contract for foreign domestic workers in Jordan stipulated a set salary and provided for medical care. New laws followed to regulate and license recruitment agencies. A steering committee involving relevant ministries, embassies and NGOs has also been established.

Textbox 13.6

Exploring the Role of Reformed Bilateral Labour Agreements: The Caribbean Community and the Temporary Movement of Less-skilled Labour

Composed largely of small island states with limited economies of scale and per capita income differentials of up to 35:1, the Caribbean Community and Common Market (CARICOM) relies in good part on intra-regional labour mobility for the realization of a Caribbean Single Market and Economy (CSME). The objective of the free movement of persons (covering the movement of skills, the movement of services and the right to establishment) is tied to a 2008 target; however, for this deadline to be met the more developed states will have to acquire confidence in their ability to manage influxes of migrants, especially when they are less-skilled.

Until this issue is fully addressed, the growth of those sectors of the economy that rely on intensive, less-skilled labour – tourism, for instance – will be constrained and least developed countries (LDCs) with a surplus of less-skilled labour will struggle to overcome intra-regional disparities (Caldentey and Schmid, 2006). In the meantime, as unmet labour demands persist and important countries of origin (e.g. Haiti) and destination (e.g. the Bahamas) remain outside the CSME, one may expect an increase in irregular intra-regional migration.

The regulation and facilitation of less skilled labour flows is also of critical significance for the management of extra-CARICOM migration, whether to the nearby Dominican Republic or farther afield to the U.S., Canada, the United Kingdom, France and the Netherlands, all the more so because of the role played by remittances in the regional economy (IADB, 2007; World Bank, 2005) and because of the current and/or projected demographic and economic profiles and associated demands for migrant workers among various countries of destination.

In the light of such unresolved concerns over how best and to what extent to integrate labour markets at the lower end of the skills spectrum, bilateral labour agreements (BLAs) may constitute promising instruments for the flexible matching of labour supply and demand, both seasonal and structural and according to national requirements and capacities, while mitigating irregular migration pressures. Several BLAs already exist, including those under the Commonwealth Caribbean Seasonal Agriculture Workers Program (SAWP) with Canada[1], and others concluded by CARICOM Member States with the U.S. for the temporary employment of farmers and hospitality workers.

If the coverage of destination countries and worker categories of such agreements is to be expanded successfully (World Bank, 2005), public education and awareness of their benefits, and significant improvements in their design to ensure feasibility, will be critical.

The benefits of well-designed BLAs for countries of origin include, among others, expanded access to the international labour market and "brain circulation". Destination countries meanwhile can gain from cooperation in ensuring that access to their territory generally remains temporary and responds more efficiently to verifiable labour shortages and sectoral shifts in demand. Effectively meeting these objectives requires that these agreements and/or accompanying unilateral initiatives incorporate incentives for temporary and circular migration; adequate quotas; and relatively low transaction costs for employers and migrants alike (Mansoor and Quillin, 2007; Ruhs, 2005).

BLAs could also potentially serve as development policy instruments by offering less-skilled nationals of LDCs preferential access to employment quotas, the impact of which may support the attainment of the Millennium Development Goals (MDGs) (Pritchett, 2006). By targeting the less-skilled, these agreements could partly address the reservation that skill-biased admission policies may exacerbate income disparities within countries of origin by raising the local skill premium (Pritchett, 2006; Caldentey and Schmid, 2006) and skewing remittance flows towards the presumably better-off. However, at the moment, Haiti, for instance, has a fairly even distribution of remittance recipients among the lowest and highest income quintiles, according to the Haiti Remittance Survey 2006 of the Inter-American Development Bank (IADB, 2007), although this could change. Nevertheless, further research is required to determine whether any such effects are offset by the human capital and/or employment generated through higher returns to education and the local investment of remittances from highly skilled workers (World Bank, 2005).[2] Such development objectives may be most realistic where the agreements address labour shortages that are of a temporary nature.

BLAs may furthermore reduce the vulnerability of migrant workers to exploitation during recruitment and employment. Beyond obliging countries of origin to better regulate recruitment agencies, the agreements could assist them in negotiating limited freedom of movement for their nationals within assigned occupational sectors, thereby also potentially raising labour market efficiency in the destination country (Ruhs, 2005).

More rigorous research on the effectiveness of such agreements in terms of their implementation and impact and, possibly, the formation of a regional consultative process (RCP) on migration to complement the CSME, where good practices and experiences can be shared, would likely assist the Member States of the Caribbean Community to develop expanded and more effective BLAs.

To conclude, well-designed BLAs can assist countries of origin and destination to cultivate the multi-stakeholder cooperation and public support necessary to address politically sensitive issues in migration management and help to bring migration policies more into line with those on trade and foreign investment (Ruhs, 2005). In so doing, BLAs may assist in securing the interests of all parties and facilitate a more equitable integration of less-developed countries of origin into the regional and global economies.

Notes:

1 Implementation of the SAWP commenced in 1966 based on negotiations between Canada and Jamaica, and the programme was subsequently extended to Trinidad and Tobago and Barbados in 1967, Mexico in 1974, and the Organization of East Caribbean States in 1976.

2 Other remittance issues under discussion include the direction of causality in the association between remittance inflows and relatively high unemployment among migrant-sending households in some countries such as the Dominican Republic, and the potential for remittances to result in exchange rate appreciation and reduced competitiveness of exports among small economies.

Source: *Jennifer Zimmermann, Darfur Coordinator, IOM Sudan (formerly Project Development Officer, IOM Haiti).*

4.3 Different Forms of Bilateral Arrangements and their Scope

As discussed above, bilateral cooperation on temporary labour migration may aim to fulfil various economic, social and political purposes and take a number of different approaches. But how does this cooperation take shape? Bilateral cooperation arrangements can be distinguished according to their legal status, the comprehensiveness or specificity of the migratory issues addressed and the categories of workers covered.

(a) Legal status

Bilateral arrangements can cover a wide variety of devices, from legally binding agreements (i.e. formal treaties) to less formal Memoranda of Understanding (MoUs) and very informal practical arrangements, such as those involving primarily the national employment agencies of the two countries concerned.

Bilateral arrangements can take the form of a treaty, i.e. a legally binding instrument between the two governments concerned governed by international law. Such agreements may or may not include a formal mechanism (e.g. arbitration) for the settlement of disputes, but where they do, the parties to the agreement are required to follow the decisions of any such body. Furthermore, bilateral agreements are often published in the official journal of laws of the countries concerned, although their method of adoption and publication will normally depend on the administrative and constitutional rules of those countries.

A country may, however, prefer to conclude MoUs or Cooperation Arrangements (CA),[57] which have a status similar to that of administrative or private "arrangements", and which are not legally binding on the state. While MoUs/CAs may also contain mechanisms for resolving disputes, these are usually in the form of further political dialogue or consultations between representatives of the parties concerned.

Memoranda of Understanding can be of the "government to government" type (e.g. MoU between Canada and Mexico or the Caribbean states on the Seasonal Agriculture Worker Program (SAWP) – see Textbox 13.6), of the "government to private sector" type (e.g. Guatemalan Ministry of Labour with FERME, an employer association in the Canadian Province of Québec on the recruitment of seasonal agriculture workers - see Textbox 10.2) or between national administrations (e.g. between Germany's and Slovenia's employment services for "guest workers"). While under a MoU, the actions or decisions taken

57 MoUs and CAs are two out of a large variety of informal arrangements used. For example, the U.K. operates a youth exchange scheme with Japan, "Japan yes", on the basis of a *Note verbale* agreed with Japan, and the Philippines has signed a "Memorandum of Agreement" with Iraq, Jordan and Qatar.

are generally not subject to public international law, they may be subject to pertinent branches of national law (e.g. administrative or labour laws).

Bilateral labour arrangements and MoUs are general framework agreements: the details for their implementation are to be found in operational guidelines often attached to the main agreement (e.g. Canada SAWP MoU, Annex 1), or to be arranged through informal cooperation directly between the parties[58] (e.g. through an exchange of letters between administrative agencies), or be left for decisions to be taken at the local level, which in turn may or may not be enshrined in administrative instruments or similar means of regulation. BLAs and MoUs may serve to establish a joint committee to manage issues arising from the application of the agreement by countries of origin and destination (e.g. under the Spain-Ecuador agreement[59] and Canada's SAWP[60]).

Flexibility is an important element of bilateral arrangements. One of the potential advantages of foreign employment schemes is their ability to adapt in a timely manner to labour market developments in terms of the number and groups of persons they wish to capture. Sometimes programmes are set up for a limited period of time, for example the time needed by a country to adapt its human resource development strategy to meet certain needs.[61] In all bilateral agreements, the possibility of amendment is included and, indeed, most existing agreements have been modified several times. Emphasis on flexibility is further expressed by the legal nature of these agreements, only a few are legally binding treaties, while most of them constitute less formal arrangements.

In summary, when formal arrangements are in place, they also require informal cooperation, in particular on the administrative details for their implementation. However, bilateral cooperation may rely on purely informal processes in the absence of written commitments, and operate through working groups, periodic discussions and annual conferences. For example, Guatemala and Mexico established a bilateral commission on migration for the exchange of information, discussions on working conditions and irregular migration, together with a sectoral working group on agriculture workers (Geronimi, 2004).

Because they are generally in a less advantageous bargaining position, countries of origin usually prefer legally binding arrangements between governments and the establishment of clear procedures. Formal agreements specify more clearly the division of responsibilities between the parties, and their binding character compels compliance while offering better guarantees regarding the protection of the interests of each party.

(b) Comprehensive labour agreements and agreements on specific issues

The different forms of bilateral cooperation may also be categorized according to the extent to which they cover the various stages and aspects of the migratory process. The content of formal bilateral labour agreements is generally more detailed than in MoUs and other less formal arrangements. ILO identifies

[58] E.g. the Model Bilateral Agreement between the Czech Republic and selected partner eastern European countries (OECD, 2004). Clause 8 stipulates that implementation mechanisms should be elaborated in cooperation with responsible authorities.

[59] The Agreement, n. 51 above, establishes a Joint Coordination Committee, which has a multifaceted role regarding follow-up, proposals for amendments where appropriate, timely dissemination of the contents of the agreement and the settlement of any difficulties that may arise in its application.

[60] Canada organizes a national meeting every year in alternation with Mexico or a Caribbean country, which includes senior officials from the source country's Ministry of Labour, Ministry of Foreign Affairs and Ministry of Health.

[61] In 2001, Canada signed MoUs with employer representatives in the construction and the tooling and machining trades of the manufacturing sector. The purpose of both MoUs was to fill immediate shortages in the sectors concerned by facilitating the temporary entry and employment of foreign workers with a view to replacing the latter with Canadian citizens and permanent residents in the medium to long terms. Consequently, both MoUs had a limited life span, although they also contained express provisions for their renewal.

24 core elements which should appear in bilateral labour agreements (Geronimi, 2004).[62]

The categories of workers covered in these agreements vary, with some referring to general employment and others being more sector or skill specific.[63] The most common categories by type of labour recruited are:

- seasonal workers (in sectors such as, for example, tourism, agriculture or construction);
- contract workers and project-tied workers (foreigners employed by a foreign-based company or a domestic firm for work abroad);
- "guest workers" (under general temporary recruitment programmes or programmes targeting skilled professionals);
- trainees (for vocational or language training); and
- working holidaymakers (access to work for young adults while in the host country on holiday).[64]

Beside agreements focusing on temporary labour migration and issues related to a specific migratory process, a number of other bilateral agreements facilitate mobility and/or the management of migration flows generally as regards the admission and return of migrant workers, as well as the prevention of irregular migration and readmission of irregular migrants. These can be broadly classified as follows:

- Bilateral agreements covering specific groups of migrant workers or other migrant categories **with a broader purpose than the management of labour mobility**:

  a. Free trade agreements (FTAs) with provisions on the mobility of workers, particularly skilled or highly skilled workers, discussed in more detail in Textbox 13.7 at the end of this chapter.
  b. Technical cooperation and development agreements, with emphasis on the development of the country of origin (e.g. return and reintegration of skilled workers, creation of job opportunities in areas of high migration pressure, and investment tools and remittances).

- Bilateral agreements covering different migrant target groups and **addressing border-crossing issues**:

  a. Agreements designed to prevent irregular migration, including readmission arrangements and the management of security threats (e.g. assistance for the manufacture of secure identity documents, information campaigns on the risks associated with irregular migration and cooperation on the return of irregular migrants).
  b. Cross-border agreements (applicable to persons residing in border areas and addressing commuting, employment, taxation and other issues of concern)
  c. Visa facilitation agreements which call for, on the basis of reciprocity, the issuance of short-stay visas (e.g. 90 days within a period of 180 days) for specific categories of persons (e.g. scientists, journalists or members of international crews).[65]

---

62 These core elements are: Identification of the competent government authority; exchange of information; situation of irregular migrants; notification of job opportunities; list of candidates; pre-selection of candidates; final selection; nomination of candidates by employers (possibility to state the name of a person of interest to the employer); medical examination; entry documents; residence and work permits; transportation; employment contract; employment conditions; dispute settlement; trade union and collective bargaining rights; social security; remittances; housing; family reunification; activities of social and religious organizations; establishment of a joint commission to monitor the implementation of the agreement; validity and renewal of the agreement; the applicable law and place of jurisdiction (Geronimi, 2004: 23-26).

63 Some agreements are not limited to temporary labour migration and may also facilitate permanent employment-based immigration, as, for instance, the agreement between Spain and Ecuador (see n. 51 above).

64 For a description of working holidaymaker schemes, see Chapter 5.

65 This is, for instance, the case for the visa facilitation agreements concluded between the EU and the Russian Federation, Ukraine and the Western Balkan countries, respectively.

- Bilateral agreements **facilitating (or addressing the consequences of) mobility**, while paying no attention to international border-crossing issues:

  a. Mutual recognition arrangements on the criteria and procedures for the recognition of diplomas, or the right to practice a profession or trade in another country.
  b. Social security and double taxation agreements (e.g. portability of pensions, prevention of double taxation).

The diversity of instruments available often implies that a wide range of actors are involved in bilateral cooperation on labour migration. The leading roles in the negotiations and discussions are typically taken by one or several ministries (for instance, the ministry of labour and social affairs, or interior or foreign affairs, or the ministry of immigration or emigration where such specific entities exist). Administrations and institutions under their umbrella (e.g. public employment agencies, universities) may also initiate bilateral agreements with a local or national scope. Some agreements are concluded between private entities and foreign public and/or private authorities. Added to this is the fact that the authorities in charge of negotiating an agreement are often not the same as those responsible for their implementation.

Given these complexities, one of the main challenges consists in achieving coherence in the framing of bilateral labour migration policies, especially as they relate to both the identification of economic and social objectives and their realization through policymaking and implementation. This requires a relatively high degree of national coordination on the part of countries of origin and destination, which is typically lacking owing to the real or perceived inability to reconcile conflicting objectives pursued by diverse public and private stakeholders at various levels (e.g. between different ministries; by businesses; and representatives of employers, workers and civil society), and/or the lack of institutional capacity and financial resources (especially when developing countries are involved).

The high degree of informality, the diversity of objectives and the variety of actors involved make it all the more difficult to track the dynamics of bilateral negotiations on facilitating and regulating labour migration; to identify the trade-offs resulting in the opening up of new channels for migrant workers from particular countries; and to weigh the importance of particular migration management issues (e.g. addressing irregular migration) and their success in securing regular openings for migrant workers.

4.4 Impediments to Bilateral Agreements

It would be mistaken to assume that the relatively limited number of bilateral labour arrangements that have been concluded and are being implemented to date are a reflection of the asymmetry of relations between countries of origin and destination, where the former would be willing to enter into bilateral arrangements but lack the capacity to convince the latter to do so. It is true that many destination countries have declined offers from countries of origin to negotiate such arrangements. Spain has declined 40 such requests (Schulman, 2003), whereas the Philippines and Moldova have not been successful in securing bilateral agreements with some major destination countries (e.g. Saudi Arabia, in the case of the Philippines; and 24 countries relying to some extent on Moldovan migrant workers in the case of Moldova[66]). However, the reasons for this lack of success are complex.

Some of the difficulties may stem from the fact that a number countries adopt a position of principle not to resort to bilateral agreements, but to pursue a

[66] These include Bosnia and Herzegovina, Bulgaria, Canada, the Czech Republic, Estonia, France, Germany, Greece, Hungary, Israel, Italy, Kuwait, Lithuania, Former Yugoslav Republic of Macedonia (FYROM), Poland, Slovakia, the then Serbia and Montenegro, and Slovenia (Sleptova, 2003).

more universal approach regarding labour migration, i.e. one that does not distinguish on the basis of nationality.[67] Other destination countries have engaged in bilateral agreements, but may be unwilling to expand the number of current beneficiaries for various reasons, such as reservations regarding countries that do not figure prominently on their list of priorities, or they may entertain other concerns (e.g. domestic labour market conditions or a source country's standards regarding governance and human rights). Obstacles may also arise from a divergence of opinions between countries of origin and destination about the terms of a bilateral agreement, or from a lack of institutional capacity to pursue the negotiation and implementation of such agreements.

(a) Preference for a unilateral/universal approach

Certain destination countries do not feel the need for bilateral agreements as foreign workers have access to their labour markets through their general immigration policy, and the rights of migrant workers are protected under national legislation. They may also have concerns that concluding bilateral agreements would result in conferring additional rights on migrants not enjoyed by local workers.

For countries that favour a universal immigration policy and offer the same access and conditions to workers of all nationalities, bilateral arrangements may be regarded as discriminatory which, by privileging nationals from one country over others, are susceptible to create political tensions. Indeed, entering into a bilateral labour agreement with one country is likely to create expectations for other countries that their nationals should similarly benefit from the favourable treatment and may, in consequence, affect the quality of diplomatic relations by generating resentment in case of refusal.

With regard to skilled and highly skilled workers, in a context where such competences are scarce and the challenge of global competition to attract such workers is acutely felt, restricting labour market access to professionals from selected nationalities may not appear advisable.

As far as **opening up access** to their labour market is concerned, most destination countries, when declining an offer to negotiate, point to the situation of their employment market and their unemployment rates. Parallel reasons include the general opposition expressed by public opinion to regular migration and fears relating to overstay and the fuelling of irregular migration. As far as **working conditions** are concerned, there may be a reluctance on the part of the government to take decisions which could translate into more obligations beyond those set down in national and international labour standards, and higher costs for the employers of foreign workers (e.g. by regulating issues such as accommodation, overtime pay, rest periods and similar concerns). Certain governments are of the view that the determination of wages and the conditions surrounding the hiring of workers more generally is essentially a private matter between employers and employees, or should be left to labour market forces to determine.

While an argument in favour of BLAs is the prevention of abuse by the private sector (e.g. overcharging of fees, contract substitution) through the involvement of the state in the recruitment process, it has also to be considered that governments or public administrations are not necessarily immune to malpractices themselves and that their involvement can be misdirected to satisfy "political patronage". Furthermore, unnecessarily bureaucratic

[67] This policy is sometimes also qualified as a unilateral approach. However, universal and unilateral approaches are not necessarily the same. Indeed, a unilateral approach suggests that one country has established a policy on its own and on the basis of objectives identified by its government. A universal policy (applying no differences in terms of migrants' origins) may result from such a unilateral process. However, there is nothing to preclude a country from entering into consultations with source countries with a view to improving its universal policy, and therefore departing from a purely unilateral approach (see also Chapter 11 and the discussion regarding the adoption of "development-friendly" policies).

administrative requirements can be an obstacle to effective implementation of the agreement.

The general tendency among major destination countries today is still concerned with the management of ports of entry on the basis of a universal system and closer cooperation with countries of origin on issues related to irregular migration at the bilateral level. Moreover, some countries believe that their commitments under GATS Mode 4 (see Textbox Int. 1), which could be invoked by non-parties on the basis of the Most Favoured Nation Clause of the GATS, preclude such a bilateral approach to admission.

(b) Negotiation and implementation problems

Destination countries usually limit their readiness to enter into bilateral agreements to countries that are potential sources of migratory flows. The number of BLAs they accept to enter into is limited for several reasons, in addition to those connected with the existence of less favourable labour market conditions. Any additional BLA a country concludes will have the effect of limiting or diluting the relative advantage of other beneficiary countries, and may create discontent. Another source of tension emerges when a BLA does not generate movements; countries of origin often regard the availability of jobs in a country of destination as an entitlement rather than a mere prospect, and quotas (where they exist) more as targets than ceilings. Some countries of destination experience this problem with their trainee programmes for foreign nationals, which are typically underused to the dissatisfaction of countries of origin, especially when the programme was negotiated together with a readmission agreement (OECD, 2004). Lack of implementation or utilization can be due to inadequacies in recruitment mechanisms; employer preferences; mismatches between admission criteria and labour force profiles in countries of origin; the balance between earning possibilities (wages, duration of stay) and the costs of migration (i.e. travel, medical examination, lodgings and such like); administrative inefficiency; and the presence of community networks from other countries acting as intermediaries for job matching for their nationals.

It may also be difficult to terminate a bilateral agreement, or to resist pressure for its expansion, even if conditions in the labour market have changed or if countries prefer to change their future immigration policy and restrict their intervention (and related costs) to visa delivery, so as not to be involved in the administration and monitoring of the entire process. Indeed, bilateral agreements are time and resource (financial and human) intensive, as they might imply extensive public administration involvement in their implementation and monitoring; the more countries involved, the higher the administrative complexity, especially if, as is often the case, the terms of the agreements vary.

Countries of destination enter into bilateral labour agreements for two main reasons: (a) normalizing a pre-existing situation with a source country by regularizing irregular flows and reorganizing them in a satisfactory manner; or (b) encouraging/ facilitating new recruitment channels for persons whose qualifications are in high demand on the basis of the resources available in **specific** countries (e.g. agreements on nurses by the U.K. with the Philippines and Spain[68]). Consequently, countries of origin that are outside the scope of these interests experience difficulties in building the bargaining capacity necessary to enter into bilateral cooperation.

Obstacles to negotiations and prospective implementation on the part of countries of origin may arise from a lack of institutional capacity to analyse the existing labour demand in destination countries, determine their priorities and pursue

[68] However, changes in the demand for certain categories of foreign labour can affect the functioning of these agreements. For instance, "general nursing" occupations were removed from the U.K. shortage occupation list in August 2006, which impacted on the recruitment of nurses from the Philippines.

a lengthy process of negotiation.[69] Countries of origin may also suffer from the absence of adequate public or private recruitment agencies to "market" their national workforce and facilitate the implementation of labour migration programmes. Further impediments include the educational level, skills and language proficiency of their nationals, whose attributes do not always correspond to those in demand in destination countries.

Countries of origin may also be reluctant to accept a bilateral arrangement requiring, in exchange for some limited market access, the return of nationals in an irregular situation in the destination country. Indeed some countries of origin may feel that it is beyond their capacity to prevent the departure of irregular migrants whose job expectations cannot be accommodated at home, and whose families rely on remittances from abroad to make ends meet. Furthermore, when wages are agreed under BLAs while other sources of foreign recruitment exist, such types of agreement may undermine their competitiveness. For some countries, bilateral agreements are of limited interest as they typically offer few mechanisms for enforcement and redress, and unequal power relationships between countries of origin and destination make it difficult to negotiate equitable agreements that truly protect migrant workers.

Even when parties are willing to enter into BLAs, the terms under discussion might put too much pressure on one party to reach an accord. It is sometimes difficult for the parties to identify common goals when each is advocating its own agenda and is unwilling to make compromises regarding its own perceived interests. Among some of the common subjects of contention are: social and medical insurance, family reunification, conditions of readmission of irregular migrants, recognition of qualifications, and mechanisms supporting circular migration between host and home country to limit disruption to families.

In the context of GATS Mode 4 negotiations and development considerations, the likelihood of bilateral agreements being a complementary tool to the multilateral framework by providing for further openings for the low and semi-skilled workforce should not be overestimated.[70]

It would nonetheless be worthwhile to explore in more depth the other ways in which bilateral agreements may assist in liberalizing the movement of workers, either through further research on examples of good practices of migration management extracted from bilateral agreements, which could lead developed destination countries to adopt a more open attitude towards them, and/or through using these examples for the elaboration of a pre-commitment mechanism which would guarantee access to the labour markets of WTO Members to any countries of origin meeting the stated criteria. Both options offer the advantage of providing solutions for all developing countries because they are not discriminatory and support efforts in the direction of the establishment of a workable global framework.

5. Conclusion

In recent years, the international community has come to recognize migration as a key global issue. There are few who would dispute that migration affects virtually every country in the world in one way or another, and frequently to a very significant degree. This has created previously unforeseen challenges for policymakers, but it has also led to the acknowledgement that no country can realistically hope to manage migration on its own; and, in turn, provided impetus for cooperation

[69] And once the agreement is signed, to discuss the modalities for its implementation and monitoring.

[70] Another issue when exploring bilateral possibilities is the fact that an agreement covering movements of persons only in the context of service provision would normally be incompatible with the Most Favoured Nation principle of the WTO which requires all Member States to be treated equally.

towards the development of common approaches to the management of international migration.

At the global level, there are elements of a normative framework "dispersed across a number of treaties, customary law provisions, non-binding agreements and policy understandings" (GCIM, 2005: 55). There are challenges for the international community in both articulating clearly these provisions and ensuring that they are implemented. The GATS Mode 4 negotiations are an ambitious worksite where advances on the access and entry of service providers is, to a large extent conditioned to progress on much larger portfolios of interest such as agriculture. For the foreseeable future however, most of the effort at the global level is likely to be applied to the Global Forum on Migration and Development, where the migration and development agenda offers a commonly acceptable discussion platform for countries of origin and destination.

At the regional level, the most significant outcomes have been achieved when migration management objectives are linked to broader economic integration endeavours supported by well-developed institutional frameworks and considerable financial resources, as best exemplified within the European Union. By providing a normative framework, such regional undertakings create predictability and a legal basis for safeguarding the rights of migrants. However, in many regions, movements of workers are still restricted, with the exception of the highly skilled in carefully defined situations, and the prospects of fuller integration of labour markets and freer movements of workers are clouded by economic disparities and fear of massive inflows by the strong economies of regional groupings. For this reason, most of the considerable activity at this level is of an informal and non-binding nature. Regional frameworks are sometimes seen as relay stations for the non-coercive implementation of standards and principles adopted at the global level. Regional cross-border movements create shared concerns and elicit interest in their management. The limited number of countries involved offers a more manageable environment for consensus building, allocation of financial resources and technical assistance, and reduction in transaction costs through joint activities. In response to the emergence or evolution of issues of interest to more than one region, inter-regional processes, such as the Bali Process or the Abu Dhabi Dialogue (see Textbox 13.4), can be established as broader consultative or cooperative platforms.

Finally, the bilateral level offers a wide range of possibilities for cooperation, including very concrete partnerships to enable the movement of targeted contingents of migrant workers. Bilateral arrangements are very diverse in form and content. In considering why and how they work, it should be noted that the principal motivations for engaging in such cooperation for the facilitation of movement may frequently be unrelated to the improved matching of labour demand and supply. Other social, economic or political considerations come into play, and the specific objectives pursued by countries influence the way these agreements/arrangements are designed and in turn their capacity to function effectively as instruments fostering labour movements. Other internal and external factors are also relevant. Internal conditions relate, for instance, to the efficiency of the mechanisms in the agreement or arrangements for matching demand and supply, the criteria outlined for migrants to participate in the scheme, the complexity of administrative procedures, and the cost of the process to workers and employers. Among external conditions are the existence of other migration routes;[71] the language and vocational skills available in the country of origin; the availability of a pool of irregular migrants;[72] the deterrent effect

[71] E.g. possibilities to enter under other migration/visa programmes for foreign workers, under family migration/reunion or even humanitarian schemes.

[72] Irregular migrants are attractive to employers because they are cheaper (employers do not respect minimum wage requirements, or pay contributions to the social security system, etc.) and allow considerable flexibility in hiring and firing according to the needs of enterprises.

of policies against unauthorized employment; and the preference of employers for workers of certain nationalities (e.g. for reasons of cultural affinity, geographical proximity).

The bilateral, regional and global levels of cooperation afford differing advantages and disadvantages to countries in terms of bargaining strategies and outcomes. The bilateral approach generally allows the more powerful party a stronger say, while offering the ability to both parties to arrive at tailor-made arrangements reflecting an agreed balance of interests. Regional cooperation, even when dominated by the stronger economies in the group, provides possibilities for countries with a weaker voice to be heard, and the commitments made in such circles tend to be measured and practicable. The global arena is a more level playing field, in theory at least, with each country having an equal voice and weaker countries being in a position to develop effective alliances with like-minded partners, bearing in mind that in global institutions developing countries are superior in number to developed countries. Countries interested in becoming more involved in international cooperation on labour mobility may explore all these available opportunities according to their respective merits.

Textbox 13.7

Skilled Migration and Regional, Bilateral and Multilateral Agreements

The flow of global talent across borders is growing continuously, spurred by such diverse factors as demographic profiles, developments in information and communication technologies, and the growing internationalization of goods and services production and delivery. Earlier, skilled labour flows were primarily directed from developed to developing countries. Increasingly, skilled migration also occurs within and among developing countries, reflecting the integration of developing economies in global markets and the growth in South-South trade and investment relations.

Today, there is a distinct shift in migration patterns towards the highly skilled, and countries of destination are pursuing various approaches to attract talent globally (see Chapter 2). In countries of origin, there has also been a shift in thinking on skilled outflows, from viewing such flows as brain drain to seeing them as sources for brain exchange and circulation, especially in view of the temporary and repeat nature of much of these flows in key source sectors like information technology and within global firms. Thus, although economic and social push and pull factors in countries of origin and countries of destination, respectively, have been and remain the primary drivers in migratory flows, changes in host country policies and shifts in source country attitudes have also played a role in driving the growth in cross-border skilled flows.

As more and more host countries compete for global talent and as more and more source countries seek to reap benefits from their skilled labour base and capitalize on their demographic dividend, labour mobility is becoming an important issue in bilateral, regional, and multilateral discussions. Several trade and investment agreements today include labour mobility provisions and commitments on movement and entry of workers among countries. Such agreements are intended to ensure an appropriate framework for managed migration among the parties, in a manner that benefits both sides and at times also go beyond to address issues of capacity building, education and training policies, as well as coordinating screening, monitoring and deployment issues. In the context of skilled migration, these agreements entail shaping the sectoral and regional dynamics of skilled labour movements so as to lower transactions costs for trade and business flows and to leverage complementarities in labour supply and demand between partner countries.

At the multilateral level, the General Agreement on Trade in Services (GATS), negotiated under WTO auspices, provides a framework for the discussion of international movements of service providers at all skill levels. However, despite a few improved offers in the Doha Round discussions that touch on certain categories of interest to developing countries and remove certain conditions on entry and stay, there has been little progress made in the Mode 4 discussions under the GATS and no commercially meaningful improvement in market access conditions so far (see Textbox Int. 1). Thus, the prospects for liberalizing skilled labour flows do not seem promising under the GATS at this time.

On the other hand, regional and bilateral approaches have been more successful in handling migration issues.[1] Regional and bilateral agreements, such as free trade agreements (FTAs), economic partnership agreements (EPAs) and comprehensive economic cooperation agreements (CECAs), generally cover labour mobility under the separate headings of labour and investment. These agreements tend to focus on skilled labour categories similar to those under GATS, as these raise fewer concerns over labour displacement and cultural and social impacts. Regional and bilateral arrangements need not be viewed separately as the approach towards liberalizing migration is not affected by the number of the participating countries or the size of the region covered by such arrangements. Several of these agreements use the GATS model with specific schedules of commitments for various categories of persons. Some, such as the U.S.-Jordan FTA, also go beyond GATS to include specific visa commitments for such categories as independent traders, treaty investors and investment-related entry.

The approach adopted by regional and bilateral agreements towards skilled labour mobility can be broadly classified into three groups.

The **first** concerns agreements such as those concluded under European Union (EU), European Economic Area (EEA) and European Free Trade Association (EFTA) auspices, as well as the Australia-New Zealand Closer Economic Relations Agreement that cover skilled movements under the broader heading of labour movements, which is a general right among member countries. Such agreements tend to be concluded among developed countries.

The **second** group consists of agreements which specifically focus on movements associated with investment and business flows, such as business visitors and investment treaty-related movements. The Asia-Pacific Economic Cooperation (APEC) Forum, for example, excludes self-employed and low or semi-skilled labour and includes arrangements to facilitate labour mobility through information exchange, business dialogue, harmonization of immigration procedures and standards, and the streamlining of procedures for entry, processing and stay for business purposes. There is an in-principle agreement to reduce the processing time for temporary entry applications for intra-corporate transferees, specialists and business visitors. An APEC Business Travel Card valid for three years provides for multiple short-term business entries and accelerated airport processing and entry for business travellers from within APEC (see Textbox 13.5). Likewise, the U.S.-Jordan FTA specifies visa commitments for independent traders and persons entering in connection with investment activities. Jordanian nationals can obtain E-1 and E-2, i.e. U.S. treaty-trader and treaty-investor visas, respectively. The Japan-Singapore Economic Partnership Agreement regulates movement for business purposes, covering business visitors, intra-corporate transferees and certain categories of professionals and investors. However, parties to such agreements continue to retain the right to refuse entry, and national laws on employment, entry and stay take precedence over the agreement provisions on mobility. The Trade in Services Agreement (TIS), concluded under the Framework Agreement on Comprehensive Economic Cooperation between China and the Association of Southeast Asian Nations (ASEAN), similarly provides for improved market access and national treatment for select service suppliers with the objective of facilitating greater investment in the region.

The **third** group of regional or bilateral agreements focuses on liberalizing market access for select business and professional categories to address skills shortages in particular areas. These agreements also discuss associated regulatory issues such as harmonization of standards and mutual recognition of professional and academic qualifications among the parties. For instance, the India-Singapore CECA relaxes visa restrictions for Indian professionals in 127 categories, including information technology (IT), medicine, engineering, nursing, accountancy and university lecturers, by introducing one-year multiple entry visas and removing economic needs tests and labour market tests together with the social security contribution requirement for these categories. By adopting this targeted approach, the agreement clearly builds on the complementarity in the supply of and demand for skilled service providers between India and Singapore, respectively. It also provides for mutual recognition of degrees issued by specified universities and technical education boards of both countries, and a framework for negotiations in other areas where there are requests for recognition. The agreement further addresses the issue of wage parity by adding special allowances paid in India and Singapore to the basic pay of Indian professionals to achieve salary equivalence requirements for market entry into Singapore. Thus, under this bilateral agreement, India has been able to address and make some headway on critical regulatory and market access issues, which the government has also raised in the context of the GATS negotiations. In turn, India hopes to use the CECA as a benchmark in negotiations on other regional trade agreements.

Two points should be noted concerning discussions on labour mobility in the context of bilateral and regional frameworks.

The first point is that, although more progress on skilled movements may be achieved in the regional and bilateral context than under the GATS, discussions have not always been easy even as regards the former. Agreement on skilled movement and labour mobility is often particularly difficult. Thus, the Japan-Philippines Economic Partnership Agreement (JPEPA) was initially unable to progress concerning the admission of Filipino nurses onto the Japanese market. This was the first free trade agreement to be negotiated by Japan to include provisions on the movement of labour. Japan's new economic strategy aims to boost the number of foreign workers in Japan and this agreement is a step in that direction. The Japanese Government has decided to introduce a new facilitated licence for nursing caretakers, which will certify those who have completed relevant courses at vocational schools, colleges and universities, but have not passed a national exam, as "practical" nursing caretakers. This will enable nurses who have not passed the state exam to work at nursing care facilities. Japan will accept 400 nurses and 600 nursing caretakers under this FTA. As a result, hundreds of Filipino nurses, caregivers and nursing care trainees are expected to enter Japan. Some organizations have already been training Filipino nurses in anticipation of this development. Other countries, such as Thailand and Indonesia, that are interested in free trade agreements with Japan are also likely to seek greater market access for skilled and semi-skilled service providers to the Japanese market. However, the Japan-Philippines FTA shows that the passage of labour mobility provisions is not a smooth one, although it could also be argued that more has been achieved by the Philippines in the bilateral than might have been possible in a multilateral context, from a traditionally closed host country like Japan.

Likewise, China's request for admission of its skilled workers to New Zealand has been a matter of debate, as New Zealand negotiators wish to protect working conditions and their local labour force in any agreement. Trade unions in New Zealand are concerned that to admit such labour would reduce incentives to train and upgrade the skills of local workers and affect their working conditions. However, some associations in New Zealand, such as the Engineering, Printing and Manufacturing Union, view such provisions as a means to fill critical skills gaps in manufacturing and other areas, and thus potentially as beneficial. New Zealand may grant access to select groups of skilled Chinese workers, such as teachers of Mandarin, specialists in Chinese medicine and working holidaymakers from China. Therefore, labour mobility issues clearly evoke a wide range of responses and raise host country sensitivities on such issues as wages, the displacement of local workers and the effect on working conditions, similar to those in the multilateral context and, therefore, progress is not easily made.

A second point worth noting is that bilateral and regional agreements may involve substantial concessions by developing countries to their partners to the agreement, particularly in sectors that are in high demand, in exchange for market access for their skilled workers. In the discussions between China and New Zealand, New Zealand has demanded major concessions from China in return for increased access for Chinese skilled workers. In the discussions taking place between India and the EU, the free movement of professionals, especially in such activities as IT, medicine and engineering, and the recognition of professional qualifications are among India's main demands. However, such access is likely to require India's commitments on investment in, for example, the financial, telecom and retail distribution services sectors, and in other areas such as tariffs for industrial products as well as competition policy and regulatory transparency. Thus, the quid pro quo, especially for countries such as India and China, which have large pools of skilled labour but are also very attractive markets for investment, is likely to be much more pronounced in bilateral and regional discussions and also a necessary condition for realizing any gains on skilled movement.

The real value of bilateral and regional agreements, however, lies beyond the market access gained through any particular agreement. Such agreements also provide developing countries with experience and the institutional and regulatory capacity to negotiate with large trading partners on issues such as visas and standards. India is expected to use the CECA concluded with Singapore as a benchmark for its mutual recognition and visa discussions with the EU. Likewise, China, which is seeking market access for its skilled workers on temporary permits as part of a planned free trade deal with New Zealand, is looking to use this agreement as a precedent in its future discussions with larger OECD economies.

Thus, bilateral and regional agreements can potentially serve as building blocks for multilateral frameworks such as the GATS by providing countries with negotiating experience, enabling regulatory capacity building and instilling confidence among policymakers to undertake commitments initially on a bilateral or regional scale before moving on to the multilateral level.

This is particularly so for complex issues such as standards, mutual recognition and labour market policies where there can be no single agreed technical formula for liberalization and where multilateral discussions are more likely to falter. Ideally, these regional and bilateral pacts should pave the way for more liberal multilateral commitments. Whether or not this will be so depends on the overall state of play and the confidence of member countries in the multilateral trading system and the intersectoral trade-offs involved. There is, of course, the frequently referred to concern that some smaller countries may be marginalized in these regional and bilateral processes. But, given the growing number of small countries that are entering into EPAs and FTAs with developed countries, and the accelerating rate of South-South pacts, such marginalization need not occur. Additional issues, such as the classification of occupations and occupational categories, could be addressed multilaterally building on the experience and successful cases of regional and bilateral pacts.

Note:

[1] Much of the discussion on bilateral and regional agreements and their typologies is based on Nielson (2003) and miscellaneous articles from the bilaterals.org website.

Source: *Rupa Chanda, Professor of Economics, Indian Institute of Management, Bangalore.*

REFERENCES

Al-Shammary, H.

2003 "Recruitment of workers from Bangladesh resumes", *The Arab News* (Saudi Arabia), 19 August.

Böhning, W.R.

2003 "The Protection of Temporary Migrants by Conventions of the ILO and the UN", paper presented to the Workshop on Temporary Migration – Assessment and Practical Proposals for Overcoming Protection Gaps, 18-19 September, International Institute for Labour Studies, International Labour Organization (ILO), Geneva, http://www.ilo.org/public/english/bureau/inst/download/bohning.pdf.

Brown, O., F.H. Shaheen, S.R. Khan and M. Yusuf

2005 "Regional Trade Agreements: Promoting conflict or building peace?", October, International Institute for Sustainable Development (IISD), Winnipeg, http://www.iisd.org/pdf/2005/security_rta_conflict.pdf.

Dommen, C.

2005 "Migrants' Human Rights: Could GATS Help?", *Migration Information Source*, March, Migration Policy Institute (MPI), Washington, D.C., http://www.migrationinformation.org/Feature/display.cfm?id=290.

European Commission

2005a *Green Paper on an EU approach to managing economic migration*, COM (2004) 811, 11 January.

2005b *Migration and Development: Some concrete orientations*, COM (2005) 390, 1 September.

2005c *Policy Plan on Legal Migration*, COM (2005) 669, 21 December.

2007a *Communication applying the Global Approach to Migration to the Eastern and South-Eastern Regions neighbouring the European Union*, COM (2007) 247, 16 May.

2007b *Communication on circular migration and mobility partnerships between the European Union and third countries*, COM (2007) 248, 16 May.

2007c *Proposal for a Directive of the European Parliament and of the Council providing for sanctions against employers for illegally staying third-country nationals*, COM (2007) 249, 16 May.

2007d *Proposal for a Council Directive on the conditions of entry and residence of third-country nationals for the purposes of highly qualified employment*, COM (2007) 637, 23 October.

2007e *Proposal for a Council Directive on a single application procedure for a single permit for third-country nationals to reside and work in the territory of a Member State and on a common set of rights for third-country workers legally residing in a Member State*, COM (2007) 638, 23 October.

Fonseca, L., J. Macaísta Malheiros and S. Silva

2005 "Portugal" in J. Niessen, Y. Schibel and C. Thompson (Eds.), *Current Immigration Debates in Europe: A Publication of the European Migration Dialogue*, September, Migration Policy Group (MPG), Brussels/Lisbon, http://www.migpolgroup.com/multiattachments/3011/DocumentName/EMD_Portugal_2005.pdf.

Geronimi, E.

2004 *Acuerdos bilaterales de migración de mano de obra: Modo de empleo*, International Migration Paper No. 65, International Migration Programme, International Labour Office, Geneva, http://www.ilo.org/public/english/protection/migrant/download/imp/imp65s.pdf.

Global Commission on International Migration (GCIM)

2005 *Migration in an Interconnected World: New directions for action*, Report of the GCIM, October, SRO-Kundig, Geneva, http://www.gcim.org/attachements/gcim-complete-report-2005.pdf.

Global Union Research Network (GURN)

2007 Bilateral and Regional Trade Agreements, GURN online discussion, http://www.gurn.info/topic/trade/.

International Confederation of Free Trade Unions (ICFTU)

2004 "The Spread of Bilateral and Regional Trade Agreements", Draft Paper, June, ICFTU, http://www.gurn.info/topic/trade/icftu_0604.pdf.

International Labour Organization (ILO)

1999 *General Survey on Migrant Workers*, Committee on the Application of Conventions and Recommendations, Report III (1B), International Labour Conference, 87th Session, June, International Labour Office, Geneva, http://www.ilo.org/public/english/standards/relm/ilc/ilc87/r3-1b.htm.

2004 *Towards a fair deal for migrant workers in the global economy*, Report VI, International Labour Conference, 92nd Session, June, International Labour Office, Geneva, http://www.ilo.org/wcmsp5/groups/public/---dgreports/---dcomm/documents/meetingdocument/kd00096.pdf.

2006 *ILO Multilateral Framework on Labour Migration: Non-binding principles and guidelines for a rights-based approach to labour migration*, International Labour Office, Geneva, http://www.ilo.org/public/english/protection/migrant/download/multilat_fwk_en.pdf.

International Organization for Migration (IOM)

2005 *World Migration 2005: Costs and Benefits of International Migration*, IOM, Geneva, http://www.iom.int/jahia/Jahia/cache/offonce/pid/1674?entryId=932.

IOM and Swiss Federal Office for Migration

2005a *International Agenda for Migration Management*, IOM/Swiss Federal Office for Migration, Geneva/Berne, http://www.iom.int/jahia/Jahia/cache/offonce/pid/1674?entryId=8005.

2005b *Interstate Cooperation and Migration*, Berne Initiative Studies, IOM/Swiss Federal Office for Migration, Geneva/Berne, http://www.iom.int/jahia/Jahia/cache/offonce/pid/1674?entryId=8008.

Ng, E. and J. Whalley

2007 "Visas and Work Permits: Possible Global Negotiating Initiatives", paper prepared for a Centre for International Governance and Innovation (CIGI) project and resubmitted to the *Review of International Organizations*, September, http://economics.uwo.ca/grad/Ng/AdditionalPaper1~Oct2007.pdf.

Organisation for Economic Co-operation and Development (OECD)

2004 *Migration for Employment – Bilateral Agreements at a Crossroads*, OECD, Paris.

Piper, N. and R. Iredale

2003 *Identification of the Obstacles to the Signing and Ratification of the UN Convention on the Protection of the Rights of all Migrant Workers: The Asia-Pacific Perspective*, United Nations Educational, Scientific and Cultural Organization (UNESCO) Series of Country Reports on the Ratification of the UN Convention on Migrants, Doc. SHS/2003/MC/1 REV, UNESCO, Paris, http://unesdoc.unesco.org/images/0013/001395/139528E.pdf.

Santestevan, A.M.

2007 "Free Movement Regimes in South America: The Experience of MERCOSUR and the Andean Community" in R. Cholewinski, R. Perruchoud and E. Macdonald (Eds.), *International Migration Law: Developing Paradigms and Key Challenges*, T.M.C. Asser Press, The Hague, 363-386.

Shulman, R.

2003 "Underage, Illegal and taking their Chances in Spain: Moroccan Girls defy Social Convention to Escape Poverty, Violence and Despair", *Washington Post*, 2 November.

Sleptova, E.

2003 "Labour Migration in Europe: Special focus on the Republic of Moldova", Institute for Public Policy (IPP), Moldova Republic, http://www.ipp.md/public/biblioteca/50/en/St~Sleptova~fin.doc.

Williams, V.

2008 "Interstate Cooperation in Migration Management in the Southern African Development Community (SADC)", revised draft paper presented at the IOM-University of Toronto Workshop on Migration and International Cooperation: South-South Perspectives, 7-8 August, Geneva.

Winters, L.A.

2005 "Developing Country Proposals for the Liberalization of Movements of Natural Service Suppliers", Working Paper T8, January, Development Research Centre on Migration, Globalisation and Poverty, University of Sussex, Brighton, http://www.migrationdrc.org/publications/working_papers/WP-T8.pdf.

Textbox 13.1 - The International Convention on the Protection of the Rights of All Migrant Workers and Members of Their Families

Office of the United Nations High Commissioner for Human Rights (OHCHR)

2008 International Convention on the Protection of the Rights of All Migrant Workers and Members of Their Families, General Assembly resolution 45/158 of 18 December 1990, OHCHR, http://www2.ohchr.org/english/law/cmw.htm.

2005 Committee on Migrant Workers, 15 December 2005; Day of General Discussion: Protecting the rights of all migrant workers as a tool to enhance development, OHCHR, http://www2.ohchr.org/english/bodies/cmw/mwdiscussion.htm.

Textbox 13.6 - Exploring the Role of Reformed Bilateral Labour Agreements: The Caribbean Community and the Temporary Movement of Less-skilled Labour

Caldentey, E.P. and K. Schmid

2006 "The Performance of CARICOM Economies in the 1990s: The Current Effect on Migration and Conflict Potential" in T. Lesser, B. Fernández-Alfaro, L. Cowie and N. Bruni (Eds.), *Intra-Caribbean Migration and the Conflict Nexus*, Human Rights Internet (in collaboration with the IOM, Association of Caribbean States and The University of West Indies), Ottawa.

Caribbean Community (CARICOM)

2007 CARICOM Secretariat Law website, http://www.caricomlaw.org/doc.php?id=557.

Cholewinski, R., J. Redpath, S. Nonnenmacher and J. Packer

2006 "The International Normative Framework with Reference to Migration in the Greater Caribbean" in T. Lesser, B. Fernández-Alfaro, L. Cowie and N. Bruni (Eds.), *Intra-Caribbean Migration and the Conflict Nexus*. Human Rights Internet (in collaboration with the IOM, Association of Caribbean States and The University of West Indies), Ottawa.

Council on Hemispheric Affairs (COHA)

2005 *Neighborly Quarrels: The Dominican Republic and the Perennial Haitian Immigrant Issue*, Memorandum to the Press, 30 June, COHA, Washington, D.C., http://www.coha.org/2005/06/30/neighborly-quarrels-the-dominican-republic-and-the-perennial-haitian-immigrant-issue/.

Ferguson, J.

2003 *Migration in the Caribbean: Haiti, the Dominican Republic and Beyond*, July, Minority Rights Group International, London, http://www.minorityrights.org/1038/reports/migration-in-the-caribbean-haiti-the-dominican-republic-and-beyond.html.

Fuchs, D. and T. Straubhaar

2003 *Economic Integration in the Caribbean: The development towards a common labour market*, International Migration Papers 61, May, Social Protection Sector, International Migration Programme, International Labour Office, Geneva, http://www.ilo.org/public/english/protection/migrant/download/imp/imp61e.pdf.

Hendrikx, M.

2006 *Appropriate social security for migrant workers: Implementation of agreements on social security*, paper prepared for the International Social Security Association (ISSA) Regional Conference for the Americas, 28-31 May, Belize City, http://www.issa.int/pdf/belize06/2hendrikx.pdf.

Inter-American Development Bank (IADB)

2007 *Haiti Remittance Survey 2006*, presented at the IADB and the Multilateral Investment Fund (MIF) Conference on Sending Money Home: Remittances to Haiti, 6 March, Port-au-Prince, http://www.iadb.org/news/docs/HaitiSurvey.pps.

International Organization for Migration (IOM)

2005 "Bilateral Labour Agreements: Effective Tools for Managing Labour Flows?", Textbox 12.2 in *World Migration 2005: Costs and Benefits of International Migration*, IOM, Geneva, 238-251.

2008 Website on Migration and Trade, http://www.iom.int/jahia/page1172.html.

Orozco, M.

2006 "Understanding the remittance economy in Haiti", final draft of the paper commissioned by the World Bank, Inter-American Dialogue 2006, 15 March, Research Consortium on Remittances in Conflict and Crises (RCRCC), Institute for the Study of International Migration (ISIM), Georgetown University, Washington, D.C., http://isim.georgetown.edu/Publications/RCRCCPubs/Orozco/Understanding%20the%20remittance%20economy%20in%20Haiti.pdf.

Pritchett, L.

2006 *Let Their People Come: Breaking the Gridlock on Global Labor Mobility*, Center for Global Development, Washington, D.C., http://www.cgdev.org/content/publications/detail/10174.

Ruhs, M.

2005 "Designing Viable and Ethical Labour Immigration Policies" in *World Migration 2005: Costs and Benefits of International Migration*, IOM, Geneva, 203-220.

United Nations, Security Council

2006 *Report of the Secretary-General on the United Nations Stabilization Mission in Haiti*, Doc. S/2006/592, 28 July, UN Security Council, New York.

World Bank

2005 *A Time to Choose: Caribbean Development in the 21st Century*, Report No. 31725-LAC, April 26, Caribbean Country Management Unit, Poverty Reduction and Economic Management Unit, Latin America and the Caribbean Region, The World Bank, http://web.worldbank.org/WBSITE/EXTERNAL/COUNTRIES/LACEXT/0,,contentMDK:20468612~pagePK:146736~piPK:146830~theSitePK:258554,00.html.

2006 *Social Resilience and State Fragility in Haiti: A Country Social Analysis*, Report No. 36069–HT, April 27, Caribbean Country Management Unit, ESSD Sector Management Unit, Latin America and the Caribbean Region, The World Bank, http://siteresources.worldbank.org/SOCIALANALYSIS/1104894-1115795935771/20938696/Haiti_CSA.pdf.

Textbox 13.7 - Skilled Migration and Regional, Bilateral and Multilateral Agreements

Bilaterals.org website

http://bilaterals.org.

Chanda, R.

2004 "Movement and Presence of Natural Persons and Developing Countries: Issues and Proposals for the GATS Negotiations", Trade-Related Agenda, Development and Equity (T.R.A.D.E.) Working Papers 19, May, South Centre, Geneva, http://www.southcentre.org/index.php?option=com_content&task=view&id=234&Itemid=67.

Docquier, F. and H. Rapoport

2004 Skilled migration: the perspective of developing countries, WPS332, The World Bank, Washington, D.C., http://www-wds.worldbank.org/servlet/WDSContentServer/WDSP/IB/2004/09/22/000160016_20040922151739/Rendered/PDF/WPS3382.pdf.

Nielson, J.

2003 "Labour Mobility in Regional Trade Agreements" in A. Mattoo and A. Carzaniga (Eds.), *Moving People to Deliver Services*, The World Bank, Washington, D.C.

United Nations Department of Economic and Social Affairs (UN DESA)

2004 *World Economic and Social Survey 2004: International Migration*, Docs. E/2004/75/Rev.1/Add.1, ST/ESA/291/Add.1, UN DESA, New York, http://www.un.org/esa/policy/wess/wess2004files/part2web/part2web.pdf.

World Trade Organization (WTO)

1994 General Agreement on Trade in Services (GATS) and Related Instruments, April, WTO, Geneva, http://www.wto.org/english/tratop_e/serv_e/gatsintr_e.htm.

CONCLUSION*

Human mobility in its many and varied forms, within and across national borders, is a major characteristic and perhaps even one of the defining features of our contemporary world. People move in ever increasing numbers and for many different purposes related to work, family, social, educational, cultural, business or personal safety concerns; sometimes within their own countries, at other times across the nearest border or perhaps across the world.

Today, a great deal of policy attention tends to fall on highly qualified workers and their needed skills, drive and energy. Developed countries are conscious of the need to offer competitive conditions of entry, residence and employment if they are to attract needed talent from abroad, as exemplified by the European Union's current debate about the proposed introduction of a "Blue Card" for highly qualified individuals (European Commission, 2007). On the other hand, low and semi-skilled workers remain a much more challenging and contested category: while their labour continues to be indispensable in many economically important areas of employment, for instance in the agriculture, construction and hospitality sectors, in many host countries their presence is the subject of persistent controversy. When community debates arise about the size of migration quotas, about the value of permanency of residence as opposed to circularity of movement, about worker rights and social entitlements and, even more generally, about the economic impact of migration, it is generally these workers who are the focus of interest.

For any analysis of contemporary mobility to be comprehensive and meaningful, however, other, often overlooked categories have to be taken into consideration. For instance, student populations in countries of destination are increasingly seen as pools of talented individuals who can be and are encouraged to stay on for work at the completion of their studies.

Tourists and business visitors account for the highest numbers of international border crossings, and their movements have perceptible impacts on broader migratory patterns: tourists may combine the pursuit of cultural and leisure activities with prospecting for employment in anticipation of subsequent migration, and business visits may be a prelude to eventual longer-term residence and employment, or the establishment of business enterprises. In

* This Conclusion was written by Gervais Appave and Ryszard Cholewinski (Editors-in-Chief), and Michele Klein Solomon, Director, Migration Policy, Research and Communications, IOM, Geneva.

addition, there is a growing trend to offer carefully tailored access to domestic labour markets to young, educated tourists through the use of working-holiday visas.

Family migrations are also changing. They have, in the past, often been seen as an adjunct to labour migration and consisting largely of economically inactive female spouses and dependent children. Without prejudice to the importance of the reunion of spouses, and parents and children in migration management, this perception needs to be adjusted to acknowledge more readily the fact that women are now migrating as heads of households, that family migrants do enter and actively participate in the workforce in countries of destination, and that family members are recruited to meet specific labour market needs.

The number of internal migrants[1] probably far exceeds that of international migrants and, in many countries – India and China for example, but they are not, by any means, the only ones – they are an established and essential part of the labour force. Their contribution to the economic, social and cultural life of both their regions of origin and destination appears to be beyond question. Internal migration may eventually lead to international migration.

Last, but no means least, there are the scattered but vast contingents of irregular migrants who remain beyond the reach of official policy and procedure, but who, albeit to different degrees, are nonetheless very much part of migration and employment patterns in countries of transit and destination.

The broad surveys of these diverse manifestations of human movement, as laid out in Part A of *World Migration 2008*, invite a number of observations. The first is that mobility is both a consequence and a constituent part of the complex and interdependent social and economic processes that are now collectively referred to as globalization; a consequence in the sense that developments towards the facilitation of the production of goods and services through global resourcing, the facilitation of the movement of capital and the facilitation of trade create a context that encourages human mobility; a constituent part in the sense that human mobility in itself gives rise to ever expanding networks of relationships and communications that are part and parcel of globalization.

Second, as one of the consequences of the choice made by the international community to facilitate the movement of capital, goods and services, human mobility or, more specifically, the movement of human resources at all skills levels is now factored into the equations intended to yield new economic gains. In other words, labour market dynamics are increasingly operating across international borders.

Third, while the motivations underlying human mobility are many and varied, work-related interests and concerns are rarely if ever entirely absent and provide a strong unifying link.

The fourth observation is that these dynamics are sustained and amplified by the large demographic differentials and wage disparities between developing and developed countries and are also operating to some degree among developing countries.

The fifth and final point that emerges is that there are strong regional dynamics in operation. The report identifies six different areas of intense or growing migratory activity: Africa, Asia, the Americas, Europe, the Middle East and Oceania, each with its own specificities worth noting and studying. Migrants from African countries move predominantly to other African countries, with Southern Africa, the Maghreb and West Africa being the sub-regions most affected by labour mobility on the African

[1] As discussed in Chapter 7, internal migrants as a class are often indistinguishable from cross-border transients in border zones.

continent. Asia is the largest source of temporary contractual migrant workers worldwide, while being characterized also by very large intra-regional flows of migrant workers, in particular the vast internal movements in China and India. Europe stands apart because of the EU objective of creating a common migratory space within far-flung but jointly managed external borders. The Americas are characterized by strong South-North migratory flows from Latin America and the Caribbean to the United States and Canada and, increasingly, Europe. The United States and Canada continue to be the major receivers of permanent settlers from across the world, but they are also faced with growing demands for temporary workers. The Middle East is by far the most important region of destination for temporary contractual workers, most of who come from Asia. Finally, Oceania includes two large destination countries, Australia and New Zealand, on the one hand and, on the other, many small island nations whose populations are increasingly interested in labour migration. All regions are significantly affected by irregular migration.

The policy implications of these evolving realities require careful exploration, but it is already apparent that neither avoidance of the issues nor a passive laissez-faire approach are likely to lead to the policy responses needed to realize the social and economic potential of mobility. The priority need is for planned and predictable ways of matching labour demand with supply in safe, legal, humane and orderly ways, with due regard to the human rights of migrants and to the social implications of migration. Given the diversity of labour market needs and of available skills, policies and procedures will have to display commensurate flexibility and adaptability to enable modes of labour mobility that may be short-term, circular, long-term or permanent.

Countries of origin and destination are increasingly engaged in the formulation of policies to meet their particular labour mobility objectives: on the one hand, to train and prepare their nationals to work at destinations abroad; on the other, to identify labour market needs and seek recruitment of appropriate personnel. Optimal outcomes will be achieved when the two sets of policies are envisaged as complementary elements of a coherent whole, directed towards the achievement of shared development goals while also ensuring that benefits continue to accrue to migrant workers and their families.

As a general rule, foreign employment policies in countries of origin and destination are established unilaterally, which is unsurprising given that every country has its own economic, political, social and cultural interests at heart. Thus, countries of origin will aim to identify and secure authorized employment opportunities abroad for their citizens, while ensuring that their human rights are protected. Countries of destination, for their part, wish to admit various categories of foreign workers to fill certain domestic labour shortages, while also ensuring the integrity of their sovereign territory and frontiers, and respect for national cultural and social core values. Nevertheless, there are signs pointing to policy convergence in this area built around the notions of human resource development and migration management.

For countries of origin, this means taking on the challenge of formulating policies and setting priorities able to both satisfy local labour market and economic needs, and nurture talent to compete for work placements abroad. This is best achieved within a comprehensive human resource development (HRD) framework. Central to such a framework is a properly resourced education system capable of providing the necessary formal learning opportunities and complemented, where necessary, by practical work experience and training, to be formally assessed and certified by recognized educational and professional authorities. Of necessity, however, HRD planning starts well upstream of educational processes, with the identification of employment opportunities in relation to both domestic and international labour market needs taking account of, inter alia, demographic projections. Policies required for the specific management of labour mobility then follow. Foremost among these are measures to uphold the integrity of recruitment processes and, more generally, protect migrant workers from exploitation and abuse. Access to authoritative, accurate and up-to-date information is of great importance, but so are welfare and support services for the workers while abroad and, when needed, appropriate arrangements to facilitate their return and reintegration in the home country.

From the perspective of countries of destination, the starting point is also the definition of explicit mobility-related objectives and desired outcomes, followed by the formulation of appropriate policies. These policies are not narrowly limited to the admission of foreign workers to fill existing labour shortages, but relate more broadly to economic and demographic planning, and cover the entire migration cycle from departure in countries of origin, the treatment and adequate protection of migrant workers (and their families) in the host society and the workplace, including appropriate integration strategies, to their return and reintegration, where appropriate, as well as possible continued movement between the country of origin and of destination. Such policies should be sufficiently flexible to be able to respond to changing labour market needs. They may need to accommodate both temporary labour migration and (permanent) employment-based immigration and, in certain instances, to provide a bridge between the two types of movement.

Both countries of origin and destination stand to benefit from securing the involvement and cooperation of the widest range of stakeholders, including employers, private recruitment agencies, trade unions, migrant and diaspora associations, and international organizations.

Bilateral cooperation offers many possibilities. Bilateral agreements are flexible instruments that can be used to match labour supply and demand in a planned, predictable and rights-based manner, while also contributing to the mitigation of irregular migration. They enable employers in countries of destination to recruit trained and competent individuals with the needed skills, while countries of origin obtain assurances that employment contracts will be adhered to and workers enjoy decent and safe working conditions. Cooperation does not stop there. Human mobility is increasingly the subject of international cooperation at the sub-regional, regional, inter-regional and global level, although it is true that progress in the management of labour migration is yet to match what has been achieved at the international level in other domains of economic and social affairs.

The discretion to determine who may or may not enter its territory remains a prerogative of the nation state, and this may limit the state's willingness to engage in cooperative endeavours. A second issue is the difficulty in achieving nationally coordinated policy positions addressing labour mobility among interested domestic agencies, such as those concerned with employment, foreign affairs, development, trade or welfare, prior to multilateral engagement. Yet another obstacle is differences in priorities among countries: while they are all affected by migratory flows, they are not all affected at the same time or in the same way, nor do they share the same circumstances or objectives. Despite these hurdles, however, numerous consultative mechanisms on migration policy have emerged over the last decade or so. The Abu Dhabi Dialogue, held in early 2008, is a good example of how consultations among countries of origin and destination can lead to the development of concrete projects to facilitate the movement of workers and improve their welfare (see Textbox 10.5). Such consultative processes, characterized by their informality and open-endedness, deserve to be further developed as forums for confidence building and information exchange and as "workplaces" where governments can meet to discuss the challenges of managing mobility, improve their grasp of issues and identify viable policy options.

Considerable amounts of time, resources and effort have been invested in non-binding consultative exercises in recent years. The Berne Initiative, IOM's International Dialogue on Migration, the UN General Assembly's High-Level Dialogue on International Migration and Development, and the Global Forum on Migration and Development have been or are, in many ways, large-scale community learning exercises. The Global Commission on International Migration (GCIM) was another parallel and intensive effort at developing a "framework for the formulation of a coherent, comprehensive and global response to the issue of international migration" (GCIM, 2005: vii). The outcomes of all these exercises are strikingly convergent. All of them take as their starting point the increasing political visibility and importance of international migration; all of them acknowledge that mobility is an unavoidable economic and social reality; all of them point to benefits that flow from properly managed flows; all of them draw attention to the risks of not managing those flows; all of them assert that it is possible to arrive at common understandings and principles, and propose remarkably consistent lines of action. They also confirm the need for clearer linkages to be established between the domain of human mobility proper and closely adjoining policy fields, especially those of development and trade.

Accordingly, the migration and development equation has become a foremost subject of research and policy debate. It has now been established beyond any doubt that migration can and does contribute to poverty reduction at both the individual and community level. Migrants can benefit directly by obtaining access to higher wages and improved living conditions, and there are follow-on benefits for the family members and communities, who are the recipients of flows of remittances that had an estimated global value of USD 337 billion in 2007 (Ratha et al., 2008). Other longer-term gains accrue from the establishment of expatriate communities. Under the right circumstances, these diasporas have demonstrated that they can develop and sustain extensive social and cultural networks, promote and conduct trade, become providers of investment funding and business know-how, offer humanitarian assistance in times of crisis and even make a meaningful contribution to democratic processes in countries of origin. There are, however, downsides to the picture. Countries of origin – especially the smaller ones – are concerned about the impact on their economies of the departure of large proportions of their highly skilled workers. Developing countries are therefore keenly interested in the development of legislative and policy frameworks that will provide a balanced set of solutions affording opportunities and rights for migrants while meeting their concerns regarding brain drain.

For all countries, progress in this continuously evolving and complex area is first and foremost subject to a better understanding of the impact of international labour mobility on domestic labour supply; the impact of migration on productivity in the domestic economy; and the impact of remittance flows on development. It will also depend on the establishment of genuine partnerships between countries of origin and destination to attain mutually satisfactory outcomes.

The migration and trade nexus is at least as complex as the migration and development equation. At the global level, tariffs and other barriers to cross-border investment and trade in goods have been very substantially reduced in recent decades with the consequent growth in the global exchanges of capital, goods and services. Facilitation of the movement of people has been identified as a potential avenue to further economic gains through trade liberalization, but the policy intersections between migration and trade need to be more clearly mapped out and more fully explored. One specific issue to be addressed is the fundamental tension between trade-oriented policy objectives driven by market dynamics and premised on planning and predictability, and approaches to migration management that favour discretion and the adaptation of policy strategies to changing circumstances. At the doctrinal level, trade theories have yet to agree whether trade and migration are substitutes (viz. supporting local economic growth and boosting exports would have the effect of easing migration pressure) or complements (viz. both trade and migration can increase, and can be mutually supportive). Trade theories need to be reviewed from the trade-migration vantage point and relevant supporting evidence gathered to better inform policies aimed at managing international labour mobility, all the more so as current globalization trends are predominantly characterized by the growth in trade in services and knowledge-based trading patterns, both of which rely heavily on the mobility of human resources. In the context of international trade negotiations, GATS Mode 4 is seen as a promising means to facilitate the temporary movement of service personnel; however, so far its scope of application has been largely limited to the international movement of highly skilled personnel, and considerable creativity and persistence are still needed to allow these negotiations to move forward. Regional and bilateral initiatives will similarly have to be nurtured and encouraged to yield the intended results. In fact, regional and bilateral trade agreements that already incorporate labour mobility may turn out to be learning stations where states acquire the confidence to work on broader approaches (see Textbox 13.7). Finally, policy coherence requires improvement in two ways: first, through the integration of worker mobility in national, regional and international employment and migration policies and strategies and, second, the definition of the particular roles and responsibilities of all key stakeholders, including the private sector.

The elucidation of the connections between migration, development and trade needs to take full account of the rights of migrant workers, in particular those who, for various reasons, such as age, gender, low-skill profile or work in unregulated sectors, are not covered by national labour laws and find themselves in vulnerable situations. Similarly, issues such as the management of change while maintaining social cohesion and adherence to core values, environmental impacts on mobility and vice versa (see Textbox Conc. 1) and migrant health should be taken into account in the development of effective migration management strategies.

Textbox Conc. 1

Climate Change and Labour Mobility

The importance of the reciprocal impact of climate change and migration is expected to grow incrementally over the coming decades. Altered rainfall patterns, rising sea levels and increasingly frequent natural disasters are all likely to exceed the absorption capacity of large areas of the world, and to critically affect problems of food and water security in marginal areas.

A number of analysts, of whom Norman Myers of Oxford University is perhaps the best known, have undertaken to estimate the number of people who will be forced to move over the long term as a direct result of climate change. Myers predicts that, by 2050, "there could be as many as 200 million people overtaken by disruptions of monsoon systems and other rainfall regimes, by droughts of unprecedented severity and duration, and by sea-level rise and coastal flooding" (Myers, 2005: 1).

This is a staggering number and, should it come to pass, some two per cent or one in forty-five people alive in 2050 would have been displaced by climate change at some point in their lives, and their total number would exceed the estimated current global migrant population of 200 million.

Such predictions are, of course, inherently speculative. There are so many and diverse factors at play – population growth, urbanization and local politics, to name just three – that establishing a causal relation between climate change and migration is difficult and fraught with uncertainties. However, it is clear that climate change will lead to large areas becoming increasingly less able to sustain peoples' livelihoods and lead to large-scale moves to areas still able to offer better opportunities.

Migration is, and always has been, an important response mechanism to climate stress. While pastoralists have since time immemorial migrated to and from water sources and grazing lands as part of their normal way of life as well as in response to climate changes, it is becoming apparent that migration as a response to environmental change is no longer limited to nomadic societies.

In Western Sudan, for example, studies have shown that one adaptive response to drought is to send an older male family member to the capital, Khartoum, to find paid work so as to tide the family over until the end of the drought (McLeman and Smit, 2004). Temporary labour migration in times of climate stress can supplement a family's income through remittances from paid work elsewhere, and reduce the demand on local resources as there will be fewer mouths to feed.

But the picture is nuanced. Recent studies in the West African Sahel have revealed the recourse to temporary labour migration as an adaptive mechanism to climate change. The region has suffered a prolonged drought for much of the past three decades. One way that households have adapted has been to send their young men and women in search of wage labour after each harvest. But **how far** they go depends on the success of the harvest.

A good harvest might give the family sufficient resources to send a member to Europe in search of work. While the potential rewards in terms of remittances are high, the journey is dangerous and the migrant is unlikely to be back in time for the next planting season. But, in a drought year, when harvests are poor, the young men and women tend to stay much closer to home and travel instead to nearby cities for paid work with which to supplement the household income. In such years the risk of losing the "migration gamble" is simply too great (McLeman, 2006).

In the past, the rich developed countries focused mainly on mitigating climate change by setting emissions targets for the OECD countries and deliberating on how to gain new adherents to an emissions control agreement after the Kyoto Protocol expires in 2012. More recently, greater attention has been paid to helping developing countries to adapt to the impacts of climate change, for instance by altering irrigation techniques, building better storm shelters and developing drought-resistant crops.

This approach to adaptation is fundamentally based on the idea of adapting "in situ". Migration is somehow viewed as a failure to adapt. The United Nations Framework Convention on Climate Change, for example, has supported the development of National Adaptation Programmes of Action (NAPA) to help the Least Developed Countries to identify and rank their priorities for adaptation to climate change. However, none of the fourteen NAPAs submitted so far mention migration or population relocation as a possible policy response. Likewise, the developed countries are very resistant to the idea of relaxing their immigration or asylum policies and to consider environmental strain as a legitimate reason for migration.

It may be said that the international community is, in fact, ignoring labour mobility as a coping strategy for climate stress. Instead, there is a collective, and rather successful, attempt to ignore the scale of future climate-induced migration. However, how the international community reacts to climate-driven labour migration will have a real effect on the larger development impacts of climate change.

Some analysts are beginning to argue that migration is both a necessary element of global redistributive justice and an important response to climate change; and that greenhouse gas emitters should accept an allocation of "climate migrants"[2] in proportion to their historical greenhouse gas emissions. Andrew Simms of the New Economics Foundation argues: "Is it right

---

2 IOM applies the term "environmental migrants" to describe persons moving primarily as a result of climate change and environmental degradation. In its 2007 Discussion Note on "Migration and the Environment", IOM defined environmental migrants as "persons or groups of persons who, for reasons of sudden or progressive changes in the environment that adversely affect their lives or living conditions, are obliged to leave their habitual homes, or choose to do so, either temporarily or permanently, and who move either within their country or abroad" (IOM, 2007: 1-2, para. 6). This term is broader than "climate migrants" and encompasses population movements that are resulting both from climate and non-climate related environmental processes and events.

that while some states are more responsible for creating problems like global climate change, all states should bear equal responsibility to deal with their displaced people?"

There is a dilemma here. Relaxing immigration rules as part of a concerted policy to "release the population pressure" in areas affected by climate change could accelerate the brain drain of talented individuals from the developing world to the developed – and thereby worsen the "hollowing out" of affected economies, which is itself a driver of migration. On the other hand, closing borders in both source and destination countries undermines remittance economies and denies developing countries the benefits of access to the international labour market.

Clearly, there has to be a balance of policies that promotes the incentives for workers to stay in their home countries, whilst not closing the door to international labour mobility. The first steps are to acknowledge, assess and plan for the role of climate change and environmental degradation in future population movements.

Source: *Oli Brown, International Institute for Sustainable Development (IISD), Geneva.*

Accurate and reliable data on migrant stocks, flows and trends are indispensable to develop, monitor and evaluate migration policies and programmes. However, the collection, sharing and management of migration data is a highly time-consuming and resource-intensive process. Data are frequently gleaned from a multitude of sources not actually designed for migration-related analysis. In addition, since migration data are frequently considered to be sensitive, the sharing of data among institutions at the national level, let alone with other governments or non-government specialists, is often avoided. Special efforts are needed to improve the reliability and comparability of existing data sources; to identify and gather new data on emerging issues; and to ensure the dissemination and utilization of data and research on labour migration.

For many countries, migration is a new administrative area, and comprehensive systems to track, process and facilitate inward and outward movements of people are weak or non-existent. What is needed is a renewed focus on building the capacity of all governments, in particular those of developing countries or of countries newly affected by migratory flows; to formulate policy and legislation; to improve labour migration and related human resource development programmes through experimentation and innovation; to properly administer them; and to monitor progress and evaluate outcomes.

A new spirit of partnership in outlook and action is both possible and essential to realizing beneficial outcomes for the international community as a whole, including countries of origin, countries of destination and the migrants and their families. Such a partnership will be the key to the success or failure of the efforts to manage the international labour mobility challenges of the twenty-first century.

REFERENCES

European Commission

2007 *Proposal for a Council Directive on the conditions of entry and residence of third-country nationals for the purposes of highly qualified employment*, COM (2007) 637, 23 October.

Global Commission on International Migration (GCIM)

2005 *Migration in an Interconnected World: New directions for action*, October, GCIM, SRO-Kundig, Geneva, http://www.gcim.org/attachements/gcim-complete-report-2005.pdf.

International Organization for Migration (IOM)

2007 "Discussion Note: Migration and the Environment", 1 November, IOM Council, 94th Session, Doc. MC/INF/288, IOM, Geneva, http://www.old.iom.int//DOCUMENTS/GOVERNING/EN/913208461788198.pdf.

Ratha, D., S. Mohapatra, K.M. Vijayalakshmi and Z. Xu

2008 *Revisions to Remittance Trends 2007*, Migration and Development Brief 5, 10 July, Migration and Remittances Team, Development Prospects Group, The World Bank, Washington, D.C., http://siteresources.worldbank.org/INTPROSPECTS/Resources/334934-1110315015165/MD_Brief5.pdf.

Textbox Conc. 1 - Climate Change and Labour Mobility

Dupont, A. and G. Pearman

2006 "Heating up the Planet: Climate Change and Security", Lowry Institute for International Policy, Paper 12, Sydney, http://lowyinstitute.richmedia-server.com/docs/AD_GP_ClimateChange.pdf.

McLeman, R.

2006 "Global warming's huddled masses", *The Ottawa Citizen*, 23 November, http://www.canada.com/ottawacitizen/news/opinion/story.html?id=f4f4a221-e39e-42ac-9d19-5f0bd4b0ee3e.

McLeman, R. and B. Smit

2004 "Climate change, migration and security", Canadian Security Intelligence Service, March, Commentary No. 86, Ottawa, http://www.csis-scrs.gc.ca/pblctns/cmmntr/cm86-eng.asp.

Myers, N.

2005 "Environmental Refugees: An emergent security issue", 13th Economic Forum, 23-27 May, Session III – Environment and Migration, Organization for Security and Co-operation in Europe (OSCE), Prague, Doc. EF.NGO/4/05, http://www.osce.org/documents/eea/2005/05/14488_en.pdf.

Pielke, R. Jr, G. Prins, S. Rayner and D. Sarewitz

2007 "Lifting the taboo on adaptation: renewed attention to policies for adapting to climate change cannot come too soon", *Nature*, 445 (8 February): 597-598.

REGIONAL OVERVIEWS

INTRODUCTION

While *World Migration 2008* lays emphasis on the global nature of contemporary migratory activity, it is nonetheless true that each major geographic region displays characteristics that distinguish it from the others. The following brief Regional Overviews are intended to complement the information provided in the rest of this Report by drawing attention to the key features typifying each region. Given the known difficulty of obtaining up-to-date, comprehensive and comparable data on migratory phenomena, the overviews are not intended to be read as statistically accurate accounts, but rather as impressionistic depictions of the migratory dynamics in operation within the regions.

Based on a review of many different and not infrequently conflicting sources, each overview offers information on the stocks and distribution of migrants; the major types of flows encountered and their magnitude and determinants; and some of the topical migration management issues to which they give rise. Wherever possible, preference has been given to graphs and illustrations over lengthy word descriptions.

AFRICA

- With an increase of just over half a million migrants from 16.3 to 16.9 million between 2000 and 2005, Africa[1] experienced the lowest growth rate in international migrants of any region in the world, and, at two per cent, the continent also registers the lowest proportion of migrants as a share of the population. Its share of the global migrant stock has remained stable at nine per cent (UN DESA, 2005).
- Migrants are widely distributed across the continent, with a disproportionate number in sub-Saharan countries. In absolute terms, it is the large West and Southern African countries that are most affected by migration, but relative to the size of their population the smallest countries or territories receive more migrants (see Figure 1).

Figure 1:

Stock of migrants in Africa, top ten destinations, 2000 and 2005

Part A: Total number of migrants

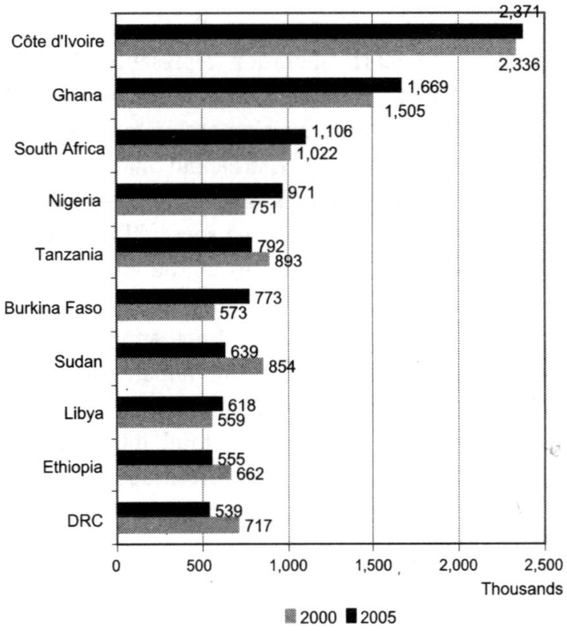

[1] **East Africa**: Burundi, Comoros, Djibouti, Eritrea, Ethiopia, Kenya, Madagascar, Malawi, Mauritius, Mozambique, Reunion, Rwanda, Seychelles, Somalia, Uganda, Tanzania, Zambia, Zimbabwe. **Central Africa**: Angola, Cameroon, Central African Republic, Chad, Congo, Democratic Republic of the Congo (DRC), Equatorial Guinea, Gabon, Sao Tome and Principe. **North Africa**: Algeria, Libya, Morocco, Sudan, Tunisia. **Southern Africa**: Botswana, Lesotho, Namibia, Republic of South Africa and Swaziland. **West Africa**: Benin, Burkina Faso, Cape Verde, Côte d'Ivoire, Gambia, Ghana, Guinea, Guinea-Bissau, Liberia, Mali, Mauritania, Niger, Nigeria, Saint Helena, Senegal, Sierra Leone, Togo (division of countries according to UN DESA, 2005). Egypt is considered in the Migration Overview on the Middle East.

Part B: As a share of total population

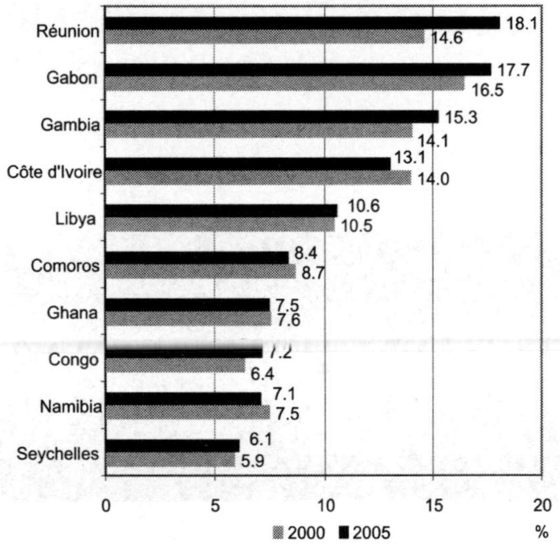

Source: UN DESA, 2005.

- Most of the recorded migration in Africa occurs within the region; out of a total of 14.5 million migrants originating in sub-Saharan Africa, 10 million migrants (or 69%) move within the region (Ratha and Shaw, 2007).
- On the other hand, data from North Africa[2] show that South-South migration represents only 19 per cent of total migration from this sub-region while South-North migration accounts for 80 per cent of total migration (Ratha and Shaw, 2007).
- Africa has the world's highest concentration of internally displaced persons (IDPs), with 12.7 million in 20 countries at the end of 2007 (IDMC, 2008), largely outnumbering the refugee population which declined from approximately six million to about three million in the 1995-2005 decade (UNHCR, 1995 and 2007).
- Refugees as a percentage of total international migrants decreased by four percentage points to 18 per cent of the current migrant population (UN DESA, 2005).
- Africa received USD 23.1 billion in remittances[3] in 2007, the smallest share of global transfers (World Bank, 2008).
- Coastal migration and environmental migration are among the emerging features of migration in Africa.

EAST AND CENTRAL AFRICA

- The four leading East African countries of destination for migrants from the sub-region registered a decline in their migrant populations between 2000 and 2005. With nearly a million migrants, Tanzania is host to the largest contingent of migrants; while migrants make up a larger share of the populations of the smaller islands. Thus, the share of migrants in the total population of La Réunion increased from 14.6 per cent to 18 per cent between 2000 and 2005, and the Comoros and Seychelles host, respectively, 8.4 and 6.1 migrants per 100 habitants (UN DESA, 2005) (see Figure 2).

Figure 2:

Stock of migrants in East Africa, top ten destinations, 2000 and 2005

Part A: Total number of migrants

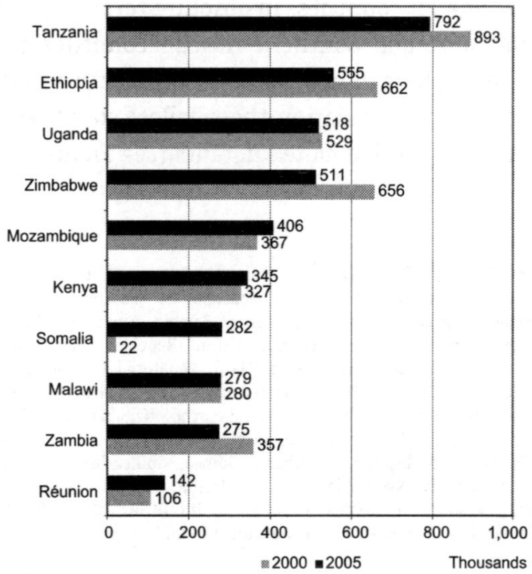

2 North Africa here includes the Middle East. While the Middle East region is analyzed in a separate overview, a reference to this region is made here because the findings cited from the South-South remittances analysis aggregate data for North Africa and the Middle East (Ratha and Shaw, 2007).

3 Unless otherwise stated, remittance figures in these overviews refer to officially recorded flows and do not capture amounts transmitted through informal channels.

Part B: As a share of total population

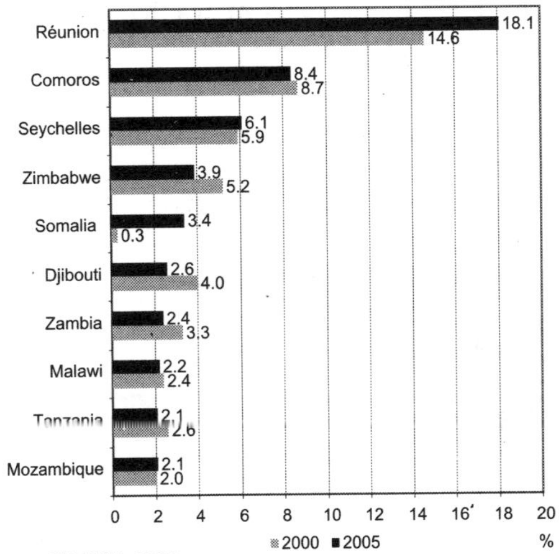

Source: UN DESA, 2005.

- Even though between 2000 and 2005 the migrant population in the Democratic Republic of the Congo (DRC) dropped from 717,000 to 539,000, at the end of that period their numbers continued to be the highest in Central Africa. As a share of the population, they represented only 1.4 per cent in 2000 and 0.9 per cent in 2005. In 2005, migrants in Gabon represented 17.7 per cent of the local population, the largest share in any Central African country (see Figure 3).

Figure 3:

Stock of migrants in Central Africa, by destination, 2000 and 2005

Part A: Total number of migrants

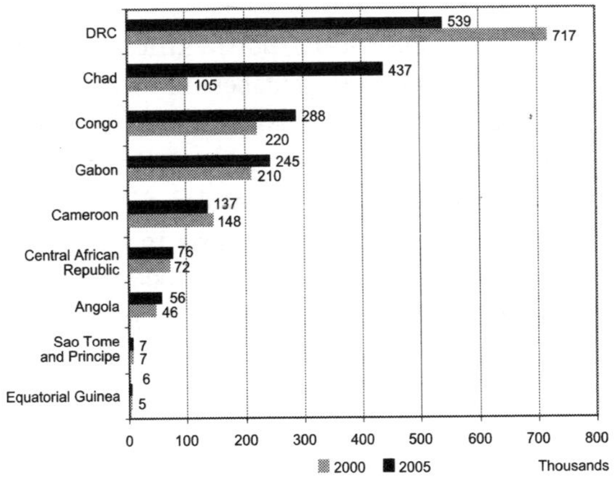

Part B: As a share of total population

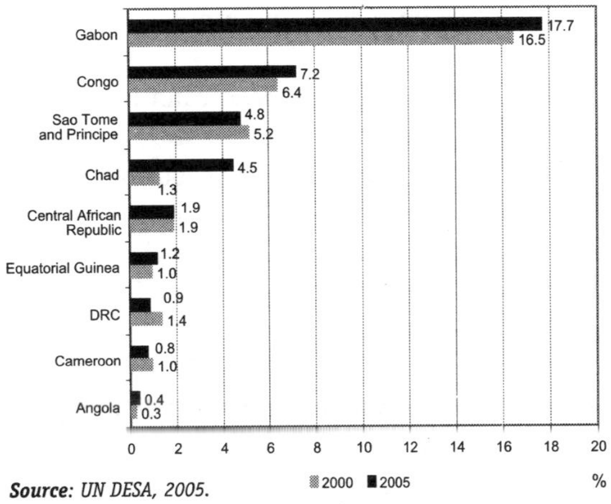

Source: UN DESA, 2005.

The number of IDPs exceeds that of refugees in East African countries

- At the end of 1995, the number of IDPs concentrated in the countries of the Greater Horn of Africa[4] (GHA) amounted to less than half of the total regional refugee population of 3.2 million (Oucho, 2006); however, by 2007, owing to the conflicts in the ten GHA countries, their numbers relative to refugees increased dramatically (see Figure 4).

Figure 4:

Greater Horn of Africa: Refugees and IDPs in 2007

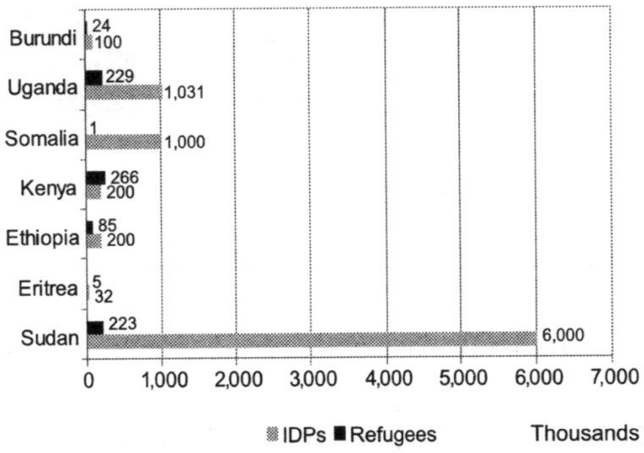

Note: Djibouti, Rwanda and Tanzania are not included in Figure 4 for lack of data on IDPs.

Sources: *UNHCR, 2008a, IDMC, 2008.*

[4] The "Greater Horn of Africa" (GHA) comprises ten countries: the two Great Lakes region states of Burundi and Rwanda; the three countries of East Africa – Kenya, Tanzania and Uganda; and the "Horn of Africa" (HOA) states of Djibouti, Eritrea, Ethiopia, Somalia and Sudan.

East Africa includes the countries with the highest number of asylum seekers in Europe

- Somalia is the leading African country of origin for asylum seekers in Europe, with 7,588 and 11,035 applications for asylum deposited in 2006 and 2007, respectively (UNHCR, 2008b). Eritrea is the second largest African country of origin with 5,956 and 6,424 asylum applications in 2006 and 2007, respectively.

The East African diaspora is growing in Australia

- While migration from Africa to Australia continues to be dominated by migrants of European stock, there has been a substantial increase in the diversity of migration from sub-Saharan Africa to Australia over the last decade, most notably with increasing numbers of migrants born in Ethiopia, Kenya and Somalia, who were mainly admitted under the Australian refugee and humanitarian programmes (Hugo, 2005) (see Figure 5).

Figure 5:

Number of migrants born in East African countries in Australia, 1991-2001

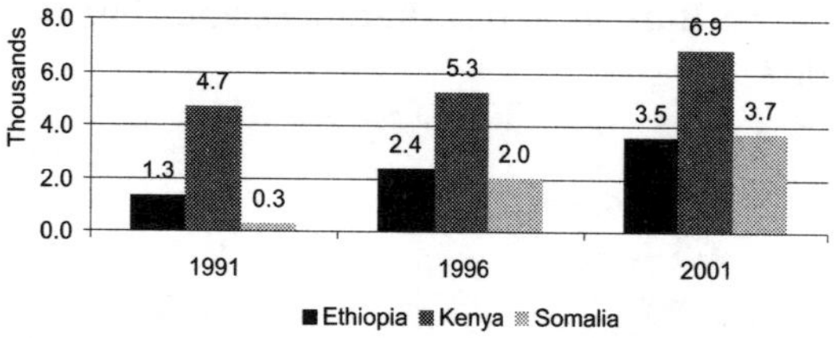

Source: Hugo, 2005.

NORTH AFRICA

- Sudan and Libya are the two leading countries of destination in North Africa in both absolute and relative terms (UN DESA, 2005) (see Figure 6).

Figure 6:

Stock of migrants in North Africa, by destination, 2000 and 2005

Part A: Total number of migrants

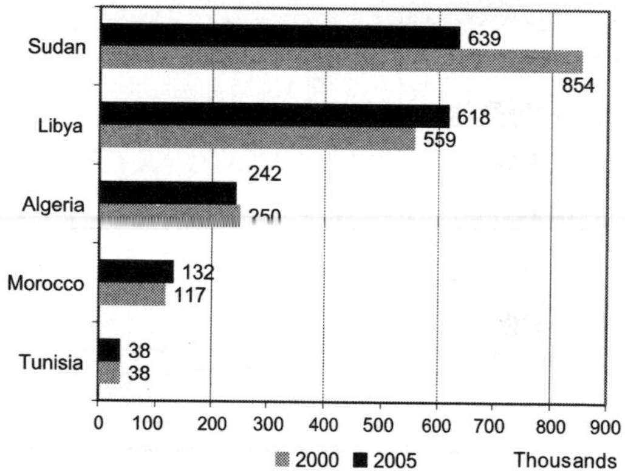

Part B: As a share of total population

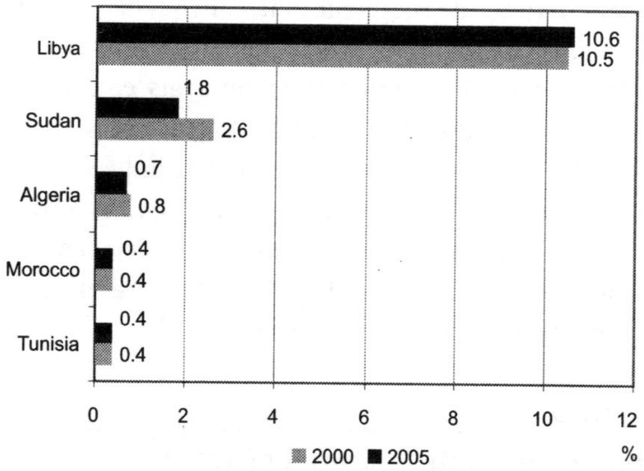

Source: UN DESA, 2005.

From transit migration to de facto migration

- For the past few years, North Africa has been receiving a growing number of sub-Saharan migrants "in transit", predominantly from West Africa, who want to enter Europe. For example, an annual average of 22,000 irregular migrants take the route from Libya and Tunisia to the Italian island of Lampedusa, although in 2006 this traffic decreased by 4.5 per cent (see Chapter 8). Owing to the gradual reinforcement of migration controls around the Mediterranean, transit migration has tended to become de facto immigration. In 2005, 10,000 West African migrants, or ten per cent of the local population, were in transit in the port of Nouadhibou in northern Mauritania, on their way to Europe. In the same year, an estimated 20,000 migrants from sub-Saharan African countries were waiting for an opportunity to cross over into Europe around the Spanish enclaves of Ceuta and Melilla, as well as in the city of Oujda on the Algerian border (OECD, 2006).

North African migrants are found widely across Europe and North America

- In 2004, France was home to the largest population of Moroccans abroad (1.1 million), but there were sizable communities of Moroccan migrants in Spain (424,000), The Netherlands (300,000), Italy (299,000), Belgium (293,000) and Germany (102,000) (de Haas, 2007a).
- Since 1995, the population of Algerian descent has increased by 18% in France, while in Spain and Italy the numbers have increased by 547% and 126% respectively (de Haas, 2007a).
- Of the seven million migrants born in Africa and living in OECD countries, nearly half are from North Africa and reside mainly in France, Belgium, Spain and the Netherlands (OECD, 2007).
- Between 2003 and 2004, the total number of Moroccan, Algerian and Tunisian citizens living in the U.S. stood at 128,000 and at 125,000 in Canada (European Commission, 2007).

SOUTHERN AFRICA

- South Africa is a major destination country in this sub-region, hosting over one million migrants. Namibia ranks first in terms of migrants as a share of the total population, although this proportion decreased slightly between 2000 and 2005 (UN DESA, 2005) (see Figure 7).

Figure 7:

Stock of migrants in Southern Africa, by destination, 2000 and 2005

Part A: Total number of migrants

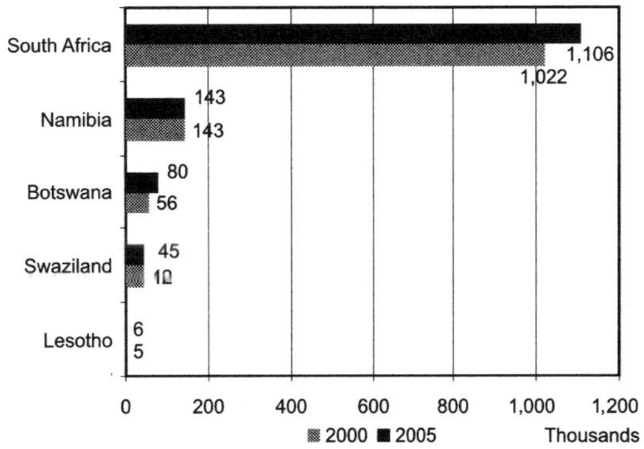

Part B: As a share of total population

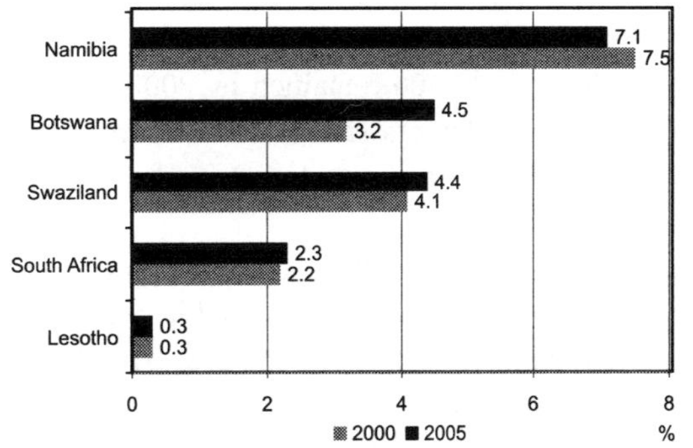

***Source:** UN DESA, 2005.*

Mobility in general is growing rapidly in Africa, in particular in Southern Africa

- Temporary regular cross-border movements from other African countries into South Africa (particularly from the Southern African Development Community, SADC) have increased significantly; for example, between 1990 and 2000:[5]
  - total visits to South Africa increased from one million to 5.1 million;

[5] The figures reflect the number of times the border is crossed, rather than the number of individuals crossing the border (Crush and Williams, 2005).

- African visits to South Africa increased from 550,000 to four million; and
- SADC visits to South Africa increased from 500,000 to 3.7 million (Crush and Williams, 2005).

Health worker migration is a growing phenomenon ...

- Medical doctors from South Africa are emigrating at an annual rate of about 1,000, and it is estimated that 30-50 per cent of all medical school graduates emigrate to the U.K. or U.S. every year. More than 75 per cent of skilled South African emigrants relocate in only five countries: the U.K., the U.S., Australia, Canada and New Zealand (IOM, 2007a). Doctors from South Africa make up 9.7 per cent of total foreign-trained doctors in Australia and seven per cent in the U.K. (IOM, 2007b).
- While Zambia had an estimated 1,600 doctors in the 1980s, only 400 remained by 2002. Similarly, of the 1,200 doctors trained in Zimbabwe in the 1990s, only 360 were practicing in the country in 2003 (IOM, 2007a).
- Between 2000 and 2004, nearly 40,000 foreign nurses registered to work in the U.K. according to the government's official statistics. Over a period of four years, 6,028 nurses left South Africa for the U.K., 1,561 left Zimbabwe, 1,496 left Nigeria, 660 left Ghana, 444 left Zambia, 386 left Kenya, 226 left Botswana and 192 left Malawi (IOM, 2007a).
- Lesotho and Namibia present a physician emigration rate[6] of over 30 per cent, while this rate rises to over 50 per cent in Malawi, Tanzania and Zambia and to 75 per cent in Mozambique. South Africa, Swaziland and Botswana (11%) are the only countries in Southern Africa with a physician emigration rate below the average for sub-Saharan Africa (IOM, 2007a).

... but South Africa is also a destination country for health professionals of all categories

- By 2003, South Africa reported 32,000 vacancies for nurses and 4,000 for doctors in the public health sector alone (IOM, 2007b).
- Even as South Africa is losing skilled health workers, the country is also the major destination for skilled health workers from other parts of Africa, most recently from Botswana, DRC, Ghana, Nigeria and Zimbabwe. In Africa, South Africa has the highest physician and nurse ratio to the population: 56.3 physicians and 471.8 nurses per 100,000 inhabitants, compared to a ratio of only 6.2 and 44.2, respectively, in the DRC, another SADC country (IOM, 2007b).
- South Africa has sought to address staff shortages in the public health sector through the hiring of Iranian and Cuban health personnel to work in rural areas (IOM, 2007b).

WEST AFRICA

- While Côte d'Ivoire is the leading destination country for migrants in West Africa (2.4 million international migrants in 2005), at 15.3 per cent, Gambia has the highest proportion of migrants in its population. Guinea is the only country in the sub-region to register a drop in the number of international migrants in both absolute and relative terms (from 8.7% in 2000 to 4.3% in 2005) (UN DESA, 2005) (see Figure 8).

[6] The **physician emigration rate** is the physician emigration stock compared to the total number of doctors originating from the source country (residents plus emigrants).

Figure 8:

Stock of migrants in West Africa, top ten destinations, 2000 and 2005

Part A: Total number of migrants

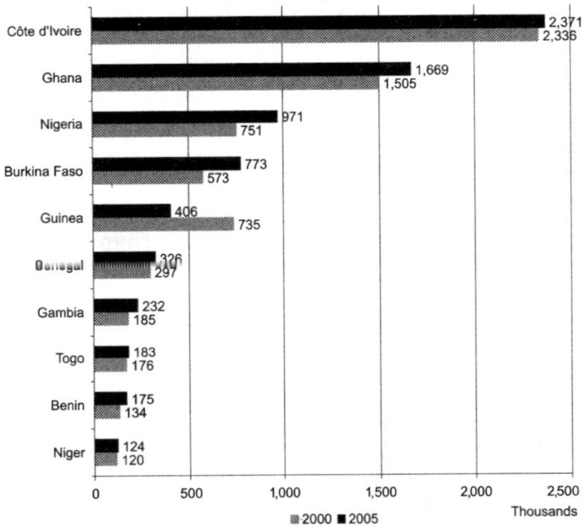

Part B: As a share of total population

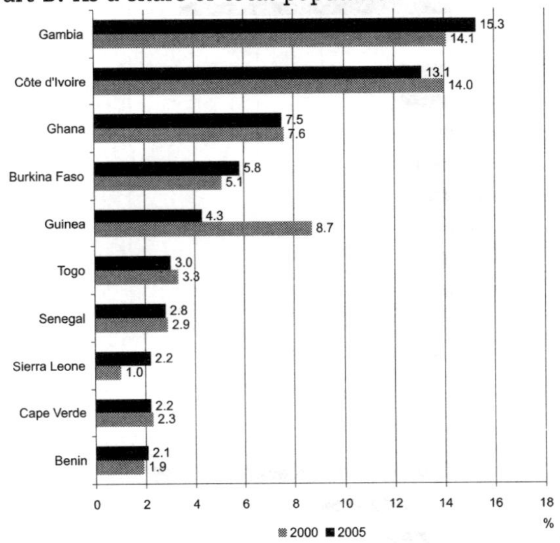

Source: UN DESA, 2005.

- Regular migration from ECOWAS[7] Member States to the EU-15[8] increased from 23,557 to 71,653 from 2000 to 2004 (European Commission, 2007).

- Recently, West African migration to North America has become more diversified. While in 1994, the inflows of citizens of ECOWAS Member States to the U.S. stood at 9,498, they had reached 24,820 in 2004. Inflows to Canada increased from 2,093 to 4,337 during that same period (see Figure 9).

Figure 9:

Diversification of West African diaspora

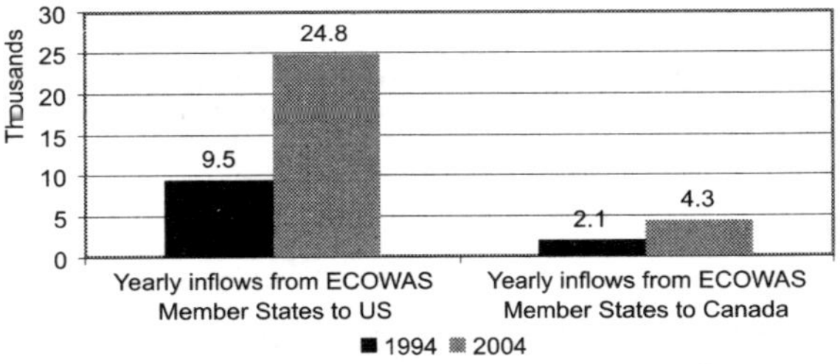

Source: European Commission, 2007.

- Currently, 56 per cent of the West African population is under 20 years of age and 66 per cent are under 25 years of age compared to 12 per cent and 15 per cent, respectively, in Europe. By the year 2020, West Africa could have about 200 million people under the age of 20 (OECD, 2006).

The outmigration of health professionals is a major concern

- According to World Health Organization (WHO) figures, over 900 physicians trained in Ghana are working in an OECD country, compared with 3,240 practicing in Ghana itself (UNECA, 2006).

Environmental migration is an emerging major issue in West Africa

- Yields from rain-fed agriculture, the most important part of sub-Saharan agriculture, are projected to fall by up to 50 per cent by 2020 (IPCC, 2007), seriously compromising agricultural production and access to food. Labour migration has already become an important part of the annual coping

---

[7] The Economic Community of West African States (ECOWAS) is a regional grouping of 16 countries: Benin, Burkina Faso, Cape Verde, Côte d'Ivoire, Gambia, Ghana, Guinea, Guinea Bissau, Liberia, Mali, Mauritania, Niger, Nigeria, Senegal, Sierra Leone and Togo.

[8] The EU-15 refers to the 15 European Union Member States before the enlargements of the EU to 25 and 27 Member States in May 2004 and January 2007, respectively.

strategy against the prolonged drought that has been affecting the West African Sahel for the past three decades (Brown, 2007).

- Under the worst climate change migration scenario, it has been estimated by the Intergovernmental Panel on Climate Change (IPCC) that more than 200 million people might be displaced globally by climate change, and the Sahelian region could become uninhabitable on a permanent basis (Brown, 2008).

SOME TOPICAL POLICY ISSUES IN MIGRATION MANAGEMENT IN AFRICA

Remittances

Remittance flows are significant but Africa receives the smallest share of global transfers

- According to World Bank estimates for 2007, the African continent received USD 23.1 billion in remittances, with USD 11.7 billion to sub-Saharan Africa and USD 11.4 billion to North Africa (World Bank, 2008) (see Figure 10).

Figure 10:

Remittances received in Africa, 2007 (billions of USD)

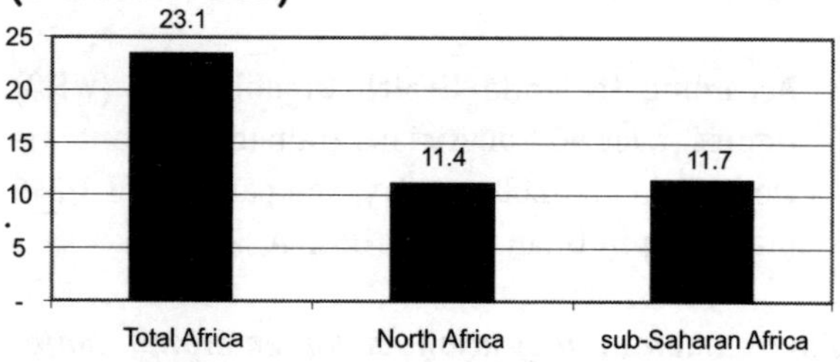

Note: Egypt is not included in these calculations.

Source: *World Bank, 2008.*

- In 2007, Africa received 6.8 per cent of global remittance flows of USD 337 billion (World Bank, 2008).

- Remittances to sub-Saharan Africa accounted for around 2.5 per cent of GDP on average between 2000 and 2005, which is considerably lower than in some other developing countries. However, there are striking exceptions such as Lesotho, where remittances represent almost 28 per cent of GDP, and Cape Verde, Guinea-Bissau and Senegal, with more than five per cent (see Figure 11). For many countries, remittances are an important source of foreign exchange: for Lesotho, Cape Verde, Uganda and Comoros, for instance, remittances have since 2000 amounted on average to more than 25 per cent of export earnings (Gupta et al., 2007).

Figure 11:

Leading ten recipients of remittances in sub-Saharan Africa, 2005-2006

Part A: Total flows (millions of USD)

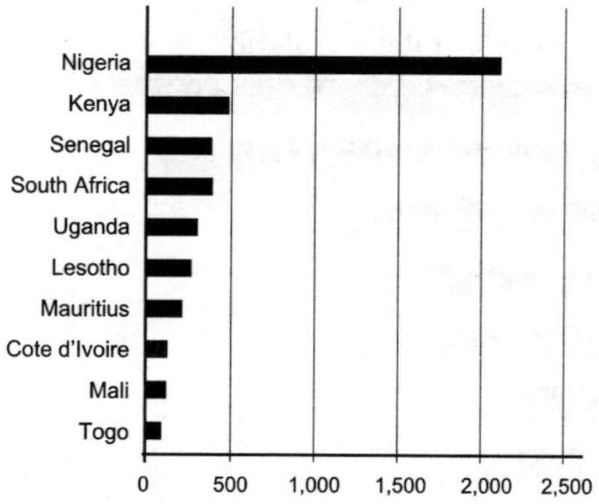

Part B: Ratio to GDP (%)

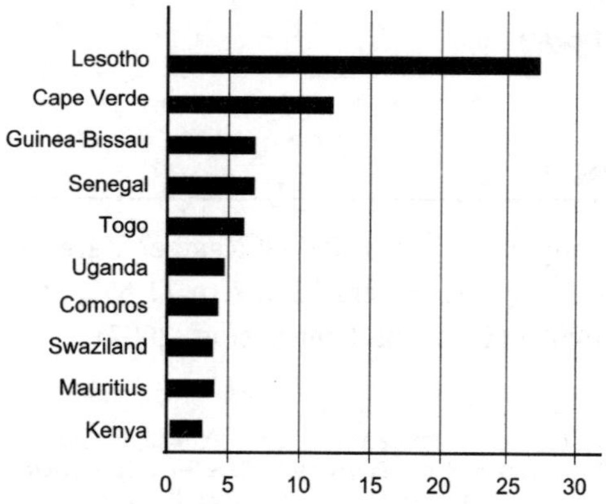

Part C: Ratio to export earnings (%)

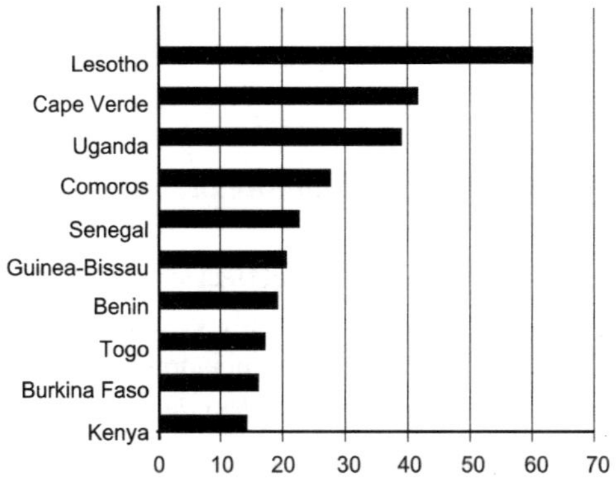

Note: Rankings are based on average remittance inflows for 2005-2006.

Source: *Gupta et al., 2007.*

- South-South remittances in Africa can be significant, a good example being the flows within the Southern Africa sub-region, where South Africa is the major remittance-sending country to other SADC countries (Genesis Analytics, 2005).

Major remittance flows in the SADC

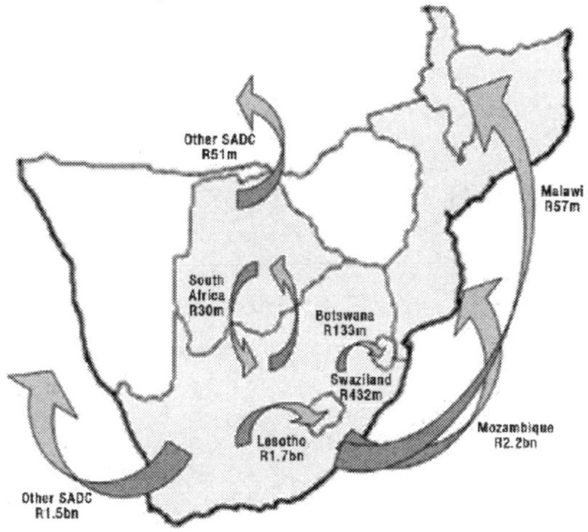

Source: *Genesis Analytics, 2005.*

Contrary to other regions, in Africa foreign direct investment flows are higher than remittance flows

- While remittances to African countries more than doubled from USD 7 billion to 17 billion between 1995 and 2005, foreign direct investment (FDI) increased fivefold from about USD 5 billion to USD 25 billion over the same period (World Bank, 2007) (see Figure 12).

Figure 12:

Total remittances and FDI received by Africa, 1995-2005 (billions of USD)

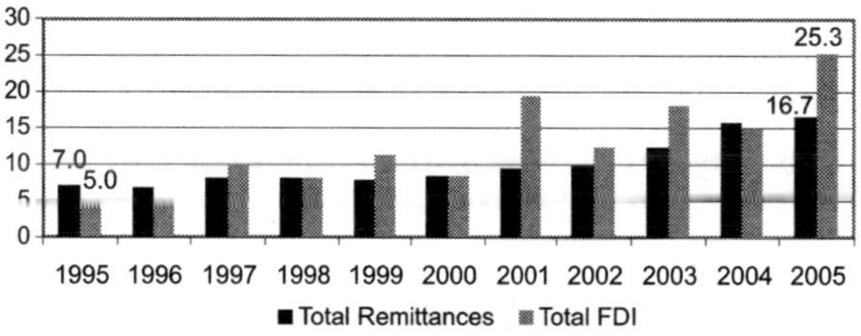

Note: Egypt is not included in these calculations.

Source: *UNCTAD, 2006 and World Bank, 2007.*

Irregular Migration

Irregular migration, both within and from Africa, is growing but still represents only a small proportion of all irregular migrants in Europe

Various locations on the West African coastline are used as staging posts for smuggling and trafficking operations into Europe

- Although the European Union has introduced extensive control operations in recent years, there are still substantial numbers of irregular migrants who attempt to cross in an irregular manner from West Africa to Italy or Spain. Some 34,000 irregular migrants were apprehended on or off the Canary Islands in 2006 (*Migration News Sheet*, February 2007), and, in 2007, increasing numbers of Asians joined Africans crossing from the West African coast to the Canary Islands (de Haas, 2007b). In 2007, however, these numbers dropped due to greater vigilance by countries of departure and surveillance missions conducted by Spain alone or within the framework of the EU border agency, FRONTEX (*Migration News Sheet*, September 2007).

Saharan routes are commonly used by Asian migrants seeking to reach southern European countries

- In recent years, migrants from Bangladesh, China, India and Pakistan have begun to migrate to the Maghreb overland via Saharan routes. Most of them fly from Asia to West African capitals, sometimes via the Gulf states. From there, they follow the common Saharan trail via Niger and Algeria to Morocco. Others enter North Africa through Egypt to Libya and Tunisia, from where they cross to Italy and Malta (de Haas, 2007b).

Some of the irregular migratory flows in Africa are intra-continental, for instance those involving migrants moving in search of life and work opportunities, whether to South Africa ...

- More than 300,000 migrants were deported from South Africa in 2007, up from approximately 250,000 in 2006 (CoRMSA, 2008).
- According to the Government of South Africa, 50,000 Zimbabweans were returned to their country between January and March 2007 (ReliefWeb, 2007).

... or to islands in the Indian Ocean

Mayotte has become the pole of attraction for between 45,000 to 60,000 irregular migrants principally from other islands of the Comoro Archipelago with smaller numbers from Madagascar (*Le Monde*, 15 August 2007).

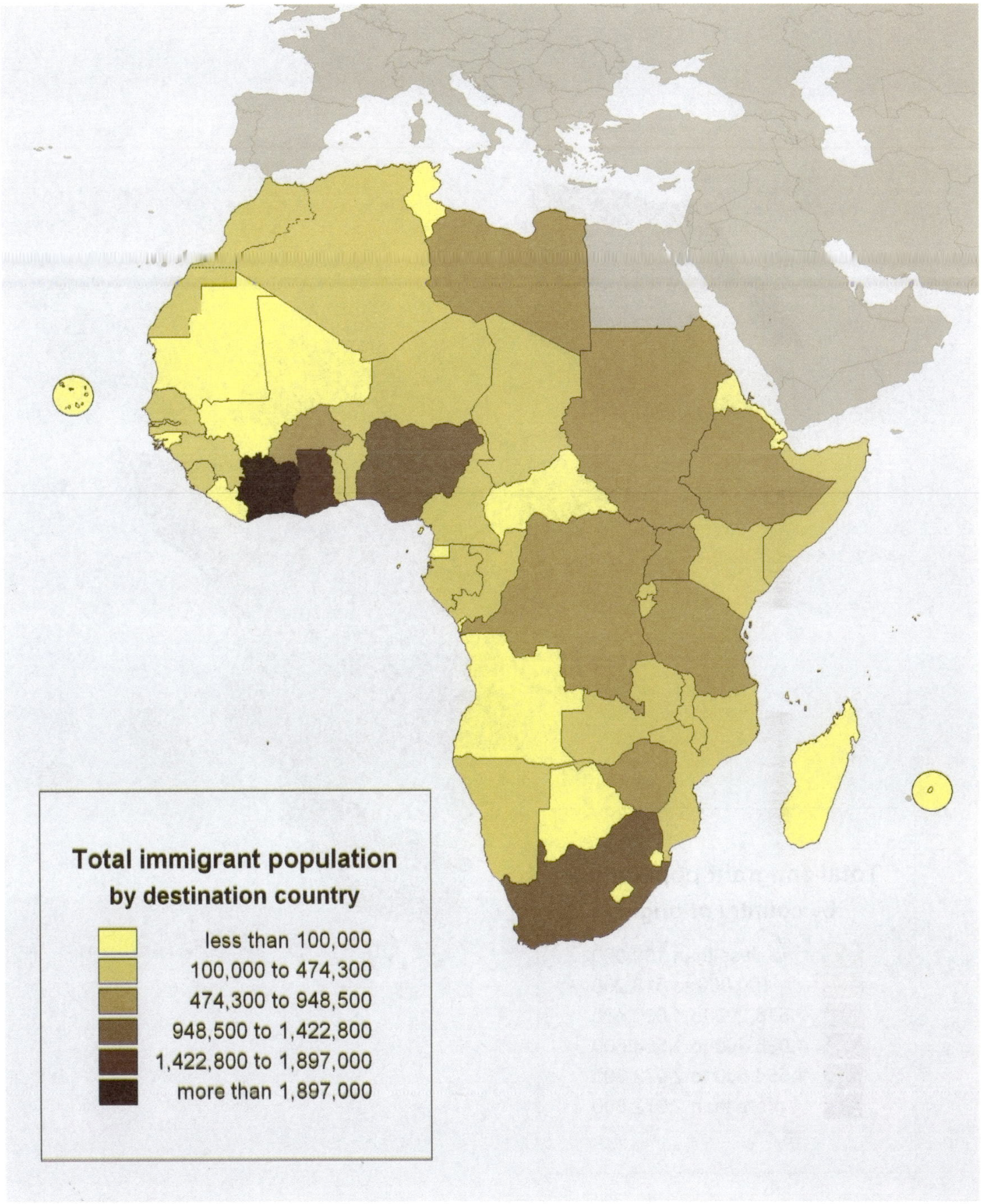
Total immigrant population
by destination country
less than 100,000
100,000 to 474,300
474,300 to 948,500
948,500 to 1,422,800
1,422,800 to 1,897,000
more than 1,897,000

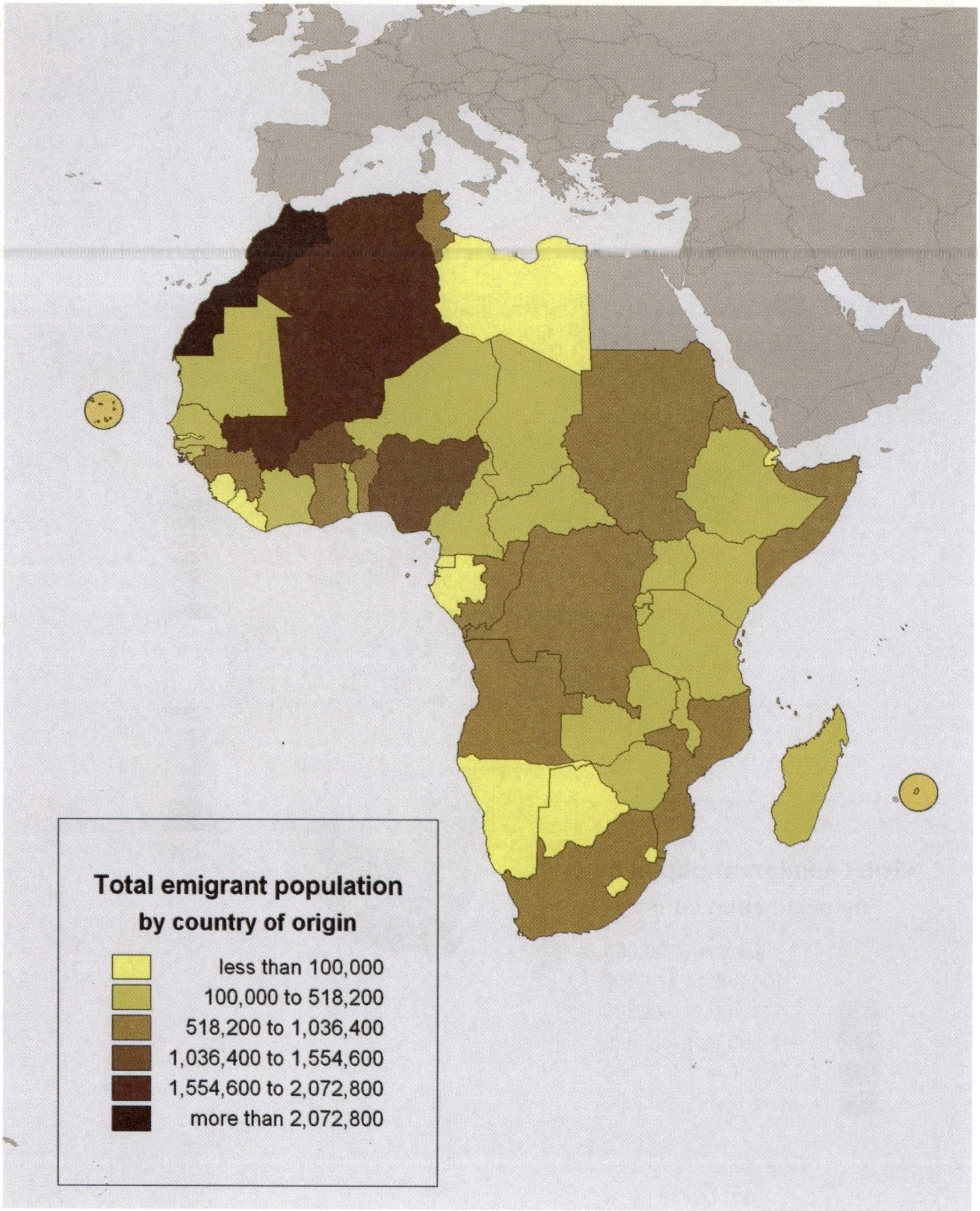
Total emigrant population
by country of origin
less than 100,000
100,000 to 518,200
518,200 to 1,036,400
1,036,400 to 1,554,600
1,554,600 to 2,072,800
more than 2,072,800

REFERENCES

Adepoju, A.

2006 "Policy-driven Research on International Migration in sub-Saharan Africa" in K. Tamas and J. Palme (Eds.), *How Migration can Benefit Development*, Institute for Future Studies, Stockholm, 69-84.

Brown, O.

2007 "Climate change and forced migration: Observations, projections and implications", background paper for the 2007 Human Development Report, http://hdr.undp.org/en/reports/global/hdr2007-2008/papers/brown_oli.pdf.

2008 *Migration and Climate Change*, Migration Research Series, No. 31, International Organization for Migration (IOM), Geneva.

Cross, C., D. Gerdelblom, N. Roux and J. Mafukukidze (Eds.)

2006 *Views on Migration in Sub-Saharan Africa: Proceedings of an African Migration Alliance Workshop*, HSRC Press, Cape Town.

Crush, J. and V. Williams

2005 "International Migration and Development: Dynamics and Challenges in South and Southern Africa", paper prepared for the United Nations Expert Group Meeting on International Migration and Development, United Nations Department for Economic and Social Affairs (UN DESA), 6-8 July, New York, Doc. UN/POP/MIG/2005/05, http://www.un.org/esa/population/meetings/ittmigdev2005/P05_Crush&Williams.pdf.

de Haas, H.

2007a "North-African Migration Systems: evolution, transformations and development linkages", International Migration Institute (IMI) Working Paper 6, University of Oxford, http://www.imi.ox.ac.uk/pdfs/WP6%20North%20African%20Migration%20Systems.pdf.

2007b "The myth of invasion – Irregular migration from West Africa to the Maghreb and the European Union", IMI Research Report, October, University of Oxford, http://www.imi.ox.ac.uk/pdfs/Irregular%20migration%20from%20West%20Africa%20-%20Hein%20de%20Haas.pdf.

European Commission

2007 "Migration from Africa: A Case Study on Root Causes and Factors Contributing to Migration from Senegal to the EU", Technical Note IPSC/TN/2007/xxx.

Genesis Analytics

2005 "Supporting Remittances in Southern Africa", Genesis Analytics, Johannesburg, http://www.microfinancegateway.com/files/27700_file_27700.pdf.

Gupta, S., C. Pattillo and S. Wagh

2007 "Making Remittances Work for Africa", *Finance and Development*, 44:2 (June).

Hugo, G.

2005 "Migration in the Asia-Pacific Region", paper prepared for the Policy Analysis and Research Programme of the Global Commission on International Migration (GCIM), September, Geneva, http://www.gcim.org/mm/File/Regional%20Study%202.pdf.

Internal Displacement Monitoring Centre (IDMC) of the Norwegian Refugee Council

2008 *Internal Displacement: Global Overview of Trends and Developments in 2007*, April, IDMC, Geneva, http://www.internal-displacement.org/8025708F004BE3B1/(httpInfoFiles)/BD8316FAB5984142C125742E0033180B/$file/IDMC_Internal_Displacement_Global_Overview_2007.pdf.

International Organization for Migration (IOM)

2005 *World Migration 2005: Costs and Benefits of International Migration*, IOM, Geneva, http://www.iom.int/jahia/Jahia/cache/offonce/pid/1674?entryId=932.

2007a "Health Workers Migration in South and Southern Africa: Literature Review", October, IOM Regional Office for Southern Africa, Pretoria.

2007b "Facilitation of the Recruitment and Placement of Foreign Health Care Professionals to Work in the Public Sector Health Care in South Africa", Assessment conducted in the Netherlands, the United Kingdom and the United States, November, IOM Pretoria in consultation with the National Department of Health, Republic of South Africa, Pretoria, http://www.iom.int/Template/health_worker_assessment_report.pdf.

Le Monde

2007 "Des Comoriens se Noient en Vue de l'Eldorado Mahorai", *Le Monde*, 15 August.

Migration News Sheet

2007a "Spain expects less 'boat migrants' in 2007", *Migration News Sheet*, February, Migration Policy Group (MPG), Brussels.

2007b "Spain: 55% drop in number of irregular migrants to the Canary Islands", *Migration News Sheet*, September, MPG, Brussels.

Organisation for Economic Co-operation and Development (OECD)

2006 "The socio-economic and regional context of West African migrations", Working Document 1, November, Sahel and West Africa Club, OECD, Paris, http://www.oecd.org/dataoecd/21/40/38481393.pdf.

2007 *International Migration Outlook*, SOPEMI 2007 Edition, OECD, Paris.

Oucho, J.O.

2006 "Migration and Refugees in Eastern Africa: A Challenge for the East African Community", in C. Cross, D. Gelderblom, N. Roux and J. Mafukidze (Eds), *Views on Migration in Sub-Saharan Africa: Proceedings of an African Migration Alliance Workshop*, HSRC Press, Cape Town, 130-147.

Quartey, P.

2006 "International Migration and Poverty Reduction", paper prepared for the Institute of Statistical Social and Economic Research (ISSER) - Merchant Bank Development Seminar Series on Does Globalisation Hurt or Enhance National Development? Ghana's Experience in the Last Two Decades, July, Accra.

Ratha, D. and W. Shaw

2007 "South-South Migration and Remittances", 19 January, Development Prospects Group, The World Bank, Washington, D.C., http://siteresources.worldbank.org/INTPROSPECTS/Resources/South-SouthmigrationJan192006.pdf.

ReliefWeb

2007 "South Africa Deports 1,800 Zimbabweans", ReliefWeb, 19 May, http://www.reliefweb.int/rw/RWB.NSF/db900SID/MCON-73E5BM?OpenDocument.

United Nations Conference on Trade and Development (UNCTAD)

2007 Major FDI Indicators, Statistics, UNCTAD, http://stats.unctad.org/FDI/TableViewer/tableView.aspx?ReportId=899.

2006 *World Investment Report 2006 – FDI from Developing and Transition Economies: Implications for Development*, UNCTAD, New York and Geneva, http://www.unctad.org/en/docs/wir2006_en.pdf.

United Nations Department of Economic and Social Affairs (DESA), Population Division

2005 *Trends in Total Migrant Stock: The 2005 Revision*, UN DESA, Population Division, New York, http://esa.un.org/migration/index.asp?panel=1.

United Nations Economic Commission for Africa (UNECA)

2006 *International Migration and Development: Implications for Africa*, Doc. ECA/SDD/06/01, September, UNECA, Addis Ababa, http://192.132.208.14/eca_resources/Publications/MigrationReport2006.pdf.

United Nations High Commissioner for Refugees (UNHCR)

1995 *Populations of Concern to UNHCR: A Statistical Overview (1995)*, UNHCR, Geneva, http://www.unhcr.org/statistics/STATISTICS/3bfa32e82.pdf.

2006 *2005 Global Refugee Trends - Statistical Overview of Populations of Refugees, Asylum-Seekers, Internally Displaced Persons, Stateless Persons, and Other Persons of Concern to UNHCR*, 9 June, UNHCR, Geneva, http://www.unhcr.org/cgi-bin/texis/vtx/events/opendoc.pdf?tbl=STATISTICS&id=4486ceb12.

2007 *Statistical Yearbook 2006: Trends in Displacement, Protection and Solutions*, UNHCR, Geneva, http://www.unhcr.org/statistics/STATISTICS/478cda572.html.

2008a *2007 Global Trends: Refugees, Asylum-seekers, Returnees, Internally Displaced and Stateless Persons*, 3 June, UNHCR, Geneva, http://www.unhcr.org/statistics/STATISTICS/4852366f2.pdf.

2008b *Asylum Levels and Trends in Industrialized Countries, 2007: Statistical Overview of Asylum Applications Lodged in Europe and Selected Non-European Countries,* 18 March, UNHCR, Geneva, http://www.unhcr.org/statistics/STATISTICS/47daae862.pdf.

World Bank

2006a *African Development Indicators 2006*, The World Bank, Washington, D.C.

2006b *Global Economic Prospects 2006: Economic Implications of Remittances and Migration*, The World Bank, Washington, D.C., http://econ.worldbank.org/WBSITE/EXTERNAL/EXTDEC/EXTDECPROSPECTS/GEPEXT/EXTGEP2006/0,,contentMDK:20709766~menuPK:1026823~pagePK:64167689~piPK:64167673~theSitePK:1026804,00.html.

2007 *2007 Remittances Dataset*, The World Bank, Washington, D.C.

2008 *Revisions to Remittance Trends 2007*, July, The World Bank, Washington, D.C., http://econ.worldbank.org/WBSITE/EXTERNAL/EXTDEC/EXTDECPROSPECTS/0,,contentMDK:21121930~menuPK:3145470~pagePK:64165401~piPK:64165026~theSitePK:476883,00.html.

World Meteorological Organization (WMO) and the United Nations Environment Programme (UNEP), Intergovernmental Panel on Climate Change (IPCC)

2007 *Climate Change 2007: Impacts, Adaptations and Vulnerability*, Contribution of Working Group II to the Fourth Assessment Report of the IPCC, April, http://www.ipcc-wg2.org/.

AMERICAS

- In 2005, there were 51.1 million migrants in the Americas, the vast majority, namely 44.5 million, in North America, and a further 6.6 million in Latin America and the Caribbean. Migrants accounted for 13.5 per cent of the total population in North America and for 1.2 per cent of the total population in Latin America (UN DESA, 2005).
- South-North migration continues to be the dominant migration trend in the Americas. According to the migration data gathered by the University of Sussex, in the United Kingdom[1] (Ratha and Shaw, 2007), South-North migration accounts for 87 per cent of total migration in the region, representing the highest rate of South-North migration in the world. Migration to other Latin American and Caribbean countries accounts for the remaining 13 per cent, which means that there is no significant migration to other developing regions beyond the Americas, such as to Africa or Asia.
- In 2005, 25 million Latin American and Caribbean citizens lived outside their country of origin, accounting for nearly four per cent of the population of their home countries, and 74 per cent of whom were thought to be living in the United States (ECLAC, 2006a).
- Between 2000 and 2005, the number of Latin American and Caribbean migrants increased by four million (UN DESA, 2005). Economic crises, social conflicts, violence, gradual economic and political change, environmental disasters and the diversification of destination countries have all shaped new migration patterns throughout the region.

NORTH AMERICA[2]

- The United States remains the principal country of destination in North America, hosting 38.3 million migrants in 2005, three million more than in 2001 (see Figure 1). However, relative to the size of its population, Bermuda has the

[1] The University of Sussex database gathers information from individual country censuses. Although available data is not up-to-date, it is the latest comparable information for the region, gathered from 2000 to 2002 country censuses, with the exception of Barbados (1990), Colombia (1993), Peru (1993) and Uruguay (1996).

[2] This section covers Canada, Mexico, the United States and three dependent territories or overseas departments (Bermuda, Greenland, and Saint-Pierre-et-Miquelon). In keeping with the UN DESA Population Division practice, Mexico is considered under the sub-region North America for reasons of geographical consistency.

highest number of migrants (29.4%), followed by Saint-Pierre-et-Miquelon (22.4%) and Greenland (21.4%). Compared to 2001, all countries and territories in North America have seen an increase in immigration in both absolute and relative terms.

Figure 1:

Stock of migrants in North America, by destination, 2000 and 2005

Part A: Total number of migrants

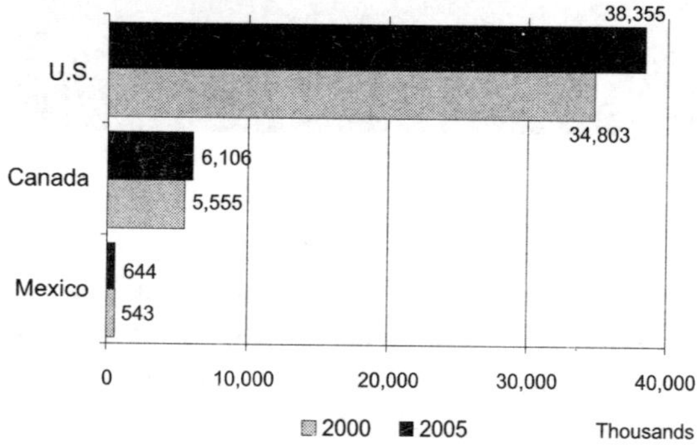

Part B: As a share of total population

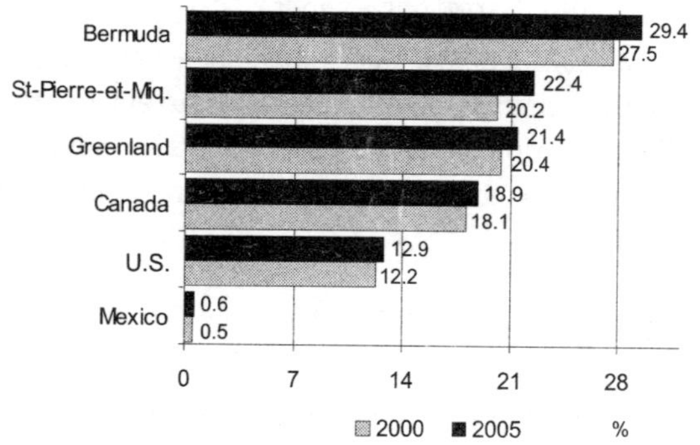

Source: UN DESA, 2005.

UNITED STATES

Intra-regional migration accounts for more than half of total immigration in the United States

- In absolute numbers, the United States remains the dominant country of destination in the Americas and in the world. In 2005, of the 38.3 million migrants living in the U.S., 55 per cent were from the Americas: 10.8 million from Mexico, 4.6 million from Latin America, 3.2 million from the Caribbean and 692,000 from Canada and other parts of North America (see Figure 2).

Figure 2:

Stock of foreign-born population in the U.S., by region of origin, 1995 to 2005

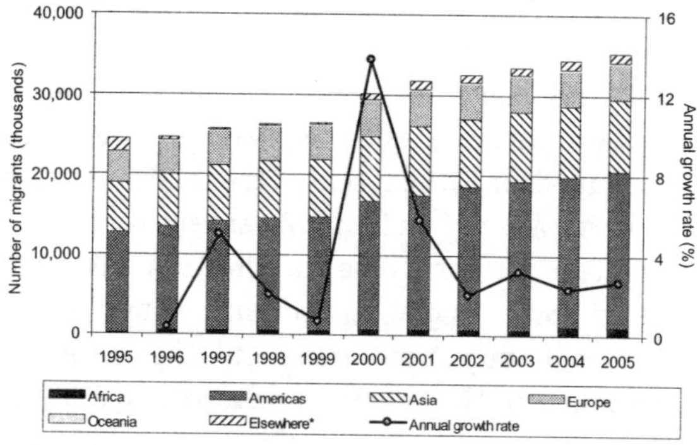

Note: *Includes region not known.

Source: *Urban Institute tabulations from public-use files from the U.S. Census Bureau, Current Population Survey, March Supplement, 1995 to 2005.*

- Persons of Hispanic origin are the fastest growing ethnic group in the U.S., becoming the largest minority group in 2004.

Changes in settlement patterns have profoundly affected migration in the U.S.

- The impact of immigration on the United States has also been influenced by changes in the settlement patterns of immigrants in recent years (MPI, 2004). California and New York continue to be the top receiving states of migrants, hosting 27 and 11 per cent of the total foreign-born population, respectively. From 1990 to 2005, however, their combined percentage of total migration fell by 9.3 per cent (California losing 6% and New York 3.3%). The loss of the big "gateway" states was partially compensated by non-traditional immigration states like Arizona, Georgia, Virginia, North Carolina, Colorado and Nevada. In these new immigration states, the foreign-born population grew on average by over 200 per cent with some states experiencing even higher growth rates (North Carolina and Georgia led with a growth rate of 412% and 382%, respectively – MPI, 2004).

- Finally, it is important to mention that while in the past agriculture was the main sector employing migrant labour, new arrivals are now distributed more widely, notably in the food and service industries.

CANADA

Canada is not only a country of destination but also has a long history of emigration to the U.S.

- Immigration trends in Canada from 2000 to 2005 show a rise in the foreign-born population of 0.55 million. Immigration to Canada has grown at a 9.2 per cent average quintennial rate since 1960. In 2005, Canada's foreign-born population of 6.1 million represented 18.9 per cent of the total population, a figure higher than in the U.S. (see Figure 3).
- Nearly one-quarter of the 235,808 new permanent residents admitted in Canada in 2004 were selected through Canada's "points system" that tests them inter alia for skills and education (see Chapter 11). Family members accompanying these migrants account for a little over another quarter of admissions, with subsequent family reunification and humanitarian migrants making up the remainder (O'Neil et al., 2005).
- Canada is not only a destination country but has a long history of emigration to the United States. In 2005, the foreign-born from Canada, 674,000 people, made up the ninth-largest immigrant group in the U.S. (U.S. Census Bureau, 2005).

Figure 3:

Estimated number of migrants in Canada by gender at mid-year and quintennial growth rate

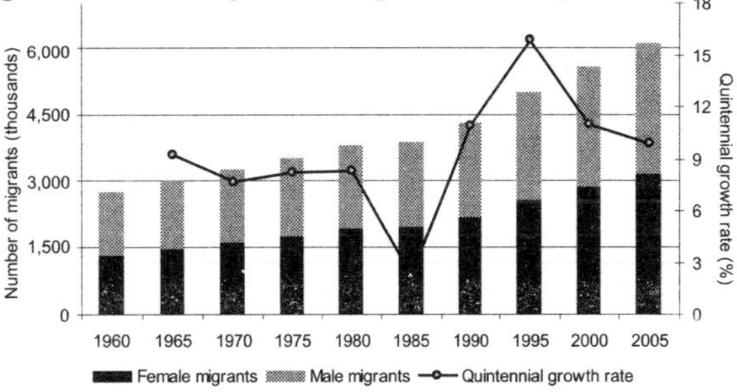

Source: *UN DESA, 2005.*

MEXICO

Mexico is not only a significant country of origin but has also become an important country of transit

- Mexico is characterized primarily by the mass emigration of Mexicans to the United States. With 10.8 million migrants, or 90 per cent of the country's total emigration, Mexico is the top country of origin of the foreign-born population in the U.S. (U.S. Census Bureau, 2005). In addition, one in every five immigrants who obtained U.S. permanent residence status in 2002 was from Mexico (Grieco, 2003).
- Immigrants do not represent a large proportion of Mexico's population. In 2005, the percentage of the foreign-born population in Mexico was around 0.6 per cent, or 644,361 (UN DESA, 2005). Of these, the majority (69% in 2000) were from the United States (Castillo, 2006). Most are thought to be

the U.S.-born children of Mexican migrants or of Mexican border residents; however, an increasing number of U.S.-born senior citizens are settling in Mexico after their retirement. In 2000, the Mexican census showed 28,247 U.S.-born senior citizens in Mexico, representing an increase of 17.3 per cent over 1990 (MPI, 2006). There are also temporary workers from Central America, for example, from Guatemala, who tend to work in border areas in sectors such as agriculture, construction and domestic service.

- Over the last two decades or so, Mexico has become a significant country of transit, especially for Central American migrants. In 2006, over 270,000 Central Americans entered Mexico through its southern border trying to reach the U.S. Around 216,000 were detained and returned to their countries of origin. A smaller number of transit migrants originate from South America (mainly Ecuador and Brazil), China, Cuba, other Caribbean countries and Africa (around 3,000 for all nationalities) (CONAPO, 2006).

LATIN AMERICA AND THE CARIBBEAN[3]

- Argentina, hosting 1.5 million migrants in 2005, is the top country of destination in Latin America and the Caribbean, followed by Venezuela (one million) and Brazil (641,000) (see Figure 4). These countries remain as the top three destination countries of the sub-region despite a decrease in the stock of migrants relative to 2000. Costa Rica, ranking fourth as country of destination in 2005, experienced the greatest increase in the stock of migrants (130,000) compared to 2000. Dependent territories or overseas departments of larger countries, have the highest number of immigrants relative to the size of their population. French Guiana is at the top of the list with 44.9 per cent, followed by Anguilla (42.5%) and the British Virgin Islands (38.3%) (UN DESA, 2005).

Figure 4:

Stock of migrants in Latin America and the Caribbean, top ten destinations, 2000 and 2005

Part A: Total number of migrants

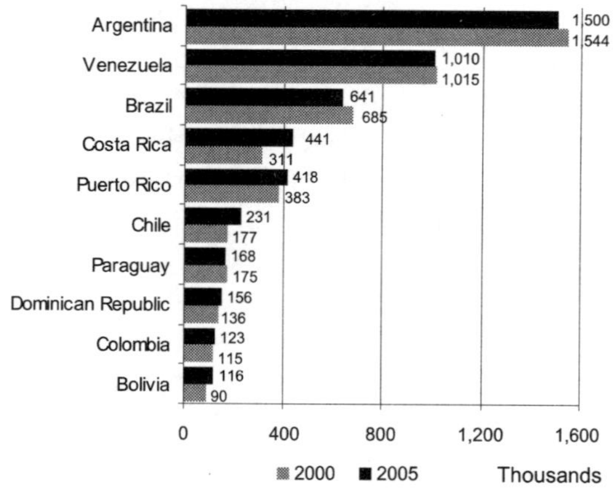

Part B: As a share of total population

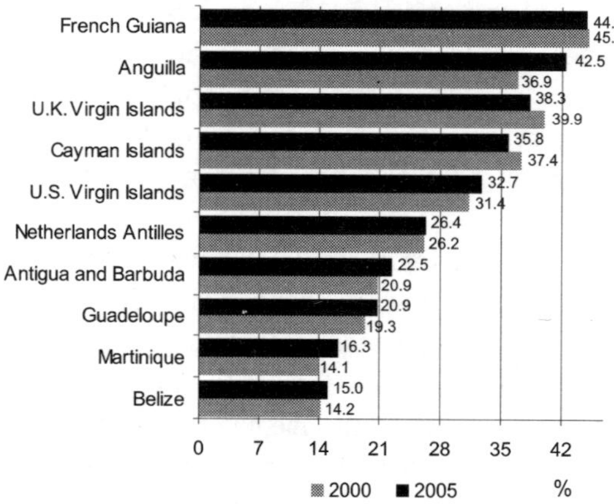

Source: *UN DESA, 2005.*

3 This section covers 14 **Caribbean countries** (Antigua and Barbuda, Bahamas, Barbados, Cuba, Dominica, Dominican Republic, Grenada, Grenadines, Haiti, Jamaica, Saint Kitts and Nevis, Saint Lucia, Saint Vincent, and Trinidad and Tobago); seven **Central American countries** (Belize, Costa Rica, El Salvador, Guatemala, Honduras, Nicaragua and Panama); 12 **South American countries** (Argentina, Brazil, Bolivia, Colombia, Chile, Ecuador, Guyana, Paraguay, Peru, Suriname, Uruguay and Venezuela), and ten **dependent territories or overseas departments** (Anguilla, British Virgin Islands, Cayman Islands, French Guiana, Guadeloupe, Martinique, Netherlands Antilles, Puerto Rico, United States Virgin Islands and Turks and Caicos Islands).

The U.S. continues to host the highest number of Latin American and Caribbean migrants ...

- According to the Population Division of the Economic Commission for Latin America and the Caribbean (ECLAC), the number of Latin American and Caribbean migrants increased considerably from an estimated total of 21 million in 2000 to 25 million in 2005,[4] accounting in 2005 for four per cent of the population of their home countries (ECLAC, 2006a). Relative to the approximately 191 million international migrants in the world in 2005 (UN DESA, 2005), this sub-region accounts for over 13 per cent of all international migrants worldwide. In 2001, half of those migrants resided in the Americas (70% in the U.S. and 30% within Latin America and the Caribbean) and half in other parts of the world.

... and yet the flow of Latin American and Caribbean migrants towards Europe has increased during the last 15 years

- In geographical terms, the destinations of Latin American and Caribbean migrants have been expanding and diversifying. Owing to push factors, the demand for specialized workers and the emergence of social networks, the flows of migrants from Latin America and the Caribbean towards Europe (particularly Spain, Portugal and Italy), as well as Japan and Canada, increased over the period 1990-2005 (ECLAC, 2006a). According to ECLAC estimates, approximately three million people from Latin America and the Caribbean are living outside the sub-region in countries other that the U.S. Figure 5 shows the evolution of Latin American and Caribbean migration as a percentage of total immigration in some of the main countries of destination.

Figure 5:

Volume of Latin American and Caribbean migrants as a percentage of total migration, by main destination, 1995-2005

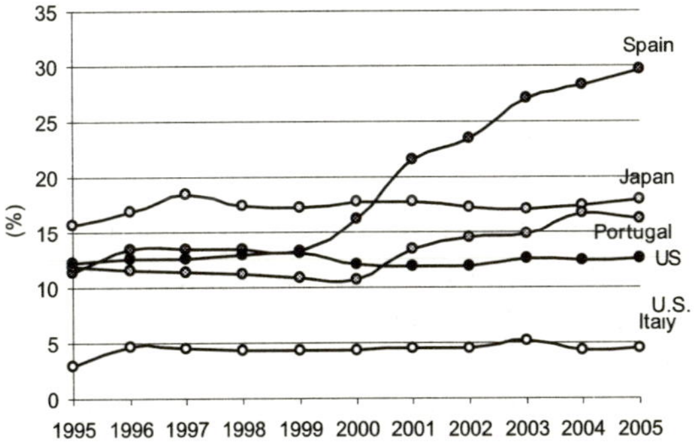

Source: *OECD, Stocks of foreign population by nationality and stocks of foreign-born population by country of origin, online database.*

- The changing migration patterns affecting Latin America and the Caribbean are complex. However, some of the larger trends in the sub-region have been shaped by natural and economic crises, gradual economic and political change, the feminization of migration flows and the diversification of countries of destination for Latin American migrants (O'Neil et al., 2005).

The importance of crises and economic change in migration trends

- Emigration trends from Latin America and the Caribbean can sometimes be traced clearly to specific crises, but flows triggered by general economic and cultural changes are more difficult to identify. Natural disasters and conflicts are the most obvious causes of migration, especially in Central America where natural disasters have

[4] The 2000 and 2005 figures of the total number of Latin American and Caribbean migrants include the number of migrants from Mexico, which accounts for around half of Latin American and Caribbean citizens living outside their country of origin. The importance of including Mexico as part of Latin American migration is that, in terms of migrant characteristics (reasons for migrating, migration conditions, living conditions in the host countries, etc.), Mexican migrants are more similar to the rest of Latin American and Caribbean citizens living outside their country of origin than to U.S. and Canadian citizens living outside their country of origin.

contributed to maintaining emigration flows, originally provoked by political violence two or three decades earlier. This migration is often between fairly close neighbouring countries, as in the case of Costa Rica, which hosted 296,461 migrants in 2000; 75 per cent of those migrants came from Nicaragua. But it can also occur at the sub-regional level as in the case of Panama, where most migrants come from South America (especially Colombia which contributed 26 per cent of the total migrant stock for 2000) and the Caribbean (O'Neil et al., 2005).

- Economic crises have played a powerful role in migration in Latin America, shaping new migration trends in some countries and even reversing migration patterns in some others. In Argentina, the economic crisis of 2001 caused a dramatic reversal in migration flows. Originally a magnet for migrants during the 1990s, Argentina experienced an exodus of 255,000 people from 2001 to 2003, nearly six times as many as during the period 1993-2000. Argentine emigration slowed down as the country recovered from the crisis (O'Neil et al., 2005).
- Two other countries, Venezuela and Brazil, show evolving migration trends due to changing economic circumstances. Venezuela, a net destination for migrant labour from other countries in the sub-region and southern Europe since the oil boom 50 years ago, has started to experience some migration outflows, especially to the U.S. and Spain. As to Brazil, the number of Brazilians in the U.S. and in Portugal has been rising to reach 356,000 in 2005 (U.S. Census Bureau, 2005) and 70,400 in 2005 (OECD, online datasets, 2007), respectively. In addition, Brazilians numbering 302,100 in 2005 accounted for the third-largest foreign group in Japan (OECD, online datasets, 2007).
- Ecuador provides another example of the importance of economic crises in shaping migration trends in Latin America, and also of the emergence of new migration patterns in the sub-region. After the crisis that began in 1998, 550,000 Ecuadorians left the country (O'Neil et al, 2005). The Ecuadorian case shows two interesting transformations in emigration that can be observed in other Latin American countries as well. First, the major country of destination of Ecuadorian migrants has changed, with Spain receiving a yearly average inflow of 69,453 Ecuadorians from 2000 to 2004, compared to fewer than 1,000 migrants per year before the crisis in 1998, replacing the U.S. as the top destination (OECD, online datasets, 2007). Other countries where emigration patterns have shifted away from the U.S. as the top destination are Argentina, Bolivia, Peru and Venezuela.
- The second significant new trend observed in Ecuador, and that can be extended throughout Latin America, is the increased importance of women in intra-regional migration. According to ECLAC estimates, on the American continent as a whole, there has been a shift replacing predominantly female migration in the 1970s and 1980s by mainly male migration thereafter (González and Sánchez, 2002). However, if the analysis is restricted to cross-border migration between Latin American countries, there is a strong increase in the number of women relative to total emigration. Figure 6 shows the trend in gender balance among international migrants in Latin America between 1970 and 2000. Latin America records the highest proportion of women among international migrants in the developing parts of the world (ECLAC, 2006a). Female migration in Latin America and the Caribbean has also been characterized by the increased participation of women in the labour market, which confirms the increase in the feminization of migration in this sub-region. In addition, according to the United Nations International Research and Training Institute for the Advancement of Women (UN INSTRAW), 54 per cent of Latin American migrants are women, and the majority of their remittances (30% of their income, compared to 10% for men)

is used for education, health care and small businesses that benefit their families. The amount of money female migrants send home accounts for more than half of total remittances transferred (LP, 2007).

Figure 6:

Gender ratio of the stock of intra-regional migration from Latin America and the Caribbean, 1970-2000

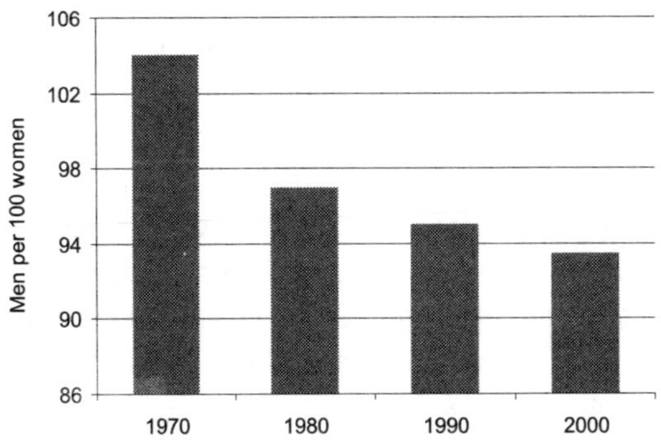

Source: ECLAC, 2006a.

SOME TOPICAL ISSUES IN MIGRATION MANAGEMENT IN THE AMERICAS

Irregular migration in the region is substantial and rising

- In the Americas, as in many other parts of the world, irregular migration is substantial and rising (see also Chapter 8). In the U.S., for example, although the irregular migration problem has been felt for some considerable time, rising numbers during the last decade have pushed the topic towards the top of the national agenda. According to the OECD (2006), net irregular immigration to the United States is estimated to be in the vicinity of 500,000 persons per year, which amounts to around 0.15-0.20 per cent of the total population per year. The Pew Hispanic Center (Passel, 2006) estimated the stock of irregular migrants at between 11.5 and 12 million persons in March 2006, and suggests that most irregular migrants arrived since 1990. These numbers concur broadly with the estimates of the U.S. Department of Homeland Security, according to which the volume of the irregular migration flow increased from 120,000 per year in the 1980s to 440,000 per year during the period 1990-1994, and to 650,000 per year during the period 1995-1999, to reach 850,000 migrants per year during the period 2000-2005 (Passel, 2006). Mexico is the major country of origin and transit for irregular migration to the U.S. (over 450,000 a year). This flow has become more pronounced since the 1990s, even though Mexico has strengthened its migration control measures. According to Mexico's National Migration Institute (Instituto Nacional de Migración, 2005), the number of apprehensions and deportations of irregular migrants increased from 215,695 in 2004 to 240,269 in 2005 but decreased to 167,437 during the first ten months of 2006.
- During the last ten years, South America has become characterized by intensive outmigration towards North America and Europe, while traditional intra-regional movements have declined. The most important source countries for irregular migration to Europe are Ecuador and Peru, but also traditional destination countries like Argentina and Brazil. In Spain, for example, in 2003 a majority of irregular migrants came from Latin America (the top three source countries being Ecuador – 20%, Colombia – 8% and Bolivia – 7%). The same is true of Portugal, where six per cent of irregular migrants came from Brazil in 2004 (Kostova Karaboytcheva, 2006).

Remittances are increasing in the region and play a central role in economic development

- An important emerging migration issue in the Americas is the increasing role of remittances in economic development. According to the World Bank (2008), in 2007 the countries of Latin America and the Caribbean received USD 60.7

billion in remittances, over 16 per cent more than in 2006, with this sub-region receiving 24.14 per cent of total remittances sent to developing countries in 2007 (World Bank, 2008) (see Figure 7). Moreover, the Inter-American Development Bank (2003) estimates that the actual impact of remittances on local economies can be enhanced by a factor of three through their multiplier effects. At the national level, the country with the highest remittance inflows in the region is Mexico (41% of total flows) (World Bank, 2008), which is estimated to have received USD 25.1 billion in 2007, making it the third largest recipient of remittances in the world, after India and China and followed by the Philippines. In addition, in 2006, in seven countries in the region remittances accounted for more than ten per cent of GDP (World Bank, 2008): Honduras (25.6%), Guyana (24.3%), Haiti (21.6%), Jamaica (18.5%), El Salvador (18.2%), Nicaragua (12.2%) and Guatemala (10.3%) (World Bank, 2008).

Figure 7:

Workers' remittances sent to developing countries, 2001-2007

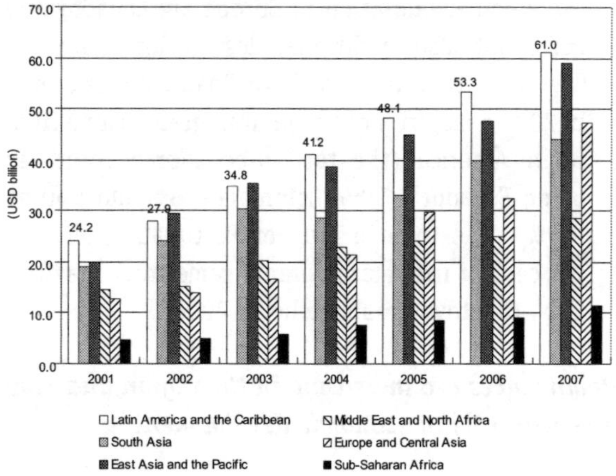

Note: Workers' remittances, compensation of employees and migrant transfers.

Source: *World Bank (2008), based on the International Monetary Fund's Balance of Payments Statistics Yearbook 2007.*

Brain drain is a growing concern in the region

- Brain drain in the Caribbean has become an issue of particular relevance, given the rate of emigration against the size of the pool of highly qualified persons. While in South America and Mexico brain drain accounts for ten and five per cent of the college and high-school educated population respectively, in the case of Caribbean countries nearly one-third of college and high-school educated citizens live in the U.S. (Lowell and Suro, 2002). Jamaica and Haiti have some of the highest rates of emigration of the highly skilled in the world, with two-thirds of their college graduates abroad (O'Neil et al., 2005). Even if the emigration of highly skilled persons is considered to yield some direct beneficial effects to countries of origin, Beine et al. (2002) argue that in the case of Jamaica and Haiti they are made unambiguously poorer.

The movement of refugees and displaced persons is no longer a concern on the scale of the previous two decades

- Finally, the movement of refugees and displaced persons in Latin America and the Caribbean, while still of significance, is no longer experienced on the scale of the previous two decades. The number of refugees leaving the sub-region has fallen considerably compared to the 1980s and 1990s. According to the Office of the United Nations High Commissioner for Refugees (UNHCR), as of the end of 2005, there were 2.51 million "persons of concern" from Latin America and the Caribbean, compared to 8.86 million in Asia, 5.17 in Africa, 3.68 million in Europe, 716,806 in North America and 82,492 in Oceania (UNHCR, 2006). However, the estimated number of displaced people in some Latin American countries is substantial. For instance, according to one reliable source, there were in 2007 between 2.39 and four million internally displaced persons in Colombia, the second highest IDP figure in the world after Sudan (IDMC, 2008). In addition, more than 400,000 Colombians have refugee status within the region and in the U.S. (O'Neil et al., 2005), and the number of asylum applications by Colombians in Ecuador has increased from 36 in 1999 to 11,388 in 2003 totalling 37,143 applications during the period 2000-2005 (UNHCR, 2006). This trend represents a significant challenge not only for Colombia, but also for all host countries in the region.

The access of migrants and mobile populations to health care is an important issue

In the Americas, as indeed in other regions, speedy and adequate access of migrants and mobile populations to HIV prevention, care and treatment is considered essential to combating the virus, and a number of interventions have been undertaken in the region to this effect (see Textbox Reg. 1).

Textbox Reg. 1

Universal Access to HIV Prevention, Care and Treatment: Targeting Migrants and Mobile Populations in the Americas

Many socio-economic and psychosocial factors that drive migration, such as poverty, unemployment, political instability and conflicts, are also closely associated with the proliferation of HIV infections, as their spread traces rural-urban migration paths within countries and subsequent return migration to areas and communities of origin. At the global level, the spread of HIV is often associated with the flow of people fleeing armed conflicts and civil unrest, but also accompanies the growth of international tourism, business travel and commercial activities, while the rise in international criminal activities, such as the smuggling and the trafficking in human beings, has also become an important factor in the spread of the disease. In the destination country, migrants can be perceived as potential sources of HIV infections, while they themselves face important obstacles in accessing health services and advice on either prevention or care and support in living with HIV, and are frequently barred from permanent residence status if mandatory tests show them to be HIV positive.

Young, lonely and isolated adult migrant men living and working far away from home, from disadvantaged socio-economic backgrounds, with little or no knowledge of the local language, frequently undocumented, are particularly vulnerable to becoming infected with HIV, a situation further compounded by exploitative working conditions, lack of access to health and social services and a high number of sexual partners, including same-sex partners and prostitutes, as well as excessive drinking, substance abuse and risky conduct under stress (Hirsch et al., 2002; Organista and Kibo, 2005). Studies have shown that on the Mexico-Guatemalan border, 70 per cent of truck drivers *(traileros)*, who are either married or in a stable relationship, neglect the use of condoms to protect themselves and their partner, even though 40 per cent would have engaged in extramarital sex, including prostitution (Bronfman-Pertzovsky and Leyva, 2000). Female migrant workers are especially vulnerable to abuse, including trafficking, forced labour and prostitution. An estimated 60 per cent of undocumented migrant women would have been exposed to some kind of sexual activity during their migration experience, ranging from sexual abuse, coerced sex or new sexual partners (Aguilar, 1996). Different cultural factors and attitudes to sexuality in the destination country contribute to a migrant's vulnerability, as do the different approaches to healthcare and medical practice, together with unfamiliar legal and administrative rules.

In the Americas, a major risk factor for HIV transmission is unprotected sex between men, though the heterosexual transmission of HIV has also become a major risk factor for the wives and female partners of returnees. In the Caribbean, the high HIV prevalence reflects the significant level of population mobility and poses a major challenge for the control of the epidemic (Borland et al., 2004).

Unmet health needs are common among migrant workers and their access to healthcare is often affected by a migrant's legal status. Some of the most frequently reported obstacles to healthcare cited by Latino migrants in the U.S. is their irregular status and fear of deportation (Brown et al., 2002; Cunningham, et al., 2000), insufficient economic means, lack of health insurance and competing essential needs (e.g. housing, food, transportation) as well as language, cultural factors and stigma (Solorio, et al., 2004). According to a 2006 New York City Department of Health report, foreign-born adults with low incomes are less likely to have Medicaid than others born in the U.S. (29% and 42%, respectively) and foreign-born adults under the age of 65 who speak only Spanish are nearly twice as likely to be unable to obtain medical care when needed as those who speak English (15% and 8%, respectively). They are also less likely to use preventive measures, and low-income migrants in New York are less likely to have tested for HIV during the past year (Kim et al., 2006).

Because of the higher vulnerability to HIV infection among migrants and other mobile populations, a number of countervailing initiatives have been launched throughout the region. Thus, since 2001, the HIV/AIDS Mobile Population Project for Central America, Mexico and the U.S., developed under the auspices of the National Institute of Public Health, Mexico, and the IMPSIDA project[1] of the United Nations, have been active at eleven border-crossing points throughout Mesoamerica with educational initiatives, access to free condoms and to HIV counselling and testing services (Bronfman-Pertzovsky and Leyva, 2000). Similar HIV-testing initiatives were launched in El Salvador at the San Cristobal border-crossing point, providing guidelines for the care of mobile populations as well as pamphlets, posters and other tools to raise general awareness and knowledge about HIV and AIDS among mobile populations (Bortman et al., 2006).

Another example of effective practice in the region is the 1990 AIDS Law in Argentina, which guarantees full access to healthcare and treatment regardless of the migrant's status (Art. 8),[2] and various programmes, services and guidelines are being offered and implemented in response to this political mandate (Vásquez et al., 2005).

Among the positive examples of prevention exercises for highly mobile populations is an innovative programme in Brazil aimed at truck drivers. As they wait for customs clearance at the Brazil-Argentina-Paraguay border, two outreach educators hand them educational material and invite them to a mobile trailer for health services, including testing and counselling for HIV and syphilis, as well as the management of sexually transmitted infection (STI) syndromes. In addition, they have their blood pressure taken, are screened for diabetes and asked to return for a follow-up visit two weeks later. Interviews were conducted with a random sample of 1,775 male truck drivers before the screening exercise and with another 2,408 eighteen months later. Of the truck drivers interviewed during the post-intervention period, half had participated in the programme; one-third had participated in HIV testing and counselling; and only around 13 per cent were unaware of the project. Nearly 2,000 truck drivers participated in pre-test counselling for HIV and syphilis. Of the 1,795 who gave blood samples, 83 per cent returned for post-test counselling and results. Only 0.3 per cent tested positive for HIV and 4.7 per cent for Syphilis.

However, examples of successful initiatives are few and far between, and regular and large-scale services for HIV/AIDS testing, prevention, care and treatment, and systematic and reliable information for mobile populations, in particular irregular migrants, on how to access them are lacking or, at best, uneven throughout the Caribbean, Latin America and North America. In order to combat and control the spread of HIV/AIDS, governments and policymakers need to devote more attention and means to the issues at stake and strive towards universal access to prevention, care and treatment for mobile and hard-to-reach populations, such as migrants. To be effective, such service outreach must also aim to breach the social isolation and stigma frequently experienced by migrants, and to gain an insight and understanding of their social networks, relationships and dynamics, and not limit itself to the mere handout of condoms and HIV/AIDS testing and education.

By the end of 2008, IOM Washington and the HIV/STI Unit of the Pan American Health Organization (PAHO) will publish research on migrants' access to health in the Caribbean, with a particular focus on HIV, as a follow-up to a Baseline Assessment on mobile populations, conducted in 2004 (Borland et al., 2004).[3]

Notes:

1 Iniciativa Mesoamericana para Prevenir la expansión del VIH-SIDA [Mesoamerican Initiative for Prevention of the Spread of HIV/AIDS].

2 Argentina, Ley Nacional de SIDA [Aids Law] No. 23.798, Republic of Argentina, Buenos Aires, 16 August 1990.

3 *HIV/AIDS in the Caribbean* (forthcoming). On the basis of a comparison between five countries (Bahamas, Dominican Republic, Guyana, Haiti and Trinidad and Tobago), the study covers the different facets of the relationship between HIV/AIDS and migration in the region. It includes an analysis of vulnerability factors in the migration process, dynamics and impact of health workers' migration, and legal and political responses to the phenomenon.

Source: *HIV/STI Unit, PAHO, Washington, D.C.*

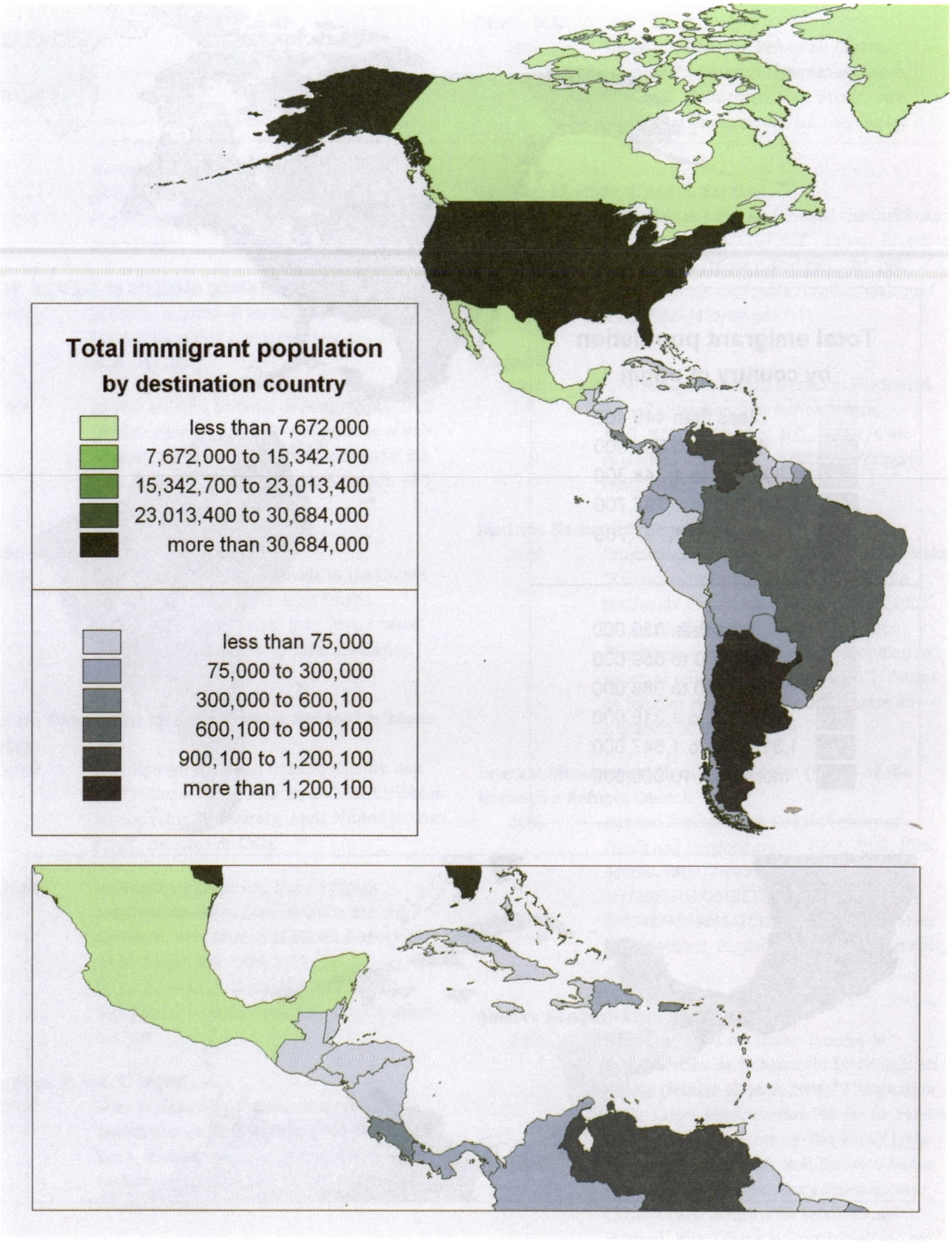
Total immigrant population
by destination country
less than 7,672,000
7,672,000 to 15,342,700
15,342,700 to 23,013,400
23,013,400 to 30,684,000
more than 30,684,000
less than 75,000
75,000 to 300,000
300,000 to 600,100
600,100 to 900,100
900,100 to 1,200,100
more than 1,200,100

Latinamerica Press (LP)

2007 http://www.latinamericapress.org/index.asp# (accessed 13 August).

Lowell, B.L. and R. Suro

2002 *The Improving Educational Profile of Latino Immigrants*, A Pew Hispanic Center Report, 4 December, Washington, D.C., http://pewhispanic.org/files/reports/14.pdf.

Migration Policy Institute (MPI)

2004 *Building the New American Community: Newcomer Integration and Inclusion Experiences in Non-Traditional Gateway Cities*, Washington, D.C.

Fact Sheet on the Foreign Born: The United States, MPI Data Hub, Online information, February, Washington, D.C., http://www.migrationinformation.org/DataHub/state.cfm?ID=US.

2006 *America's Emigrants: US Retirement Migration to Mexico and Panama*, MPI, Washington, D.C., http://www.migrationpolicy.org/pubs/americas_emigrants.pdf.

O'Neil, K., K. Hamilton and D. Papademetriou

2005 "Migration in the Americas", paper prepared for the Policy Analysis and Research Programme of the Global Commission on International Migration (GCIM), September, Geneva, http://www.gcim.org/attachements/RS1.pdf.

Organisation for Economic Co-operation and Development (OECD)

2006 *International Migration Outlook*, SOPEMI 2006 Edition, OECD, Paris.

Passel, J.S.

2006 *Changing Dynamics and Characteristics of Immigration to the United States*, June, Pew Hispanic Center, Washington, D.C..

Ratha, D. and W. Shaw

2007 "South-South Migration and Remittances", 19 January, Development Prospects Group, The World Bank, Washington, D.C., http://siteresources.worldbank.org/INTPROSPECTS/Resources/South-SouthmigrationJan192006.pdf.

United Nations, Department of Economic and Social Affairs (UN DESA), Population Division

2002 *International Migration Report 2002*, UN DESA, Population Division, New York, http://www.un.org/esa/population/publications/ittmig2002/ittmigrep2002.htm.

2005 *Trends in Total Migrant Stock: The 2005 Revision*, UN DESA, Population Division, New York, http://esa.un.org/migration/index.asp?panel=1.

United Nations High Commissioner for Refugees (UNHCR)

2006 *Statistical Yearbook 2005*, UNHCR, Geneva, http://www.unhcr.org/statistics/STATISTICS/464478a72.html.

United States Census Bureau

2006 Urban Institute tabulations from public-use files from the Current Population Survey, March Supplement, 1995 to 2005.

Van Hook, J., F.D. Bean and J. Passel

2005 "Unauthorized Migrants Living in the United States: A Mid-Decade Portrait", *Migration Information Source*, September, MPI, Washington, D.C., http://www.migrationinformation.org/feature/display.cfm?ID=329.

World Bank

2006 *Global Economic Prospects 2006: Economic Implications of Remittances and Migration*, The World Bank, Washington, D.C., http://econ.worldbank.org/WBSITE/EXTERNAL/EXTDEC/EXTDECPROSPECTS/GEPEXT/EXTGEP2006/0,,contentMDK:20709766~menuPK:1026823~pagePK:64167689~piPK:64167673~theSitePK:1026804,00.html.

2008 *Revisions to Remittance Trends 2007*, July, The World Bank, Washington, D.C., http://econ.worldbank.org/WBSITE/EXTERNAL/EXTDEC/EXTDECPROSPECTS/0,,contentMDK:21121930~menuPK:3145470~pagePK:64165401~piPK:64165026~theSitePK:476883,00.html.

Textbox Reg. 1 - Universal Access to HIV Prevention, Care and Treatment: Targeting Migrants and Mobile Populations in the Americas

Aguilar, H.S.

1996 *VIH/SIDA en Guatemala. Una Bibliografía anotada*, Mimeo, Julio, Guatemala, Guatemala.

Bolland, B., L. Faas, D. Marshall, R. McLean, M. Schroen, M. Smit and T. Valerio

2004 *HIV/AIDS and Mobile Populations in the Caribbean: A Baseline Assessment. Final Report*, June, International Organization for Migration (IOM), Santo Domingo, Dominican Republic, http://www.iom.int/jahia/webdav/site/myjahiasite/shared/shared/mainsite/published_docs/books/hiv_mobile_carribbean.pdf.

Bortman, M., L.B. Saenz, I. Pimenta, C. Isern, A.E. Rodríguez, M. Miranda, L. Moreira and D. Rayo

2006 *Reducing HIV/AIDS Vulnerability in Central America: El Salvador: HIV/AIDS Situation and Response to the Epidemic*, December, Latin America and the Caribbean Region and The Global HIV/AIDS Program, The World Bank, Washington, D.C.

Bronfman-Pertzovsky, M. and R. Leyva

2000 *Traileros en la frontera México-Guatemala. Impacto de una intervención informativa sobre ETS/VIH/SIDA y promoción del uso del condón*, SSA Instituto Nacional De Salud Pública.

Brown, E.R., N. Ponce, T. Rice and S.A. Lavarreda

2002 *The State of Health Insurance in California: Findings from the 2001 California Health Interview Survey*, June, University of California, Los Angeles (UCLA) Center for Health Policy Research, Los Angeles, http://www.healthpolicy.ucla.edu/pubs/files/shic062002.pdf.

Cunningham, W.E., D.M. Mosen, L.S. Morales, R.M. Andersen, M.F. Shapiro and R.D. Hays

2000 "Ethnic and racial differences in long-term survival from hospitalization for HIV Infection", *Journal of Health Care for the Poor and Underserved*, 11(2): 163-178.

Hirsch, J.S., J. Higgins, M.E. Bentely and C.A. Nathanson

2002 "The Social Construction of Sexuality: Marital Infidelity and Sexually Transmitted Diseases – HIV Risk in a Mexican Migrant Community", *American Journal of Public Health*, 92: 1227-1237.

Kim, M., G. Van Wye, B. Kerker, L. Thorpe and T.R. Frieden

2006 *The Health of Immigrants in New York City*, A Report from the New York City Department of Health and Mental Hygiene, June, New York, http://www.nyc.gov/html/doh/downloads/pdf/episrv/episrv-immigrant-report.pdf.

Organista, K. and A. Kubo

2005 "Pilot Survey of HIV Risk and Contextual Problems and Issues in Mexican/Latino Migrant Day Laborers", *Journal of Immigrant Health*, 7(4): 269-281.

Solorio, M.R., J. Currier and W. Cunningham

2004 "HIV health care services for Mexican migrants", *Journal of Acquired Immune Deficiency Syndromes*, 37(Supp. 4): S240-S251.

Vásquez, M., G. Wald and K. Frieder

2005 *Guía para promotores comunitarios Prevención del VIH/SIDA en Población Migrante*, 2nd Ed., Fundación Huésped, Buenos Aires.

ASIA

- Over the past three decades, international labour mobility has become an increasingly important feature of the Asian economic landscape. The estimated current stock of Asian migrant workers abroad may be around 25 million (Hugo, 2005), including both within and beyond the Asian region.[1] Much of these movements are undocumented and are not included in the available official statistics.
- Asian migration has become an increasingly intra-regional phenomenon. In mid-2000, a quarter of the 25 million international migrants worked in East and Southeast Asia – and their number increases to 7.5 million if unauthorized workers are included (Hugo, 2005).
- From 2000 to 2005, the estimated number of international migrants in South-Central Asia dropped from 15 to 13 million, while it increased in both East Asia (from 5.7 to 6.5 million) and Southeast Asia (from 4.7 to 5.6 million) (UN DESA, 2005).
- Some of the countries/areas that are most affected by international migration are in Asia. For instance, approximately 56 percent of the total population of Macao SAR is foreign-born, while the proportion of foreign-born in Hong Kong SAR and Singapore is nearly 43 per cent. In Brunei, about one-third of the population is foreign-born (Hugo, 2005).
- Countries/areas in Asia can be roughly classified according to their international labour migration situation as "mainly emigration" (Bangladesh, Cambodia, China, India, Indonesia, Laos, Myanmar, Nepal, Pakistan, the Philippines, Sri Lanka, Viet Nam); "mainly immigration" (Brunei, Hong Kong SAR, Japan, Macao SAR, Malaysia, Singapore, Republic of Korea (South Korea), Taiwan Province of China) and "both significant immigration and emigration" (Thailand) (Hugo, 2005). Some countries, such as Cambodia, China, Indonesia, the Philippines and Thailand, are also transit countries.

EAST ASIA

- The two Special Administrative Regions of China, Hong Kong and Macao, have the highest

[1] For the purpose of this Migration Overview, Asia includes: **East Asia** (China (China mainland, Hong Kong Special Administrative Region of China, Macao Special Administrative Region of China – hereafter Hong Kong SAR and Macao SAR, respectively - and Taiwan Province of China), the Democratic People's Republic of Korea (North Korea), Japan, Mongolia and the Republic of Korea (South Korea)); **Southeast Asia** (Brunei, Cambodia, Indonesia, Laos, Malaysia, Myanmar, the Philippines, Singapore, Thailand, Timor-Leste, Viet Nam); and **South-Central Asia** (Afghanistan, Bangladesh, Bhutan, India, Iran, Maldives, Nepal, Pakistan and Sri Lanka). Countries in Western Asia and Central Asia are addressed in the Migration Overviews on the Middle East and Europe, respectively.

concentration of international migrants in East Asia (43% and 56% of their total population, respectively). With about three million international migrants, Hong Kong SAR is also the major destination in the sub-region, followed by Japan with two million international migrants (UN DESA, 2005) (see Figure 1).

Figure 1:

Stock of migrants in East Asia, by destination, 2000 and 2005

Part A: Total number of migrants

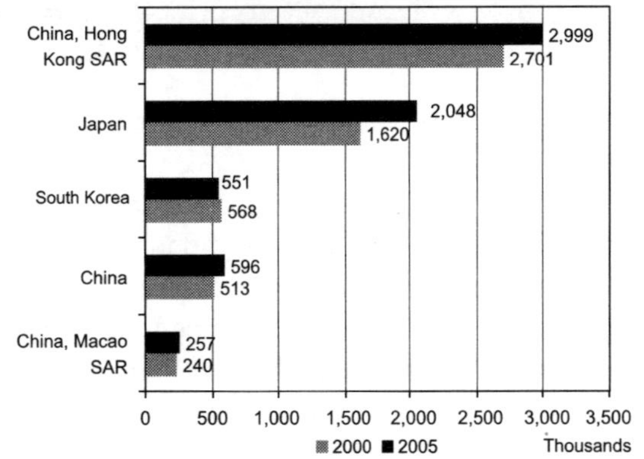

Part B: As a share of total population

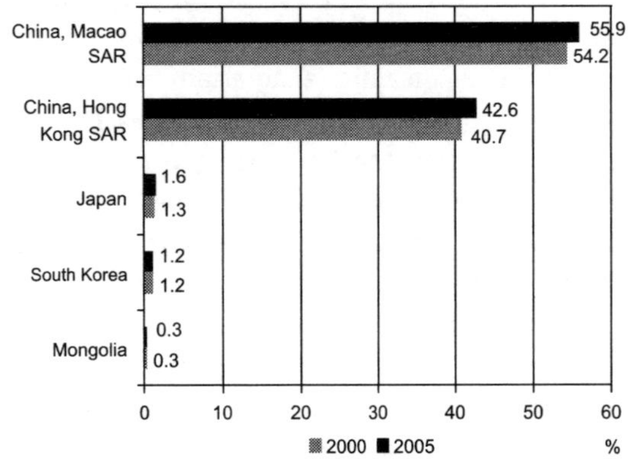

Note: East Asian countries showing negligible values on the scale are not included in this table.

Source: *UN DESA, 2005.*

Many East Asian countries/areas, together with Thailand and Singapore, show a high dependence on foreign labour

- The Migrant Labour Dependency Ratio (MLDR)[2] has significantly increased in recent years in all East Asian countries/areas with the exception of Hong Kong SAR, which experienced a decrease from 95 in 1993 to 72 in 2000 but still shows the highest MLDR in the region (Athukorala, 2006).

Japan receives migrant workers from less-developed Asian countries ...

- Japan hosts the third largest number of overseas Filipino workers (258,977), after the U.S. (2.7 million) and Saudi Arabia (one million), representing nearly a third of all foreign workers in Japan, totalling 910,000 in 2005 (POEA, 2006).
- In Japan, migrants from China make up almost one-quarter of new arrivals (*Financial Times*, 9 July 2007).

... and also from Russia

- The growing presence of Russians in Japan's northern provinces had hardly been researched until recently. Japanese Government statistics put the number of Russians entering Japan at around 37,000 per year, and the number of Russians residing in the country for 90 days or longer at a little over 6,000. Also, several tens of thousands of Russian seafarers and tourists visit Japanese port cities each year on a temporary landing permit while their ships are at anchor (Akaha, 2004).

China depends on its internal migrant workers ... and domestic remittances

- Labour migration in China has been characterized by the large outflow of agricultural labourers from

2 The Migrant Labour Dependency Ratio is defined as the number of migrant workers per 1,000 workers in the labour force.

inland villages to work in the manufacturing and service sectors in the coastal provinces, mostly on a temporary basis. This pattern of domestic and temporary migration has helped to generate a very large inflow of money from migrant workers to their families at home that has contributed to raise the income and welfare of farmers, and to reduce poverty. On average, a migrant worker remits between ¥500-1,000 (EUR 50-100[3]) three to six times a year. In 2006, domestic remittances averaged ¥331 billion[4] (EUR 33 billion). Approximately 75 per cent of the total domestic remittance volume of ¥223 billion in 2004 was captured by formal financial institutions. The remaining 25 per cent were either hand-carried home or sent through other channels (Cheng and Zhong, 2005).

Highly skilled emigration from East Asia is still an issue ...

- South Korean professionals continue to emigrate, with 4,600 leaving for Canada and 4,200 for the U.S. in 2003. Some 188,000 South Koreans were studying abroad in April 2004 (*Migration News*, 2005), a step that often leads to permanent settlement abroad.
- It is estimated that more than half of the graduating class of Beijing University's engineering students will seek opportunities overseas. Between 1979 and 1998, only about a third of all Chinese students benefiting from government assistance to study abroad returned home. The return rate, at around 10 per cent, is lowest for students going to the United States (from Canada the rate is around 50%) (Asia Pacific Foundation of Canada, 2000).

... but there are also signs that talent can be encouraged to return home

- Incentives schemes have been launched to encourage the return of highly skilled diaspora both to Taiwan Province of China and to South Korea.
- In China, the number of returned students jumped from less than 10,000 in 2000 to about 25,000 in 2004. However, returnees, as a percentage of persons going overseas, have not increased, as liberalization of the policy on travelling abroad on the basis of own funds has resulted in a very significant increase in the number of persons going abroad (Zweig, 2006).

SOUTH–CENTRAL ASIA

- Though India is the main destination country in South-Central Asia, the 5.7 million international migrants living there account for only 0.5 per cent of the total population. At the other extreme, the 818,582 international migrants living in Nepal represent three per cent of the local population, the highest share in this part of the world (UN DESA, 2005) (see Figure 2).

Figure 2:

Stock of migrants in South-Central Asia, by destination, 2000 and 2005

Part A: Total number of migrants

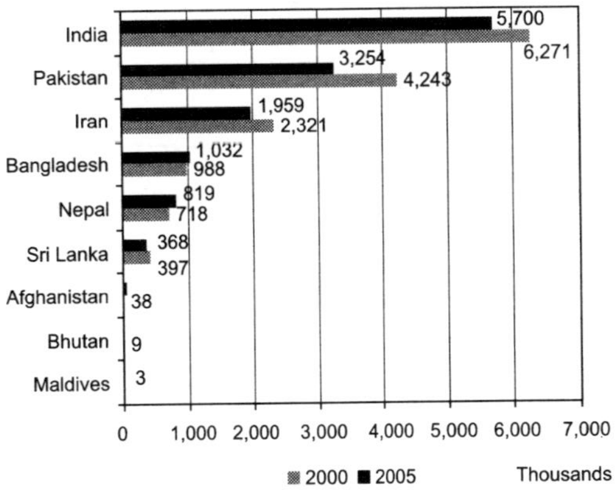

[3] One China Yuan Renminbi = EUR 0.099 (exchange rate, August 2008).

[4] The above estimate is based on the assumption that 75 per cent of the 126 million migrant workers in China in 2006 sent on average ¥3,500 home per year (Cheng and Zhong, 2005).

Part B: As a share of total population

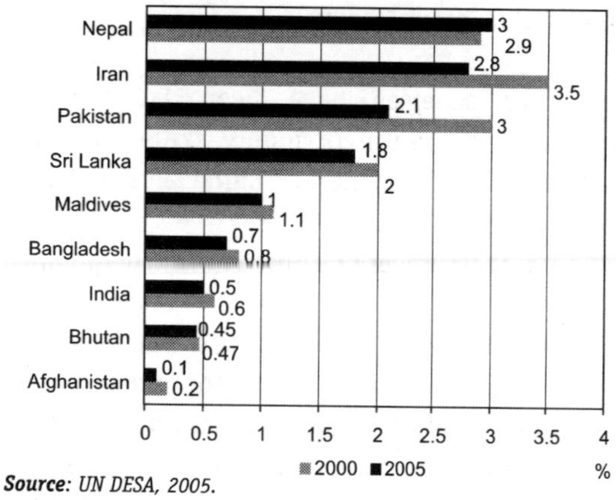

Source: UN DESA, 2005.

Many South-Central Asian countries are major sources of migrant workers

- Bangladesh, India, Nepal and Sri Lanka are major countries of origin of migrant workers (see Figure 3).
- While India is also a country of destination and transit, its levels of emigration increased in 2005 and accounted for almost eight per cent of total inflows in Australia (compared to 5% for the period 1990-2004), 11 per cent in Canada (8%) and eight per cent in the United States (5%) (OECD, 2007).

Figure 3:

Labour migration outflows for South-Central Asia, 2001-2005

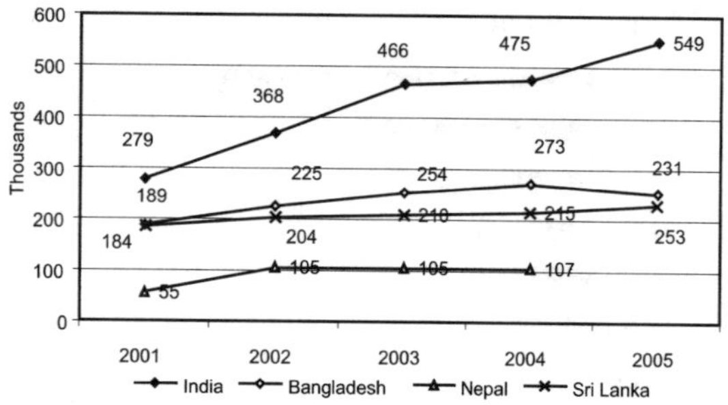

Note: Figures based on official statistics for the South-Central Asian region and the Nepal Institute of Development Studies (NIPS).

Source: *IOM, 2005.*

- According to research conducted in 2002 by the Nepal Institute for Development Studies (NIDS) for the United Nations Women's Fund (UNIFEM), approximately 170,000 Nepalese were in East and Southeast Asia,[5] nearly 36,000 in Europe and over 10,000 in North America. However, most Nepali workers abroad were to be found in the Gulf states; over 465,000 Nepalese were working in countries such as Saudi Arabia (42% of all Nepali expatriate workers) and Qatar (11%) (Seddon, 2005).

These movements continue to comprise mainly low-skilled workers ... and involve women

- The majority of Nepali women migrant workers present outside of India, mainly in the Middle East, East Asia, and Southeast Asia, were concentrated in two destinations – Hong Kong SAR (44%) and Japan (9%) – with 56.5 per cent in East and Southeast Asia. The remainder were employed in the U.K. (12%), the U.S. (9%), Australia (6%), Bahrain (4%) and other countries. Most of them were working in domestic service or in other areas of the services sector (Seddon, 2005).

South-Central Asia is also characterized by large outflows of students

- Indian students in the U.S. accounted for 13.9 per cent of all foreign students in the period 2003-2004, the largest percentage for the third year in a row, followed by students from China, South Korea, Japan, Canada, and Taiwan Province of China. In 2004-2005, India continued to be the main country of origin for students leaving to study in the U.S., with 80,466 students (Khadria, 2006).

5 In February 2001, the Malaysian Government officially "opened" its labour market to workers from Nepal. Within six months, over 12,000 migrant workers had left for Malaysia and, a year later, Malaysia was hosting some 85,000 Nepali migrant workers.

During the last decade, labour migration flows from South-Central Asia have become more diverse: while Asian destinations now receive many more migrants, the Middle East continues to be the most popular destination

- An estimated 8.7 million temporary contractual workers from different Asian countries live and work in the Middle East (Hugo, 2005) (see Figure 4).

Figure 4:

Estimated stock of Asian origin temporary contractual workers in the Middle East

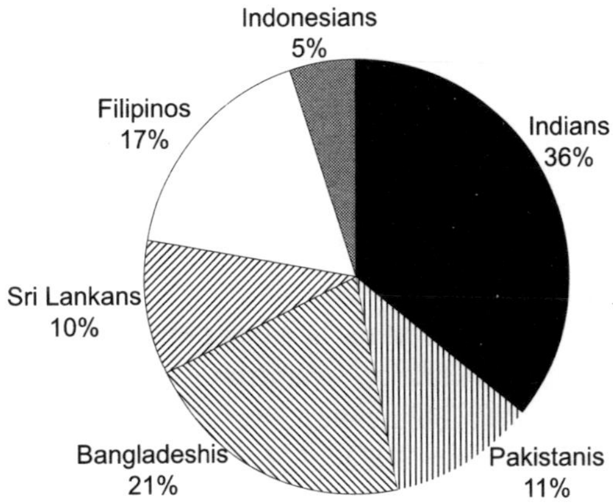

Source: *Hugo, 2005.*

- Bangladesh, India and Pakistan supply workers to realize infrastructure projects in the Gulf states, while Indonesia and Sri Lanka have secured the greatest part of the labour market for domestic workers, which has also spurred the feminization of migration in the Gulf region (Asis, 2005).
- Outflows of Pakistani workers to the Gulf countries fluctuate from year to year. The number of Pakistani workers who moved to Kuwait was 400 in 2001, but reached 12,087 in 2003 and then declined to 6,895 in 2005. Likewise, 18,421 Pakistani workers went to the United Arab Emirates (UAE) in 2001, whereas in 2003 the number was 61,329, then 47,441 in 2005. Around 90 per cent of Pakistani temporary contractual workers to the Gulf countries are in semi to low-skilled employment categories (IDB, 2006).

SOUTHEAST ASIA

- Southeast Asian countries are grouped in the ASEAN[6] regional block and most of their migrant populations originate within this system (Battistella, 2002). In Southeast Asia, Singapore has the highest number of international migrants on its territory (1.8 million), followed by Malaysia with 1.6 million. In terms of concentration, Singapore still leads with nearly 43 migrants per 100 inhabitants, while Malaysia has a much lower migrant share of 6.5 per cent. The country of Brunei Darussalam ranks second in concentration with about 33 migrants per 100 habitants (UN DESA, 2005) (see Figure 3).

Figure 5:

Stock of migrants in Southeast Asia, by destination, 2000 and 2005

Part A: Total number of migrants

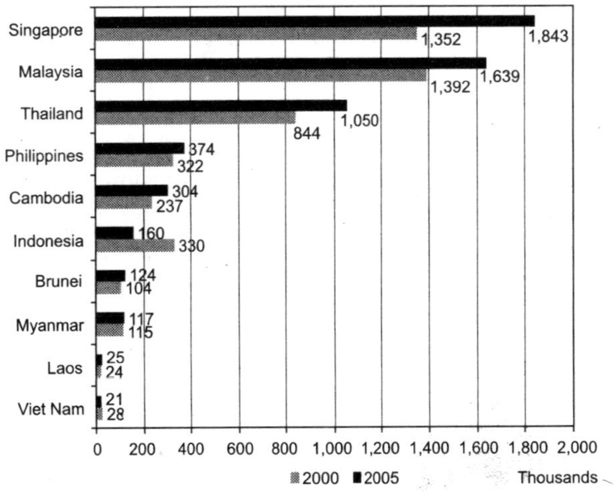

[6] ASEAN is the Association of Southeast Asian Nations and comprises 10 countries: Brunei, Cambodia, Indonesia, Laos, Malaysia, Myanmar, Philippines, Singapore, Thailand and Viet Nam.

Part B: As a share of total population

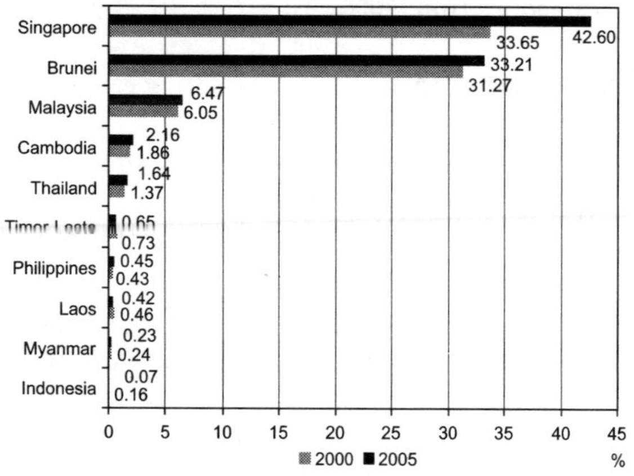

Source: *UN DESA, 2005.*

Although Malaysia, Thailand and Singapore show a dependence on foreign labour, ...

- Singapore's non-resident workforce increased 170 per cent, from 248,000 in 1990 to 670,000 in 2006. About 580,000 foreign workers are lower-skilled workers (Yeoh, 2007).
- The number of regular foreign workers in Malaysia, as per official sources, was reported to be as high as 2.2 million[7] in 2008 or up to 2.5-3 million if irregular migrant workers are included.[8] In 2006, Indonesians made up 65 per cent of all regular migrants, followed by Nepalese (11%) and Indian nationals (7%). About 32 per cent of migrants were employed in manufacturing and the remainder in the services, construction and plantation sectors (EIU, 2006).
- The Economist Intelligence Unit (EIU, 2006) forecast suggests that between 2005 and 2015 Singapore and Thailand (along with Hong Kong SAR and Taiwan Province of China) will face a situation where the growth in labour demand will exceed growth in the working age population. Thailand's MLDR increased from 5 in 1990 to 15 in 2003 (Athukorala, 2006). These countries/areas are thus expected to face incremental pressure on the demand for labour in connection with continued economic growth. The problem is most acute in Singapore (EIU, 2006).

... many Southeast Asian countries are major sources of migrant labour

- A newcomer to labour migration, Viet Nam, has expanded its overseas employment programme, with the result that over 70,000 workers go abroad per annum (Asis, 2005). Some 75,000 migrants went abroad in 2003, when there was a stock of 350,000 Vietnamese migrants abroad, including 75,000 in Malaysia and 40,000 in Taiwan Province of China; other destinations are Japan, South Korea and the Middle East (*Migration News*, 2004).
- The Philippines have the largest stock of migrant workers in foreign countries. Official figures from the Philippine Overseas Employment Administration (POEA, 2006) reveal that, as at the end of 2006, the total stock of overseas Filipinos was 8.2 million distributed as follows: 3.6 million permanent residents, 3.8 million temporary residents and 875,000 irregular migrants.
- Indonesia is a quintessential labour-surplus country. At the end of 2006, an estimated 11 per cent of Indonesian workers (11.6 million) were unemployed, and underemployment stood at over 20 per cent (i.e. 45 million workers) (Hugo, 2007). Official governmental sources in July 2006 reported that two million Indonesians worked abroad, 70 per cent of whom were low-skilled (*Migration News*, 2006).
- On the other hand, the number of Thai nationals officially in employment overseas fell steadily from 202,000 in 1999 to about 150,000 in 2003, owing to increased competition from more populous countries and their large supply of low-wage

[7] Malaysia showed the highest dependency on migrant workers in the region with about 220 migrants per 1,000 workers in 2003, having experienced an increase of 65 per cent since 1994 (Athukorala, 2006).

[8] The discrepancy with the UN DESA estimates provided in Figure 3 and those reported by the Malaysian government is likely to be due to the different reference year of the two sources.

labour, and to stricter labour migration regulations in Thailand and in destination countries (Huguet and Punpuing, 2005).

These outflows are also directed to non-ASEAN destinations

- The vast majority of Filipino workers abroad is to be found either in the Middle East or in other Asian countries (see Figure 6).

Figure 6:

Deployment of overseas Filipino workers, by destination, (new employees and returnees, excluding seafarers), 1998-2006

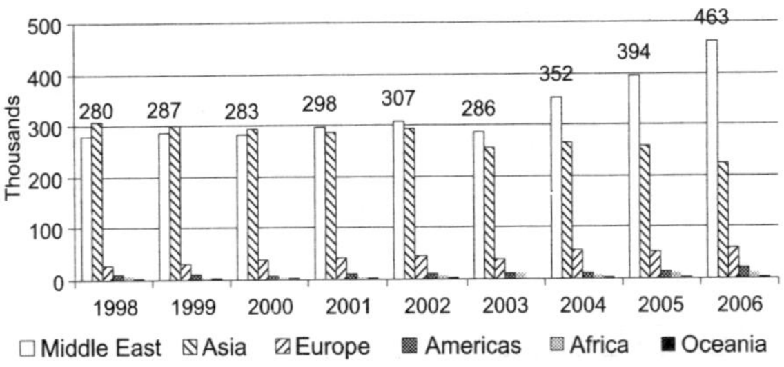

Source: POEA, 2006.

- Out of some 200,000 migrant workers in the Lebanon, about 34,000 were from the Philippines in mid-2006, mostly in domestic service (*Migration News*, 2006).
- Since 2001, the Middle East has again become the leading destination for Indonesian overseas workers, with their number peaking at over 226,000 in 2006 (Hugo, 2007).
- Taiwan Province of China is the major destination for Thais migrating for employment, followed by Singapore. While Israel has been steadily attracting Thai workers during the last decade, South Korea has emerged as a new top destination only during the last five years and is now the third largest destination for Thai temporary migrant workers. Brunei is also becoming another significant destination for Thais and migration of Thais to non-Asian destinations, such as Europe, is steadily increasing (TOEA, 2007) (see Figure 7).

Figure 7:

Thai workers abroad, by destination, 1995-2007

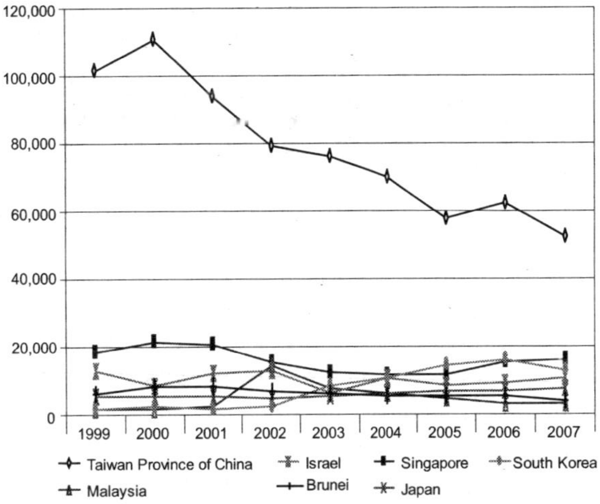

Source: TOEA, 2007.

... but there are signs that talent can be encouraged to return home

- Malaysia has introduced a programme under which the estimated 10,000 Malaysian professionals abroad can apply to return with the government guaranteeing their previous foreign salary. In 2004, 250 out of 650 applications to return had been accepted (*Migration News*, 2004).

SOME TOPICAL ISSUES IN MIGRATION MANAGEMENT IN ASIA

Increasing numbers of Asian migrants are leaving to work in African countries

- The number of Filipino nationals working in Africa has steadily increased over the last years (see Figure 8).

Figure 8:

Overseas Filipino workers in Africa, (new employees and returnees), 1998-2006

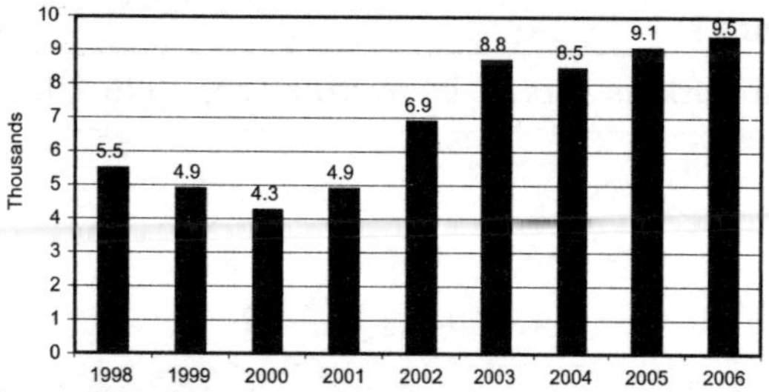

Source: POEA, 2006.

- China is also rapidly becoming an important country of origin for migrants going to Africa, especially to South Africa where an estimated 100,000 to 200,000 Chinese migrants are working either as regular or irregular entrants (*SAMP Migration News*, January 2006).
- Lesotho is home to about 5,000 Chinese nationals (mainly investors in the textile industry) both from Taiwan Province of China and the mainland, making it the largest foreign community ever to reside there (MPI, 2004).

South-Central and Southeast Asian migration is increasingly feminized

- With employment opportunities and the number of destinations increasing worldwide, many more women are joining the migrant flows from Asian countries to Europe, the Middle East and North America, and also within the Asian region itself.

Figure 9:

Selected Asian countries of origin: proportion of women in international labour migration flows

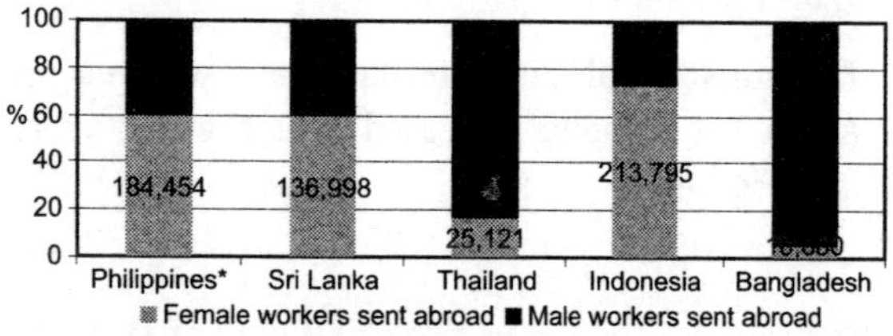

*Sources: POEA, 2006 (*only new employees); Sri Lanka Bureau of Foreign Employment 2005; Chalamwong, 2005 for Thailand; Soeprobo, 2004 for Indonesia; Bangladesh Bureau of Manpower, Employment and Training (BMET), 2006.*

- Women represent about 60 per cent of all migrants from the Philippines, Sri Lanka and Indonesia (POEA, 2006; Sri Lanka Bureau of Foreign Employment 2005; Soeprobo, 2005) (see Figure 9).
- Women make up just over 15 per cent of Thai migrant workers, but the actual number may be considerably higher given that much female migration is undocumented (Hugo, 2005) and that most women migrant workers from Thailand work in the domestic sector which is not a recognized category of employment.
- Countries with a traditionally higher proportion of female migrants, such as Sri Lanka and the Philippines, have experienced a slower rate of increase in the number of female migrants than countries where women have only relatively recently joined the migration flows and where their numbers are still relatively low, for instance, Bangladesh (POEA, 2006; Sri Lanka Bureau of Foreign Employment, 2005) (see Figures 10 and 11).

Figure 10:

Trends in female labour migration from the Philippines and Sri Lanka

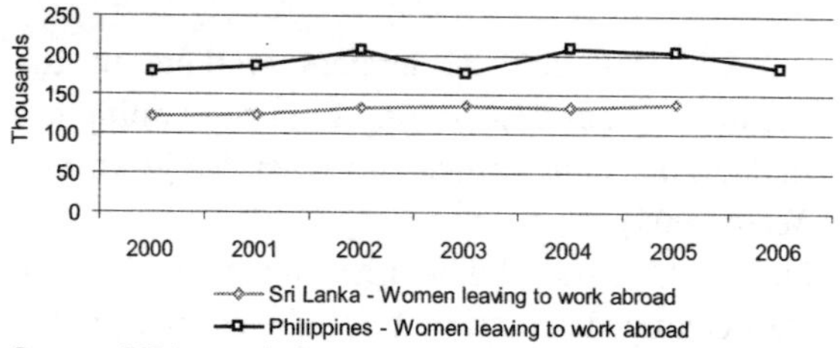

Sources: POEA, 2006 (only new employees) and Sri Lanka Bureau of Foreign Employment, 2005.

Figure 11:

Trends in female labour migrant flows from Bangladesh

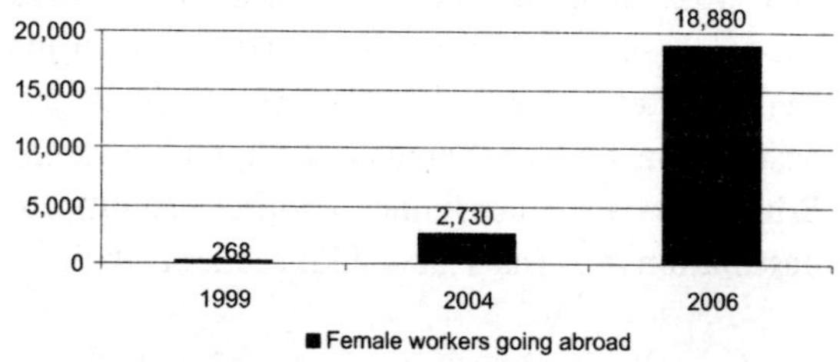

Source: BMET, 2006.

- Although Bangladesh did introduce a selective ban on female migration owing to cases of abuse and sexual exploitation of women migrants abroad, according to the recently adopted overseas employment policies by the Government of Bangladesh, both men and women are free to migrate abroad to work and the earlier ban on female migration is being reviewed on a case-by-case basis.[9]
- The evidence provided by Blanchet (2008) suggests that the official statistics on both male and female Bangladeshi migrant workers have been significantly underestimated. In sharp contrast to the official figure of 18,880 for 2006, this study provides an estimate of 430,000 Bangladeshi women migrant workers abroad. On the other hand, while the official statistics indicate that there are 3.8 million male migrant workers, the paper gives an estimate of 2.9 million. Given these new estimates, the proportion of female migrants as compared to their male counterparts stands at approximately 15 per cent.
- The majority of the ten main destinations for Bangladeshi women between mid-2004 and mid-2007 are in the Middle East (BMET, 2007) (see Figure 12).

Figure 12:

Top destinations for Bangladeshi women, mid-2004-mid-2007

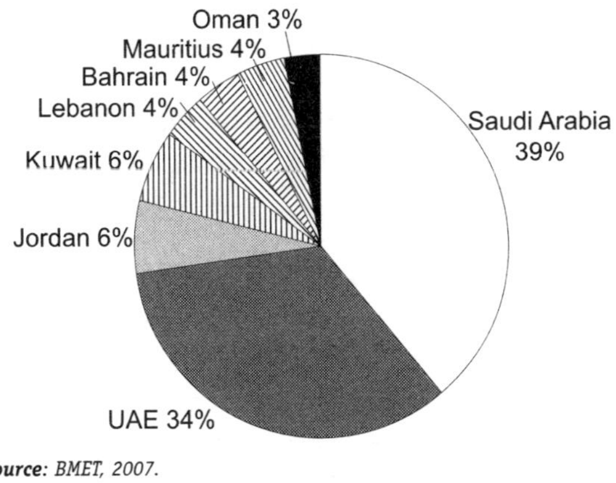

Source: *BMET, 2007.*

Asia is increasingly attracting highly trained individuals from more developed countries/areas within and outside Asia

- ASEAN-6[10] countries have been net destinations for skilled individuals in recent years: Malaysia, Singapore and Thailand have attracted some 60,000-70,000 foreign workers, with some 10,000 to 20,000 migrants also working in Indonesia and the Philippines in 2002-2003 (Bathnagar and Manning, 2005). Professional posts requiring greater skills and experience are largely filled by workers from Singapore, the G-8 countries and Australia and New Zealand (EIU, 2007).
- Indonesia is also experiencing an influx of skilled expatriates owing to the inability of Indonesian training institutions to supply a sufficient number of professionals (in particular engineers, scientists, managers and accountants) commensurate with the country's structural changes and economic growth. Experts have come from Australia and other developed countries, as well as the Philippines and India (Hugo, 2007).
- While India can generally meet its need for skilled workers from its large pool of university graduates, there has been a recent trend to hire foreign nationals already working with Indian companies around the world. Foreigners are being employed in India's information technology (IT) sector, and this trend is likely to continue (EIU, 2007).
- Many Hong Kong SAR residents work outside their territory, particularly in mainland China. According to a survey conducted in Hong Kong SAR in early 2004, close to 80 per cent out of a total of 240,000 held administrative and professional positions in mainland China. Chinese authorities offer three-year multiple-entry visas to visiting third-country nationals who are permanent residents in Hong Kong SAR. Most of those working in China do so on a temporary basis; annual departures from the territory as a whole are relatively low at just 9,800 in 2004 (EIU, 2007).

9 Information obtained via personal email contact with Shahidul Haque (IOM).

10 ASEAN-6 refers to those countries that are long-standing members of the World Trade Organization (WTO): Brunei-Darussalam, Indonesia, Malaysia, the Philippines, Singapore and Thailand.

Diasporas from Asia are some of the largest in the world

- With 30 to 40 million overseas Chinese (Chinese nationals as well as those who have acquired citizenship of host countries), the Chinese diaspora is the largest (2.9% of the population), followed by the Indian diaspora with around 20 million, or 1.9% of the population. The Philippines diaspora is some 8.2 million strong (over 10% of the population[11]), and the number of Pakistanis abroad stands at around four million or 2.8 per cent of the population (Hugo, 2005; POEA, 2006).
- As a general rule, the Asian diasporas maintain close and active relationships with their home countries, and this is particularly evident during crisis times, as demonstrated by the vast relief efforts undertaken by the members of the expatriate communities abroad in the wake of the Tsunami in 2004 (IOM, 2007a).

Irregular migration movements exist throughout the region

- The Malaysian Home Affairs Minister estimated the number of unauthorized migrant workers in Malaysia at around 600,000 in late 2006, the majority from Indonesia, notwithstanding periodic repatriation campaigns, deportations and amnesties (Hugo, 2007).
- While the majority of Filipinos in the five leading destination countries generally hold regular status, more than 70 per cent (125,000) of Filipinos working in Malaysia are in an irregular situation (Commission on Filipinos Overseas, 2006) (see Figure 13). Unauthorized migration from the Philippines to Malaysia is primarily to Sabah province (Battistella, 2002).

[11] The total population of 76.5 million in the Philippines is taken from the 2002 census data.

Figure 13:

The five destination countries with the largest estimated stocks of Filipinos overseas as of end 2006

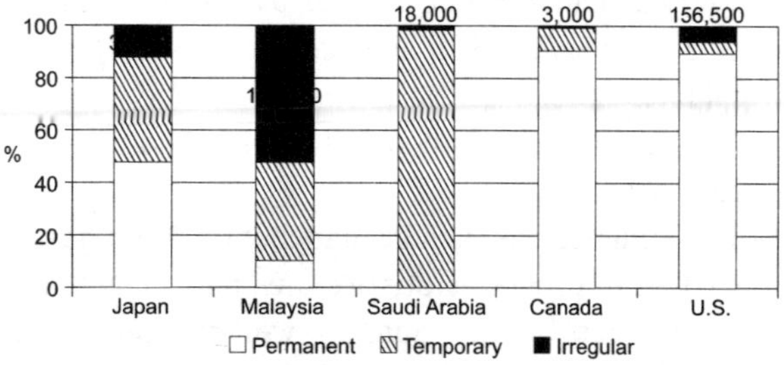

Sources: *POEA, 2006. Data were prepared by the Commission on Filipinos Overseas from CFO, DFA, POEA and other sources covering 194 countries / territories.*

- According to the Ministry of Labour, there were at least 360,000 migrants working in South Korea in June 2006, some 1.5 per cent of the total workforce. Of this total, at least 189,000 were irregular migrant workers (Amnesty International, 2006).
- Data from the Immigration Detention Centre in Bangkok for 2003 show that 58,322 migrants from East and Southeast Asia were detained and 58,719 were deported, the majority from Myanmar and Cambodia. In the same year, a further 2,344 from South-Central Asia were detained and 2,224 deported (Huguet and Punpuing, 2005).
- Of the two million foreigners living in Japan, well over 200,000 are estimated to be irregular residents (*Financial Times*, 9 July 2007).

Internal displacements caused by natural disasters are a major and recurring issue in South-Central Asia

- Frequent floods, earthquakes, cyclones and, more recently, tsunamis have led to the massive displacement of local populations. As of July 2005, official figures put the number of displaced persons due to the 2004 Tsunami in the Indian Ocean region at over 1.7 million. Indonesia's

Aceh province was particularly hard hit and, according to the Indonesian Government's disaster coordinating agency, BAKORNAS, by the end of 2005, a total of 532,898 people had been displaced in Aceh alone (Rofi and Robinson, 2006).

- Chronic flooding in Bangladesh is provoking the repeated major displacements of populations, as occurred again in 2007 when over eight million people were estimated to having been displaced due to the monsoon rains (Li, 2007).
- Cyclone Sidr in November 2007, one of the worst natural disasters in Bangladeshi history, resulted in an estimated 4,000 deaths and the displacement of over three million people (U.S. Embassy, Dhaka, 2007).
- The 2004 Tsunami displaced large population segments in Sri Lanka and some parts of India, with estimates of the number of people displaced in Sri Lanka alone ranging from 500,000 to one million persons (Haque, 2005).

Remittances

- Between 2000 and 2007, remittance flows to East Asia grew at a faster rate than to Southeast and South-Central Asia, although the latter received the largest share overall (World Bank, 2008) (see Figure 14).

Figure 14:

Global flows of international migrant remittances to Asia, 2000-2007 (USD billions)

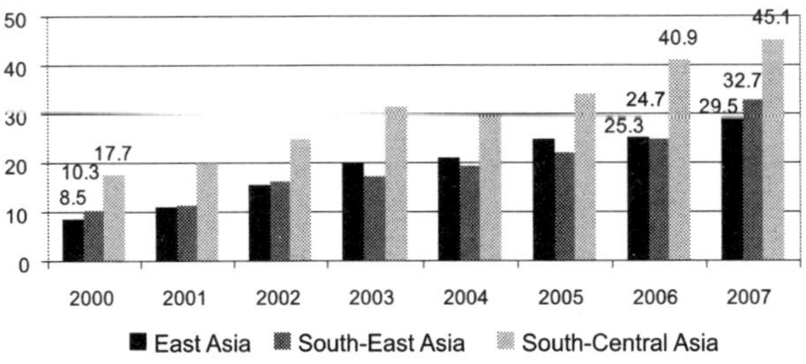

Source: World Bank, 2008.

- India remained the leading recipient of global remittance flows, which reached USD 27 billion in 2007, accounting for about three per cent of the GDP or close to 11 per cent of all remittance flows to developing countries (see Figure 15). Remittances to India have risen steadily over the last 15 years, and dramatically so over the last decade (Muzaffar Chisti, 2007).
- Bangladesh Bank statistics revealed that remittance inflows continue to increase and reached approximately 6.4 billion USD in 2007-08[12] surpassing the previous fiscal year's total of USD 5 billion (Bangladesh Bank, 2008).
- World Bank estimates for 2007 show that Bangladesh, Philippines and Pakistan continue to grow robustly in Asia underscoring the global growth in remittances inflows (World Bank, 2008).

Figure 15:

Remittances received in Asia by main countries of origin, 2007 (USD billions)

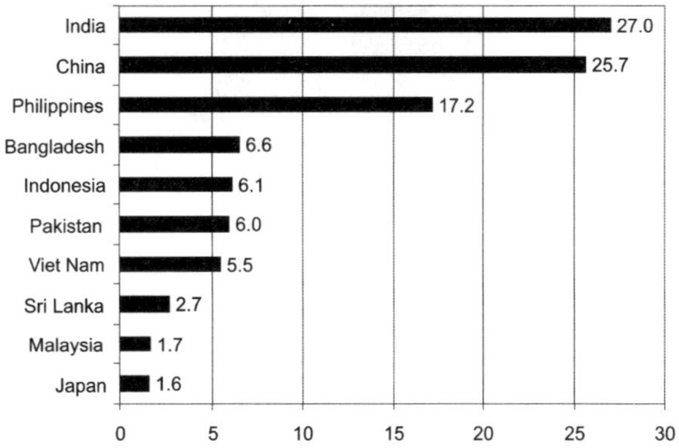

Source: World Bank, 2008.

- Most remittance flows generated within Asia remain in the region. As shown in Figure 16, more than 90 per cent of the remittance outflows from Malaysia, India and Singapore remain within Asia. For India, the share of remittances generated that

[12] Data up to April of financial year 2007-08.

remains within Asia is around 80 per cent and, for Singapore, this share is over 70 per cent (IOM calculations based on the World Bank bilateral remittances dataset, 2006).

Figure 16:

Selected Asian sending and receiving countries of remittances (%, estimates in USD millions)

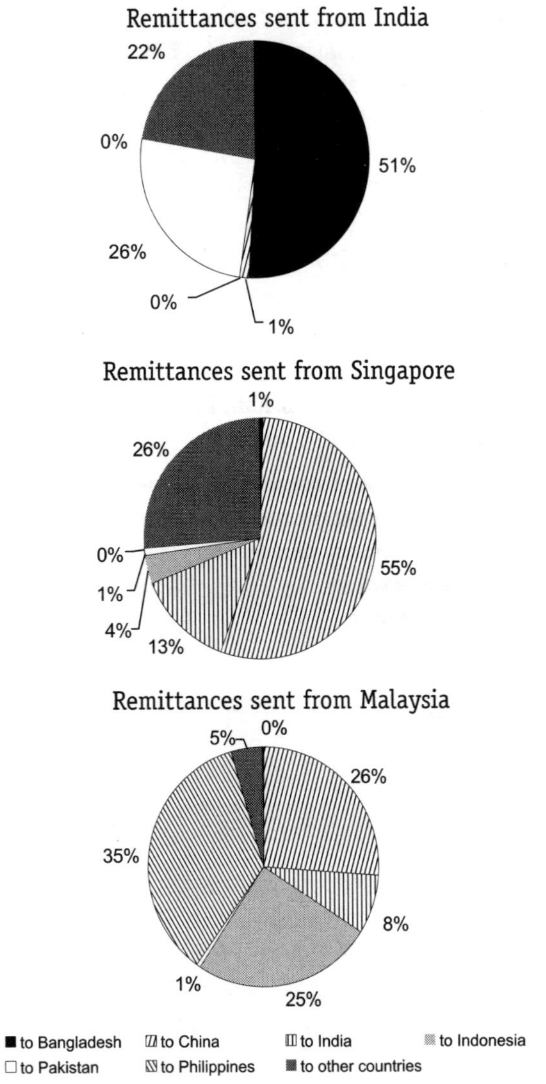

Note: IOM calculations using figures from the "Bilateral Remittance Flows using Migrant Stocks" dataset by Ratha and Shaw (World Bank, 2006).

Source: *IOM, 2007b.*

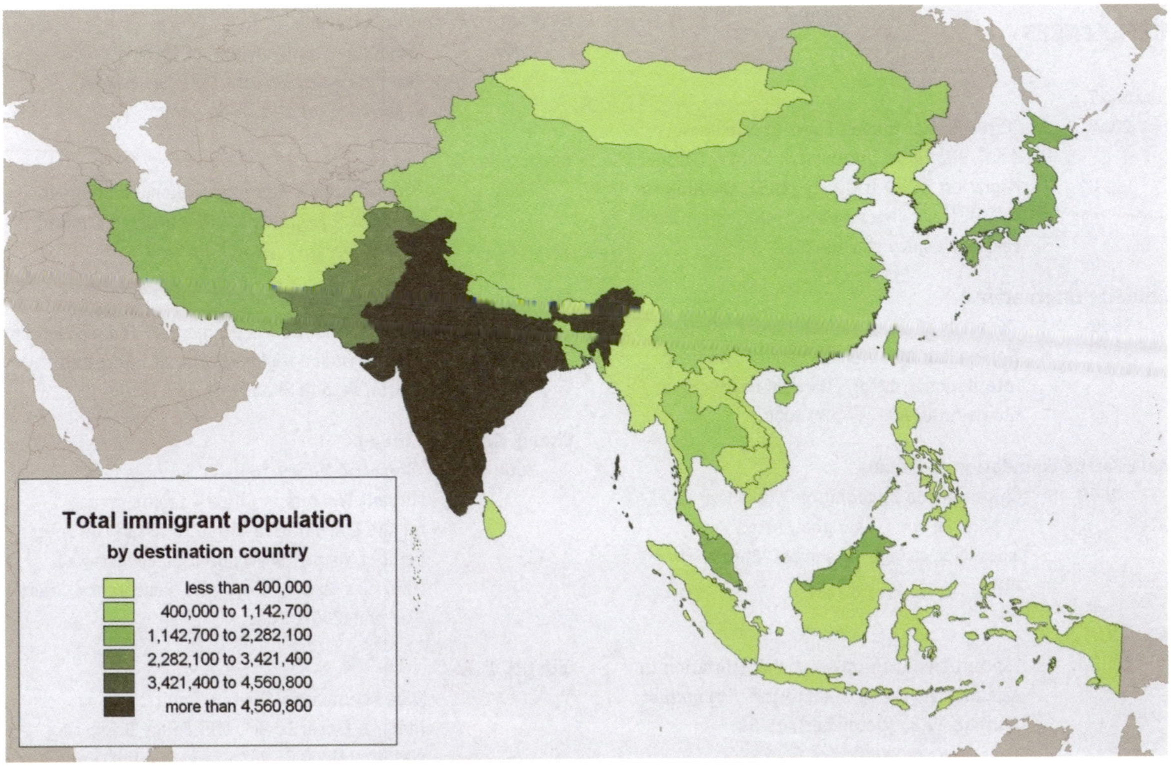
Total immigrant population
by destination country
less than 400,000
400,000 to 1,142,700
1,142,700 to 2,282,100
2,282,100 to 3,421,400
3,421,400 to 4,560,800
more than 4,560,800

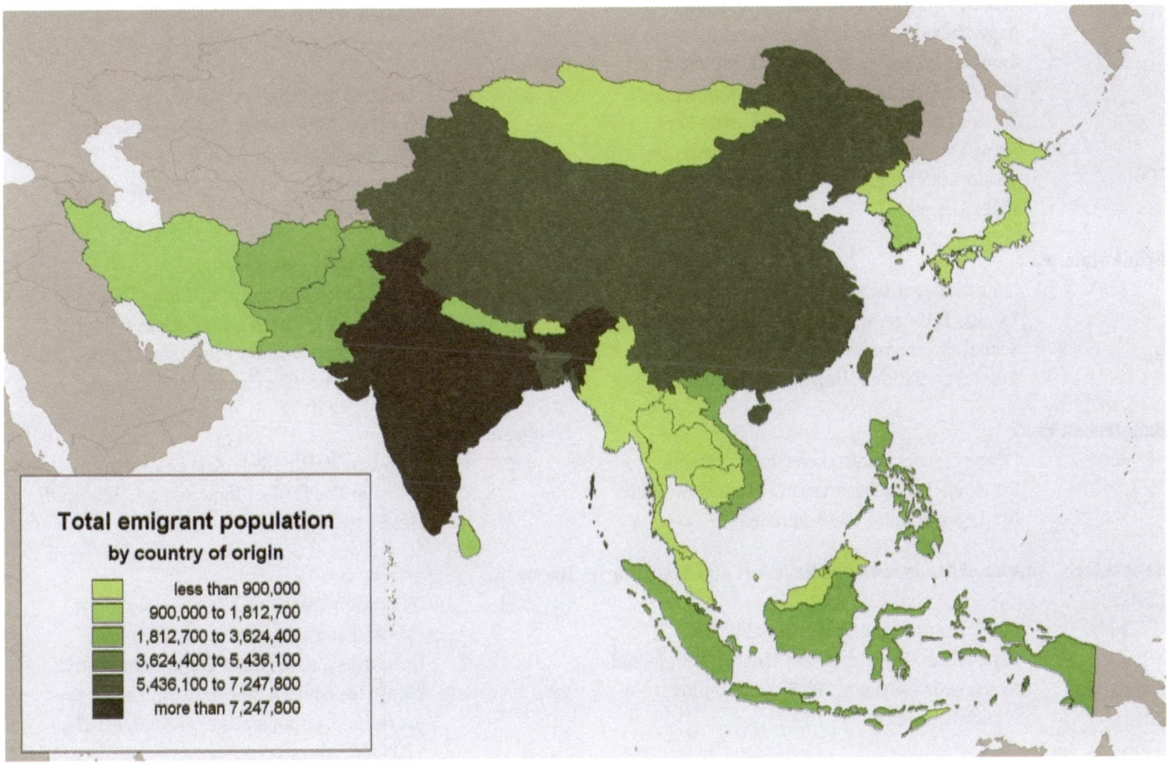
Total emigrant population
by country of origin
less than 900,000
900,000 to 1,812,700
1,812,700 to 3,624,400
3,624,400 to 5,436,100
5,436,100 to 7,247,800
more than 7,247,800

REFERENCES

Akaha, T.
2004 "Cross-Border Human Flows in Northeast Asia", *Migration Information Source*, October, Migration Policy Institute (MPI), Washington, D.C., http://www.migrationinformation.org/Feature/display.cfm?id=257.

Amnesty International
2006 "Republic of Korea (South Korea): Migrant Workers are Also Human Beings", Amnesty International, http://www.amnesty.org/en/library/info/ASA25/007/2006.

Asia Pacific Foundation of Canada
2000 China-Canada Immigration Workshop, Final Report, 28 June, Shanghai, http://www.asiapacific.ca/analysis/pubs/28jun00-shanghai.html.

Asis, M.M.B.
2005 "Recent Trends in International Migration in Asia and the Pacific", *Asia-Pacific Population Journal*, 20(3) (December): 15-38.

2006 "Gender Dimensions of Labor Migration in Asia", paper submitted to the High-Level Panel on The Gender Dimensions of International Migration, UN Commission on the Status of Women, 50th Session, 27 February - 10 March, New York, http://www.un.org/womenwatch/daw/csw/csw50/statements/CSW%20HLP%20Maruja%20MB%20Asis.pdf.

Athukorala, P.
2006 "International Labour Migration in East Asia: Trends, Patterns and Policy Issues", Asia-Pacific School of Economics and Government, The Australian National University, Canberra.

Bangladesh Bank
2007 "Wage Earners Remittance Flows", Foreign Exchange Policy Department, Bangladesh Bank, http://www.bangladesh-bank.org/.

Bangladesh, Bureau of Manpower, Employment and Training (BMET)
2007 Government of the People Republic's of Bangladesh, Ministry of Expatriates Welfare and Overseas Employment, BMET website, http://www.bmet.org.bd/.

Bathnagar, P. and C. Manning
2005 "Regional Arrangements for Mode 4 in the Services Trade: Lessons from the ASEAN Experience", *World Trade Review*, 4(2): 171-199.

Battistella, G.
2002 "Unauthorized Migrants as Global Workers in the ASEAN Region", *Southeast Asian Studies*, 40(3): 350-371.

Blanchet, T., A. Razzaque and H. Biswas
2008 *Documenting the Undocumented: Female Migrant Workers from Bangladesh*, Drishti Research Centre, Pathak Shambesh, Dhaka.

Cheng, E. and X. Zhong
2004 "Domestic Money Transfer Services for Migrant Workers in China", report prepared for the Consultative Group to Assist the Poor, October, http://www.microfinancegateway.com/files/28874_file_China_Remittance_Study_Workshop20Oct_.doc.

Chishti, M.A.
2007 "The Phenomenal Rise in Remittances to India: A Closer Look", MPI Policy Brief, May, Washington, D.C., http://www.migrationpolicy.org/pubs/MigDevPB_052907.pdf.

Cobbe, J.
2004 "Lesotho: Will the Enclave Empty?", *Migration Information Source*, September, MPI, Washington, D.C., http://www.migrationinformation.org/Profiles/display.cfm?ID=248.

Economist Intelligence Unit (EIU)
2007 "Labour Mobility and Migration - Trends in the Asia Region", EIU Research Paper prepared for the Asia-New Zealand Foundation, http://www.asianz.org.nz/files/labour_mobility.pdf.

Financial Times
2007 "The New Melting Pot: Asia Learns to Cope with a Rise in the Flow of Immigrants", *Financial Times*, 19 July.

Haque, S.
2005 "Migration Trends and Patterns in South Asia and Management Approaches and Initiatives", *Asia-Pacific Population Journal,* 20(3) (December): 39-60, http://www.unescap.org/esid/psis/population/journal/Articles/V20N3A2_Ab.asp.

Hugo, G.

2005 "Migration in the Asia-Pacific region", paper prepared for the Policy Analysis and Research Programme of the Global Commission on International Migration (GCIM), September, Geneva, http://www.gcim.org/mm/File/Regional%20Study%202.pdf.

2007 "Indonesia's Labor Looks Abroad", *Migration Information Source*, April, MPI, Washington, D.C., http://www.migrationinformation.org/Profiles/display.cfm?ID=594.

Huguet, J.W and S. Punpuing

2005 *International Migration in Thailand*, International Organization for Migration (IOM), International Labour Organization (ILO), United Nations Children's Fund (UNICEF), United Nations Development Programme (UNDP), UN Economic and Social Commission for Asia and the Pacific (UNESCAP), World Bank, World Health Organization (WHO), Bangkok, http://www.iom.int/jahia/webdav/site/myjahiasite/shared/shared/mainsite/published_docs/books/iom_thailand.pdf.

International Organization for Migration (IOM)

2005 "In-house Workshop on Labour Migration and Project Development", 29-31 May, IOM Dhaka.

2007a "Migration, Development and Natural Disasters: Insights from the Indian Ocean Tsunami", IOM *Migration Research Series*, No. 30, Geneva, http://www.iom.int/jahia/Jahia/cache/offonce/pid/1674?entryId=14556.

2007b "Migration Dynamics in South Asia: Overview of Labour Migration in Bangladesh, India, Nepal and Sri Lanka", presentation, 29 May, IOM Dhaka.

Islamic Development Bank (IDB)

2006 *Brain Drain in IDB Member Countries: Trends and Development Impact,* IDB Occasional Paper No. 12, May.

Khadria, B.

2006 "Uncharted Contours of a Changing Paradigm - Skilled Migration and Brain Drain in India", *Harvard International Review*, July 17, http://hir.harvard.edu/articles/1445/.

Li, K.

2007 "Millions affected by floods in Bangladesh face a 'desperate situation'", 7 August, UNICEF, http://www.unicef.org/infobycountry/bangladesh_40538.html.

Migration News

2004 "South-East Asia", *Migration News*, 11(4) (October), University of California at Davis.

2005 "Japan-Korea", *Migration News*, 12(1) (January), University of California at Davis.

2006 "Philippines, Indonesia", *Migration News*, 13(4) (October), University of California at Davis.

Migration Policy Institute (MPI) and Globalization, Urbanization and Migration (GUM) Project

2007 "Global City Migration Map, 2007", MPI/GUM, http://www.migrationinformation.org/datahub/gcmm.cfm#map1.

Philippine Overseas Employment Administration (POEA)

2006 "OFW Global Presence – A Compendium of Overseas Employment Statistics", POEA, http://www.poea.gov.ph/stats/2006Stats.pdf.

Rofi, A. and C. Robinson

2006 "Tsunami Mortality and Displacement in Aceh Province, Indonesia", *Disasters* 30(3): 340-350.

Seddon, D.

2005 "Nepal's Dependence on Exporting Labour", *Migration Information Source*, January, MPI, Washington, D.C., http://www.migrationinformation.org/Feature/display.cfm?id=277.

Siddiqui, T.

2005 "International Labour Migration from Bangladesh: A Decent Work Perspective", Working Paper No. 66, November, Policy Integration Department, National Policy Group, ILO, Geneva.

Skeldon, R.

2004 "China: From Exceptional Case to Global Participant", *Migration Information Source*, April, MPI, Washington, D.C., http://www.migrationinformation.org/Profiles/display.cfm?id=219.

Soeprobo, T.B.
2004 "Recent Trends in International Migration in Indonesia", paper prepared for the Workshop on International Migration and Labour Market in Asia, organized by the Japan Institute for Labour Policy and Training (JILPT), Japan Institute of Labour, 5-6 February, Tokyo.

Southern African Migration Project (SAMP)
2006 "South Africa", *SAMP Migration News*, January, http://www.queensu.ca/samp/migrationnews/article.php?Mig_News_ID=2339&Mig_News_Issue=13&Mig_News_Cat=8.

Sri Lanka Bureau of Foreign Employment
2007 http://www.slbfe.lk/.

Thailand Overseas Employment Administration (TOEA)
2007 http://www.overseas.doe.go.th:8081/overseas/index.php?lang=en.

United Nations Department of Economic and Social Affairs (UN DESA), Population Division
2005 *Trends in Total Migrant Stock: The 2005 Revision*, UN DESA, Population Division, New York, http://esa.un.org/migration/index.asp?panel=1.

United States Embassy, Dhaka
2007 "U.S. Response to Cyclone Sidr: Operation Sea Angel II", Embassy of the United States, Dhaka, Bangladesh, http://dhaka.usembassy.gov/cyclone_sidr.html.

World Bank
2006 "Bilateral Remittance Flows using Migrant Stock" dataset by D. Ratha and W. Shaw, The World Bank, Washington, D.C., http://www.worldbank.org/prospects/migrationandremittances.

2008 *Revisions to Remittance Trends 2007*, July, The World Bank, Washington, D.C., http://econ.worldbank.org/WBSITE/EXTERNAL/EXTDEC/EXTDECPROSPECTS/0,,contentMDK:21121930~menuPK:3145470~pagePK:64165401~piPK:64165026~theSitePK:476883,00.html.

Yeoh, B.S.A.
2007 "Singapore: Hungry for Foreign Workers at All Skill Levels", *Migration Information Source*, January, MPI, Washington, D.C, http://www.migrationinformation.org/Profiles/print.cfm?ID=570.

Zweig, D.
2006 "Learning to compete: China's efforts to encourage a 'reverse brain drain'" in C. Kuptsch and P. Eng Fong (Eds.), *Competing for Global Talent*, International Labour Office, Geneva, 187-213.

EUROPE

- In 2005, western and central Europe hosted 44.1 million migrants, a significant proportion of whom came from neighbouring countries.[1]
- In 2005, migrants accounted for 7.6 per cent of the total population in the region and 23.2 per cent of international migrants worldwide (UN DESA, 2005). Furthermore, in 2005 net migration contributed almost 85 per cent of Europe's population growth (Münz, 2006), while labour migration made up a substantial share of total migration flows.
- In the majority of western European countries, the foreign-born population represents between seven and 15 per cent of the total population, while in most new European Union (EU) Member States the share of foreign-born in 2005 was still below five per cent (Münz, 2006; see also Map 6).
- The Russian Federation, with 12 million migrants in 2005, ranks as the leading country of destination in eastern Europe (UN DESA, 2005).

[1] Thirty per cent of migrants living in western and central European countries are originally from other western and central European countries (UN DESA, 2005).

WESTERN AND CENTRAL EUROPE[2]

- Germany, host to 10.1 million migrants in 2005, is the principal country of destination, followed by France (6.5 million), the U.K. (5.4 million), Spain (4.8 million) and Italy (2.5 million) (see Figure 1). The ten countries reviewed in this Figure all show positive rates of growth in the stock of migrants from 2000 to 2005, with Spain and Italy recording the most important increases of 194.2 per cent, or 3.1 million migrants, and 54.1 per cent, or 884,000 migrants, respectively. Relative to population size, Luxembourg and Liechtenstein are host to the highest migrant stocks (37.3% and 33.5%, respectively), followed by Switzerland (22.9%) and the Baltic states of Latvia and Estonia (19.5% and 15.2%, respectively) (UN DESA, 2005). In three countries the immigration/population ratio actually contracted between 2000 and 2005, for

[2] This section covers the 27 **EU Member States** (Austria, Belgium, Bulgaria, Cyprus, Czech Republic, Denmark, Estonia, Finland, France, Germany, Greece, Hungary, Ireland, Italy, Latvia, Lithuania, Luxembourg, Malta, the Netherlands, Poland, Portugal, Romania, Slovakia, Slovenia, Spain, Sweden and the United Kingdom), the three **European Economic Area (EEA) countries** (Iceland, Liechtenstein and Norway) as well as Switzerland, and two **EU candidate countries**, Croatia and Turkey. However, the latest data available in respect of EU countries relates to the EU-25 (i.e. minus Bulgaria and Romania, which acceded to the EU on 1 January 2007).

various reasons: the number of migrants dropped in Latvia and Estonia during this five-year period, while in Liechtenstein immigration actually increased, but at a lower rate than population growth.

Figure 1:

Stock of migrants in western and central Europe, top ten destination countries, 2000 and 2005

Part A: Total number of migrants

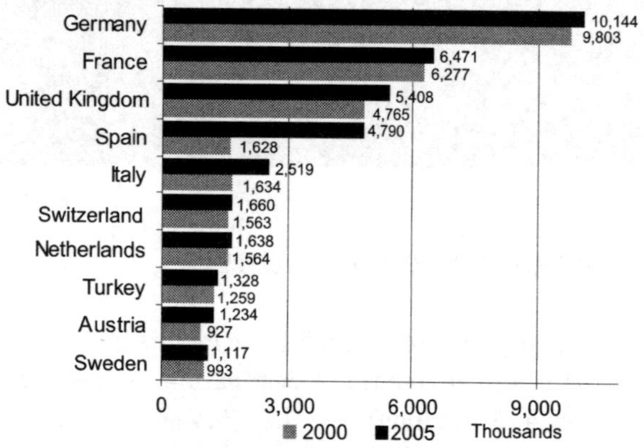

Part B: As a share of total population

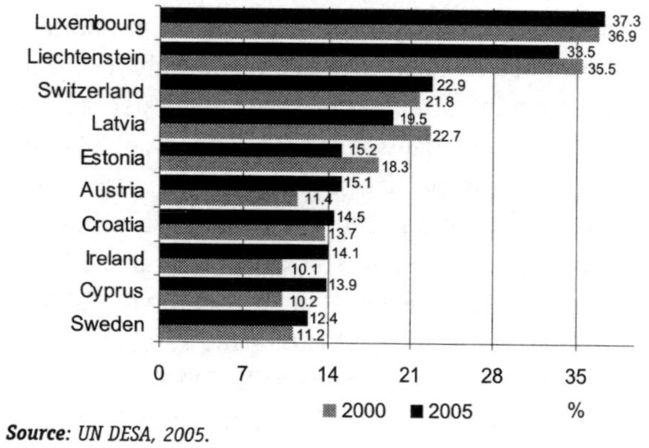

Source: UN DESA, 2005.

Western and central Europe is one of the most important regions of destination for migratory flows ...

- While most regions of the world experienced fluctuations in migratory flows over the last 50 years, nowhere have the changes been as pronounced as in Europe. Having been primarily countries of emigration for more than two centuries, most countries in the region became countries of immigration in the late 20th century. Many reasons have been advanced to account for this reversal, covering factors as diverse as economic disparities between Europe and its neighbours to the south and east, the large humanitarian inflows of the 1980s and 1990s, and the emergence of organized trafficking and smuggling networks. The role of growing demand for migrant workers to fill gaps in local labour markets is also widely acknowledged.

... leading to a steady growth of its migrant population

- As the membership of the EU grew from 12 to 25 between 1990 and 2004, the number of migrants across the combined territories of EU Member States and other countries in western and central Europe likewise increased from 14.5 to 44.1 million. Migration to this sub-region has grown on average at a 14.5 per cent quintennial rate since 1990. In 2005, the foreign-born living in western and central Europe represented 7.6 per cent of its total population, and 23.2 per cent of all international migrants worldwide (see Figure 2).

Figure 2:

Estimated number of migrants in western and central Europe, by gender and as a percentage of total population

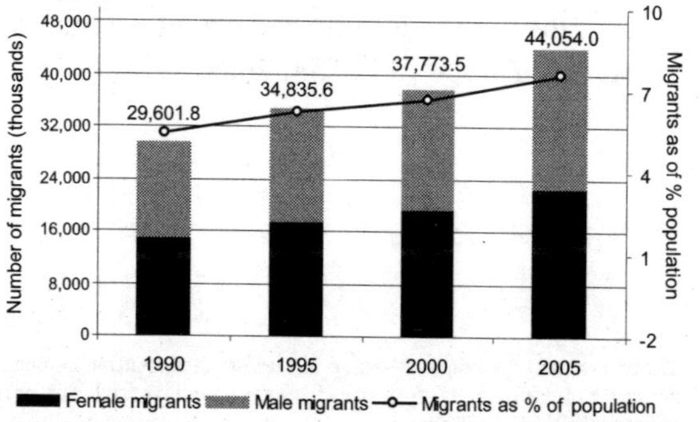

Source: UN DESA, 2005.

- The former EU-15 (except the Netherlands), Norway and Switzerland have a positive migration balance, as do six of the 10 new EU Member States (Cyprus, the Czech Republic, Hungary, Malta, Slovenia and Slovakia). Several countries, in particular the Czech Republic, Italy, Greece, Slovenia and Slovakia, registered population growth only in 2005, and that because of migration. In Germany and Hungary, the population decline would have been much larger without a positive migration balance (see Figure 3). In absolute numbers, the EU-25 registered a net gain of 1.8 million people in 2005 owing to international migration, accounting for almost 85 per cent of Europe's total population growth.

Figure 3:

Net migration in Europe per 1,000 population, 2005

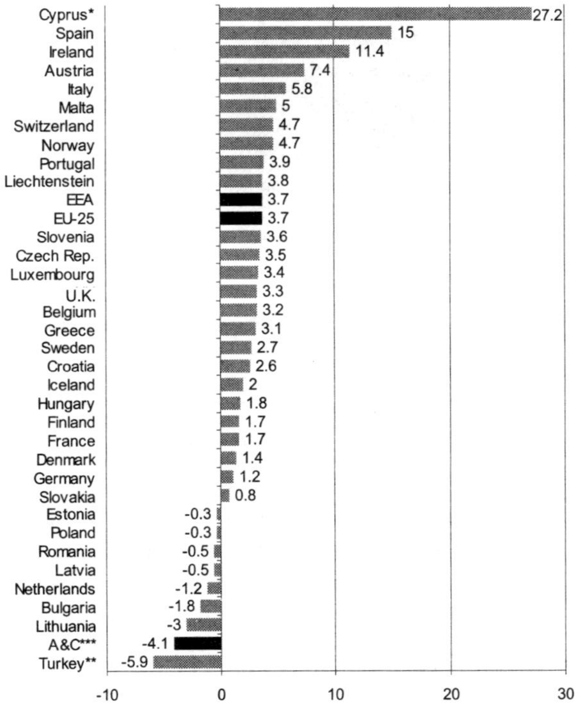

Notes: *Area under the effective control of the Government of the Republic of Cyprus.
**Data for Turkey on net migration are from 2003.
***Accession and Candidate countries excluding the Former Yugoslav Republic of Macedonia.

Source: *Eurostat. Data taken from Münz, 2006.*

The majority of migrants come from within the region or adjacent countries

- One interesting but often overlooked feature of the migratory patterns in Europe is the prevalence of intra-regional movements. The OECD online datasets on migration show that intra-regional movements in Europe represented around 30 per cent of total migration in the period 1998-2004. Figure 4 shows the stock of intra-regional migrants as a percentage of total migration in EU-25 countries, Switzerland and Norway. In most of the countries analyzed, the bulk of migrants from the EU-25 accounts for at least 25 per cent of total migration. In some countries (e.g. Belgium, Ireland, Luxembourg, the Slovak Republic and Switzerland), migrants from within the region equal or exceed 50 per cent of total migration. However, in all countries reviewed besides Italy, the contribution of intra-regional migration to total migration has decreased over time. Yet, in absolute terms, with the exception of Germany and the Czech Republic, the European foreign population in these countries increased, but by less than the number of migrants from outside Europe.

Figure 4:

Stock of intra-regional migrants as a percentage of total migration in OECD European countries, 2000 and 2004*

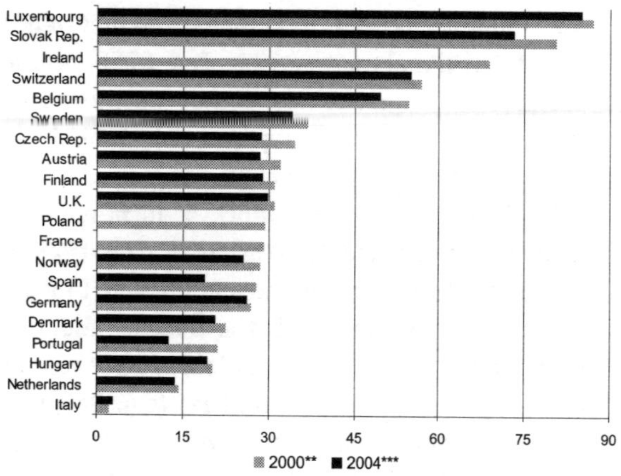

Notes: *Data for Austria, Belgium, Denmark, Finland, Hungary, Ireland, the Netherlands, Norway, Poland, the Slovak Rep. and Sweden correspond to the stock of foreign population by country of birth; while data for the Czech Rep., France, Germany, Italy, Luxembourg, Portugal, Spain, Switzerland and the U.K. are stocks of foreign population by nationality.

**Figures for France correspond to 1999 data; Slovak Rep. (2001); Poland (2002); and Ireland (2002).

***Figures for Italy and Belgium use 2003 data.

Source: *OECD online datasets.*

- Looking at the origins of the migratory flows, the pattern is one of relative stability (see Figure 5), although a number of differences are noticeable between 2000 and 2005. Over that period, Ecuador lost its place in the top ten countries of origin for OECD EU countries, while The Russian Federation and Ukraine became significant providers of migrants. The large 2005 influxes from Poland, Romania and Bulgaria reflect Poland's accession to EU membership the year before and Romania and Bulgaria's status as candidate countries at that time.

Figure 5:

Major countries of origin of migrants in OECD European countries, 2000 and 2005 (thousands)

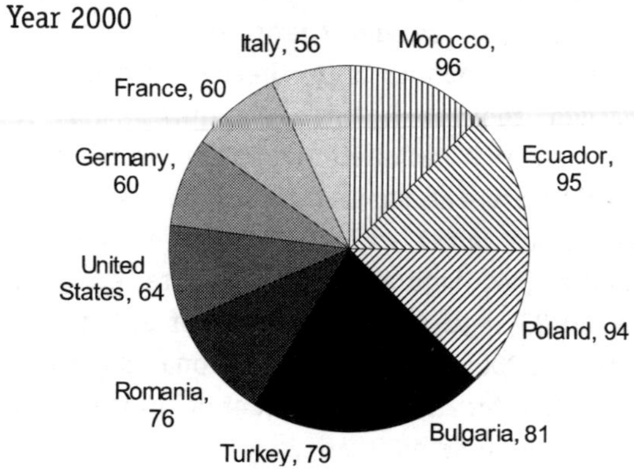

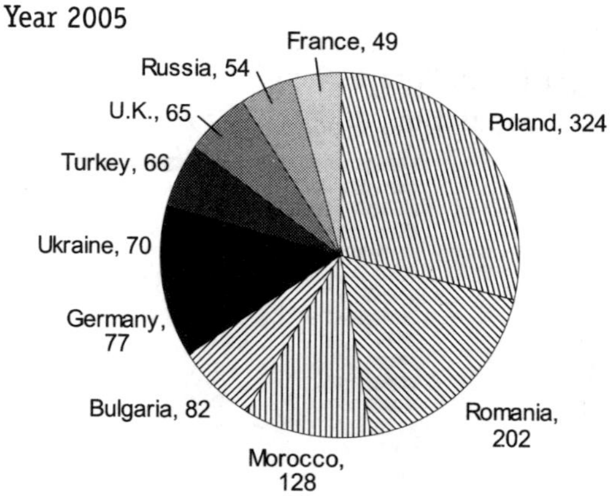

Note: Data are not harmonized. Statistics from some countries may include many short-term flows.

Source: *OECD, 2007.*

- A newly developing trend is the emergence of Latin America as a significant source region. Migration from Latin America to Europe has increased from a negligible base in 1995 to between 150,000 and 250,000 persons annually since 2000. The main countries of destination are Spain, Portugal and Italy. Spain, the leading country of destination for Latin American migrants, registered a stock of 813,200 migrants in 2004, mostly from Ecuador (357,100) and Colombia (204,300), and the remaining migrants originated mainly from Peru, Argentina, the Dominican Republic and Cuba (see Figure 6).

Figure 6:

Stock of foreign population in Spain, 1995, 2000 and 2005 (thousands)

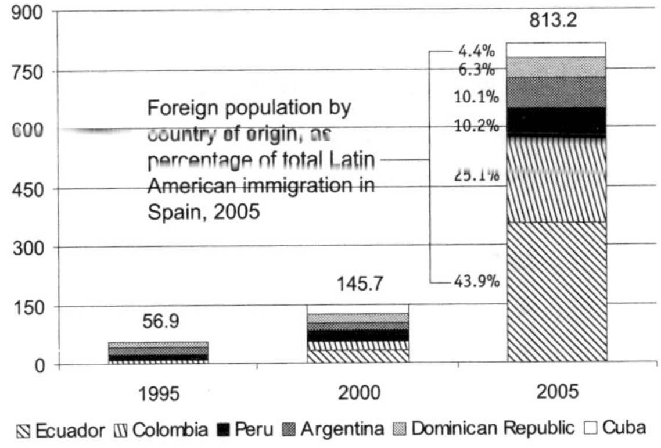

Source: *OECD, Stock of foreign population by nationality, online database.*

Figure 7:

International migration by category of entry in selected European countries as a percentage of total inflows, harmonized data, 2005

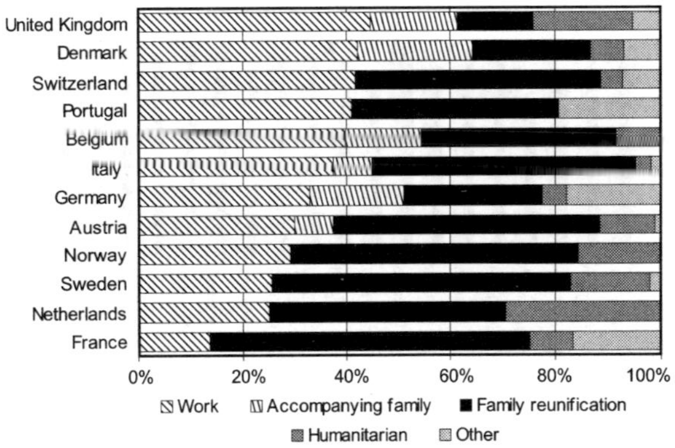

Source: *OECD, 2007.*

Work-related migration is substantial

- Work-related migration (workers and accompanying family members) is responsible for a substantial share of migrant inflows, accounting for over 40 per cent of all migrants in Belgium, Denmark, Germany, Italy, Portugal, Switzerland and the U.K. Elsewhere, including Switzerland and Italy, family reunification accounts for the highest proportion of migration (see Figure 7). However, Figure 7, just as the overall harmonized statistics on migrant flows, does not include irregular labour movements, which, according to OECD (2007), have been substantial in southern Europe in recent years (see also Chapter 8).

- In 2005, migrants accounted for a large and growing proportion of the total labour force in European countries. The size of the foreign-born population has increased by over 20 per cent from 2000 to 2005 in almost all the countries reviewed, except in France and the Netherlands. In just under half of the countries, the labour force participation rate of the foreign-born was equivalent or higher than for the native-born (see Figure 8). Moreover, during the last decade the difference in the labour force participation rate between the foreign-born and the native-born has tended to decrease in most countries, although in 2004 and 2005 the unemployment rate of migrants continued to be higher, except in Hungary and Poland (OECD, 2007).

Figure 8:

Labour force participation rate of foreign-born and native-born population in selected European countries, 2005

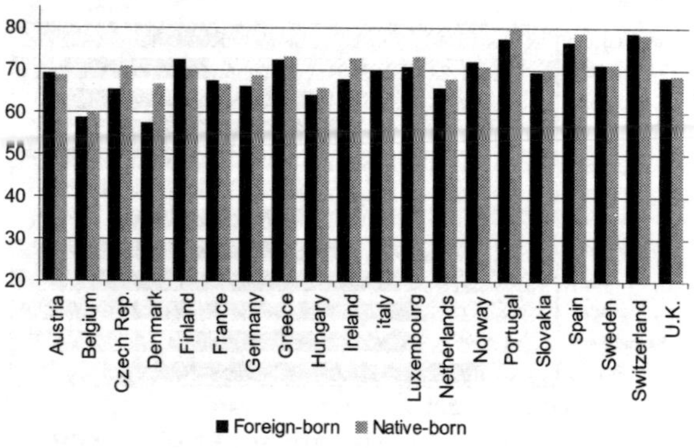

Source: *European Community Labour Force Survey (data provided by Eurostat) except for Denmark (Population Register), taken from OECD, 2007.*

Figure 9:

Stock of migrants in eastern Europe and Central Asia, top ten destinations, 2000 and 2005

Part A: Total number of migrants

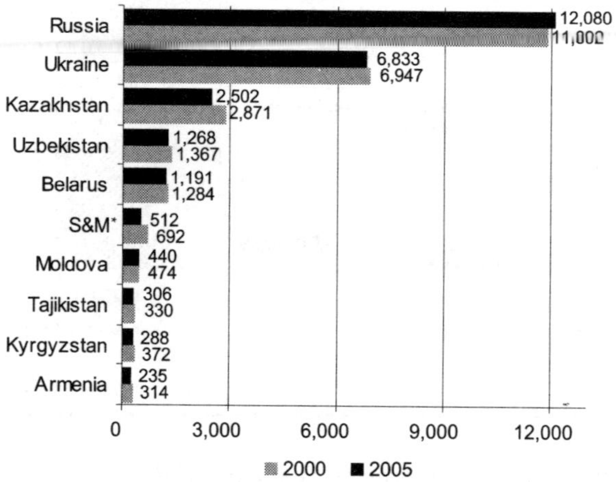

Note: * The then Serbia and Montenegro.

Part B: As share of total population

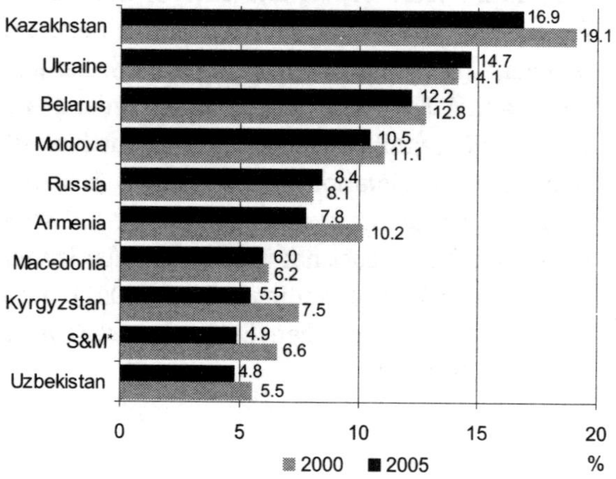

Note: * The then Serbia and Montenegro.

Source: *UN DESA, 2005.*

EASTERN EUROPE AND CENTRAL ASIA[3]

- As host to 12 million migrants in 2005, the Russian Federation is the leading country of destination in this region, followed by Ukraine (6.8 million) and Kazakhstan (2.5 million) (see Figure 9). While Russia registered a 1.6 per cent increase in the stock of migrants from 2001 to 2005, the other nine countries reviewed saw their stock of migrants fall over the same period. With the exception of Ukraine and Russia, the number of migrants as a share of their total populations fell in all countries.

[3] Albania, Armenia, Azerbaijan, Belarus, Bosnia and Herzegovina, Georgia, Kazakhstan, Kyrgyzstan, Former Yugoslav Republic of Macedonia (FYROM) (granted EU candidate country status in December 2005), Moldova, the Russian Federation, the then Serbia and Montenegro, Tajikistan, Turkmenistan, Ukraine and Uzbekistan.

Two broad migration systems operate in this sub-region

- The nature and patterns of migratory movements in this sub-region since 1990 have been shaped by the combined effects of economic transition, political and social liberalization, and the break-up of two federal countries (the former Soviet Union, and former Federal Republic of Yugoslavia). They also account for the difficulty of accessing and compiling reliable migration data concerning this sub-region. The direction and magnitude of migration flows have changed significantly following the lifting of political constraints on movement, as has the emergence of 22 new countries and the resulting diversification of migratory flows throughout the region. Finally, with the break-up of the former Soviet Union a new category of migrants, the "statistical" migrants, emerged, who may not have moved physically, but were defined as migrants under UN practice (World Bank, 2006).
- According to Mansoor and Quillin (2006), two broad migration systems have developed in the region: the first concerns migrants from eastern European countries who move to western Europe; and the second involves the majority of migrants from Central Asia who travel to the wealthier countries of the Commonwealth of Independent States (CIS), particularly the Russian Federation and Kazakhstan. Figures 10a and 10b clearly show this bipolar migration system, with Russia registering by far the largest population gain from migration. Most of the migration to Russia is shaped by migrants leaving the other countries of the former Soviet Union.

Figure 10:

Net migration in eastern Europe and Central Asia as a percentage of total population, 1989-1999 and 2000-2003

10a: In the CIS

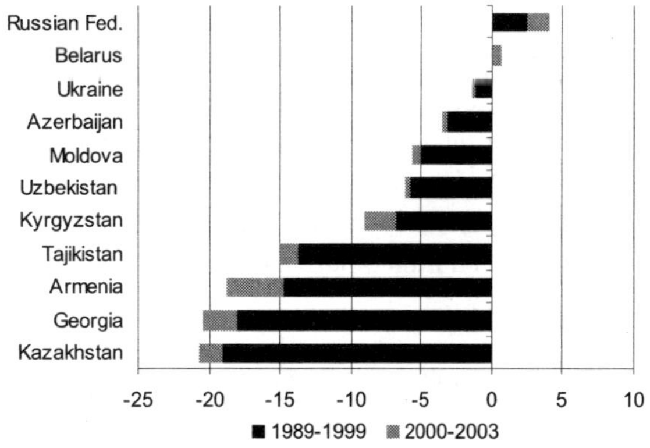

10b: In Eastern Europe

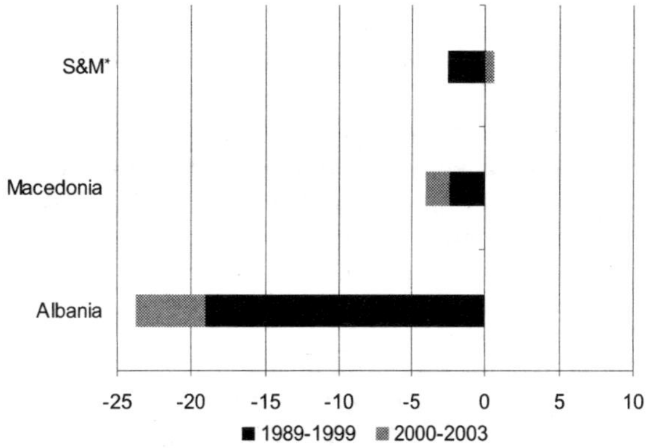

Note: * The then Serbia and Montenegro.
Turkmenistan and Bosnia and Herzegovina are not included owing to migration data difficulties.

Source: *National statistical offices and UNICEF, TransMONEE Database, Mansoor and Quillin (2006).*

- Yet, the two migration systems in the sub-region are not exclusively bipolar. Indeed, there are significant subsidiary flows from the poorer CIS economies, particularly from Moldova, to western European countries; and from Central Asia towards the EU and Turkey.

- There is a considerable migration flow from Western European and Central Asian (WECA)[4] countries to western Europe (73% of total emigration from WECA countries), as well as in the opposite direction (17% of total emigration from western Europe), accounting for 62 per cent of total immigration to WECA countries (Mansoor and Quillin, 2006). Flows from Germany to Poland, the then Serbia and Montenegro and Turkey are among the major contributors to such migratory movements from western Europe.
- Regarding flows involving the CIS countries, the Russian Federation is both a source and destination of such flows. The largest flows that do not include Russia are from Ukraine and Kazakhstan to Germany. The first can be explained by proximity and large per capita income differentials, the second by the fact that Kazakhstan hosted the largest concentration of persons of German ancestry in the former Soviet Union (Mansoor and Quillin, 2006).
- Since the break-up of the former Soviet Union, there have been significant flows of migrant workers to the Russian Federation, mainly from neighbouring countries. Concerns about the levels of these movements and their irregularity has resulted in the formulation and implementation of a new Russian migration law and policy to better manage these flows and the status of migrants once in the country (see Textbox Reg. 2).

[4] In this paragraph, Western European and Central Asian (WECA) countries consist of Albania, Bosnia and Herzegovina, Bulgaria, Croatia, Czech Republic, Estonia, FYROM, Hungary, Latvia, Lithuania, Poland, Romania, the then Serbia and Montenegro, Slovakia, Slovenia and Turkey. This is a specific classification used in Mansoor and Quillin (2006).

Textbox Reg. 2

The New Russian Migration Legislation

At the time the new Russian migration legislation[1] came into force on 15 January 2007, the vast majority of foreign workers had neither residence nor work permits that would have allowed them to live and work in the Russian Federation. The number of irregular migrants, primarily originating from the Commonwealth of Independent States (CIS) region and coming to Russia for the purpose of temporary employment, was variously estimated at between 5.5 and 10 million, and felt to pose a threat not only to the country's public order and security, but also to the safety of migrant workers themselves. Legal and administrative impediments to the acquisition of work and residence permits were generally seen to be one of the main causes for the rise in irregular migration.

While it remains virtually impossible to fully resolve the problem of irregular migration, the new legislation is intended to improve policy effectiveness and coherence.

The two key elements of the new legislation with a direct impact on the regulation of labour migration in Russia are: (1) **the introduction of a simplified registration procedure** – covering all foreigners who come to Russia for short visits; and (2) **the simplification of the procedures for obtaining work permits** – covering migrants originating from countries benefiting from visa-free arrangements.

The new legislative provisions introduce the following significant reforms in procedure:

- **Temporary migrant workers may register their stay in Russia through a simplified procedure**[2]

Under this new procedure, all migrants, including temporary migrant workers, are required to present their personal identification and migration card, stamped by the border guard authorities at the point of entry to Russia, to the "sponsor" (i.e. the party who invited the migrant, which may include the whole range of natural persons and legal entities – e.g. employers, landlords, officials, etc.); the sponsor is then responsible for notifying the authorities (either at their office/s or by post) about the arrival of the migrant. If there is no sponsor, the migrant is responsible for notifying the authorities him/herself.

In addition, the legislation further simplifies registration of all migrants, including temporary migrant workers, by establishing a notification-based procedure (in contrast to the previous system that provided considerable discretion to the authorities and under which registration could be refused). It is now also possible for migrant workers to register at the place of employment, thus addressing an important objective, namely that of retaining the existing pattern of predominantly **circular or temporary labour migration**, which is considered by many to be the preferred type of labour migration for Russia. Finally, the legislation intends to lay the foundations for a migration registration scheme on which to base an official system for the collection of immigration statistics.

In view of the scope and the protection offered by the new registration procedures, the vast majority of migrants may be expected to comply with this law and duly register as required.

- **The procedures for obtaining a work permit for temporary migrants are much simplified and more time-efficient**

The migrant from a country benefiting from a visa-free regime can now apply for a work permit him/herself (previously only the employer could do so) and should be issued with a work permit within a 10-day period (the only basis for the authorities to refuse the permit, if all the papers are in order, would be the exhaustion of quotas).

By allowing migrants to apply for the work permit themselves, this provision also has the effect of protecting migrant workers against exploitative working conditions as it enables them to choose and change employers and encourages them to take into consideration their rights. The legislation can therefore be seen to contribute to the ongoing efforts to combat human trafficking and forced labour. As such, it is expected to address the shadow economy and, by the same token, increase the tax revenue for the Russian treasury.

The progressive nature of the new legislation is also demonstrated by the granting of significant privileges to foreign workers from countries with which the Russian Federation has concluded visa-free entry agreements, viz. Armenia, Azerbaijan, Belarus, Kazakhstan, Kyrgyzstan, Moldova, Tajikistan, Ukraine and Uzbekistan.[4]

Moreover, employers of temporary workers from those countries do not have to comply with the general requirement to obtain a permit to employ foreign workers, an arrangement having the effect of promoting closer cooperation with CIS countries with a view to the eventual creation of a common CIS-wide labour market.

This approach was supported by the huge 2007 quota of six million work permits for visa-free migrants. This quota was considered to be more than enough to cover the entire labour migration flow from those countries and to legalize the employment of irregular migrants already in Russia before the new legislation came into force.[5]

With the major legal obstacles to the legalization of foreign workers removed, it is now largely up to migrants themselves to regularize their status in Russia. Accordingly, the new legislation foresees heavier penalties for unauthorized residence and employment in Russia, with fines between 2,000 and 5,000 Russian roubles.[6]

Persons aiding and abetting migrants to live and work in Russia in violation of the law, or who exert pressure on them to do so, face fines of up to 8,000 times the statutory minimum monthly wage (2,000-5,000 Russian roubles for physical persons, 25,000-50,000 for officials and 250,000-800,000 Russian roubles for organizations). The severity of these sanctions is intended to make the unauthorized employment of a migrant unattractive and to discourage employers from doing so and, by the same token, to enhance the protection of migrants' human and labour rights. Since the legislation came into effect, many companies employing irregular migrants have had to pay heavy fines, which, by the end of May 2007, already totalled around 60 million Russian roubles.

At the same time, the penalty procedures for migrants have in practice worked as a de facto regularization process. Migrants originating from countries with a visa-free regime and already present in Russia could pay a fine and then apply for a work permit. This is especially important for the very large number of foreign workers who were in Russia without authorization prior to the new legislation coming into force.

However, effective implementation of this legislation has not been easy and many challenges remain to be overcome. One shortcoming has been the lack of information dissemination about the new legal procedures.[7] Another has been the absence of sufficient administrative personnel. Finally, a network of officially certified employment agencies is yet to be established.

Such initial difficulties notwithstanding, there is evidence[8] of the legislation's positive impact as demonstrated by: (a) the rise in the share of foreign nationals lawfully present in Russia; and (b) the increase in the percentage of migrant workers holding work permits. If just over 700,000 work permits were issued in Russia in 2005 and a little more than one million in 2006, that figure rose to nearly one million work permits (997,500) issued during the first five months of 2007 alone (i.e. as of 31 May 2007). Thus, based on the same estimated overall total of migrants, the percentage of migrant workers holding valid work permits has nearly doubled.

Notes:

1 This legislation consists of five Federal laws (No. 109-FZ of 18 July 2006, No. 110-FZ of 18 July 2006, No. 121-FZ of 18 July 2006, No. 189-FZ of 5 November 2006, No. 2-FZ of 6 January 2006) as well as various implementing decrees and orders issued by the Federal Migration Service (FMS).

2 Federal Law No. 109-FZ and Federal Law No. 110-FZ.

3 Federal Law No. 110-FZ.

4 Ibid.

5 The 2008 quota is 1,828,245. The rationale for this lower quota is that migrants who have worked in Russia without authorization had an opportunity to regularize their status during 2007.

6 Approximately USD 85-205 as at August 2008.

7 However, IOM, in conjunction with the FMS, has since conducted such an information campaign, which included the preparation and printing of a large number of information materials (reference books, leaflets and posters) for distribution within Russia as well as individual countries of origin.

8 In conjunction with the FMS, IOM Moscow recently launched a study monitoring implementation of the new migration legislation.

Source: *IOM Moscow.*

SOME TOPICAL ISSUES IN MIGRATION MANAGEMENT IN EUROPE

Labour migration is now at the centre of debates about migration management in EU Member States

- There is growing recognition that migration is one of the possible answers to problems of demographic ageing and welfare system sustainability. There is therefore an ongoing search for effective policy formulation and programme management strategies covering, inter alia, identification of needs, skill recognition, selection, recruitment and integration arrangements (see Chapter 11). Many Member States have introduced or are considering introducing schemes to attract highly qualified professionals in the face of growing international competition for skilled migrants (see Chapter 2). A bigger challenge lies in the development of cooperative approaches and partnerships with countries of origin (see Chapter 13).

Student mobility continues to increase in response to policies in destination countries

- Recent years have seen a large increase in the numbers of international tertiary students studying in European countries (see Figure 11). From 1998 to 2003, their numbers increased by some 38.5 per cent, with much of the increase occurring since 2001, resulting in a 24 per cent growth rate between 2001 and 2003. According to UNESCO (2006), the total number of international tertiary students leaving their countries of origin to study in western European countries stood at a little more than 1.5 million in 2004. The top destination countries in that year were the U.K. (300,100 international students), Germany (260,300) and France (237,600), with 54 per cent of international students concentrated in these three countries (UNESCO, 2006). The increase in the number of international students seems to be a response to signals sent by destination countries concerning possibilities for work and residence following the completion of study, especially in fields where there is a shortage of labour. For more detailed explanations of these trends and a definition of student migration, see Chapter 4; for a visual distribution of students by country of destination, see Map 2.

Figure 11:

Stock of international tertiary students in selected European countries, 1998, 2003

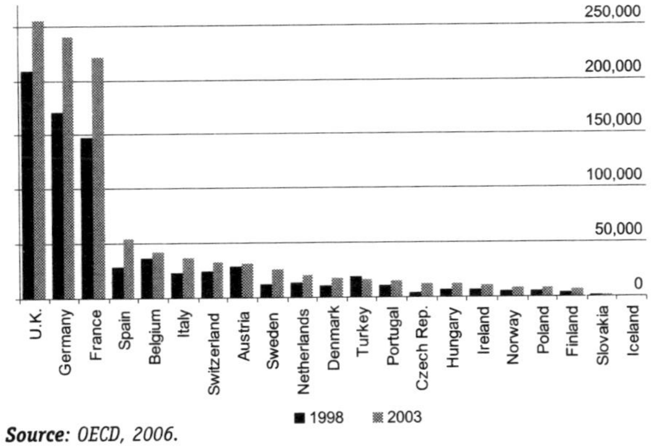

Source: *OECD, 2006.*

Europe is increasingly an attractive destination for young sportspersons

- The growing migration of young football (soccer) players from Africa and Latin America to Europe is giving rise to concerns regarding the welfare of the young persons concerned and the impact on countries and regions of origin. But if the football player is successful, there also appear to be clear benefits to this mobility (see Textbox Reg. 3).

Textbox Reg. 3

A Very Long Shot

All over the world, millions of boys dream of becoming football[1] stars as a gateway to fame and fortune and an escape from poverty and need. They pursue their dream in the dust, on bare feet, with footballs made out of rags. They hear stories about the millions earned by the superstars in Europe, which further adds to their determination. But only a lucky few will ever get a real shot at a professional career and at breaking out of the economic realities they face in their countries.

The issue of mobility and top sport has gained prominence over the past few years. It was recently the topic of scientific debate at the International Conference "Globalised Football: Nations and Migration, The City and the Dream", held in Lisbon in May 2006.

The global mobility of human talent is at its most visible in the world of football, but it can equally be seen in other highly competitive sports where a lot of money is at stake. Out of the 14 teams in the most recent Cricket World Cup, ten had foreign coaches and training staff, something that would have been unheard of even a decade earlier (Kapur and McHale, 2005). Professional sports in North America – baseball, basketball, American football and ice hockey – show a similar migration of talent.

But football is by far the most important international market for elite players from developing countries. Most of the players from developing countries in the 2006 Football World Cup play abroad, the majority of them in Europe where the sport is most competitive and lucrative. Every player on the national team from Côte d'Ivoire, for example, plays for a club outside his country (Pratt, 2006). Conversely, some European teams, like London's Arsenal, may be composed entirely of foreigners (Milanovic, 2006). Another London club, Chelsea, had 17 players on 10 different national teams in the 2006 World Cup.[2]

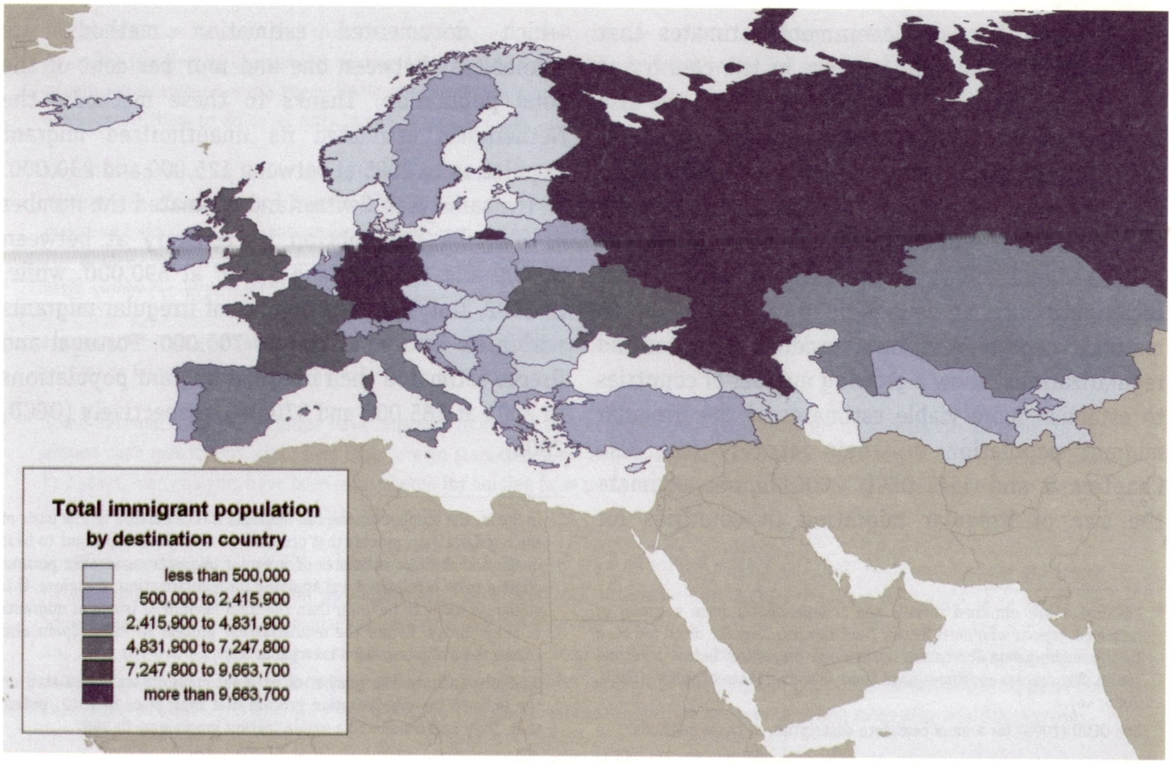
Total immigrant population
by destination country
less than 500,000
500,000 to 2,415,900
2,415,900 to 4,831,900
4,831,900 to 7,247,800
7,247,800 to 9,663,700
more than 9,663,700

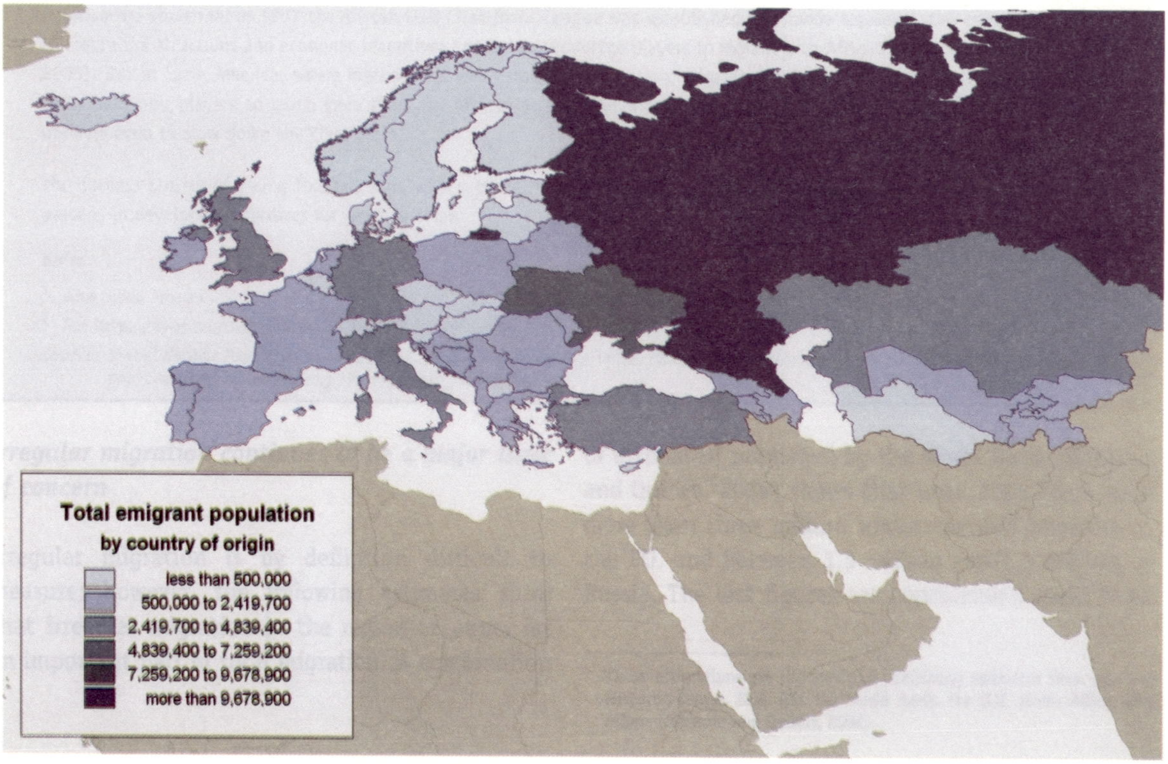
Total emigrant population
by country of origin
less than 500,000
500,000 to 2,419,700
2,419,700 to 4,839,400
4,839,400 to 7,259,200
7,259,200 to 9,678,900
more than 9,678,900

REFERENCES

Drew, C. and D. Sriskandarajah

2007 "EU Enlargement in 2007: No Warm Welcome for Labor Migrants", *Migration Information Source*, January, Migration Policy Institute (MPI), Washington, D.C., http://www.migrationinformation.org/feature/display.cfm?ID=568.

Jandl, M.

2003 "Estimates on the Numbers of Illegal and Smuggled Immigrants in Europe", presentation of the International Centre for Migration Policy Development (ICMPD) at the Eighth International Metropolis Conference, 17 September, Vienna, http://www.mighealth.net/eu/images/5/5b/Icmpd.pdf.

2004 "The Estimation of Illegal Migration in Europe", *Studi Emigrazione/ Migration Studies*, 61(153) (March): 141–155.

Mansoor, A. and B. Quillin (Eds.)

2006 *Migration and Remittances: Eastern Europe and Former Soviet Union*, Chapter 1: "Overview of Migration Trends in Europe and Central Asia, 1990-2004", The World Bank, Washington, D.C.

Münz, R.

2004 "Towards a Common European Migration Regime?", *Migration Information Source*, February, MPI, Washington, D.C., http://www.migrationinformation.org/events/021804_sum.php.

2006 "Europe: Population and Migration in 2005", *Migration Information Source*, June, MPI, Washington, D.C., http://www.migrationinformation.org/feature/display.cfm?ID=402.

Organisation for Economic Co-operation and Development (OECD)

2006 *International Migration Outlook*, SOPEMI 2006 Edition, OECD, Paris.

2007 *International Migration Outlook*, SOPEMI 2007 Edition, OECD, Paris.

Ratha, D. and W. Shaw

2007 "South-South Migration and Remittances", 19 January, Development Prospects Group, The World Bank, Washington, D.C., http://siteresources.worldbank.org/INTPROSPECTS/Resources/South-SouthmigrationJan192006.pdf.

Russian News and Information Agency (Novosti)

2006 "Russia loses over $9 bln/yr from illegal immigration govt.", Novosti, 3 November http://en.rian.ru/russia/20061103/55351198.html.

United Nations, Department of Economic and Social Affairs (UN DESA), Population Division

2002 *International Migration Report 2002*, Doc. ST/ESA/SER.A/220, UN DESA, Population Division, New York, http://www.un.org/esa/population/publications/ittmig2002/2002ITTMIGTEXT22-11.pdf.

2005 *Trends in Total Migrant Stock: The 2005 Revision, Population Database*, UN DESA, Population Division, New York, http://esa.un.org/migration/index.asp?panel=1.

United Nations Economic and Social Council (UN ECOSOC)

2006 *World population monitoring, focusing on international migration and development*, Report of the Secretary-General, Doc. E/CN.9/2006/3, UN ECOSOC, Commission on Population and Development, 39th Session, 3-7 April, New York.

United Nations Educational, Scientific and Cultural Organization (UNESCO)

2007 *Global Education Digest 2006: Comparing Education Statistics Across the World*, UNESCO Institute for Statistics, Montréal, http://www.uis.unesco.org/TEMPLATE/pdf/ged/2006/GED2006.pdf.

World Bank

2006 *Global Economic Prospects 2006: Economic Implications of Remittances and Migration*, The World Bank, Washington, D.C., http://econ.worldbank.org/WBSITE/EXTERNAL/EXTDEC/EXTDECPROSPECTS/GEPEXT/EXTGEP2006/0,,contentMDK:20709766~menuPK:1026823~pagePK:64167689~piPK:64167673~theSitePK:1026804,00.html.

Textbox Reg. 3 - A Very Long Shot

BBC News Online

2003 "Blatter condemns European clubs", BBC News, 17 December, http://news.bbc.co.uk/sport2/hi/football/africa/3326971.stm.

Kapur, D. and J. McHale

2005 "African Soccer Goes Global", *The Globalist*, 21 November, http://www.theglobalist.com/StoryId.aspx?StoryId=4915.

Migration News

2001 "EU: Immigration, Co-Development, Soccer", *Migration News*, 7(4) (March), University of California at Davis, http://migration.ucdavis.edu/mn/more.php?id=2326_0_4_0.

Milanovic, B.

2006 "Learning About Globalization by Watching A Soccer Game", *Taipei Times*, 12 February, http://www.carnegieendowment.org/publications/index.cfm?fa=view&id=18064&prog=zgp&proj=zted.

Pratt, T.

2006 *The Match of the Day Guide to the 2006 World Cup*, Interact Publishing, London.

MIDDLE EAST

- With nearly 19 million international migrants in 2005, the Middle East[1] has experienced an increase of 3.2 million migrants since 2000 (UN DESA, 2005).
- Together with the Mediterranean basin, the Middle East is characterized by highly contrasting labour market features, with certain countries experiencing surplus labour supply and other exhibiting labour shortages.
- Temporary workers from overseas are the most prominent migration feature in the Middle East region, especially in the Gulf Cooperation Council (GCC) States.
- Saudi Arabia is the largest source country of remittances, with an outflow of USD 14 billion in 2005 (World Bank, 2006).
- Egypt and Lebanon, with USD 5.9 billion and USD 5.8 billion, respectively, were the two major recipients of remittances in 2007 (World Bank, 2008).

[1] Following the regional classification used in IOM (2005), this section examines the **Arab Mashrek** (Egypt, Iraq, Jordan, Lebanon, the Occupied Palestinian Territories (OPT), Syria and Yemen), the **Gulf Cooperation Council (GCC) States** (Bahrain, Kuwait, Oman, Qatar, Saudi Arabia and the United Arab Emirates (UAE)) and **Israel.**

ARAB MASHREK

- From 2000 to 2005, migrant stocks increased in all Arab Mashrek countries, apart from Iraq, which experienced a drastic decrease of its migrant population after the outbreak of the second Gulf War in 2002, which also had an important impact on internal migration in Iraq. Jordan is the major destination for migrants in the region, with 2.2 million immigrants in 2005, 80 per cent of whom are refugees (UN DESA, 2005) (see Figure 1).

Figure 1:

Stock of migrants in the Arab Mashrek, by destination, 2000 and 2005

Part A: Total number of migrants

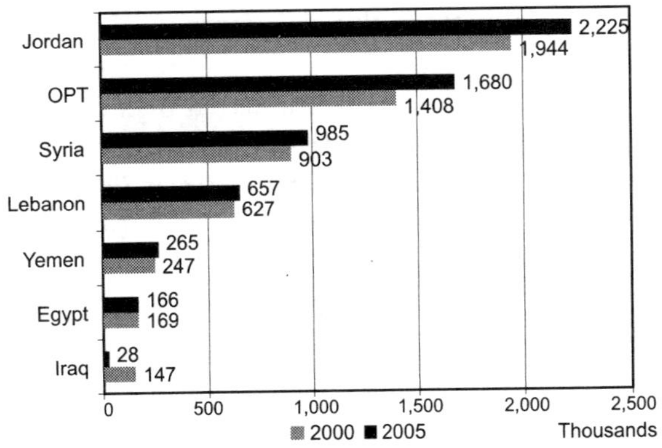

Part B: As a share of total population

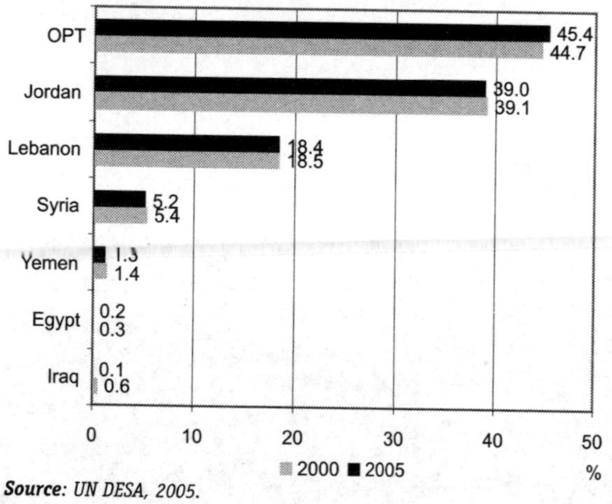

Source: UN DESA, 2005.

- The number of migrants as a proportion of the total population has remained stable in all countries except Iraq: the Occupied Palestinian Territories (OPT) are in first place with international migrants making up 45 per cent of their population, followed by Jordan (39%) and Lebanon (18%) (UN DESA, 2005) (see Figure 1).
- The figures for the OPT consist of Palestinian refugees coming under the mandate of the United Nations Relief and Works Agency for Palestine Refugees in the Near East (UNRWA). As at 30 June 2008, the total registered refugee population in the Gaza Strip and the West Bank stood at 1.06 million and 754,263, respectively (UNRWA, 2008).

People flows from the Arab Mashrek to GCC States are considerable, but mobility between Arab Mashrek countries is also significant

- In 2005, 461,211 Syrian citizens left their country to go to Saudi Arabia, the second most popular destination for Syrians after Lebanon (in 2005, 2.45 million Syrian citizens entered Lebanon) (CARIM, 2005).
- In 2003, an estimated 400,000 Syrians were cross-border commuters, who lived in Syria and worked in Lebanon (Sadeldine, 2005).
- In 2005, 1.68 million Lebanese citizens, or 29 per cent of all annual arrivals, came to Syria, followed by Jordanians, whose numbers increased from 609,000 to 940,000 over the 2001-2005 period (CARIM, 2005).

Lately, the Arab Mashrek has also been characterized by significant migration to destinations further afield, especially from Lebanon and Egypt ...

- Recent data indicate that Europe is increasingly becoming a destination for migrants from Egypt and Lebanon, with stocks of 127,060 and 111,691 migrants, respectively, followed by Syria with 70,879 migrants (Fargues, 2006) (see Figure 2).
- Italy has become a popular destination for Egyptians. In 2006, there were 46,834 Egyptians regularly residing[2] in Italy, compared to 32,381 in 2001 (ISTAT, 2006).
- The U.S. is another popular destination for Arab Mashrek migrants, with Egypt and Lebanon ranking first and second among countries of origin (113,995 and 105,920 migrants, respectively) (Fargues, 2006) (see Figure 2).

Figure 2:

Emigrants from the Arab Mashrek

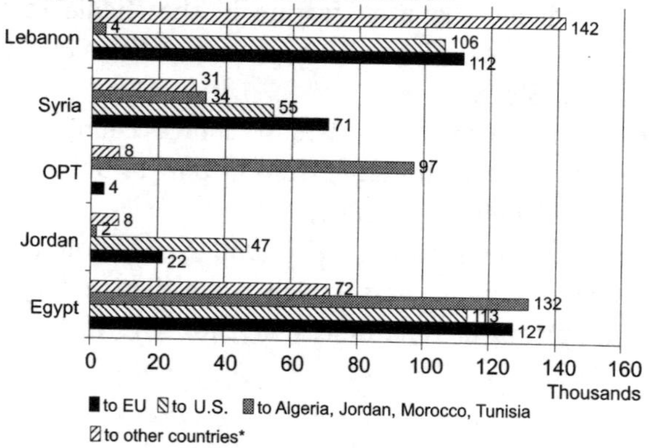

Note: * Data for countries of destination were collected from countries providing the latest available census data on foreign residents by country of nationality/birth. Some of the world's major destination countries for overseas temporary workers, such as Saudi Arabia, the UAE and other Gulf states could not be included for lack of accurate data.

Source: *Fargues, 2006.*

[2] i.e. all migrants who hold a residence permit.

... leaving more room for low-skilled workers from Asian countries

- Lebanon, together with Jordan and Egypt, are destinations for increasing numbers of workers mainly from Sri Lanka and the Philippines. More than 55,000 work permits are issued in Lebanon each year to East Asians, mostly to women (Fargues, 2006).

Arab Mashrek countries are a source of both highly skilled and low-skilled migrants

- The active migrant workforce originating from the Middle East Arab countries is predominantly low or semi-skilled, but some countries, such as Lebanon, Jordan and Egypt, also experience a high degree of highly skilled emigration. While migrants from Jordan, for instance, are predominantly hired as service workers (35%), lawyers and managers account for 33 per cent of migrants leaving the country (Fargues, 2006) (see Figure 3).

Figure 3:

Migrants from Jordan, according to occupation

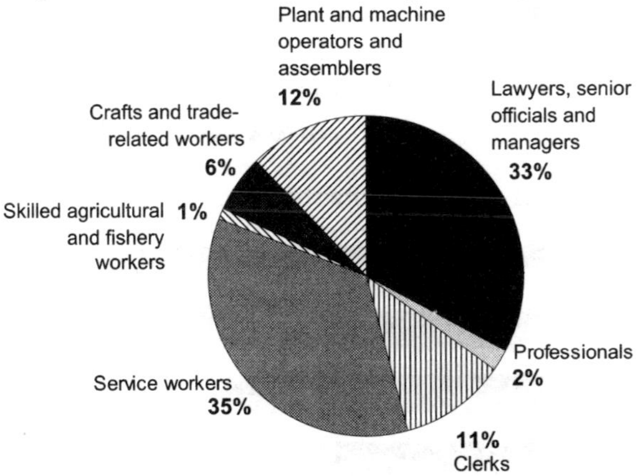

Note: *Only the following countries of residence providing the distribution by occupation of Jordanian migrants are included in the Figure: Austria, Canada, France, Spain and the U.S.*

Source: *Fargues, 2006.*

The region is strongly affected by the presence of refugees and IDPs

- At mid-2005, Jordan was host to 1.8 million refugees (UN DESA, 2005). Most of them were Palestinians (on 30 June 2008, 1.93 million Palestinians refugees were registered in Jordan with UNRWA[3]) constituting 31 per cent of the total population of the country (5.7 million), the highest ratio in any of UNRWA's operational regions.
- Syria also has a sizable Palestinian refugee population, estimated at 424,650 or 2.2 per cent of its total population in 2005 (UNRWA, 2006; UN DESA, 2005).
- Nearly one million people were displaced at the height of the Middle East conflict in the summer of 2006 – the vast majority of them in Lebanon. Some 200,000 are estimated to remain in a situation of displacement (IDMC, 2006).

Arab Mashrek countries are important sources of remittances ...

- The remittances sent from the Arab Mashrek countries were estimated at USD 3.7 billion in 2007, with USD 2.8 billion from Lebanon alone (World Bank, 2008).

... but they are mostly significant recipients of remittances

- The total amount of remittances sent to Arab Mashrek countries reached USD 17.2 billion in 2007 (World Bank, 2008). Egypt and Lebanon received almost USD 6 billion each and alone

[3] See UNRWA (2008). Under UNRWA's operational definition, Palestinian refugees are persons whose normal place of residence was Palestine between June 1946 and May 1948, and who lost both their homes and means of livelihoods as a result of the 1948 Arab-Israeli conflict (http://www.un.org/unrwa/refugees/whois.html). UNRWA's definition of a refugee also covers the descendants of persons who became refugees in 1948 and, as a consequence, the number of registered Palestinian refugees continues to rise due to natural population growth.

accounted for two-thirds of remittances received in the sub-region (see Figure 4).

- Remittances sent to Egypt rose sharply from USD 2.9 billion in 2000 to USD 5.9 billion in 2007 (World Bank, 2008).

Figure 4:

Remittances to the Arab Mashrek, 2007 (billions of USD)

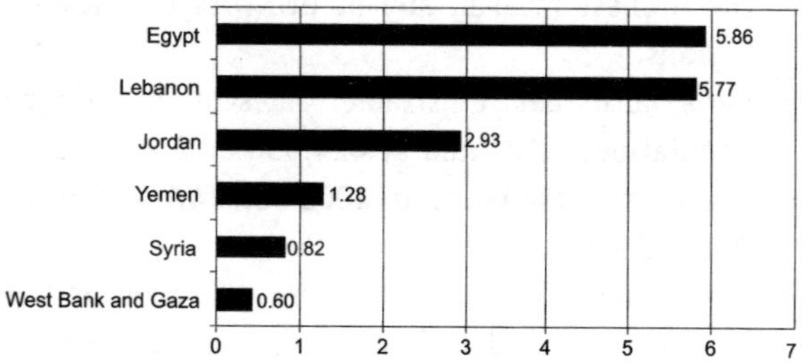

Note: Iraq is not included in the Figure as data are unavailable.
Source: *World Bank, 2008.*

- In Lebanon and Jordan, remittances represent an important source of income. They increased, respectively, from USD 1.58 and USD 1.84 billion in 2000 to USD 5.8 and USD 2.9 billion in 2007 and, at 22.9 per cent, Lebanon received the highest share in relation to GDP in the Mediterranean region. In Jordan, net remittances accounted for 20.4 per cent of GDP, while in Egypt they accounted for five per cent (World Bank, 2008).
- Remittances have significantly improved Lebanon's creditworthiness and access to international capital markets. When remittances are included, debts as a proportion of exports decrease from 732 per cent to 355 per cent (World Bank, 2006).

GULF COOPERATION COUNCIL STATES

- Gulf Cooperation Council (GCC) States are the third-largest region of destination in the world after North America and Europe. They host a total of 12.8 million non-nationals, representing over a third (36%) of their population of 36 million (UN DESA, 2005).
- Between 2000 and 2005, the stock of non-nationals in the GCC States, as a share of their total populations, increased by an annual average of 0.4 per cent (UN DESA, 2005).
- Saudi Arabia has the largest absolute numbers of non-nationals, while Qatar, the UAE and Kuwait are the countries with the highest numbers of non-nationals as a share of their total populations (UN DESA, 2005; http://www.kuwaittimes.net/, February 2007) (see Figure 5).

Figure 5:

Stock of non-nationals in individual GCC countries, 2000 and 2005

Part A: Population of non-nationals

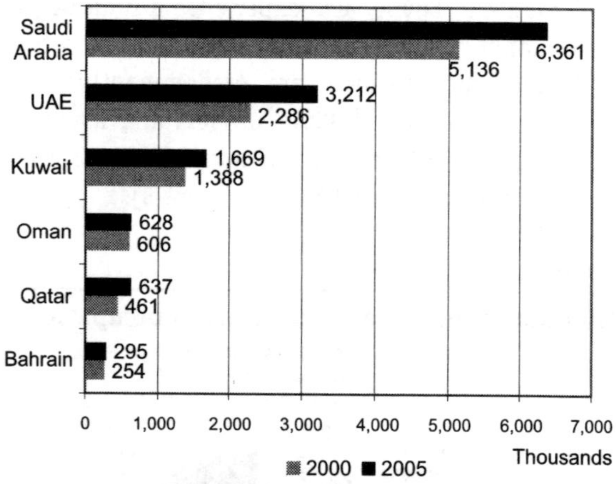

Part B: As a share of total population

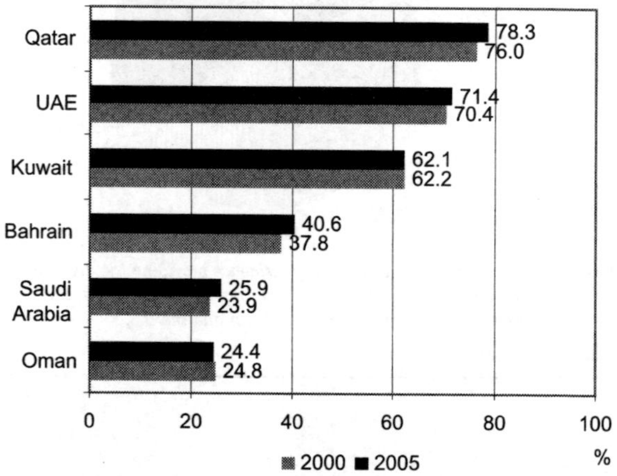

Source: *UN DESA, 2005.*

GCC economies continue to rely heavily on temporary workers from overseas

- The six GCC States[4] experienced a sharp increase in the inflow of overseas workers from one million in 1970 to four million in 1980, and 9.6 million in 2000, of whom 5.1 million lived in Saudi Arabia (UN DESA, 2002), and the numbers have since continued to rise.
- The largest groups of overseas temporary workers in GCC States in 2002 were Indian nationals, with 3.2 million, followed by Pakistanis, Egyptians and Yemenis (Baldwin-Edwards, 2005).
- In 2002, there were approximately 1.35 million Egyptian temporary contractual workers in Saudi Arabia and, in 2005, out of 250,244 contracts issued to Egyptians to work in Gulf countries, 136,468 contracts were from Saudi Arabia, including 38,657 for highly qualified Egyptian nationals (IDB, 2006).

As the number of expatriates of Arab origin in GCC States decreased, workers have been recruited from more distant origins

- In all GCC States, Arabs now constitute only a minority of the expatriate population: 38 per cent in Saudi Arabia, 46 per cent in Kuwait, 25 per cent in Qatar, 10 per cent in the UAE and less than five per cent in Oman, where non-Arabs account for 95.6 per cent of the non-national labour force in the public and private sectors combined (Fargues, 2006). On the other hand, GCC States host 7.5 million Asians (Baldwin-Edwards, 2005), who account for 74 per cent of non-nationals residing on their territory. An increasing part of the Asian labour force is female. The global trend towards the feminization of labour mobility, especially of Asian overseas workers, may therefore also be observed in the GCC States, where women constitute 30 per cent of the foreign labour force. Most female workers, however, are still concentrated in the domestic services sector (UN DESA, 2006; ILO, 2006).

Over the next two decades, the national labour force in the GCC and Arab Mashrek countries is expected to grow dramatically

- Due to rapid demographic growth and rising labour market participation rates, especially of women, the labour force in GCC States is expected to increase from 11.6 million in 2000 to 20.7 million by 2020 (see Figure 6).[5] Estimates for the Arab Mashrek countries foresee an increase from 37 to 66 million over the same period. Substantial labour market, economic and labour force policy reforms will be needed to respond to these major changes (Baldwin-Edwards, 2005).

Figure 6:

Labour force growth in the GCC, 1990-2020

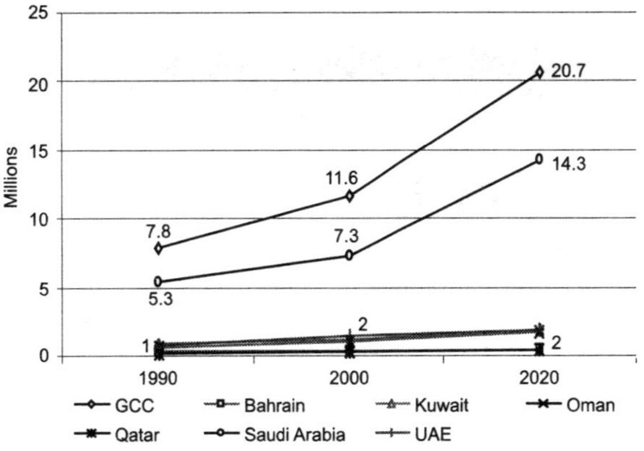

Source: Baldwin-Edwards, 2006.

[4] Bahrain, Kuwait, Oman, Qatar, Saudi Arabia and the United Arab Emirates (UAE).

[5] Estimates reported here were calculated using the total fertility rate (TFR) and life expectancy data estimated by the UN.

ISRAEL

- From 2000 to 2005, the number of international migrants in Israel increased by about 20 per cent from 2.3 million in 2000, or 37 per cent of the population, to 2.7 million in 2005, or 40 per cent of the population (UN DESA, 2005) (see Figure 7).

Figure 7:

Stock of migrants in Israel, 2000 and 2005

Part A: Total number of migrants

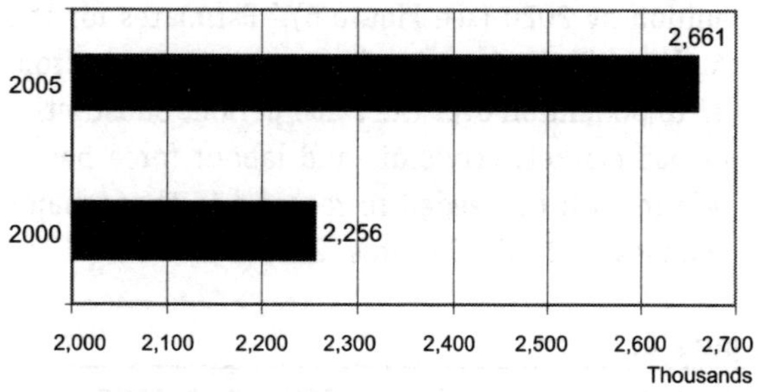

Part B: As a share of total population

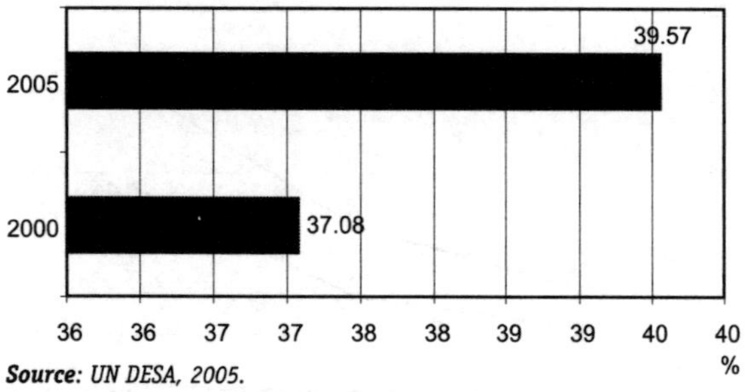

Source: *UN DESA, 2005.*

- Persons of Jewish ancestry account for a large share of total immigration to Israel, facilitated by the "Law of Return" of 1950 and its subsequent amendments. Ethiopian Jews, or *Falasha*, constitute another important migrant group, estimated in 2005 by the Israel Association for Ethiopian Jews to number around 85,000, of whom some 20,000 were already born in Israel. The largest immigration flow of the last 20 years occurred in the wake of the dissolution of the former Soviet Union, when approximately 900,000 Soviet Jews settled in Israel (Kruger, 2005).
- In addition, non-Jewish and non-Palestinian temporary migrant workers have lately been accepted by Israel to support its prosperous economy. 2003 estimates put the number of migrant workers at about 189,000. They come mainly from Southeast Asia and eastern Europe and are hired as low-skilled workers. The largest groups are from the Philippines (around 50,000) working mainly as home health carers, followed by Thai migrant workers (some 30,000) who work in agriculture, and Chinese (15,000) active in construction. Another approximately 65,000 foreign workers are from eastern Europe (over half of whom are from Romania) who work mainly in construction. Women constitute around one-third of all migrants and are mainly employed in the 24-hour home healthcare sector (Kruger, 2005).

United Nations Relief and Works Agency for Palestine Refugees in the Near East (UNRWA)

2008 "Total Registered Refugees per Country and Area (as at 30 June, 2008)", UNRWA, http://www.un.org/unrwa/publications/pdf/rr_countryandarea.pdf.

World Bank

2004 *Unlocking the Employment Potential in the Middle East and North Africa: Toward a New Social Contract*, The World Bank, Washington, D.C., http://web.worldbank.org/WBSITE/EXTERNAL/COUNTRIES/MENAEXT/0,,contentMDK:20260961~pagePK:146736~piPK:146830~theSitePK:256299,00.html.

2006 *Global Economic Prospects 2006: Economic Implications of Remittances and Migration*, The World Bank, Washington, D.C., http://econ.worldbank.org/WBSITE/EXTERNAL/EXTDEC/EXTDECPROSPECTS/GEPEXT/EXTGEP2006/0,,contentMDK:20709766~menuPK:1026823~pagePK:64167689~piPK:64167673~theSitePK:1026804,00.html.

2008 *Revisions to Remittance Trends 2007*, July, The World Bank, Washington, D.C., http://econ.worldbank.org/WBSITE/EXTERNAL/EXTDEC/EXTDECPROSPECTS/0,,contentMDK:21121930~menuPK:3145470~pagePK:64165401~piPK:64165026~theSitePK:476883,00.html.

OCEANIA

- Oceania[1] is host to five million international migrants (UN DESA, 2005), representing 15.2 per cent of its population, the largest share in any region in the world, and accounting for 2.6 per cent of the global migrant stock.
- Migration accounts for one-quarter of population growth in Australia, New Zealand and Pacific Ocean island countries, with the number of migrants in the Oceania region increasing from 4.8 million to five million over the period 1990-2005 (UN, 2005).
- Women migrants in Oceania have outnumbered men since 2000, when they constituted 50.6 per cent of international migrants. Their share has since risen to 51.3 per cent of total international migrants (UN, 2005).

AUSTRALIA AND NEW ZEALAND

- Migrants make up a fifth of the population of Australia, the highest proportion for any country in the world with a population of 20 million or more.[2] While in Australia the migrant population has increased since 1995, in New Zealand the number of migrants decreased from 708,000 to 642,000 (UN DESA, 2005).

Figure 1:

Stock of migrants in Australia and New Zealand, 2000 and 2005

Part A: Total number of migrants

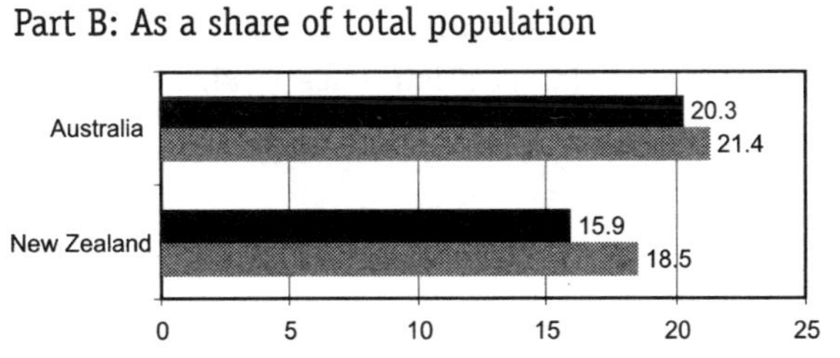

Part B: As a share of total population

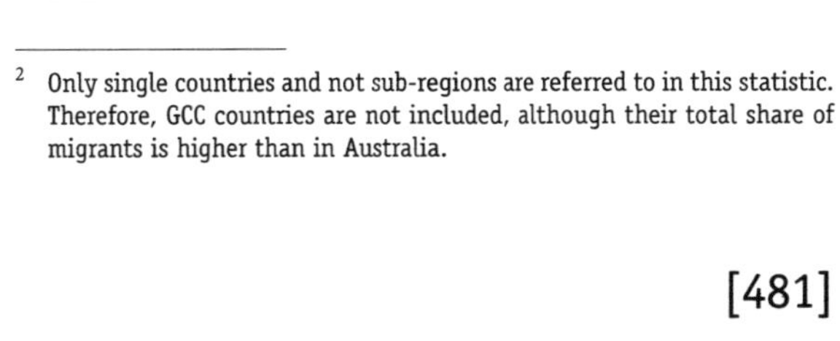

Source: *UN DESA, 2005.*

[1] Oceania includes the following countries and territories: Australia, New Zealand, **Melanesia** (Fiji, New Caledonia, Papua New Guinea, Solomon Islands, Vanuatu), **Micronesia** (Guam, Kiribati, Marshall Islands, Micronesia (Federated States of), Nauru, Northern Mariana Islands, Palau) and **Polynesia** (American Samoa, Cook Islands, French Polynesia, Niue, Pitcairn, Samoa, Tokelau, Tonga, Tuvalu, Walis and Futuna Islands).

[2] Only single countries and not sub-regions are referred to in this statistic. Therefore, GCC countries are not included, although their total share of migrants is higher than in Australia.

- In both Australia and New Zealand the number of migrants as a share of the total population declined between 2000 and 2005 (UN DESA, 2005) (see Figure 1). Three main factors may explain this development.[3] First, from 2000 to 2005, the rules concerning migration for family reunion, which in the past had accounted for a substantial share of immigration to both countries, have been tightened. Second, while skilled immigration continued to grow significantly, much of it was, in fact, of a temporary nature of between six months and two years, and therefore does not show up in some statistics. Third, though of less immediate impact, particularly in Australia, the numbers of the older post-World War II immigrants are declining as old age takes its toll (Connell, 2007).

Australia and New Zealand are among the few countries in the world to have active immigration programmes and are the major destinations in the region for both migrants and refugees

- The U.K. has traditionally been the leading country of origin for immigrants in Australia. In 1996, however, arrivals from New Zealand, outnumbered British immigrants, reaching 25,000 in 2001. In 2003, the U.K. regained its first position until 2005, when the differential between these two top groups of migrants decreased with 18,220 and 17,345 arrivals from the U.K. and New Zealand, respectively (MPI, 2005).
- In 1996, China became the third country of origin for migrants arriving in Australia, and has maintained this position since (MPI, 2005) (see Figure 2).

[3] Email communication with Professor John Connell, University of Sydney, Australia.

Figure 2:

Australia – leading countries of origin, by country of birth, 1991-2005

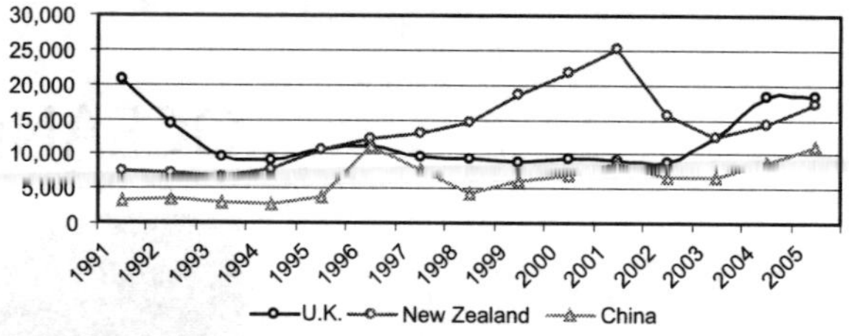

Source: MPI, 2005.

- The stock of foreign-born workers in Australia increased steadily from 1995 to 2005, while, as a proportion of the total labour force, it declined slightly during the period 2003-2004 (OECD, 2007) (see Figure 3).

Figure 3:

Stock of foreign workers in Australia

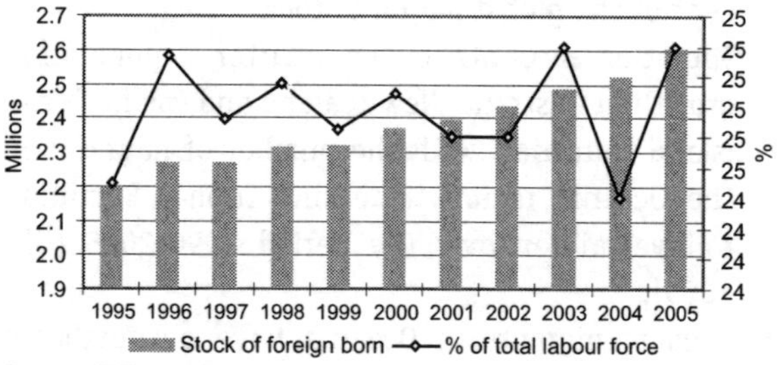

Source: OECD, 2007.

Family reunification has been the traditional cornerstone of migration policies ...

- During the period 1990-2002, family reunification accounted for 37 per cent of immigrant entries to Australia. For New Zealand, the share of admissions for family reasons was lower and continued to decline over the same period (UN, 2005).

... but many more highly skilled migrants are now admitted under the "points system" ...

- Between 2006-2007, 97,920 permanent residents were granted permanent residence in Australia under the skills programme, compared to 50,079 under the family reunification programme (DIAC, 2007).

... and the student population remains large

- In 2006-2007, a total of 228,592 student visas were granted, which represents a significant increase of almost 20 per cent over the 2005-2006 figure of 190,674 visas. The two leading source countries were China and India with 28,949 and 24,915 visa grants, respectively (DIAC, 2007).
- In 2004-2005, foreign graduates of Australian Universities accounted for 20 per cent of Australian immigrants under the skills programme, led by Chinese and Indians (*Migration News*, January 2006).

Temporary migration for work is gaining in importance

- The number of temporary workers in Australia has increased noticeably since 1996, when the government introduced a new temporary business entry visa that allows employers to sponsor skilled workers from overseas for a stay of up to four years (OECD, 2007) (see Figure 4).

Figure 4:

Inflows of foreign workers to Australia, 1995-2005 (thousands)

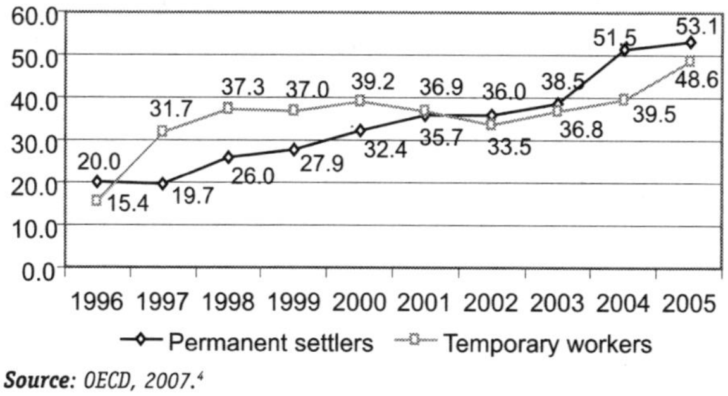

Source: OECD, 2007.[4]

- Temporary migration also increased in New Zealand over the last ten years (see Figure 5). In line with this general trend, a pilot programme for seasonal workers from Vanuatu was launched in April 2007 (IMF, 2007).

Figure 5:

Inflows of foreign workers into New Zealand, 1998-2005 (thousands)

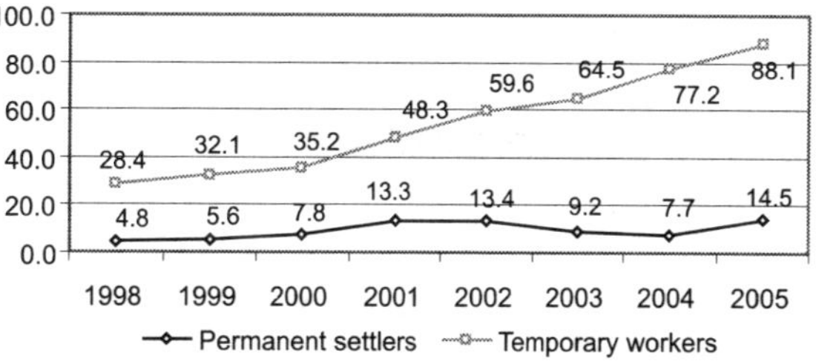

Source: OECD, 2007.

Female migration is also gaining greater prominence

- Recent data show that women are migrating to Australia to take up managerial, professional and other positions that cannot be filled locally. For example, Australia is projecting nursing deficits of 40,000 during the next four to five years (UNFPA, 2006). According to the New Zealand nurse registry figures for 2002, 23 per cent of nurses were foreign-born.

The relatively high emigration levels from Australia and New Zealand primarily reflect the desire of educated young citizens to seek work experience abroad

- Australia has an overall emigration rate[5] of 1.75 and New Zealand 10.7. The highly skilled emigration rate[6] is 3.68 and 17, respectively (OECD, 2005).

---

[4] **Permanent settlers**: Skilled workers including the following categories of visas: employer nominations, business skills, occupational shares system, special talents and independent, including accompanying dependants. Period of reference: Fiscal year (July to June).
Temporary workers: Skilled temporary resident programme, including accompanying dependants. Includes Long-stay Temporary Business Programme as from 1996-97. Period of reference: Fiscal year (July to June).

[5] The emigration rate is calculated by dividing the expatriate population from that country by the total native-born population of the country (native-born = expatriates + resident native-born) (OECD, Database on Immigrants and Expatriates, 2005).

[6] The emigration rate of highly educated persons is calculated by dividing the highly educated expatriate population from that country by the total highly educated native-born population.

MELANESIA, POLYNESIA AND MICRONESIA

Figure 6:

Stock of migrants in Melanesia, Polynesia and Micronesia, 2000 and 2005

Part A: Total number of migrants

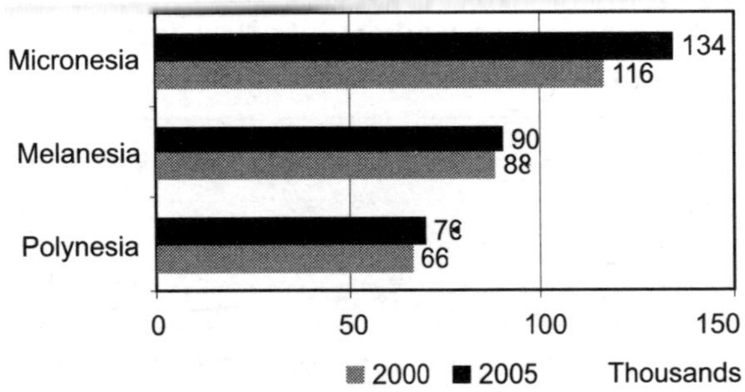

Part B: As a share of total population

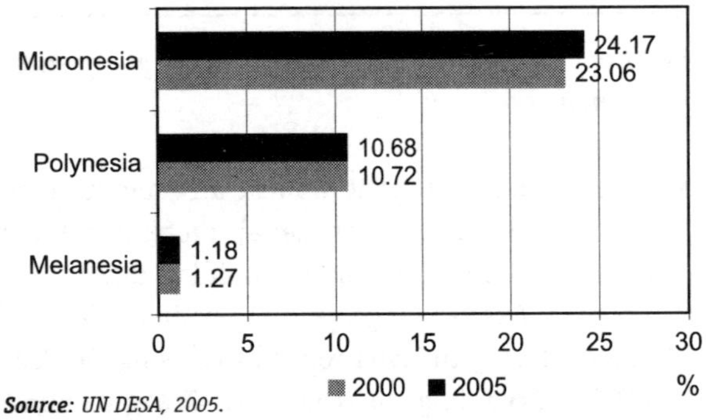

Source: UN DESA, 2005.

- All sub-regions of Micronesia, Melanesia and Polynesia experienced an increase in their migrant population between 2000 and 2005 (see Figure 6). Micronesia leads with 134,000, or 24 per cent of its population (UN DESA, 2005).

Under the influence of globalization, Fiji has become a source of temporary skilled migrants in response to specific opportunities abroad, especially in the Middle East and in other Pacific countries

- Between 2000 and 2004, 27,000 Fijian citizens emigrated. A breakdown of these figures reveals that the vast majority were of Indo-Fijian origin and that more than 3,800 had a professional or technical background (Mohanty, 2006) (see Figure 7).

Figure 7:

Emigration of Fijian citizens by ethnic group and profession, 1987-2004

Year	Fijians	Indo-Fijians	Others	Total	Average annual emigration rate	Professionals**	
						Total	Annual average
1987-1999	3,926	57,159	3,124	64,209	4,939	6,869	528
2000-2004*	2,373	23,585	1,126	27,084	5,413	3,826	765
1987-2004*	6,299	80,744	4,250	91,293	5,070	10,695	594

Notes: * The figure for 2004 is from January to September.
** Includes professionals, technical and related workers.
Source: *Mohanty, 2006.*

- In addition to continuing permanent Indo-Fijian emigration from the country, Fiji has also witnessed new trends in temporary migration of mostly indigenous Fijians, as members of peacekeeping forces, security personnel, nurses, sportspeople and students to distant parts of the world.

  - Fijian soldiers have been deployed to Iraq, continuing a long-standing tradition of Fijian soldiers working in multinational peace-making and peace-keeping operations. Many Fijians are also employed in security, engineering and IT occupations in major cities in Iraq.

  - Estimates of the number of temporary contractual workers recruited to the Middle East from Fiji are variable but are as high as 20,000, though such figures relate to those who applied and paid fees of more than FJD 150 to private recruitment agencies, rather than those who were finally selected for employment overseas, which might be about 2,500 (Connell, 2006).

- Nurses from Fiji have also migrated to the U.K. and to other Pacific countries such as the Marshall Islands (Rokoduru, 2006).

Overseas remittances play a crucial role in Fiji's foreign exchange earnings

- Fiji's economy has relied historically on sugar and gold mining and, more recently, also on tourism and garment manufacturing; but, in the decade between 1994 and 2004, the amount of remittances has increased to a level where they bring in more foreign exchange than all other sectors except tourism (Maclellan and Mares, 2006) (see Figure 8).

Figure 8:

Increase in foreign exchange earnings in Fiji, 1994-2004 (millions of Fijian Dollars)

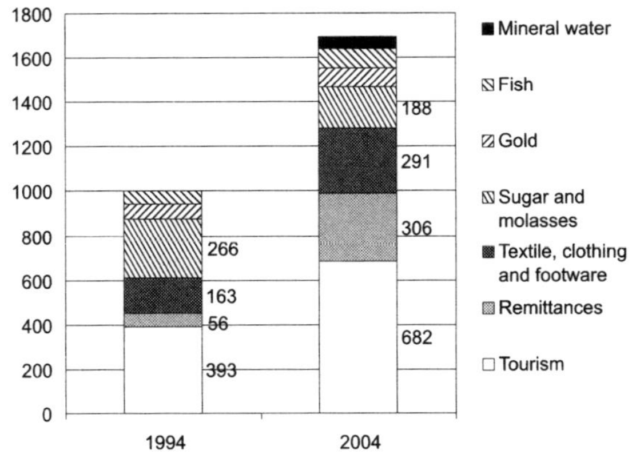

Note: 1 Fiji Dollar (FJD) equals about 0.63 U.S. Dollar as of August 2008.

Source: *Maclellan and Mares, 2006.*

- The small Pacific island states do not feature prominently in an analysis of global migratory processes, but they are nonetheless confronted increasingly by migratory concerns

- Niue is currently seeking immigration from Tuvalu, as its population has declined sharply after being hit by Cyclone Heta in 2004, continuing a long-term "culture of migration" (Connell, 2006). Niue's declining population has been of concern to successive governments and currently stands at around 1,500. Over 20,000 Niueans live in New Zealand and despite government attempts to encourage them to return home, migration patterns persist (Department of Foreign Affairs and Trade, Australian Government, 2007).
- Many, but by no means all, South Pacific economies rely heavily on remittances from migrants abroad. Tonga is among the Pacific nations that have been identified since the 1980s as MIRAB economies, that is, sustained principally by Migration, Remittances, Aid and Bureaucracy.[7] In 2006, Tonga was globally the second main recipient country (after Moldova and Liberia) of remittances as a share of GDP (32.2%) (World Bank, 2008). According to Small and Dixon (2004), in the case of Tonga, "it is migration, along with the remittances of cash and goods from migrants who live and work overseas, that keeps the Tongan economy afloat". Remittances are its major source of foreign exchange.
- On the other hand, Vanuatu experiences almost no emigration and receives few remittances, in marked contrast to Samoa and Tonga (IMF, 2007).

All countries in this sub-region will experience an oversupply of labour by 2015

- According to World Bank projections, Melanesia, Polynesia and Micronesia will register an excess labour supply by 2015. This large increase (except in Fiji, where the increase is expected to be more

[7] The acronym was developed originally by Bertram and Watters (1985) in relation to Pacific states linked to New Zealand, and expanded to include other Pacific nations in similar economic situations.

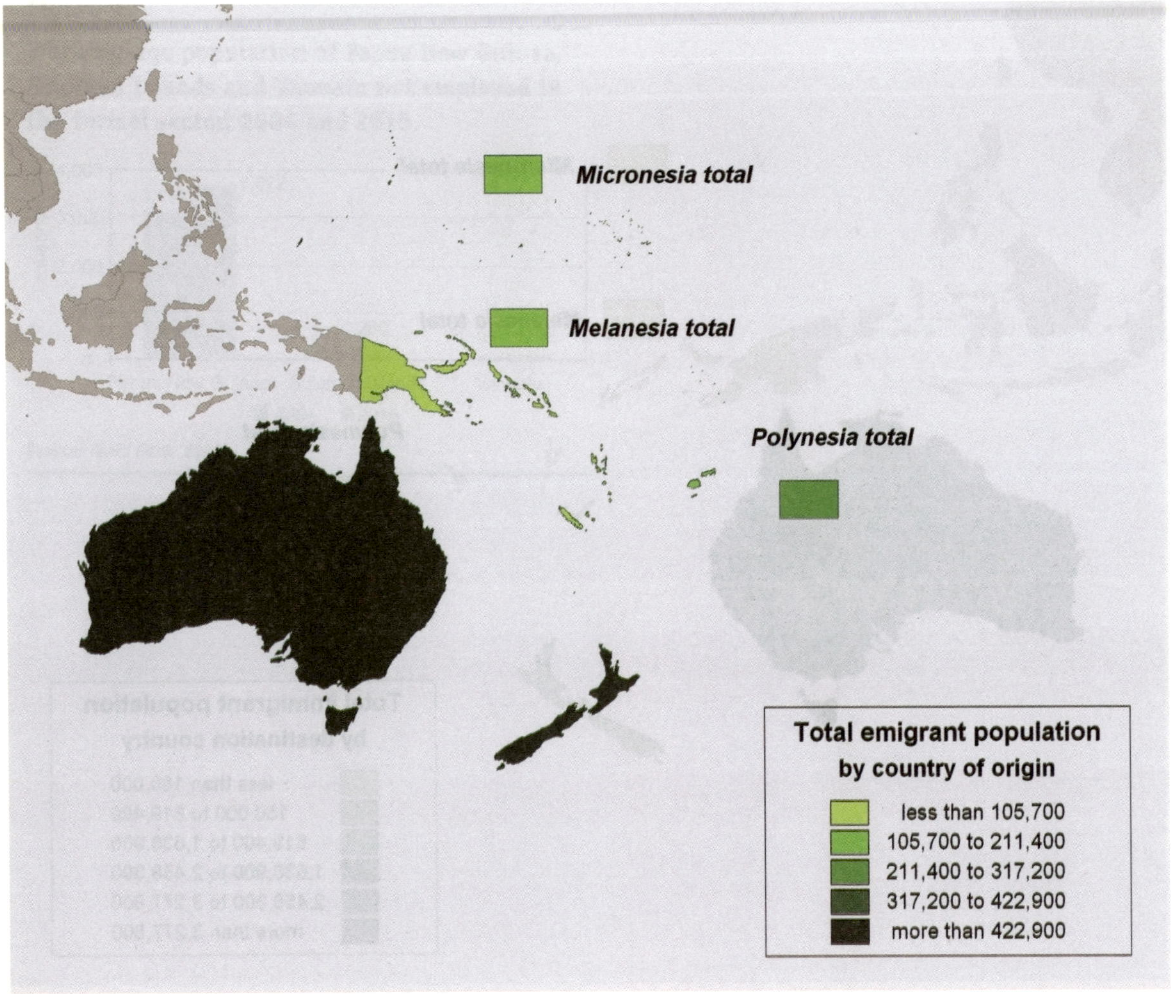
Micronesia total
Melanesia total
Polynesia total
Total emigrant population
by country of origin
less than 105,700
105,700 to 211,400
211,400 to 317,200
317,200 to 422,900
more than 422,900

REFERENCES

Australia, Department of Foreign Affairs and Trade

2007 "Niue Country Brief", Department of Foreign Affairs and Trade, http://www.dfat.gov.au/geo/niue/niue_brief.html.

Australia, Department of Immigration and Citizenship (DIAC)

2007 *Annual Report 2006-07*, November, DIAC, http://www.immi.gov.au/about/reports/annual/2006-07/pdf.htm.

Bertram, G. and R. Watters

1985 "The MIRAB Economy in Pacific Microstates", *Pacific Viewpoint* 26(3): 497-519.

Connell, J.

2006 "Migration, Dependency and Independency in the Pacific: Old Wines in Bigger Bottles? (Part 1)" in S. Firth (Ed.), *Globalisation and Governance in the Pacific Islands*, Australian National University (ANU) E Press, Canberra, 59-80, http://epress.anu.edu.au/ssgm/global_gov/pdf_instructions.html.

Haberkorn, G.

2004 "Current Pacific population dynamics and recent trends", July, Secretariat of the Pacific Community (SPC) Demography/Population Programme, http://www.spc.int/demog/en/stats/2004/2004%20Current%20Pacific%20population%20dynamics.doc.

Hugo, G.

2005 "Migration in the Asia Pacific Region", paper prepared for the Policy Analysis and Research Programme of the Global Commission on International Migration (GCIM), Geneva, http://www.gcim.org/mm/File/Regional%20Study%202.pdf.

Inglis, C.

2004 "Australia's Continuing Transformation", *Migration Information Source,* August, Migration Policy Institute (MPI), Washington, D.C., http://migrationinformation.com/Profiles/display.cfm?ID=242.

International Monetary Fund (IMF)

2007 "Vanuatu", Staff Report for the 2006 Article IV Consultation, IMF Country Report No. 07/92, March, IMF, Washington, D.C., http://www.imf.org/external/pubs/ft/scr/2007/cr0792.pdf.

Maclellan, N. and P. Mares

2006 "Labour Mobility in the Pacific: Creating seasonal work Programs in Australia" in S. Firth (Ed.), *Globalisation and Governance in the Pacific Islands*, ANU E Press, Canberra, 137-171, http://epress.anu.edu.au/ssgm/global_gov/pdf_instructions.html.

Migration News

2006 "Australia, New Zealand: Riots, Migrants, Students", *Migration News*, 13:1 (January), University of California at Davis, http://migration.ucdavis.edu/MN/more.php?id=3170_0_5_0.

Migration Policy Institute (MPI)

2005 "Global Data Center. Australia: Top Ten sending countries, by country of birth, 1991 to 2005", *Migration Information Source,* MPI, Washington, D.C., http://www.migrationinformation.org/DataHub/countrydata/data.cfm.

Mohanty, M.

2006 "Globalisation, New Labour Migration and Development in Fiji" in S. Firth (Ed.), *Globalisation and Governance in the Pacific Islands*, Australian National University (ANU) E Press, Canberra, 107-120, http://epress.anu.edu.au/ssgm/global_gov/pdf_instructions.html.

New Zealand Statistics

2007 Population Indicators, Statistics New Zealand, http://www.stats.govt.nz/tables/population-indicators.htm.

Organisation for Economic Co-operation and Development (OECD)

2005 Database on immigrants and expatriates, Directorate for Employment, Labour and Social Affairs, OECD, Paris, http://www.oecd.org/document/51/0,3343,en_2649_33931_34063091_1_1_1_1,00.html.

2007 *International Migration Outlook*, SOPEMI 2007 Edition, OECD, Paris.

Rokoduru, A.

2005 "Contemporary Migration within the Pacific Islands: the Case of Fijian Skilled Workers in Kiribati and Marshall Islands" in S. Firth (Ed.), *Globalisation and Governance in the Pacific Islands*, ANU E Press, Canberra, 173-186, http://epress.anu.edu.au/ssgm/global_gov/pdf_instructions.html.

Small, C.A. and D.L. Dixon

2004 "Tonga: Migration and the Homeland", *Migration Information Source*, February, MPI, Washington, D.C., http://www.migrationinformation.org/Profiles/print.cfm?ID=198.

United Nations (UN)

2005 "International Migration and Development", Regional Fact Sheet on Oceania, UN, Department of Public Information, in cooperation with the Population Division of the UN Department of Economic and Social Affairs (UN DESA), http://www.un.org/migration/presskit/factsheet_oceania.pdf.

United Nations Department of Economic and Social Affairs (DESA), Population Division

2005 *Trends in Total Migrant Stock: The 2005 Revision*, Population Database, UN DESA, Population Division, New York, http://esa.un.org/migration/index.asp?panel=1.

United Nations Population Fund (UNFPA)

2006 "Migration by Region: Oceania", UNFPA, http://www.unfpa.org/swp/2006/presskit/docs/factsheet_oceania.doc.

World Bank

2006 *Global Economic Prospects 2006: Economic Implications of Remittances and Migration*, The World Bank, Washington, D.C., http://www-wds.worldbank.org/external/default/WDSContentServer/IW3P/IB/2005/11/14/000112742_20051114174928/Rendered/PDF/343200GEP02006.pdf.

2007 *At Home and Away: Expanding Job Opportunities for Pacific Islanders through Labor Mobility*, The World Bank, Washington, D.C., http://web.worldbank.org/WBSITE/EXTERNAL/COUNTRIES/EASTASIAPACIFICEXT/PACIFICISLANDSEXTN/0,,contentMDK:21020027~pagePK:141137~piPK:141127~theSitePK:441883,00.html.

2008 *Revisions to Remittance Trends 2007*, July, The World Bank, Washington, D.C., http://econ.worldbank.org/WBSITE/EXTERNAL/EXTDEC/EXTDECPROSPECTS/0,,contentMDK:21121930~menuPK:3145470~pagePK:64165401~piPK:64165026~theSitePK:476883,00.html.

MIGRATION TERMINOLOGY*

admission: The granting of entry into a state.

alien: *See non-national.*

amnesty: A general pardon, "regularization" or "legalization" that is extended to people who can show residence in a country for which the amnesty is granted, despite the fact that such residence was unauthorized.

assimilation: Adaptation of one ethnic or social group – usually a minority – to another, involving the subsuming of language, traditions, values and behaviour or even fundamental vital interests.

assisted voluntary return: Logistical, financial and reintegration support to rejected asylum seekers, victims of trafficking in human beings, stranded migrants, qualified nationals and other migrants unable or unwilling to remain in the host country, who volunteer to return to their countries of origin. *See also voluntary return.*

asylum seeker: A person who seeks safety from persecution or serious harm in a country other than her/his own and awaits a decision on the application for refugee status under relevant international and national instruments. *See also refugee.*

best (effective) practices: Means to further the application of the existing norms and principles, both at the international and the national levels. Best practices may be translated into operational directives, codes of conduct or other manifestations of soft law, but should not lead to a weakening or erosion of positive law. They are characterized by: being innovative, developing creative solutions; showing a positive impact on the level of implementation of the rights of migrants; having a sustainable effect, especially by involving migrants themselves; and having potential for replication.

bilateral labour migration agreements: Formal mechanisms concluded between states, which are essentially legally binding treaty commitments concerned with inter-state cooperation on labour migration. The term is also used to describe less formal arrangements regulating the movement of workers between countries entered into by states as well as a range of other actors, including individual ministries, employer organizations, etc.

biometrics: The study of measurable biological characteristics. "Biometric identifiers" (BIs) are pieces of information that encode a representation of a person's unique biological make up (e.g. fingerprints, facial recognition photographs, retinal scans or voice scans).

bonded labour: Service rendered by a worker under condition of bondage arising from economic considerations, notably indebtedness through a loan or an advance. Where debt is the root cause of bondage, the implication is that the worker (or dependents or heirs) is tied to a particular creditor for a specified or unspecified period until the loan is repaid.

border control: A state's regulation of the entry of persons to its territory, in the exercise of its sovereignty.

* Many of the terms in this section are drawn or adapted from the terms found in a similar section in *World Migration 2005* and IOM's *Glossary on Migration*, November 2004.

border management: Facilitation of authorized flows of persons across a border and the detection and prevention of irregular entry of non-nationals into a given country.

brain drain: Emigration of trained and talented persons from the country of origin to another country resulting in a depletion of skills resources in the former.

brain gain: Immigration of trained and talented persons into a destination country. Also called "reverse brain drain".

business migrant: A person who is granted entry for a limited term to take up a pre-nominated position with approved national sponsor-employers, generally in a professional or managerial capacity.

business visitor: A person who is granted entry under a business visa or for the purposes of conducting business.

capacity building: Building capacity of governments and civil society by increasing their knowledge and enhancing their skills. Capacity building can take the form of substantive direct project design and implementation with a partner government, training opportunities, or in other circumstances the facilitation of a bilateral or multilateral agenda for dialogue development put in place by concerned authorities. In all cases, capacity building aims to build towards generally accepted benchmarks of management practices.

change/switching of status: Procedure whereby a non-national present in a state may seek a different immigration status.

circular migration: The fluid movement of people between countries, including temporary or long-term movement which may be beneficial to all involved, if occurring voluntarily and linked to the labour needs of countries of origin and destination.

citizen: *See national.*

citizenship: *See nationality.*

clandestine migration: Secret or concealed migration in breach of immigration requirements. The generic term "irregular migration" should preferably be used. *See irregular migration.*

consular officers: Government officials representing the state abroad in visa and residency issues (*Art. 1(d), Vienna Convention on Consular Relations, 1963*).

consular protection: Consular functions aiming at helping nationals abroad, including assisting in the protection of their rights and interests before local courts. In particular, protection extended to migrants arrested or committed to prison or custody pending trial or detained in any other manner; such migrants must be informed without delay of the right to communicate with consular authorities.

contractual labour: Labour supplied by a contractor.

country of destination: The country that is a destination for migratory flows (regular or irregular). *See also host country and receiving country.*

country of origin: The country that is a source of migratory flows (regular or irregular). *See also sending country and source country.*

country of transit: The country through which migratory flows (regular or irregular) move.

cross-border migration: A process of movement of persons across international borders.

debt bondage: The status or condition arising from a pledge by a debtor of his/her personal service or those of a person under his/her control as security for a debt, if the value of those services as reasonably assessed is not applied toward liquidation of the debt or the length and nature of those services are not respectively limited and defined (*Art. 1(a), United Nations Supplementary Convention on the Abolition of Slavery, the Slave Trade and Abolition of Practices Similar to Slavery, 1956*).

demography: The study of human populations, especially with reference to size and density, distribution and vital statistics.

dependant: A person who relies on another for support. In the migration context, a spouse and minor children are generally considered "dependants", even if the spouse is not financially dependent.

deportation: The act of a state in the exercise of its sovereignty in removing a non-national from its territory to his/her country of origin or a third country after refusal of admission or termination of permission to remain. *See also expulsion, refoulement.*

detention: Restriction on freedom of movement, usually through enforced confinement, of a person by government authorities.

diaspora: Diasporas are broadly defined as individuals and members of networks, associations and communities who have left their country of origin, but maintain links with their homelands. This concept covers more settled expatriate communities, migrant workers based abroad temporarily, expatriates with the citizenship of the host country, dual citizens, and second-/third-generation migrants.

discrimination: A failure to treat all persons equally where no objective and reasonable distinction can be found between those favoured and those not favoured. Discrimination is prohibited in respect of "race, sex, language or religion" (*Art. 1(3), United Nations Charter, 1945*) or "of any kind, such as race, colour, sex, language, religion, political or other opinion, national or social origin, property, birth or other status" (*Art. 2, Universal Declaration of Human Rights, 1948*).

displaced person: A person who flees his/her state or community due to fear or dangers other than those which would make him/her a refugee. A displaced person is often forced to flee because of international or non-international armed conflicts, or natural or man-made disasters. *See also internally displaced persons, refugee.*

documented migrant workers: Migrant workers or members of their families authorized to enter, to stay and to engage in a remunerated activity in the state of employment pursuant to the law of that state and to international agreements to which the state is a party (*Article 5(a), International Convention on the Protection of the Rights of All Migrant Workers and Members of Their Families, 1990*).

dual/multiple nationality: Simultaneous possession of the nationality of two or more countries by the same person. *See also nationality.*

economic migrant: A person leaving his/her habitual place of residence to settle outside his/her country of origin in order to improve his/her quality of life. This term is often loosely used to distinguish from refugees fleeing persecution and is also similarly used to refer to persons attempting to enter a country without legal permission and/or by using asylum procedures without *bona fide* cause. It may equally be applied to persons leaving their country of origin for the purpose of employment. *See also frontier worker, migrant worker, seasonal migrant worker.*

emigration: The act of departing or exiting from one state with a view to settling in another.

entry: Any entrance of a non-national into a foreign country, whether voluntary or involuntary, authorized or unauthorized.

environmental migrant: Environmental migrants are persons or groups of persons who, for reasons of sudden or progressive changes in the environment that adversely affect their lives or living conditions, are obliged to leave their habitual homes, or choose to do so, either temporarily or permanently, and who move either within their country or abroad.

exclusion: The formal denial of a non-national's admission into a state.

exploitation: The act of taking advantage of something or someone, in particular the act of taking unjust advantage of another for one's own benefit (e.g. sexual exploitation, forced labour or services, slavery or practices similar to slavery, servitude or the removal of organs). *See also forced/compulsory labour, slavery, trafficking in persons.*

expulsion: An act by an authority of the state with the intention and with the effect of securing the removal of a person or persons (non-nationals or stateless persons) against their will from the territory of that state. *See also deportation, refoulement.*

family reunification/reunion: Process whereby family members separated through forced or voluntary migration regroup in a country other than the one of their origin.

family migration A more general concept covering family reunification, the migration of a family unit as a whole and family formation.

feminization of migration: The growing participation of women in migration (some 49 per cent of all migrants globally are women). While the proportion of migrants who are women has not changed greatly in recent decades, their role in migration has changed considerably. Women are now more likely to migrate independently, rather than as members of a household, and they are actively involved in employment.

forced/compulsory labour: All work or service which is exacted from any person under the menace of any penalty and for which the said person has not offered himself/herself voluntarily (*Art. 2(1), ILO Convention No. 29 on Forced Labour, 1930*).

forced migration: A migratory movement in which an element of coercion exists, including threats to life and livelihood, whether arising from natural or man-made causes (e.g. movements of refugees and internally displaced persons as well as people displaced by natural or environmental disasters, chemical or nuclear disasters, famine or development projects).

forced return: The compulsory return of a person to the country of origin, transit or third country, on the basis of an administrative or judicial act. Also referred to as mandatory return.

foreigner: A person belonging to, or owing an allegiance to, another state. *See also alien and non-national.*

freedom of movement: A human right which comprises three basic elements: the freedom of movement within the territory of a country (*Article 13(1), Universal Declaration of Human Rights, 1948*: "Everyone has the right to freedom of movement and residence within the borders of each state"); the right to leave any country; and, the right to return to his or her own country (*Article 13(2), Universal Declaration of Human Rights, 1948*: "Everyone has the right to leave any country, including his own, and to return to his country."). Freedom of movement is also referred to in the context of freedom of movement arrangements between states at the regional level (e.g. European Union).

frontier worker: A migrant worker who retains his or her habitual residence in a neighbouring state to which he or she normally returns every day or at least once a week (*International Convention on the Protection of the Rights of All Migrant Workers and Members of Their Families, 1990, Article 2(2)(a)*). *See also migrant worker.*

globalization: A process of interaction and integration among the people, corporations, and governments of different states; a process driven by international trade and investment and aided by information technology. This process has effects on the environment, culture, political systems, economic development and prosperity, and human well-being in societies.

green card: An identity card issued by the U.S. Government to non-nationals who have been granted permanent resident status in the United States. Also called a Permanent Resident Card, it is evidence of a non-national being a lawful permanent resident with a right to live and work permanently in the United States.

highly skilled/qualified migrant: While there is no internationally agreed definition, two overlapping meanings are often intended. In very general terms a highly skilled migrant is considered to be a person with tertiary education, typically an adult who has completed a formal two-year college education or more. In a more specific sense, a highly skilled migrant is a person who has earned, either by tertiary level education or occupational experience, the level of qualifications typically needed to practice a profession.

host country: *See country of destination, receiving country, state of employment.*

human rights: Those liberties, benefits and entitlements, which, by accepted contemporary values, all human beings should be able to claim "as of right" in the society in which they live; e.g. as contained in the *Universal Declaration of Human Rights, 1948* and the *International Covenants on Economic, Social and Cultural Rights*, and *on Civil and Political Rights*, 1966 (together frequently referred to as the "International Bill of Rights"), and developed by other treaties from this core.

illegal/irregular/unauthorized entry: Act of crossing borders without complying with the necessary requirements for legal entry into the receiving state (*Art. 3(b), Protocol Against the Smuggling of Migrants by Land, Sea and Air, supplementing the United Nations Convention against Transnational Organized Crime, 2000*).

illegal migrant/migration: *See irregular migrant/migration.*

immigration: A process by which non-nationals move into a country for the purpose of settlement.

immigration status: Status which a migrant is accorded under the immigration law of the host country.

integration: While the term is used and understood differently in different countries and contexts, "integration" can be defined as the process by which migrants become accepted into society, both as individuals and as groups. It generally refers to a two-way process of adaptation by migrants and host societies, while the particular requirements for acceptance by a host society vary from country to country. Integration does not necessarily imply permanent settlement. It does, however, imply consideration of the rights and obligations of migrants and host societies, of access to different kinds of services and the labour market, and of identification and respect for a core set of values that bind migrants and host communities in a common purpose.

internal migration: A movement of people from one area of a country to another for the purpose or with the effect of establishing a new residence. This migration may be temporary or permanent. Internal migrants move but remain within their country of origin (e.g. rural to urban migration). *See also internally displaced persons.*

internally displaced persons (IDPs): Persons or groups of persons who have been forced or obliged to flee or to leave their homes or places of habitual residence, in particular as a result of or in order to avoid the effects of armed conflict, situations of generalized violence, violations of human rights or natural or human-made disasters, and who have not crossed an internationally recognized state border (*Para. 2, Guiding Principles on Internal Displacement, UN Doc. E/CN.4/1998/53/Add.2*).

international law: The legal principles governing relationships between states. The contemporary law of international relations embraces not only states, but also such participants as international organizations and even individuals (such as those who invoke their human rights or commit war crimes). Also termed law of nations, public international law, *jus gentium*.

international migration: Movement of persons who leave their country of origin, or the country of habitual residence, to establish themselves either permanently or temporarily in another country.

international migration law: Instruments of international law applicable to migration.

international minimum standard: A state is required to observe minimum standards set by international law with respect to treatment of non-nationals present on its territory (or the property of such persons) (e.g. denial of justice, unwarranted delay or obstruction of access to courts are in breach of international minimum standards required by international law).

intra-corporate transferee: An employee of a firm who is temporarily transferred to a foreign affiliate of that firm (branch, subsidiary, office, joint venture, etc.).

irregular migrant: A person who, owing to unauthorized entry, breach of a condition of entry, or the expiry of his or her visa, lacks legal status in a transit or host country. The definition covers inter alia those persons who have entered a transit or host country lawfully but have stayed for a longer period than authorized or subsequently taken up unauthorized employment. *See also undocumented migrant, illegal migrant, clandestine migration.*

irregular migration: Movement that takes place outside the regulatory norms of the origin, transit and destination countries.

***jus sanguinis* (Latin):** The rule that a child's nationality is determined by its parents' nationality, irrespective of the place of its birth.

***jus soli* (Latin):** The rule that a child's nationality is determined by its place of birth (although it can also be conveyed by the parents).

labour migration: Movement of persons from their home state to another state or within their own country of residence for the purpose of employment.

lawful admission: Legal entry of a non-national into the country, including under a valid immigrant visa.

legalization: The act of making lawful; authorization or justification by legal sanction. *See also amnesty, regularization.*

less/low-skilled and semi-skilled migrant worker: There is no internationally agreed definition of a less or low-skilled and semi-skilled migrant worker. In broad terms, a semi-skilled worker is considered to be a person who requires a degree of training or familiarization with the job before being able to operate at maximum/optimal efficiency, although this training is not of the length or intensity required for designation as a skilled (or craft) worker, being measured in weeks or days rather than years, nor is it normally at the tertiary level. Many so-called "manual workers" (e.g. production, construction workers) should therefore be classified as semi-skilled. A less or low-skilled worker, on the other hand, is considered to be a person who has received less training than a semi-skilled worker or, having not received any training, has still acquired his or her competence on the job.

long-term migrant: A person who moves to a country other than that of his or her usual residence for a period of at least a year, so that the country of destination effectively becomes his or her new country of usual residence. From the perspective of the country of departure, the person will be a long-term emigrant and from that of the country of arrival, the person will be a long-term immigrant. *See also short-term migrant.*

migrant flow: The number of migrants counted as moving, or being authorized to move, to or from a given location in a defined period of time.

migrant/worker in an irregular situation: *See irregular migrant, undocumented migrant/worker.*

migrant stock: The number of migrants residing in a given location at a particular point in time.

migrant worker: A person who is to be engaged, is engaged or has been engaged in a remunerated activity in a state of which he or she is not a national (*Art. 2(1), International Convention on the Protection of the Rights of All Migrant Workers and Members of Their Families, 1990*).

migration: A process of moving, either across an international border, or within a state. It includes migration of refugees, displaced persons and migrants moving for other purposes.

migration management: A term used to encompass numerous governmental functions within a national system for the orderly and humane management of cross-border migration, particularly managing the entry and presence of foreigners within the borders of the state and the protection of refugees and others in need of protection. It refers to a planned approach to the development of policy, legislative and administrative responses to key migration issues.

mixed flows: Complex population movements including refugees, asylum seekers, economic migrants and other migrants.

multilateral: In relation to treaties and negotiations, multilateral (or multipartite) connotes the involvement of more than two states in the process. *See also treaty.*

national: A person, who, either by birth or naturalization, is a member of a political community, owing allegiance to the community and being entitled to enjoy all its civil and political rights and protection; a member of the state, entitled to all its privileges. A person enjoying a nationality of a given state. *See also citizen, nationality, naturalization.*

nationality: Legal bond between a person and a state. Under *Art. 1, Hague Convention on Certain Questions Relating to the Conflict of Nationality Laws, 1930*, "it is for each state to determine under its own laws who are its nationals. This law shall be recognized by other states in so far as it is consistent with international conventions, international custom, and the principles of law generally recognized with regard to nationality".

naturalization: Granting by a state of its nationality to a non-national through a formal act on the application of the person concerned.

net migration: *See total migration.*

non-admission: Refusal to permit entry to the territory of a state. *See also admission.*

non-discrimination: The refusal to apply distinctions of an adverse nature to human beings simply because they belong to a specific category. Discrimination is prohibited by international law, for example in *Art. 26, International Covenant on Civil and Political Rights, 1966*, which states: "All persons are equal before the law and are entitled without any discrimination to the equal protection of the law. In this respect, the law shall prohibit any discrimination and guarantee to all persons equal and effective protection against discrimination on any ground such as race, colour, sex, language, religion, political or other opinion, national or social origin, property, birth, or other status". *See also discrimination.*

non-national: A person who is not a national or citizen of a given state. *See also alien, foreigner.*

non-refoulement: A principle laid down in the *Geneva Convention Relating to the Status of Refugees, 1951*, according to which "no contracting state shall expel or return ("*refouler*") a refugee in any manner whatsoever to the frontiers of territories where his life or freedom would be threatened on account of his race, religion, nationality, membership of a particular social group or political opinion." (*Art. 33(1), Geneva Convention Relating to the Status of Refugees, 1951*). Non-refoulement has also been recognized as a principle of customary international law. *See also refoulement.*

orderly migration: The movement of a person from his/her usual place of residence to a new place of residence, in keeping with the laws and regulations governing exit from the country of origin and travel, transit and entry into the destination or host country.

offshoring: The relocation of business activities of an entity to another country. *See also outsourcing.*

outsourcing: The sub-contracting by an entity of specific business processes such as design or manufacturing to another company. Also referred to as global resourcing.

overstay: To remain in a country beyond the period for which entry was granted. Persons who overstay are referred to as "overstayers".

permanent residence: The right, granted by the authorities of the destination country to a non-national, to live and work therein on a permanent (unlimited or indefinite) basis.

petition: *See sponsorship.*

policy: General principles by which a government is guided in its management of public affairs.

project-tied worker: A migrant worker admitted to a state of employment for a defined period to work solely on a specific project being carried out in that state by his or her employer (*Art 2(2)(f), International Convention on the Protection of the Rights of All Migrant Workers and Members of Their Families, 1990*). *See also migrant worker.*

protection: All activities aimed at securing respect for individual rights in accordance with the letter and spirit of the relevant bodies of law (namely, International Human Rights Law, International Humanitarian Law, International Labour Law, International Migration Law and International Refugee Law).

push-pull factors: Migration is often analysed in terms of the "push-pull model," which looks at the push factors, which drive people to leave their country, and the pull factors, which attract them to a new country.

qualified national: Expatriate national with specific professional skills in demand in the country or region of origin. *See also highly skilled migrant, skilled migrant.*

quota: In the migration context, a quantitative restriction on the number of migrants to be admitted each year.

ratification: Ratification refers to the "acceptance" or "approval" of a treaty. In an international context, ratification "is the international act so named whereby a state establishes on the international plane its consent to be bound by a treaty" (*Art. 2(1)(b), Vienna Convention on the Law of Treaties, 1969*). Instruments of ratification establishing the consent of a state take effect when exchanged between contracting states, deposited with a depositary or notified to the contracting states or to the depositary, if so agreed (*Art. 16, Vienna Convention on the Law of Treaties, 1969*). In a domestic context, it denotes the process whereby a state puts itself in a position to indicate its acceptance of the obligations contained in a treaty. A number of states have in their Constitutions procedures which have to be followed before the state considers itself bound by a treaty. *See also treaty.*

readmission: Act by a state accepting re-entry of a person (own national, third-country national or stateless person).

readmission agreement: Agreement which addresses procedures, on a reciprocal basis, for one state to return non-nationals in an irregular situation to their home state or a state through which they have transited.

receiving country: Country of destination (host country). In the case of return or repatriation, also the country of origin. *See also host country, country of destination, state of employment.*

refoulement: The return by a state of an person to the territory of another state in which his/her life or liberty would be threatened, or s/he may be persecuted for reasons of race, religion, nationality, membership of a particular social group or political opinion; or would run the risk of torture. *See also non-refoulement.*

refugee (mandate): A person who meets the criteria of the UNHCR Statute and qualifies for the protection of the United Nations provided by the High Commissioner, regardless of whether or not s/he is in a country that is a party to the Convention Relating to the Status of Refugees, 1951 or the 1967 Protocol Relating to the Status of Refugees, or whether or not s/he has been recognized by the host country as a refugee under either of these instruments.

refugee: A person, who "owing to well-founded fear of persecution for reasons of race, religion, nationality, membership of a particular social group or political opinion, is outside the country of his nationality and is unable or, owing to such fear, is unwilling to avail himself of the protection of that country" (*Article 1A(2), Convention relating to the Status of Refugees, 1951 as modified by the 1967 Protocol*).[1]

regional consultative processes: Non-binding consultative fora, bringing representatives of states and international organizations together at the regional level to discuss migration issues in a cooperative manner. Some regional consultative processes (RCPs) also allow the participation of other stakeholders (e.g. NGO or other civil society representatives).

regular migration: Migration that occurs through recognized, authorized channels. *See also irregular migration.*

regularization: Any process or programme by which the authorities of a country allow non-nationals in an irregular or undocumented situation to stay lawfully in the country. *See also amnesty, legalization.*

reintegration: Re-inclusion or re-incorporation of a person into a group or a process, e.g. of a migrant into the society of his/her country of origin. *See also integration.*

---

[1] In Africa, the term "refugee" also applies to a person who "owing to external aggression, occupation, foreign domination or events seriously disturbing public order in either part or the whole of his [her] country of origin or nationality, is compelled to leave his [her] place of habitual residence in order to seek refuge in another place outside his [her] country of origin or nationality" (*Article I(2) OAU Convention Governing the Specific Aspects of Refugee Problems in Africa 1974*). In Central America, the term applies equally to persons "who have fled their country because their lives, safety or freedom have been threatened by generalized violence, foreign aggression, internal conflicts, massive violation of human rights or other circumstances which have seriously disturbed public order" (*Conclusion 3, Cartagena Declaration on Refugees, 22 November 1984*).

remittances: Monies earned or acquired by non-nationals that are transferred back to their country of origin.

removal: *See deportation, expulsion.*

repatriation: The return of a refugee or a prisoner of war to his/her country of nationality under specific conditions laid down in various international instruments (*Geneva Conventions, 1949 and Protocols, 1977, Regulations Respecting the Laws and Customs of War on Land, Annexed to the Fourth Hague Convention, 1907,* the human rights instruments as well as in customary international law).

replacement migration: Internal migration that occurs where the vacuum created by workers departing for another country is filled by workers from other parts of the country, or international migration that a country would need to offset population decline and population ageing resulting from low fertility and mortality rates (see Chapter 7).

resettlement: The relocation and integration of people (refugees, internally displaced persons, etc.) into another geographical area and environment, usually in a third country.

residence: The act or fact of living in a given place for some time; the place where one actually lives as distinguished from a domicile. Residence usually just means bodily presence as an inhabitant in a given place, while domicile usually requires bodily presence and an intention to make the place one's home. A person thus may have more than one residence at a time but only one domicile.

residence permit: A document issued by a state to a non-national, confirming that s/he has the right to live in the state concerned. *See also residence.*

return migration: The movement of a person returning to his/her country of origin or habitual residence usually after at least one year in another country. The return may or may not be voluntary. *See also circular migration, forced return, voluntary return.*

reverse brain drain: *See brain gain.*

right to leave: "Everyone has the right to leave any country, including his own..." (*Art. 13(2), Universal Declaration of Human Rights, 1948*). This right was set down in other international law instruments, for example in *Art. 12(2), International Covenant on Civil and Political Rights, 1966,* which states: "Everyone shall be free to leave any country, including his own." Some restrictions on this right can be legitimately imposed however (Art. 12(3), *International Covenant on Civil and Political Rights, 1966*: "The above-mentioned [right] shall not be subject to any restrictions except those which are provided by law, are necessary to protect national security, public order (*ordre public*), public health or morals or the rights and freedoms of others, and are consistent with the other rights recognized in the present Covenant"). The right to leave is an aspect of the right to freedom of movement, and it applies to all persons without distinction. There is however, no corollary right to enter the territory of a foreign country under international law. *See also freedom of movement, international minimum standard, repatriation, return.*

seafarer: Migrant worker employed on board a vessel registered in a state of which he or she is not a national (includes fishermen) (*Art. 2(2)(c), International Convention on the Protection of the Rights of All Migrant Workers and Members of Their Families, 1990*). *See also migrant worker.*

seasonal migrant worker/migration: A migrant worker whose work, or migration for work that, by its character is dependent on seasonal conditions and is performed only during part of the year (*Art. 2(2)(b), International Convention on the Protection of the Rights of All Migrant Workers and Members of Their Families, 1990*). *See also migrant worker.*

self-employed migrant worker: A migrant worker who is engaged in a remunerated activity otherwise than under a contract of employment and who earns his or her living through this activity normally working alone or together with members of his or her family, and any other migrant worker recognized as self-employed by applicable legislation of the state of employment or bilateral or multilateral agreements. (*Art. 2(2)(h), International Convention on the Protection of the Rights of All Migrant Workers and Members of Their Families, 1990*). *See also migrant worker.*

sending country: A country from which people leave to settle abroad permanently or temporarily. *See also country of origin.*

short-term migrant: A person who moves to a country other than that of his or her usual residence for a period of at least three months, but less than a year, except in cases where the movement to that country is for purposes of recreation, holiday, visits to friends or relatives, business or medical treatment. For the purpose of international migration statistics, the country of usual residence of short-term migrants is considered to be the country of destination during the period they spend in it. *See also long-term migrant, temporary migrant workers.*

skilled migrant: A migrant worker who, because of his/her skills or acquired professional experience, is usually granted preferential treatment regarding admission to a host country. *See also highly skilled migrant, qualified national.*

slavery: The status or condition of a person over whom any or all the powers attaching to the right of ownership are exercised (*Art. 1, Slavery Convention, 1926, as amended by the 1953 Protocol*)

smuggler (of migrants): An intermediary who is moving people by agreement with them, in order to transport them in an unauthorized manner across an internationally recognized state border. *See also smuggling, trafficking.*

smuggling: The procurement, in order to obtain, directly or indirectly, a financial or other material benefit, of the illegal [or unauthorized] entry of a person into a state party of which the person is not a national or a permanent resident (*Art. 3(a), Protocol Against the Smuggling of Migrants by Land, Sea and Air, supplementing the United Nations Convention against Transnational Organized Crime, 2000*).

sovereignty: As a concept of international law, sovereignty has three principal aspects: external, internal and territorial. The external aspect of sovereignty is the right of the state freely to determine its relations with other states or other entities without the restraint or control of another state. This aspect of sovereignty is also known as independence. The internal aspect of sovereignty is the state's exclusive right or competence to determine the character of its own institutions, to enact laws of its own choice and ensure their respect. The territorial aspect of sovereignty is the exclusive authority which a state exercises over all persons and things found on, under or above its territory. In the context of migration, this means the sovereign prerogative of a state to determine which non-citizens should be admitted to its territory subject to the limitations of the *non-refoulement* principle, human rights and provisions in bilateral or regional agreements (e.g. free movement or integration agreements). *See also non-refoulement, human rights.*

specified-employment worker: A migrant worker: (i) Who has been sent by his or her employer for a restricted and defined period of time to a state of employment to undertake a specific assignment or duty; or (ii) Who engages for a restricted and defined period of time in work that requires professional, commercial, technical or other highly-specialized skill; or (iii) Who, upon the request of his or her employer in the state of employment, engages for a restricted and defined period of time in work whose nature is transitory or brief; and who is required to depart from the state of employment either at the expiration of his or her authorized period of stay, or earlier if he or she no longer undertakes that specific assignment or duty or engages in that work (*Art. 2(2)(g), International Convention on the Protection of the Rights of All Migrant Workers and Members of Their Families, 1990*). *See also migrant worker.*

sponsorship: The act of promising support, in particular financial support, for a non-national seeking entry to the state, generally for a defined period of time. Some states require either sponsorship or proof of adequate income as a condition of entry for certain categories of migrants as well as visitors.

source country: *See also country of origin, sending country.*

state: A political entity with legal jurisdiction and effective control over a defined territory, and the authority to make collective decisions for a permanent population, a monopoly on the legitimate use of force, and an internationally recognized government that interacts, or has the capacity to interact, in formal relations with other entities.

state of employment/state of origin/state of transit: *See country of destination, country of origin, country of transit.*

stateless person: A person who is not considered a national by any state under the operation of its law (*Art. 1, United Nations Convention Relating to the Status of Stateless Persons, 1954*). As such, a stateless person lacks those rights attributable to nationality: the diplomatic protection of a state, the inherent right of sojourn in the state of residence and the right of return in case s/he travels.

step migration: Where a person moves to one or more locations within the country before emigration to another country, or from one country to another before moving to his/her ultimate or final country of destination.

technical cooperation: The sharing of information and expertise on a given subject usually focused on public sector functions.

temporary (labour) migration: Migration of workers who enter a foreign country for a specified limited period of time before returning to the country of origin.

temporary migrant workers: Skilled, semi-skilled or low-skilled workers in the destination country for definite periods, for example under a work contract with an individual employer or a service contract with an enterprise.

terrorism: Any act intended to cause death or serious bodily injury to a civilian, or any other person not taking an active part in the hostilities in a situation of armed conflict, when the purpose of such act is to intimidate a population, or compel a government or an international organization to do or abstain from doing an act (*Art. 2(1)(b), International Convention for the Suppression of Financing of Terrorism, 1999*).

third country: A country other than the country of origin of a person. In the context of the European Union, third country refers to non-EU Member States. *See also country of destination, country of origin, country of transit.*

total migration/net migration: Total migration is the sum of the entries or arrivals of immigrants, and of exits or departures of emigrants; net migration is the balance resulting from the difference between arrivals and departures.

trafficker, human: An intermediary who is moving people in order to obtain an economic or other profit by means of deception or coercion for the purpose of exploitation.

trafficking in persons: The recruitment, transportation, transfer, harbouring or receipt of persons, by means of the threat or use of force or other forms of coercion, of abduction, of fraud, of deception, of the abuse of power or of a position of vulnerability or of the giving or receiving of payments or benefits to achieve the consent of a person having control over another person, for the purpose of exploitation (*Art. 3(a), Protocol to Prevent, Suppress and Punish Trafficking in Persons, Especially Women and Children, supplementing the United Nations Convention against Transnational Organized Crime, 2000*).

transit: A stopover of passage, of varying length, while travelling between two or more countries, either incidental to continuous transportation, or for the purposes of changing planes or joining an ongoing flight or other mode of transportation. *See also country of transit, state of transit.*

transnational identity/transnationalism: The process whereby people establish and maintain socio-cultural connections across geopolitical borders.

treaty: An international agreement concluded between states in written form and governed by international law, whether embodied in a single instrument or in two or more related instruments and whatever its particular designation. (*Art.2(1)(a), Vienna Convention on the Law of Treaties, 1969*).

travel documents: All documents which are acceptable proof of identity for the purpose of entering another country. Passports and visas are the most widely used forms of travel documents.

unaccompanied minors: Persons under the age of majority who are not accompanied by a parent, guardian, or other adult who by law or custom is responsible for them.

unauthorized/unlawful entry/admission: Act of crossing borders without complying with the necessary requirements for legal entry into the receiving state (*Art. 3(b), Protocol against the Smuggling of Migrants by Land, Sea, and Air, supplementing the United Nations Convention against Transnational Organized Crime, 2000*). *See also irregular migration.*

undocumented migrant workers/migrant workers in an irregular situation: Migrant workers or members of their families not authorized to enter, to stay or to engage in employment in a state. *See also irregular migrant/migration.*

victim of human trafficking: A person who is a victim of the crime of trafficking in persons. *See also trafficker, trafficking in persons.*

visa: An endorsement by a consular officer in a passport or a certificate of identity that indicates that the officer, at the time of issuance, believes the holder to fall within a category of non-nationals who can be admitted under the state's laws.

violence against (migrant) women: Any act of gender-based violence that results in, or is likely to result in physical, sexual, or psychological harm or suffering to women, including threats of such acts, coercion or arbitrary deprivation of liberty, whether occurring in public or private life (*Art. 1, Declaration on the Elimination of Violence against Women, 1993*).

voluntary return: The assisted or independent return to the country of origin, transit or another third country based on the free will of the returnee.

vulnerable group: Any group or sector of society at higher risk of being subjected to discriminatory practices, violence, natural or environmental disasters, or economic hardship than other groups within the state; any group or sector of society (such as women, children, the elderly, persons with disabilities, indigenous peoples or migrants) that is at higher risk in periods of conflict and crisis.

work permit: A legal document giving authorization for employment of migrant workers in the host country.

xenophobia: While no universally accepted definition of xenophobia exists, it can be described as attitudes, prejudices and behaviour that reject, exclude and often vilify persons based on the perception that they are outsiders or foreigners to the community, society or national identity.

ALPHABETICAL INDEX

I

MAP 1: Total Immigrant and Emigrant Population by Region*

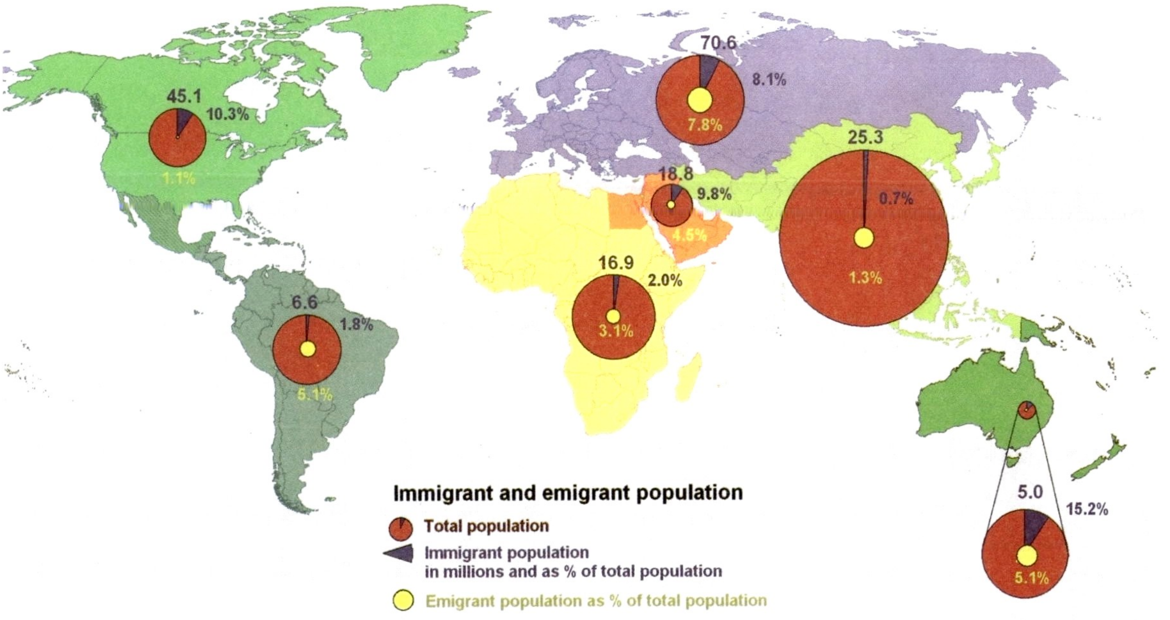

Sources: *Population Division of the Department of Economic and Social Affairs of the United Nations Secretariat, Trends in Total Migrant Stock: The 2005 Revision, New York, http://esa.un.org/migration; University of Sussex, U.K., Global Migrant Origin Database, Dataset 4, updated March 2007, http://www.migrationdrc.org/research/typesofmigration/global_migrant_origin_database.html.*

In 2005, Europe (including the countries from Central Asia as explained on p. 439) hosted the largest immigrant population of all world regions, over 70.5 million, followed by North America with just over 45.1 million immigrants and Asia with nearly 25.3 million. Among these three regions, North America (including Mexico) had the highest proportion of immigrants in the population, 10.3 per cent, and Asia the lowest with only 0.7 per cent. Among all regions, Oceania, with five million immigrants, presented the highest share at 15.2 per cent of the total population of the region.

Regarding the number of emigrants as a percentage of total population by regions in 2000, Europe (including the countries from Central Asia) has the largest share with 7.8 per cent, followed by Oceania and Latin America and the Caribbean (including Mexico**), each with 5.1 per cent.

Note: These global statistics on immigration for 2005 and on emigration for 2000 show the same regional constellations used in the Regional Migration Overviews. This differs from the breakdown by regions used in Maps 5 and 8, which follows the regional distributions of the sources used.

* The Global Migrant Origin Database used for the emigration stock data presented in the map is a Bilateral Migrant stock matrix that was created using the 2000 round of population censuses. For a detailed elaboration of the methods and limitations of the construction of the database, see: Parsons, C.R., R. Skeldon, T.L. Walmsley and L.A. Winters, 2007, "Quantifying International Migration: A Database of Bilateral Migrant Stocks", World Bank Policy Research Working Paper 4165, March, The World Bank, Washington, D.C., http://www-wds.worldbank.org/external/default/WDSContentServer/IW3P/IB/2007/03/06/000016406_20070306151900/Rendered/PDF/wps4165.pdf.

** The 2005 figures of the total number of Latin American and Caribbean migrants include the number of migrants from Mexico, which accounts for around half of the citizens of Latin America and the Caribbean living outside their country of origin. The importance of including Mexico as part of Latin American migration is that, in terms of migrant characteristics (reasons for migrating, migration conditions, living conditions in destination countries, etc.), Mexican migrants are more similar to Latin American and Caribbean citizens living outside their country of origin than to U.S. and Canadian citizens living outside their country of origin.

MAP 2: Foreign Students in Higher Education in Selected Countries, 2004*

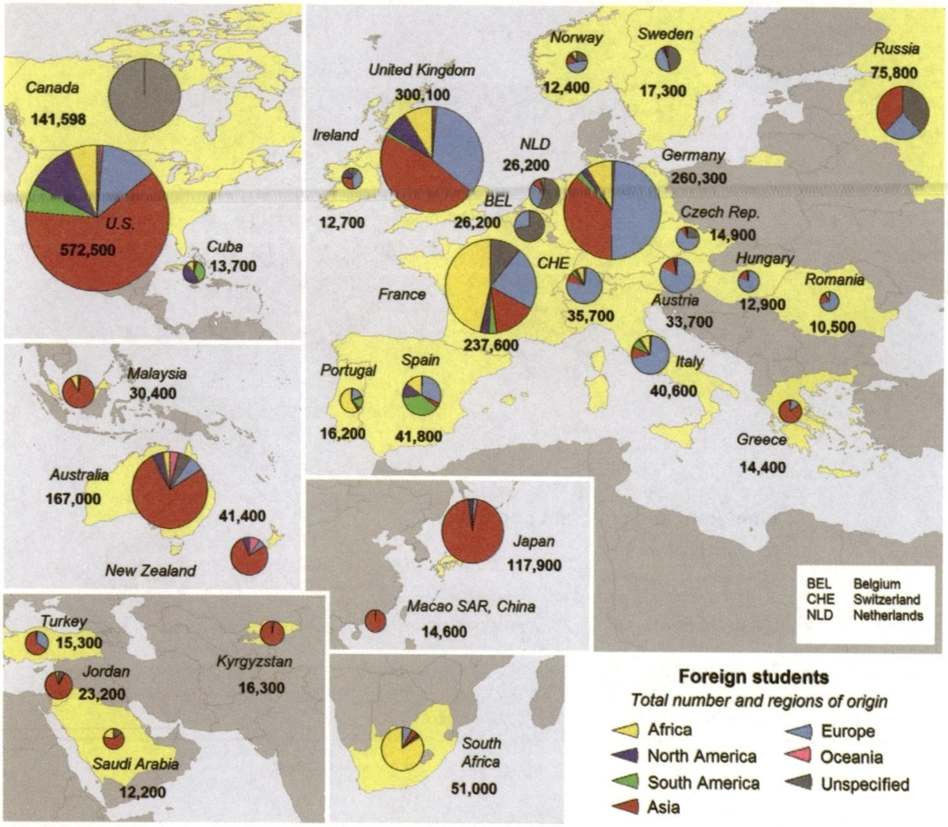

Note:
The size of each pie chart shown on this map is proportional to the total number of foreign students hosted by the relevant country, while the size and colours of each pie slice highlight the importance of the different regions of origin in numerical terms. The data for Canada, drawn from Citizenship and Immigration Canada statistics, did not allow a breakdown by region although it did list the ten top places of origin, namely (in order of magnitude): China, South Korea, U.S., Japan, France, India, Taiwan Province of China, Hong Kong SAR, Mexico, Germany, U.K.

Sources: *UNESCO, Global Education Digest 2006: Comparing Education Statistics Across the World, Paris. For Canada: Citizenship and Immigration Canada, Stocks of Foreign Students 2004, http://www.cic.gc.ca/english/resources/statistics/facts2006/temporary/10.asp.*

Map 2 shows the global distribution of international students in tertiary education by region of origin. The data in this map primarily refer to the 2004 school year and only countries hosting more than 10,000 students have been selected in each region.

The U.S. and the U.K. had the largest number of foreign students in 2004, hosting 572,500 and 300,100 individuals, respectively. Germany, France, Australia, Canada and Japan follow with totals ranging from about 260,300 students (Germany) to 100,000 (Japan). While the U.S. figure is more than twice that of France and Germany, and nearly twice that of the U.K, Europe considered as a whole is the largest recipient of foreign students globally. Most of them come from within Europe as students from the European Union (EU) finding it convenient and cheaper to study in another EU Member State. Half, or more than half, of the foreign students in Austria, Germany, Hungary, Italy, Norway, Romania, Sweden and Switzerland are from the EU. On the other hand, nearly half of the foreign students in France and more than half in Portugal are from Africa, and these two countries are globally the largest recipients of African students after South Africa, while in the U.K. and Greece most international students come from Asia. Spain is the country hosting the highest proportion of foreign students from South America (37%).

Globally, Asia produces the highest number of students going abroad to pursue higher education. Within Asia, more than 90 per cent of foreign students in Japan and Macao SAR are from within the region, while in Malaysia they account for 89 per cent. In Australia and New Zealand, Asians account for about 77 per cent of all the overseas students. Students from Asia also make up the majority in Saudi Arabia and Jordan. With a total of 12,200 and 23,200 foreign students, respectively, these two countries are the largest poles of attraction in the Middle East.

Finally, with a total of 51,000 international students, South Africa is the most significant country of destination for foreign students in Africa with the majority (43,176) coming from countries within the continent.

MAP 3: Internally Displaced Persons, 2007

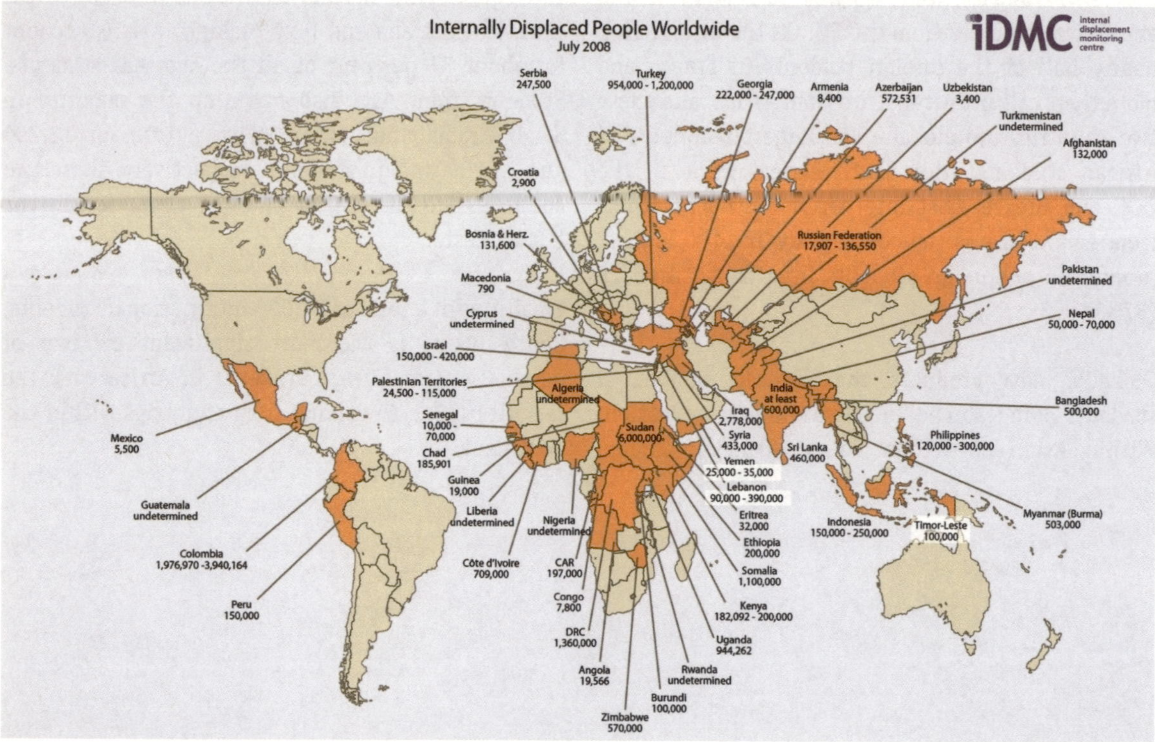

Source: *Global IDP Project, Norwegian Refugee Council, Geneva. Updated versions of the map can be downloaded from the following website: http://www.internal-displacement.org/8025708F004CE90B/httpWorldMap?ReadForm&count=1000.*

In recent years the estimated global figure for internally displaced persons (IDPs) has grown to 26 million, the highest figure since the early 1990s. While at least 52 countries worldwide were affected by internal displacement in 2007, close to half of the people displaced by conflict were in Africa (12.7 million), spread across 20 countries. If individual countries are considered, then three in particular had the largest internally displaced populations: Colombia, Iraq and Sudan. Together, these countries accounted for nearly 50 per cent of the world's IDPs. The region with the largest relative increase in the IDP population during 2007 was the Middle East, with a rise of nearly 30 per cent.

MAP 4: World's Refugees by Region of Origin and Region of Asylum, 2006

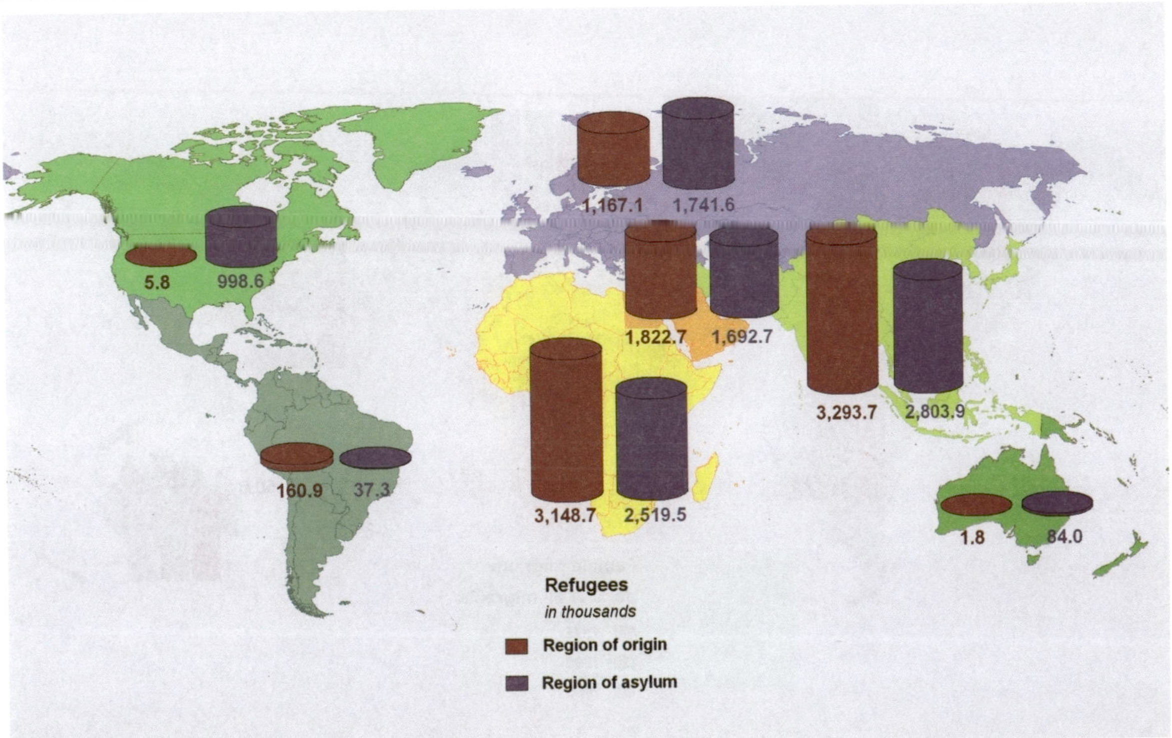

Source: *UNHCR, Statistical Yearbook 2007, Geneva, http://www.unhcr.org/statistics.html. Data are provisional and subject to change.*

Complementing Map 3 on IDPs, Map 4 shows that most of the world's refugees stay in the same region after having fled from their countries. Most refugees can be found in the developing world. Thus, Africa and Asia, while being the source of significant numbers of refugees in other continents, were also host to large refugee populations, with over 2.5 million each in 2006. North America and Europe are the most important net destinations for refugees.

MAP 5: Proportion of Women Migrants by Region, 1975, 1990, 2005

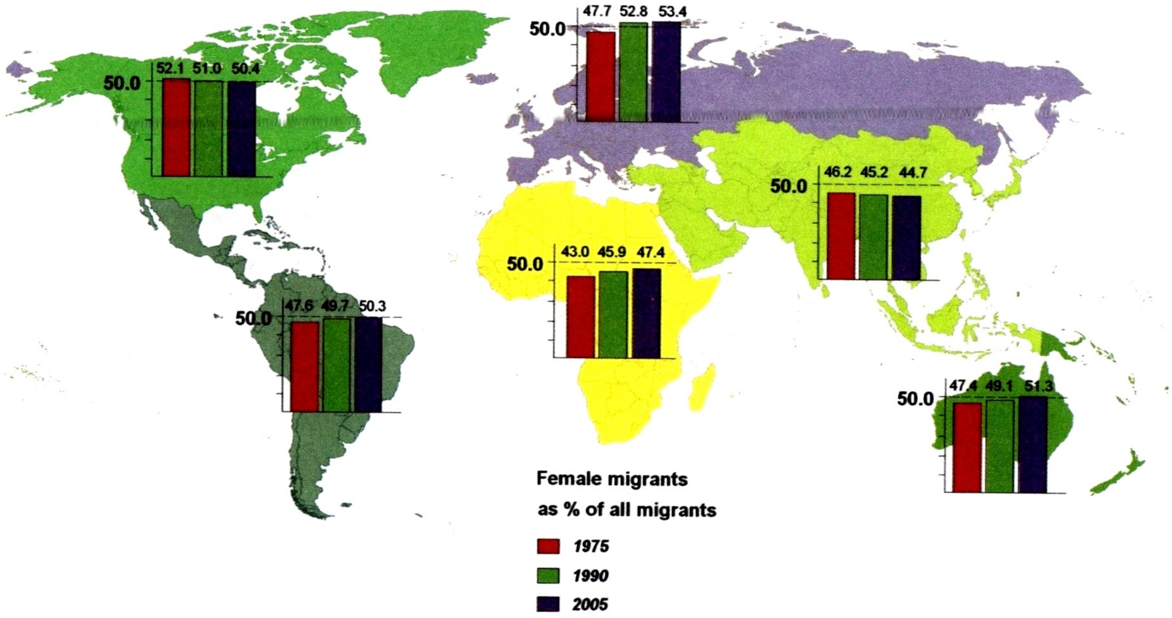

Source: *Population Division of the Department of Economic and Social Affairs of the United Nations Secretariat, Trends in Total Migrant Stock: The 2005 Revision, New York, http://esa.un.org/migration.*

Map 5 shows the proportion of women migrants residing in different world regions in the period 1975 to 2005. This proportion rose globally by more than two per cent from 47.4 to 49.6 per cent, the steepest increases being recorded in Europe and the Russian Federation, with a rise of about six per cent. Asia and North America were the only two regions where the share of female migrants declined during this period from 46.2 to 44.7 and 52.1 to 50.4 per cent, respectively.

In all regions the share of female migrants is higher than 50 per cent, except for Africa and Asia (including the Middle East).

MAP 6: Population Change in the EU-27, EEA and Switzerland, 2005

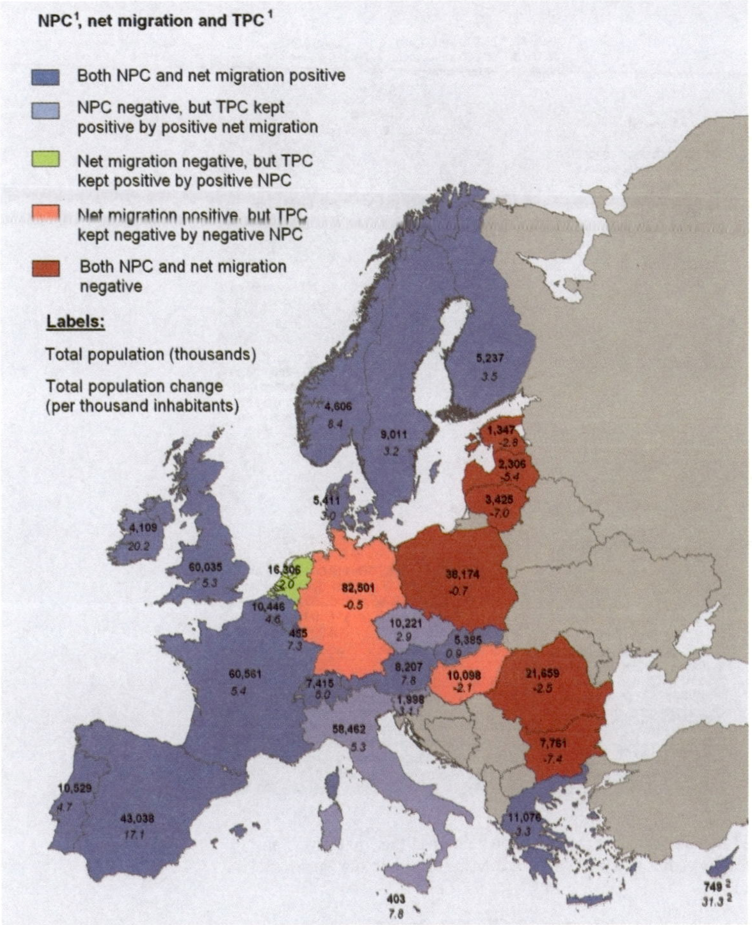

Notes:

¹ NPC refers to "natural population change"; TPC refers to "total population change"

² Figures refer to the area under the effective control of the Government of the Republic of Cyprus.

Source: *Münz, R. 2006, "Europe: Population and Migration in 2005", Migration Information Source, June, Migration Policy Institute (MPI), Washington, D.C., http://www.migrationinformation.org/feature/display.cfm?ID=402.*

Map 6 presents the demographic indicators for the EU-27 Member States, the European Economic Area (EEA) countries and Switzerland in the year 2005. The map shows that both the natural population change (births minus deaths) and the net migration were positive in 15 of the countries analyzed in 2005. In three of the countries examined (Czech Republic, Italy and Slovenia), the natural population change was either zero or negative, but the total change was positive through net migration. In The Netherlands, the total population change was kept positive on the strength of a positive natural population change, despite negative net migration. For Germany and Hungary, the strongly negative natural change kept the total population change negative, in spite of the clearly positive net migration. Finally, for Bulgaria, Estonia, Latvia, Lithuania, Poland and Romania, both natural population change and net migration were negative for that year.

MAP 7a: Main Regularizations and Amnesty Programmes in the Americas and Europe

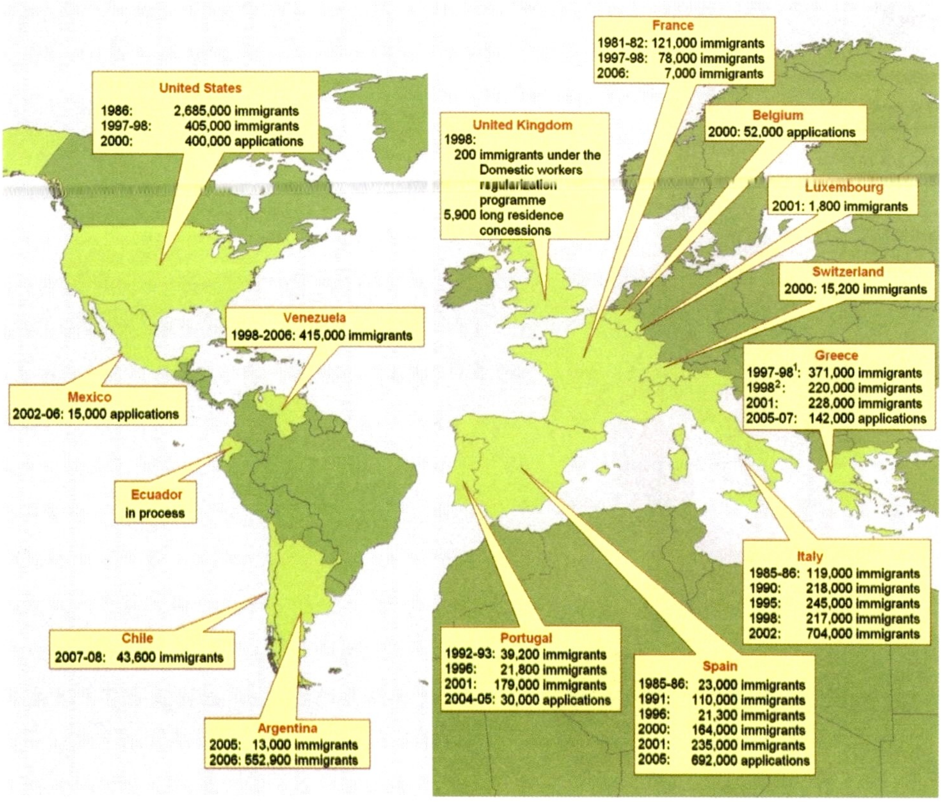

Notes:

[1 and 2] In 1997-98 371,000 immigrants in Greece obtained a "white card". Of these, 220,000 obtained the "green card" in 1998. The "white card" provided a six-month residence permit and was a prerequisite for obtaining the "green card", which provided a one-to-five year residence permit.

Sources for both Maps 7a and 7b: *OECD 2004, Trends in International Migration, SOPEMI 2003, Paris; OECD 2007, International Migration Outlook, SOPEMI 2007, Paris; Government of New Zealand; Government of Portugal; Thailand, Ministries of Labour and Interior; the Philippines, Ministry of Labour; Republic of Korea, Ministry of Justice; Government of Malaysia; Levinson, A. 2005, The Regularization of Unauthorized Migrants: Literature Survey and Country Case Studies, Centre on Migration, Policy and Society (COMPAS), University of Oxford, http://www.compas.ox.ac.uk/publications/papers/Regularisation%20Report.pdf.*

Obtaining accurate estimates of the number of irregular or undocumented migrants in a country is problematic and prone to a considerable margin of error. The estimates quoted in Maps 7a and 7b are compiled from a variety of sources. While it is difficult to state estimates with confidence, it is possible to at least identify the different indicators used to calculate these estimates (Levinson, 2005).

One useful indicator is the number of persons participating in regularization or amnesty programmes, which enable irregular migrants to acquire lawful status. Not all irregular migrants can benefit from these measures, as regularization often depends on the number of years a person has lived in a country or whether he or she is in employment. Therefore, the figures in Maps 7a and

MAP 7b: Main Regularizations and Amnesty Programmes in Asia and Oceania

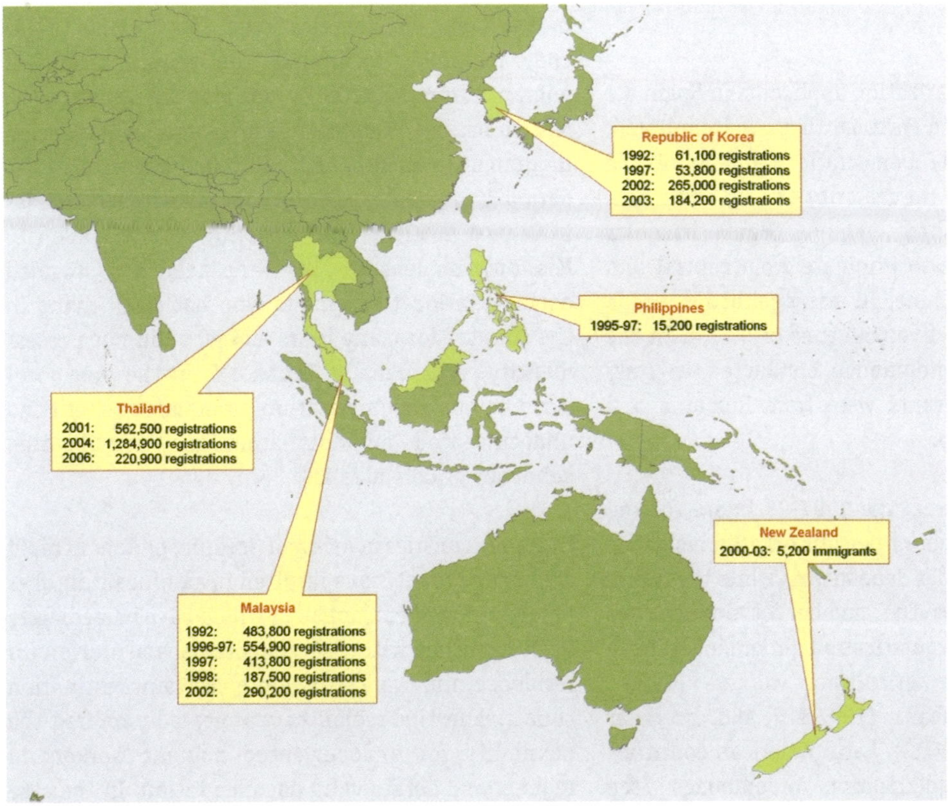

7b can only be indicative of the number of irregular migrants residing in a country at a particular point in time. Other factors limiting participation in such programmes are that employers may not wish to reveal their recourse to unauthorized labour, or may prefer to keep workers in an irregular situation so that they can pay lower wages. Furthermore, regularization frequently does not offer permanent residence status. Many of these migrants fall back into an irregular situation, owing to the insecurity or short duration of the status offered under certain programmes and the burdensome administrative procedures involved in renewing their regular status (OECD, 2004). Whatever the merits of regularization in the different regions of the world, the process itself does allow the movements due to unauthorized entry or overstay to enter the immigration statistics and thus to provide some idea of the scale of such movements (OECD, 2007).

Comparability of Data

It is important to note that the regularization figures published by governments can refer either to the number of applications for, or the number of persons granted, regular status. Each country has its own individual system for collecting data. For instance, the figures for Belgium and Switzerland for 2000 count the number of applications received and the dependants named therein, and include asylum seekers. Countries on the northern shores of the Mediterranean (France, Greece, Italy, Portugal,

Spain) have carried out successive regularization programmes, which principally target undocumented migrant workers.

The majority of regularization applicants in Spain are from Latin America; in Portugal they are from Brazil; in Belgium from the Democratic Republic of the Congo; and in France the majority of such applicants are from the Maghreb region. Many irregular migrants in Europe also originate from central and eastern Europe and China. In many countries, China ranks among the top five countries of origin. In the last regularization programme conducted in Italy in 2002, most applicants were from Romania and Ukraine (OECD, 2004).

Regarding the Americas, the 1997-98 figure for the U.S. counts the number of persons granted residence permits, which excludes dependants, while the figure for 2000 only shows the number of applications received. The U.S. regularization programmes have principally targeted agricultural workers (1986), Nicaraguans and Cubans (1997-98) and irregular migrants generally (2000). Latin American countries also implement regularization programmes (see Textbox 8.3). In Argentina, the National Programme for the Regularization of Migrants *"Patria Grande"* in its first phase (2005) granted residence status to migrants who were not citizens of countries belonging to the Common Market of the South (MERCOSUR) and, in 2006, facilitated the regularization of migrants from MERCOSUR and associated countries. Mexico has been implementing a large regularization programme, which benefited 15,000 migrants in the period 2002-2006, most of whom came from countries in Central America. The *"Mision Identidad"* (Identity Mission), implemented by Venezuela, has provided documentation to migrants who had been living in the country for many years and who did not possess identity cards. Finally, Ecuador is in the process of carrying out a regularization programme benefitting undocumented migrants from the neighbouring countries of Colombia and Peru.

In many countries in Asia and Oceania, periods of rapid economic growth have resulted in significant intakes of migrant workers, not all of whom have immediately been furnished with the requisite documentation for residence and work. Therefore, certain destination countries in this region have repeatedly offered the possibility for undocumented migrant workers to register and obtain valid documentation. In the case of New Zealand's regularization programme, carried out in 2000-2003, 5,200 overstayers were identified.

MAP 8: Remittances and Foreign Aid by Region, 2006

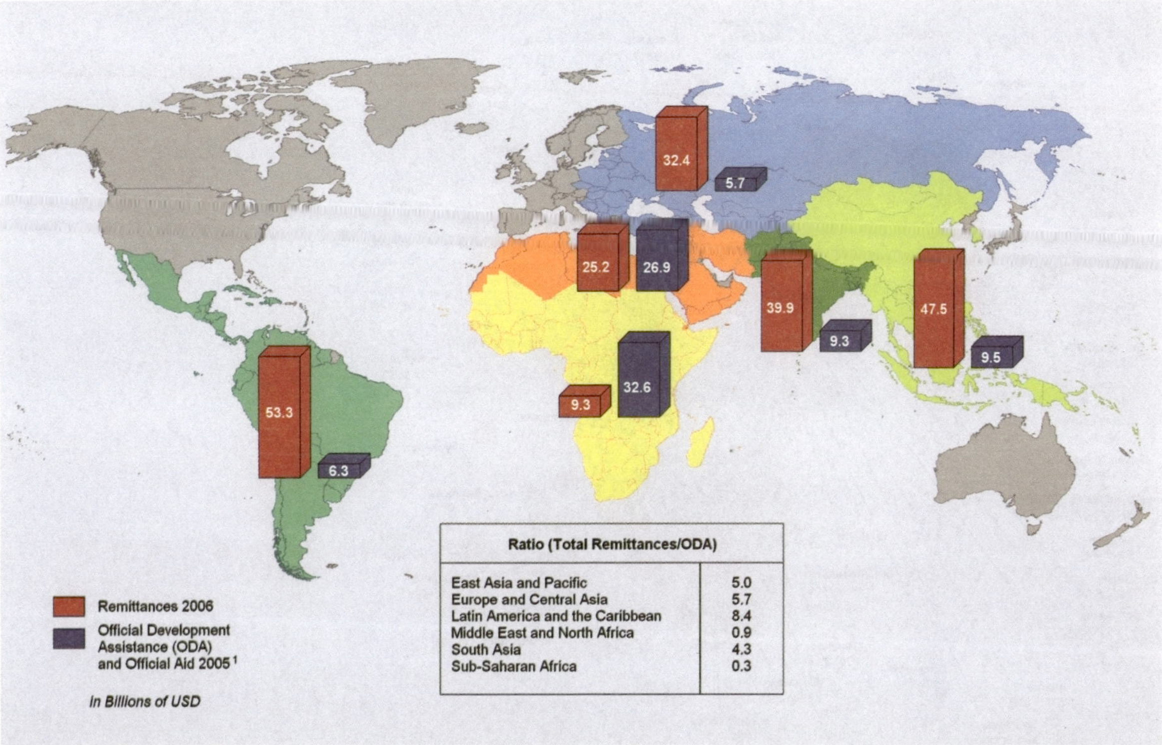

Note:

[1] Foreign aid includes Official Development Assistance (ODA) and official aid.

Sources: *World Bank Staff Estimates based on the International Monetary Fund's Balance of Payments Statistics Yearbook 2007; World Development Indicators 2007, The World Bank, Washington, D.C.*

In 2006, officially recorded remittances amounted to USD 281 billion. Of that amount, USD 207 billion was sent back to developing countries. In 2005, foreign aid (Official Development Assistance (ODA) and official aid) was less than half that amount (USD 90.4 billion), which underscores the importance of remittances as a source of income for developing countries.

The economic importance of migrant remittances varies across the globe. Some developing countries and regions receive considerably higher amounts of remittances than foreign aid, while in other regions foreign aid plays a larger role in development. In the Latin American and Caribbean region, remittances were 8.4 times higher than foreign aid received in 2005. The Middle East and Africa were the only two regions where foreign aid exceeded remittances in 2005-2006. As in previous years (see *World Migration 2005*), sub-Saharan Africa received the smallest nominal amount of remittances, but the region received the highest percentage of foreign aid (32.6%). Total remittances accounted for only 0.4 times the amount of all the foreign aid.

Note: Maps 8 to 12 have been produced on the basis of the World Bank 2006 remittance figures. The World Bank released new figures on remittance trends in July 2008, and the Regional Migration Overviews include such data, but the trends indicated in these maps remain essentially the same.

MAP 9: Remittances to Select African and Middle East Countries, 2006

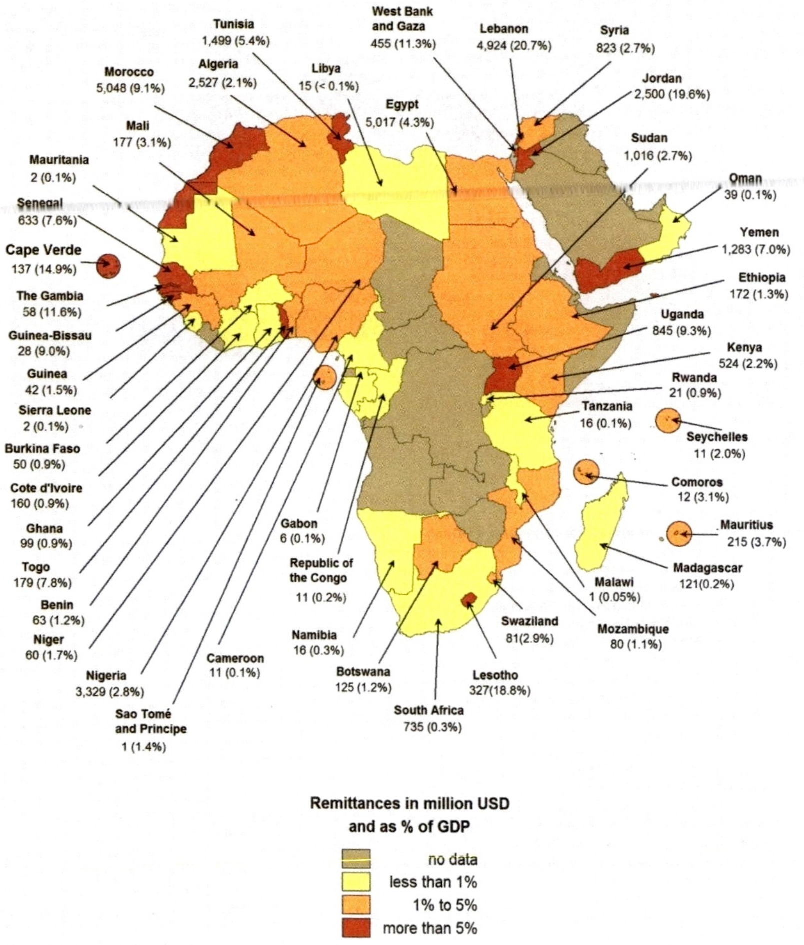

Source: *World Bank Staff Estimates based on the International Monetary Fund's Balance of Payments Statistics Yearbook 2007.*

Total migrant remittances in 2006 to Africa (including all the Maghreb countries but not Egypt) amounted to USD 18.3 billion, while in the Middle East in 2006 they reached USD 16 billion. With USD 5 billion, Egypt received the largest amount of remittances in the Middle East, followed by Lebanon with USD 4.9 billion. However, taken as a proportion of GDP, remittances received by Egypt represented only 4.3 per cent, while in Lebanon and Jordan they were equal to almost 21 and 19.6 per cent of GDP, respectively. In North Africa, Morocco was the foremost recipient of remittances in 2006, receiving USD 5.05 billion, representing nine per cent of the country's GDP. Sub-Saharan Africa is still the African sub-region receiving the lowest amount of remittances in absolute terms. At USD 3.3 billion, Nigeria is the only country in this sub-region where remittances exceeded one billion U.S. dollars. Measured against annual GDP in 2006, remittances were highest in the smallest countries with Lesotho in the lead (equal to almost 19% of GDP), followed by Cape Verde (nearly 15%) and The Gambia (12%).

MAP 10: Remittances to Select Latin American and Caribbean Countries, 2006

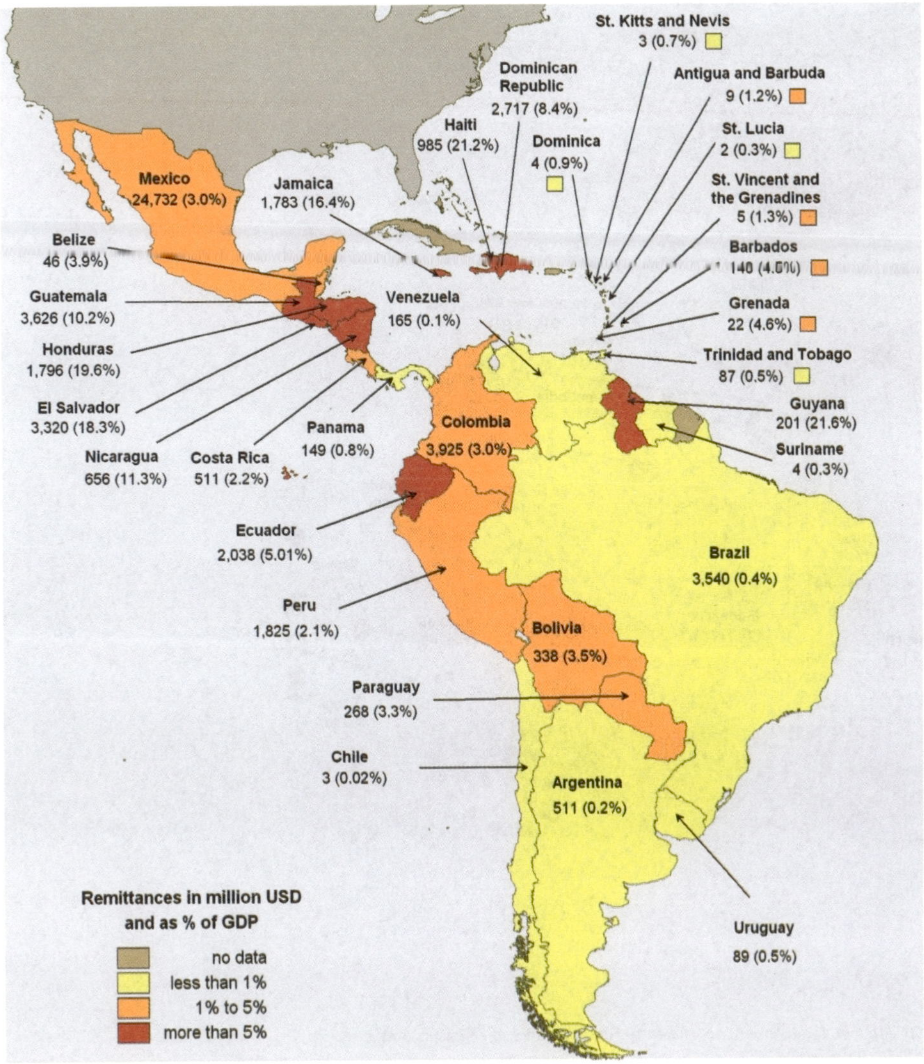

Source: *World Bank Staff Estimates based on the International Monetary Fund's Balance of Payments Statistics Yearbook 2007.*

Total migrant remittances to the Latin American and Caribbean region in 2006 amounted to USD 53.5 billion, of which more than 46 per cent were received by Mexico, the world's second largest receiver of migrant money transfers after India. Mexico's officially registered annual amount of USD 24.7 billion equalled three per cent of its GDP in 2006. The next largest receivers in the region were Colombia (USD 3.9 billion), Guatemala (USD 3.6 billion) and Brazil (USD 3.5 billion). Remittances accounted for the highest proportion of GDP in El Salvador, Honduras, Haiti and Guyana, where the share of remittances as a percentage of GDP ranged between 18 and 22 per cent.

MAP 11: Remittances to Select Countries in Asia and Oceania, 2006

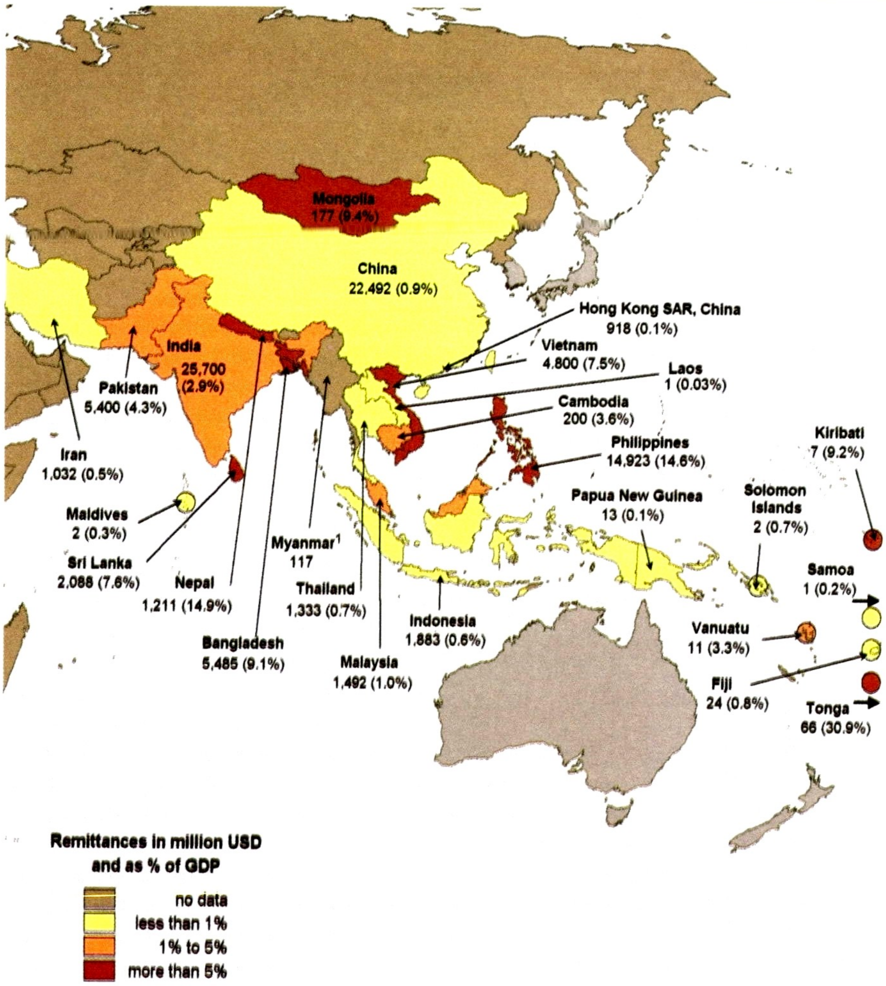

Source: *World Bank Staff Estimates based on the International Monetary Fund's Balance of Payments Statistics Yearbook 2007.*

In 2006, the Asia-Pacific region received a total of USD 91 billion in migrant remittances, with South-Central Asia in the lead with a total of USD 41 billion and East Asia and Southeast Asia each receiving a total of USD 25 billion. India has consistently been one of the foremost receivers of remittances and, in 2006, ranked first in Asia and the world as a whole with USD 25.7 billion (nearly 3% of its GDP). At USD 22.5 billion, China was the second largest recipient of remittances in Asia in absolute terms, but as a percentage of GDP they account for less than one per cent. The Philippines, on the other hand, was not only one of the foremost receivers of remittances (USD 14.9 billion) in absolute terms, but also as a percentage of GDP (14.6%), which in the region was only surpassed by Nepal (with USD 1.2 billion, the equivalent of 14.9% of its GDP). Remittances account for more than five per cent of GDP in Bangladesh, Sri Lanka and Viet Nam.

MAP 12: Remittances to Countries in Transition in Europe and Central Asia, 2006

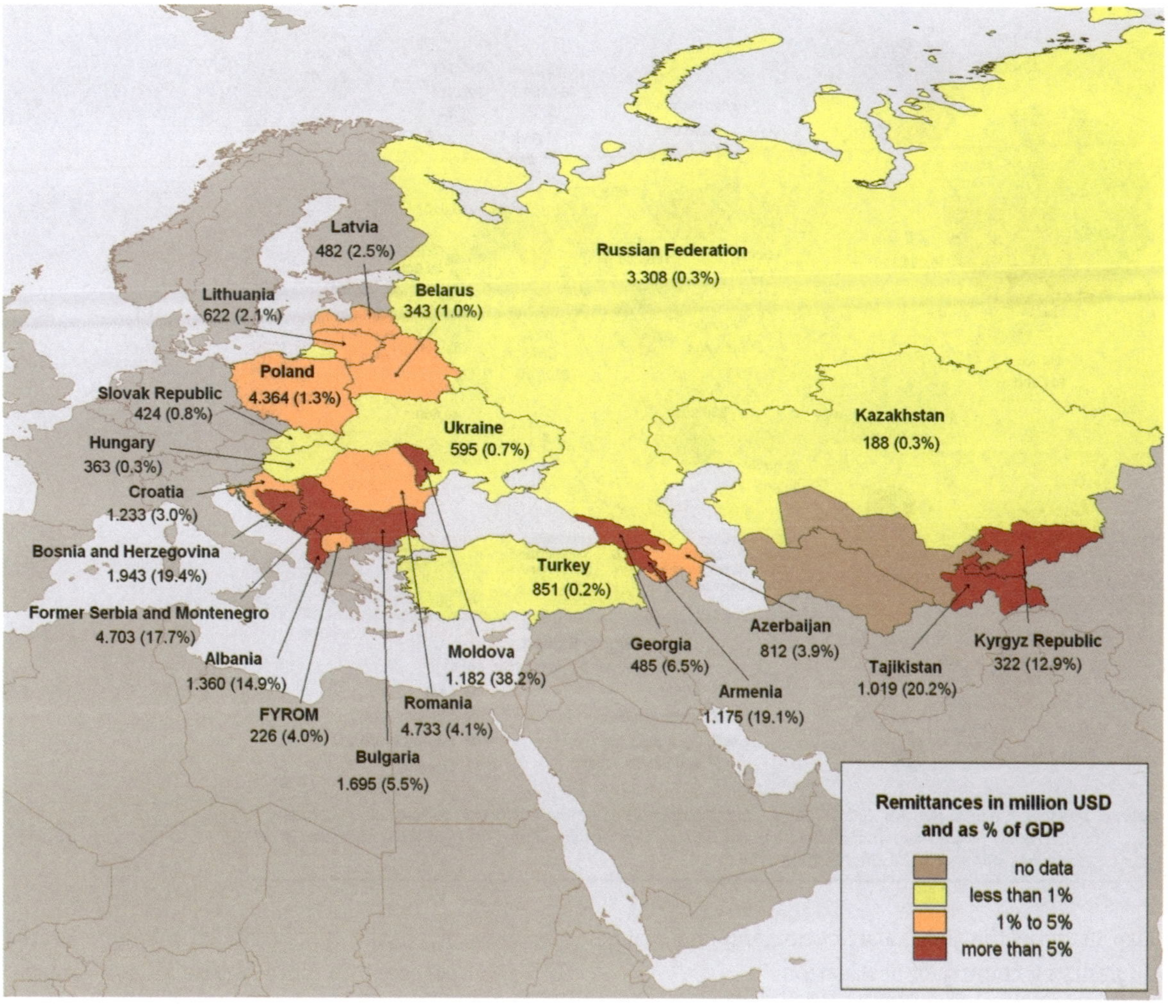

Source: *World Bank Staff Estimates based on the International Monetary Fund's Balance of Payments Statistics Yearbook 2007.*

Total migrant remittances to countries in transition in Europe and Central Asia in 2006 amounted to USD 32.4 billion, an increase of 11.1 per cent from 2005. The largest receivers in the region were Romania, the then Serbia and Montenegro and Poland, with all three recording absolute remittance figures of over USD 4 billion. In terms of remittances as a share of GDP, the highest proportions were to be found in Armenia, Bosnia and Herzegovina, Tajikistan and Moldova, with shares of GDP ranging between 19 and 39 per cent.

Only the countries considered by the United Nations as "countries in transition from centrally planned to market economies", and for which information is available, have been taken into account for the purpose of this map.

MAP 13: Highly Skilled Migrants by Destination Country, 2000

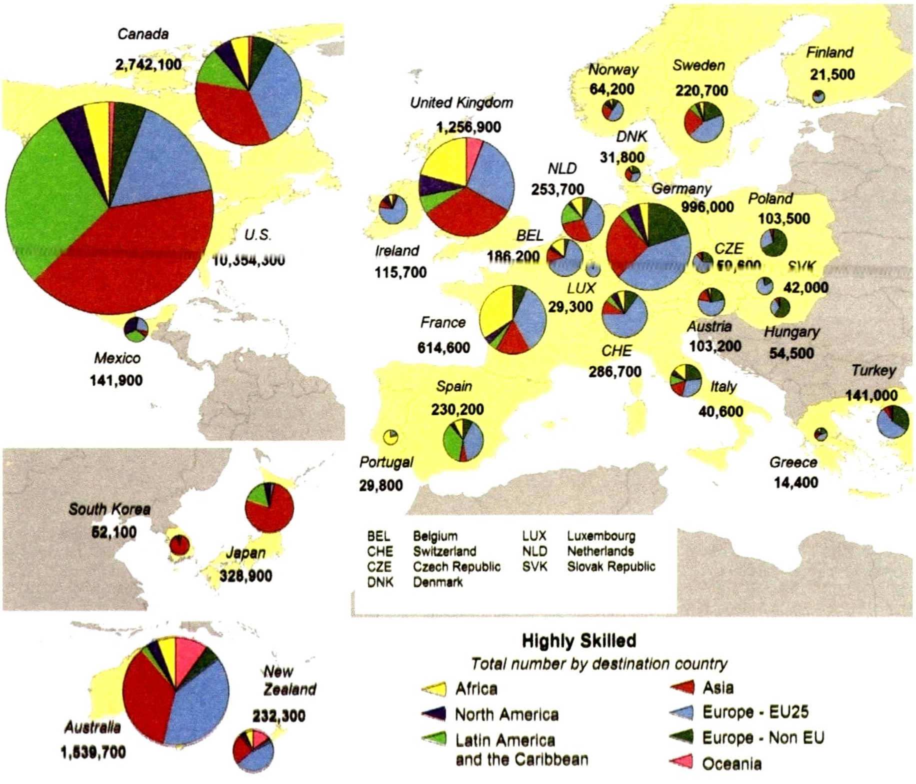

Source: *Docquier, F. and A. Marfouk. 2006, "International Migration by Education Attainment, 1990-2000" in C. Özden and M. Schiff (Eds.), International Migration, Remittances, and the Brain Drain, The World Bank and Palgrave Macmillan, Washington D.C./New York, 151-199.*

Map 13 shows the global distribution of highly skilled migrants by country of destination.

The map clearly shows that, with more than ten million, the U.S. is the most important recipient of highly skilled migrants, followed by Canada and Australia, with 2.7 and 1.5 million, respectively. Even though each individual OECD country in Europe, with the exception of the U.K., shows figures below one million, when considered as an entity, Europe is the second largest destination, hosting five million highly skilled migrants.

Highly skilled Asian migrants are well represented across the regions of the world, accounting for 41 per cent of all the highly skilled migrants in the U.S., 35 per cent in both Australia and Canada, and 33 per cent in the U.K. Latin America and the Caribbean rank second, accounting for 29 per cent of the highly skilled migrants to the U.S., and 35 per cent to Spain, while Mexico has the highest share of highly skilled migrants from Latin America and the Caribbean (34%). Highly skilled migrants from Africa are mostly found in Europe, where they account for 79 per cent of all highly skilled immigrants in Portugal and 34 per cent in France. European highly skilled migrants are most likely to move among European countries, accounting for 43 per cent of all highly skilled migrants in Germany and 39 per cent in Spain.

MAP 14: Highly Skilled Migrants by Region of Origin, 2000

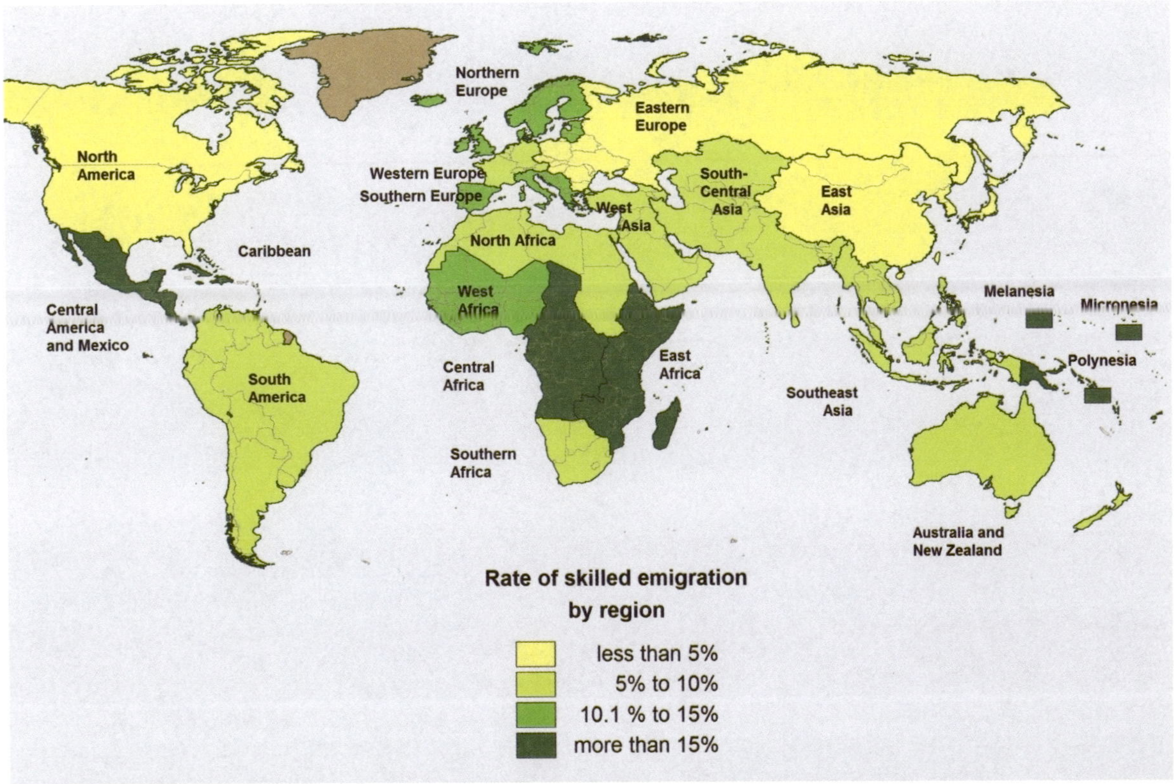

Source: *Docquier, F. and A. Marfouk. 2006, "International Migration by Education Attainment, 1990-2000" in C. Özden and M. Schiff (Eds.), International Migration, Remittances, and the Brain Drain, The World Bank and Palgrave Macmillan, Washington, D.C./New York, 151-199.*

To complement Map 13, Map 14 shows the global distribution of highly skilled migrants by region of origin.

The map shows that, in relative terms, East Africa, Central America and Mexico, and the Caribbean, together with the Pacific Islands, are the most affected sub-regions with more than 15 per cent of their highly skilled nationals migrating abroad. On the other hand, the sub-regions least affected by the emigration of their highly skilled nationals in 2000 are North America, eastern Europe and East Asia.